合规风险已日益成为金融机构面对的主要风险，认真研究相关案例，无论对规避监管风险还是完善合规体系建设都非常必要。

田国立
中国建设银行董事长

美国反洗钱合规监管

美国监管机构处罚案例集

MEIGUO FANXIQIAN HEGUI JIANGUAN

风暴

岳留昌◎编著

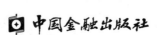

中国金融出版社

责任编辑：张智慧　王雪珂
责任校对：潘　洁
责任印制：陈晓川

图书在版编目(CIP)数据

美国反洗钱合规监管风暴/岳留昌编著.—北京：中国金融出版社，2019.1

ISBN 978-7-5049-9746-3

I.①美…II.①岳… III.①洗钱罪—案例—美国　IV.①D971.24

中国版本图书馆CIP数据核字（2018）第210907号

出版
发行　中国金融出版社

社址　北京市丰台区益泽路2号
市场开发部　　(010) 63266347，63805472，63439533 (传真)
网 上 书 店　http://www.chinafph.com
　　　　　　　(010) 63286832，63365686 (传真)
读者服务部　(010) 66070833，62568380
邮编　100071
经销　新华书店
印刷　保利达印务有限公司
尺寸　169毫米×239毫米
印张　30.75
字数　497千
版次　2019年1月第1版
印次　2019年1月第1次印刷
定价　89.00元
ISBN 978-7-5049-9746-3
如出现印装错误本社负责调换　联系电话(010) 63263947

序 一

2008年全球金融危机后，金融业处于"风口浪尖"，一时之间，华尔街、伦敦金融城沦为了邪恶、贪婪的代名词，备受民众的唾弃和指责，"占领华尔街""占领法兰克福"等运动此起彼伏。金融业成为众矢之的，全球监管纷纷提高监管标准，强化监管要求，加大执法力度和对系统性金融风险的防范，全球监管趋严趋同和"严管重罚"成为了国际监管的主基调。

美国次贷危机引发全球金融海啸以后，国际大型银行在美国的经营面临越来越大的合规监管压力，其中反洗钱合规更是"压力山大"。据不完全统计，2012年至2017年，因反洗钱合规问题被美国监管机构罚款1亿美元以上的银行就有13家，金额达到176.22亿美元。汇丰银行、法国巴黎银行、摩根大通银行、德意志银行等国际知名大行赫然在榜单上。在竞争激烈的国际金融市场上，这些银行可都是业中翘楚或业界标杆。

国际知名银行如此，中资银行的海外拓展之路亦非平坦，反洗钱合规已成为中资银行国际化经营之路上一道"绕不开"但又必须"迈过去"的坎儿。从国家层面看，中国已成为全球第二大经济体，中国企业的国际化、人民币的国际化、中资银行的国际化，使得中国银行业扩张国际金融版图已成必然。中资银行的国际影响力正与日俱增，相应地也引起了国际监管机构的重点关注。在这个过程中，中资银行必然，或者说，已经遭遇到国际社会合规和反洗钱的软性约束。2014年以后，随着国有四大银行陆续成为全球系统重要性银行（G-SIBs），中资银行的反洗钱合规风险开始凸显，以反洗钱/反恐融资、制裁合规、反逃税为主要内容的反洗钱监管特别是美国的反洗钱监管更是成为各家银行跨国经营中不得不直面的首要压力。现在，四大行均因反洗钱问题受到过境外监管处罚，以后处罚会不会更严，甚至是否会出现因反洗钱不过关而像巴基斯坦最大的银行——哈比银行那样被迫退出美国市场的情况？这种可能并非完全不存在。如果不能突破反洗钱合规这一发展瓶颈，中国金融机构国际化必将受阻，甚至会付出高昂的代价。

反洗钱合规是商业银行合规体系建设中不可或缺的重要组成部分，是检验一家银行合规管理水平的"试金石"，更是中资银行国际化运营能力高低的"校准器"。有效防范和化解反洗钱合规风险，需要中资银行从思想认识上转过弯来，从骨子里认可反洗钱合规是一个全球化的趋势，尽快将反洗钱合规的短板补齐，并且将反洗钱合规能力建设作为商业银行核心能力建设的重要一环，以久久为功的信心和矢志不移的决心持续加以推进和实施。

反洗钱合规工作的开展需要良好的合规文化为前提和基础。一个合规文化缺失、合规意识缺位的机构是无法做好反洗钱合规工作的。中资银行应该持续推进合规文化的建设和合规意识的培养，使合规真正成为每位员工自觉、自愿、自发的行为。在这方面，境内外各级金融机构的"一把手"要切实承担起倡导员工主动合规的责任。巴塞尔商业银行合规指引强调"合规从高层做起"（Compliance starts at the top），强调"高层为合规定调"（Tone from the top），都是从不同角度诠释了自上而下推动和培养良性合规文化的重要性。以主动合规为前提的良性合规文化还意味着我们要主动平衡好业务发展与合规管理的关系，主动对合规工作进行必要的支持和投入，以确保合规资源分配与本机构风险状况相匹配。在这方面，提前主动的投入永远比接受监管处罚后被动整改和投入所付出的代价和成本要小得多。合规肯定是要付出成本的，但不合规的成本会更高！

合规无小事。做好反洗钱工作要求我们必须紧跟监管大势，从大局着眼，从小处入手，千万不能抱侥幸心理。欧美大银行都被处罚过了，一个最重要的原因就是违规行为、反洗钱管理不严和规避金融制裁规定。2016年6月，美国披露的巴拿马开户文件拉开了全球反对利用离岸中心避税和洗钱的序幕。在这出剧中，许多国家政要纷纷出场，其中冰岛总理京勒伊格松因隐藏海外资产被迫辞职，英国前首相卡梅伦被曝出以离岸基金的方式蓄意隐瞒海外资产；2017年7月，巴基斯坦总理谢里夫也因为家族海外资产案受到调查而辞职。从合规和反洗钱角度讲，巴拿马文件几乎涵盖了所有高风险洗钱因素，比如：巴拿马本身就是高风险司法管辖区，一度还被国际金融行动特别工作组（FATF）列入了洗钱"灰名单"。此外，股权结构、透明度问题、政要人物（PEP）、最终受益人（UBO）、离岸资产、空壳公司、逃避税等因素哪一个都没落下。

反洗钱合规是一门科学。做好反洗钱工作不仅需要从业人员具备丰富的专业技能，还需要诚信正直的职业操守和坦诚良好的沟通能力，这是赢得监管信任和认可的基本前提。当然，在具体的监管过程中，有的监管者可能会因为民族、种族、宗教信仰、意识形态的不同以及地缘政治等原因，存在一些偏差甚至歧视情况，但这不能成为商业银行不做好反洗钱合规工作的挡箭牌和借口。一个机构合规工作没做好，不能总找客观原因，不能简单地说监管机构不讲理，更不能动辄以"阴谋论""唯发展论"等来掩盖自身的反洗钱合规缺陷和不足。我们必须面对现实，指尖向内，认真进行自我剖析、自我反省、自我纠错和自我修复。要明白"苍蝇不叮无缝的蛋"的道理，在反洗钱合规上一定要做到态度端正、尽职尽责、查漏补缺，同时与监管者做好沟通与交流，对于监管指出的问题，即知即改、立行立改。

反洗钱合规不仅仅是商业银行海外分支机构的事，更多的工作需要境内分支机构去做。境外机构做的很多跨境业务和联动业务来自境内，了解你的客户（KYC）或客户尽职调查（CDD）等反洗钱关键环节只有境内分支机构做扎实了，境外分支机构的压力和合规风险才会减少。跨境汇款、外币清算、贸易融资、代理行业务等反洗钱合规要求高的业务种类，更需要境内外一体化的反洗钱合规机制到位，同时也对境内外统一的反洗钱/反恐融资和制裁名单系统建设提出了更高的要求。

唐太宗说"以古为鉴，可知兴替"，《晋书》说"前车之覆轨，后车之明鉴"，这些都表明要以历史的前车之鉴，作为当今的后事之师。显然，本书中国际大型商业银行因涉嫌洗钱或反洗钱合规不力被监管机构处罚的案例和事例，将为我们做好反洗钱合规工作提供有益的借鉴。

丰习来

2019年1月

序　二

中资银行（尤其是拥有大量海外分支机构的大行）为应对国际上（主要是美国）的反洗钱合规监管，纷纷根据监管机构要求，正在构建包括树立反洗钱合规为先的理念，建立反洗钱政策制度框架和治理结构，成立强有力的内控合规监督管理部门，完善相关的法律规章制度，将反洗钱合规管理嵌入业务流程之中，设立独立的不受干扰的反洗钱合规官，举办反洗钱合规管理的培训、职业技能考试、持证上岗以及全员反洗钱合规文化建设等多位一体的反洗钱合规控制体系，以期能尽快满足反洗钱合规监管的要求，稳步推进海外业务发展，融入国际金融市场之中。

作为中国银行业代理业务的一群从业人员，我们最先感受到国际上反洗钱合规监管方面的压力并积极参与到相关反洗钱合规项目之中。虽然国际上反洗钱合规监管法律条文和相关书籍汗牛充栋，但中文方面的材料却比较稀少。在百度上以"反洗钱"作为关键词搜索，发现都是碎片化的信息和支离破碎的文章以及关于反洗钱培训的广告等，专业的书籍和完整的好文档真的不好找。所幸，在中国金融出版社见到《银行保密法/反洗钱检查手册》和《国际视角：反洗钱渠道研究》两本专业的书籍。2016年11月美国纽约州金融服务局对中国某银行及纽约分行开出2.15亿美元的天价反洗钱合规罚单后，某银行将《银行保密法/反洗钱检查手册》作为业务教材。如果不是特殊原因使然，这样的专业书籍估计会乏人问津。

2018年中国金融出版社准备出版新的《银行保密法/反洗钱检查手册》（2015年版），我们遂萌生以案例和讲故事的方式配合《银行保密法》的出版，以快速传播反洗钱合规文化。

为此，我们挑选了2012年至2017年间、罚款金额在1亿美元以上、具有震慑性的11个典型洗钱合规案例，以监管机构和银行达成的《和解令》公布的时间为序和核心进行详细解读。罗英燕、姜福晓、李拓、王淼、杨慧、于雯、叶小琳、杨志华、刘洁、黄颖、王盛楠、郭芊、韩磊、李紫燕等分别负责了相关篇节的写作和翻译，我对全书篇章结构进行总纂和体例的统一与筹划。在阅读这些案例的过程中，我有些许的认识和体会，在此和读者共勉。

1.关于反洗钱概念的发展及演进

反洗钱概念有一个渐进的过程。从开始反毒品走私交易的洗钱，到打击逃税漏税和金融犯罪以及行贿腐败和反恐融资及金融制裁等，内涵不断丰富、外延不断扩大。反洗钱的概念本身有一个不断发展的过程。

反洗钱作为一个法律概念最早正式出现在1988年12月《联合国反对非法交易麻醉品和精神病药物公约》。该公约把洗钱定义为"为隐瞒或掩饰因制造、贩卖、运输任何麻醉品或精神药物所得非法财产的来源，而将该财产转换或转移"。2000年10月，加拿大皇家骑警和美国海关在加拿大温哥华主办召开了"太平洋周边地区打击反洗钱及金融犯罪会议"，进一步将反洗钱犯罪涉及的非法所得来源从隐瞒毒品犯罪扩大到黑社会性质的组织犯罪、走私犯罪、贪污贿赂犯罪、破坏金融秩序犯罪所得及收益的来源。同时把犯罪收益洗白为合法收入这一模式扩大到：合法资金洗成黑钱用于非法用途，如把银行贷款通过洗钱变成默认在赌场的资金（白钱洗黑）；把一种合法资金洗成另外一种表面也合法的资金，如把公有或共有的资产通过洗钱转移到个人账户达到侵占的目的（洗钱本身就是犯罪过程），把非法收入通过洗钱合法化，如企业把偷漏税款通过洗钱转移到境外（黑钱洗白）。"9·11"以后，打击资助恐怖活动也纳入打击洗钱犯罪的总体框架之中。

本书案例之中，有的因为协助毒品走私交易被罚，有的因为违反金融秩序犯罪被罚，更多的是因为反恐融资和金融制裁不力被罚，反映出反洗钱合规监管的发展变化。

2.美国双线多重的银行监管体系

翻开案例，很多银行因反洗钱被问责和处罚时，往往是多家政府监管机构一起出手进行惩戒，原因是美国实行双线多重的银行监管体系。

由于历史原因，美国的银行监管体制相当复杂。由于银行实行国法银行（指依照联邦法律登记注册的银行）和州法银行（指按照各州法律登记注册的银行，而并非州立银行）并存的双重银行体制，因此法律不仅赋予联邦政府以监管商业银行的职能，而且也授权各州政府行使监管职责。因此，除美国财政部下设的货币监理署（OCC）以外，各州政府均设立了银行监管机构—金融服务局（DFS），形成了联邦和州政府的双线监管体制。OCC和DFS成为美国银行最主要的两个基本监管者。

美国所有国法银行都是联邦储备体系（Federal Reserve System）的成员，而州法银行则可自主选择是否成为联储的成员。选择成为联储成员的被称为州成员银行，否则被称为州非成员银行。2012年，在全美9000多家商业银行中，有3700多家是联储成员银行。美联储对所有成员银行均负有直接的、基本的监管职能。如联储对州法银行申请成为联储成员的，要进行审查，以确定其是否符合联储成员标准，因此联储对于州成员银行来说是基本监管者，除了美联储和州联储银行、财政部货币监理署、各州的金融服务局外，涉及反洗钱合规监管的机构主要包括司法部（DOJ）、联邦存款保险公司（FDIC）、储贷监理署（OTS）、国家信用联盟监督局（NCUA）、海外资产控制办公室（OFAC）、金融犯罪执法网（FinCEN）。

可以说，美国实行的这种双线多重式银行监管体制既是美国联邦制度高度分权所要求的，也是多次出现金融危机以后不断总结经验教训、不断修正监管体制的结果。这种纵横交错的立体监管模式从多个方面监督、控制和调整着银行的经营行为，比较有效地防范和化解了银行领域的风险。然而，在双线多重的监管模式下，即使是一家规模不大的州非成员银行，也要接受至少两家监管机构的监管——州银行管理当局和FDIC。至于像花旗银行这样的大机构，监管者更是来自方方面面，联储、OCC、FDIC、OTS、SEC以及多达50个州的监管部门都对之实施监管。这些机构职能重叠现象严重又不相互协调，存在竞争性监管现象。可以看到，一家银行机构违规，各家监管机构会群起而攻之。

3. 有法可依、重事实和实际行为的、透明的监管

美国反洗钱的内控合规监管不是一来就罚款的，而是会先检查反洗钱的

规章制度是否完善、反洗钱是否嵌入业务流程之中、合规官否能履职，等等。根据检查的具体情况（事实），讨论哪个程序有问题，哪个岗位有问题，哪个流程有问题，为什么会出现问题，最后提出整改意见。整改意见分为参考建议（suggestion）、有益忠告（recommendation）和必须建议（enforcement）三个等级。对屡教不改、屡查屡犯的银行，监管机构才会给出请外聘的独立审计检查机构帮助整改和罚款决定。整改和罚款决定作出后，银行会进一步反馈其意见，并与监管机构磋商达成最后的《和解令》。《和解令》是公开透明的，就挂在监管机构的官网上，任何人都可以阅读、下载。其内容非常翔实，包括违规背景、适用法规、违规事实、整改措施和罚金，监管机构和银行的责任人签字等。有了这份公开透明的《和解令》，既不用听金融机构息事宁人、大事化小片面之词，也不用听媒体的聒噪、夸大其词、唯恐天下不乱的宣扬。

4. 反洗钱合规的重点

风险为本的反洗钱原则就是根据风险状况及程度配置反洗钱资源，要将最多的反洗钱合规资源投入到洗钱风险大的业务领域。在风险为本的反洗钱原则下，金融机构应当审视哪些区域或领域更具洗钱威胁，分析哪些产品或服务类型存在薄弱环节，识别哪些客户洗钱概率更大，要求金融机构根据自身对风险和危害程度的判断，灵活地选择实施与风险程度相应的反洗钱措施，确保以有限的资源实现洗钱危害最小化的目标。根据风险为本的反洗钱原则，目前中资大行反洗钱合规的重点是：区域上在美国的分支机构、业务上跨境支付清算、币种上是美元。

5. 反洗钱合规的三道防线和全员反洗钱合规文化的建设

有成效的反洗钱制度要有"五大支柱"：（1）书面的规章制度；（2）指定的反洗钱合规官；（3）独立的测试；（4）培训；（5）以风险为基础的客户尽职调查。搭建反洗钱合规管理的框架、深刻理解了反洗钱合规的三道防线制度落实和反洗钱合规嵌入业务流程是做好反洗钱合规的第一步。

银行反洗钱合规内控的三道防线体系大致如下：客户经理在将客户录入系统前，一定要按照内控合规的要求，将KYC、CDD和AML工作按步骤一步步落实好后，通过合规官的审查，交由管理层最后批准客户准入。客户经理、主管合规官以及管理层每年有不同层级的网上考试，考试成绩由专门的协会记录在案。第一道防线是客户的准入调查，注重事前的防范。第二道防线是风险与合规，负责合规内控体系的建设、管理、监督检查和评价前台客户与产品部门按照反洗钱合规流程做尽职调查并对模糊不清反洗钱合规进行解读和最终确认等，属于体系建设和事中监控。第三道防线是审计和监管，注重事后的重检。显然最重要的是第一道防线，也就是客户和产品部门。前台和产品部门只要一放松，等于足球比赛中的罚点球，没有球员在拱卫球门了，只靠合规一个守门员，球门很容易被攻破，审计和监管最后就是判定有多少个进球，违了多少规，怎么进行处罚的事。

6. 全面落实银行客户和产品部门反洗钱合规的主体责任

从让我合规到我要合规，就不会出现百密一疏、智者千虑必有一失，而会出现愚者千虑必有一得。做与不做是态度问题，做好与做坏是能力问题。

很多客户管理部门谈合规而色变，互相推诿，甚至希望与合规划清界限，认为合规是合规部门的事情，以为对合规不闻不问，就可以做到免责；以为把合规管理推到别的部门，出了事也可以脱得了干系。其实，这样的想法不免有些掩耳盗铃。客户是客户部门的核心，是客户部门的根本。客户合规出了问题，就是客户出了问题，第一责任人当然是客户部门，并不是想推就能推得掉的。就像父母是孩子的监护人，孩子触犯了法律，父母肯定是第一责任人，没有父母会怪法律部门没有把孩子管好，去找法律部门问责的。搞清了这个关系，就不会再有部门说合规不是客户部门的职责了，他们反而会第一时间把客户的合规管理职责揽过来，充分地做好尽职调查和反洗钱合规管理工作。因为他们清楚地知道，今天的尽职是为了明天的免责。

另外，要落实客户反洗钱合规主体责任，实现从合规是成本到合规是利润的转变。合规不单单是关乎机构声誉风险，而是机构存亡的生死线，必须付出的成本也是效益和盈利。有位汇丰银行的相关专家曾表示，合规审查在实际业务操作中没有给业务造成障碍，反而给该行代理行管理带来了利润收入。因为：第一，进行合规审查时，该行根据风险、互惠信息、重要性等一系列指标，识别出一些高风险且业务量很小的代理行，对其予以关闭，减少了风险的同时也减少了代理行管理维护成本。第二，对于风险较低且盈利较多的客户，该行通过反洗钱合规审查，加强了对客户的了解，进一步挖掘了客户的潜在业务机会，对客户实现了精细化管理，这部分客户盈利提高了近30%，从根本上扭转了合规是成本的管理困境。把反洗钱合规管理落到实处，与业务真正地结合起来，就可以转变成本为盈利。

由此可见，合规管理和业务发展之间并不矛盾，它们从来都是相辅相成的关系，合规管理并不是业务发展的桎梏，而是业务发展的铠甲。

7. 反洗钱合规文化建设至关重要

全员反洗钱合规文化的建设至关重要。在美国监管机构与各家银行的《和解令》中，高频出现的词语是"蓄意""姑息""纵容""隐瞒""欺诈"等，表明有的银行是明知故犯，有的银行是睁一只眼闭一只眼，有的银行是熟视无睹。造成这种情况的原因有的是因为业绩冲动，有的是为了特定的客户群体，有的是因为地缘政治。然而隐藏在背后最深层次的原因却是反洗钱合规文化建设的缺失。巴塞尔商业银行合规指引强调"合规从高层做起"（Compliance starts at the top），强调"高层为合规定调"（Tone from the top），都是从不同角度诠释了自上而下推动和培养良性合规文化的重要性。

合规是机构和个人职业生涯的生命线，全员反洗钱合规文化建设至关重要。监管机构在对机构进行处罚的同时，也有对未尽职个人的处罚，比如进监狱、禁止从事金融机构业务、罚金等，不一而足。可以说，反洗钱合规与个人的职业生涯密切相关。在境外，银行合规官和税务官是两个可能因为没有尽职或隐瞒而被投入监狱的两个岗位。由此可见反洗钱合规文化建设的重要性。譬如，某行马德里分行的例子。如果仅仅是处罚和解，没有人入狱，这些员工可以调回总行或国内重新安排工作，但一旦入狱，其家庭会怎样？出狱后工作如何安排？除了个人面临的困境之外，银行机构也将面临窘境，重新安置这些员工，银行机构将背负"有组织的违法犯罪"的名声；不重新安置这些员工，银行机构有推卸责任之嫌疑，就像过去媒体报道的很多案例，一旦是坏事和不好的事情，就说是"临时工""保安"干的。为生计、为职业生涯、为机构声誉，商业银行必须重视反洗钱、反恐融资和金融制裁合规文化的建设工作。

8. 坚做批发不碰零售的海外发展策略

除中国银行外，其他中资银行的海外业务发展策略只做批发、不碰零售和现金，以免除中资银行海外分支机构反洗钱合规风险的最大隐患，这里的海外不包括香港、澳门和台湾地区。中国银行海外分行因特殊的历史原因和在海外华人中的影响不得不做一些零售和现金业务。事实上，中国银行的海外零售业务也是块"鸡肋"，食之无味、弃之可惜！后来者的其他中资银行发展海外业务时应该慎重对待零售业务。

目前国际大行海外零售业务的收缩和痛苦退出的实践经验表明，在和当地金融机构竞争零售业务的过程中，外资银行没有任何优势可言，也无利可图，有的只是教训。而外资银行在拓展海外批发业务上的收益则是有目共睹的事实。想当年，苏格兰皇家银行吞并ABN AMRO，海外业务发展一时风头无两，更有做大零售业务的雄心。然而，如今的苏格兰皇家银行的主要业务集中在西欧，零售业务只在本土经营。在业务全球化过程中，做得最出色的汇丰银行和花旗银行均开始收缩其海外零售业务，不断撤并网点，出售零售业务。大通银行、美国银行和富国银行的零售业务焦点在美国本土，其海外业务主要是以机构业务和公司业务为主的批发业务，现在看来其策略是成功的。国内某大行要做世界最大的零售银行，境外并购与自设机构并举，在境外大举布点，并将零售业务作为其分支机构的标配，必须有街边的店铺。结果呢？并购的整合步履维艰，一些海外机构的零售业务涉嫌反洗钱正被监管和法院追责。因此，在海外业务发展策略上，一定要坚持做批发业务，绝不碰零售和现金业务。

9. 反洗钱合规必须掌握一个"度"

这里的"度"有两层含义：一是指完成规定动作，而不能像警察那样跟踪调查客户。在反洗钱合规过程中，我们一定要完成所有规定动作，制定各项反洗钱规章制度，并严格执行这些规章制度，把反洗钱合规嵌入业务流程之中。二是指"亲"与"清"的隔离。与客户关系密切，KYC和CDD做得清楚明白，为客户提供解决方案等做到了"亲"，但在"亲"的同时，一定要做到"清"，银行内部关于反洗钱合规政策、大额交易以及当地现金交易报告的具体内容严格与客户隔离开，不能因为维护客户关系而传授客户规避检查的技巧方法等，更不能为了发展业务和完成经营业绩而故意引导客户规避反洗钱检查。很多员工违规都是因为这个"度"没有把握好。

最后，在编写这些案例的过程中，我们也有困惑和不明白的地方，譬如：罚款数字是怎么计算出来的？监管机构和银行是如何达成妥协的？监管执法人员是否有奖金激励措施？如果有，是如何激励的？是否有潜规则，这些潜规则又是如何运作的？

关于罚款的金额，说法不一。有的说是按该业务收益的倍数处罚，有的说是将机构这么多年的利润来个"一勺烩"。还有，大笔的罚金收缴国库，对监管执法人员是否有激励措施？据说，有些监管人员平时比较拮据，一旦办个大案，就会出去度假或购置奢侈品。其具体情况到底是怎样呢？

我们期望更多的有识之士能去挖掘和探索并能分享出来，以促进我国金融业稳健合规地发展。

反洗钱合规永远在路上。反洗钱合规是一个不断变化和深入的过程，其内容和实质会随着社会政治经济科技的发展而不断演变。

囿于知识和视野，书中难免有错漏之处，敬请批评指正。

岳留昌

于北京金融大街

2019年1月

目　录

3. 不认真整改的后果很严重
——渣打银行洗钱案例 / 077

4. 欲盖弥彰搞小动作的后果
——三菱日联银行反洗钱合规案例分析 / 115

引言

美国反洗钱合规监管风暴概述

　　2007—2009 年美国次贷危机引发全球金融海啸，是一个重要分界线，从此以后，美国对涉嫌洗钱或反洗钱、反恐融资和金融制裁履职不力的银行进行了"震慑性"的巨额罚款，"严管重罚"成为美国金融监管的新常态。

美国反洗钱的"严管重罚"新常态

2012年至2017年，因反洗钱合规问题被美国监管机构罚款1亿美元以上的银行有13家（见表1），金额达到176.22亿美元。

2007—2009年美国次贷危机引发全球金融海啸，是一个重要分界线，从此以后，美国对涉嫌洗钱或反洗钱、反恐融资和金融制裁履职不力的银行进行了"震慑性"的巨额罚款，"严管重罚"成为美国金融监管的新常态。

表1 2012—2017年因反洗钱合规问题被美国监管机构罚款1亿美元以上的银行表

日期	金融机构	相关政府部门	总罚款
2012年6月	ING银行（ING Bank N.V）	OFAC、司法部、纽约州检察官	6.19亿美元
2012年12月	汇丰银行（HSBC Holdings Plc/ HSBC Bank USA N.A.）	OFAC、司法部、联储行、金融犯罪执法局、金融服务局	19.2亿美元
2012年12月 2014年8月	渣打银行（Standard Chartered Bank）	OFAC、司法部、联储行、金融犯罪执法局、货币监理署纽约州检察官、金融服务局	3.27亿美元 3.00亿美元
2013年6月 2014年11月	三菱东京日联银行（Bank of Tokyo-Mitsubishi UFJ.Ltd）	金融服务局	2.50亿美元 3.15亿美元
2013年12月	苏格兰皇家银行（Royal Bank of Scotland）	OFAC、联储行、金融服务局	1.00亿美元
2014年1月	大通银行（JPMorgan Chase Bank, N.A.）	司法部、货币监理署、金融犯罪执法局	20.5亿美元

2014 年 6 月	法国巴黎银行（BNP Paribas）	OFAC、司法部、联储行、纽约州检察官、金融服务局	89 亿美元
2015 年 3 月	德国商业银行（Commerzbank AG）	金融服务局、司法部、纽约州检察官、联储行、OFAC	14.5 亿美元
2016 年 8 月	兆丰银行（Mega Bank）	金融服务局	1.80 亿美元
2016 年 11 月	中国农业银行（Agricultural Bank of China）	金融服务局	2.15 亿美元
2016 年 12 月	意大利联合圣保罗银行（Intesa Sanpaolo）	金融服务局	2.35 亿美元
2017 年 1 月	德意志银行（Deutsche Bank）	金融服务局、联储行	4.25 亿美元 4.100 万美元
2017 年 8 月	哈比银行（Habib Bank Limited）	金融服务局	2.25 亿美元

此表会持续扩大延展吗？答案是肯定的。

2018年3月12日，美联储又对中国××银行纽约分行发布《停止和中止经营令》。2018年3月15日，美国财政部宣布对俄罗斯实施新一轮的制裁，制裁黑名单新增加了19个个人和5家实体机构。随着美国反洗钱合规监管力度的不断加大，将会有越来越多的银行卷入，反洗钱、反恐融资和制裁的合规监管成为悬在各大国际金融机构头上的达摩克利斯之剑。

美国反洗钱合规监管的历史演进

1970年，美国国会通过了《货币和对外交易报告法案》，又称《银行保密法》（BSA）。该法案目的是协助国家确定流入、流出美国或存放于金融机构的现金和其他货币工具的来源、数量和变动情况。为达至该目标，该法案要求个人、银行和其他金融机构必须向美国财政部提交识别个人交易行为的报告，并通过保存适当的交易记录来保留文件线索。这些报告和交易记录能够让监管和执法机构对犯罪、逃税和其他违反监管法规的行为进行调查、取证。

《银行保密法》确立了个人、银行和其他金融机构交易记录保存和报告制度的要求。从根本上确立了美国金融机构以提交货币交易报告的形式协助美国政府机构侦查和打击洗钱犯罪。它详细地规定了合规检查的范围、计划和程序、合规核心监管要求（客户身份识别、客户尽职调查、可疑交易报告、现金交易报告等）的具体内容和检查程序、对产品和服务（代理行、账户行、运钞、汇票、贸易融资、私人银行、信托和资产管理等）的扩展检查的内容和程序以及适用于自然人和实体（国外人、政治敏感人物、使领馆、非银行金融机构、专业服务提供者、非政府组织和慈善机构、商业实体、现金密集型行业等）的扩展检查的内容与程序。

1986年的《洗钱控制法案》进一步提升了《银行保密法》的效力。该法案对故意协助洗钱或构造交易而逃避报告义务的个人和金融机构追究刑事责任，来杜绝逃避《银行保密法》要求的行为。

在反洗钱作为一个法律概念正式出现在1988年12月《联合国反对非法交易麻醉品和精神病药物公约》以后，《银行保密法》被通俗地称为美国反洗钱法。它建立了美国反洗钱监管制度基本框架，是美国最重要的、最基础的反洗钱法律。其后美国国会通过所有关于反洗钱方面的法律、法规都是对它的修改和扩充。

1992年《阿农齐奥—怀利反洗钱法案》、2001年《爱国者法案》以及2017年《以制裁反击美国敌人法案》。这些法案不但宣布恐怖融资犯法还提高了原《银行保密法》对在客户身份识别程序上的要求，同时要求金融机构具备尽职调查程序、建立反洗钱项目、加重对洗钱的民事和刑事处罚、将行业制裁名单编纂成法加以固化，还不断更新其反洗钱、反恐融资和制裁的黑名单，如特别指定国民和被阻禁者（SDNs）名单和行业制裁识别（SSIs）名单，以及实施50%规则：SDN名单上的实体或个人拥有50%或以上所有者权益的实体被视为SDN或SSI。

美国反洗钱合规监管风暴的广阔时代背景

近年来美国在全球范围内展开的反洗钱、反恐融资与制裁风暴的背景和渊源，可以追溯到美国政府为应对2008年全球金融危机措施上。

2008年美国次贷危机引发全球金融海啸。为应对危机，美国开始实行量化宽松的货币政策和严监管政策。美联储不断减息和扩大资产负债表向市场提供充足的流动性，《多德—弗兰克法案》加强对银行金融衍生品交易的监管，降低了系统性金融风险和大型金融机构倒闭带来的损害，催生了消费者金融保护局的诞生，消费者金融保护局和美国其他金融监管机构一起进一步强化了反洗钱、反恐融资和金融制裁的监管功能。2015年以后，随着美国经济的复苏，美联储2015年12月7日启动金融危机以来的首次加息，开始了缓慢的货币政策正常化进程，2016年12月、2017年3月、2017年6月、2017年12月加息，并在2017年10月开始缩减资产负债表，特朗普上台后酝酿缩减《多德—弗兰克法案》，意在放松对华尔街的监管，然而美国监管机构的反洗钱、反恐融资和制裁功能并没有随着货币政策的变化而减弱，相反却在特朗普让美国在伟大的民粹主义、贸易保护主义的旗帜下得到进一步固化和增强。

2007年至2009年的金融危机是一个重要分界线，虽然此前美国也有反洗钱、反恐融资和金融制裁的措施和功能，但从来没有像那次金融危机后，在长臂管辖法则的支持下，反洗钱、反恐融资和制裁成为美国挥舞着的大棒和重型武器。

经济上，贸易保护主义抬头，逆全球化浪潮出现。

贸易保护主义抬头和"去全球化"思潮泛起的根本原因就在于全球经济增长的放缓，而金融危机的出现更是引起了人们对全球化和自由贸易的反思。最近二十年来，"全球化""经济自由化"曾经是非常时髦的词汇，人们认为它们给世界经济带来了活力，把它们看作是世界经济未来的不可逆转的趋势。然而在出现金融危机的时候，人们马上就发现了它们的弊端。首先，美国金融危机为什么会波及全世界？这次危机的源头是美国的"次贷危机"，而"次贷危机"最终却通过"次级债"演化成全球金融危机，这其中金融全球化被认为是罪魁祸首。如果没有金融全球化，美国的"次贷危机"就会被局限于美国的范围内，不会波及全球。其次，亚洲金融危机期间国际热钱未受约束的自由流动可以说就是亚洲金融危机的主要原因之一。亚洲金融危机之所以爆发，相关亚洲经济存在一定问题固然是原因之一，但更重要的原因就是规模巨大的国际热钱的自由跨境流动。如果没有后者，许多亚洲经济，尤其是状况较好的经济本来不会受到冲击，比如中国香港、中国台湾和新加坡。再次，"全球化"被认为减少了发达国家的就业机会。在发达国家看来，贸易的存在和扩张被认为挤压了本国同类企业的生存空间，减少了本国在这些行业的就业机会，尤其是这些国家"夕阳行业"的就业机会。而要素的自由流动被认为也有同样的效果。比如，对外投资的扩张导致本国资金流入发展中国家，而这些资金如果投在本国，就会增加本国的生产能力，为本国创造更多的就业机会，这实际上就是对本国就业的一种抑制，而有些对外投资甚至同时导致了产业转移，本来在本国生产的一些产品被转移到了生产成本低廉的发展中国家，劳动力的流动往往也会导致外来劳动力对本国劳动力的替代，等等。最后，"全球化"客观上使发达国家面临更为强烈的低生产成本的发展中国家的竞争和产业相应的转移，从而使各国宏观经济政策的效果大打折扣。目前世界各国在宏观调控中主要采取需求管理政策，也就是通过财政政策或货币政策来调节总需求。但在全球化的情况下，一个国家辛辛苦苦创造出来的总需求却可能是对外国产品的总需求，从而使得本国宏观经济政策的效果减小。比如说，如果政府减税，老百姓的消费需求就可能增加，但老百姓消费的可能是本国产品也可能是外国产品，如果老百姓买的外国货更多，那实际上是在自己花钱帮外国政府，这是哪个政府都不愿意看到的结果。如果世界经济运行良好，没有金融危机，现有的制度安排就不会受到质疑，贸易保护主义也就不会抬头。在出现金融危机的情况下，各国政府为了自身的利益，就不得不对现存的各种现象重新思考，于是贸易自由主义就受到人们的怀疑，贸易保护主义就会抬头。

政治"娱乐化"，民粹主义、分裂化倾向出现。

2010年6月，澳大利亚总理陆克文的工党党魁位置被副党魁吉拉德发动党团投票式"党内政变"，吉拉德成为工党党魁和澳大利亚总理，随后吉拉德又被陆克文搞掉，重新夺回党魁和总理宝座，2013年救生员出身的阿博特当选自由党党魁和总理，刚两年时间就被特恩布尔利用党团投票式的政变拿下。美国政府更是因为财政赤字，面临经常性关门的风险，奥巴马医改半途而废，希拉里与特朗普总统大选打得一塌糊涂、不可开交，最终，美国总统大选选上一个最不靠谱的"推特"总统——特朗普，他要让美国再次伟大；英国首相卡梅伦"玩"脱欧公投游戏，结果真的把英国"公投"出了欧洲，甩下烂摊子挥挥手走人，欧盟虽然面临前所未有的解体危机，更不放弃对英国的碾压。面对欧盟咄咄逼人态势，英国新任首相特蕾莎·梅还是启动脱欧程序；韩国总统朴槿惠的"闺蜜门"让这个"嫁给韩国的女人"黯然失色，为韩国民众唾弃，最终国会弹劾后，锒铛入狱；意大利总理伦奇发起修宪公投，结果公投高票否决伦奇的修宪决定，伦奇辞职，反欧元民粹党派五星运动支持率最高，意大利政局风雨飘摇，欧盟面临被进一步打击的危险。从澳洲政府总理走马灯般的更迭，到"推特治国"的特朗普、英国公投脱欧、朴槿惠闺蜜门、伦奇修宪等一系列的黑天鹅事件显示出政治正在被娱乐化，也昭示民粹主义抬头，分裂化的迹象。特朗普的一系列政策措施都深深打上贸易保护主义的烙印，美墨边境的墙（wall）、美国减税政策、重回制造大国以及对中国重启301条款的贸易调查等，英国脱欧，欧盟一体化进程受阻就是欧洲民粹主义抬头和分裂化倾向。

国际金融格局悄然改变，金融乱象纷呈。

经济与政治的变化映射在国际金融体系上，使得国际金融格局悄然改变。国际金融的新趋势、新现象与新科技重叠交织，美国加息、美联储缩表与欧洲、日本等负利率和量化宽松货币政策相互纠结缠绕，国际金融乱象纷呈。

为对应2008年美国次贷危机引发的金融海啸，美联储在2007年9月至2008年12月接连降息10次，将联邦基准利率由5.25%降至0.25%的"零利率"水平。在利率措施无计可施之时，美联储在2009—2014年先后推出了三轮大规模货币量化宽松（QE），通过购买美国国债、按揭支持证券（MBS）和政府机构债券形式，扩张资产负债表，履行作为金融市场最后贷款人的角色，缓解市场危机，导致资产负债表从危机前的不到1万亿美元，扩大到4.5万亿美元。在美联储史无前例的货币量化宽松之下，美国长期利率得以被快速地降低，美国经济逐渐实现了复苏，失业率由危机时10%的峰值降至目前的4.5%，通胀水平也逐渐接近美联储的目标值2%。随着美国经济复苏的推进，2015年12月美联储实施了危机后的首次加息25个基点（BPS），美国货币政策开始反转。继2016年12月加息25个基点后，2017年3月、6月、12月美元分别加息25个基点，全年加息75个基点。同时，美联储在2017年9月的议息会议上宣布2018年还将加息3~4次。与此同时，美联储已开启渐进式缩表进程。2017年10月，美联储宣布了缩减资产负债表计划，2017年将缩表300亿美元，2018年为4 200亿美元。美元加息和美联储缩表意味着美联储要从市场抽出流动性，意味着市场存在大量美元回流美国本土的预期，必然会带来全球流动性紧缩，造成新兴国家投资减少、资产价格下跌、汇率下跌。

反应慢半拍的欧洲、日本等国却在美元开始加息的时候开始大规模的量化宽松和负利率的货币政策，2015年以欧洲央行和日本央行为代表，瑞典、丹麦、瑞士也纷纷调降了基准利率至负利率。负利率直接导致全球主要发达经济体国债收益率下降，甚至进入负利率区间。根据惠普评级数据，截至2016年6月27日，全球负利率资产规模达到11.7万亿美元。另据摩根大通统计，截至2016年6月10日，在摩根大通国债指数中，收益率为负的国债为8.3万亿美元，在整个指数中占31%。负利率为金融机构资产配置带来了挑战，整个金融市场面临着"资产荒"。

一方面是资金回流美国，市场出现流动性问题，另一方面却是大量的负利率资产，整个金融市场面临资产荒。国际金融市场乱象纷呈。

欧洲银行收缩，亚洲银行扩张，美资银行在跨境投资银行领域独领风骚。2016年初，英国前五家大银行，即汇丰银行、巴克莱银行、渣打银行、劳里德银行、苏格兰皇家银行都在纷纷出售亚洲、非洲、南美和中东的机构和资产，收缩其业务范围和经营区域，表现在全球机构数目减少、收缩资产负债表，即收缩经营规模、裁员降薪、海外利润对集团的盈利贡献度下降等方面。亚洲方面以中国银行业的崛起为代表的亚洲大银行在全球兼并和设立分支机构和营业网点，在全球机构的数目、覆盖的范围、资产规模和海外利润的贡献度持续和爆发式的增长，无论资产规模、利润、净资产、人员、机构数目等为标准，中国四大银行都在世界10大银行之列。跨国性投资银行业务几乎全部集中到了美资银行手中。曾经想在投资银行领域分一杯羹的英国巴克莱银行、德国德意志银行、瑞士联合银行都在市场屡屡碰壁，不得不回到商业银行和财富管理上来。据Dealogic统计发布的数据，2017年全球前五大投资银行悉数为美资银行，JP摩根、高盛、美银美林、摩根士丹利和花旗投资无论是业务规模，还是收入和利润，均稳居前五。

金融科技（Fintech）创新进一步加剧金融乱象。全球金融游戏规则正在改变，谁拥有了领先的金融科技，谁就会将在未来的竞争中占有先机。大数据分析（big data analytics）、区块链（block chain technology）、分布式账本技术（mutual distributed ledger）、人工智能（AI）、云计算（cloud computing）、支付清算系统（payment and transaction system）、网络安全技术（cyber security）、直接借贷系统（Peer to Peer lending）等，金融与科技的深度融合，冲击着传统金融业。任何科技都是中性的，可以更好、也可以更坏。譬如区块链是比特币的底层技术，信息技术专家们把区块链称为创造信任的机器，在区块链的系统中，参与者无须了解其他人的背景、也不需要借助任何第三方的担保或增信，就可以直接交易，成本低、方便快捷等，但在过去一段比特币大火的日子里，交易比特币一度成为洗钱的新方式和通道。另外据参考资料说，在全球的比特币炒家中，来自中国大陆的占到85%，而八成的比特币资源掌握在5%的大炒家手上。很多人渴望在比特币和区块链中攫取一笔新时代的"红利"，投资机会的金融衍生化似乎让每一个人都有机会分享科技变革的红利，但事实上，它更多的属于为投机者设置的圈套。

曝光的巴拿马文件和瑞士银行保密制度标志着反洗钱合规达到了新的高度和标准。

巴拿马文件揭开国际离岸中心洗钱和避税的黑幕。2016年6月，美国披露的巴拿马开户文件拉开了全球反对利用离岸中心避税和洗钱的序幕，在这出剧中，许多国家政要纷纷出场，其中冰岛总理因隐藏海外资产被迫辞职；英国首相卡梅伦被曝出以离岸基金的方式蓄意隐瞒海外资产；2017年7月，巴基斯坦总理谢里夫也因为家族海外资产案受到调查而辞职。从合规和反洗钱角度讲，巴拿马文件几乎涵盖了所有高风险洗钱因素——比如，巴拿马本身就是高风险司法管辖区，一度还被国际金融行动特别工作组（FATF）列入了洗钱"灰名单"。除此之外，透明度问题、政要人物（PEP）、最终受益人（UBO）、离岸资产、空壳公司、逃避税等因素哪一个都没落下。

瑞士银行保密体系终结。一直以来，瑞士的银行业以严格的保密制度著称于世，瑞士银行体系向来以保护隐私拒绝透露客户信息，也因此在全球金融体系中占据了重要位置。依仗这一利器，瑞士成为了世界上最大的离岸金融中心。

但在美国的强横面前，中立、高傲的瑞士银行不得不低下高贵的头颅，臣服于美国的长臂管辖法则之下，2014年5月7日，瑞士政府发表声明，宣布支持与经济合作与发展组织（OECD）国家签署《实施银行间自动交换信息标准》（AEOI）。与瑞士一起签署宣言的还包括其他经合组织国家、G20成员国以及开曼群岛和泽西岛等离岸中心。

这份在巴黎经合组织签署的宣言，要求各国收集外国人的银行账户、公司的实益拥有权等信息，并自动与其他国家分享。瑞士政府表示，宣言的签署显示了瑞士打击逃税行为和税务欺诈的决心。同时瑞士银行家协会表示，瑞士的银行愿意与其他国家交换信息，只要信息与税收有关。此次宣言的签署，将宣告瑞士银行保密制度的终结。

综上所述，全球政治经济金融格局的新趋势和新变化，民粹主义抬头、贸易保护主义甚嚣尘上、逆全球化浪潮兴起、国际金融发展的新趋势、新变化与金融科技创新相互交织，国际金融乱象纷呈大的背景下，为维护金融机构系统的稳定，防止金融危机对民众的影响，打击国际恐怖组织、地区和国家、打击漏税、避税等和金融犯罪等展示美国促使各国政府，尤其是美国政府对反洗钱、反恐融资和制裁合规标准不断提高，使得国际金融监管日趋严苛，国际金融机构面临的反洗钱合规压力空前。

中资银行面临美国反洗钱合规压力空前

目前，中资大行面临国际上尤其是美国的反洗钱的压力却是空前的。

先出一道多项选择题：

2013年前中资银行很少因为反洗钱合规被各国金融监管机构罚款的原因如下：

A.中资银行反洗钱合规工作比汇丰银行、大通银行等国际大行做得好

B.2013年前，中资银行对全球金融系统重要性的影响有限

C.2013年前，中资银行的海外规模和影响有限

D.2013年前，国际监管机构无暇顾及中资银行

显然，2013年以前，中资银行还不是国际监管机构处罚对象，并不是中资银行的反洗钱合规工作做得好或各国监管机构无暇顾及。而是因为中资银行在全球金融系统的影响力不够，其国际业务、海外业务的规模小，还未引起各国监管机构的重视。

为防止2008年美国雷曼兄弟倒闭导致金融危机这一类似情况的发生，金融稳定委员会（Financial Stability Board，FSB）在2011年7月21日圈定了28家具有"全球系统重要性的银行"并建议对其实施1%~2.5%的附加资本要求，在特定的条件下，最具系统重要性的银行可能面临最高3.5%的附加资本。当时，中资四大银行中只有国际化程度较高的中国银行成为全球系统重要性银行。而且只是入门级即第一档（1%附加资本要求）。

直到2年后，中资其他三大银行才陆续成为去全球系统重要性银行，2013年中国工商银行、2014年中国农业银行、2015年中国建设银行成为全球系统重要性银行。而且在刚加入时，中资银行在系统重要性5档榜单中都仅仅是入门级的第一档序列之内（5档全球系统重要性榜单和酒店的5星级宾馆分类相似，1档入门，5档最高，只不过酒店是按豪华程度和服务安排的舒服度来定义的，全球系统重要性榜单是按规模和复杂性来定义的。银行全球系统重要性评估指标包括：调整后的表内外资产余额、金融机构间资产、金融机构间负债、发行证券和其他融资工具、通过支付系统或代理行结算的支付额、托管资产、有价证券承销额、场外衍生产品名义本金、交易类和可供出售证券、跨境债权、跨境负债等）。

然而，到了2017年11月，金融稳定理事会（FSB）更新了银行名单时，除中国农业银行还在入门级第一档序列之内，中国工商银行、中国建设银行和中国银行均进入了第二档，这意味着中资银行对全球金融系统重要性的影响在进一步加大，也意味着中国作为世界第二大经济体在全球金融系统中重要性的增长。今非昔比，原来不入各国监管者法眼的中资银行，已经成为各国监管者密切监控的对象。

表 2　2016 年和 2017 年全球系统重要性银行名单

	2016 年全球系统重要性银行名单	2017 年全球系统重要性银行名单
5（3.5%）		
4（2.5%）	花旗银行 摩根大通银行	摩根大通银行
3（2.0%）	美国银行 法国巴黎银行 德意志银行 汇丰银行	美国银行 花旗银行 德意志银行 汇丰银行
	巴克莱银行 瑞士信贷银行 高盛 中国工商银行 东京三菱日联银行 富国银行	中国银行 巴克莱银行 法国巴黎银行 中国建设银行 高盛 中国工商银行 东京三菱日联银行 富国银行
1（1.0%）	中国农业银行 中国银行 纽约梅隆银行 中国建设银行 法国人民储蓄银行 法国农业信贷银行 荷兰国际银行 瑞穗银行 摩根士丹利 北欧银行 苏格兰皇家银行 桑坦德银行 法国兴业银行 渣打银行 美国道富银行 三井住友银行 瑞士联合银行 意大利联合信贷银行	中国农业银行 纽约梅隆银行 瑞士信贷银行 法国农业信贷银行 荷兰国际银行 瑞穗银行 摩根士丹利 北欧银行 加拿大皇家银行 苏格兰皇家银行 桑坦德银行 法国兴业银行 渣打银行 美国道富银行 三井住友银行 瑞士联合银行 意大利联合信贷银行

　　2013年以前，四大银行中除国际化程度较高的中国银行海外业务初具规模外，其他三家银行海外业务规模和影响有限。2013年以后，除中国银行和农业银行保持自设分支机构策略外，中国工商银行和中国建设银行则实施了购并与自设并举的大规模扩张的海外发展战略，到2016年底海外扩张战略初见成效，全球网络布局基本完成。中资四大银行的海外资产和利润从2011年的3.9万亿元和409亿元人民币增长到2017年的10.2万亿元和910亿元人民币，中资银行的海

外资产、海外盈利、海外分支机构数目、海外覆盖国家和地区和海外员工的数量达到各国监管不容忽视的程度。

表3　四大银行海外机构布局比较

机构	各级机构总数		覆盖国家和地区		海外员工人数	
	2011年	2017年	2011年	2017年	2011年	2017年
中国银行	586	545	35	53	21 212	22 927
工商银行	239	419	33	45	5 135	15 021
建设银行	64	214	13	29	2 584	6 336
农业银行	10	23	8	17	334	812

表4　四大银行海外资产和盈利比较　　　　　单位：亿元人民币

机构	海外资产		海外利润	
	2011年	2017年	2011年	2017年
中国银行	25 742	54 451	292	551
工商银行	7 893	23 333	87	255
建设银行	4 432	17 260	21	72
农业银行	1 247	7 952	9	33

注：数据来源于四大银行的年报。

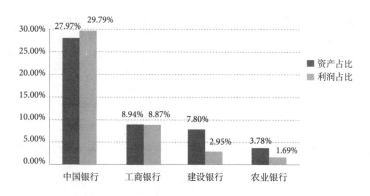

图1　四大银行海外资产利润集团占比比较（2017年末）

　　正是在这样的背景下，中资银行面临的国际监管压力空前。2015年6月，中国银行米兰分行因涉嫌洗钱遭意大利检察院控告，并于2017年2月达成和解。中行为此支付了60万欧元罚款，4名员工因洗钱罪获刑2年，缓期执行。2016年2月，中国工商银行西班牙马德里分行因涉嫌洗钱被当地警方调查，6名员工被临时羁押，案件还在审理中。2016年11月，农行纽约分行因违反该州反洗钱法及掩盖可疑金融交易，被美国纽约州金融服务局处以2.15亿美元罚款。2018年2月，建行约翰内斯堡分行未能遵守南非的《金融情报中心法案（2001年第38号法）》（Financial Intelligence Centre Act，FIC法案），在反洗钱、反恐融资和制裁的控制措施存在弱点而被南非央行罚款7 500万兰特。南非央行还特别指出，这一行政处罚并不是因为发现CCB参与了洗钱或恐怖融资交易，而是因为该行在这方面的控制措施上存在弱点。2018年3月美联储又对中国工商银行纽约分行发出了《停止和中止经营令》。

　　中国四大行境外均已因反洗钱、反恐融资和金融制裁问题受到监管处罚，以美国为首的国际反洗钱、反恐融资和金融制裁的监管风暴并没有减弱的趋势，未来的监管处罚将会更严苛，甚至会出现因合规反洗钱不过关而像巴基斯坦哈比银行那样被迫退出美国市场的情况，中资大行的海外经营面临国际反洗钱合规监管尤其是美国的监管的压力是空前的。

美国反洗钱监管案例

从此以后，美国对涉嫌洗钱或反洗钱、反恐融资和金融制裁履职不力的银行进行了"震慑性"的巨额罚款，"严管重罚"成为美国金融监管的新常态。

1.

制裁国家的业务碰不得
——荷兰安智银行洗钱案例

　　2012年6月13日，荷兰安智银行（ING BANK）宣布，将向美国财政部支付6.19亿美元的创纪录罚款，原因是美国指控该行触犯了美国外国资产控制办公室（OFAC）的法规，此事主要与该行在古巴的运营有关。此外，荷兰安智银行还被控触犯了限制与伊朗、缅甸、苏丹和利比亚进行交易的法规。6.19亿美元的罚款创下了当时OFAC制裁历史上开出罚单的最高纪录。

荷兰安智银行概述

　　荷兰安智银行全称为Internationale Nederlanden Groep N.V.，简称ING，属于控股集团，是由NMB Postbank groep NV（荷兰邮政银行集团）与荷兰最大的保险公司Nationale-Nederlanden NV（荷兰国民人寿保险公司）于1991年合并而成。

　　成立之后，该集团开展了一系列的并购活动。1995年，集团收购了英国商人银行Baring Brothers& Co Ltd的大部分业务、资产和负债，并将其转移到ING Bank名下。1997年，集团将ING Bank 的国际批发和投资银行业务转移至ING Barings名下。

　　1998年1月，集团收购了比利时第三大私有商业银行——Banque Bruxelle Lambert（BBL）。同年，为进入德国的直销银行市场收购法兰克福的ADD银行49%的股权；同年9月，又收购了德国第六大商人银行——BHF-BANK的大量股票，自1999年9月，集团控股BHK-BANK达97.1%（后于2004年卖出）；同年，在美国收购联合生命保险公司，以拓展在美国的保险业务。

　　2008年金融危机发生之后，集团与荷兰政府和欧盟达成协议，承诺对集团进行拆分，重新回归基本的银行业务，对旗下的保险、资产管理、财富管理、房地产投资、融资租赁等非银行业务，及部分的非核心银行业务进行出售或者IPO：2009年12月29日，集团将所持有的太平洋安泰50%的股权正式转让给建行，后改名为建信人寿；2013年，集团在北美的保险业务以Voya的名义进行IPO；2014年，集团在欧洲和日本的保险业务以NN的名义进行IPO；2016年4月，集团完成最后一笔对荷兰国民人寿保险公司价值14亿欧元的减持，成功转型并重新定位成为一家领先的欧洲银行。

荷兰安智银行秉承前瞻性思维战略（Think Forward Strategy），致力于通过让客户在生活和业务中领先一步的方式支持社会可持续发展。安智银行在集团中主营银行业务，大致分为零售银行和批发银行两个板块。

零售银行——为个人客户、中小企业客户和中型公司客户提供产品和服务，截至2015年底拥有超过3 400万客户，按照市场区分为领先市场（Market Leaders），挑战者市场（Challengercountries）和发展市场（Growth Markets）。安智银行在零售银行领域追求电子渠道优先的策略，辅以咨询服务，以及全渠道接触和分销策略，在大多市场均提供全套零售银行产品及服务，涵盖支付、储蓄、投资、担保及无担保贷款等。其中领先市场包括荷兰、比利时和卢森堡；挑战者市场包括澳大利亚、奥地利、捷克、法国、德国、意大利和西班牙，以较强的存款吸纳能力配合低成本的电子渠道分销；发展市场指的是处于发展中的经济体，对安智银行意味着争取可持续的市场份额的良好机遇，包括波兰、罗马尼亚、土耳其，以及安智集团在北京银行和泰国的TMB银行持有的股份，以及在印度Kotak Mahindra Bank的投资。

批发银行——安智银行的批发银行网络覆盖欧洲、亚洲和美洲共40多个国家，为公司客户、跨国企业、金融机构、政府和多边组织等提供行业贷款、一般贷款、交易服务、金融市场等产品和服务。

案件回顾

2012年6月12日，美国财政部下设的外国资产控制办公室（OFAC）宣布与荷兰ING银行达成了6.19亿美元的和解协议，以此作为对荷兰ING银行违反美国相关制裁法令的处罚。这笔处罚金额是OFAC当时开出的所有类型罚单中最大的一笔。OFAC查明，自2002年至2007年，ING银行采用对相关信息进行人为操纵和删减的方式，使用美国境内的第三方银行，处理了超过20 000笔金融和贸易交易，违反了美国对古巴、伊朗、缅甸、苏丹以及利比亚等国家的制裁法令。

ING银行上述违规交易的总金额高达16亿美元，涉及ING银行批发金融业务部的多家分支机构。但是该行在美国的保险或银行业务并没有成为此次调查的对象。从20世纪90年代开始，经ING银行的高级管理层指示，该行库拉索分行（Curacao）的员工开始在发往美国的付款信息中有意去掉古巴的相关信息，从而防止美国的代理行发现并阻止这些交易。而且，ING银行在法国、比利时、荷兰的分支机构也使用了此种操作方式。此外，ING银行的法国分行向古巴的金融机构提供虚假印章供他们在处理旅行支票时使用。同时，OFAC还发现ING银行违反了对伊朗等相关国家的制裁法令。

1994年8月，ING银行成立了荷兰加勒比银行（NCB），这是一家与古巴的合资银行。ING银行的批发业务部（ING批发业务部）也在哈瓦那成立了代表处（ING哈瓦那）。ING批发业务部设在库拉索（Curacao，一座位于加勒比海的岛，属于荷兰王国的自治领土）的分行（ING Curacao）代表NCB和ING哈瓦那处理所有的付款指令，并提供支持服务。

ING哈瓦那和NCB制作的付款处理操作手册指示员工对在付款明细上涉及与古巴相关的人名或公司要给与特别关注，从而防止被无关联的美国银行没收款项。ING Curacao高级管理层经常通过邮件或口头方式提醒员工在付款指示中不要提及古巴。对于不遵从上述指示的员工，将会受到口头或者书面批评，甚至是解雇。NCB对于那些使用美元支付给NCB账户的客户也会提供相似的指令。

从1998年开始，ING Curacao使用一套标准流程来筛查与古巴相关的付款信息，这些汇款将可能被美国阻止。如果筛查到与古巴相关的信息，ING Curacao、ING哈瓦那和NCB有时会修改这一信息——在向美国代理行发出汇款指令前删除或者掩饰相关信息，这样，美国代理行就不会发现相关交易涉及被禁止的古巴利益。ING Curacao的单证贸易融资部门也制定了一套标准程序，要求付款行和客户只提及ING Curacao的相关交易参考号而不用提及古巴受益人的名字。在高管的授意下，ING Curacao的员工使用代码来描述古巴相关交易，这些交易信息被发送到ING批发业务部的纽约代表处。

从2001年开始，ING Curacao不断使用MT202银行间头寸调拨方式向美国代理行发送与古巴相关的交易信息，这样就不必再包含发起人或受益人等与古巴相关的交易方信息。在多个场合，当美国代理行成功拦截了与古巴相关的付款后，ING Bank的员工，包括管理层和其合规部门的律师，会作出虚假陈述，告诉美国代理行，ING Curacao本来是打算使用另外一个币种汇款，从而试图收回（被拦截的）款项。

2004年，在得知上述行为后不久，ING批发业务部的一个员工写了一封邮件，最终到了ING集团的法律部。其中写道：美国政府对几个国家实施制裁……我们不能与这些国家的机构进行任何以美元计价的收付款交易，因为所有的美元交易都要通过曼哈顿来进行清算，这样就会受美国司法管辖……如果不能遵守这些限制，将会违反美国法律。然而，ING集团法律部的一名律师并不接受这一观点，他回复道：我们与古巴做交易已经有很多年了，我非常确信我们知道怎么做来避免罚款……因此不用担心，今后有什么疑虑可以直接写给我，这样我们就可以在影响整体业务之前好好沟通。

ING批发业务部的法国分行（ING FRANCE）还为一家古巴银行提供了美元旅行支票结算服务。这项服务使得这家古巴银行可以向ING FRANCE发送没有背书印章的美元旅行支票，收到这些支票后，ING FRANCE将使用自己的背书印章为支票做背书。2000年3月和6月，这家古巴银行询问如何制造ING FRANCE的背书印章来供自己用于古巴的旅行支票。ING FRANCE的一名部门负责人授权这家古巴银行自己制造并使用一枚背书印章。这家古巴银行在ING FRANCE的一名高级经理和其他人员的帮助下制造了这枚印章。印章上面没有古巴或古巴银行的信息，这样古巴的介入就不明显。2004年8月，ING FRANCE使用相似流程为另一家古巴银行办理了旅行支票服务，并为这家银行签发了一枚新印章。尽管在2003年和2005年，ING FRANCE的付款部门审计报告提出了这种允许一家古巴银行使用ING FRANCE的背书印章的做法有问题，但并无迹象表明ING FRANCE为此采取了行动，这种行为至少直到2006年才停止。

ING批发业务部的荷兰分行（ING Netherlands）在发送美元SWIFT信息时谨慎地不加入美国制裁国家相关信息，是因为他们认为只有这样做，才能避免被美国代理行根据OFAC的政策对汇款进行拦截。ING Netherlands设在鹿特丹的贸易和商品融资部（TCF Rotterdam）保留了为Curef Metal Processing B.V.和Nickel Refining and Trading B.V.开设的账户，这两家公司都在对古巴制裁的SDN名单上。从1994年到2006年，TCF Rotterdam的员工使用一个暂记账户以及另外不在SDN名单上的两家客户来为上述两家SDN客户提供服务。在TCF Rotterdam

管理层知晓的情况下，其中一家非SDN客户被当作"一家特殊目的前台办公室"来为Curef提供交易服务。TCF Rotterdam的一位员工写到，这一安排属于"高度机密"。这种付款方式是按照TCF Rotterdam后台部门的操作指示来进行的，目的是避免被美国代理行拦截汇款。而且，ING Bank法律部门、TCF Rotterdam的风险管理部门以及相关的信贷委员会都明显知悉这种做法。

2003年11月，伊朗的Bank Tejarat代表伊朗航空开出了一笔155万美元的信用证，用来从一家罗马尼亚贸易公司购买一台飞机发动机。信用证要求"一份原产地证明表明该发动机是美国制造"并注明"飞机发动机经过德国到伊朗的梅赫拉巴德机场"。

2003年11月，这家罗马尼亚贸易公司联系ING批发业务部在罗马尼亚的分行（ING Romania），希望将信用证转让给该公司的"美国交易伙伴"。随后，Bank Tejarat对信用证进行了修改，由该贸易公司转让给其美国供货商；同时修改了对货物的描述以模糊其原产地；将货物最终目的地从伊朗修改为德国，并去掉了原产地证明的要求以及所有涉及伊朗的表述。Bank Tejarat所做的修改取得了效果——去掉了所有对伊朗的描述并模糊货物的原产地来自美国。2004年2月，ING Romania转让该信用证给美国出口商，金额为120.5万美元。

2004年3月，一家美国银行在索偿函中发现了上述信用证的一个不符点并告知ING Romania拒付。信用证通知行联系了ING批发业务部在阿姆斯特丹的分行来帮助解决这一拒付问题。此后，索偿行要求提供"开证行的详细信息"。ING批发业务部阿姆斯特丹分行的一名员工就此事通知另一名员工，"对通知行的付款延误只是因为他们写错了信用证号码，并无其他原因。对整个交易结构，索偿行本来不应该有不同意见。我认为美国的银行知道游戏规则"。ING Romania的一名员工单独告知了通知行该信用证与Bank Tejarat相关，通知行将这一信息告知了OFAC。

发现上述违规事实后，在荷兰央行的指导下，ING BANK立即采取行动，通过全面的全球性措施进行补救。这些措施包括在所有ING BANK的业务单元执行一套统一的针对制裁国家的相关政策，以及制定针对美国原产货物向制裁国家再出口的合规方案；在ING BANK的内部进行了广泛的针对制裁的培训；采用新的业务软件系统检查ING BANK的全球机构的国际汇款和客户信息库；不再从事与古巴、伊朗、缅甸、朝鲜、苏丹和叙利亚相关的任何币种的交易；

关闭了哈瓦那办事处；下发了一套新的政策指引，加强现有业务的透明度并强调了ING BANK在汇款和贸易融资业务的标准和透明度。

案件的影响及教训

美国OFAC在2012年对荷兰ING BANK开出的6.19亿美元的罚单，是当时OFAC开出的各种类型罚单中金额最大的一笔。

ING BANK在2002年至2007年，使用删除相关受制裁方信息、设立空壳公司以及其他欺骗手段等有意识的人为操纵行为，使用在美国的第三方银行机构，经办了超过2万笔的汇款和贸易融资等业务，违反了美国对古巴、伊朗、缅甸、苏丹等国家的制裁法令。在此期间，为完成交易，ING BANK使用了其多家分支机构，涉案金额高达16亿美元。

值得注意的是，ING BANK在美国的分支机构并没有卷入本案，也没有成为被调查对象。

通过本案，我们应该体会到，即使一家银行的纽约分支机构没有卷入违规行为，但只要交易违反美国相关制裁规定并且使用了在美国的银行机构，就会受美国司法管辖，都会面临美国监管当局的处罚。因此，不能心存侥幸，受制裁国家的业务碰不得。同时，从本案中我们也应该注意加强自身的合规建设，防患于未然。主要包括以下几点：

（1）对受制裁国家（包括联合国、美国、欧盟等发布的制裁名单）的相关业务要制定明确的、全行统一的业务政策和指引，受制裁业务碰不得；

（2）在执行层面和技术手段上加强投入，比如开发（引进）先进的反洗钱系统，保证将全行的统一政策落到实处；

（3）加强对员工的反洗钱合规培训，使"合规办业务"的思想深入人心。

附录：

《和解令》英文原文

MUL-565595

SETTLEMENT AGREEMENT

This Settlement Agreement (the "Agreement") is made by and between the U.S. Department of the Treasury's Office of Foreign Assets Control and ING Bank, N.V.

I. PARTIES

1. The Office of Foreign Assets Control ("OFAC") of the U.S. Department of the Treasury administers and enforces economic sanctions against targeted foreign countries, regimes, terrorists, international narcotics traffickers, and persons engaged in activities related to the proliferation of weapons of mass destruction, among others. OFAC acts under Presidential national emergency authorities, as well as authority granted by specific legislation, to impose controls on transactions and freeze assets under U.S. jurisdiction.

2. ING Bank, N.V. and its predecessor banks (collectively, "ING Bank") is a financial institution registered and organized under the laws of The Netherlands. The Netherlands' De Nederlandsche Bank N.V. ("DNB") is ING Bank's primary regulator.

II. FACTUAL STATEMENT

3. In August 1994, ING Bank opened the Netherlands Caribbean Bank N.V. ("NCB"), a joint venture with Cuba. The Wholesale Banking Division of ING Bank ("ING Wholesale Banking") also opened a representative office in Havana ("ING Havana"). ING Wholesale Banking's branch in Curacao ("ING Curacao") processed all payment instructions on behalf of, and performed support functions for, NCB and ING Havana.

4. Payment processing manuals developed at ING Havana and NCB instructed employees to give special attention to payment details for any name or company related to Cuba in order to avoid confiscation by unaffiliated U.S. banks. Senior management within ING Curacao, with the knowledge of ING Groep Compliance and Legal, regularly reminded ING Curacao staff, by email and verbally, to avoid Cuba references in payment instructions. Staff members who failed to comply with the instructions were subject to oral reprimands, warning letters, or termination. NCB also provided similar instructions to its customers on sending U.S. dollar ("USD") payments (which would have transited the United States) to their NCB accounts, directing the customers to: (i) reference NCB, and not the customer, as the beneficiary, (ii) make reference to the customer's name or account number elsewhere in the same message and (iii) refrain from making any references to Cuba.

5. Beginning in 1998, ING Curacao employed a standard practice of screening information on payment instructions for Cuba-related references that might have resulted in wires becoming blocked in the United States. If the filter identified a reference to Cuba, ING Curacao, NCB, or ING Havana sometimes would modify the message to eliminate or camouflage the Cuban reference

or other information that caused the "hit" before sending the payment to unaffiliated U.S. banks without references that would have caused U.S. financial institutions to identify transactions as involving a blocked Cuban interest. ING Curacao's Documentary Trade Department also instituted a standard practice of sending settlement instructions to paying banks and clients requesting they mention only an ING Curacao reference number and not the names of the Cuban beneficiaries. At the instruction of senior management, ING Curacao employees used coded references to describe Cuba-related information that was sent to, or accessible by, ING Wholesale Bank's representative office in New York.

6. Beginning in 2001, ING Curacao increasingly used MT 202 cover payments to send Cuba-related payments to unaffiliated U.S. banks, which would not have to include originator or beneficiary information related to Cuban parties. For serial payments, up until the beginning of 2003, NCB populated field 50 of the outgoing SWIFT MT 103 message with its own name or Bank Identifier Code. Beginning in the second quarter of 2003, NCB populated field 50 with its customer's name, but omitted address information. ING Curacao also included its customer's name, but no address information, in field 50 of outgoing SWIFT messages. Additionally, while in 2004 the use of International Bank Account Number ("IBAN") codes in field 50 of MT 103 payment messages was instituted across ING Bank, outgoing payments for non-Cuban customers of ING Curacao also included the customers' names and addresses, whereas payments for Cuban customers of ING Curacao contained only the customers' names and the IB AN. On multiple occasions when unaffiliated U.S. institutions successfully interdicted Cuba-related payments, ING Bank personnel, including management and a lawyer in ING Legal and Compliance, falsely stated to the U.S. institution that ING Curacao had intended to make the payment in another currency in an attempt to recover the funds.

7. In 2004, shortly after learning of this conduct, an employee in ING Wholesale Banking wrote in an email that ultimately reached ING's Groep Legal Department, in part:

There are several countries which are subject to sanctions by the US government... We

must not carry out any transactions involving payments to or from entities in these

countries denominated in US dollars, as all dollar payments are cleared through

Manhattan and thus fall under US jurisdiction ... Any failure to observe this restriction

could place ING in breach of US law.

An attorney in ING Groep's Legal Department was not receptive to this view, however, responding:

...we have been dealing with Cuba ... for a lot of years now and I'm pretty sure that

we know what we are doing in avoiding any fines ...So don't worry and direct any

future concerns to me so that we can discuss before stirring up the whole business.

8. In addition to maintaining and distributing an explicit policy of omitting the name and BIC of Cuban banks in payment messages sent to the unaffiliated U.S. correspondent banks, ING Wholesale Banking's branch in France ("ING France") also provided a USD traveler check processing service to a Cuban bank. The service entailed the Cuban bank sending USD travelers checks to ING France without an endorsement stamp. Upon receiving the checks, ING France would then endorse the checks using an ING France endorsement stamp. In March and June 2000, the Cuban bank inquired about the creation of an ING France endorsement stamp for its own use

on travelers checks from Cuba. A department head from ING France authorized the Cuban bank to create and use such a stamp. The Cuban bank manufactured the stamp with the advice of a senior manager at ING France and other personnel. There were no references to Cuba or the Cuban bank's name on the stamp so that the Cuban involvement was not apparent. Rather, it appeared as if only ING France was, involved. In August 2004, ING France approved a similar procedure to process travelers checks for and issued a new stamp to a second Cuban bank. Although in 2003 and 2005, ING France's Payment Department Audit Reports raised questions regarding the propriety of the practice of allowing a Cuban bank to use an ING France- style endorsement stamp, there is no indication that ING France acted on this information, or that the activity had ceased until at least 2006.

9. Although understanding among employees at ING Wholesale Banking's branch in Belgium ("ING Belgium") varied regarding whether the use of cover payments differed from methods used to process non-OFAC sanctioned country payments, the employees, with the knowledge of senior employees in multiple ING Belgium departments, took care to ensure that there was no reference to OFAC-sanctioned countries in payment messages sent to the United States. The Head of ING Belgium's Compliance Department stated that the use of cover payments in connection with payments involving OFAC sanctioned countries had been in place for about 40 years, beginning with Cuban transactions, and was subsequently used for transactions involving other OFAC-sanctioned countries. Awareness among employees at ING Belgium of this cover payment method was widespread and included, specifically, senior employees from the Financial Institutions, Payments, Documentary Trade, and Financial Markets departments.

10. ING Wholesale Banking's branch in The Netherlands ("ING Netherlands") used care not to include references to U.S. sanctioned countries in USD SWIFT messages because they believed doing so was necessary to avoid the payments being blocked by unaffiliated U.S. correspondent banks in accordance with OFAC regulations. ING Netherlands's Trade and Commodity Finance business in its Rotterdam location ("TCF Rotterdam") maintained USD accounts bn behalf of Curef Metal Processing B.V. and Nickel Refining and Trading B.V.,Cuban SDNs, and, from at least 1994 up to 2006, employees of TCF Rotterdam processed transactions on behalf of these entities using suspense accounts and two other companies that were also clients of TCF Rotterdam and not listed on the SDN list. One of the non-SDN entities was used, with TCF Rotterdam management's knowledge, to act as "a special purpose front office" for Curef for certain transactions. One TCF Rotterdam employee wrote that this arrangement was "Highly confidential." This payment method was initiated to avoid the blocking of the clients' USD payments by unaffiliated U.S. correspondent banks and implemented according to "standing instructions to the TCF Rotterdam back office."Furthermore, this practice was apparently known within ING Bank Legal, TCF Rotterdam Risk Management, and the relevant credit committees.

11. In November 2003, Bank Tejarat, Iran issued a $1,550,000 letter of credit ("LC") on behalf of Iran Air to finance the purchase of an aircraft engine from a Romanian trading company. The LC required "a certificate of origin for the engine indicating that it was U.S. origin," and stated that "the aircraft engine was to be transported to 'Tehran via Mehrabad Airport' through Germany."

12. In November 2003, the Romanian trading company contacted ING Wholesale Banking's branch in Romania ("ING Romania") about transferring the LC to the trading company's "USA Partner." Subsequently, Bank Tejarat amended the LC to make it transferable by the trading company to its U.S. supplier; changed the description of the goods to obscure their origin, changed

the final destination of the goods from Tehran to Germany; and deleted the U.S. certificate of origin document requirement and all references to Iran. Amendments directed by Bank Tejarat had the effect of removing all references to Iran and obscuring the-U.S. origin of the goods. In February 2004, ING Romania transferred the LC, then in the amount of $1,205,000, to the U.S. exporter.

13. In March 2004, a U.S. bank noted a discrepancy in a reimbursement claim related to the LC and informed ING Romania that it therefore was not authorized to pay the claim. The advising bank contacted ING Wholesale Banking in Amsterdam for assistance in resolving the reimbursement claim problem. Later that month, the claiming bank employee requested "the complete details of the issuing bank..." One ING Wholesale Banking employee in Amsterdam advised another, however, that "the delay in payments with [the advising bank] was done only because they gave a wrong L/C number. I would advise you to say this ... and nothing more. [F]or the whole structure, [the claiming bank] should not have in writing anything. I think US banks know how the game is played..." After an ING Romania employee separately informed the advising bank that the LC related to Bank Tejarat, the advising bank disclosed the transaction to OFAC.

14. OFAC has reason to believe that ING Bank's conduct resulted in transactions prohibited by Executive Orders and/or regulations promulgated pursuant to the International Emergency Economic Powers Act ("DEEPA"), 50 U.S.C. §§ 1701-06, and the Trading With the Enemy Act ("TWEA"), 50 U.S.C. App. §§ 1-44.

15. From on or about October 22,2002, to on or about July 6,2007, ING Bank processed 20,452 electronic funds transfers, trade finance transactions, and travelers checks in which Cuba had an interest, in the aggregate amount of $1,654,657,318, through financial institutions located in the United States in apparent violation of the prohibition against "[a]ll transfers of credit and all payments between, by, through, or to any banking institution or banking institutions wheresoever located, with respect to any property subject to the jurisdiction of the United States," 31 C.F.R. § 515.201(a).

16. From on or about December 26, 2003, to on or about September 6,2007, ING Bank processed a combined 41 electronic funds transfers and trade finance transactions, in the aggregate amount of $15,469,938, through financial institutions located in the United States, in apparent violation of the prohibitions against (i) "the exportation or re-exportation of financial services to Burma, directly or indirectly, from the United States...," of the Burmese Sanctions Regulations ("BSR"), 31 C.F.R. § 537.202, and/or (ii) dealing in property and interests in property that "come within the United States" of persons listed in the Annex to Executive Order 13310,31 C.F.R. § 537.201.

17. From on or about January 14,2004, to on or about December 11, 2006, ING Bank processed a combined 44 electronic funds transfers and trade finance transactions, in the aggregate amount of $1,976,483, to the benefit of the Government of Sudan and/or persons in Sudan, through financial institutions located in the United States in apparent violation of the prohibitions against (i) the "exportation or re-exportation, directly or indirectly, to Sudan of.. .services from the United States," 31 C.F.R. § 538.205, and/or (ii) dealing in property and interests in property of the Government of Sudan that "come within the United States," 31 C.F.R. § 538.201.

18. From on or about January 13,2004, to on or about April 27, 2004, ING Bank processed three electronic funds transfers in the aggregate amount of $26,803, to the benefit of the Government of Libya and/or persons in Libya, through financial institutions located in the United States in apparent violation of the now-repealed prohibition against the exportation of "...goods,

technology ...or services ...to Libya from the United States..31 C.F.R. § 550.202.

19. On or about October 27,2004, ING Bank processed one $153,000 electronic funds transfer to the benefit of the Government of Iran and/or persons in Iran, through a financial institution located in the United States in apparent violation of the prohibition against the "exportation ..., directly or indirectly, from the United States ... of any ... services to Iran or the Government of Iran," 31 C.F.R. § 560.204. In addition, from on or about February to March 2004, ING Bank processed, through financial institutions located in the United States, one $1,205,000 transferable export letter of credit, including a related reimbursement claim, issued by an Iranian Bank related to the export of an aircraft engine from the United States to Iran in apparent violation of the prohibition against the "exportation ..., directly or indirectly, from the United States, ...of any ... services to Iran or the Government of Iran," 31 C.F.R. § 560.204.

20. The apparent violations of the CAGE, BSR, SSR, the now-repealed LSR, and one of the apparent violations of the ITR described above were voluntarily self-disclosed to OFAC within the meaning of OFAC's Economic Sanctions Enforcement Guidelines (the "Guidelines"). The February to March, 2004, apparent violation of the ITR was not voluntarily self-disclosed to OFAC within the meaning of the Guidelines. See 31 C.F.R. part 501, App A.

21. The apparent violations by ING Bank described above undermined U.S. national security, foreign policy, and other objectives of U.S. sanctions programs.

22. Upon discovering the apparent violations, and under the direction of the DNB, ING Bank took prompt and thorough remedial action through extensive, global measures, including adopting a consolidated sanctioned countries policy for all ING Bank business units and an export compliance program focusing on U.S. regulations concerning the re-export of U.S. origin goods to sanctioned countries; instituting broad-based training sessions on sanctions policy at ING Bank's offices; implementing new software for the screening of international payments and customer databases for all ING Bank entities worldwide; disengaging from any new business in any currency involving Cuba, Iran, Burma, North Korea, Sudan and Syria; closing its representative office in Havana; purchasing the non-ING Bank interests in NCB, closing its Havana office, and placing it into liquidation; and circulating a set of policy guidelines reinforcing existing business principles regarding transparency and emphasizing in greater detail ING Bank's commitment to, and minimum standards for, transparency in payment processing and trade transactions among others.

23. ING Bank cooperated with OFAC by conducting an historical review to identify weaknesses in its compliance program and providing substantial arid well-organized information regarding the apparent violations for OFAC's assessment; signing a tolling agreement with OFAC; and by responding to multiple inquiries and requests for information. ING Bank did not consistently cooperate with OFAC with regard to explicit requests for information, however. The requested information was ultimately provided, but only after multiple submissions to OFAC of information that was heavily redacted.

24. OFAC had not issued a penalty notice or Finding of Violation against ING Bank in the five years preceding the apparent violations.

III. TERMS OF SETTLEMENT

IT IS HEREBY AGREED by OFAC and ING Bank that:

25. ING Bank has terminated the conduct described in paragraphs 3 through 13 above and

has put in place, and agrees to maintain, policies and procedures that prohibit, and are designed to minimize the risk of the recurrence of, similar conduct in the future.

26. After a period of one year from the date of this Agreement, ING Bank shall conduct a review of its policies and procedures and their implementation, and an appropriate risk-focused sampling of USD payments, to ensure that its OFAC compliance program is functioning effectively to detect, correct, and report OFAC-sanctioned transactions when they occur. The review, which shall commence one year after the date of this Agreement, shall be conducted by ING Bank's Corporate Audit Services. The review will be conducted in accordance with generally accepted auditing standards and the results will be submitted to OFAC within six months of the one-year anniversary date of this Agreement.

27. Without this Agreement constituting an admission or denial by ING Bank of any allegation made or implied by OFAC in connection with this matter, and solely for the purpose of settling this matter without a final agency finding that a violation has occurred, ING Bank agrees to a settlement in the amount of $619,000,000 arising out of the alleged violations of IEEPA, TWEA, the Executive Orders, and the Regulations referenced in this Agreement. ING Bank's obligation to pay such settlement amount to OF AC shall be satisfied by its payment of an equal amount in satisfaction of penalties assessed by U.S. federal, state, or county officials arising out of the same pattern of conduct.

28. Should OFAC determine, in the reasonable exercise of its discretion, that ING Bank has willfully and materially breached its obligations under paragraphs 26 or 27 of this Agreement, OFAC shall provide written notice to ING Bank of the alleged breach and provide ING Bank with 30 days from the date of ING Bank's receipt of such notice, or longer as determined by OFAC, to demonstrate that no willful and material breach has occurred or that any breach has been cured. In the event that OFAC ultimately determines that a willful and material breach of this Agreement has occurred, OFAC will provide notice to ING Bank of Its determination, and this Agreement shall be null and void, and the statute of limitations applying to activity occurring on or after October 19,2002, shall be deemed tolled until a date 180 days following ING Bank's receipt of notice of OFAC's determination that a breach of the Agreement has occurred.

29. OFAC agrees that, as of the date that ING Bank satisfies the obligations set forth in paragraphs 26 through 27 above, OFAC will release and forever discharge ING Bank from any and all civil liability, under the legal authorities that OFAC administers, in connection with any and all violations arising from or related to the conduct disclosed during the course of the investigation, including that described in paragraphs 3 through 13 above and the alleged violations described in paragraphs 15 through 19 above.

30. ING Bank waives any claim by or on behalf of ING Bank, whether asserted or unassorted, against OFAC, the U.S. Department of the Treasury, and/or its officials and employees arising out of the facts giving rise to this Agreement, including but not limited to OFAC's investigation of the apparent violations and any possible legal objection to this Agreement at any future date.

IV. MISCELLANEOUS PROVISIONS

31. The provisions of this Agreement shall not bar, estop, or otherwise prevent OFAC from taking any other action affecting ING Bank with respect to any and all violations not arising from or related to the conduct described in paragraphs 3 through 13 above or the investigation, or violations occurring after the date of this Agreement. The provisions of this Agreement shall not bar, estop, or

otherwise prevent other U.S. federal, state, or county officials from taking any other action affecting ING Bank.

32. Each provision of this Agreement shall remain effective and enforceable according to the laws of the United States of America until stayed, modified, terminated, or suspended by OFAC.

33. No amendment to the provisions of this Agreement shall be effective unless executed in writing by OFAC and by ING Bank.

34. The provisions of this Agreement shall be binding on ING Bank and its successors and assigns.

35. No representations, either oral or written, except those provisions as set forth herein, were made to induce any of the parties to agree to the provisions as set forth herein.

36. This Agreement consists of 9 pages and expresses the complete understanding of OFAC and ING Bank regarding resolution of the alleged violations arising from or related to the conduct described in paragraphs 3 through 19 above. No other agreements, oral or written, exist between OFAC and ING Bank regarding resolution of this matter.

37. OFAC, in its sole discretion, may post on OFAC's website this entire Agreement or the facts set forth in paragraphs 3 through 19 of this Agreement, including the identity of any entity involved, the satisfied settlement amount, and a brief description of the alleged violations. OFAC also may issue a press release including this information.

38. Use of facsimile signatures shall not delay the approval and implementation of the terms of this Agreement. In the event any party to this Agreement provides a facsimile signature, the party shall substitute the facsimile with an original signature. The Agreement may be signed in multiple counterparts, which together shall constitute the Agreement. The effective date of the Agreement shall be the latest date of execution.

39. All communications regarding this Agreement shall be addressed to:

ING Bank N.V.
P.O. Box 810
1000 AV Amsterdam
The Netherlands

Office of Foreign Assets Control
U.S. Department of the Treasury
Attn. Sanctions Compliance & Evaluation
1500 Pennsylvania Avenue, N.W., Annex
Washington, DC 20220

AGREED:

_____
Jan-Willem Vink
General Counsel
ING Bank, N.V.

_____
Adam J. Szubin
Director
Office of Foreign Assets Control

DATED: 8 June 2012

DATED: June 11, 2012

_____
J.V. Koos Timmermans
Vice Chairman, Management Board Banking
ING Bank, N.V.

DATED: 8-6-2012.

《和解令》中文译文[①]

财政部华盛顿特区 20220
MUL-565595

和解令

本和解协议（以下简称协议）由美国财政部下设的外国资产控制办公室和荷兰ING银行签署。

I. 协议签署方

1. 美国财政部下设的外国资产控制办公室（OFAC）负责管理和执行对目标国家、政权、恐怖分子、国际贩毒分子以及从事大规模杀伤性武器扩散人员的经济制裁行动。OFAC依据总统国家紧急授权以及其他特别授权，对美国管辖权以内的交易进行控制并冻结资产。

2. ING银行以及其前身（统称ING 银行）是一家按照荷兰法律注册成立的金融机构。荷兰中央银行是ING银行的主要监管机构。

① 本书和解令以英文为准，并适用于全书。

II. 认定事实

3. 1994年8月，ING银行成立了荷兰加勒比银行（NCB），这是一家与古巴的合资银行。ING银行的批发业务部（ING批发业务部）也在哈瓦那成立了代表处（ING哈瓦那）。ING批发业务部设在库拉索（Curacao，是一座位于加勒比海的岛，属于荷兰王国的自治领土）的分行（ING Curacao）代表NCB和ING哈瓦那处理所有的付款指令，并提供支持服务。

4. ING哈瓦那和NCB制作的付款处理操作手册指示员工对在付款明细上涉及与古巴相关的人名或公司要给与特别关注，从而防止被无关联的美国银行没收款项。ING Curacao高级管理层经常通过邮件或口头方式提醒员工在付款指示中不要提及古巴。对于不遵从上述指示的员工，将会受到口头或者书面批评，甚至是解雇。NCB对于那些使用美元支付给NCB账户的客户也会提供相似的指令（使用美元将会通过美国进行），要求客户：（1）将NCB而不是客户作为受益人；（2）在同一条信息的其他地方显示客户的姓名与账号；（3）不要提及古巴。

5. 从1998年开始，ING Curacao使用一套标准流程来筛查与古巴相关的付款信息，这些汇款将可能被美国阻止。如果筛查到与古巴相关的信息，ING Curacao、ING哈瓦那和NCB有时会修改这一信息——在向美国代理行发出汇款指令前删除或者掩饰相关信息，这样，美国代理行就不会发现相关交易涉及被禁止的古巴利益。ING Curacao的单证贸易融资部门也制定了一套标准程序，要求付款行和客户只提及ING Curacao的相关交易参考号而不用提及古巴受益人的名字。在高管的授意下，ING Curacao的员工使用代码来描述古巴相关交易，这些交易信息被发送到ING批发业务部的纽约代表处。

6. 从2001年开始，ING Curacao不断使用MT202银行间头寸调拨方式向美国代理行发送与古巴相关的交易信息，这样就不必再包含发起人或受益人等与古巴相关的交易方信息。一直到2003年，NCB在汇出的SWIFT MT103信息第50栏输入其自己的名字或者银行识别号码。从2003年第二季度开始，NCB在第50栏输入其客户的名字，但是却省略了地址信息。ING Curacao也在汇出的SWIFT信息的第50栏加入了客户的名字，但没有地址信息。而且，尽管ING Bank在2004年规定在MT103报文第50栏中使用国际银行账户号码（IBAN），ING Curacao汇出汇款中非古巴相关客户的信息包括了客户的名称和地址，但是古巴客户的汇款信息中则只包括客户名称和国际银行账户号码（IBAN）。在多个场合，当美国代理行成功拦截了与古巴相关的付款后，ING Bank的员工，包括管理层和其合规部门的律师，会作出虚假陈述，告诉美国代理行，ING Curacao本来是打算使用另外一个币种汇款，从而试图收回（被拦截的）款项。

7. 2004年，在得知上述行为后不久，ING批发业务部的一个员工写了一封邮件，最终到了ING集团的法律部。其中写道：

美国政府对几个国家实施制裁……我们不能与这些国家的机构进行任何以美元计价的收付款交易，因为所有的美元交易都要通过曼哈顿来进行清算，这样就会受美国司法管辖……如果不能遵守这些限制，将会违反美国法律。然而，ING集团法律部的一名律师并不接受这一观点，他回复道：

……我们与古巴做交易已经有很多年了，我非常确信我们知道怎么做来避免罚款……因此不用担心，今后有什么疑虑可以直接写给我，这样我们就可以在影响整体业务之前好好沟通。

8. 除了保持一个明确的政策——在发送给美国代理行的付款信息上略去古巴银行的名称和BIC代码之外，ING批发业务部的法国分行（ING FRANCE）还为一家古巴银行提供了美元旅行支票结算服务。这项服务使得这家古巴银行可以向ING FRANCE发送没有背书印章的美元旅行支票。收到这些支票后，ING FRANCE将使用自己的背书印章为支票做背书。2000年3月和6月，这家古巴银行询问如何制造ING FRANCE的背书印章来供自己用于古巴的旅行支票。ING FRANCE的一名部门负责人授权这家古巴银行自己制造并使用一枚背书印章。这家古巴银行在ING FRANCE的一名高级经理和其他人员的帮助下制造了这枚印章。印章上面没有古巴或古巴银行的信息，这样古巴的介入就不明显。2004年8月，ING FRANCE使用相似流程为另一家古巴银行办理了旅行支票服务，并为这家银行签发了一枚新印章。尽管在2003年和2005年，ING FRANCE的付款部门审计报告提出了这种允许一家古巴银行使用ING FRANCE的背书印章的做法有问题，但并无迹象表明ING FRANCE为此采取了行动，这种行为至少直到2006年才停止。

9. 尽管ING批发业务部的比利时分行（ING Belgium）的员工对于（上面提到的）银行间头寸划拨方式是否与处理非OFAC制裁国家的付款方式有区

别没有达到共识，但是ING Belgium的员工，特别在一些资深雇员知情的情况下，谨慎操作以确保在向美国发送OFAC制裁国家的付款信息时，不会涉及相关信息。ING Belgium的合规部门负责人表明ING对OFAC制裁国家的头寸划拨方式的使用已经持续了近40年左右，从古巴的交易开始，后来又被用于其他OFAC制裁国家。ING Belgium的员工对这种付款方式广泛知情，特别是那些来自金融机构部、付款、单证结算以及金融市场部的资深员工。

10. ING批发业务部的荷兰分行（ING Netherlands）在发送美元SWIFT信息时谨慎地不加入美国制裁国家相关信息，是因为他们认为只有这样做，才能避免被美国代理行根据OFAC的政策对汇款进行拦截。ING Netherlands设在鹿特丹的贸易和商品融资部（TCF Rotterdam）保留了为Curef Metal Processing B.V.和 Nickel Refining and Trading B.V.开设的账户，这两家公司都在对古巴制裁的SDN名单上。从1994年到2006年，TCF Rotterdam的员工使用一个暂记账户以及另外不在SDN名单上的两家客户来为上述两家SDN客户提供服务。在TCF Rotterdam管理层知晓的情况下，其中一家非SDN客户被当作"一家特殊目的前台办公室"来为Curef提供交易服务。TCF Rotterdam的一位员工写到，这一安排属于"高度机密"。这种付款方式是按照TCF Rotterdam后台部门的操作指示来进行的，目的是避免被美国代理行拦截汇款。而且，ING Bank法律部门、TCF Rotterdam的风险管理部门以及相关的信贷委员会都明显知悉这种做法。

11. 2003年11月，伊朗的Bank Tejarat 代表伊朗航空开出了一笔155万美元的信用证，用来从一家罗马尼亚贸易公司购买一台飞机发动机。信用证要求"一份原产地证明表明该发动机是美国制造"并注明"飞机发动机经过德国到伊朗的梅赫拉巴德机场"。

12. 2003年11月，这家罗马尼亚贸易公司联系ING批发业务部在罗马尼亚的分行（ING Romania），希望将信用证转让给该公司的"美国交易伙伴"。随后，Bank Tejarat对信用证进行了修改，由该贸易公司转让给其美国供货商；同时修改了对货物的描述以模糊其原产地；将货物最终目的地从伊朗修改为德国，并去掉了原产地证明的要求以及所有涉及伊朗的表述。Bank Tejarat所做的修改取得了效果——去掉了所有对伊朗的描述并模糊货物的原产地来自美国。2004年2月，ING Romania转让该信用证给美国出口商，金额为120.5万美元。

13. 2004年3月，一家美国银行在索偿函中发现了上述信用证的一个不符点并告知ING Romania拒付。信用证通知行联系了ING批发业务部在阿姆斯特丹的分行来帮助解决这一拒付问题。此后，索偿行要求提供"开证行的详细信息"。ING批发业务部阿姆斯特丹分行的一名员工就此事通知另一名员工，"对通知行的付款延误只是因为他们写错了信用证号码，并无其他原因。对整个交易结构，索偿行本来不应该有不同意见。我认为美国的银行知道游戏规则"。ING Romania的一名员工单独告知了通知行该信用证与Bank Tejarat相关，通知行将这一信息告知了OFAC。

14. OFAC有理由确认ING BANK的行为导致这些交易违反了《国际紧急经济权利法案》以及《与敌人交易法案》等行政命令和相关制度。

15. 从2002年10月22日左右开始直到2007年7月6日左右，ING BANK处理了与古巴利益相关的20 452笔电子资金转账、贸易融资业务、旅行支票业务，金额共计1 654 657 318美元。上述交易都是通过美国的金融机构来完成，明显违反了"信贷和款项的转让（收付）经由（到）银行机构，不管这个银行机构位于何地，只要有归美国政府管辖的资产……"

16. 从2003年12月26日到2007年9月6日，ING BANK处理了41笔电子资金转账和贸易融资，金额共计15 469 938美元。这些交易都通过美国的金融机构完成，明显违反了缅甸制裁规定"从美国向缅甸出口或再出口金融服务，直接或间接……"和/或与总统令中所列人员进行财产交易，而这些财产来自美国。

17. 从2004年1月14日至2006年12月11日，ING BANK处理了44笔电子资金转账和贸易融资，金额共计1 976 483美元。这些交易有利于苏丹政府以及苏丹有关人员，且通过美国的金融机构完成，明显违反了苏丹制裁规定"从美国向苏丹出口或再出口金融服务，直接或间接……"和/或与苏丹政府进行财产交易，而这些交易来自美国。

18. 从2004年1月13日至2004年4月27日，ING BANK处理了3笔电子资金转账，金额共计26 803美元。这些交易有利于利比亚政府以及利比亚有关人员，且通过美国的金融机构完成，明显违反了利比亚制裁（现在已撤销）规定"从美国向利比亚出口货物、技术或服务……"

19. 2004年10月27日，ING BANK处理了1笔金额为153 000美元的电子资金转账，这笔交易有利于伊朗政府和/或伊朗有关人员，且通过美国的金融机构完成，明显违反了伊朗制裁规定"从美国向伊朗或伊朗政府出口任何服务，直接或间接……"（C.F.R法案31条）。除此以外，2004年2月到3月，ING BANK通过美国金融机构办理了一笔金额为1 205 000美元的可转让出口信用证，包括相关联的索偿函。该信用证由一家伊朗银行开出，服务于从美国向伊朗出口飞机发动机，这明显违反了相关制裁规定"从美国向伊朗或伊朗政府出口任何服务，不论直接或间接……"

20. 上述违反CACR、BSR、SSR、LSR（现在已撤销）、ITR法案的交易都是由ING BANK根据OFAC的经济制裁执行指引自愿提供给OFAC的。2004年2月到3月明显违反ITR的交易不是按照该指引的规定自愿披露的。

21. ING BANK上述的违规行为损害了美国的国家安全、外交以及其他的制裁目标。

22. 发现上述违规事实后，在荷兰央行的指导下，ING BANK立即采取行动，通过全面的全球性措施进行补救。这些措施包括在所有ING BANK的业务单元执行一套统一的针对制裁国家相关政策，以及制定针对美国原产货物向制裁国家再出口的合规方案；在ING BANK的内部进行了广泛的针对制裁的培训；采用新的软件系统检查ING BANK的全球机构的国际汇款和客户信息库；不再从事与古巴、伊朗、缅甸、朝鲜、苏丹和叙利亚相关的任何币种的交易；关闭了哈瓦那办事处；下发了一套新的政策指引，加强现有业务的透明度并强调了ING BANK在汇款和贸易融资业务的标准和透明度。

23. ING BANK与OFAC合作对其合规方案进行了历史回顾和重检以确定合规缺陷并就违反OFAC制裁方面提供了大量组织良好的信息；与OFAC签署了收费协议；对于OFAC的问询和要求提供信息比较合作。然而，ING BANK并非一贯地对于提供信息的要求十分合作。有些信息经过了多次反复与修改才最终提供给OFAC。

24. OFAC在上述违规发生之前5年内没有签发过罚款单或违规确认书。

III. 和解协议

ING BANK与OFAC在此约定：

25. ING BANK 已经终止了上述从第3条至第13条描述的行为，而且已经采取并将持续实施有关政策和措施，来禁止类似事情再次发生并将相关风险降至最低。

26. 自本协议签字之日一年起，ING BANK将对其相关政策和执行情况进行重检，并建立一个适当的美元付款风险样本，以确保有效地执行OFAC合规政策，准确识别并向OFAC报告相关制裁交易情况。上述重检将从本协议签字之日1年后由ING BANK的 审计部门执行。该重检将按照通行审计标准进行，重检结果在协议签字日的1年半以内提交给OFAC。

27. 本协议不构成ING BANK承认或否认与此相关的OFAC的指控，仅仅是为了在没有一家最终机构确认违法的情况下达成和解，ING BANK同意支付由于指控违反IEEPA、TWEA、总统命令以及其他相关规定而产生的6.19亿美元。ING BANK向OFAC的付款责任在其支付由美国联邦、州以及县级官员确认的罚款之后解除。

28. 如果OFAC有合适的理由自主确定，ING BANK故意且本质上违反了其在第26条和第27条的责任，OFAC将书面通知ING BANK该违约行为，并给他30天时间（或者由OFAC确定的更长的时间）来证明没有发生违约行为或者违约行为已经得到补救。如果OFAC最终确定ING BANK故意且实质违反了该协议，OFAC将通知ING BANK，该协议将确认无效，同时，在2002年10月19日之后发生的交易的诉讼时效将被视为延长到ING BANK收到OFAC的违反协议通知之日起的180天以内。

29. OFAC同意，当ING BANK满足第26条和第27条的义务之后，OFAC将在其职权范围内解除ING BANK的相关民事义务。这些义务涉及调查期间披露的违规行为，包括从第3条至第13条所描述的内容以及第15条至第19条指控的违规。

30. ING BANK放弃对OFAC、美国财政部以及/或这些部门的官员和雇员的任何与此协议相关的主张或要求，包括但不限于OFAC对违规的调查以及对本协议将来的任何反对意见。

IV. 其他事项

31. 本协议的规定将不影响OFAC对ING BANK不在上述第3条至第13条描述的内容之外的其他违规采取行动，也不影响OFAC对本协议签字日之后的违规采取行动。本协议规定将不影响其他的美国联邦、州或县级官员采取针对ING BANK的行动。

32. 除非被OFAC修改或废止，本协议的每一项条款都持续有效且可执行。

33. 除非经OFAC和ING BANK书面修改，本协议的条款将不得变更。

34. 本协议条款对ING BANK和其继承人有效。

35. 除本协议的条款之外，没有任何声明，不管是书面还是口头。

36. 本协议为9页，对解决第3条至第19条的违规行为作出了完整的表述。OFAC和ING BANK之间不存在任何其他与本违规事项相关的口头或书面协议。

37. OFAC可以自己决定将本协议整体或本协议的第3条至第19条的内容放到其网站上，包括任何介入方的身份，和解金额以及对违规的简要描述。OFAC也可以就相关内容对媒体公布。

38. 使用传真签字将不会延迟本协议条款的批准与执行。如本协议的任何一方提供传真签字页，则须用原始签字页替代。本协议可以签署多份，整体上构成本协议。本协议的生效日期将为最后签字日。

39. 本协议项下的通讯将寄往下述地址：

ING Bank N.V.
P.O. Box 810
1000 AV Amsterdam
The Netherlands

Office of Foreign Assets Control
U.S. Department of the Treasury
Attn. Sanctions Compliance & Evaluation
1500 Pennsylvania Avenue, N.W., Annex
Washington, DC 20220

2.

塞耳盗钟大福不再
——汇丰银行洗钱案

　　2012年12月汇丰银行与美国监管机构达成和解令（见附录），最终支付了19.21亿美元的巨额罚单，并签订了一份为期5年的延期诉讼协议。汇丰银行因违反了《银行保密法（BSA）》《国际紧急经济权利法（IEEPA）》以及《敌国贸易法（TWEA）》三部法案而分别被美国司法部、海外资产控制办公室、美国货币监理署和金融犯罪网络局以及美联储处以8.81亿美元、3.75亿美元、5亿美元、1.65亿美元的罚款。

　　汇丰银行洗钱案牵涉的监管主体之多、涉及法律之繁、罚款金额之大、整改时间之久，一度空前。"蓄意"（willfully）一词在和解令中多次出现，汇丰银行明知自己的一些经营行为会触碰监管和法律的底线，但却抱有侥幸心理，因为业绩冲动，选择了"迎难而上""绕道而行"，最终为此付出了惨痛的代价。汇丰银行洗钱案曾在国际金融市场上引起震动，留下许多可资思考借鉴的空间。

汇丰银行概述

汇丰银行，这家总部设于伦敦的老牌金融机构，在世界60多个国家和地区设有约3 900个分支机构，时至今日仍是世界规模最大的银行及金融服务机构之一。根据2017年年报，该行总资产约为1.1万亿美元，按资产规模排名国内第三，世界第二十五位。"The world's local bank"，凭借当年成功的市场营销和扎实高效的服务基础，汇丰银行甚至曾一度蝉联世界500大银行品牌之首。

从发展战略来看，汇丰银行主要奉行两大长期策略：一是拓展国际网络。致力于服务不同地区的企业，促进国际贸易和资金流，帮助客户拓展业务。二是投资具有本土实力的财富管理和零售银行业务。立足选定的零售银行和财富管理业务市场，充分把握全球社会流动、财富增值和人口结构变化带来的机遇。在具体经营上，该行将全球业务分为四大板块，包括零售和财富管理业务、工商金融服务、环球银行及资本市场服务、私人银行服务。根据2017年年报披露的数据，除私人银行业务营收略有下降之外，其他板块业务同比均有较快增长。

2015年6月，汇丰集团高调宣布将要采取一系列重要行动，着重提升资源利用效率，推进投资以促进业务增长。这些措施主要围绕调整规模及精简集团架构，重新部署资本及投资两个方面进行，共提出了包括减少集团2 900亿美元风险加权资产、在英国设立分离运作银行、实现约50亿美元成本节约、透过人民币国际化推动业务增长、重新评定总部所在地等十大目标。据悉，该行各项措施目前正在有序推进，截至2017年底，十大目标中已达成八个。

从组织结构来看，汇丰银行的母公司是汇丰控股有限公司（HSBC

Holdings Plc），作为控股管理型公司，不负责具体业务运营，其麾下主要机构包括：香港最大的银行——香港上海汇丰银行有限公司（Hong Kong and Shanghai Banking Corp. Ltd）、英国第三大银行——汇丰银行（HSBC Bank Plc）、控股62%的香港第二大银行——恒生银行（Hang Seng Bank）、美国（HSBC Bank USA N.A.）、法国（HSBC France）、汇丰中东银行（HSBC Middle East）及其在中国的全资子银行汇丰银行（中国）有限公司等。2011年，汇丰银行一度在88个国家和地区设立机构，遍布全球的服务网络虽是该行非常显著的竞争优势，但在某些高风险国家设立的分支机构，因缺乏有效监管，也为洗钱案件的爆发埋下了伏笔。

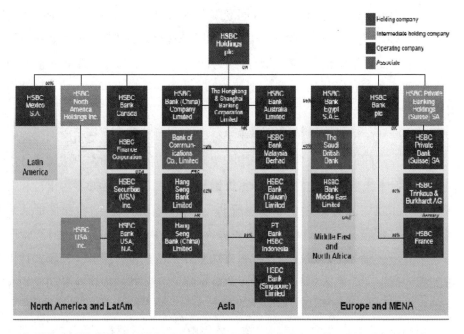

1. As at 31 December 2017, showing entities in Priority markets, wholly-owned unless shown otherwise (part ownership rounded down to nearest per cent). Excludes other Associates, insurance companies and Special Purpose Entities.

图1 汇丰集团组织结构图

案件回顾

事件背景

2012年7月，美国参议院发布了一份针对汇丰银行的长达300多页的调查报告，指出该行涉嫌参与洗钱、贩毒和恐怖融资，并无视美国OFAC制裁令，与古巴、叙利亚、伊朗等受制裁实体发生业务往来。参议院调查委员会负责人卡尔·莱文曾警告，如果此事不能被彻查，参议院将动议吊销汇丰在美国的营业执照。

在报告发布的第二天，汇丰银行首席合规官戴维·巴格利（David Bagley）便宣布引咎辞职。巴格利在7月17日举行的美国参议院听证会上表示"我们辜负了监管机构的期望"，承认了汇丰银行涉嫌为毒贩洗钱、为恐怖分子融资，随后作出了上述辞职决定。在参加听证会的过程中，巴格利多次坦承自己忽视了同事的谏言。例如，2008年汇丰墨西哥分行反洗钱主管曾告知巴格利，"有人指出墨西哥70%洗钱活动是通过汇丰进行""汇丰迟早将面临法律指控"；2010年，汇丰北美的反洗钱主管也曾反映职权不够的问题。但巴格利同时也辩解称，作为首席合规官他职权有限，他无权管理或控制汇丰全球所有合规部门，"某种情况下，根本不知情汇丰北美的洗钱活动"。虽为辩解，但也透露出当时合规条线的无奈，当时汇丰银行的业务范畴一度覆盖80多个国家和地区，庞大的组织构架令信息横向的传递与沟通变得非常困难。

然而，巴格利的下台并未能止住洗钱丑闻的扩散，参议院声称要对汇丰银行就防范洗钱不力全面问责。曾担任汇丰首席执行官的英国贸易与投资大臣葛霖（Lord Stephen Green）也因此面临巨大政治压力，工党要求他说明掌管汇丰时对洗钱案的了解。葛霖于2003年6月至2006年5月担任汇丰集团执行官，之后便出任汇丰集团总裁，直至2010年12月。2011年1月受英国政府延揽，开始担任贸易与投资大臣，积极为英商争取海外投资机会，同时也是财政大臣奥斯本的顾问。

根据美国参议院的调查，2005年曾有汇丰银行员工告知葛霖，墨西哥分行未遵守反洗钱法，合规部员工伪造交易记录，可能涉及为毒枭洗钱，但他未能及时发现问题。2008年葛霖升任总裁后，再次被告知，墨西哥政府发现洗钱证据，并警告汇丰银行可能要负法律责任，但该行直到2009年中才开始进行内部调查。工党财政事务发言人Chris Leslie表示，美国参议院报告所揭发的内容十分重要，情节也很严重，葛霖也应就洗钱案他所知道的内容及何时知道等重要问题作出答复。

在拿到参议院的报告后，美国司法部介入，对汇丰银行的行为开展刑事调查。同年12月，历经一番周折，汇丰银行与美国司法部达成和解，最终支付了19.21亿美元的巨额罚单，并签订了一份为期5年的延期诉讼协议。其中美国司法部（DOJ）分得8.81亿美元，美国财政部海外资产控制办公室（OFAC）分得3.75亿美元；汇丰银行同时需支付6.65亿美元的民事犯罪赔偿，分别为美国货币监理署（OCC）及金融犯罪执法网络局（FinCEN）5亿美元，美联储（FD）1.65亿美元，罚款金额总计19.21亿美元。

细数汇丰银行当时存在的九大漏洞

监管部门出具的和解令以及参议院发布的调查报告，对汇丰银行当时的不当行为和洗钱证据进行了详细列述，从集团文化到具体操作环节，内容涉及方方面面。笔者试将其主要缺陷概括如下：

（1）集团层面未对合规官权责进行明确

汇丰银行虽然表面上设有反洗钱与合规流程，但各个角色的权责界定不够明确，流程执行不够到位。比如，汇丰集团的合规官无权直接责令其分支机构进行整改，而在分支机构层面，对于涉及反洗钱和制裁问题，到底是由合规官还是业务人员来最终决策负责，一直也都没有定论。当时的部分高管又普遍存在侥幸心理，在业绩与利润的诱惑下，不顾合规人员的提示与劝谏，对于一些潜存洗钱风险的可疑交易一再纵容，置之不理。

（2）人力资源配置不足

为了降低成本和提高资本回报，汇丰美国从2007年起便严格控制其反洗钱部门的员工数量，导致其根本无力监控经手的可疑交易。据内部人士透露，当时的反洗钱部门加班加点也无法处理完应接不暇的反洗钱问题，保守估计也应增加35个正式编制。而汇丰美国还尝试推行一人多岗，身兼多职，比如汇丰美国的合规部总经理身兼反洗钱主管，汇丰北美的法律总顾问身兼地区合规官角色。这一政策，更是令原本便已苍白脆弱的反洗钱体系雪上加霜。

事实证明，再先进的系统也无法完全替代人力的投入，任何精细、科学的参数设置一旦被人掌握利用，便可找到办法，设计出绕过系统监控的交易结构。其实在案件泄露前，汇丰美国也意识到了这一点，在2011年便投入了2亿多美元，扩充和完善合规条线。在2010年1月，该行反洗钱部门仅有92名全职员工和25名顾问，等到2012年5月，已增加至约880名全职员工和267名顾问，负责监测可疑交易的员工数量，也增加了10倍达到430名。

（3）对集团内部的交易不做监控

汇丰银行在全球众多国家和地区开展经营，每个司法辖区的监管完备情况和各机构反洗钱合规执行情况都不尽相同。但根据集团内部政策，汇丰美国无须对集团内分支机构的汇款交易进行监控，这种盲目信赖也成为了该行反洗钱链条上的最大漏洞。根据司法部的报告，自2006年至2010年，汇丰美国未能执行有效的反洗钱流程监控墨西哥的可疑交易，未对汇丰墨西哥的汇款进行筛查监控，使得墨西哥锡纳罗亚犯罪集团和哥伦比亚的卡特尔贩毒集团成功从汇丰美国至少完成了8.81亿美元的涉毒洗钱。

（4）国别风险控制不当

美国货币监理署的调查报告显示，汇丰银行的反洗钱流程对来自"标准"和"中等"国别风险国家客户的电汇不做监控，而此类汇款在汇丰美国的占比高达三分之二。虽然该行对这些业务采用了其他替代性的监控手段，但覆盖面有限，效果不佳，不能实际减少反洗钱风险。值得一提的是，"标准"是该行国别风险评级中最低的一档，而墨西哥在2006年至2009年，被该行分类定位为"标准"。松懈的评判标准和系统监控，让不法集团和洗钱组织成功利用了汇丰银行的渠道，将大量非法所得汇回美国。

（5）客户信息收集不充分

美国货币监理署在此前的检查中发现，与集团内分支机构间的汇款无须监控的策略类似，汇丰美国对汇丰集团其他分支机构的不要求开展客户普通型尽调（CDD）和加强型尽调（EDD），客户资料无须收集和保存。而尽职调查一般包含客户的注册信息、经营状况、关联企业、资金往来对象、营业范围、风险控制措施等重要信息，充分翔实的尽调是对客户进行风险评定的重要依据，客户信息的缺少使得汇丰美国无法对其他分支机构账户的可疑交易进行识别。

（6）积压大量未处理的系统预警

各行的反洗钱系统虽不尽相同，但一般都会根据行内的政策和标准设置预警指标，如受益人名称、所在地址、大额交易、高频交易、敏感行业、制裁名单筛查等。某笔交易若触发相关指标，则会发出系统预警，需要进行人工落地处理，待合规人员收集额外信息并进行确认后方可放行。对于可疑交易，还需要及时上报监管机构。美国货币监理署在2009年10月开展的检查中，发现该行积压了大量未处理的预警，而且该行对积压预警的后续重检过于简单，甚至不作处理直接关闭预警，不能完全满足监管要求，造成了大量的可疑交易向监管机构迟报、漏报。该行在2010年漏报了890份可疑报告，总金额高达63.4亿美元。

（7）客户风险分类不够严格

根据国际监管惯例，政治敏感人物（PEP）一般会被视为洗钱高风险类别，金融机构为保持反洗钱力度，应加强对此类客户的监察，设置更高的审查程序和风险分类。与之相应，一旦客户群体中出现此类人物，就意味着要面临更多的监管审查和后续的人力物力投入，出于种种考虑，汇丰银行并未将政治敏感人物列为高风险客户，也为洗钱风险埋下了潜在问题。

（8）代理清算业务监控力度不足

除对集团内分支机构的账户不做监控外，汇丰银行在代理清算业务合作机构的筛选上也存在一定问题。例如，拉吉哈银行因涉嫌恐怖主义融资，在2004年被美国政府列入黑名单，而汇丰银行只是象征性地发了声明表示已与其"一刀两断"。2006年拉吉哈银行以取消全部业务合作为要挟，重新建立了在汇丰美国的现钞账户，据说从汇丰美国买入了约10亿美元现金。汇丰香港也在2009年拿到汇丰美国的授权，为拉吉哈银行开立账户，每月为其提供大量非美元货币现钞，包括泰铢、印度卢比和港元。

（9）有意规避OFAC制裁

根据美国司法部的报告，2000年至2006年，汇丰集团有意违反美国的制裁，开展古巴、伊朗、利比亚、苏丹和缅甸等实体的代理清算业务。为规避OFAC监管，汇丰银行变通采用了掉头交易（U-turn transactions）的方式进行直接拨付。具体方式为，直接发送披露详情的MT103给受益行，同时向代理行发送MT202报文，但只指示拨划，不提供详情，通过改变汇款信息和路径，隐藏了被制裁实体的身份，从而确保这些交易没法被汇丰美国和美国其他金融机构监测到。此段时期发生的交易大约有6.6亿美元。

案件的影响及教训

和解令的签署并不代表着事件的终了，根据延期诉讼协议的要求，汇丰银行在罚款之余，还要疲于应对监管的后续检查与严苛要求，美国政府派驻了专门的检查官，负责督导、检查汇丰银行的整改情况，并需按季度向法院提供落实情况报告。值得庆幸的是，在和解宣布的5年之后，美国司法部已于2017年底向纽约东区法院提起诉讼，撤回对该行实行的暂缓起诉协议（DPA），汇丰银行履行了协议规定的整改要求并通过了监管验收，本案终于尘埃落定。

除去支付的巨额罚款，汇丰银行在这五年间还投入了大量的人力物力，加强合规建设，落实监管要求，合规人员数量与2012年相比增加了超过10倍，采纳了更严苛的反洗钱监控系统和预警参数设置，加大各条线的合规培训力度，甚至一度暂停了代理美元清算新增业务。汇丰内部人员称，在遭受罚款之后的几年里，普通员工的绩效也因此严重缩水，收入基本停止增长。正所谓"塞翁失马，焉知非福"，股价受挫，利润受损，汇丰银行的的确确为自己的疏忽付出了沉重的代价。但反而观之，经过本次事件洗礼，该行的反洗钱、反恐怖融资能力得到了迅速提升，基础系统配套设施明显升级，更重要的是合规意识在集团每位员工的心中牢固树立，"业务绑架合规"的现象大大减少。从汇丰集团2017年年报来看，虽然该集团在近年来从一些高风险国家撤并了部分机构，但其四大业务板块均保持良好的发展势头，营业收入和净利润均比2016年有了明显提升。

面对证据凿凿的犯罪事实，汇丰银行从一度面临吊销执照，到迅速和美国司法部支付罚款达成和解，其实除了自身诚恳的认错态度之外，背后政治势力的参与和斡旋也起到了至关重要的作用。

2016年7月，英媒报道称，在美国官员拒绝对洗钱罪行成立的汇丰银行进行司法起诉后，美国国会于7月11日公布了一份报告，指责前美国司法部长埃里克·霍尔德误导了国会决策。国会报告称，调查结果并不缺乏汇丰犯罪行为的证据，但司法部高层拒绝了起诉汇丰的建议，因为这些官员担心起诉这家银行会"导致全球金融灾难"。2013年，霍尔德在出席国会听证时表示，一些金融机构大到难以进行司法起诉，他认为"如果我们发现银行或金融机构做错了什么，且错误超过了合理的范围，他们将受到起诉"。国会报告指责称，当时有人建议对汇丰进行起诉，但霍尔德的这些言论明显误导了最终决定。

美国司法部的决定显然是受到了来自英国政府的压力。据悉，英国的监管部门"阻碍"调查并"影响"了最终结果。"英国财政大臣奥斯本对调查进行了干涉，他写信给美联储主席伯南克，对美国调查一家英国银行表示了担心"。在这封信中奥斯本说，起诉汇丰"可能严重影响金融和经济稳定，尤其是对欧洲和亚洲市场"。

回到事件本身，纵观整个案例，"蓄意"与"纵容"可谓是汇丰银行所犯下的最大错误。知法犯法，不仅暴露了集团内部对于合规工作的漠视本质，也给监管机构和政府部门的处罚决定提供了最好的证据和理由。汇丰银行的有意为之体现在多个方面。

第一，故意修改和隐藏汇款信息。早在20世纪90年代，汇丰英国就对受制裁实体采取了谨慎对待，他们会在这些客户的付款报文中添加诸如"小心，受制裁国家""不要向纽约提及我们的名字""不要提及伊朗"等说明，汇丰欧洲的系统可以自动识别出这些有修改痕迹的汇款，他们的员工会在手动删除受制裁实体的相关信息后再发往汇丰美国，这样便可确保这些汇款不会因OFAC制裁的因素而遭到延期处理或退回。汇丰集团在2000年发现了这一问题，集团的首席合规官意识到"修改报文信息，为违背集团制裁政策的行为提供了基础和便利"，并责令汇丰欧洲停止这一做法。但汇丰欧洲则辩驳道"受制裁客户的汇款给汇丰带来巨大的业务机会"，迫于业务的压力，首席合规官给予了汇丰欧洲特赦，允许其继续这种处理，在后续的几年里，汇丰欧洲和汇丰中东还从合规部拿到了类似的多次授意。尽管汇丰美国一直要求对于受制裁实体的付款需提供全套透明的客户信息，甚至拿到了汇丰集团一位高级合规官的承诺——"集团不会允许分支机构通过修改报文信息的方式，刻意回避美国的制裁筛查"，但这一承诺并未得到有效落实，汇丰的其他分支机构向汇丰美国刻意隐藏了修改信息的事实，并在那段时间开展了大量的美元清算业务。

第二，掉头交易并教授其他银行直通指令。2001年4月，汇丰欧洲告知了伊朗的一家银行如何规避和突破OFAC制裁筛查，确保汇款不受延迟和拒付。汇丰欧洲的员工曾写下"我们找到了一个甚至不太需要手工调整的汇款处理办法……关键就是要确保报文52栏填有信息——如果实在没有付款人，就写上'我们的一位客户'……汇丰英国不会在报文里引上'伊朗银行'是汇款方，只会显示汇丰英国……这样自然也就不必加上'不要提及我们名字'的说明，汇丰美国也就不会对这类的汇款进行落地筛查了"。如前文提到，汇丰银行此段时期仅通过掉头交易发生的汇款大约就有6.6亿美元。

业务与合规本是同一链条上相辅相成的两个环节，绝不能将两者对立起来，"业务绑架合规"或者"合规限制业务开办"都不是上策，将合规要求吃透摸透并有机融入到业务办理的每一环节，才是银行长远发展的立足之本。了解监管规则，绝不能出于"绕道而行""挑战底线"的动机，闭目塞听，塞耳盗钟的行为或许可以赢得一些短期的蝇头微利，但错误终究会带来处罚，幸运的事情不可能永远只降临在同一个人的身上。

随着全球化进程的深入，金融双向开放的步伐不断加快，中国银行业在加速"走出去"，融入国际市场的过程中也面临着越来越严峻的挑战。切实增强反洗钱合规管理能力，有效防范反洗钱监管风险，牢固树立全员参与的合规文化，真正实现属地合规、集团合规，既是适应国际金融环境的首要前提，又是商业银行国际竞争力的重要体现。

附录1：

《和解令1》英文原文

#2012-262

UNITED STATES OF AMERICA
DEPARTMENT OF THE TREASURY
COMPTROLLER OF THE CURRENCY

In the Matter of: HSBC Bank USA, N.A McLean, Virginia	AA-EC-12-112

CONSENT ORDER FOR THE
ASSESSMENT OF A CIVIL MONEY PENALTY

The Comptroller of the Currency of the United States of America ("Comptroller"), through his national bank examiners and other staff of the Office of the Comptroller of the Currency ("OCC"), has conducted an examination and investigation of the Payments and Cash Management ("PCM"), Global Banknotes, and foreign correspondent operations of HSBC Bank USA, N.A., McLean, Virginia ("Bank"). The OCC has identified deficiencies in the Bank's internal controls for these areas as well as in its overall program for Bank Secrecy Act/anti- money laundering ("BSA/AML") compliance. These findings were the subject of a Consent Cease and Desist Order issued on October 6, 2010 ("Consent Order"). Upon issuance of the Consent Order, the OCC deferred a decision with regard to the assessment of a civil money penalty ("CMP") against the Bank based on deficiencies addressed in the Consent Order, pending additional investigation.

The Bank, by and through its duly elected and acting Board of Directors ("Board"), has executed a "Stipulation and Consent to the Issuance of a Consent Order for the Assessment of a Civil Money Penalty," dated December ___11___, 2012 ("Stipulation"), that is accepted by the Comptroller. By this Stipulation, which is incorporated by reference, the Bank has consented to the issuance of this Consent Order for the Assessment of a Civil Money Penalty ("CMP Order") by the Comptroller.

On December ___11___, 2012, the Bank entered into a Deferred Prosecution Agreement ("DPA") with the United States Department of Justice ("DOJ"). In the DPA, the Bank admitted it had violated 31 U.S.C. § 5318(h)(1), which makes it a crime to willfully fail to establish and maintain an effective AML program, and 31 U.S.C. § 5318(i)(1), which makes it a crime to willfully fail to establish due diligence for foreign correspondent accounts. The Bank further consented to DOJ's findings in connection with these violations.

ARTICLE I
COMPTROLLER'S FINDINGS

The Comptroller finds the following:

The Comptroller incorporates the following findings in Article I of the Consent Order:

（1）The OCC's examination findings identified deficiencies in the Bank's BSA/AML compliance program. These deficiencies resulted in a BSA/AML compliance program violation under 12 U.S.C. § 1818(s) and its implementing regulation, 12 C.F.R. § 21.21 (BSA Compliance Program). In addition, the Bank violated 12 C.F.R. § 21.11 (Suspicious Activity Report Filings); and 31 U.S.C. § 5318(i) and its implementing regulation, 31 C.F.R. § 1010.610 (Correspondent Banking) (formerly 31 C.F.R. § 103.176).

The Bank failed to adopt and implement a compliance program that adequately covers the required BSA/AML program elements, including, in particular, internal controls for customer due diligence, procedures for monitoring suspicious activity, and independent testing. The Bank's compliance program and its implementation were ineffective, and accompanied by aggravating factors, such as highly suspicious activity creating a significant potential for unreported money laundering or terrorist financing.

Some of the critical deficiencies in the elements of the Bank's BSA/AML compliance program included the following:

（A）The Bank excluded from automated BSA/AML monitoring wire transfers initiated by customers domiciled in countries risk rated as "standard" or "medium," representing two-thirds of total dollar volume for PCM. While the Bank employed other methods for monitoring wire transactions for customers located in countries risk rated standard or medium, these alternatives provided limited coverage, were not effective, and did not mitigate the BSA/AML risks posed;

（B）During mid-2006 through mid-2009, the Bank did not perform BSA/AML monitoring for banknote (or "bulk cash") transactions with Group Entities (defined as the Bank's foreign affiliates in which the Bank's parent, HSBC Holdings plc, London, England ("HSBC Group"), holds a majority interest);

（C）The Bank did not collect or maintain customer due diligence ("CDD") or enhanced due diligence ("EDD") information for Group Entities. The Bank transacted extensive wire transfers and purchases of United States bulk cash with Group Entities. The lack of due diligence information inhibited the Bank's assessment of customer risk and the identification of suspicious activity in Group Entity accounts;

（D）The Bank failed to disposition its alerts appropriately or to comply fully with its obligation to report suspicious activity on time. As part of the 2009-10 examination, the OCC cited the Bank for its backlog of unprocessed alerts. The Bank's subsequent review of the backlogged alerts led it to file a substantial number of late Suspicious Activity Reports ("SARs") with law enforcement authorities; and

（E）The Bank did not appropriately designate customers as "high-risk" for purposes of BSA/AML monitoring, even where a customer's association with politically-exposed persons ("PEPs") could have harmed the Bank's reputation.

(2) The above violations and failures were the result of a number of factors, including, among others, (i) inadequate staffing and procedures in the alert investigations unit that resulted in a significant backlog of alerts; (ii) the closure of alerts based on ineffective review; (iii) inadequate monitoring of Group Entities' correspondent accounts for purpose and anticipated activity, anti-money laundering record, or consistency between actual and anticipated account activity; (iv) unwarranted reliance on Group Entities' following HSBC Group BSA/AML policies; (v) inadequate monitoring of funds transfers; (vi) inadequate procedures to ensure the timely reporting of suspicious activity; (vii) failure to adequately monitor Group Entities' banknote activity, (viii) inadequate monitoring of correspondent funds transfer activity; and (ix) inadequate collection and analysis of CDD information, including inadequate monitoring of PEPs.

The Comptroller further finds, for purposes of this CMP Order:

(3) The Bank has not fully complied with Article IX (Wire Monitoring) of the Consent Order. In relevant part, the Consent Order required the Bank to fully install, test, and activate a new wire monitoring system within 180 days. The Bank installed and activated a new wire monitoring system for its PCM unit without adequately testing the system. The Consent Order further required the Bank to conduct validation (gap) testing of the new system after installation. The Bank did not complete this testing within a reasonable period after installing the new system at its PCM unit. These instances of noncompliance exposed the Bank to a material risk of failing to report suspicious activity, including suspicious international wire transfers, to law enforcement.

(4) Pursuant to Article XI (Account/Transaction Activity Review ("Look-Back")) of the Consent Order, the Bank retained a consultant to conduct a look-back to review certain account and transaction activity specified by the OCC. The look-back, and the prior review during 2010 of the Bank's backlog of unprocessed alerts, together resulted in the Bank's late-filing 890 SARs addressing suspicious activity in the amount of $6.34 billion.

(5) The foregoing violations of law and noncompliance with the Consent Order meet the requirements for a "Tier II" civil money penalty, pursuant to 12 U.S.C. § 1818(i)(2)(B). The violations of law formed a pattern of misconduct. The BSA/AML compliance program violation began by January 1, 2007, and continued through 2010. The remaining violations of law lasted for three years or longer.

(6) During 2007-10, the Bank benefited from the foregoing violations of law by conserving funds that it should have expended in order to maintain a robust BSA/AML compliance program, as required by law. In this case, it is necessary to assess a civil money penalty in excess of the benefit amount to promote compliance with statutory and regulatory requirements and deter future misconduct.

Pursuant to the authority vested in him by the Federal Deposit Insurance Act, as amended, 12 U.S.C. § 1818, the Comptroller hereby ORDERS that:

ARTICLE II
ORDER FOR A CIVIL MONEY PENALTY

(1) The Bank shall pay a civil money penalty of five hundred million dollars ($500,000,000.00) to the United States Treasury upon execution of this CMP Order.

(a) The Bank shall pay the penalty by wire transfer to the United States Treasury, as instructed by the OCC.

(b) Upon payment of the penalty, the Bank shall send photocopies of the confirmation of the wire transfer by e-mail and overnight delivery to the Director of Enforcement and Compliance, Office of the Comptroller of the Currency, 400 Seventh Street SW, Washington, DC 20219.

(2) This CMP Order shall be enforceable to the same extent and in the same manner as an effective and outstanding order that has been issued and has become final pursuant to 12 U.S.C. § 1818(h), (i) (as amended).

ARTICLE III
<u>CLOSING</u>

(1) If, at any time, the Comptroller deems it appropriate in fulfilling the responsibilities placed upon him by the several laws of the United States to undertake any action affecting the Bank, nothing in this CMP Order shall in any way inhibit, estop, bar, or otherwise prevent the Comptroller from so doing.

(2) This CMP Order is and shall become effective upon its execution by the Comptroller, through his authorized representative whose hand appears below. The CMP Order shall remain effective and enforceable against the Bank and its successors in interest, except to the extent that, and until such time as, any provisions of this CMP Order shall have been amended, suspended, waived, or terminated in writing by the Comptroller.

(3) This CMP Order is intended to be, and shall be construed to be, a final order issued pursuant to 12 U.S.C. § 1818(i)(2), and expressly does not form, and may not be construed to form, a contract binding the Comptroller or the United States.

(4) The terms of this CMP Order, including this paragraph, are not subject to amendment or modification by any extraneous expression, prior agreements, or prior arrangements between the parties, whether oral or written.

IT IS SO ORDERED, this __11__ day of December, 2012.

UNITED STATES OF AMERICA
DEPARTMENT OF THE TREASURY
COMPTROLLER OF THE CURRENCY

In the Matter of:

HSBC Bank USA, N.A McLean,
Virginia

AA-EC-12-112

STIPULATION AND CONSENT TO THE
ISSUANCE OF A CONSENT ORDER FOR
THE ASSESSMENT OF A CIVIL MONEY PENALTY

The Comptroller of the Currency of the United States of America ("Comptroller") intends to initiate a civil money penalty proceeding against HSBC Bank USA, N.A., McLean, Virginia ("Bank") pursuant to 12 U.S.C. § 1818(i)(2), for violations of 12 U.S.C. § 1818(s); the Bank Secrecy Act, 31 U.S.C. §§ 5311 *et seq,* including 31 U.S.C. § 5318(i); and Bank Secrecy Act regulations 12 C.F.R. §§ 21.11 and 21.21, and 31 C.F.R. § 1010.610 (formerly 31 C.F.R. § 103.176), and for noncompliance with Article IX (Wire Monitoring) of the Consent Cease and Desist Order issued on October 6, 2010 ("Consent Order").

The Bank, in the interest of compliance and cooperation, enters into this Stipulation and Consent to the Issuance of a Consent Order for the Assessment of a Civil Money Penalty ("Stipulation") and consents to the issuance of a Consent Order for the Assessment of a Civil Money Penalty, dated December __11__ , 2012 ("CMP Order");

In consideration of the above premises, the Comptroller, through his authorized representative, and the Bank, through its duly elected and acting Board of Directors, stipulate and agree to the following:

ARTICLE I
JURISDICTION

(1) The Bank is a national banking association chartered and examined by the Comptroller pursuant to the National Bank Act of 1864, as amended, 12 U.S.C. § 1 *et seq.*

(2) The Comptroller is "the appropriate Federal banking agency" regarding the Bank pursuant to 12 U.S.C. §§ 1813(q) and 1818(i).

(3) The Bank is an "insured depository institution" within the meaning of 12 U.S.C. § 1818(i).

ARTICLE II
AGREEMENT

(1) The Bank consents and agrees to issuance of the CMP Order by the Comptroller.

(2) The Bank consents and agrees that the CMP Order shall (a) be deemed an "order issued with the consent of the depository institution" pursuant to 12 U.S.C. § 1818(h)(2), become effective upon its execution by the Comptroller through his authorized representative, and (c) be fully enforceable by the Comptroller pursuant to 12 U.S.C. § 1818(i).

(3) Notwithstanding the absence of mutuality of obligation, or of consideration, or of a contract, the Comptroller may enforce any of the commitments or obligations herein undertaken by the Bank under his supervisory powers, including 12 U.S.C. § 1818(i), and not as a matter of contract law. The Bank expressly acknowledges that neither the Bank nor the Comptroller has any intention to enter into a contract.

(4) The Bank declares that no separate promise or inducement of any kind has been made by the Comptroller, or by his agents or employees, to cause or induce the Bank to consent to the issuance of the CMP Order and/or execute the CMP Order.

(5) The Bank expressly acknowledges that no officer or employee of the Comptroller has statutory or other authority to bind the United States, the United States Treasury Department, the Comptroller, or any other federal bank regulatory agency or entity, or any officer or employee of any of those entities to a contract affecting the Comptroller's exercise of his supervisory responsibilities.

(6) The Office of the Comptroller of the Currency ("OCC") releases and discharges the Bank from all potential claims and charges that have been or might have been asserted by the OCC based on the Comptroller's Findings set forth in Article I of the CMP Order, to the extent known to the OCC as of the effective date of the CMP Order. However, the violations described in Article I of the CMP Order may be utilized by the OCC in future enforcement actions (a) against the Bank, to establish a pattern of violations or the continuation of a pattern of violations, or (b) against the Bank's institution-affiliated parties. This release shall not preclude or affect any right of the OCC to determine and ensure compliance with the terms and provisions of this Stipulation or the CMP Order.

(7) The terms and provisions of this Stipulation and the CMP Order shall be binding upon, and inure to the benefit of, the parties hereto and their successors in interest. Nothing in this Stipulation or the CMP Order, express or implied, shall give to any person or entity, other than the parties hereto, and their successors hereunder, any benefit or any legal or equitable right, remedy or claim under this Stipulation or the CMP Order.

ARTICLE III
WAIVERS

(1) The Bank, by consenting to this Stipulation, waives:

(a) the issuance of an Assessment of a Civil Money Penalty pursuant to 12 U.S.C. § 1818(i)(2) (as amended);

(b) any and all procedural rights available in connection with the issuance of the CMP Order;

(c) all rights to a hearing and a final agency decision pursuant to 12 U.S.C. § 1818(h), (i)(2) (as amended), and 12 C.F.R. Part 19;

(d) all rights to seek any type of administrative or judicial review of the CMP Order;

(e) any and all claims for fees, costs or expenses against the Comptroller, or any of his agents or employees, related in any way to this enforcement matter or the CMP Order, whether arising under common law or under the terms of any statute, including, but not limited to, the Equal Access to Justice Act, 5 U.S.C. § 504 and 28 U.S.C. § 2412; and

(f) any and all rights to challenge or contest the validity of the CMP Order.

ARTICLE IV
CLOSING

(1) The provisions of this Stipulation shall not inhibit, estop, bar, or otherwise prevent the Comptroller from taking any other action affecting the Bank if, at any time, it deems it appropriate to do so to fulfill the responsibilities placed upon him by the several laws of the United States of America.

(2) Nothing in this Stipulation shall preclude any proceedings brought by the Comptroller to enforce the terms of the CMP Order, and nothing in this Stipulation constitutes, nor shall the Bank contend that it constitutes, a waiver of any right, power, or authority of any other representative of the United States or an agency thereof, including, without limitation, the United States Department of Justice, to bring other actions deemed appropriate.

(3) The terms of this Stipulation and the CMP Order are not subject to amendment or modification by any extraneous expression, prior agreements or prior arrangements between the parties, whether oral or written.

IN TESTIMONY WHEREOF, the undersigned, authorized by the Comptroller as his representative, has hereunto set her hand on behalf of the Comptroller.

《和解令》中文译文

UNITED STATES OF AMERICA
DEPARTMENT OF THE TREASURY
COMPTROLLER OF THE CURRENCY

In the Matter of:

AA-EC-12-112

HSBC Bank USA, N.A.
McLean, Virginia

民事犯罪评定和解令

美国货币监理署调派国有银行检查官和其他职员，对汇丰美国的支付和现金管理、环球银票以及代理行业务展开了一次专项调查，发现该行在相关业务的内部管理以及对银行保密法和反洗钱合规的整体执行上存在漏洞。这些发现已在2010年10月6日颁布的和解令中列明，在发布之后，OCC决定延迟开展对汇丰银行的民事犯罪评定，并暂停了其他相关调查。

经在任的董事会授意，汇丰银行执行了"关于同意发布民事犯罪和解令协议"。此份协议于2012年12月11日签订，并被货币监理署接受。

2012年12月11日，该行正式执行与美国司法部的暂缓起诉协议。根据协议，该行承认自己主观故意未建立一套有效的反洗钱流程，且有意未对境外代理行账户开展尽职调查，均违背了相关法律。该行也同意司法部发现的其他相关犯罪事实。

第一章

货币监理署将如下检查结果写入和解令第一章

（1）OCC的检查发现了汇丰银行在反洗钱合规程序上的缺陷，这些漏洞违反了银行保密法及相关执行规定，此外该行还违反了可疑交易报告规定。

该行采用的合规程序，未能涵盖银行保密法和反洗钱流程所要求的基本要素，包括客户尽职调查内控、可疑交易监测以及独立测试。该行的合规流程和执行效果不佳，加之大量严重的可疑交易，都有可能导致洗钱和恐怖融资行为的漏报。

该行反洗钱合规流程的主要问题如下：

A.该行的反洗钱流程对来自"标准"和"中等"国别风险国家客户的电汇不做监控，而此类汇款占比高达三分之二。虽然该行对这些业务采用了其他替代性的监控手段，但覆盖面有限，效果不佳，不能减少反洗钱风险。

B.在2006年中至2009年中，该行未对集团内分支机构的银行票据交易实施监控。

C.该行未对汇丰集团内客户的普通型尽调和加强型尽调资料进行收集和保存。而该行确与集团内分支机构开展电汇和美国银行票据交易，尽调的缺失使得该行无法对客户风险进行评定，也无法对汇丰分支机构账户的可疑交易进行识别。

D.该行未能合理处置预警，没有按义务及时报告可疑交易。在2009年10月开展的检查中，OCC已指出该行积压了大量未处理的预警。而该行对积压预警的后续重检不当，造成了大量的可疑交易向法律执行机构晚报。

E.该行未合理评定"高风险"客户，仅仅是客户与PEP（政治人物）存在关联就可能影响到银行的声誉。

（2）造成上述违法行为的原因有很多，主要包括：（i）预警处理方面人员配备不足、流程不畅导致了大量的预警积压；（ii）预警重检敷衍无效，甚至直接关闭预警；（iii）未对集团分支机构的代理行账户进行合理监控，包括交易预估、反洗钱记录以及当前账户使用与预估交易的一致性；（iv）集团分支机构对汇丰集团反洗钱政策的执行情况无法保证；（v）电汇业务监控不当；（vi）集团内部银行票据交易监控不当；（vii）缺少合理流程来确保及时报告可疑交易；（viii）代理行汇款业务监控不当；（ix）普通型尽职调查的收集分析不足，未对政治人物进行监控。

（3）该行未能完全满足和解令第九章（电汇）的要求。根据和解令相关要求，该行需在180天之内完成新的电汇监控系统的安装、测试和激活使用，尤其是要求要在新系统安装后，要进行有效性测试，而该行实际上未经测试就上线了新系统。这些不合规的行为使得该行面临无法及时报告可疑交易的巨大风险。

（4）根据和解令第十一章（账户/交易重检），该行需聘用一名顾问，对货币监理署发现的账户和交易行为进行重检。重检不当加之积压的未处理预警，导致该行在2010年漏报了890份可疑报告，总金额高达63.4亿美元。

（5）根据有关法律，上述的违法行为以及对和解令的非合规执行，符合二级民事犯罪的标准。对银行保密法和合规流程的违反开始于2007年1月1日，一直持续到2010年，整个持续了3年甚至更多的时间。

（6）在2007年至2010年，该行从上述违法行为中获益良多，并且节省了本该投放于增强合规流程的经费。鉴于此种情况，有必要给予该行一份超过其获益金额的民事犯罪罚款，以此督促该行改进合规以符合监管要求并杜绝后续的不当行为。

根据联邦存款保险法案赋予的权力，货币监理署在此宣判：

第二章

民事犯罪判罚书

（1）在落实和解令之余，汇丰银行需向美国财政部支付5亿美元的民事犯罪罚款。

（a）该行需根据货币监理署的要求，以电汇形式向美国财政部支付罚款。

（b）支付罚款后，该行需通过邮件发送汇款确认书复印件，并于第二天向货币监理署合规执行办公室寄送原件。

（2）根据相关法律，本判罚书和此前发布的和解令具有同等法律效力和强制执行力，并且为最终定论。

第三章

（1）除判罚书中明文禁止事项之外，若货币监理署认为有必要行使美国有关法律赋予其的权责，可以在任何时间采取措施干预该行的经营。

（2）本判罚书一经货币监理署执行，即刻生效，并对该行及其继任者保有法律效力和强制执行力，除非货币监理署对其内容进行了修改、暂停、终止或免除。

（3）本判罚书为根据相关法律颁布的最终判罚，并不是该行与货币监理署或美国政府缔结的协议。

（4）本判罚书的条款，不因任何外部解释而改变，不因先前协议或双方先前任何口头或书面安排而受影响。

2012年12月11日，宣判如上。

附录2：

《解令2》英文原文

UNITED STATES DISTRICT COURT
EASTERN DISTRICT OF NEW YORK

<table>
<tr><td>

UNITED STATES OF AMERICA,

    - versus -

HSBC BANK USA, N.A. AND HSBC
HOLDINGS PLC,

              Defendants.

</td><td>

MEMORANDUM
AND ORDER
12-CR-763

</td></tr>
</table>

JOHN GLEESON, United States District Judge:

On December 11, 2012 the government filed an Information charging HSBC Bank USA, N.A. ("HSBC Bank USA") with violations of the Bank Secrecy Act ("BSA"), 31 U.S.C. § 5311 *et. seq.*, including, *inter alia*, willfully failing to maintain an effective anti-money laundering ("AML") program. *See* Information, ECF No. 3-1. The Information also charges HSBC Holdings plc ("HSBC Holdings") with willfully facilitating financial transactions on behalf of sanctioned entities in violation of the International Emergency Economic Powers Act ("IEEPA"), 50 U.S.C. §§ 1702 & 1705, and the Trading with the Enemy Act ("TWEA"), 50 U.S.C. App. §§ 3, 5, 16. *See id.*

On the same day the government filed the Information, it also filed a Deferred Prosecution Agreement ("DPA"), a Statement of Facts, and a Corporate Compliance Monitor agreement. The government filed these documents as exhibits to a letter application requesting that the Court hold the case in abeyance for five years in accordance with the terms of the DPA and exclude that time pursuant to 18 U.S.C. § 3161(h)(2) from the 70-day period within which trial must otherwise commence.[①] Gov't Letter, Dec. 11, 2012, ECF No. 3. The DPA provides that if HSBC Bank USA and HSBC Holdings (collectively, "HSBC") comply with its terms and provisions, the government will seek to dismiss the Information after five years.

On December 20, 2012 the parties appeared before the Court for a status conference. At the conference, I indicated that this Court has authority to accept or reject the DPA pursuant to Federal Rule of Criminal Procedure ("Fed. R. Crim. P") 11(c)(1)(A) and United States Sentencing Guideline ("U.S.S.G.") § 6B1.2.[②] Accordingly, I inquired as to whether, under the rubric of U.S.S.G. § 6B1.2, the DPA adequately reflects the seriousness of the offense behavior and why accepting the DPA would yield a result consistent with the goals of our federal sentencing scheme. I granted the parties leave to respond to these queries in writing.

For the reasons set forth herein, I approve the DPA pursuant to the Court's supervisory power and grant the parties' application to place the case in abeyance for five years pursuant to the Speedy

---

①   HSBC Bank USA and HSBC Holdings joined in the government's application.

②   The parties expressed their agreement with this characterization of the Court's authority at the status conference. Dec. 20, 2012 Tr. 5:20-6:17.

Trial Act. The Court will maintain supervisory power over the implementation of the DPA and directs the government to file quarterly reports with the Court while the case is pending.

A. *The Authority of the Court*

1. *Fed. R. Crim. P. 11(c)(1)(A) and U.S.S.G. § 6B1.2*

In their written submissions to the Court, the parties contest the applicability of Fed. R. Crim. P. 11(c)(1)(A) and U.S.S.G. § 6B1.2 to the DPA.[1] Gov't Mem. in Supp. DPA 2 n.1, ECF No. 14; Defs.' Letter in Supp. DPA 1-2, ECF No. 15. The parties assert that these provisions apply to cases where a defendant pleads guilty or nolo contendere to a charged (or lesser-included) offense and the plea agreement provides that the government will not bring, or will move to dismiss, other criminal charges. Gov't Mem. in Supp. DPA 2 n.1; Defs.' Letter in Supp. DPA 2. They submit that this scenario is not presently before the Court because HSBC has not agreed to plead guilty. Rather, HSBC has entered into an agreement to defer prosecution, whereby the government agrees to dismiss the Information if HSBC complies with the terms and provisions of the DPA. Gov't Mem. in Supp. DPA 2 n.1; Defs.' Letter in Supp. DPA 2.

The parties have a sound textual basis for their position. Fed. R. Crim. P. 11(c)(1)(A) states:

> (c) Plea Agreement Procedure.
>
> > (1) In General. An attorney for the government and the defendant's attorney . . . may discuss and reach a plea agreement. The court must not participate in these discussions. If the defendant pleads guilty or *nolo contendere* to either a charged offense or a lesser or related offense, the plea agreement may specify that an attorney for the government will:
> >
> > > (A) not bring, or will move to dismiss, other charges

The parties have not reached a plea agreement within the meaning of Fed. R. Civ. P. 11(c)(1) (A). HSBC has not agreed to plead guilty or *nolo contendere* to any of the charged offenses; it entered pleas of not guilty at the arraignment and expects that the charges will eventually be dismissed. Minute Entry, Dec. 20, 2012, ECF No. 13. Nor has the government agreed to dismiss other charges in exchange for a plea of guilty. Accordingly, neither Fed. R. Crim. P. 11(c)(1)(A) nor U.S.S.G. § 6B1.2 is applicable here.[2]

2. *The Speedy Trial Act*

The parties assert that 18 U.S.C. § 3161(h)(2) of the Speedy Trial Act "provides the applicable legal standard for the Court's review, as it requires the Court's approval for the exclusion of time." Defs.' Letter in Supp. DPA 2; *see also* Gov't Mem. in Supp. DPA 2 n. 1 ("In connection with a DPA, once a defendant has made an appearance and the speedy trial clock has begun to

---

[1] The government nevertheless addresses why the DPA adequately reflects the seriousness of the offense behavior and why accepting the DPA would yield a result consistent with the goals of our federal sentencing scheme. Gov' t Mem. in Supp. DPA 2 n.1.

[2] U.S.S.G. Chapter Six, Section B sets forth "[p]olicy statements governing the acceptance of plea agreements under Rule 11(c), Fed. R. Crim. P. . . . . to ensure that plea negotiation practices (1) promote the statutory purposes of sentencing prescribed in 18 U.S.C. § 3553(a); and (2) do not perpetuate unwarranted sentencing disparity." U.S. Sentencing Guidelines Manual ch. 6, pt. B, introductory cmt. (2012).

run, as it has here, the Court has the authority to determine whether to grant or deny a speedy trial waiver . . . .). Pursuant to 18 U.S.C. § 3161(h)(2), "[a]ny period of delay during which prosecution is deferred by the attorney for the Government pursuant to written agreement with the defendant, with the approval of the court, for the purpose of allowing the defendant to demonstrate his good conduct" "shall be excluded . . . in computing the time within which the trial of any such offense must commence." As HSBC observes, "subsection (h)(2) does not itself set forth a standard for the exclusion of time in the deferred prosecution context." Defs.' Letter in Supp. DPA 2. HSBC argues, however, that "subsection (h)(7), the Act's catch-all provision, provides that time should be excluded if the interests of justice served by the exclusion outweigh the best interests of the defendant and the public in a speedy trial." Id. (citing 18 U.S.C. § 3161(h)(7)).

I disagree with HSBC's assertion that the standard for excluding time pursuant to 18 U.S.C. § 3161(h)(2) is the ends-of-justice balancing inquiry articulated by 18 U.S.C. § 3161(h)(7). In Zedner v. United States, the Supreme Court explained:

> [T]he [Speedy Trial] Act recognizes that criminal cases vary
> widely and that there are valid reasons for greater delay in
> particular cases. To provide the necessary flexibility, the Act
> includes a long and detailed list of periods of delay that are
> excluded in computing the time within which trial must start. See

---

neither engaged in plea discussions nor entered a plea agreement, U.S.S.G. § 6B1.2, which articulates "Standards for Acceptance of Plea Agreements," is similarly inapplicable.

> § 3161(h). For example, the Act excludes "delay resulting from
> other proceedings concerning the defendant," § 3161(h)([1]),
> "delay resulting from the absence or unavailability of the
> defendant or an essential witness," § 3161(h)(3)(A), "delay
> resulting from the fact that the defendant is mentally incompetent
> or physically unable to stand trial," § 3161(h)(4), and "[a]
> reasonable period of delay when the defendant is joined for trial
> with a codefendant as to whom the time for trial has not run and no
> motion for severance has been granted," § 3161(h)([6]).
> Much of the Act's flexibility is furnished by § 3161(h)([7]), which
> governs ends-of-justice continuances . . . . This provision permits
> a district court to grant a continuance and to exclude the resulting
> delay if the court, after considering certain factors, makes on-the-
> record findings that the ends of justice served by granting the
> continuance outweigh the public's and defendant's interests in a
> speedy trial. This provision gives the district court discretion -
> within limits and subject to specific procedures - to accommodate
> limited delays for case-specific needs.

547 U.S. 489, 497-99 (2006). The Court's interpretation makes clear that 18 U.S.C. § 3161(h)(7) is not a "catch-all provision;" rather, it describes one specific type of exclusion - i.e., when the ends of justice served by the exclusion outweigh the best interests of the public - permitted

by the Speedy Trial Act.[①] This interpretation accords with a straightforward reading of the provision, which nowhere suggests that this balancing inquiry applies to the myriad other types of exclusion enumerated in 18 U.S.C. § 3161(h).

Returning then to 18 U.S.C. § 3161(h)(2), the exclusion applies to that "delay during which prosecution is deferred by the attorney for the Government pursuant to written agreement with the defendant, with the approval of the court, for the purpose of allowing the defendant to demonstrate his good conduct." Thus, under a plain reading of this provision, a court is to exclude the delay occasioned by a deferred prosecution agreement.

approval of the agreement by the court. This interpretation is buttressed by the legislative history of the provision. The Report of the Senate Judiciary Committee on the Speedy Trial Act states that this provision "assures that the court will be involved in the decision to divert and that the procedure will not be used by prosecutors and defense counsel to avoid the speedy trial time limits." S. Rep. No. 93-1021, at 37 (1974).

The Speedy Trial Act is silent as to the standard the court should employ when evaluating whether to grant "approval" to a deferred prosecution agreement under 18 U.S.C. § 3161(h)(2). Case law on this point is barren both in the Second Circuit and in other Circuits. However, the Report of the Senate Judiciary Committee suggests that such approval is grounded in a concern, to put it bluntly, that parties will collude to circumvent the speedy trial clock. S. Rep. No. 93-1021, at 37. 18 U.S.C. § 3161(h)(2) appears to instruct courts to consider whether a deferred prosecution agreement is truly about diversion and not simply a vehicle for fending off a looming trial date.

The DPA at issue here is, without a doubt, about diverting HSBC from criminal prosecution. But approving the exclusion of delay during the deferral of prosecution is not synonymous with approving the deferral of prosecution itself. As I discuss in greater detail below, the parties erroneously assume that the Court lacks authority to consider the latter question, and therefore need only decide the former. They are wrong. As such, the question of whether to exclude the duration of the DPA from the speedy trial clock hinges on a determination of whether the Court approves the DPA.

3. The Court's Supervisory Power

This Court has authority to approve or reject the DPA pursuant to its supervisory power. "The supervisory power . . . permits federal courts to supervise 'the administration of criminal justice' among the parties before the bar." United States v. Payner, 447 U.S. 727, 735 n.7 (1980) (quoting McNabb v. United States, 318 U.S. 332, 340 (1943)); Bank of Nova Scotia v. United States, 487 U.S. 250, 264 (1988) (Scalia, J., concurring) ("[E]very United States court has an inherent supervisory authority over the proceedings conducted before it . . . ."). The courts have wielded this authority substantively, that is, to provide a remedy for the violation of a recognized right of a criminal defendant. See McNabb, 318 U.S. at 345 (holding that "a conviction resting on evidence secured through . . . a flagrant disregard of the procedure which Congress has commanded [then 18 U.S.C. § 595, now Fed. R. Crim. P. 5(a)(1)] cannot be allowed to stand without making the courts themselves accomplices in willful disobedience of law"); see also United States v. Hasting, 461 U.S. 499, 505

---

① 18 U.S.C. § 3161(h)(7) does operate as a "catch-all provision" in the sense that "[t]he exclusion of delay resulting from an ends-of-justice continuance is the most open-ended type of exclusion recognized under the Act." Zedner, 547 U.S. at 508. Indeed, the parties could have chosen to request the exclusion of delay on ends-of- justice grounds in addition to or in lieu of the 18 U.S.C. § 3161(h)(2) exclusion.

(1983) (recognizing the "implementation of] a remedy for violation of recognized rights" as one of the proper uses of the supervisory power). They have also wielded this authority to fashion "civilized standards of procedure and evidence" applicable to federal criminal proceedings. McNabb, 318 U.S. at 340; see, e.g., McCarthy v. United States, 394 U.S. 459 (1969) (establishing procedure for accepting guilty plea); Elkins v. United States, 364 U.S. 206 (1960) (overruling "silver platter" doctrine, which permitted federal courts to receive evidence illegally seized by state officials without the involvement of federal officials); Ballard v. United States, 329 U.S. 187 (1946) (holding that jurors must be selected from fair cross-section of community).

One of the primary purposes of the supervisory power is to protect the integrity of judicial proceedings. Hasting, 461 U.S. at 526 ("[Our] cases have acknowledged the duty of reviewing courts to preserve the integrity of the judicial process."); Payner, 447 U.S. at 735 n.8 ("[T]he supervisory power serves the 'twofold' purpose of deterring illegality and protecting judicial integrity."); Elkins, 364 U.S. at 216, 222-23 (discussing "the imperative of judicial integrity" in invoking the supervisory power). Justice Louis Brandeis eloquently articulated this distinct duty to uphold judicial integrity:

> The governing principle has long been settled. It is that a court
> will not redress a wrong when he who invokes its aid has unclean
> hands. The maxim of unclean hands comes from courts of equity.
> But the principle prevails also in courts of law. Its common
> application is in civil actions between private parties. Where the
> government is the actor, the reasons for applying it are even more
> persuasive. Where the remedies invoked are those of the criminal
> law, the reasons are compelling.
>
> . . . The court's aid is denied only when he who seeks it has
> violated the law in connection with the very transaction as to
> which he seeks legal redress. . . . It is denied in order to maintain
> respect for law; in order to promote confidence in the
> administration of justice; in order to preserve the judicial process
> from contamination. . . . The court protects itself.

Olmstead v. United States, 211 U.S. 438, 483-85 (1928) (Brandeis, J., dissenting), overruled by Katz v. United States, 389 U.S. 341 (1961), and Berger v. New York, 388 U.S. 41 (1961). Justice Brandeis's words have since resonated throughout the Supreme Court's supervisory power jurisprudence. See Elkins, 364 U.S. at 223 (stating that federal courts will not be "accomplices in the willful disobedience of a Constitution they are sworn to uphold"); Mesarosh v. United States, 352 U.S. 1, 14 (1956) ("This is a federal criminal case, and this Court has supervisory jurisdiction over the proceedings of the federal courts. If it has any duty to perform in this regard, it is to see that the waters of justice are not polluted."); McNabb, 318 U.S. at 341 ("We are not concerned with law enforcement practices except in so far as courts themselves become instruments of law enforcement.").

Both parties assert that the Court lacks any inherent authority over the approval or implementation of the DPA. They argue that the Court's authority is limited to deciding, in the present, whether to invoke an exclusion of time under the Speedy Trial Act and, in the distant future, whether to dismiss the charges against HSBC. Gov't Mem. in Supp. DPA 2 n.1; Defs.' Letter in Supp. DPA 2. I conclude that the Court's authority in this setting is not nearly as cabined as the parties contend it is.

The government has absolute discretion to decide not to prosecute. ICC v. Brotherhood of Locomotive Engineers, 482 U.S. 270, 283 (1987) ("[I]t is entirely clear that the refusal to prosecute cannot be the subject of judicial review."). Even a formal, written agreement to that effect, which is often referred to as a "non-prosecution agreement," is not the business of the courts.[①] In addition, the government has near-absolute power under Fed. R. Crim. P. 48(a) to extinguish a case that it has brought. See United States v. Pimentel, 932 F.2d 1029, 1033 n.5 (2d Cir. 1991) ("Rule 48(a) provides that prosecutors may, 'by leave of court,' file a dismissal of an indictment, information or complaint. A court is generally required to grant a prosecutor's Rule 48(a) motion unless dismissal is 'clearly contrary to manifest public interest.'"). In my view, if the government were now moving to dismiss this case, it would be an abuse of discretion to deny that motion.

The government has chosen neither of those paths. Rather, it has built into the DPA with HSBC a criminal prosecution that will remain pending (assuming all goes well) for at least five years. DPA ^ 3, ECF No. 3-2. Just as a non-prosecution agreement is perceived as a public relations benefit to a company,[②] perhaps the filing and maintenance of criminal charges was intended to produce a public relations benefit for the government.[③] But for whatever reason or reasons, the contracting parties have chosen to implicate the Court in their resolution of this matter. There is nothing wrong with that, but a pending federal criminal case is not window dressing. Nor is the Court, to borrow a famous phrase, a potted plant.[④] By placing a criminal matter on the docket

---

① See Memorandum from Craig S. Morford, Acting Deputy Att'y Gen., U.S. Dep't of Justice, to Heads of Department Components, U.S. Att'ys re: Selection and Use of Monitors in Deferred Prosecution Agreements and Non-Prosecution Agreements with Corporations (Mar. 7, 2008), available at http://www.justice.gov/dag/morford-useofmonitorsmemo-03072008.pdf (last visited June 28, 2013) ("In the nonprosecution agreement context, formal charges are not filed and the agreement is maintained by the parties rather than being filed with a court.").

② The major distinction between a deferred prosecution agreement and a non-prosecution agreement appears to be the stigma associated with the former (i.e., filing a criminal charge). See Peter J. Henning, The Organizational Guidelines: R.I.P.?, 116 Yale L.J. Pocket Part 312, 314 n.9 (2007), http://yalelawjournal.org/ images/pdfs/528.pdf ("A deferred prosecution agreement involves the filing of criminal charges that will be dismissed after an agreed term so long as the company fulfills all the requirements of the agreement. A nonprosecution agreement is similar except that the charges are not filed, thus giving a small public relations benefit to the company, which can truthfully assert it was never prosecuted for the misconduct.").

③ On the day that the government filed the Information and DPA in this case, it issued a press release, in which the United States Attorney for the Eastern District of New York, Loretta E. Lynch, stated: "Today we announce the filing of criminal charges against HSBC, one of the largest financial institutions in the world. . . . Today's historic agreement, which imposes the largest penalty in any BSA prosecution to date, makes it clear that all corporate citizens, no matter how large, must be held accountable for their actions." Press Release, U.S. Dep't of Justice, HSBC Holdings Plc. and HSBC Bank USA N.A. Admit to Anti-Money Laundering and Sanctions Violations, Forfeit $1.256 Billion in Deferred Prosecution Agreement (Dec. 11, 2012), available at http://www.justice.gov/opa/pr/2012/December/12-crm-1478.html (last visited June 28, 2013).

④ See Attorney Brendan Sullivan, Counsel for Lieutenant Colonel Oliver North, Tells the Iran- Contra

of a federal court, the parties have subjected their DPA to the legitimate exercise of that court's authority.

The courts "are not concerned with law enforcement practices except in so far as courts themselves become instruments of law enforcement." McNabb, 318 U.S. at 347. The inherent supervisory power serves to ensure that the courts do not lend a judicial imprimatur to any aspect of a criminal proceeding that smacks of lawlessness or impropriety. "The court protects itself." Olmstead, 277 U.S. at 485. The parties have asked the Court to lend precisely such a judicial imprimatur to the DPA, by arranging for its implementation within the confines of a pending case. The Court will therefore exercise its supervisory authority over the DPA.

I recognize that the exercise of supervisory power in this context is novel. In the typical supervisory power case, the defendant raises a purported impropriety in the federal criminal proceeding and seeks the court's redress of that impropriety. See United States v. Johnson, 221 F.3d 83, 96 (2d Cir. 2000) ("[G]enerally the exercise of supervisory power arises in the context of requests by defendants to vacate convictions, dismiss indictments, or invalidate sentences . . . .") (internal citations omitted). In the deferred prosecution context, the defendant is presented with the opportunity for diversion from the criminal proceeding altogether. For obvious reasons, a defendant in these circumstances is less likely to raise a purported impropriety with the process, let alone seek the court's aid in redressing it, given the risk of derailing the deferral of prosecution.

Nevertheless, it is easy to imagine circumstances in which a deferred prosecution agreement, or the implementation of such an agreement, so transgresses the bounds of lawfulness or propriety as to warrant judicial intervention to protect the integrity of the Court. For example, the DPA, like all such agreements, requires HSBC to "continue to cooperate fully with the [government] in any and all investigations." DPA ^ 6. Recent history is replete with instances where the requirements of such cooperation have been alleged and/or held to violate a company's attorney-client privilege and work product protections,[①] or its employees' Fifth[②] or Sixth Amendment rights. [③]The DPA

---

① For nearly ten years - from 1999 to 2008 - the Department of Justice's corporate charging policies, as articulated in the Holder, Thompson, McCallum, and McNulty Memos, emphasized the importance of corporate cooperation, including a willingness to waive the attorney-client and work product protections. See Memorandum from Eric H. Holder, Jr., Deputy Att'y Gen., U.S. Dep't of Justice, to All Component Heads and U.S. Att'ys (June 16, 1999), available at http://www.justice.gov/criminal/fraud/documents/reports/1999/charging- corps.PDF (last visited June 28, 2013) [hereinafter Holder Memo]; Memorandum from Larry D. Thompson, Deputy Att'y Gen., U.S. Dep't of Justice, to Heads of Dep't Components and U.S. Att'ys (Jan. 20, 2003), available at http://www.albany.edu/acc/courses/acc695spring2008/thompson%20memo.pdf (last visited June 28, 2013) [hereinafter Thompson Memo]; Memorandum from Robert D. McCallum, Jr., Acting Deputy Att'y Gen., U.S. Dep't of Justice, to Heads of Dep't Components and U.S. Att'ys (Oct. 21, 2005), available at http://lawprofessors.typepad. com/whiteconarcrime_blog/files/AttorneyClientWaiverMemo.pdf (last visited June 28, 2013); Memorandum from Paul J. McNulty, Deputy Att'y Gen., U.S. Dep't of Justice, to Heads of Dep't Components and U.S. Att'ys (Dec. 12, 2006), available at http://www.justice.gov/dag/speeches/2006/ mcnulty_memo.pdf (last visited June 28, 2013).these policies engendered an enormous backlash. They catalyzed the formation of the Coalition to Preserve the Attorney-Client Privilege, composed of a broad swath of organizations including the American Civil Liberties Union, the Association of Corporate Counsel, the National Association of Criminal Defense Lawyers, and the United States Chamber of Commerce. Answers to Questions About the Attorney-Client Privilege, ABANOW (Dec. 1, 2006), http://www.abanow.org/2006/12/answers-to-questions-about-the-attorney-client-privilege/ ("The Coalition to Preserve the Attorney-Client Privilege represents a remarkable political and philosophical diversity, demonstrating just how widespread concerns about government policy in this area have become in the business, legal, and public policy communities."). It also led the American Bar Association ("ABA") to create the Presidential Task Force on Attorney-Client Privilege to study and address the erosion of attorney-client privilege. ABA President Robert Grey Creates Task Force to Advocate for Attorney-Client Privilege, ABANOW (Oct. 6, 2004), http://www.abanow.org/2004/10/aba-president-robert-grey-creates-task-force-to-advocate-for-attorney- client-privilege/. In August 2005, the ABA House of Delegates approved Recommendation 111, submitted by the Task Force, which held:

② The DOJ's corporate charging policies, as articulated in the Holder and Thompson Memos, also instructed federal prosecutors to consider the extent to which a cooperating company makes witnesses available to the government. Holder Memo, supra note 9, at 5; Thompson Memo, supra note 9, at 6. In United States v. Stein, the United States District Court for the Southern District of New York held that by pressuring the corporate defendant to use its power over its employees to coerce them to make statements to the government, such coercive tactics were attributable to the government, and suppressed some of the statements made by employees. 440 F. Supp. 2d 315, 337-38 (S.D.N.Y. 2006).

③ The DOJ's corporate charging policies, as articulated in the Holder and Thompson Memos, also instructed federal prosecutors to consider a company's advancing of legal fees to employees, except as required by law, as potentially indicative of an attempt to shield culpable individuals, and therefore a factor weighing in favor of indictment of the company. Holder Memo, supra note 9, at 6; Thompson Memo, supra note 9, at 7-8. In United States v. Stein, the United States District Court for the Southern District of New York held in another opinion that the government, in "tak[ing] into account, in deciding whether to indict [the corporate defendant], whether [the corporate defendant] would advance attorneys' fees to present or former employees in the event they were indicted .

also contemplates, in the event of a breach by HSBC, an explanation and remedial action, which the government will consider in determining whether to prosecute the pending charges and/or bring new ones. DPA ^ 16-17. What if, for example, the "remediation" is an offer to fund an endowed chair at the United States Attorney's alma mater? Or consider a situation where the current monitor needs to be replaced. See Gov't Letter, June 5, 2013, ECF No. 22 (advising the Court of the selection of an independent compliance monitor). What if the replacement's only qualification for the position is that he or she is an intimate acquaintance of the prosecutor proposing the appointment? See DPA ^ 10 ("The Department may also propose the names of qualified Monitor candidates for consideration.").

I do not intend to catalog all of the possible situations that might implicate the Court's supervisory power in this case. I couldn't even if I wanted to; the exercise would amount to looking through a glass, darkly, at five years of potential future developments in the case. What I can say with certainty is that by placing the DPA on the Court's radar screen in the form of a pending criminal matter, the parties have submitted to far more judicial authority than they claim exists.

B. Approval of the DPA

I approve the DPA. However, for the reasons set forth above, my approval is subject to a continued monitoring of its execution and implementation.

In approving the DPA, I am as mindful of the limits of the supervisory power as I am of its existence. For the most part, "when supervisory powers have been invoked the Court has been faced with intentional illegal conduct." Payner, 447 U.S. at 746 (Marshall, J., dissenting). My review of the DPA, and my knowledge of the actions that have been taken pursuant to the DPA thus far, reveal no impropriety that implicates the integrity of the Court and therefore warrants the rejection of the agreement.

I am aware of the heavy public criticism of the DPA. See, e.g. Editorial, Too Big to Indict, N.Y. TIMES, Dec. 11, 2012; Jesse Singal, HSBC Report Should Result in Prosecutions, Not Just Fines, Say Critics, The Daily Beast, July 18, 2012; Matt Taibbi, Gangster Bankers: Too Big to Jail, Rolling Stone, Feb. 14, 2013. Indeed, I have received unsolicited input from members of the public urging me to reject the DPA. See ECF Nos. 16, 17, 18, 21. These criticisms boil down to the argument that the government should seek to hold HSBC criminally liable, rather than to divert HSBC from the criminal process. But even if I were to reject the DPA, I would have no power to compel the government to prosecute the pending charges against HSBC to adjudication. To the contrary, as mentioned above, if the government moved under Fed. R. Crim. P. 48(a) to dismiss the Information, it would be an abuse of discretion not to grant that motion.

Significant deference is owed the Executive Branch in matters pertaining to prosecutorial discretion. The Executive Branch alone is vested with the power to decide whether or not to prosecute. United States v. Bonnet-Grullon, 212 F.3d 692, 701 (2d Cir. 2000) ("It is well established that the decision as to what federal charges to bring against any given suspect is within the province

---

interfered with the rights of such employees to a fair trial and to the effective assistance of counsel and therefore violated the Fifth and Sixth Amendments to the Constitution." 435 F. Supp. 2d 330, 382 (S.D.N.Y. 2006). The Second Circuit affirmed this decision, finding that the government had "unjustifiably interfered with [employees'] relationship with counsel and their ability to mount a defense, in violation of the Sixth Amendment," but did not reach the lower court's Fifth Amendment ruling. United States v. Stein, 541 F.3d 130, 136 (2d Cir. 2008).

of the Executive Branch of the government."), superseded by statute on other grounds by United States v. Levia-Deras, 359 F.3d 183, 188 (2d Cir. 2004). The decision whether to seek a criminal conviction implicates a complex of factors that "do not lend themselves to resolution by the judiciary." Inmates of Attica Correctional Facility v.

Rockefeller, 477 F.2d 375, 380 (2d Cir. 1973) (stating that "the task of supervising prosecutorial decisions" would place reviewing courts "in the undesirable and injudicious posture of becoming 'superprosecutors.'"). The Supreme Court has observed that a prosecutor's

> broad discretion rests largely on the recognition that the decision to
> prosecute is particularly ill-suited to judicial review. Such factors
> as the strength of the case, the prosecution's general deterrence
> value, the government's enforcement priorities, and the case's
> relationship to the government's overall enforcement plan are not
> readily susceptible to the kind of analysis the courts are competent
> to undertake. Judicial supervision in this area, moreover, entails
> systemic costs of particular concern.

Wayte v. United States, 470 U.S. 598, 607 (1985). With respect to cases of corporate misconduct, prosecutors must consider such factors as the nature and seriousness of the conduct, the pervasiveness of the conduct within the company, and the company's reaction to its own misconduct. They must also consider the ripple effects a conviction might have on innocent parties, such as employees (present and former) and shareholders. I have no doubt resource allocations concerns within the Department of Justice ("DOJ") play a legitimate role as well. Judges (even, and perhaps especially, judges who themselves once exercised prosecutorial discretion) need to be mindful that they have no business exercising that discretion and, as an institutional matter, are not equipped to do so.

I observed many years ago that although the Supreme Court's language in Wayte addressed "the decision of whether to prosecute, it is equally applicable to the decision of how aggressively to prosecute, and specifically to whether an arguably reasonable sentence bargain is appropriate." John Gleeson, Sentence Bargaining Under the Guidelines, 8 Fed. Sent'g Rep. 314, 315 (1996) ("[T]he judicial policing of sentence bargaining is unrealistic. The prosecutor may defend a plea agreement by reference to an office policy on such cases, but the probation officer may conclude that the AUSA is simply too lazy to try the case, or overly intimidated by the defense attorney. The probation officer may be right, but courts have no business engaging in that inquiry and have no ability to do so."). I add here that this language is just as applicable to the decision to enter into a deferred prosecution agreement.

Bearing in mind the appropriate degree of deference that is owed to the Executive Branch, the decision to approve the DPA is easy, for it accomplishes a great deal.

1. HSBC's Offense Conduct

According to the Statement of Facts, incorporated as part of the DPA, from 2006 to 2010, HSBC Bank USA failed to implement an effective AML program to monitor suspicious transactions from Mexico. Statement of Facts $ 9, ECF No. 3-3. During the same period, Grupo Financiero HSBC, S.A. de C.V. ("HSBC Mexico"), one of HSBC Bank USA's largest Mexican customers, had its own significant AML failings. Id. These collective AML failures permitted Mexican and Colombian drug traffickers to launder at least $881 million in drug trafficking proceeds through

HSBC Bank USA undetected. Id. HSBC Holdings was aware of HSBC Mexico's AML compliance problems as early as 2002, but failed to inform HSBC Bank USA of these problems or their potential impact on HSBC Bank USA's AML program. Id. $$ 9, 42-45; see also Gov't Mem. in Supp. DPA 6.

In addition, from at least 2000 to 2006, HSBC Group[1] knowingly and willfully engaged in practices outside the United States that caused HSBC Bank USA and other U.S. financial institutions to process payments on behalf of banks and other entities located in Cuba, Iran, Libya, Sudan, and Burma, in violation of U.S. sanctions. Statement of Facts $ 63. HSBC Group Affiliates[2] ensured that these transactions went undetected in the U.S. by altering and routing payment messages in a manner that hid the identities of these sanctioned identities from HSBC Bank USA and other U.S. financial institutions. Id. The total value of these transactions during this period was approximately $660 million. Id.

The government identifies three major causes for the failures in HSBC's AML and sanctions programs. Gov't Mem. in Supp. DPA 6-9. First, there was an "an institution-wide lack of accountability and diffusion of responsibility." Id. at 7. "At the HSBC Holdings level,

HSBC Group Compliance lacked the authority to mandate corrective or other action by any HSBC Group Affiliate." Id. And "[a]t the Affiliate level, HSBC's internal policies about whether AML officers or business executives were ultimately responsible for the AML and sanctions programs were unclear." Id. The result was that AML compliance and sanctions problems, even when identified at the HSBC Holdings level, went unresolved.

Second, HSBC Bank USA failed to provide adequate staffing and other resources to maintain an effective AML program. Statement of Facts ^ 25-28. Beginning in 2007, HSBC Bank USA began to "freeze" staffing levels in its AML department "as part of a bank-wide initiative to cut costs and increase the bank's return on equity." Id. ^ 25. As a result of this policy, HSBC Bank USA and HSBC North America Holdings, Inc. ("HSBC North America"[3]) did not replace departing compliance and AML staff, even senior officers such as HSBC Bank USA's AML Director and HSBC North America's Regional Compliance Officer (who oversaw compliance and AML at HSBC Bank USA). Id. ^ 25-26. HSBC Bank USA also combined multiple positions into one, for example, charging HSBC Bank USA's Head of Compliance with the responsibilities of HSBC Bank USA's AML Director, and charging HSBC North America's General Counsel with the responsibilities of HSBC North America's Regional Compliance Officer. Id. Finally, "requests for additional resources were discouraged and, ultimately [AML] employees stopped making staffing requests." Id. ^ 28.

Third, the corporate culture of HSBC "discouraged sharing of information within the organization." Gov't Mem. in Supp. DPA 8. At the HSBC Holdings level, a philosophy that "HSBC does not 'air the dirty linen of one affiliate with another,'" defined the approach to compliance. Statement of Facts ^ 45 (quoting HSBC's Head of Compliance). As a result, HSBC Holdings failed to inform HSBC Bank USA about HSBC Mexico's AML compliance problems or their potential impact on HSBC Bank USA's AML program. Id. ^ 42-45. At the HSBC Bank USA level, it adhered

---

[1] HSBC Group refers collectively to HSBC Holdings and its subsidiaries. Statements of Facts $ 3.

[2] HSBC Group Affiliates "refer to financial institutions throughout the world . . . that are owned by various intermediate holding companies and ultimately, but indirectly, by HSBC Holdings." Id.

[3] HSBC Bank USA is a subsidiary of HSBC North America, which, in turn, is an indirect subsidiary of HSBC Holdings. Id.

to a formal policy not to conduct due diligence on other HSBC Group Affiliates, which "impeded [its] ability to assess its money laundering vulnerabilities, including the extensive AML problems at HSBC Mexico." Gov't Mem. in Supp. DPA 8-9; Statement of Facts ^ 15. "With respect to U.S. sanctions, despite HSBC Bank USA's request for full details in transactions processed by HSBC Group Affiliates, some Group Affiliates structured transactions so that . . . HSBC Bank USA could not properly review the transactions to determine whether they violated U.S. sanctions." Gov't Mem. in Supp. DPA 9; Statement of Facts ^ 65-67.

2. The Deferred Prosecution Agreement

The DPA requires HSBC to undertake (or continue to undertake) remedial measures that address these systemic failures. HSBC Holdings and HSBC North America have overhauled their leadership teams. HSBC Holdings installed a new Chief Executive Officer ("CEO"), Chairman, Chief Legal Officer, and Head of Global Standards Assurance; HSBC North America installed a new CEO, General Counsel, Chief Compliance officer, AML Director, Deputy Chief Compliance Officer, and Deputy Director of Global Sanctions. DPA ^ 5(a), (m).

HSBC Holdings and HSBC Bank USA have taken steps to address the lack of accountability over their AML and sanctions compliance programs. HSBC Holdings elevated the Head of HSBC Group Compliance to the status of a Group General Manager, one of the 50 most senior positions at HSBC globally, and granted him direct oversight over every HSBC compliance and AML officer. Id. ^ 5(q)-(r); Gov't Mem. in Supp. DPA 12. It also restructured its senior executive bonus system so that bonuses are dependent on meeting compliance and AML standards. DPA ^ 5(v). HSBC Bank USA reorganized its AML department "to strengthen its reporting lines and elevate its status within the institution as a whole" by, inter alia, requiring that the AML Director report directly to the Board and senior management regarding HSBC Bank USA's AML program. Id. ^ 5(e).

HSBC Bank USA has made significant investments in its AML program, spending $244 million in 2011. Id. ^ 5(c). It increased its AML department staff from 92 fulltime employees and 25 consultants in January 2010 to approximately 880 full-time employees and 267 consultants as of May 2012. Id. ^ 5(d). Whereas in 2008, it had only four employees to review suspicious wire transactions, it now employs approximately 430 individuals to undertake this task. Gov't Mem. in Supp. DPA 8.

Finally, HSBC has taken steps to promote the sharing of information within the organization. HSBC Holdings "implemented procedures that require the sharing of information pertaining to AML weaknesses at one Group Affiliate horizontally throughout the HSBC Group." Gov't Mem. in Supp. DPA 13-14 (citing DPA ^ 5(t)). HSBC Bank USA has reformed its due diligence and risk-rating policies so as to subject HSBC Group Affiliates to a heightened level of scrutiny. DPA ^ 5(f)-(g). And it has implemented a new monitoring system, which allows it to track the originator, sender, and beneficiary of every wire transaction that moves through HSBC Bank USA. Id. ^ 5(j).

The DPA requires a corporate compliance monitor to supervise HSBC's remedial measures, as well as evaluate HSBC's ongoing compliance with the BSA, IEEPA, and TWEA, during the pendency of the agreement. Id. ^ 5; see also Corporate Compliance Monitor, ECF No. 3-4. The monitor will report regularly to the DOJ regarding HSBC's compliance with and/or violation of the DPA. Corporate Compliance Monitor ^ 3, 8. The monitor is charged with making recommendations for improving HSBC's effectiveness in implementing compliance and remedial measures; HSBC is required, under the DPA, to comply with such recommendations. Id. ^ 5.

In addition to remedial measures, the DPA also requires HSBC to forfeit $1.256 billion and to admit to criminal wrongdoing, as set forth in the Statement of Facts. Id. ^ 1-2, 7; see also Statement of Facts. Considered together, the DPA imposes upon HSBC significant, and in some respect extraordinary, measures. Indeed, taking into account the fact that a company cannot be imprisoned, it appears to me that much of what might have been accomplished by a criminal conviction has been agreed to in the DPA. In any event, in light of the broad deference owed by the Court to the prosecutor's actions, I approve without hesitation both the DPA and the manner in which it has been implemented thus far.

C. The Court Retains Supervisory Power over the Implementation of the DPA

As long as the government asks the Court to keep this criminal case on its docket, the Court retains the authority to ensure that the implementation of the DPA remains within the bounds of lawfulness and respects the integrity of this Court. Accordingly, the parties are directed to file quarterly reports with the Court to keep it apprised of all significant developments in the implementation of the DPA. Doubts about whether a development is significant should be resolved in favor of inclusion. The Court will notify the parties if, in its view, hearings or other appearances are necessary or appropriate.

So ordered.

John Gleeson, U.S.D.J.

Dated: July 1, 2013
Brooklyn, New York

《和解令》中文译文
美国地区法院纽约东区法院和解备忘录节译

美国政府起诉汇丰美国和汇丰控股

2012年12月11日，美国政府向汇丰美国提出控告，指控其违反了银行保密法（BSA），主观疏于使用有效的反洗钱流程。此外，还指控汇丰控股蓄意支持受制裁实体的金融交易，违反了国际紧急经济权利法（IEEPA）和敌国贸易法（TWEA）。

同一天，美国政府还提交了一些其他信息，包括延期追溯协议、事实陈述和公司合规监控协议。政府将这些文件作为书面申请书的附件，要求法院依据DPA的条款暂时搁置此案5年，而相关法律一般要求必须于70天内开庭审理。DPA有关条款规定，若汇丰美国和汇丰控股能够遵守条款和相关规定，政府可于5年后撤回控告。

参照后述理由，本人根据法院的监查权准许通过此份DPA，并根据STA法案，同意双方申请将此案停审5年。在停审期间，法院仍具有对DPA执行情况的监查权，并要求政府按时提交季度报告。

1.HSBC的犯罪行为

根据DPA中所附的事实陈述，自2006年至2010年，汇丰美国未能执行有效的反洗钱流程监控来自墨西哥的可疑交易。这些反洗钱上的疏漏，使得墨西哥和哥伦比亚的毒贩成功从汇丰美国至少完成了8.81亿美元的涉毒洗钱。而汇丰控股实际上早在2002年就获悉了汇丰墨西哥在反洗钱和合规管理方面的问题，但却并没有将这些问题和其他潜在影响告知汇丰美国。

另外，从2000年至2006年，汇丰集团知晓并有意利用汇丰美国和美国其他金融机构，违反美国的制裁，开展古巴、伊朗、利比亚、苏丹和缅甸等实体的代理清算业务。汇丰集团及其分支机构通过改变汇款信息和路径，隐藏了被制裁实体的身份，从而确保这些交易无法被汇丰美国和美国其他金融机构监测到。此段时期发生的交易大约有6.6亿美元。

美国政府指出了汇丰在反洗钱和制裁程序上存在问题的三点主因。

首先，整个机构内部存在严重的不可靠性和责任模糊。在汇丰控股层面，汇丰集团的合规官无权责令其分支机构进行整改或采取其他行动；在分支机构层面，对于反洗钱和制裁流程最终是由合规官还是业务决策人员来负责，汇丰集团也一直都没有明确。

其次，汇丰美国未能配置充足的人力物力资源来保证反洗钱流程的有效性。从2007年开始，出于降低成本和提高资本收益率的考虑，汇丰美国便严格控制其反洗钱部门的员工数量和级别。这一政策，直接造成汇丰美国和汇丰北美在合规人员离职后，没有及时补充替代，甚至包括反洗钱主管和地区合规官等重要岗位。汇丰美国还尝试进行岗位合并，一人多岗，比如汇丰美国的合规部总经理要同时身兼反洗钱主管职责，汇丰北美的总法律顾问身兼地区合规官角色。反洗钱职员提出的增配资源的要求都被驳回并且不被倡导，最终也不再有员工为此发声。

最后，汇丰的企业文化并不倡导在机构间分享信息。甚至在总行层面也盛行着对待合规问题"家丑不外传"、"汇丰不允许恶习在机构间互相渐染"的观念。这样一来，汇丰控股并未将汇丰墨西哥在反洗钱和合规管理方面的问题和其他潜在影响告知汇丰美国也就不足为奇了。而且汇丰美国也一直不对汇丰集团自己的分支机构开展尽职调查，这也限制了其侦别出汇丰墨西哥等洗钱行为的能力。对于美国的制裁规定，尽管汇丰美国已要求其他兄弟机构执行全套交易信息审查，但汇丰的部分分支机构设计了一些交易结构，使得汇丰美国无法正常监测和判断这些交易到底是否违法了美国制裁。

2.暂缓起诉协议（DPA）

DPA要求汇丰银行采取弥补措施来改善这些系统性缺陷。汇丰控股和汇丰北美已经更换了高层领导团队，汇丰控股认命了新的CEO、主席、首席法务官，全球标准保障主管；汇丰北美认命了新的CEO、总法律顾问、首席合规官、反洗钱主管、副首席合规官和国际制裁副主管。

汇丰控股和汇丰北美已采取措施并重视其在反洗钱、制裁筛查及合规流程上的缺陷与问题。汇丰控股将集团合规主管提升至集团总经理级别，成为汇丰集团全球50位最重要的高管层之一，并且授予其直接管理汇丰集团每一位合规官和反洗钱官的权力，此外汇丰控股还相应调整了高管激励机制，只有满足合规和反洗钱标准才可获得激励。汇丰北美重组了其反洗钱部以加强条线工作汇报和机构融合，要求反洗钱主管直接向汇丰北美的董事会和高管层汇报。

汇丰美国已于2011年花费244亿美元，对其反洗钱流程做了重要投资。在2010年1月，反洗钱部门仅有92名全职员工和25名顾问，等到2012年5月，已增加至约880名全职员工和267名顾问。在2008年，汇丰美国仅有4名员工负责监测可疑交易，而目前从事这一方面工作的员工已高达430名。

最后，汇丰银行还采取了一系列措施促进机构内的信息共享。汇丰控股通过流程控制，要求某一分支机构的反洗钱相关方面的缺陷，能够在集团范围内横向分享。汇丰美国修改了尽职调查和风险分类政策，对集团内的分支机构也进行高等级的审查，并且采用了一套全新的监控系统，可以对汇丰美国经手的每笔电汇的汇款人、受益人进行跟踪监测。

DPA要求在停审期间设有一名合规检查员，负责督察汇丰银行的弥补措施落实情况，并对汇丰银行日常持续性合规工作进行评估，评判其是否满足

BSA，IEEPA和TWEA法案的要求。合规检察员将定期向美国司法部汇报汇丰银行对DPA的执行情况，并可就如何提高整改效果、落实合规要求向汇丰银行提出建议或提示，而根据DPA相关条款，汇丰银行对此必须遵守并执行。

除此之外，DPA还要求汇丰银行支付12.56亿美元的罚款，并承认事实陈述里所列的违法事实。综合来看，DPA已强制对汇丰银行采取了一系列影响巨大的举措，并且考虑到汇丰银行作为一家公司无法入狱，DPA与刑事定罪的效果几乎无异。

3.

不认真整改的后果很严重
——渣打银行洗钱案例

    2012年和2014年，渣打银行与美国监管机构分两次达成《和解令》（见附录）。渣打银行由于反洗钱合规不力，涉及伊朗、沙特、苏丹和利比亚等中东及北非敏感国家客户交易，连续两次被美国纽约州金融服务管理局分别处以3.4亿美元和3亿美元的罚款。很少有其他国际银行像渣打银行一样，在洗钱领域的同一个地方连续跌倒两次，即两次被处罚的原因基本相同，金额也很接近，这种特殊的洗钱案例引起我们无数的好奇和思考。

渣打银行概述

渣打银行集团有限公司的主体是渣打银行。渣打银行①（Standard Chartered Bank）是一家国际领先的银行集团。按照2017年底资产排名，该银行以6 479亿美元位列全球大银行第50位。穆迪对该银行的长期债务评级为A1，标普外币评级为A。

1863年成立的不列颠南非标准银行②（The Standard Bank of British South Africa）与1853年成立的印澳中注册银行③（the Chartered Bank of India, Australia and China）两家机构均致力于在贸易方面进行扩张，并从欧洲、亚洲和非洲的货物贸易融资中获利。这两家银行于1969年合并成为了渣打银行。

因此，渣打银行在全球一些最有活力的市场上已经经营超过了150年，其90%以上的营运收入和利润来自亚洲、非洲和中东市场。渣打银行选择性地投入市场以及坚持发展与客户深厚关系的承诺，推动该银行在近年以来取得强劲增长。渣打银行除在伦敦及中国香港的交易所上市外，还在印度的孟买以及印度国家证券交易所上市。

渣打银行的主要业务单元分为：零售银行业务、批发银行业务、中小企业银行业务、伊斯兰地区银行业务、私人银行业务和网上银行业务。

渣打银行在海外发展的战略十分清晰，核心是以"客户为中心"，一般分四步走。金融机构业务（FI Business）：一般先从设立代表处开始，初步了解

---

① 渣打银行。
② 不列颠南非标准银行。
③ 印澳中注册银行。

和熟悉当地市场，发展同当地金融机构的联系，这是进入市场的第一步；跨国公司业务（Multinational Corporate Business）：根据本土的跨国公司的需要，到客户发展业务的海外开设分支机构；当地业务（Local Business）：随着海外分支机构在当地站稳脚跟，慢慢吸收当地客户，发展当地业务。例如渣打银行收购韩国本土的韩一银行就是遵循这样的发展轨迹：先是渣打银行跟随客户的需要在韩国当地开设分支机构，发现当地的许多客户群体有业务需求，但苦于没有足够的分支机构与当地银行竞争，于是后来根据发展当地业务的需要兼并了韩一银行；零售业务（Retail Banking）：发展零售银行业务的第一步是开展财富管理业务（Wealth Management），针对当地的富裕客户，走高端服务路线。后面再根据市场需要以合适的途径接触普通大众客户。

整个渣打银行集团在英国本土，以及亚太、南亚、中东、非洲、美洲等68个国家和地区拥有1 700多家分支机构，雇员人数达到86 000余名。渣打银行的发展战略是：产品上，以零售银行业务、公司业务、中小企业业务、私人银行业务和伊斯兰银行业务为核心；地域上，力争成为亚洲、非洲及中东地区最重要的国际性银行。正是由于渣打银行客户的地域分布特点，导致该银行面对受国际制裁的中东及北非客户群体庞大，客户类型多样，再加上反洗钱系统设计不够精准，难免出现百密一疏的失误。

渣打银行与美国监管机构的第一次对峙和妥协

2012年，多年以来顺风顺水的渣打银行遭受到一次意外的打击。渣打银行经过数个月与监管机构的拉锯战最终达成和解（和解令相关内容参见附录）在这一年，华盛顿检方指控称，渣打银行在美国的分行帮助受制裁国家洗钱，卷入伊朗等多个国家的洗钱案，而这些国家都名列美国政府的"黑名单"。纽约州金融服务管理局（Department of Financial Services，NYDFS）提出可能吊销渣打银行在美银行执照，美国司法部、美联储以及曼哈顿地区检察署等机构也参与进来，让事态骤然紧张，一场看似生死存亡的危机向渣打银行袭来。

美国纽约州金融局指控渣打这家英国资产第五大银行在过去10年间秘密与

伊朗机构进行了6万多笔金融交易，涉及2 500亿美元，并以可能吊销渣打在美国的银行执照相威胁。纽约州金融局认为，渣打的行为违反了此前制裁伊朗的相关规定和美国银行法，同时对投资者构成了欺骗。与此同时，美国司法部等其他机构也对此事进行了调查。事态瞬间恶化，受此影响，渣打股价一天之内下跌了16%。而就在事件发酵的一个礼拜间，该银行股票跌幅最多时曾接近25%，为1988年有记录以来的最大跌幅。消息发出后，渣打银行董事会主席庄贝思（Sir John Peace）在第一时间奔赴纽约寻求对策，而行政总裁冼博德（Peter Sands）也随时待命，准备飞往纽约。

随后，渣打银行正式向美国政府等相关监管部门发起"反击"，对上述指控予以坚决否认，表示产生矛盾的原因只是"小小的笔误"。市场不断传出渣打管理层对此事的应对措施，包括反起诉、向母国层面的监管机构求助等。庄贝思还在当时接受英国《金融时报》采访时说："渣打银行因为上述指控被伤害是完全错误的，我们将与控方进行沟通甚至是辩论以证明渣打银行的清白。"与此同时，渣打银行在母国的游说也起到了效果，一些英国政界人士参与进来，异于寻常地公开反对美国此举，称这是肆意动摇伦敦金融中心地位的阴谋。

但是渣打银行的反击终究力量有限，到了2012年8月，提出指控的纽约州金融局检察官本杰明·洛斯基（Benjamin Lawsky）在官网发布公告称，双方已达成和解，代价是渣打银行需向纽约州金融局支付3.4亿美元的民事赔偿金，该金额远高于渣打原先设想的500万美元。洛斯基同时强调此事并未完结，国际层面的调查将继续进行。由于协商成功，原定于在曼哈顿纽约州监管机构办公室进行的听证会被取消。渣打银行首席执行官冼博德随后声称，违规与2007年集团的交易后监督系统的更新报告相关，当时的报告将这个系统形容为"实施不力"。因此渣打银行的反洗钱系统未能发现可疑，甚至是可能违法的付款。

至此，闹得沸沸扬扬的渣打银行洗钱风波也算告一段落。

这一结果并不令人意外。细究起来，其实并没有看起来这么可怕。吊销执照的"威胁"仅仅是一种谈判技巧，从历史上看，这也并非首例。因此，尽管双方都剑拔弩张，但走上谈判桌达成和解协议似乎是唯一选择。

面对双方剑拔弩张的情形，英国《每日电讯报》曾引述消息称，渣打和金融局都不希望在听证答辩会上"兵戎相见"，都希望以罚款来和解，只是对罚款金额存在巨大分歧。尽管双方一度互不相让，但最终还是回到了谈判桌上。在他来看，罚款和解就是一个讨价还价的过程，渣打原先想以区区500万美元了结此事的愿望太不切实际。事实证明，最后3.4亿美元的"量刑"正好是个中间值。

另据纽约州金融局官网公布的声明，和解在三个方面基本达成。首先，渣打支付3.4亿美元的民事赔偿金给纽约州金融局；其次，该行同意建立一个监控系统，利用这一系统对纽约州分行的洗钱风险进行评估，并将系统设置为直接汇报给纽约州金融局检察官，期限不得少于两年；最后，渣打总部需在纽约州分行永久性设置专门负责监管和审计境外洗钱活动的职位，以监控和审计该行所有涉及离岸洗钱的行为。

监管机构对渣打吊销执照的"威胁"是危机升级的关键点。从历史上看，上一次美国当局撤销一家大型银行执照还是20年前的事。这家银行是当时在全球排名439位的国际商业信贷银行，其重要性远不及入选全球系统重要性金融机构的渣打银行，单从这个意义上说，吊销渣打这样的大型银行的执照在美国金融史上非常罕见，美国方面也不会轻易作此决定。不仅如此，既然纽约州金融局敢开出3.4亿美元的和解砝码，就说明只要支付这样的罚单，渣打便不会失去其美国银行执照，甚至由于罚款附带的保密协议，渣打洗钱丑闻的过多细节也不会为世人所知。而对渣打而言，若没有和解协议，监管机构很可能将此事披露给媒体，从而对其声誉造成重大的负面影响，这也是他们所不能接受的。因此，双方多次交涉的根本目的还在于对罚款数额的讨价还价。至于如此众多的监管机构也加入其中，无非是想在巨额罚款中分得一杯羹罢了。

在刚刚过去的2012年6月，荷兰银行国际集团（ING）就类似事件被罚款6.19亿美元。由于相关保密协议，监管机构向外界披露的信息也非常少，从而避免了ING的声誉受到太多负面影响。当时另外一家同样深处洗钱丑闻的大型银行——汇丰银行也已经拨出7亿美元的准备金应对洗钱风波的罚款。

最终，渣打集团宣布就2001年至2007年遵守美国制裁问题及美元支付操作与若干美国当局达成和解，当中涉及由纽约州金融局发出的同意令、美国联邦储备委员会（联储局）发出的终止及停止指令、与美国司法部及纽约郡地方检察官办公室分别签订的延迟检控协议，以及与美国外国资产控制办公室签订的和解协议（统称"和解"），民事罚款总计6.67亿美元，其中3.4亿美元支付给纽约州金融局，其余部分由上述其他监管机构分享。

美国监管机构对渣打银行的第二次处罚

2014年，美国检方对包括渣打银行在内的几大银行再次展开调查，理由是检方怀疑几大银行违反了先前达成的和解协议。

美国检察官认为：遭调查的几大银行早前接受和解，仅仅是为了避免刑事诉讼而支付罚款，但并没有在银行内部实施改革。

对于渣打银行，检察官们提出质疑称，该银行向政府隐瞒了自己的错误行径，并且已经破坏了先前约定的协议。纽约州金融服务局表示，渣打银行存在数百万未申报的可疑交易。

虽然在两年之前已经因为违反制裁法案被纽约州金融局及美国当局罚款而取得了和解协议，并承诺改善其内部流程，不过源自该行未能依照2012年协议的要求落实监控机制以发现可疑交易，渣打银行自2014年的年中开始，就一直在与纽约银行业监管机构进行谈判，当时外界估计渣打银行可能以至多3亿美元的金额和解该行未能发现有问题交易的相关指控。

这样金额的惩戒对于一个后续和解协议而言是相当高的数额，这凸显了纽约州金融服务局负责人本杰明·洛斯基（Benjamin Lawsky）的强硬立场，那就是，银行同意了和解协议中的某些条款，就必须严格遵守它们。

渣打银行还要同意纽约州金融服务局其他的额外惩戒措施，包括延长一个独立监察方的合约，帮助该行发现有问题的交易。

这一组调查是渣打银行在2012年与包括纽约州金融服务局在内的美国当局所达成的一组和解协议的后续，该行在当时被指控违反美国制裁法案，与苏丹，伊朗，利比亚以及缅甸开展业务。在当时的6.67亿美元和解金中，有3.4亿美元归纽约州监管机构所有，渣打银行在当时同意聘用独立监察方来评估银行对和解协议的执行，并确保停止处理被禁止的交易。

渣打银行自2012年的制裁相关和解以来就与美国当局争议不断。渣打银行董事会主席庄贝思爵士曾表示，虽然该行承认了违反制裁措施的责任，但是这些违规行为只是"文书错误"，而不是"故意"破坏规则。这一说法让监管机构非常不满。

庄贝思爵士的上述发言导致他本人，行政总裁冼博德，以及时任财务主管的理查德-梅丁斯（Richard Meddings）被美国当局传召至华盛顿，三人均被严厉训斥。庄贝思爵士之后被迫向投资者和银行职员道歉，承认他的言论"在法律和事实上均不正确"。

渣打银行的亚洲业务负责人白承睿（JaspalBindra）曾抱怨说，监管机构将银行的失误当作刑事犯罪一样对待。他在接受路透社访问时说，"银行业被要求在反洗钱事务中扮演监察者的执法角色，但是一旦我们有疏失，我们并没有被当作执法者来对待，而是被视作一名罪犯"。

2014年8月，纽约州金融服务局宣布，渣打银行将因未能遵守2012年与纽约州洗钱和解条约规定，解决其洗钱问题，已同意支付3亿美元的罚金，并对业务流程进行多项调整以和解针对该行反洗钱合规失当的指控。（和解令相关内容参见附录）

纽约州金融服务局表示，作为该行与纽约州银行业监管机构3亿美元和解协议的一部分，和解协议将要求渣打银行采取多项措施，包括解除部分特定的，与阿拉伯联合酋长国业务中存在的高风险客户关系。渣打银行还同意停止其香港子公司对部分高风险零售客户的美元结算业务，渣打银行还被禁止在未经纽约州金融服务局批准的情况下，不能接受新的美元清算业务客户。此前该行未能改善工作流程以发现可疑的交易活动。

纽约州金融服务局的媒体声明稿指出，香港和阿拉伯联合酋长国业务中有"大量具有潜在高风险的交易"，而渣打银行之前的反洗钱系统未能及时发现。

本次的和解是2012年渣打银行与多家美国监管机构之间和解协议的后续，当时的和解协议允许纽约州金融服务局在该行内部设立了一个独立监察机制。

纽约州金融服务局主管本杰明·洛斯基指出，"如果一家银行无法兑现自己的承诺，那么应该为其行为而承担相应的严重后果。在反洗钱合规这样的严肃领域尤其是如此，这一方面的要求能够有效地帮助防止恐怖主义和侵犯人权的行为"。

而渣打银行在一份书面声明中表示，其将承担责任，并且为该行在纽约分行反洗钱交易监测系统中出现的漏洞深表歉意，将为打破洗钱条约规定而支付另一笔罚金。渣打银行声称已经开始采取深度广泛的补救措施，并致力于解决那些极端紧急的问题。声明表示，该协议将影响有限数量的客户："本集团愿意为纽约分行反洗钱交易监控系统的不足之处负责，并为它们感到遗憾。本集团已启动大范围补救努力，并致力于把完成这些任务当做头等大事。"中止客户关系及后续的罚金为在纽约州开展业务的银行设置了新的标杆，这些银行都要受纽约州金融服务局负责人本杰明·洛斯基的监督。对渣打银行来说，它此次上缴的罚金几乎与纽约州金融服务局当初征收的罚金相等。

最终，在2014年8月19日，渣打集团纽约分行就反洗钱交易监测系统的不足之处与纽约州金融局达成最终和解方案，支付为数3亿美元的民事罚款。按要求，该系统独立于制裁名单筛选程序，将成为渣打集团整体金融罪行监控的一部分，旨在提醒纽约分行须于交易后作进一步调查客户的不寻常交易模式，以便发现可能存在的隐患。之后，在2017年11月，渣打集团宣布同意将其美国延迟检控协议进一步延长，直至2018年7月28日为止。

两次制裁的影响及教训

（1）两次制裁对渣打银行自身造成的影响。两次制裁对渣打银行造成的影响除了沉重的罚款负担，核查及整改内部流程也要付出一笔巨款之外，该事件对于该行高管层造成的压力也颇大。

这两次打击引发了部分最大股东对过去十年以来该行高速扩张策略的质疑。他们认为，2006年上任的该行首席执行官冼博德（Peter Sands）和2009年成为公司主席的庄贝思爵士（Sir John Peace）应该承担主要责任。

在2012年至2014年的两年里，冼博德因该行的糟糕业绩及下滑股价而受到多次批评。几乎毫发无损地渡过了2008年的金融危机，并有超过十年的年均两位百分数盈利增长之后，受反洗钱事件影响，渣打股价一天之内下跌了16%。而就在事件发酵的一个礼拜间，该银行股票跌幅最多时曾接近25%，为1988

年有记录以来的最大跌幅。此后，渣打银行在2014年上半年又经历了严重下行——税前利润指标有20%的降幅，股价在18个月中下跌了约三分之一。该行大机构投资者表示："冼博德只有最后一次机会，如果业绩持续不好的状态，他就得离职。"

两次制裁不仅对渣打银行自身造成了严重的影响，与该银行相关的机构也受到波及。当银行聘用知名顾问公司来参与调查，并要求监管部门相信调查结果时，这样的处罚通常会引发利益冲突。

（2）两次制裁对相关机构造成的影响。2015年8月，当初被渣打银行聘用的华盛顿咨询公司Promontory金融集团，如今搬起石头砸了自己的脚。纽约金融监管机构声称，Promontory曾在针对渣打的调查中协助后者掩盖真相，并因此勒令 Promontory暂停为国企贷款商提供顾问服务。这种处罚可能会制造冲突，并且带来比罚款更多的刺痛。

2012年，涉嫌2 500亿美元洗钱案的渣打银行与美国监管机构进行和谈，以期实现缴纳罚款和解。但因纽约州金融服务局与联邦监管机构在此问题上的分歧，和谈采取了渣打与联邦监管机构、纽约州金融服务局分开谈判的形式。渣打认为，纽约州金融服务局指控的2 500亿美元与伊朗业务往来中，99.9%符合美国的"掉头交易"规则。该银行聘用了Promontory咨询公司。该咨询公司帮渣打作出的估计是，渣打纽约州分行与伊朗交易中违反联邦禁令的交易共1 400万美元，不到纽约州金融服务局指控的0.1%。但纽约州金融服务局对该调查结果并不接受。

Promontory咨询公司的高管包括前通货监理官、美联储前副主席和前美国官员。因为高管是德高望重的大人物，所以Promontory咨询公司在业界的知名度很高。因为名气大，这家咨询公司瞄准的都是大企业。

纽约州金融服务局指控Promontory咨询公司在针对渣打洗钱案的调查中协助渣打稀释相关数据。纽约州金融服务局声称，比如说，当渣打的律师问及是否能将报告做得"更温和"时，Promontory咨询公司欣然答应。

纽约州金融服务局认为，在准备工作中，Promontory咨询公司缺少"独立的判断"。处罚是：禁止Promontory咨询公司获得未来为银行提供咨询服务所需的机密监管信息。

显然，这个处罚很严苛，尤其是在被处罚者并无违法行为的情况下。全球知名的德勤会计师事务所也因在渣打洗钱事件中未能尽到自己的职责，而同意向美国监管部门递交总计1 000万美元的罚金，并接受长达一年的禁业处罚。

经验教训的总结和借鉴

（1）及时设立高规格的内部监督机构。在遭受处罚后，渣打银行痛定思痛，随即成立了最高规格的董事会合规监督委员会，确定了最高管理层对于处罚的直接整改和监督机制。

渣打银行董事会合规监督委员会于2013年成立，履行重要职责，代表董事会监督全集团履行与美国当局所达成和解的责任相关事宜。这包括对美国任何联邦或州机构或其他相关机构就有关和解或该集团过往及现时遵守美国制裁法规所发出的其他要求、传票及命令作出响应。该委员会由执行董事及独立非执行董事成员组成，其中执行董事负责监督与美国当局所达成和解的责任履行情况。

除独立非执行董事外，委员会也包括监督该等责任履行的执行董事。委员会不定时进行会晤，并接收有关纽约州金融服务整治方案（Financial Services Remediation Programme）的报告。该集团致力于证明其在打击金融罪行方面领先业界，同时向客户提供优质服务。为达到此目标，该集团制订了减低金融罪行风险计划；该计划为持续多年的全面计划，旨在检讨该集团现有反洗黑钱及制裁合规方法的多个方面，并在适当情况下加以改进以达到此目标。减低金融罪行风险计划的一项主要工作是应对2012年与美国当局就过往制裁合规问题达成的和解。这项工作称为美国监督整治计划，并列入委员会2013年重点关注的范围。监督整治计划包括一系列工作流程，旨在确保所有和解协议所载的整治要求均得以遵守。2014年，鉴于审核委员会的角色，其将代表董事会从内部监控方面监督减低金融罪行风险计划（包括监督整治计划）。在2014年全年的时间里，委员会专注于就该集团过往及现时遵守美国制裁法规有关的其他要求、传票及命令作出响应。

（2）启动内部复核措施以表明态度。在进行处罚后，监管机构首先关注的是被处罚机构对于历史问题的态度，即以往的错误事项是否被重新反思和处理，而不仅仅是未来业务不犯错误就可以搪塞的。因此，渣打银行就以往已发生业务进行了认真的重检复核工作。

由于在2001年至2007年间，渣打银行进行了伊朗相关业务，因此该银行就有关遵守美国制裁复核了2001年1月至2007年12月期间该集团的美元所有交易，以及该复核涵盖期内受美国制裁所规限的所有国家。

这项复核由美国及英国的外聘律师及外部顾问执行。复核的事实结果以32份详尽报告呈交美国当局。在整个复核过程中，美国当局、本集团的主要英国监管机构金融服务管理局、该集团董事会及审核委员会，均定期获得有关的最新数据。鉴于复核之性质，由该集团主席、集团行政总裁及高级独立董事组成的董事会监督小组实施额外监督。于复核过程中，项目指导委员会定期与董事会监督小组会面，并告知其有关重大进展的最新消息。渣打银行外聘律师的高级代表与集团公司秘书一样，出席了董事会监督小组的大部分会议。审核委员会及董事会也定期获得最新数据。

（3）采取多种配套措施开展合规工作。满足监管要求的合规整改是一项系统性工程，单独一项或两项整改措施的实施是不能让监管机构信服的。需要一家银行从整体和流程的全方面进行考虑。

2012年8月，在接获金融局指令后，作为内部管治安排对金融局指令的响应，该集团刊发了一份声明，声明中除了订立和解协议并支付民事罚款外，作为该和解的一部分，该集团同意采取多项整治措施，包括根据纽约州金融局同意在渣打银行纽约分行委任一名独立监察员。集团也已成立专责项目团队，确保遵守该等整治措施。审核委员会将负责监督工作，并会确保整治计划有效实行。

此外，和解的条款也包括有关加强制裁以及反洗钱及银行保密法监控措施的多项条件及持续责任，例如整治方案、申报规定、合规审查及计划、银行透明度要求、培训措施、审核计划、披露责任等。该等责任由一个名为美国监督整治计划的工作计划所管理。渣打银行明确监督整治计划包括为确保有关方面遵守所有和解内的整治规定而设的工作流程。

（4）积极进行公关活动取得投资人谅解。尽管渣打银行在2008年的金融危机中毫发无损，但从2012年起，由于受到监管处罚和糟糕业绩的双重影响，渣打银行股价严重下滑。为避免投资者的信心受到打击，渣打银行多次发布高规格的解释和说明。

其中，包括对于避免关于事件严重性的推测及已采取措施的准确描述，渣打银行指出被罚款事项是早已发生并已经停止的声明：在2001年至2007年间，本集团进行伊朗相关业务。2006年底，本集团决定一律停止与伊朗实体进行以美元结算的新业务，而截至2007年8月，本集团决定一律停止与伊朗实体进行以任何货币结算的新业务。此后，本集团持续减少遗留业务。2010年1月，我们联系并通知了美国当局，于2009年初，我们已就有关遵守每股制裁开始复核2001年1月至2007年12月期间本集团的美元交易。渣打银行于2006年后期已终止其伊朗美元支付业务，并于翌日停止与伊朗机构的任何新的业务往来，此等行动还在美国当局实施相关要求之前。

另一份声明强调该银行主体业务是谨慎而合规的，不合规的业务比例很小：外国资产控制办认定"大约60 000宗与伊朗有关的付款，总值达2 500亿美元，其中的绝大部分看来没有违反《伊朗交易条例》"。在2001年至2007年底整个期间，外国资产控制办认定渣打银行为伊朗人士处理约2 400万美元交易款项，以及为其他国家（缅甸、苏丹和利比亚）的其他被制裁机构处理总值1.09亿美元款项，该等交易看来违反制裁法律。但渣打纽约分行在同期处理的支付款项高达139万亿美元。潜台词就是违规业务不到万分之一，比例相当小。

再例如，几乎是在渣打银行与纽约州金融服务局达成和解令的同时，该银行董事会即发布公告声称，董事会于和解期（自2012年8月6日至12月10日）内举行七次会议以讨论情况，并决定采取何种风险措施能够符合股东的最佳利益："我们已于2012年8月13日专门成立董事会监督委员会，且董事会授权其对谈判进行监督。该董事会监督委员会在组成方面类似于先前的董事会监督小组，不同的是加入我们的董事会风险委员会主席作为候补成员。"

与此同时，不断就集团高管对于处罚的看法与公众沟通，说明利害关系："在整个复核与和解期内，董事会行事力求符合我们股东、客户及员工的最佳利益，以圆满解决此事。经咨询我们的美国及英国法律顾问后，董事会作出评价，结果指出不与美国当局达成和解的潜在代价远远高于和解成本。我们已就有关美国和解的情况广泛接洽我们的机构股东，他们亦认同我们的做法。"

（5）亡羊补牢为时未晚。2014年，美国检方对包括渣打银行在内的几大银行再次展开调查，认为渣打银行实施的改革力度不够，其依据在于新的可疑交易。涉及伊朗的交易倒是没有了，但涉及中国香港、阿联酋特定客户的交易同样要遭到处罚。根据笔者的分析，这次处罚的根本原因仍在于系统问题，即渣打银行自动化的交易监测系统没有识别特定可疑的反洗钱交易。

为此，渣打银行除了支付罚款外，进一步细化了合规反洗钱工作的具体目标，包括：

①改进纽约分行的交易监测系统；

②将监察员任期延长两年，预期将进一步延长；

③以下一系列临时整治措施将持续生效，直至交易监测系统的检测情景按监察员批核的标准运作为止：

（a）未经纽约州金融局事先批准及与监察员磋商，纽约分行不得为无纽约分行账户的任何客户开设美元活期存款账户。

（b）就透过纽约分行发出的部分关联方及第三方支付信息，要求加入识别发起人及受益人的数据。

（c）对若干香港个人客户业务的客户施加美元结算服务限制。

（d）加强对阿联酋的若干中小型企业客户的监管。集团决定退出该业务，作为努力加强策略重点的一部分，退出或重新调整非策略性业务，包括该等监管成本增加而影响经济可行性的业务，确保退出流程完成。而按照和解协议，美元结算限制自2014年11月17日起实施监督整治计划的职权范围已扩大至涵盖内部管理责任。

此外，在2014年12月，司法部、纽约郡地方检察官办公室及渣打集团已同意将延迟检控协议的期限再延长三年，直至2017年12月10日为止，并继续聘任一名监察员，以评价渣打银行集团的制裁合规计划及作出推荐建议。最终司法部协议确认渣打集团已采取多项步骤，以遵从原有延迟检控协议的规定，并加强及优化其制裁合规，包括实施更严谨的美国制裁政策及程序、安排获认证的员工培训、雇用高级法律及金融罪行合规人员以及最近推行额外措施以封锁受美国制裁法律及法规限制的国家所发出的付款指示。

总结

2014年和解相关的事件到今天已经过去了四年的时间，渣打银行没有再次受到监管对于合规方面的指责。渣打银行已完成其合规制度和程序的全面检讨及提升。已采取的措施包括加强关于制裁规定与客户尽职调查的审查制度、增设驻任纽约的人员处理制裁法律合规及金融罪行汇报事项、聘任一名独立顾问评估其《银行保密法》/反洗钱计划，以及设立强有力的《银行保密法》/反洗钱规定测试、审计和质量保证的规章及程序。渣打银行进行广泛内部调查后，主动向美国有关部门报告调查结果，说明渣打银行过往遵守制裁法律的情况，并且花费了近三年的时间与监管机构和检控部门大力合作，而达致和解。渣打集团声称将与当局紧密合作，务求对其美国制裁计划作出额外实质改善以达到延迟检控协议规定的标准。该集团与所有相关当局一起实施该等方案及履行和解所规定的责任。

附录1：

《和解令1（2012）》英文原文

STANDARD CHARTERED PLC

(Incorporated as a public limited company in England and Wales with registered number 966425)

(Stock Code: 02888)

New York State Department of Financial Services' Consent Order Relating to Standard Chartered

Standard Chartered PLC (the "Group") confirms that it has now finalised the terms of the settlement with the New York State Department of Financial Services ("DFS") as outlined on 14th August which included a payment USD340m. The DFS Consent Order documenting the settlement is attached.

The Group continues to engage with the other US agencies on their review of the Group's historical US sanctions compliance. The Group cannot predict when this review and these discussions will be completed or what the outcome will be and therefore potential liabilities cannot be reasonably quantified at this point.

The details of any resolution will be communicated in due course.

By Order of the Board

Annemarie Durbin

Group Company Secretary

Hong Kong, 23 September 2012

As at the date of this announcement, the Board of Directors of Standard Chartered PLC comprises:

Chairman:

Sir John Wilfred Peace

Executive Directors:

Mr Peter Alexander Sands; Mr Stefano Paolo Bertamini; Mr Jaspal Singh Bindra; Mr Richard Henry Meddings; Mr Alun Michael Guest Rees and Mr Viswanathan Shankar

Independent Non-Executive Directors:

Mr Richard Delbridge; Mr James Frederick Trevor Dundas; Ms Valerie Frances Gooding, CBE; Dr Han Seung-soo, KBE; Mr Simon Jonathan Lowth; Mr Rudolph Harold Peter Markham (Senior Independent Director); Ms Ruth Markland; Mr John Gregor Hugh Paynter; Mr Paul David Skinner and Mr Oliver Henry James Stocken

NEW YORK STATE DEPARTMENT
OF FINANCIAL SERVICES

In the Matter of:

STANDARD CHARTERED BANK,
New York Branch

CONSENT ORDER UNDER
NEW YORK BANKING LAW § 44

WHEREAS, on August 6, 2012, the Department of Financial Services (the "Department") issued an order pursuant to Banking Law § 39, charging Standard Chartered Bank ("SCB"), a wholly owned subsidiary of Standard Chartered plc, with certain apparent violations of law and regulation, and directing that SCB appear before the Department on August 15, 2012 to explain those charges (the "August 6th Order");

WHEREAS, the charges contained in the August 6th Order relate primarily to transactions that SCB conducted on behalf of Iranian parties with a value of approximately $250 billion that were settled through SCB's New York branch ("SCB NY") during the period 2001 through 2007. These transactions were identified by SCB through its review of its U.S. dollar transactions during the review period;

WHEREAS, on August 14, 2012, prior to appearing before the Department as directed by the August 6th Order, SCB and the Department (collectively, the "Parties") agreed to resolve this matter without formal proceedings or hearings;

NOW, THEREFORE, the Parties are willing to resolve the matters cited herein. The Department finds as follows:

1. Throughout the period relevant to the Department's investigation, Iran was subject to U.S. economic sanctions for, among other things, sponsoring international terrorism and attempting to build nuclear weapons.

2. From at least January 2001 through 2007, SCB provided U.S. dollar clearing services to Iranian state and privately owned banks, corporations, and individuals. In processing transactions on behalf of its Iranian customers, SCB removed or omitted Iranian information from U.S. dollar wire payment messages through a practice known internally at SCB as "repair," which was designed to help SCB compete for Iranian business and to avoid potential processing delays.

3. The removal or omission of Iranian information, by the use of cover payments or by "repair," occurred with respect to approximately 59,000 transactions totaling approximately $250 billion.

4. It is the position of the Department that SCB's policies and procedures during the relevant period, pursuant to which certain wire transfers evidencing the transactions did not contain information regarding Iranian parties when sent through SCB NY, prevented New York State regulators from performing complete safety and soundness examinations, and from identifying suspicious patterns of activity, which could, among other things, allow regulators to assist law enforcement authorities.

5. In 2004, SCB consented to a formal enforcement action and executed a written agreement ("Written Agreement") with the New York Banking Department ("NYSBD"), a predecessor agency of

the Department, and the Federal Reserve Bank of New York ("FRBNY") regarding flaws in anti-money-laundering risk controls at SCB NY. The Written Agreement required SCB to adopt sound anti-money laundering practices with respect to foreign bank correspondent accounts and to hire an independent consultant to conduct a historical transaction review for the period July 2002 to October 2004. On July 10, 2007, the NYSBD and FRBNY terminated the Written Agreement and ended the ongoing enforcement action.

6. In 2011, the Department conducted an examination of SCB NY, which identified BSA/AML findings, including: (1) weaknesses in the customer risk rating methodology and documentation of certain customer due diligence ("CDD") information; (2) insufficient documentation of decisions to waive potential OF AC matches to customers and associated parties; and (3) offshoring portions of SCB NY's transaction monitoring process to SCB's Global Shared Services with insufficient evidence of oversight or communication between them.

7. SCB NY is undertaking remediation actions to address those examination findings and has hired a third-party consultant to validate corrective measures and the sustainability of the BSA AML program at SCB NY, the report of which has been provided to the Department.

SETTLEMENT PROVISIONS

Monetary Payment:

8. SCB will pay a civil monetary payment to the Department pursuant to Banking Law §§ 44 and 44-A in the amount of three hundred and forty million U.S. dollars ($340,000,000). SCB will pay the entire payment of $340,000,000 within ten (10) days of executing the Consent Order.

BSA/AML and OFAC Compliance Review:

9. Within thirty (30) days of executing the Consent Order, SCB will identify an independent on-site monitor acceptable to the Department (the "Compliance Monitor") who will report directly to the Department to conduct a comprehensive review (the "Compliance Review") of the BSA/AML and OFAC compliance programs, policies, and procedures now in place at SCB's New York Branch (the "SCB NY Program"). The Compliance Monitor will have authority, to the extent legally permissible, to examine and assess SCB's existing BSA/AML operations that are performed outside the United States on behalf of SCB's New York Branch. Based on the Compliance Review, the Compliance Monitor will identify needed corrective measures to address identified flaws, weaknesses or other deficiencies in the SCB NY Program, and oversee their implementation. The Compliance Monitor will also examine and assess SCB's New York Branch's compliance with those corrective measures.

10. SCB agrees to cooperate fully with the Compliance Monitor by, including but not limited to, providing the Compliance Monitor access to all relevant personnel and records to the extent legally permissible. The term of the Compliance Monitor will extend for two years from the date of formal engagement. Any dispute as to the scope of the Compliance Monitor's authority will be resolved by the Department in the exercise of its sole discretion after appropriate consultation with SCB and/or the Compliance Monitor.

11. Within thirty (30) days of executing the Consent Order, SCB will submit to the Department for approval the proposed terms of the Compliance Monitor's engagement ("Engagement Letter").

12. Within ninety (90) days of SCB's receipt of the Department's written approval of such

terms, the Compliance Monitor will submit to the Parties a written report of findings, including proposed corrective measures from the Compliance Review (the "Compliance Review Report"). Thereafter, the Compliance Monitor will submit written monthly progress reports ("Progress Reports") to the Parties.

BSA/AML and OFAC Compliance Programs:

13. Within sixty (60) days of the receipt of the Compliance Review Report, SCB will submit to the Department for approval a written plan that is designed to improve and enhance the current SCB NY Program, incorporating the Compliance Review Report (the "Action Plan"). The Action Plan will provide for enhanced internal controls and updates and/or revisions to current policies, procedures and processes of SCB's New York Branch in order to ensure full compliance with all applicable provisions of the BSA, the rules and regulations issued thereunder, OFAC requirements and the requirements of the Consent Order. Upon receipt of written approval by the Department, SCB will begin to implement the changes.

Management Oversight:

14. Within sixty (60) days following the receipt of the Compliance Review Report, SCB is to submit to the Department for approval a written plan to improve and enhance management oversight of SCB NY's Program ("Management Oversight Plan"). The Management Oversight Plan will address all relevant matters identified in the Compliance Review Report, provide a sustainable management oversight framework, and will take effect within thirty (30) days of receipt of written approval.

15. The Management Oversight Plan will include, among other things, SCB's New York Branch's employment of a permanent Anti-Money Laundering Auditor ("AMLA"), who will be located on-site at SCB's New York Branch, and who will audit SCB's New York Branch's BSA/AML and OFAC compliance, including compliance work conducted by SCB outside the United States on behalf of SCB's New York Branch. The AMLA will have full access to all personnel and records involved in SCB's BSA/AML compliance, transaction screening, and customer due diligence functions, to the extent legally permissible, and will further generate quarterly status reports for the Parties. In addition, Department examiners will remain on-site at SCB's New York Branch, as deemed appropriate by the Department.

16. The Parties agree that SCB's full compliance with paragraphs 9 through 15 of the Consent Order will constitute adoption of adequate corrective measures to address all violations identified by the Department in its 2011 examination of SCB NY.

Breach of the Consent Order:

17. In the event that the Department believes SCB to be materially in breach of the Consent Order ("Breach"), the Department will provide written notice to SCB of the Breach and SCB must, within ten (10) business days from the date of receipt of said notice, or on a later date if so determined in the sole discretion of the Department, appear before the Department to demonstrate that no Breach has occurred or, to the extent pertinent, that the Breach is not material or has been cured.

18. The Parties understand and agree that SCB's failure to make the required demonstration within the specified period is presumptive evidence of SCB's Breach. Upon a finding of Breach, the Department has all the remedies available to it under the New York Banking and Financial Services Laws and may use any and all evidence available to the Department for all ensuing hearings,

notices, orders and other remedies that may be available under the Banking and Financial Services Laws.

Waiver of Rights:

19. The Parties further understand and agree that no provision of the Consent Order is subject to review in any court or tribunal outside the Department.

Parties Bound by the Consent Order:

20. It is further understood that the Consent Order is binding on the Department and SCB, as well as their successors and assigns that are within the supervision of the Department, but it specifically does not bind any federal or other state agencies or any law enforcement authorities.

21. No further action will be taken by the Department against SCB for the conduct set forth in the Consent Order or the Department's August 6th Order, including the investigation referenced in footnote 1 of the August 6th Order, provided that SCB complies with the terms of the Consent Order. Notwithstanding any other provision contained in the Consent Order, however, the Department may undertake enforcement action against SCB for transactions or conduct that SCB did not disclose to the Department in the written materials that SCB submitted to the Department in connection with this matter.

22. During the period in which the Consent Order remains in effect, the approved Program, Plans, and Engagement Letter as referenced herein will not be amended or rescinded without the prior written approval of the Department, other than amendments necessary to comply with applicable laws and regulations.

23. Within ten (10) days after the end of each quarter following the execution of the Consent Order, SCB will submit to the Department written progress reports detailing the form and manner of all actions taken to secure compliance with the provisions of the Consent Order and the results thereof. SCB's responses to any audit reports covering BSA/AML matters prepared by internal and external auditors will be included with the progress report. The Department may, in writing, and in its discretion, discontinue the requirement for progress reports or modify the reporting schedule.

Notices:

24. All communications regarding this Order shall be sent to:

Mr. Gaurav Vasisht
Executive Deputy Superintendent
Banking Division
New York State Department of
Financial Services
One State Street
New York, NY 10004

Dr. Tim Miller
Director, Property, Research & Assurance
Standard Chartered Bank
1 Basinghall Avenue
London EC2V 5DD
United Kingdom
Mr. Edward Kowalcyk

Regional Head of Compliance, Americas
Standard Chartered Bank
1095 Avenue of the Americas
New York, NY 10036

Miscellaneous:

25. Each provision of the Consent Order will remain effective and enforceable until stayed, modified, terminated or suspended in writing by the Department.

26. No promise, assurance, representation, or understanding other than those contained in the Consent Order has been made to induce any party to agree to the provisions of the Consent Order.

《和解令》中文译文

根据纽约《银行法》第44条发出的同意令

鉴于在二〇一二年八月六日，纽约州金融局（"金融局"）依据《银行法》第39条发出一项指令，指控渣打集团有限公司的全资附属公司渣打银行（"渣打银行"）存在违反有关法律及规例的若干表象，并指令渣打银行于二〇一二年八月十五日到金融局就该等指控作出解释（"八月六日之指令"）；

鉴于八月六日之指令所包含的指控主要涉及渣打银行在二〇〇一年至二〇〇七年期间代表伊朗人士进行并通过渣打银行纽约分行（"渣打纽约分行"）结算价值约为2 500亿美元的交易。该等交易是渣打银行通过自行对其在有关审查期内美元交易作出的审查发现的；

鉴于在二〇一二年八月十四日，在按八月六日之指令中的指示到金融局进行解释之前，渣打银行与金融局（合称"双方"）同意在不经正式程序或聆讯的情况下解决此事；

因此，双方现在愿意解决本同意令中提及的事项。金融局认定：

1. 在整个受金融局调查的有关期间内，伊朗因支持国际恐怖活动及试图制造核武器等理由而受到美国经济制裁。

2. 渣打银行至少于二〇〇一年至二〇〇七年期间向伊朗国有及私营银行、企业及个人提供美元结算服务。在为伊朗客户处理交易时，渣打银行透过在其内部称为"修复"的做法从美元电汇付款讯息删除或省略有关伊朗的资料。该做法旨在帮助渣打银行争取伊朗业务及避免潜在的处理延误。

3. 以使用覆盖支付或"修复"方式省略有关伊朗的资料之情况涉及约59 000宗交易，总值约为2 500亿美元。

4. 金融局的立场是渣打银行在有关期间实施令可证明有关交易的若干电汇讯息通过渣打纽约分行时不包含有关伊朗人士的资料的政策和程序，妨碍纽约监管机构进行完整的安全及可靠性审查以及识别可疑的活动模式，而该等审查及识别可以起到包括让监管机构协助执法在内的功效。

5. 在二〇〇四年，渣打银行同意一项正式执行行动，并与金融局的前身——纽约州银行监管部（"纽约银行部"）及纽约联邦储备银行（"纽约联邦储备银行"）就渣打纽约分行在反洗钱风险控制方面的不足之处签署了一份全面书面协议（"该书面协议"）。该书面协议规定渣打银行就外国银行代理行账户采纳健全的反洗钱措施，以及聘请独立顾问就二〇〇二年七月至二〇〇四年十月期间进行的交易作出检讨。在二〇〇七年七月十日，纽约银行部与纽约联邦储备银行终止该书面协议，并结束当时正在进行中的执行行动。

6. 在二〇一一年，金融局对渣打纽约分行进行了一项审查，得出对有关《银行保密法》/反洗钱规定的审查结果包括：（1）客户风险评级方法及若干客户尽职调查（"客户尽职调查"）资料文件证明方面存在弱点；（2）就客户及关联人士可能属外国资产控制办指定国籍人士作出豁免决定的相关文件证明不足；（3）将渣打纽约分行的部分交由监控程序交由离岸的渣打银行环球共享服务中心负责而没有充分证明显示两者之间的监督或交流。

7. 渣打纽约分行正就该等审查结果采取补救行动，并已聘请第三方顾问认证纠正措施及渣打纽约分行与《银行保密法》/反洗钱规定相关的计划的可持续性；该第三方的报告已向金融局提供。

和解条款

付款：

8. 渣打银行将会依据《银行法》第44及44-A条向金融局支付一笔三亿四千万美元（$340 000 000）的民事款项。渣打银行将于签署本同意令后十（10）天内支付整笔三亿四千万美元的款项。

《对银行保密法》/反洗钱及外国资产控制办规定的合规检讨：

9. 在签署本同意令后三十（30）天内，渣打银行将指定一名金融局可接受的、直接向金融局汇报的驻银行独立监察员（"合规监察员"），以对渣打银行纽约分行现行的与《银行保密法》/反洗钱及外国资产控制办规定相关的合规计划、政策及程序（"渣打纽约分行计划"）进行全面检讨（"合规检讨"）。合规监察员将有权在法律许可范围内审查及评估现时渣打银行代表渣打银行纽约分行在美国境外进行的、与《银行保密法》/反洗钱规定相关的工作。根据合规检讨，合规监察员将指出必需采取的纠正措施，以处理检讨中找到的渣打纽约分行计划中存在的不足之处，并将监督该等纠正措施的执行。合规监察员亦将审查及评估渣打银行纽约分行遵行该等纠正措施的情况。

10. 渣打银行同意与合规监察员全面合作，其中包括但不限于在法律许可范围内让合规监察员接触所有有关人员及查阅所有有关记录。从正式聘任日期起计，合规监察员的任期为两年。有关合规监察员权力范围的任何争议将由金融局在与渣打银行及/或合规监察员进行适当协商后行使全权酌情决定权予以解决。

11. 在签署本同意令后三十（30）天内，渣打银行将会把合规监察员聘书（"聘书"）之建议条款提交金融局审批。

12. 在渣打银行收到金融局对该等条款的书面批准后九十（90）天内，合规监察员将向双方提交检讨结果的书面报告，包括根据合规检讨提出的建议纠正措施（"合规检讨报告"）。其后，合规监察员将会每月向双方提交书面进行报告（"进行报告"）。

与遵守《银行保密法》/反洗钱及外国资产控制办规定有关的合规计划:

13. 在收到合规检讨报告后六十（60）天内，渣打银行将会把旨在改善及加强现有的渣打纽约分行计划并将合规检讨报告纳入其中的书面方案（"行动方案"）提交金融局审批。行动方案内容将包括加强内部控制，以及更新及/或修订渣打银行纽约分行的现有政策、程序及工作流程，以确保完全遵守《银行保密法》的所有适用规定及根据该法颁布的规则及规定、外国资产控制办的要求以及本同意令的要求。在收到金融局的书面批准后，渣打银行将开始实施有关变更。

管理监督:

14. 在收到合规检讨报告后六十（60）天内，渣打银行须把有关改善及加强对渣打纽约分行计划的管理监督的书面方案（"管理监督方案"）提交金融局审批。管理监督方案将处理在合规检讨报告中指出的所有有关问题、提供一个可持续的管理监督框架，并将在收到书面批准后三十（30）天内生效。

15. 管理监督方案的内容包括渣打银行纽约分行聘用一名驻渣打银行纽约分行的常任反洗钱核数师（"反洗钱核数师"）；该反洗钱核数师将会就渣打银行纽约分行对《银行保密法》/反洗钱及外国资产控制办规定的合规情况，包括渣打银行代表渣打银行纽约分行在美国境外进行的合规工作进行审核。反洗钱核数师将有权法律许可范围内接触及查阅渣打银行在遵守《银行保密法》/反洗钱规定、交易甄别及客户尽职调查方面所涉及的所有人员及记录，并将为双方进一步编制季度情况报告。此外，金融局审查员将在金融局视为适当的情况下留在渣打银行纽约分行现场。

16. 双方同意，渣打银行完全遵守本同意令第9至15段，即构成针对金融局在二〇一一年对渣打纽约分行完全遵守本同意的审查中发现的所有违规事项采纳了充分的纠正措施。

违反本同意令：

17. 倘若金融局相信渣打银行重大违反本同意令（"违反事项"），金融局将会就违反事项向渣打银行发出书面通知，而渣打银行必须在收到上述通知日期后十（10）个营业日内或在金融局行使全权酌情决定权所决定的较后日期到金融局去证明没有发生违反事项或（在恰当情况下）违反事项并不重大或已被纠正。

18. 双方了解并同意，渣打银行如未能在指明期限内作出所需的证明，即可被推定为渣打银行作出违反事项的证据。当认定发生违反事项时，金融局可采取其根据纽约州《银行法》及《金融服务法》可以采取的所有补救方法，并且可就随后根据《银行法》及《金融服务法》可有的所有聆讯、通知、命令及其他补救方法，使用金融局可获得的任何及所有证据。

放弃权利：

19. 双方进一步了解并同意，本同意令之条款并不受制于金融局以外的任何法院或审裁机构复核。

双方受本同意令约束：

20. 双方进一步了解本同意令对金融局及渣打银行以及其在金融局监管范围内的继承人及受让人有约束力，但明确地对任何联邦或其他州的机关或任何执法机构并无约束力。

21. 只要渣打银行遵守本同意令的条款，金融局将不会就本同意令或金融局八月六日之指令中列明的行为（包括八月六日之指令脚注1中提及的调查）

对渣打银行采取进一步行动。然而，即使本同意令另有任何其他规定，金融局仍可就渣打银行没有在其就本案向金融局提交的书面材料中向金融局披露的交易或行为采取执行行动。

22. 在本同意令有效期间，未经金融局事先书面批准，不得修改或撤销本同意令中所提及的经批准之计划、方案及聘书，但为遵守适用法律及规定而作出的修改除外。

23. 在签署本同意令后每一季度结束后十（10）日内，渣打银行将会向金融局提交书面进行报告，其中将详细说明为确保遵守本同意令的规定而采取的所有行动的形式及方式以及其结果。渣打银行对内部及外部核数师编制的、涉及《银行保密法》/反洗钱事宜的任何审查报告的回应将收录在进行报告中。金融局可以书面形式及酌情决定终止有关进行报告的要求或修改报告时间表。

通知：

24. 与本同意令有关的所有通知应送交：

（此处略去涉及机构及个人）

其他：

25. 本同意令的每一项规定将持续有效并可强制执行，直至被金融局以书面形式搁置、修改、终止或暂停为止。

26. 除本同意令中所载的允诺、保证、陈述或谅解外，不存在任何旨在诱使任何一方同意本同意令中的任何规定的允诺、保证、陈述或谅解。

为证明本同意令的订立，双方代表已于本日，即二〇一二年九月二十一日，签署本同意令。

（此处略去涉及机构及个人）

附录2:

《和解令2》英文原文

NEW YORK STATE DEPARTMENT OF FINANCIAL SERVICES

_____X

In the Matter of

                           CONSENT ORDER UNDER
                           NEW YORK BANKING LAW §§ 39 and 44

Standard Chartered Bank,
New York Branch

_____X

The New York State Department of Financial Services ("the Department" or "DFS") and Standard Chartered Bank ("SCB" or the "Bank") (collectively the "Parties") stipulate that:

WHEREAS, SCB is a foreign bank with complex operations and multiple business lines and legal entities in many countries worldwide; and

WHEREAS, SCB conducts global operations through various subsidiaries and entities including its branch in New York, New York ("SCB NY"); and

WHEREAS, the Department is the licensing agency of SCB NY, pursuant to Article II of the New York Banking Law and is responsible for its supervision and regulation; and

WHEREAS, on September 21, 2012, the Parties stipulated and agreed in a consent order (the "September 21, 2012 Order") to resolve and remediate the Department's findings of certain deficiencies and apparent violations of laws and regulations; and

WHEREAS, pursuant to the September 21, 2012 Order, and State and Federal laws and regulations, SCB's compliance risk management program required an anti-money laundering ("AML") program to identify and manage compliance risks related to the Bank Secrecy Act (the "BSA") and all applicable AML regulations (the "BSA/AML Requirements"); and

WHEREAS, pursuant to the September 21, 2012 Order, SCB also agreed to engage an on-site independent monitor ("SCB Monitor") for a period of twenty-four (24) months to examine and evaluate SCB NY's BSA/AML operations, including SCB NY's transaction monitoring system; and

WHEREAS, in connection with implementation of its transaction monitoring system, SCB NY designed multiple detection scenarios which were set forth in a rulebook ("SCB Rulebook"); and

WHEREAS, the SCB Monitor gathered historical data and attempted to test the detection scenarios using the procedures provided in the SCB NY Rulebook; and

WHEREAS, the SCB Monitor determined that SCB's Rulebook was not consistent with the majority of the actual detection scenarios, and such detection scenarios contained errors or were incomplete resulting in the SCB NY transaction monitoring system failing to detect a significant number of potentially high-risk transactions for further review; and

WHEREAS, SCB failed to detect errors within the detection scenarios because of a lack of adequate testing and analysis both pre- and post- implementation of the transaction monitoring system and failed to adequately audit the transaction monitoring system; and

WHEREAS, a significant number of the potentially high-risk transactions the system has failed to detect originated from SCB's branches in the United Arab Emirates ("SCB UAE") and subsidiary in Hong Kong ("SCB Hong Kong"), among others; and

WHEREAS, the SCB Monitor discovered and reported these significant failures in SCB NY's transaction monitoring system to the Department; reporting further that these failures prevent SCB NY from effectively identifying potentially high-risk customers and transactions for further review in multiple areas of the Bank and hinder SCB's ability to assess and monitor transactions and client relationships on a bank-wide basis; and

WHEREAS, SCB NY is operating with certain ineffective compliance risk management systems for the identification and management of compliance risks related to compliance with BSA/AML laws, rules, and regulations, including BSA/AML risk related to U.S. Dollar clearing for clients of SCB UAE and SCB Hong Kong, among others; and

WHEREAS, SCB has initiated measures to remediate failures identified by the SCB Monitor;

NOW, THEREFORE, the Parties agree and stipulate that, in order to settle the instant matter without a formal proceeding, SCB will take the following measures to ensure compliance with the September 21, 2012 Order and all applicable BSA/AML Requirements:

Settlement Provisions

Payment of a Civil Monetary Penalty:

1. Within ten (10) days of the effective date of this Order, SCB shall make payment of a civil monetary penalty to the Department pursuant to Banking Law § 44 in the amount of $300,000,000.00. SCB agrees that it will not claim, assert, or apply for a tax deduction or tax credit with regard to any U.S. federal, state or local tax, directly or indirectly, for any portion of the civil monetary penalty paid pursuant to this Order.

Remediation Measures:

The SCB Transaction Monitoring System

2. SCB NY will implement an effective transaction monitoring system that operates in accordance with all BSA/AML Requirements and is acceptable to the Department.

3. Approval by the Department of the transaction monitoring system will be in writing and in the sole discretion of the Superintendent upon consultation with the SCB Monitor.

4. Within thirty (30) days of the effective date of this Order, in furtherance of remediation of its transaction monitoring system, SCB will:

A. provide a comprehensive remediation action plan with appropriate deadlines and benchmarks;

B. further integrate the SCB Monitor in the remediation process;

C. provide a clear organizational structure of the employees involved in the remediation; and

D. appoint a competent and responsible SCB Executive who will report directly to the

SCB CEO to oversee the remediation and to report on its progress on a monthly basis to the SCB CEO and continue to report to the SCB Monitor in a manner consistent with its current reporting process.

Extension of the SCB Monitor

5. SCB will extend the period of its engagement of the SCB Monitor for a period of two (2) additional years. In addition to the duties set forth under the terms and conditions of the September 21, 2012 Order, the SCB Monitor will also test and evaluate SCB's remediation efforts, and oversee SCB NY's implementation of a fully functioning transaction monitoring system and SCB NY's suspension of U.S. Dollar clearing as set forth in this Consent Order, and all other provisions set forth in this Consent Order.

Timing of Prohibition

6. The prohibitions set forth below in paragraphs 7, 8 and 9 will remain in effect until such time as SCB NY's detection scenarios are operating to a standard approved by the SCB Monitor.

New U.S. Dollar Denominated Accounts Prohibited:

7. SCB NY will not, without prior approval of the Department in consultation with the SCB Monitor, open a U.S. Dollar demand deposit account for any customer who does not already have such an account with SCB NY.

New Policies for U.S. Dollar Transactions - Originator/Beneficiary Information:

8. SCB will undertake the following:

A. Affiliate U.S. Dollar Clearing Transactions

For "Affiliate U.S. Dollar Clearing Transactions," which are defined as U.S. Dollar clearing transactions involving: (a) a payment originated from the account of a customer held at a non-U.S. SCB branch or majority-owned subsidiary, and (b) in an amount of $3,000.00 or more, the following will apply:

- Originator Identity Information: SCB NY will require that SCB affiliates provide the identity (name and address, including country) of the originator with respect to all such transactions. If SCB NY determines through post-transaction monitoring that the originator's address, including country, was not received by SCB NY and cannot be derived from the transaction information, SCB NY, posttransaction, will acquire the address, including country, of the originator. SCB will utilize this additional information for transaction monitoring.

- Beneficiary Identity Information: SCB NY will require that SCB affiliates provide any beneficiary identification information received with the transaction instruction with respect to all such transactions, and that SCB NY and SCB affiliates will undertake good faith efforts to obtain beneficiary identification information at the time of the transaction.

- SCB NY will flag, in post-transaction monitoring, transactions that do not contain the country of the beneficiary and will undertake an enhanced review protocol to be agreed upon with the SCB Monitor with respect to those transactions. SCB NY will agree to the enhanced review protocol with the SCB Monitor within thirty (30) days from the effective date of this Consent Order.

B. Third Party (Non-Affiliate) Transactions:

A "Third-Party (Non-Affiliate) Transaction" is defined as a U.S. Dollar clearing transaction involving (a) a payment originated from the account of a third party's customer held at a third party financial institution, and (b) in an amount of $3,000.00 or more.

- Communication to Third Parties: SCB will communicate to its Third-Party (Non-Affiliate) clients that SCB NY requires the country of the originator and beneficiary for all Third-Party (NonAffiliate) Transactions.

- Missing Originator Information: SCB NY will flag, in posttransaction monitoring, Third-Party (Non-Affiliate) Transactions where the country of the originator was not received and cannot be derived from address information, and undertake an enhanced review protocol to be agreed upon with the SCB Monitor.

- Missing Beneficiary Information: SCB NY will flag, in posttransaction monitoring, Third-Party (Non-Affiliate) Transactions where the country of the beneficiary was not received by SCB NY and cannot be derived from address information, and undertake an enhanced review protocol to be agreed with the SCB Monitor.

Suspension of U.S. Dollar Clearing:

9. SCB NY will suspend its U.S. Dollar clearing services as described in this section (the "Suspension"):

- Hong Kong:

  Within forty-five (45) days from the effective date of this Order, SCB NY will not process U.S. Dollar transactions for SCB Hong Kong high-risk retail business clients. This Suspension will remain in effect until such time as SCB NY's detection scenarios are operating to a standard approved by the SCB Monitor. The criteria for the selection of those high-risk clients who will be subject to the U.S. Dollar clearing suspension has been agreed upon between the SCB Monitor and SCB. In addition, the SCB Monitor will carry out a monthly review of the risks associated with U.S. Dollar transactions from the SCB Hong Kong retail business clients and determine whether additional monitoring or de-risking is necessary.

- UAE:

  SCB has commenced a process of exiting its small and medium business clients ("SME") at SCB UAE, excluding certain clients who may be retained after a requalification process in consultation with the SCB Monitor. Within thirty (30) days from the effective date of this Order, SCB NY will implement heightened monitoring of certain high-risk clients in the SCB UAE SME portfolio. The criteria for the selection of those high-risk clients will be agreed to between the SCB Monitor and SCB. The terms of the heightened monitoring will also be agreed through consultation between the SCB Monitor and SCB. SCB will make good faith efforts to exit SME clients at SCB UAE other than clients who are re-qualified.

  If exiting of the SME clients at SCB UAE is not completed within ninety (90) days from the effective date of this Order, SCB will suspend all U.S. Dollar clearing through SCB NY for those clients of SCB UAE, unless SCB has sought and obtained an extension of time from the Department, which extension will be at the sole discretion of the Superintendent.

Avoidance of Suspension:

10. SCB shall not avoid or circumvent the Suspension by using any SCB branch, affiliate, subsidiary or entity in which SCB has a controlling interest in the United States for U.S Dollar clearing.

11. SCB shall not avoid or circumvent the Suspension by moving, or causing to be moved, any client relationship or business to any other business line, branch or affiliate of SCB.

Breach of the Consent Order:

12. In the event that the Department believes SCB to be materially in breach of the Consent Order ("Breach"), the Department will provide written notice to SCB of the Breach and SCB must, within ten (10) business days from the date of receipt of said notice, or on a later date if so determined in the sole discretion of the Department, appear before the Department to demonstrate that no Breach has occurred or, to the extent pertinent, that the Breach is not material or has been cured.

13. The Parties understand and agree that SCB's failure to make the required demonstration within the specified period is presumptive evidence of SCB's Breach. Upon a finding of Breach, the Department has all the remedies available to it under New York Banking and Financial Services Law and may use any and all evidence available to the Department for all ensuing hearings, notices, orders and other remedies that may be available under the New York Banking and Financial Services Laws.

Waiver of Rights:

14. The Parties further understand and agree that no provision of the Consent Order is subject to review in any court or tribunal outside the Department.

Parties Bound by the Consent Order:

15. It is further understood that the Consent Order is binding on the Department and SCB, as well as their successors and assigns that are within the supervision of the Department, but it specifically does not bind any federal or other state agencies or any law enforcement authority.

16. No further action will be taken by the Department against SCB for the conduct set forth in the Consent Order, provided that SCB complies with the terms of the Consent Order.

17. Notwithstanding any other provision contained in the Consent Order, however, the Department may undertake action against SCB for any misconduct that SCB knew about and failed to disclose to the Department in connection with this matter.

Notices:

18. All communications regarding this Order shall be sent to:

Elizabeth Nochlin
Megan Prendergast
Banking Division
New York State Department of Financial Services
One State Street New York, NY 10004

Scott Corrigan
General Counsel, Americas
Standard Chartered Bank
1095 Avenue of the Americas, 37th Floor
New York, NY 10036

Miscellaneous:

19. Each provision of the Consent Order will remain effective and enforceable until stayed, modified, terminated or suspended in writing by the Department.

20. No promise, assurance, representation, or understanding other than those contained in the Consent Order has been made to induce any party to agree to the provisions of the Consent Order.

IN WITNESS WHEREOF, the parties hereto have caused this Consent Order to be executed as of this 19th ,day of August,2014.

《和解令》中文译文

纽约州金融局

_____X

有关

渣打银行纽约分行事宜

_____X

根据纽约《银行法》第39条及第44条发出的同意令

纽约州金融局（"金融局"）与渣打银行（"渣打银行"或"该行"）（统称为"双方"）提出：

鉴于渣打银行是一间在全球多个国家拥有复杂业务、多重业务线以及法律实体的海外银行；及

鉴于渣打银行透过多间附属公司及实体，包括位于纽约州纽约市的分行（"渣打纽约分行"）经营全球性业务；及

鉴于根据纽约《银行法》第Ⅱ条，金融局是渣打纽约分行的发牌机构并对其监督和监管事宜负责；及

鉴于在二〇一二年九月二十一日，双方在同意令（"二〇一二年九月二十一日之指令"）中订明及同意解决并修正金融局对若干不足之处以及明显违反法律及规例情况的调查结果；及

鉴于根据二〇一二年九月二十一日之指令以及州及联邦法律及规例，渣打银行的合规风险管理计划规定要制定一项反洗钱（"反洗钱"）计划，以识别并管理与《银行保密法》（"《银行保密法》"）有关的合规风险以及所有适用的反洗钱规例（"《银行保密法》/反洗钱规定"）；及

鉴于根据二〇一二年九月二十一日之指令，渣打银行亦同意聘用一个驻银行的独立监察员（"渣打银行监察员"），为期二十四（24）个月，以审查及评估渣打纽约分行的《银行保密法》/反洗钱业务，包括渣打纽约分行的交易监察系统；及

鉴于渣打纽约分行就实施其交易监察系统设计了多项检测情景，并将这些检测情景载入守则（"渣打银行守则"）内；及

鉴于渣打银行监察员收集了过往的数据并试图利用渣打银行守则载明的程序测试检测情景；及

鉴于渣打银行监察员确定，渣打银行守则与大部分实际检测情景并不一致，而有关检测情景存在误差或不完整情况，导致渣打纽约分行的交易监察系统未能侦测到大量潜在高风险交易以供进一步审查；及

鉴于渣打银行基于在实施交易监察系统前后缺乏充分测试和分析，导致未能侦测到检测情景内的错误以及未能充分地核对交易监察系统；及

鉴于系统未能侦测到的大量潜在高风险交易乃源于渣打银行位于（其中包括）阿拉伯联合酋长国的分行（"渣打阿联酋分行"）以及香港的附属公司（"渣打香港"）；

及

鉴于渣打银行监察员在渣打纽约分行的交易监察系统中发现这些重大失误并将之汇报金融局，并作出进一步汇报，称这些失误妨碍渣打纽约分行有效地在该行的多个范畴内识别潜在高风险客户和交易以供进一步审查，并阻碍渣打银行在整体银行基准上评估和监察交易和客户关系；及

鉴于渣打纽约分行在识别和管理与《银行保密法》/反洗钱法律、规则及规例有关的合规风险，包括（其中包括）为渣打阿联酋分行及渣打香港的客户进行与美元结算有关的《银行保密法》/反洗钱风险时，以若干低效的合规风险管理系统运作；及

鉴于渣打银行已开始实施措施以修正渣打银行监察员所识别的失误之处；

因此，双方现在同意并订明，为了在没有提出正式诉讼的情况下解决当前事项，渣打银行将会采取以下措施确保遵守二〇一二年九月二十一日之指令以及所有适用的《银行保密法》/反洗钱规定：

和解条款

支付民事罚款：

1. 在本同意令有效日期后十（10）天内，渣打银行须根据《银行法》第44条向金融局支付为数 300 000 000.00 美元的民事罚款。渣打银行同意，对于根据本同意令支付的民事罚款的任何部分，其将不会直接或间接就任何美国

联邦、州或地方税项作出申索、提出或申请税项减免或税项抵免。

修正措施：

渣打银行交易监察系统

2. 渣打纽约分行将会实施一项有效的交易监察系统，该系统按照所有《银行保密法》/反洗钱规定运作并属金融局可接受的系统。

3. 金融局将以书面方式并由金融局局长于咨询渣打银行监察员后全权酌情决定批核交易监察系统。

4. 在本同意令生效日期后三十（30）天内，为对交易监察系统作出修正的缘故，渣打银行将会；

A. 提供附有适当期限和基准的全面性修正行动计划；

B. 在修正过程中进一步整合渣打银行监察员；

C. 提供修正行动中所涉及雇员的清晰组织结构；及

D. 委任一名合资格兼负责的渣打主管人员，该名人员将向渣打银行的行政总裁直接汇报以监督修正行动以及每月向渣打银行的行政总裁汇报有关进度，并持续按与现时的汇报过程一致的方式向渣打银行监察员作出汇报。

延长渣打银行监察员任期

5. 渣打银行将会把渣打银行监察员的聘用期延长额外两（2）年。除根据二〇一二年九月二十一日之指令的条款和条件所列载的职责外，渣打银行监察员也将测试和评估渣打银行在修正行动上作出的努力，并对本同意令所列载的渣打纽约分行实施全面运作的交易监察系统及渣打纽约分行暂停美元结算，以及本同意令所列载的所有其他条款的实施情况进行监督。

禁止事项的时限

6. 下文第7、第8及第9段列明的禁止事项将会持续有效，直至渣打纽约分行的检测情景按渣打银行监察员批核的标准运作为止。

禁止开设新美元账户：

7. 在金融局未咨询渣打银行监察员并作出事先批准的情况下，渣打纽约分行将不会为尚未于渣打纽约分行开设美元活期存款账户的任何客户开设此类账户。

关于美元交易的新政策－汇款人／受益人资料：

8. 渣打银行将会采取下列各项措施：

A. 联系人的美元结算交易

就"联系人美元结算交易"（其定义是涉及下列各项的美元结算交易：

（a）一名客户持有的非美国渣打银行的分行或多数股权附属公司账户汇出的款项；及

（b）金额为3 000.00美元或以上）而言，下列各项将适用：

汇款人身份资料：渣打纽约分行将会规定渣打银行联属公司就所有该等交易提供汇款人身份（姓名及地址，包括国家）。倘若渣打纽约分行在交易后监察过程中确定渣打纽约分行未有收到汇款人的地址（包括国家）数据、而且未能从事务数据中获得此项资料，渣打纽约分行将在交易后要求取得汇款人的地址（包括国家）数据。渣打银行将会利用这些额外数据以进行交易监察。

• 受益人身份资料：渣打纽约分行将会规定渣打银行联属公司就所有该等交易提供其与交易指示一并收到的任何受益人身份资料，而渣打纽约分行与渣打银行的联属公司将作出真诚努力，务求在交易时获得受益人身份资料。

• 渣打纽约分行将在交易后的监察中对一些未包含受益人国家资料的交易加上标记，并会就该等交易进行将与渣打银行监察员商定的加强审查方案。渣打纽约分行将于本同意令的生效日期后三十（30）天内与渣打银行监察员商定加强审查方案。

B. 第三方（非联系人）交易

"第三方（非联系人）交易"的定义是涉及下列各项的美元结算交易：（a）从第三方的顾客于第三方金融机构持有的账户汇出的款项及（b）金额为3 000.00美元或以上。

• 与第三方沟通：渣打银行将通知其第三方（非联系人）客户，渣打纽约分行需要就所有第三方（非联系人）交易获得汇款人和受益人的国家资料。

• 汇款人资料缺漏：渣打纽约分行将在交易后的监察中对未有收到汇款人国家数据、而且未能从地址数据获得有关信息的第三方（非联系人）交易加上标记，并进行将与渣打银行监察员商定的加强审查方案。

• 受益人资料缺漏：渣打纽约分行将在交易后的监察中对渣打纽约分行未收到受益人国家数据、而且未能从地址数据获得有关信息的第三方（非联系人）交易加上标记，并进行将与渣打银行监察员商定的加强审查方案。

暂停美元结算服务：

9. 诚如本节所述，渣打纽约分行将会暂停美元结算服务（「暂停措施」）：

• 中国香港：

在本同意令生效日期后四十五（45）天内，渣打纽约分行不会为渣打香港的高风险小企客户处理美元交易。此项暂停措施将继续生效，直至渣打纽约分行的检测情景按渣打银行监察员核准的标准运作为止。至于哪些高风险客户将受制于此项暂停美元结算措施，其筛选条件已由渣打银行监察员与渣打银行相互协定。此外，渣打银行监察员每月会就渣打香港小企客户所涉及的美元交易相关风险进行审查，并确定是否需要采取额外监控或降低风险措施。

• 阿联酋：

渣打银行已于渣打阿联酋分行开展其中小型企业客户（"中小企"）的撤出程序，但这项程序不包括在咨询渣打银行监察员并进行重新鉴定程序后可被保留的客户。在本同意令生效日期后三十（30）天内，渣打纽约分行将对渣打阿联酋分行中小企业务组合内的若干高风险客户实施加强监控。至于哪些高风险客户将受制于此项加强监控措施，其筛选条件将由渣打银行监察员与渣打银行相互协议，有关加强监控的条款亦将由渣打银行监察员与渣打银行相互磋商后协议。渣打银行将作出真诚努力撤出渣打阿联酋分行的中小企客户（但重新取得资格的客户除外）。倘若撤出渣打阿联酋分行中小企客户的程序未能于本同意令生效日期后九十（90）天内完成，除非渣打银行已寻求并获得金融局批准延长有关期限，否则渣打银行将会暂停透过渣打纽约分行为渣打阿联酋分行的客户办理所有美元结算服务。

延长有关期限将由金融局局长全权酌情决定。

回避暂停措施：

10. 渣打银行不得在美国境内利用任何渣打银行分行、联属公司、附属公司或渣打银行在其中拥有控股权益的实体进行美元结算，以回避或绕过暂停措施。

11. 渣打银行不得将任何客户关系或业务转移或促使转移至渣打银行的任何其他业务线、分行或联属公司，以回避或绕过暂停措施。

违反本同意令：

12. 倘若金融局相信渣打银行重大违反本同意令（「违反事项」），金融局将会就违反事项向渣打银行发出书面通知，而渣打银行必须在收到上述通知日期后十（10）个营业日内或在金融局行使全权酌情权所确定的较后日期到金融局去证明没有发生违反事项或（在恰当情况下）违反事项并不重大或已被纠正。

13. 双方了解并同意，渣打银行如未能在指明期限内作出所需的证明，即可被推定为渣打银行作出违反事项的证据。当认定发生违反事项时，金融局可采取其根据纽约州《银行法》及《金融服务法》可以采取的所有补救方法，并且可就随后根据《银行法》及《金融服务法》可有的所有聆讯、通知、命令及其他补救方法，使用金融局可获得的任何及所有证据。

放弃权利：

14. 双方进一步了解并同意，本同意令之任何条款并不受制于金融局以外的任何法院或审裁机构复核。

双方受本同意令约束：

15. 双方进一步了解本同意令对金融局及渣打银行以及其在金融局监管范围内的继承人及受让人有约束力，但明确地对任何联邦或其他州的机关或任何执法机构并无约束力。

16. 金融局将不会就本同意令中列明的行为对渣打银行采取进一步行动，前提是渣打银行须遵守同意令的条款。

17. 即使同意令另有任何其他规定，然而，金融局或会对渣打银行知悉以及未能向金融局作出披露的任何不当行为采取行动。

通知：

18. 与本同意令有关的所有通知应送交：

（此处略去涉及机构及个人）

其他：

19. 本同意令的每一项规定将持续有效并可强制执行，直至被金融局以书面形式搁置、修改、终止或暂停为止。

20. 除本同意令中所载的允诺、保证、陈述或谅解外，不存在任何旨在诱使任何一方同意本同意令中的任何规定的允诺、保证、陈述或谅解。

为证明本同意令的订立，双方代表已于本日，即二〇一四年八月十九日，签署本同意令。

4.

■ **欲盖弥彰搞小动作的后果**
——三菱日联银行反洗钱合规案例分析

"9·11事件"以后，2002年，时任美国总统小布什提出将伊朗列入"邪恶轴心国"，从而对伊朗开启了长达数年的经济制裁。然而伊朗凭借其自身原油输出国的独特优势，与相关国家形成了石油利益链。其中，日本受自身资源匮乏的影响，进口石油就成为其经济发展的必要手段。在此背景之下，伊朗的石油贸易背后需要有金融机构进行资金清算方面的支持，而日本的第一大银行三菱日联银行（原三菱东京日联银行，于2018年4月1日正式更名为三菱日联银行，英文名为MUFG Bank Ltd.）在日本的国家战略中首当其冲地充当了这一角色，由于受到伊朗的恐怖主义威胁，美国在制裁伊朗并切断其经济命脉的同时，必然会从石油进口国的利益链条着手，虽然日本在极力保持与美国的依附关系，但美国为了让日本唯命是从，也时而会对其进行鞭策，本篇三菱日联银行被处罚事件正是在这一背景下发生的。

罚款事件始末

2013年被罚款2.5亿美元

由于三菱日联银行与伊朗、苏丹和缅甸等受到美国制裁的国家进行汇款交易，违反了美国纽约州银行法，该行于2013年6月同意向纽约州金融服务局（DFS）支付2.5亿美元的罚款（和解费）。

纽约州金融服务局是2011年成立的监管机构，融合了州银行和保险业务的监管，作为该部门的负责人，本杰明·洛斯基（Benjamin Lawsky）由于对金融不当行为的积极跟踪和独立态度获得关注，并在一段时间内让其他监管者感到不快。监管部门表示，根据估算，三菱日联银行在2002—2007年，经由纽约处理了2.8万笔非法交易，总金额涉及1 000亿美元，交易主体涉及伊朗等国家的政府和机构以及美国财政部黑名单上的实体。自此，三菱日联银行成为第三家因为涉嫌违反美国制裁法令而遭到纽约州金融服务局审查的金融机构。

2014年被追加罚款3.15亿美元

2014年11月18日，美国纽约州金融服务局宣布，有关三菱日联银行为伊朗等受到美国经济制裁对象国非法汇款一事，将追加3.15亿美元罚款，理由是该行向出具相关审计报告的会计师事务所施压，涉嫌掩饰与受制裁国家之间的交易。据纽约州金融服务局介绍，三菱日联银行的律师与高管曾向出具审计报告的美国普华永道会计师事务所施压，要求篡改报告内容，从轻记录有关账目。对此，普华永道于2014年8月同意支付2 500万美元罚款（和解费），并在两年内不得在纽约开展特定业务。

三菱日联银行在2002年至2007年为遭受美国经济制裁的国家非法汇款，在操作过程中系统性删除收款方信息。该行在内部调查中被指控存在不正当交易，于2007年主动向美国有关部门报告。根据纽约州金融服务局局长本杰明·洛斯基和三菱日联银行行长平野信行签署的和解令，这份被认为是客观的报告删除了关键信息，"误导"纽约州金融服务局达成2013年的和解协议，因此在此基础上追加罚款3.15亿美元。

纽约州金融服务局发表声明称，根据最新协议，三菱日联银行将把美国制裁合规和反洗钱部门迁往纽约。三菱日联银行也发布声明表示，对此遭到指控深表遗憾，并表示将努力遵守有关法规，切实做好内部管理，该银行已经解决自愿调查中向普华永道发出指令，以及对纽约监管机构的信息披露涉及的问题。

对于外部审计机构如本次被监管处罚的普华永道也并非第一家被处罚的会计师事务所，同为"四大"之一的德勤也于2013年6月，同意支付1 000万美元和解金，同时接受一年内不得向纽约州监管下的银行提供咨询服务的禁业处罚，以和解美国监管机构对该会计师事务所涉及英国渣打银行相关反洗钱工作的指控。纽约州金融服务局在调查渣打银行的洗钱案中，发现提供金融咨询的德勤公司有"不当行为，违反法律，并缺乏自律"。

三菱日联银行历史背景

三菱日联银行是一家拥有百年历史的国际著名金融机构，也是日本规模最大、竞争能力最强、国际化程度最高的银行。三菱日联银行在业内地位较高，声誉良好，客户基础雄厚，该行在国内网点数约为1 100个，工作人员约9万人，国际评级机构穆迪对该行外部评级为A1，标普为A+，根据2017年报显示，该行总资产约为20 447亿美元。

三菱日联银行成立于2006年1月1日（时称东京三菱日联（UFJ）银行），其前身是东京三菱银行和日联银行，在合并当时成为世界上最大的银行。三菱日联银行是三菱日联金融集团设立的全资子银行，除银行外，该集团旗下还设有信托银行、证券公司、租赁公司、信用卡公司、消费金融公司、资产管理公司等机构。

三菱日联银行有着较为复杂的合并历史。1996年4月1日，东京银行和三菱银行合并组成了东京三菱银行。合并前的东京银行是日本唯一的专业外汇银行，核心业务是外汇交易和贸易结算；三菱银行是上百家交叉持股公司的金融服务中心，核心业务是企业银行业务，提供固定资产融资，协助企业开拓海外市场，并积极在海外发展商人银行和投资银行业务。合并后的东京三菱银行秉承了上述两家银行的优势，成为日本首屈一指的大银行之一。2002年1月，原三和银行和东海银行合并成立了日联银行。三和银行的历史可追溯到1656年，在日本的各个银行中历史最为悠久。三和银行在1933年由3家银行（三十四银行、山口银行、鸿池银行）合并而成，经过多年努力，成长为日本具有代表性的城市银行。

三菱日联银行长期盈利增长情况良好，其资金来源渠道多元，除一般存款外还有发债、股票融资以及其他金融机构融资等，流动性风险较小。该行资本实力强大，2017年3月末资本充足率15.28%，资本回报率5.83%，维持在较好水平。总体上看，该银行财务稳健，业务模式稳定，违约概率极低。

近年来，随着日本银行间市场利差收益的走低，三菱日联银行努力开拓国际市场，目前该行在全球40个国家以上、100多个城市设有分支机构，海外分行约有1 150个。截至2017年6月，该行已进驻全球主要金融市场，如纽约、伦敦、法兰克福、中国香港等，此外，该行还在澳大利亚、新西兰、土耳其等国家设有分支机构。三菱日联银行于2007年7月在中国全额出资成立了外商独资银行三菱东京日联（中国），总部设在上海，其业务范围包括存贷款业务、人民币及外汇业务、进出口及贸易融资衍生产品业务、信用调查和咨询业务等，目前在国内设有近20个网点。

三菱日联银行的国际化道路

面对日本低增长、低利率、低息差、高强度竞争的严峻市场环境，三菱日联银行近年来积极探索国际化、综合化、数字化、集约化转型发展道路，在保持稳健经营的基础上，海外收入占比、非商业银行收入占比、非利息收入占比等指标取得突破性进展。

由于国内市场长期处于"低增长"形势，日本经济在20世纪90年代进入"失去的20年"，虽然整体发展稳定，但增长疲弱。2009年至2016年，日本实际GDP平均增速仅0.88%，占GDP约60%的私人消费年均增长0.53%，投资年均增长0.24%，贸易出口年均增速为1.93%。2016年，日本失业率降至22年来最低水平，但日本总人口已连续6年减少，65岁以上老年人口的占比高达27.3%，且呈上升趋势，当年新生儿数连续10年低于死亡数，老龄少子化成为日本经济停滞的重要原因之一。日本经济的低迷导致企业和个人的贷款需求都不旺盛。2008年金融危机后，日本国内金融机构国内贷款规模从危机前的年均增幅4%迅速回落到负增长3%左右，2012年以来才逐渐恢复到目前约2%的增速。

"低利率、低息差"挤压收益空间。日本曾长期实行零利率政策，而2016年1月起实施的负利率政策，更使得银行业短期利率、中长期利率乃至长期和超长期利率都大幅下降，2016财年日本银行业长期和短期新发生贷款年化利率已分别降至0.68%和0.73%，日本大型银行平均利差则下降到1%以下。自2016年末起，面向日本中央和地方政府以及政府系独立行政法人的贷款中标利率已降为零，但仍有10倍以上的银行参与竞标。

"高强度竞争"压缩了日本银行的生存空间。日本金融机构密度高，呈现"过度银行化"特征。据统计，2015财年日本每万平方公里的金融机构网点数接近3 000个，在主要发达国家中居首位。造成日本银行业激烈竞争的主要原因有：第一，法律允许实体企业投资设立银行子公司（可全资控股）；第二，日本对外资银行在日经营基本给予国民待遇，对其经营范围和经营行为没有特殊限制；第三，新兴非银行类金融企业也对传统商业银行业务带来一定的挤压。在较为严峻的外部环境下，三菱日联银行逐渐探索出一条以国际化、综合化、数字化、集约化为主要特征的转型道路。

2008年金融危机后，欧美大行海外业务收缩，日资银行则抓住机遇向海外拓展，其在全球银行业国际授信中的份额直线上升，至2016年已达16%，约为2009年的两倍。三菱日联银行拓展海外业务主要有以下三大策略：

一是扩大重点区域覆盖。金融危机后，日资银行重点拓展了经济复苏较快的美国和增长潜力较大的亚太地区，至2016年已分别占到这两个地区国际授信的三成和两成。日资银行"走出去"的主力军正是前文介绍的三菱日联银行。截至2016财年末，三菱日联银行覆盖国家和地区数已增至51个。其中，三菱日联银行的海外网点数（1 200个）已超过国内（1 100个），海外员工数占比达41%。

二是注重拓展非日资客户。例如，在三菱日联的贸易融资客户中，非日资客户占比已超过三分之二，其中，美国的这一比重高达80%，亚洲为78%，欧洲、中东和非洲均在70%左右。在中国，三菱日联的非日资客户占比约为45%。

三是拓展方式更加多元。除新设海外机构外，并购、参股、资产收购成为重要手段。金融危机以来，三菱日联银行的海外并购的投入力度大增。例如，于2008年收购摩根士丹利21%的股份，2013年收购泰国排名第五的大城银行75%的股份，2016年收购菲律宾信安银行20%的股份，此后又宣布将分阶段收购印度尼西亚金融银行73.8%的股份等。

在上述举措推动下，三菱日联银行2016财年业务条线收入中海外业务平均贡献度已达31.84%，是2009年的2.1倍。面对低息差环境和更高的资本监管压力，三菱日联银行将推行银证信融合、创新商业模式作为转型重点。积极探索"完全不消耗资本的全新商业模式"，即利用自身多元化优势为客户量身订制组合化金融商品，而实际资金从他行或机构投资人筹集。

综合化业务的发展显著改变了集团收入结构和盈利结构。三菱日联银行非利息收入占比不断提升，2016财年平均已高达57.66%，较2009财年提升18.47个百分点，非银行部门的资产占比由危机后的不足9%提高到18%，净利润贡献度由8%左右提高到25%。

如何进入美国市场

说起三菱日联银行进军美国市场还要从兼并加州联合银行（UBOC）说起。加州联合银行最早可以追溯到1864年成立的加州银行，1984年，加州银行被三菱银行兼并，成为三菱银行的全资子公司，东京银行加州分行于1975年兼并了南加州第一圣地亚哥国民银行，并更名为加州第一银行；1988年加州第一银行兼并了联合银行公司，合并后的公司更名为联合银行。1996年，三菱银行和东京银行合并，加州银行也和联合银行合并，成立加州联合银行，三菱日联银行拥有其大部分股权，2007年虽然加州联合银行因经营不善导致破产清算，但东京三菱日联银行已借助其经营网络在美国市场占据了一席之地。

2008年次贷危机以后，就在欧美银行业忙于冲销金融危机造成的不良资本和疲于应对行业新规给资本带来的压力之际，日资银行已经日益成为欧美企业重要的信贷资金来源。受日本经济衰退影响，在1995年到2005年间的10年中，日本银行业将大部分精力都放在了清理不良贷款和充实银行资本方面。而就在全球大型银行疲于应对2008年金融危机的时候，日本银行业的资产清理过程也恰恰完成，日资银行也阴差阳错地跻身于全球最健康的金融机构之列。此外，由于本国经济疲软使得企业不愿举债，日资银行手中有大量现金急于投放到海外，在此轮全球金融危机中，日本金融机构虽未能幸免，但面对日本国内增长疲软的金融市场，日本银行业再次选择扩张海外业务。

2008年后，三菱日联UFJ金融集团投资摩根士丹利，也是在经历了泡沫经济时期的海外扩张与泡沫破灭后的收缩战略后，日本银行业再次"出海"的典型案例。此后，三菱日联UFJ金融集团宣布购买苏格兰皇家银行（RBS）的项目融资资产投资组合，包括该行在欧洲、中东和非洲的基础设施项目。这一并购数目非凡，在苏格兰皇家银行资产组合中关键贷款资产的价值就达38亿英镑。创下日本历史上自三菱日联UFJ金融集团在2008年收购摩根士丹利部分资产以来规模最大的跨境交易。此前，三菱日联UFJ金融集团共斥资90亿美元收购了摩根士丹利21%的股份。

普华永道在三菱日联银行罚款事件中充当的角色

在会计界，即使是知名的四大会计师事务所一样会因出现违规行为而被处罚。2014年8月19日，纽约州金融服务局宣布，普华永道会计师事务所（以下简称普华永道）将支付2 500万美元的罚款并被禁止在纽约从事特定咨询服务两年，以和解其为日本三菱日联银行提供咨询服务时有不当行为的指控。

纽约州金融服务局指控普华永道在为三菱日联银行准备一份提交给监管机构的反洗钱事务报告中刻意淡化了问题的严重性。普华永道已经在周日晚些时候表示，同意接受罚款和禁业命令，其名下一组业务将不得为接受纽约州监管的银行提供特定咨询服务，为期两年。

纽约州金融服务局局长本杰明·洛斯基当时正将为银行提供评估服务并帮助银行应对监管事务的咨询顾问作为调查的目标，并就这些咨询顾问对银行提供评估服务，同时银行又为其雇佣服务支付相应费用所构成的利益冲突表示了疑虑。

根据纽约金融服务局的调查结果，普华永道在就三菱东京日联银行为伊朗等其他正在被美国经济制裁的国家所处理业务提交给监管机构的报告中存在多处改动，应该是淡化了所存在的问题。纽约州金融服务局称，普华永道在报告的最初版本中叙述，如果确知银行所遵循的一般性原则，为了加以验证，在这个项目上将会使用一个不同的方式进行评估。但是在最终提交给监管机构的报告中，普华永道称两种评估方式的结论不会有差别。普华永道坚称对报告的修改是回应银行以及银行的律师们所提出的意见，最终提交监管机构的报告已经包括了所有必要的实质性信息。事后，时任普华永道美国咨询业务主管迈尔斯-艾弗森（Miles Everson）在一份声明中说，和解协议事关事件发生之前完成的一项独立工作，普华永道在当时查找并确认了相关的交易，银行也已经就此向监管机构做出了汇报。

普华永道（Price Waterhouse Coopers Consulting，PwC）是全球及中国最大的专业服务机构之一，它由两大国际会计师事务所Price Waterhouse（普华）及Coopers & Lybrand（永道）于1998年7月1日全球合并而成，为世界最大的会计师事务所及专业服务机构，命名为PricewaterhouseCoopers。在152个国家中设有860余家分公司和办事处，超过155 000名的专业人才，普华永道向全球主要公司提供全方位的业务咨询服务。

普华永道管理咨询公司是业内发展最快的咨询公司之一。目前，普华永道的策略咨询已成为世界第三大策略咨询业务，普华永道的主要服务包括战略变革，流程优化和技术解决方案。主要竞争对手有美国管理系统公司、安达信咨询公司、德勤咨询公司、安永咨询公司、毕马威咨询公司、AT Kearney、Booz-

Allen & Hamilton以及麦肯锡咨询公司等。

除了在世界主要城市建立成员事务所以外，普华和永道在每个国家都会吸收并购当地的会计师事务所。这就导致在同一个国家的不同地区会产生很多的会计师事务所并达到其分布范围的临界点，从而无论快速增长的跨国公司在何处开展贸易，都可以为他们提供咨询服务。会计师事务所的成长同样受到来自于不断增长的审计需求，为了进一步利用大型会计师事务所的规模效益，普华和安达信（Arthur Andersen）曾在1989年商讨合并事宜，但最终没有达成协议。这主要是由于两者在重大领域存在利益冲突（此处专指同一会计师事务所不得兼任同一企业的审计和咨询业务）。例如，安达信为IBM公司提供强大的商务咨询服务，而普华则担任IBM的审计师。在1998年，普华（Price Waterhouse）和永道（Coopers & Lybrand）合并为普华永道（Price -waterhouse Coopers），使得新事务所成为一种不同的联盟，以获取更大的规模效益。在随后的几年里，普华永道和Grant Thornton之间的合并谈判以失败告终。因为主要的大型会计师事务所正在不断减少，新的合并已很难获得监管机构的批准。

在2002年安然（Enron）事件、世通（WorldCom）事件以及随后安达信的倒闭，导致美国证券交易委员会（U.S. Securities and Exchange Commission）对审计师的独立性提出了更为严苛的规定。随后出台的《萨班斯-奥克斯莱法案》（Sarbanes-Oxley Act）便是上述规定的结果之一。该法案强调了审计师的独立性要求，并规定核心审计必须与总体咨询业务相分离。这导致四大会计师事务所不得不剥离他们的商务咨询业务。然而，事务所的主要业务仍是在审计服务之外，诸如在税务及公司财务领域提供商业建议等。

美国对伊朗的制裁

从上述三菱日联银行由于涉伊问题被纽约州金融服务局处罚，进而挖掘更深层次的原因，就不得不谈到美国对伊朗的制裁。

自2003年伊朗核问题成为国际焦点以来，美国持续加大对伊朗的经济制裁力度。迄今，美国已推动联合国安理会通过四个制裁伊朗决议，即2006年第1737号、2007年第1747号、2008年第1803号与2010年第1929号决议。此外，美欧还出台单边制裁法案，并敦促日本、韩国、中国与印度跟进对伊朗制裁。美国加大制裁力度，集中在能源、金融两大关键领域进一步打击伊朗。

第一，为了强化对伊朗原有制裁措施的效果，2011年12月31日，美国公布《2012财政年度国防授权法》，重点强化对伊朗中央银行及相关银行的金融制裁。法案第1245条规定，自2012年6月28日起，如果某个国家的金融机构继续通过伊朗央行从伊朗购买石油，美国就切断该国所有金融机构与美国银行体系的联系，这是美国第一次将金融制裁扩大到所有外国金融机构，目的是切断伊朗中央银行与全球金融体系的联系。

第二，2012年7月12日，美国财政部再次推出新制裁措施，将制裁范围从金融扩展至贸易、能源和人员等多个领域。同年7月31日，时任美国总统奥巴马下令对伊朗能源和石化部门采取额外制裁措施，同时还对向伊朗国家石油公司、朗蒂夫国际贸易公司和伊朗中央银行提供物质支持，或者向伊朗政府提供金融帮助的个人和实体实施制裁，目的是进一步深化细化制裁措施，阻挠伊朗采用其他途径规避制裁。

第三，2013年1月2日，美国公布新财年《国防授权法》，不但加强在能源、船运、造船领域的制裁外，还将限制伊朗在贵金属、石墨、铝、钢铁、冶金用煤和一些商业软件领域的贸易，并特别规定限制易货交易，防止伊朗规避制裁。

根据以上时间点，不难看出三菱日联银行被纽约州金融服务局处罚正式是穿插在当时的制裁法案中，在伊朗对抗美国的制裁过程中，美国监管机构从与伊朗有关的金融机构下手也就变得合乎逻辑了。

其实，在两次处罚之前，三菱日联银行曾于2012年5月接到过纽约地区法院的命令，当时，在收到纽约地区法院的命令后，三菱日联银行冻结了伊朗央行和政府在该行的26亿美元资产，并在收到这个命令后提出了反驳，称美国法院对在日本的资产没有司法权。伊朗央行在处理伊朗原油的国际支付中发挥着关键作用，冻结其资产可能会导致石油供应遭到破坏。

目前在日本三大银行中，只有三菱日联银行收到了来自纽约地方法院的判令，主要因为三菱日联银行几乎负责处理与伊朗银行间的所有资产交易，其中，关于日本进口伊朗石油的交易结算，大部分也由三菱日联银行负责。

三菱日联银行为70%~80%日本的伊朗石油交易做清算。目前从伊朗进口的石油占日本石油进口的10%。日本2011年"3·11福岛核泄漏事故"以后关闭多家核电站后更加依赖进口燃料。但之后屈服于美国的压力，同意削减从伊朗的石油进口。

处罚案例得到的启示

三菱日联银行处罚案开创了美国监管机构对日资银行反洗钱合规处罚的先河，时隔仅17个月的时间，纽约州金融服务局再次向三菱日联银行开出了罚单，由此不难看出，美国监管机构对于外资金融机构监管的持续性，这也颇有点合规检查回头看的意思，在掌握了第一次罚款被隐瞒事实的证据后，第二次罚款的间隔时间更短、处罚金额更大，想必应该能够引起被处罚对象的足够重视了。

美国规则就是反洗钱的国际规则。各国银行均应当认识到这一客观现实，在反洗钱问题上，不仅要满足本国的监管要求，还要满足美国的监管要求，否则就会遭受美国政府的巨额罚款。虽然美国OFAC名单在法理上不具有国际效力，但其事实上的威力绝不亚于联合国制裁名单。各国银行特别是海外分支机构接到OFAC名单后，要及时更新自己的名单数据库，尽量避免与名单客户发生交易。此外，国外监管机构实施处罚往往有一定的时机考虑。银行存在反洗钱违规，监管机构不处罚并不等于没发现，很可能是因为处罚的时机不成熟。因此，各国银行平时就应高度关注反洗钱合规，严格控制风险，不要留下"小辫子"。遇有同美国出现贸易摩擦、政治争端等问题的敏感时期，更要加强合规管理，避免撞到"枪口"上。

监管机构（如美国参议院）对本国和外国机构不可能一视同仁。银行既要遵循本国法规，也要遵循业务国法规，能否在国内合规与国际和柜上找到平衡点是关乎银行国际业务拓展的大事，金融危机后，中资银行在国际金融领域中崭露头角，但要处处谨慎、时时提防，尽量少走弯路。银行应当意识到，为客户提供存款和结算服务的风险不比资产业务的风险低。除了对客户的自然属性进行尽职调查外，还要关注客户的生产经营是否明显违规。如果客户的产品和市场涉及美国时更要特别注意，要考虑产品知识产权、网上销售真实性以及制裁名单等复杂情况。

私人银行应参照著名的《沃尔夫斯堡集团私人银行业务全球反洗钱指引》接纳客户。如果是居于或资金来自高风险国家和地区的人士、从事某类高风险商业活动或行业的人士、政治公众人物等，可能对银行构成高风险，还要进行额外审查，并应考虑有高层管理人员审批建立的业务关系。

近年来，美国政府以违反《爱国者法》、OFAC规定为由频繁对一些跨国金融机构开展反洗钱调查、处罚或是制裁，所涉及的范围广、力度大、影响深、色彩浓，给一些金融机构不仅带来巨大损失，而且还严重影响国际声誉，甚至是相关海外分支机构的正常经营。除美国外，近年来一些FATF成员加大了本国跨境银行的反洗钱管制力度，开展所谓的反洗钱调查。

美国对国际金融业反洗钱的严厉监管。长期以来，美国对外国金融机构的制裁均援引国内法或使用美国总统行政令，其制裁名单不依据联合国安理会发布的制裁决议，一旦金融机构交易对手涉及OFAC名单，就有可能遭到美国的制裁。此外，美国还援引国内法的"长臂管辖"原则，只要美国认为某一外国人或外国金融机构参与了洗钱活动，即使该机构在美国没有分支机构，也会受到美国的制裁。

各金融机构、特定非金融机构应加强对反洗钱人员培训，提高综合知识水平与专业知识水平，利用国内反洗钱监管机构、国际机构等提供的资源，做好反洗钱专业资质认证工作，组织相关人员参加人民银行反洗钱岗位准入培训，按照"人岗匹配"和"证岗相适"原则，推行持证上岗制度。鼓励有关机构组织反洗钱人员开展国际公认反洗钱师（CAMS）资格认证，为开展反洗钱工作提供人才保障和智力支持。加大反洗钱专职合规人员的配备力度，保持核心骨干成员稳定，实施境外涉敏报警信息集中甄别机制，实现对跨境汇款业务涉敏风险的集中控制和专业化管理。

加强境外机构合规管理。各金融机构应科学合规制定境外发展规划，确保合规管理能力与业务范围、经营规模、风险特征以及监管要求相适应，保障国际化战略实施。深入了解、全面融入东道国环境，加强与监管当局的沟通，及时准确掌握当地监管规则，严格遵照相关法律法规开展业务。提升集团各机构和各部门间的信息共享和管理联动效率。加强境外反洗钱管理信息系统建设，及时全面掌握境外机构反洗钱工作动态，强化对境外机构反洗钱工作的非现场管理和考核。完善关联银行洗钱风险评估工作，对有业务往来关系的银行实施洗钱风险评估，强化风险管理。加强外派人员管理，做好外派人员行前培训工作，包括内控合规管理和境外保密、反洗钱常识等内容。

附录1:

《和解令》英文原文

NEW YORK STATE DEPARTMENT OF FINANCIAL SERVICES

In the Matter of:
The Bank of Tokyo Mitsubishi-UFJ, Ltd.,
New York Branch

CONSENT ORDER UNDER
NEW YORK BANKING LAW S 44

WHEREAS, from at least 2002 to 2007, The Bank of Tokyo-Mitsubishi UFJ, Ltd., ("BTMU") moved billions of dollars through New York for State and privately-owned entities in Iran;

WHEREAS, from at least 2002 to 2007, BTMU engaged in a practice under which BTMU's employees in Tokyo routed U.S. dollar payments through New York after first removing information from wire transfer messages that could be used to identify the involvement of sanctioned parties;

WHEREAS, BTMU established written operational instructions for its employees in Tokyo, which, translated from Japanese into English read, "...in case of a P/O addressed to the U.S., attention should be paid in order to avoid freezing of funds, e.g., the 'ORDERING BANK' field should be filled in with the name of [BTMU], while the entry of the name of the final receiving bank (in an enemy country) and the particulars of remittance should be omitted";

WHEREAS, using these means and other non-transparent means, from 2002 through 2007, BTMU estimates that it cleared approximately 28,000 U.S. dollar payments through New York worth close to $100 billion involving Iran, and additional payments involving Sudan and Myanmar, and certain entities on the Specially Designated Nationals list issued by the U.S. Treasury Department's Office of Foreign Asset Control ("OFAC");[①]

WHEREAS, after learning of these practices (described above) in 2007 and conducting an internal review of these practices, BTMU reported its findings to the U.S. authorities, and has represented that it has ceased such practices and undertaken remediation efforts;

NOW THEREFORE, the Department of Financial Services (the "Department") and BTMU (the "Parties") are willing to resolve the matters cited herein as follows:

SETTLEMENT PROVISIONS

Monetary Payment:

1. BTMU will pay a civil monetary payment to the Department pursuant to Banking Law § 44 and 44-A in the amount of two hundred and fifty million U.S. dollars ($250,000,000). BTMU will pay the entire amount of $250,000,000 within ten (10) days of executing the Consent Order.

---

① During this time period, Iran, Sudan and Myanmar were subject to U.S. economic sanctions.

Compliance Review:

2. Within thirty (30) days of executing the Consent Order, BTMU will identify an independent consultant acceptable to the Department who will report directly to the Department to conduct a comprehensive review (the "Compliance Review") of the BSA/AML related sanctions compliance programs, policies, and procedures now in place at the Bank's New York Branch (the "New York Program"). The Consultant will have authority, to the extent legally permissible, to examine and assess the Bank's existing BSA/AML operations that are performed outside the United States on behalf of the Bank's New York Branch. Based on the Compliance Review, the Consultant will identify needed corrective measures to address identified flaws, weaknesses or other deficiencies in the New York Program, and oversee their implementation. The Consultant will also examine and assess the Bank's New York Branch's compliance with those corrective measures.

3. BTMU agrees to cooperate fully with the Consultant by, including but not limited to, providing the Consultant access to all relevant personnel and records to the extent legally permissible. The term of the Consultant will extend for one year from the date of formal engagement. Any dispute as to the scope of the Consultant's authority will be resolved by the Department in the exercise of its sole discretion after appropriate consultation with BTMU and/or the Consultant.

4. Within thirty (30) days of executing the Consent Order, BTMU will submit to the Department for approval the proposed terms of the Consultant's engagement ("Engagement Letter").

5. Within ninety (90) days of BTMU's receipt of the Department's written approval of such terms, the Consultant will submit to the Parties a written report of findings, including proposed corrective measures from the Compliance Review (the "Compliance Review Report"). Thereafter, the Consultant will submit written progress reports ("Progress Reports") to the Parties.

Compliance Programs:

6. Within sixty (60) days of the receipt of the Compliance Review Report, BTMU will submit to the Department for approval a written plan that is designed to improve and enhance the current New York Program, incorporating the Compliance Review Report (the "Action Plan"). The Action Plan will provide for enhanced internal controls and updates and/or revisions to current policies, procedures and processes of the New York Branch in order to ensure full compliance with all applicable provisions of the BSA, the rules and regulations issued thereunder, OFAC requirements and the requirements of the Consent Order. Upon receipt of written approval by the Department, BTMU will begin to implement the changes.

Management Oversight:

7. Within sixty (60) days following the receipt of the Compliance Review Report, BTMU is to submit to the Department for approval a written plan to improve and enhance management oversight of BTMU NY's program ("Management Oversight Plan"). The Management Oversight Plan will address all relevant matters identified in the Compliance Review Report, provide a sustainable management oversight framework, and will take effect within thirty (30) days of receipt of written approval.

Breach of the Consent Order:

8. In the event that the Department believes BTMU to be materially in breach of the Consent Order ("Breach"), the Department will provide written notice to BTMU of the Breach and BTMU must, within ten (10) business days from the date of receipt of said notice, or on a later date if so

determined in the sole discretion of the Department, appear before the Department to demonstrate that no Breach has occurred or, to the extent pertinent, that the Breach is not material or has been cured.

9. The Parties understand and agree that BTMU's failure to make the required demonstration within the specified period is presumptive evidence of BTMU's Breach. Upon a finding of Breach, the Department has all the remedies available to it under the New York Banking and Financial Services Laws and may use any and all evidence available to the Department for all ensuing hearings, notices, orders and other remedies that may be available under the Banking and Financial Services Laws.

Waiver of Rights:

10. The Parties further understand and agree that no provision of the Consent Order is subject to review in any court or tribunal outside the Department.

Parties Bound By the Consent Order:

11. It is further understood that the Consent Order is binding on the Department and BTMU, as well as their successors and assigns that are within the supervision of the Department, but it specifically does not bind any federal or other state agencies or any law enforcement authorities.

12. This Consent Order resolves all matters before the Department relating to the conduct set forth in the Consent Order or disclosed to the Department in connection with this matter, provided that BTMU complies with the terms of the Consent Order. The Consent Order does not apply to conduct that BTMU did not disclose to the Department in connection with this matter.

13. During the period in which the Consent Order remains in effect, the approved Program, Plans, and Engagement Letter as referenced herein will not be amended or rescinded without the prior written approval of the Department, other than amendments necessary to comply with applicable laws and regulations.

14. Within ten (10) days after the end of each quarter following the execution of the Consent Order, BTMU will submit to the Department written progress reports detailing the form and manner of all actions taken to secure compliance with the provisions of the Consent Order and the results thereof. BTMU's responses to any audit reports covering BSA/AML matters prepared by internal and external auditors will be included with the progress report. The Department may, in writing, and in its discretion, discontinue the requirement for progress reports or modify the reporting schedule.

Notices:

15. All communications regarding this order shall be sent to:

Gaurav Vasisht
Executive Deputy Superintendent
Banking Division
New York State Department of Financial Services
One State Street
New York, NY 10004

Eiji Sumi
General Manager
Compliance & Legal Division
The Bank of Tokyo-Mitsubishi UFJ, Ltd.

2-7-1 Marunouchi, Chiyoda-ku
Tokyo, 100-8330, Japan

Irwin Naclc
Chief Compliance Officer & General Manager
Compliance Division for the Americas
The Bank of Tokyo-Mitsubishi UFJ, Ltd.
Headquarters for the Americas
1251 Avenue of the Americas
New York, NY 10020-1104

Miscellaneous:

16. Each provision of the Consent Order will remain effective and enforceable until stayed, modified, terminated or suspended in writing by the Department.

17. No promise, assurance, representation, or understanding other than those contained in the Consent Order has been made to induce any party to agree to the provisions of the Consent Order.

IN WITNESS WHEREOF, the parties hereto have caused this Consent Order to be executed as of this 19th day of June, 2013.

《和解令》中文译文

纽约州金融服务局在三菱东京UFJ银行有限公司纽约分行事件

和解令 基于纽约银行法第44条

鉴于至少从2002年到2007年,三菱东京UFJ银行有限公司(BTMU)为伊朗的国家和私营实体通过纽约分行转移了数十亿美元;

鉴于至少从2002年到2007年,BTMU的员工在第一次把信息从电报移除可以被用来识别参与制裁的对象信息之后,BTMU在从事在东京通过纽约的美元支付线路的实践;

鉴于BTMU为它在东京的员工建立书面操作说明,从日语翻译成英语,"……在P/O通向美国的情况下,应注意避免资金冻结,如"汇款银行项应填入[BTMU]的名称,而对最终收款银行名称(在敌国)和特殊的汇款将被删除";

鉴于使用这些手段和其他非透明手段,从2002年到2007年、BTMU通过纽约大约清算了将近28000笔美元支付价值近1000亿美元,涉及伊朗,额外的支付含盖苏丹和缅甸,并在特别指定国民某些实体名单由美国财政部外国资产控制办公室发布("OFAC");

鉴于在学习了这些实践之后(如上所述)在2007年实施这些做法的内部审查,BTMU报告给美国当局,并表示它已经停止这种做法并开展努力纠正;

基于以上,金融服务局("服务局")和BTMU("当事方")将就解决该问题在此声明如下:

和解条款

货币支付:

1. BTMU将依据银行法第44和44-A条承担民事赔偿向服务局支付金额二亿五千万美元(250 000 000美元)。BTMU将在本和解令生效后10天内支付250 000 000美元的全部金额。

合规性审查:

2. 在执行和解令后30天内,BTMU将指定一名被服务局接受的独立顾问将直接汇报给服务局进行全面审查（"合规性审查"），BSA／AML相关制裁合规计划，政策和程序现在该银行的纽约分行（纽约计划）。这名顾问将在法律上拥有授权，允许的，检查和评估银行在美国以外的代表银行纽约分行执行现有的BSA/AML操作。根据遵约审查，顾问将确定必要的纠正措施，以解决纽约计划中发现的缺陷、弱点或其他不足，并监督其执行情况。顾问还将审查和评估该银行纽约分行对这些纠正措施的遵守情况。

3. BTMU同意与顾问充分合作，包括但不限于提供咨询获得所有相关人员和记录在法律允许的范围内。顾问的任期从正式聘用之日起延长一年。任何争议的顾问的权力范围将在服务局全权行使与BTMU和/或顾问适当协商后得到解决。

4. 在执行和解令后30天内，BTMU将向服务局提交批准聘请顾问的意见（和约书）。

5. 在BTMU收到服务局书面批准的90天内，该顾问将提交给双方一个调查结果的书面报告，包括提出整改措施的合规性审查（合规审查报告）。此后，顾问将向双方提交书面进度报告（进度报告）。

合规程序：

6. 在收到合规检查报告的60天内，BTMU将向服务局提交书面计划，旨在改善和提高目前的纽约项目，包括合规审查报告（行动计划）。该行动计划将提供增强的内部控制和更新和/或修改目前的政策，以纽约分行的程序和流程以确保完全遵守所有适用的BSA的规定，规定发行以外，交流的要求和和解令的要求。在由部门书面批准后，BTMU将开始实施整改。

管理监督：

7. 在收到合规审查报告的60天内，BTMU提交给审批部门的书面计划，改善和提高BTMU纽约项目的管理监督（管理监督计划）。管理监督计划将解决所有相关事项的合规性审查报告确定，提供一个可持续的管理监督框架，并将在书面批准后的30天内生效。

违反和解令：

8. 在事件中服务局认为BTMU违反了和解令（"违约"），服务局将就

BTMU违约向BTMU提供书面通知，在自收到通知起10日内或在服务局自行确定的等候时期，出现在服务局证明没有违约的发生以前，只在一定程度上相关的，可以认为没有违反的或已经改正。

9. 双方理解并同意BTMU没有被要求证明在特殊的时期假定BTMU的违约证据，在发现违反的情况下，服务局拥有纽约银行和金融服务法所规定的所有补救办法，并可利用服务局提供的任何和所有证据，提供银行和金融服务法下可采取的所有听证会、通知、命令和其他补救办法。

放弃权利：

10. 双方进一步理解并同意，在任何服务局以外的任何法院或法庭都不接受和解令的规定。

受和解令约束的当事人：

11. 进一步理解为和解令在服务局和BTMU间有约束力，以及他们的继承人和服务局内部指定的监督，但具体不绑定任何联邦或其他国家机关或执法机关。

12. 本和解令解决所有事项有关规定的和解令或披露与这件事联系，但BTMU符合了和解令的条款。同意不适用于行为，BTMU并未透露与此有关的部门。

13. 在同意书有效期内，未经本部门事先书面批准，除符合适用法律和法规所需的修正外，未经该部门事先书面批准，将不得修改或撤销所引用的程序、计划和聘用信函。

14. 在每个季度结束后的十（10）天内和解令BTMU将向商务部提交书面进度报告，详细说明的形式以及为确保遵守《和解令》规定而采取的一切行动的方式及其结果。任何审计报告涉及事项BTMU BSA／AML的反应由内部和外部审计员准备的报告将包括在进度报告中。在写作中，并在其自由裁量权，不再要求提供报告或修改报告时间表。

注意事项：

15. 有关此订单的所有通信均应发送至：

Gaurav Vasisht

执行副主管

银行部门

纽约州金融服务局

第一州大街

纽约，纽约10004

Eiji Sumi

总经理

法律合规部

东京三菱日联UFJ银行有限公司

2-7-1丸之内，千代田区

东京，100-8330，日本

Irwin Naclc

首席合规官兼总经理

美洲合规部

三菱东京日联UFJ银行有限公司

美洲总部

1251美洲大道

纽约，纽约10020-1104

杂项：

16. 和解令的每一项规定将继续有效并可强制执行至由本服务局书面停留、修改、终止或暂停。

17. 没有承诺、保证、代表或理解已在和解令中提出，诱使任何一方同意和解令。

兹证明，双方当事人已于2013年6月19日提出此项和解令。

（此处略去涉及机构及个人）

附录2：

《和解令》英文原文

NEW YORK STATE DEPARTMENT OF FINANCIAL SERVICES

_____X

In the Matter of

CONSENT ORDER UNDER

NEW YORK BANKING LAW §§ 39 and 44

The Bank of Tokyo-Mitsubishi UFJ, Ltd.

New York Branch

_____X

The New York State Department of Financial Services (the "Department" or "DFS") and The Bank of Tokyo-Mitsubishi UFJ, Ltd. ("BTMU" or the "Bank") (collectively, the "Parties") stipulate that:

WHEREAS, BTMU is a foreign bank with complex operations and multiple business lines and legal entities in many countries worldwide; and

WHEREAS, BTMU conducts operations in the United States through various subsidiaries and entities including its branch in New York, New York (the "New York Branch"); and

WHEREAS, the Department is the licensing agency of the New York Branch, pursuant to Article II of the New York Banking Law ("NYBL") and is responsible for its supervision and regulation; and

WHEREAS, BTMU wrongfully misled the Department in connection with its understanding of BTMU's U.S. dollar clearing services on behalf of sanctioned Sudanese, Iranian, and Burmese parties ("Sanctioned Parties"), the transactions of which were settled through the New York Branch and other New York-based financial institutions.

WHEREAS, the Department finds that BTMU's conduct raised serious safety and soundness concerns and constituted violations of law and regulation.

NOW, THEREFORE, to resolve this matter, the Parties agree to the following:

Introduction

1. From approximately 2007 through 2008, the Bank engaged a team from the advisory practice of PricewaterhouseCoopers LLP (the "PwC Engagement Team") to undertake a historical transaction review (the "HTR") for BTMU to analyze the Bank's U.S. dollar clearing activity between April 1, 2006 and March 31, 2007. The stated purpose of the HTR was to: (a) identify any U.S. dollar transactions that potentially should have been frozen, blocked or reported under

applicable OFAC requirements, and (b) investigate the relevant transaction set for compliance with OFAC requirements.

2. In June 2008, BTMU submitted the PwC Engagement Team's HTR report (the "HTR Report") to the Department's predecessor agency (the New York State Banking Department), as well as to other U.S. regulators (collectively, the "Regulators"). The HTR Report purported to be the product of an "objective" and "methodologically sound" process.

3. In 2012, during the investigation into BTMU's past U.S. dollar clearing activities, BTMU notified the Department that many of the payment messages for the time period of 20022007 were not available.[1] As an alternative solution, BTMU suggested that the Parties use the HTR's findings, as set forth in the HTR Report, as a basis to extrapolate the approximate number of improper transactions processed by BTMU through the New York Branch and other New York-based financial institutions between 2002 and 2007. DFS required that information in order to accurately assess the scope of the Bank's misconduct and thereby fix an appropriate penalty.

4. In reliance on the HTR Report, as well as the Bank's representations to the Department, BTMU and the DFS executed a consent order on June 20, 2013 (the "2013 Consent Order"), pursuant to New York Banking Law § 44.

5. As set out in the 2013 Consent Order, the Parties agreed that from at least 2002 through 2007, BTMU unlawfully cleared through the New York Branch and other New York- based financial institutions an estimated 28,000 U.S. dollar payments, valued at approximately $100 billion, on behalf of certain Sanctioned Parties and for entities on the Specially Designated Nationals ("SDNs") list issued by the U.S. Treasury Department's Office of Foreign Asset Control ("OFAC").[2] The 2013 Consent Order required BTMU to make a civil monetary payment of $250 million and to hire an independent consultant to conduct a comprehensive review of the BSA/AML and sanctions related compliance programs, policies, and procedures currently in place at the New York Branch.

6. After entering into the 2013 Consent Order, the Department investigated PwC's involvement in this matter. To that end, DFS reviewed voluminous documents, including correspondence between PwC and the Bank, and took sworn testimony from eight current and former PwC professionals who had been members of the PwC Engagement Team.

7. The aforementioned investigation revealed that BTMU successfully convinced the PwC Engagement Team, including two principals from PwC's advisory group, to remove excerpts from drafts of the HTR Report that would have cast doubt upon the thoroughness, objectivity and reliability of the findings contained in the HTR Report submitted to Regulators on behalf of the Bank.

---

① U.S. dollar clearing is the process by which U.S. dollar-denominated transactions are satisfied between counterparties through a U.S. bank. The Society of Worldwide Interbank Financial Telecommunications ("SWIFT") is a vehicle through which banks exchange wire transfer messages with other financial institutions, including U.S. correspondent banks. SWIFT messages contain various informational fields.

② SDNs are individuals and companies specifically designated as having their assets blocked from the U.S. financial system by virtue of being owned or controlled by, or acting for or on behalf of, targeted countries, as well as individuals, groups, and entities, such as terrorists and narcotics traffickers, designated under sanctions programs that are not country-specific.

Statement of Facts

8. In March 2007, BTMU hired PwC for the purpose of (a) conducting a year-long historical transaction review of BTMU's international remittance and trade finance activity for compliance with OFAC regulations and (b) presenting PwC's "key findings and results" to the Regulators.

9. On May 1, 2008, after more than a year of review, and prior to completion of the HTR Report, the Bank and the PwC Engagement Team made an interim presentation to the Regulators. At this presentation, according to PwC's notes of the meeting, Regulators asked, in connection with Iranian transactions, whether as a common approach "BTMU removed information such as originating bank, originating party or beneficiary party from [ ] wire messages." The notes reflect that, in response to this direct question from the Regulators, a very senior BTMU official "emphatically" denied that the Bank did so. The Department accepted this denial as an assurance that there existed at BTMU no special written procedures to strip U.S. dollar denominated SWIFT wire messages of information that, if detected, would have triggered screening alerts for potential OFAC violations.

10. On May 23, 2008, just one month prior to completion of the HTR Report, the Bank disclosed to the PwC Engagement Team for the first time a written BTMU procedure to strip and/or falsely populate SWIFT data fields with the Bank's identifying information instead of that of the Bank's clients (and its clients' clients) from OFAC sanctioned "enemy countries." These instructions were included in the Bank's *GSC (Global Service Center) Administrative Procedures Manual for Foreign Transfers* and read:

> Banks located in countries designated by the U.S. as enemy countries hold their U.S. dollar accounts outside of the U.S. Upon receipt of U.S. do liar-denominated payment orders of which the ordering or receiving bank is such bank, use the cover payment method and not the one payment method.

> The method for filling out vouchers is the same as in "Section 2 - Payments to Other Banks Located in Japan." However, exert care to avoid the funds being frozen by, among other means, providing our Bank as the ordering bank and not specifying the final receiving bank (the name of the enemy country).

11. With an understanding of the value that this translation would have to the Department in evaluating the HTR, the PwC Engagement Team inserted it into drafts of the HTR Report upon receipt of it.

12. In the same week of May 2008, the Bank informed the PwC Engagement Team that BTMU employed its sanctions screening filter in Tokyo to stop U.S. dollar denominated SWIFT wire messages that contained language capable of triggering screening alerts in New York so that Bank employees were able to and did strip language identifying Sanctioned Entities before those messages were transmitted to New York and resubmitted the messages without the identifying language. In this way, payment messages that would have required further review - and potentially blocking or freezing - in New York, instead bypassed OF AC filters in New York.

13. PwC's Engagement Team understood that improper data manipulation could significantly compromise the HTR's integrity. Accordingly, the PwC Engagement Team inserted an express acknowledgement into a draft of the HTR Report informing the Regulators that "had PwC know[n]

about these special instructions at the initial phase of the HTR then we would have used a different approach in completing this project," a reference to the fact that PwC's Engagement Team would have recommended at the beginning of the HTR that BTMU undertake a forensic review of the Bank's wire transfers.

14. At a meeting on June 13, 2008, some of the Bank's most senior Anti-money Laundering, Compliance & Legal Division managers objected to this statement appearing in the HTR Report and requested its removal. Accordingly, the PwC Engagement Team removed it and inserted in its place "[W]e have concluded that the written instructions would not have impacted the completeness of the data available for the HTR and our methodology to process and search the HTR data was appropriate."

15. Upon its discovery of the special written procedures and the improper use of the sanctions screening filter in Tokyo, the PwC Engagement Team recommended to BTMU that PwC conduct a forensic investigation into the Bank's U.S. dollar denominated payment processes and wire transfer messages. The Bank rejected this advice and instead insisted that the BTMU investigation into wire-stripping would be conducted internally by BTMU's Internal Audit Office (the "IAO").

16. Due to BTMU's request that PwC remove its recommendation for a forensic review, the Department never learned of the PwC Engagement Team's opinion in that regard.

17. Approximately one week before the HTR Report was finalized and submitted to the Department, a manager of the Bank's Anti-money Laundering Office, Compliance & Legal Division (the "BTMU Compliance Manager") reviewing drafts of the Report wrote to the PwC Engagement Team with reference to a draft paragraph describing "the problem" of PwC's inability to review un-linked MT 202 wire payment messages. Linking such payments was at the core of PwC's review methodology. The BTMU Compliance Manager, however, asked that PwC "consider deleting the above mentioned sentence because we do not want to give the impression to the reader of the report that there are some important MTs that were not successfully reviewed." The PwC Engagement Team removed the paragraph from the HTR Report, and accordingly, from scrutiny by the Department.

18. The PwC Engagement Team suggested in its draft HTR Report that the Bank's IAO investigate the genesis of the special written procedures, the possible existence of other "similar instructions," and the Bank's "intentional omission of search terms" from payment messages. The PwC Engagement Team cautioned that "*[t]he potential impact from the findings from [any such] investigation will need to be considered when evaluating this [HTR] Report.*" (emphasis supplied). In response, the BTMU Compliance Manager forwarded the following request on behalf of the Bank: "[C]an you possibly delete this sentence?" PwC's Engagement Team complied, removing the recommendation on how an internal BTMU audit should proceed. PwC further removed questions that PwC had raised to be addressed by such an investigation.

19. At the request of the Bank, the PwC Engagement Team removed other information from drafts of the HTR Report. The revisions included:

- Deleting the English translation of BTMU's wire stripping instructions, which referenced the Bank doing business with "enemy countries" of the U.S.;[①]

---

① The BTMU Compliance Manager requested that the PwC Engagement Team delete the English translation of the written procedures for wire stripping, writing, "it is the opinion of our NY people, also

- Deleting a regulatory term of art that PwC used throughout the report in describing BTMU's wire-stripping instructions ("Special Instruction") and replacing it with a nondescript reference that lacked regulatory significance ("Written Instruction");

- Deleting most of PwC's discussion of BTMU's wire-stripping activities;

- Deleting information concerning BTMU's potential misuse of OFAC screening software in connection with its wire-stripping activities;

- Deleting several forensic questions that PwC identified as necessary for consideration in connection with the HTR Report; and

- Deleting a section of the HTR Report that discussed the appearance of special characters (such as   and in wire transfer messages, which had prevented PwC's filtering system from detecting certain transactions involving Sudan and Myanmar.

20. The Bank's IAO investigated the special written procedures and stripping of information from wire messages. BTMU's "Report on the Additional Investigation related to the Historical Transaction Review" was prepared by the IAO and issued to the Regulators in October 2008. This Report was misleading to the Department in that it was, in the face of the undisclosed PwC findings, inadequate, too limited in scope, and did not employ the type of forensic review originally recommended by PwC.

Violations of Law and Regulation

21. Due to the aforementioned conduct, BTMU misled the Department in reaching the settlement terms of the 2013 Consent Order. BTMU also:

- failed to maintain or make available at its New York Branch true and accurate books, accounts and records reflecting all transactions and actions in violation of Banking Law § 200-c; and

- knowingly violated the Department's regulation 3 NYCRR § 300.1, which requires BTMU to submit a report to the Superintendent immediately upon the discovery of fraud, dishonesty, making of false entries and omissions of true entries, and other misconduct, whether or not a criminal offense, in which any BTMU employee was involved; and

- knowingly made or caused to be made false entries in its books, reports and statements and omitted to make true entries of material particularly pertaining to the U.S. dollar clearing business of BTMU through its New York Branch or other New York-based financial institutions, misleading the Superintendent and examiners of the Department who were lawfully appointed to examine BTMU's conditions and affairs.

[our Bank's counsel] is also basically agreeing on this as well, that mentioning the exact wordings of the Instructions, especially the words 'to avoid the funds being frozen by,' might cause unnecessary concern to the regulators. From what we understand now is the real purpose of these instructions was not to have the funds [avoid] being frozen but not to have delayed by a few days because the wire contained simple words such as 'Iran.' " The PwC Engagement Team complied, and removed the English translation.

Settlement Provisions

Monetary Penalty:

22. Within ten (10) business days of executing this Consent Order, BTMU shall make full payment of a civil monetary penalty in the amount of three hundred and fifteen million U.S. dollars ($315,000,000). BTMU will not claim, assert, or apply for a tax deduction or tax credit with regard to any U.S. federal, state or local tax, directly or indirectly, for any portion of the civil monetary penalty paid pursuant to this Consent Order.

Employee Discipline and a Permanent Ban on Involvement with Licensees:

23. The Department's investigation has resulted in the resignation from BTMU of the BTMU Compliance Manager, who played a central role in the improper conduct discussed in this Consent Order.

24. BTMU shall not in the future directly or indirectly retain the individual referenced in the paragraph above, as either an officer, employee, agent, consultant or contractor of BTMU, or any affiliate of BTMU, or in any other capacity.

25. As promptly and expeditiously as possible but no later than sixty (60) days from the date of this Consent Order, the Bank shall take all steps necessary to ensure that its then- General Manager of BTMU's Anti-money Laundering Office, Compliance & Legal Division and its then- Executive Officer & General Manager of BTMU's Global Planning Division, who each played central roles in the improper conduct discussed in this Consent Order but who are still employed by the Bank's affiliated companies, shall engage in no duties, responsibilities or activities while employed at the Bank's affiliated companies that involve in any way the business of any licensee of this Department, including, but not limited to, the New York Branch.

26. BTMU shall not in the future permit the individuals referenced in the above paragraph to engage, directly or indirectly, in any duties, responsibilities or activities at or on behalf of BTMU or the Bank's affiliated companies that involve their banking business in the United States, including the business of any licensee of this Department.

Extension of Independent Consultant:

27. The Bank, the New York Branch and the Department entered into the 2013 Consent Order to, *inter alia*, install an independent consultant ("IC") to conduct a review of the Bank's existing BSA/AML related sanctions compliance programs, policies and procedures in place at the Branch. The parties now agree that, at the conclusion of the IC's engagement in March 2015, the Department shall in its sole discretion, determine if an extension of the engagement is required. If the Department determines that an extension of the IC is necessary, the extension shall be for a period of up to eighteen (18) months. The Bank further agrees to relocate its U.S. BSA/AML and OFAC sanctions compliance programs to New York, and agrees that these programs will have U.S. compliance oversight over all transactions affecting the New York Branch, including those transactions performed outside the U.S. that affect the New York Branch. The IC will oversee, evaluate, and test the implementation of those programs, as well as the BSA/AML and OFAC sanctions compliance programs that operate outside the U.S. and relate to transactions affecting the New York Branch. For the avoidance of doubt, it shall not be the responsibility of the IC to oversee, evaluate and test compliance with the laws of any jurisdiction other than those of the United States and any jurisdiction within the United States.

Breach of the Consent Order:

28. In the event that the Department believes BTMU to be materially in breach of this Consent Order ("Breach"), the Department will provide written notice to BTMU of the Breach and BTMU must, within ten (10) business days from the date of receipt of said notice, or on a later date if so determined in the sole discretion of the Department, appear before the Department to demonstrate that no Breach has occurred or, to the extent pertinent, that the Breach is not material or has been cured.

29. The Parties understand and agree that BTMU's failure to make the required demonstration within the specified period is presumptive evidence of BTMU's Breach. Upon a finding of Breach, the Department has all the remedies available to it under New York Banking and Financial Services Law and may use any and all evidence available to the Department for all ensuing hearings, notices, orders and other remedies that may be available under the New York Banking and Financial Services Laws.

Waiver of Rights;

30. The Parties further understand and agree that no provision of this Consent Order is subject to review in any court or tribunal outside the Department.

Parties Bound by the Consent Order:

31. It is further understood that this Consent Order is binding on the Department and BTMU, as well as their successors and assigns that are within the supervision of the Department, but it specifically does not bind any federal or other state agencies or any law enforcement authority.

32. No further action will be taken by the Department against BTMU for the conduct set forth in this Consent Order, provided that BTMU complies with the terms of this Consent Order.

33. Notwithstanding any other provision contained in this Consent Order, however, the Department may undertake action against BTMU for transactions or conduct that BTMU did not disclose to the Department in the written materials that BTMU submitted to the Department in connection with this matter.

Notices:

34. All communications regarding this Order shall be sent to:

> Elizabeth Nochlin
> Assistant Counsel
> Banking Division
> New York State Department of Financial Services
> One State Street
> New York, NY 10004

> Megan Prendergast
> Assistant Counsel
> Banking Division
> New York State Department of Financial Services
> One State Street
> New York, NY 10004

> Eiji Sumi
> Executive Officer & General Manger
> Compliance Division

The Bank of Tokyo-Mitsubishi UFJ, Ltd.
2-7-1 Marunouchi, Chiyoda-ku
Tokyo, 100-8330, Japan

Yasuhiko Shibata
Senior Manager
Anti-money Laundering Office
Compliance Division
The Bank of Tokyo-Mitsubishi UFJ, Ltd.
2-7-1 Marunouchi, Chiyoda-ku
Tokyo, 100-8330, Japan

Miscellaneous:

35. Each provision of this Consent Order will remain effective and enforceable until stayed, modified, terminated or suspended in writing by the Department.

36. BTMU shall continue to be subject to the terms and conditions set forth in the 2013 Consent Order by and among the Parties.

37. No promise, assurance, representation, or understanding other than those contained in this Consent Order has been made to induce any party to agree to the provisions of this Consent Order.

IN WITNESS WHEREOF, the parties hereto have caused this Consent Order to be executed as of this _18_ th day of November 2014.

《和解令》中文译文

纽约州金融服务局与三菱日联银行（UFJ）有限公司纽约分行根据纽约银行法第39条和第44条达成的和解令。

纽约州金融服务局（以下简称服务局或DFS）和三菱日联银行（UFJ）有限公司（以下简称BTUM或此银行）（双方共同）达成以下协议：

BTMU是一家具有综合服务能力和多重业务条线且在全球多个国家拥有合法实体的国外银行；

鉴于BTMU通过不同的分支机构和实体包括在纽约的分支机构（纽约分行）在美国进行管理操作；及

鉴于服务局是纽约分行的经营主管部门，依照纽约银行法（NYBL）第二部分并履行监管和控制的职责；及

鉴于BTMU错误地误导了服务局对BTMU美元清算服务获益于制裁的苏丹、伊朗和缅甸等受制裁对象的理解，这种交易是通过纽约分行或其他纽约当地的金融机构清算完成的。

鉴于服务局发现BTMU的行为提升了严重的安全性、声誉的担忧并且构成违反法律和监管。

基于以上，为解决这一问题，双方同意如下：

引言

1.大约2007年至2008年，这家银行从负责咨询实践的律师事务所团队普华永道（"普华永道审计工作组"），进行交易的历史回顾（HTR），分析银行从2006年4月1日至2007年3月31日之间的美元清算活动。指定HTR的目的在于：（a）在OFAC允许的要求下识别任何的潜在将被冻结、阻止的美元交易（b）服从OFAC的要求调查有关的交易。

2.在2008年6月，BTUM将普华永道审计工作组的 HTR报告（HTR 报告）提交给服务局的前身机构（纽约银行局），同美国其他的管理部门（统称监管者），HTR的报告的意义在于提供一种客观而且有正确方法的过程。

3.在2012年，在调查BTMU过去美元清算活动的期间，BTMU向服务局声明许多在2002—2007年支付信息已不存在。作为一种替代方案，BTMU建议双

方利用HTR的研究发现，作为HTR报告的前提，作为基础来推断近似数的在2002年至2007年之间BTMU通过纽约分行和纽约金融机构的不正当交易进行。

美元结算是指通过美国银行在美国交易对手之间满足美国美元交易的过程。世界银行同业金融电信协会（SWIFT）是一家通过银行与其他金融机构（包括美国银行）交换电汇信息的银行。SWIFT消息包含各种信息字段。

为了准确评估银行的不当行为的范围，从而确定适当的处罚。

4.依赖于HTR的报告，以及银行与服务局的交涉，BTMU和DFS执行2013年6月20日和解令（2013和解令），根据纽约银行法第44条。

5.在2013年的和解令中限定，双方同意至少从2002年到2007年，BTMU非法通过纽约分公司和纽约的其他金融机构估计28 000笔美元支付，价值约为1 000亿美元，受益于美国财政部外国资产控制办公室（OFAC）发布的在一定的认可和各方代表在特别指定国民实体（SDNs）的名单。2013年的和解令要求BTMU作出民事货币支付的2.5亿美元，雇用独立顾问对于纽约分公司目前程序进行BSA/AML的全面审查和批准相关的合规计划，政策。

6.在进入2013年和解令后，服务局调查普华永道参与此事。为此，DFS审查了大量文件，包括普华永道和银行之间的信件，并从普华永道成员中的八位现任和前任普华永道专业人员宣誓过的证词。

7.上述调查显示，BTMU成功说服了普华永道审计工作组，包括来自普华永道顾问团的两名负责人，从HTR的报告中清除掉了彻底会导致质疑的摘录。

SDN是指个人和公司特别定义为美国金融系统所拥有或控制的资产被阻止，或代理或代表特定的国家，以及个人、群体和实体，如恐怖分子和毒品走私、制裁方案，不针对具体国家的指定。

代表银行利益方面的客观性和可靠性的结果包含在提交给监管机构的HTR的报告中。

陈述事实

8.2007年3月，BTMU聘请普华永道的目的在于（a）对于BTMU由OFAC监管规定的国际汇款和贸易融资活动进行长达一年的历史交易审查；（b）向监管部门展示普华永道的"关键调查和结果"。

9.2008年5月1日，经过一年多的审查后，对HTR报告完成之前，银行和普华永道审计工作组为监管机构制作了一份临时报告。在这份报告中，根据普华永道的会议纪要，监管机构问询，在与伊朗有关系的交易中，是否作为一个通用的方式"BTMU从［ ］报文信息中删除信息如发起行、发起方或受益人方。"纪要中反映，在应对这一问题的直接监管中，一位BTMU的高管官方"着重"否认银行这样做。该服务局接受这种否定作为一种保证存在于BTMU没有特殊的书面程序删除以美元命名的SWIFT报文信息，如果检测到，会触发潜在的OFAC违反行为的警报。

10.2008年5月23日，短短一个月的HTR报告完成之前，该银行披露普华永道参与第一次编写BTMU程序为了从OFAC批准"敌对国家"去掉和/或伪造的填充SWIFT数据项并用银行的识别信息代替银行的客户（和客户的客户），这些指令被包含在银行的GSC（全球服务中心）管理，国外翻译的程序手册标注：

位于美国指定为敌国的国家的银行在收到美国美元账户后，在美国以外的美元支付订单上，即订购或收款银行是此类银行，采用支付方式而不是一种付款方式。

填写凭证的方法与"第2部分支付给位于日本的其他银行"相一致。

但是，要小心避免资金被冻结，按照其他的方式，提供给我们的银行作为指令银行的并且未指定最终收款银行（敌国名称）。

11.这样翻译会使服务局在评价HTR时具有一个有价值的理解，普华永道审计工作组在收到HTR报告的时候把它作为了一个草稿。

12.在2008年5月的同一周，该银行通知了普华永道审计工作组BTMU在东京聘请其制裁筛查过滤器停止了在纽约的以美元命名的包含能够触发警报的SWIFT报文，以致银行雇员能够在这些信息被发送到纽约，重新提交没有可识别的语言之前剔除可识别认可实体的语言。这样，付款信息将需要在纽约进一步审查潜在的阻塞或冻结，以代替在纽约OFAC的过滤。

13.普华永道审计工作组理解对于不当的数据操作可以有目的地解决HTR的完整性问题。因此，普华永道审计工作组在通知监管机构时在HTR报告的草稿中加入了表达感谢的内容"，普华永道知道这些特殊指令在HTR的初始阶段使用不同的方法完成这个项目，"指的是普华永道审计工作组会建议在HTR的开始，BTMU对银行电汇进行司法审查。

14.在2008年6月13日的一个会议上，一些银行的最高级的反洗钱合规与法律服务局经理反对这个声明出现在HTR的报告并要求将其删除。因此，普华永道审计工作组移动并把它插在这个地方"我们决定书面指令不会影响完整性的数据可用于HTR和我们的方法来处理和搜索的HTR数据是适当的"。

15.对发现的特殊的书面程序和在东京使用不当的制裁过滤筛选，普华永道审计工作组推荐BTMU，普华永道掌管着一项用于银行的美元计价的支付流程和资讯传递消息的法庭调查。该银行拒绝了这个建议，而是坚持BTMU调查报文剥离将由BTMU的内部审计办公室（IAO）进行。

16.由于BTMU要求普华永道将其推荐为司法审查，该服务局没有采纳普华永道审计工作组在这方面的意见。

17.在HTR报告最终提交给服务局约一个星期前，一个银行的反洗钱办公室经理，合规与法律部门（BTMU合规经理）审查报告的初稿给普华永道审计工作组参考草稿段落描述的"问题"，普华永道审计工作组无法审查没有关联的MT 202线支付信息。像这样的连接付款是普华永道的核心审查方法。BTMU的合规经理，要求普华永道"考虑删除上述句子，因为我们不想给读者的印象是，有一些重要的MTs没有成功接收"。于是，普华永道审计工作组从服务局的监视中删除HTR中的段落报告。

18.普华永道审计工作组在草案报告，银行的IAO研究的特殊成因提出书面程序，其他类似的指令可能存在的"银行"故意省略搜索术语"付款信息"。普华永道介入小组警告说，"他可能会对调查结果产生影响。当评价这份[HTR]报告时从[任何]调查将会被考虑。"（强调提供）。对此，该BTMU合规经理转发银行利益方面的以下要求："你可能删除这句话吗？"普华永道审计工作组遵照执行，BTMU内部审计往下进行的时候删除了这个建议。普华永道进一步删除了提出的此类调查所要解决的问题。

19.在银行的要求下，普华永道参与团队的报告草稿删除HTR等信息。修订包括：

　　• 删除涉及BTMU与美国"敌对国家"开展业务剥离报文指令的英文翻译，

　　• 删除一个调整的技巧，普华永道在描述BTMU的剥线指令报告使用

（特殊指令），取而代之的是一个不起眼的参考，缺乏监管的意义（书面指令）；

the BTMU合规经理要求普华永道审计工作组删除的书面程序，剥线、英语翻译写作，"这是我们许多人认为，银行的律师也基本同意这一点，这一指示确切的字眼，尤其是"避免资金被冻结，可能造成不必要的关注，监管机构。从我们现在了解的情况来看，这些指令的真正目的不是让资金（避免）被冻结，而不是延迟几天，因为电报中包含诸如"伊朗"这样的简单词汇。

- 删除最普华永道审计工作组讨论BTMU的剥离活动；
- 删除有关BTMU的潜在滥用OFAC筛选软件与剥离活动连接；
- 删除普华永道认定为与HTR报告连接必须考虑几个法律的问题；和
- 删除一段论述了特殊字符出现的HTR的报告（如"#""-"和"，"）在电汇信息，阻碍了普华永道的过滤系统检测某些涉及苏丹和缅甸的交易。

20.银行的IAO调查了特殊的书面程序和从电报中提取信息。BTMU的报告的额外调查有关交易的历史回顾"是由IAO准备在2008年10月向监管机构发布。本报告对该部有误导性，因为它在未公开的普华永道调查结果面前，不充分，范围太有限，没有采用普华永道最初建议的司法审查类型。

违反法律和法规

21.由于上述行为，BTMU误导服务局达到2013年同意的结算秩序的条款。BTMU也：

- 未能保持或提供其在纽约的分公司真实准确的书籍、账目和记录反映在银行法§200-c违反所有的交易及行动；及
- 故意违反服务局规定3NYCRR§300.1，这就要求BTMU提交报告给管理者立即发现欺诈，不诚实，制造虚假的条目和遗漏点条目，和其他不当行为，是否有犯罪行为，在任何BTMU员工参与；及
- 明知而作出或导致其书作虚假记载、报表和略使材料特别是属于美国的美元结算业务BTMU通过其纽约分行或纽约的其他金融机构真正的条目，误导性的服务局管理者和主考者被依法指定检查BTMU的条件和事务。

结算规定

罚款：

22.在十（10）营业日执行本和解令，BTMU将全额支付三亿一千五百万美元民事罚款（315 000 000美元）。BTMU将不申诉，坚持，或要求扣税或根据任何美国联邦，政府或当地税项扣除税额，直接或间接，作为本和解令民事罚款了结依据的任意一部分。

雇员纪律和永久禁止参与被许可人：

23.服务局的调查已导致从BTMU的BTMU合规经理辞职，谁发挥的不当行为在这同意为了讨论的核心作用。

24.BTMU今后不得直接或间接地保留在上述个人引用，作为一个官员，雇员、代理、顾问或承包商BTMU，或任何附属机构BTMU，或任何其他能力。

25.尽可能迅速，但不迟于六十（60）天本和解令的日期，银行应采取所有必要的步骤来确保其总经理BTMU反洗钱办公室、合规与法律部和随后的执行官、总经理BTMU全球规划部，都曾在不当的行为在这个和解令讨论中心的角色却仍然采用由银行的关联公司，不得从事职务、职责或活动，而在银行的关联公司，包括以任何方式任何持牌人本部，业务包括，但不限于，纽约分公司。

26.BTMU今后不得允许个人参照前款的参与，直接或间接的任何义务，责任或活动，或在BTMU或银行的关联公司，包括其在美国的业务代表，包括任何被许可方本服务局业务。独立顾问的延伸：

27.银行，纽约分行和服务局进入2013年同意为中心外安装一个独立的顾问（IC）进行银行现有BSA／AML相关制裁合规审查程序，在分支的地方政策和程序。双方现在一致认为，在2015年3月IC接触结束后，该部应自行决定是否需要延期。如果该部确定有必要延长该IC的延展期，则延长期应长达十八（18）个月。该银行还同意将其美国BSA／AML和OFAC制裁合规计划到纽约，并认为这些项目将有美国的合规性监管影响纽约分公司的所有交易，包括交易外，影响纽约分行。IC将监督、评估和测试这些程序的实现，以及

BSA／AML和OFAC制裁合规程序，运行在美国和涉及影响纽约分行的交易。为免存疑，本次级方案不应负责监督、评估和检验除美国和美国管辖权以

外的任何司法管辖区的法律的遵守情况。违反和解令：

28.在事件的服务局认为BTMU是实质上在本和解令违约（违约），该服务局将对BTMU的违约和BTMU必须提供书面通知，在十（10）日自收到日期通知营业日，或在稍后的日期，如果在服务局自行确定，出现在服务局证明没有违约的发生，在一定程度上相关，认为违反的不重要或已整改。

29.双方理解并同意，BTMU未能在规定的时间内作出必要的示范是BTMU的违约行为，推定证据。在发现违反的情况下，该部拥有纽约银行和金融服务法所规定的所有补救办法，并可利用该部提供的任何和所有证据，以便在纽约银行和金融服务法下可获得的所有听证、通知、命令和其他补救办法。

放弃权利：

30.双方进一步理解并同意，在任何服务局以外的任何法院或法庭都不接受这种和解令的规定。

受和解令约束的当事人：

31.这是进一步的了解结合部的和解令，BTMU，以及他们的继承人和受让人，在监管的服务局，但具体不绑定任何联邦或其他国家机关或任何执法机构。

32.没有采取进一步行动将由服务局对BTMU在这个和解令的规定的行为，但BTMU符合本和解令的条款。

33.尽管有其他的规定包含在本和解令，但服务局可以承担对BTMU交易的行动或行为，BTMU并未透露该部在书面材料，BTMU与此有关的服务局提交。

注意事项：

34.有关此订单的所有通信均应发送至：

Elizabeth Nochlin

律师助理

银行业务部

纽约州金融服务局

第一州街

纽约，NY 0004

Megan Prendergast

律师助理

银行业务部

纽约州金融服务局

第一州街

纽约，NY 0004

Eiji Sumi

总裁及总经理

合规部三菱东京日联UFJ银行有限公司

2-7-1丸之内，千代田区

东京，100-8330，日本

Yasuhiko Shibata

高级经理

反洗钱局办公室

合规部

三菱东京日联UFJ银行有限公司

2-7-1丸之内，千代田区，

东京，100-8330，日本

杂项：

35.这项和解令的每一项规定将继续有效并可强制执行至由本服务局书面停留、修改、终止或暂停。

36.BTMU将继续遵守的条款及条件的规定2013年当事人和当事人之间的和解令。

37.没有承诺、保证、代表或理解本同意书中所载的内容，是为了诱使任何一方同意和解令。

兹证明，双方当事人已将此和解令定为2014年11月18日执行。

（此处略去涉及机构及个人）

5.

蓄意遮挡号牌的后果
——苏格兰皇家银行洗钱案例

　　2013年12月，英国老牌银行苏格兰皇家银行因内部共谋为美国制裁国家提供金融服务而受到美国监管机构的处罚，最终苏格兰皇家银行集团同意向美联储和纽约州金融服务局各支付5 000万美元。苏格兰皇家银行踩红线、挡号牌的行为，既反映了其合规部门管理上的薄弱，也折射出苏格兰皇家银行并购后迷乱的战略导向。

苏格兰皇家银行集团概况

苏格兰皇家银行集团成立于1727年，总部设在英国爱丁堡，是英国历史最为悠久的银行之一。2000年，苏格兰皇家银行收购了国民西敏寺银行（National Westminster Bank），从一个地区性银行发展成为世界排名第五的国际商业银行。

苏格兰皇家银行集团拥有两家主要子银行，即苏格兰皇家银行公众有限公司(The Royal Bank of Scotland Plc，英国)和国民西敏寺银行公众有限公司(NatWest Plc，英国)。集团其他成员还包括爱尔兰阿尔斯特商业银行（Ulster Bank）以及著名的私人银行顾资银行（Coutts Bank）等。

2005年8月，苏格兰皇家银行与美林（Merrill Lynch）等出资31亿美元购得中行10%股权。2009年初解禁期结束后，以协议转让方式出售了其持有的中行108.09亿股H股，占中行总股本的4.26%。2007年，富通银行、苏格兰皇家银行等组成的财团成功收购了荷兰银行（ABN AMRO BANK N.V.）。

但成也并购，败也并购，2008年苏格兰皇家银行集团报亏241亿英镑，创下英国银行最大亏损纪录。为保存集团的金融实力，该集团自2009年起不断剥离非核心资产，保留资产主要集中在其核心市场和业务单元。2014年，苏格兰皇家银行集团可通过5000多个系统向38个国家和地区的客户提供多达几百种金融产品和服务，但目前该银行已退出其中的26个国家和地区，维护系统缩减至一半。2016年，苏格兰皇家银行（中国）有限公司解散。苏格兰皇家银行集团管理层重新调整了发展战略，定位于打造一家更简洁、更安全、更以客户为中心的银行。经过几年结构调整，该集团已初步达到预期目标，2017年实现税前营业收入22.39亿英镑，同时利润高达7.52亿英镑，较上年同期增长了6.32亿英镑，为近十年来最好业绩。苏格兰皇家银行集团也因此得到了投资人的广泛认可，2017年股价上涨20%，远高于其他英国同业。

通过不断消化不良资产，剥离非核心业务，缩减分支机构，目前苏格兰皇家银行集团主要保留了四个核心业务板块：

（1）个人银行业务（Personal Banking）：主要包括英国本土的个人银行业务和爱尔兰阿尔斯特商业银行（Ulster Bank）提供的个人银行业务。英国本土个人银行业务服务区域覆盖英格兰和威尔士，住房抵押贷款市场占有率较高，也是英国第一家向客户提供无纸化抵押贷款的银行；爱尔兰阿尔斯特商业银行（Ulster Bank）服务区域为爱尔兰，是爱尔兰主要的商业银行之一，也是最早介入个人电子支付领域的银行。

（2）商业银行和私人银行业务（Commercial Banking & Private Banking）：商业银行板块可以通过企业服务中心为企业搭建筹资平台，私人银行业务也一直致力于推动高效无纸化移动服务。

（3）苏格兰皇家银行国际业务（RBS International）：苏格兰皇家银行集团经过调整，已退出部分区域国际业务，目前在十余个地家和地区设有分支机构。

（4）西敏寺银行业务（NatWest Markets）：苏格兰皇家银行集团并购的西敏寺银行办理的各类业务，包括处置因其核心业务带来的历史遗留资产等。

案件概况及背景

2013年12月11日，美国财政部海外资产控制办公室、美联储及纽约州金融服务局分别对苏格兰皇家银行集团采取监管措施。该案件的起源是上述监管机构认为苏格兰皇家银行及其附属机构的行为违反了美国对伊朗、缅甸、苏丹、古巴等国家的制裁令。该案件最终以苏格兰皇家银行同意支付共计1亿美元的罚金而告终。经和解谈判，苏格兰皇家银行同意向美联储和纽约州金融服务局各支付5 000万美元（其中支付海外资产控制办公室的罚金包含在美联储5 000

万美元罚金内）。该案件表明，纽约金融服务局对在纽约运营的金融机构的监管发挥着举足轻重的作用。同时，该案件中三个监管机构的联合执法也表明，跨政府部门金融执法将可能成为趋势。

美国反洗钱法规包括国会制定的反洗钱法律、相关政府部门制定的法规以及行业监管机构发布的行业准则等。目前美国金融监管体制以"双线多头"为主要特征。"双线"是指联邦政府和州政府两条主线，"多头"指有多个金融监管职责机构以及交叉管辖权。从联邦政府层面来看，主要的金融监管部门包括美联储以及美国财政部及其下设机构，财政部下设机构主要包括货币监理署（OCC）、海外资产控制办公室（OFAC）、金融犯罪执法网络（FinCEN）、联邦存款保险公司（FDIC）等。从州政府层面看，各个州均有独立的金融监管机构，如州立金融服务局（DFS）等州一级的银行监管机构，对在本州注册的金融机构进行监管。

美国为支持反恐活动，2001年布什总统签署了《爱国者法案》，进一步扩大美国打击洗钱活动的范围。其中第三部分为《2001年消除跨国洗钱和反恐融资法》，该法案内容不仅包括金融机构对交易者身份进行识别和保存交易记录义务，还涉及司法"长臂管辖"原则、代理行账户尽职调查原则等。

近几年美国对金融机构协助受制裁国家、客户或个人或共谋违法交易予以严惩，反洗钱处罚案例涉及的罚金屡创新高，显示出美国政府反洗钱、反恐怖融资和反扩散融资力度的不断加大。

事件分析及影响

成也萧何败也萧何的并购

国民西敏寺银行因1997年利率期货交易中的失误导致巨额亏损，经过系统收缩和调整，财务状况未见明显好转，国民西敏寺银行转而通过出售改变困境。当时苏格兰皇家银行还是一家世界排名200开外的"地区性银行"，但刚上任的首席执行官已将眼光投向英国以外的市场，在跨入国际一流商业银行的战略指引下，苏格兰皇家银行抓住机遇，击败竞争对手，以342亿美元成功收购了资产规模是自身3倍的国民西敏寺银行，进而跻身世界著名商业银行之列，成为世界排名第五的国际商业银行。

得益于清晰的收购方案和整合策略，苏格兰皇家银行的核心竞争力得到有效提升，并购后的溢出效应也超出预期，不仅稳定了原有客户，还吸引了大批新客户。此后，苏格兰皇家银行开始踏上了"并购旅程"。

2000年至2007年，苏格兰皇家银行并购目标指向美国市场，先后以11亿英镑收购Churchill保险集团，22亿美元收购Mellon金融集团的地区零售及商业银行业务，105亿美元收购美国零售银行Charter One等。

2007年荷兰银行因利润和收入的增幅相差悬殊引起部分机构投资者不满，股东建议或分拆业务，或将银行整体出售。在荷兰银行并购中，巴克莱银行和苏格兰皇家银行、西班牙国际银行、比利时富通银行财团成为终局对手，最终苏格兰皇家银行财团以高出巴克莱银行100亿欧元以及高现金比例胜出，收购价达到了711亿欧元。苏格兰皇家银行顺利接收了荷兰银行的亚洲业务，同时荷兰银行在中国的17家分支机构并入苏格兰皇家（中国）。

但随即而来的金融危机以及庞大的并购重组支出，使苏格兰皇家银行陷入困顿。2008年苏格兰皇家银行全年亏损达到241亿英镑（约合343亿美元），创下了英国企业有史以来最大亏损纪录。为扶持苏格兰皇家银行渡过难关，2008年以来，英国政府对该行实施了纾困行动，先后对其增加持股比例，事实上苏格兰皇家银行已成为一家国有银行，英国政府曾一度持有该行接近80%的股权。

苏格兰皇家银行对荷兰银行亚洲业务的收购并没有达到预期的地区规模效应和协同效应，反而将苏格兰皇家银行财务状况拉入持续亏损的境地。英国金融服务管理局（FSA）2011年公布调查报告称，因管理决策混乱以及监管不力，苏格兰皇家银行（Royal Bank of Scotland）做出并购荷兰银行（ABN Amro）的赌博性决定，并因此濒临破产边缘。这份长达452页的报告指出，苏格兰皇家银行收购荷兰银行部分股份是在其资本状况不佳和融资不足的情况下做出的错误决定。

此后，苏格兰皇家银行不断调整重组策略，但受金融危机影响，资产问题爆发，始终未能扭转亏损局面。2009年，该行开始收缩亚洲业务，2010年，将中国零售银行业务及中小企业业务以一美元对价出让给了星展银行。

对新兴市场的最终放弃，是苏格兰皇家银行在错误时点高价买入后无法回避的选择，2016年中国银监会批复同意苏格兰皇家银行（中国）有限公司解散。

并购是快速提升自身规模，补缺短板，扩大市场份额的捷径，但一个成功的并购业务不仅需要的是充分的尽职调查、良好的买入时机以及并购后有效的整合策略。而在苏格兰皇家银行并购荷兰银行的这起案例上，苏格兰皇家银行恰恰是在金融危机前夜高价揽入，加上后期缺乏整合后清晰的战略目标，同时受到金融危机后问题资产层层暴露等多重影响，一家老牌英国商业银行最终走向破产的边缘。

雪上加霜的监管罚款

美国监管机构和英国监管机构近几年对苏格兰皇家银行陆续开出了高额罚单，其中因涉嫌在全球外汇交易市场试图操纵交易标准，2014年苏格兰皇家银行等全球五家跨国银行被开出金额高达34亿美元的巨额罚单，苏格兰皇家银行罚款金额达到6.34亿美元（FCA罚款3.44亿美元，CFTC罚款2.90亿美元）；2014年，英国金融监管机构对苏格兰皇家银行因计算机系统崩溃导致客户无法正常使用账户处以5 600万英镑（约合人民币5.4亿元）罚款；2016年，苏格兰皇家银行向美国监管机构支付了11亿美元，就2008年金融危机期间两项抵押贷款支持证券相关的民事诉讼达成和解；苏格兰皇家银行还面临着美国司法部和美国联邦住房金融局等美国政府部门约10余项诉讼赔偿，其中2017年7月12日，美国联邦住房金融局向其开出了高达55亿美元的巨额罚单。

案件的影响及教训

熟知监管政策，依法合规经营，这种合规理念已获得越来越多的国际商业银行普遍认可，我们有必要对苏格兰皇家银行违反美国制裁令的这起案件进行深入分析并从中吸取经验和教训。

从和解令中看到，苏格兰皇家银行此次被罚的主要原因是银行内部相关部门共谋为受制裁国家提供金融服务，苏格兰皇家银行除了同意缴纳罚金外，还同意实施新措施以确保不再违反制裁令，同时罢免了部分部门主管及区域负责人。

苏格兰皇家银行此次被认为违规的汇款业务总计约5.23亿美元，在这些通过SWIFT系统进行美元清算的业务中，远在美国以外的苏格兰皇家银行相关人员通过隐匿汇款敏感信息，或是所谓的U型账户等来绕开监管。监管机构特别强调的一项指控为，苏格兰皇家银行在2000年收购的国民西敏寺银行，作为伊朗银行的代理行通过SWIFT系统进行美元清算，而且该行在明确知道相关制裁规定的前提下，有意漏掉涉及制裁的相关信息，以便通过系统完成交易。同时，苏格兰皇家银行有关人员还设计了一套系统，包括书面的指示，通过第三国银行来对伊朗提供美元支付服务，而他们发往美国金融机构的头寸指令里都省略了涉伊的相关信息。苏格兰皇家银行起初仅对伊朗提供上述服务，随后将服务延伸至其他受制裁国家和机构。

对于金融机构而言，一旦与受美国制裁的机构或国家发生业务，则会面临未来罚款的潜在风险。随着中资银行国际化布局的拓展，部分中资银行已经因涉嫌洗钱或存在反洗钱漏洞而被当地监管机构立案调查，中资银行国际化进程中反洗钱合规等方面的压力不断加大。结合苏格兰皇家银行被美国监管机构联合处罚的案例，我国中资银行可以得到以下借鉴和启示：

第一，增强反洗钱意识，建立合规制度，培育合规文化。

中资银行反洗钱意识普遍淡薄，自身管理约束与所在国监管机构反洗钱体系差距较大，同时银行金融机构缺乏有效的反洗钱文化氛围。国际化进程中的中资银行应借鉴领先同业的优秀经验，吸取其失败教训，优化跨境业务操作流程，出台有效内控合规制度，在内部创建知行合一，合规发展业务的企业文化，提高境内外人员反洗钱风险防范意识。

第二，知己知彼，不断加强对监管政策的学习。

中资银行应对全球及所在国监管趋势保持敏锐的洞察力和判断力，加强对美国经济金融制裁相关法律的学习，把握好技术标准。被美国监管机构处罚的业务主要集中在美元汇款业务，中资银行应对关联度较大的国际结算等业务予以充分重视并加强对OFAC等制裁政策的不断学习，了解美国"长臂管辖原则"对金融机构的境内外经营带来的巨大影响，避免因不熟悉相关法律制度而陷入被动，导致银行蒙受声誉和经济损失。

第三，设立专门反洗钱合规团队并充分发挥其作用。

美国监管机构处罚的部分案例系由于金融机构内部管理漏洞所致，在本案和解令中，美联储要求苏格兰皇家银行在和解令下发90天内提交一份全面合规实施方案，包括风险评估、交易过滤、人员培训、年度评估以及对美元清算方面的独立审计报告等，这充分反映了苏格兰皇家银行在反洗钱内控方面的短板和漏洞。目前中资银行总部均已设立合规部门从事反洗钱等合规管理工作，其海外机构也都聘用了当地资深的合规人员。对客户身份、行为、交易金额、资金流向等存在的异常情形，合规部门需提出"可疑交易报告"，这是预防洗钱最主要的措施之一，同时合规部门还应对商业银行承受洗钱的能力及受到洗钱冲击后的损失弥补及恢复能力予以合理的预计和评估。中资银行应选拔和聘用合格的合规人员，建立有效的反洗钱内控制度，确保合规团队上述工作内容正常开展，避免因人员及制度缺失不能有效执行相关制裁要求。

第四，做好尽职调查，提升信息透明度。

客户尽职调查是反洗钱体系中的重要环节，包括信息收集和信息确认两方面内容。大部分处罚案例均涉及美元交易信息不透明，信息披露不充分的问题。中资银行应按所在国监管制度，认真核实客户提供的相关信息，对于不能满足监管要求的，应及时请客户补充，未能补充完善的，应终止与该客户建立业务关系。中资银行还应对客户进行风险分类管理，在客户风险评级体系中考虑到客户类别、产品、服务类别、交易额度和所处国家地区等因素的影响。在办理代理行业务时予以特别关注，对于嵌套账户、U型账户、过手账户等高洗钱风险账户类型须加强尽职调查。

第五，重视所在国监管部门的意见，积极落实整改措施。

商业银行应对所在国监管机构的建议予以足够重视，同时对监管机构提出的整改建议要采取积极有效的措施予以落实，避免未来面临更为严厉的处罚。在数起国际商业银行被罚案例中，我们看到，在起诉前积极进行和解谈判、确保采取有效举措回应监管意见是降低处罚的理性选择。

第六，做好系统支持，提升反洗钱机控能力。

部分中资银行采用系统自动监测和人工手动监测相结合的方式对交易信息进行管理，但随着业务量的增多，自动识别并预警的系统可以大大提高作业处理效率。在提升内部人员业务及合规素质，做到了解客户、熟悉业务的同时，中资银行还应持续加强反洗钱的科技系统建设，保证反洗钱数据完整，通过清算等系统优化手段强制性确保反洗钱法规的有效实施。

附录：

《和解令》英文原文

NEW YORK STATE DEPARTMENT OF FINANCIAL SERVICES

In the Matter of:

THE ROYAL BANK OF SCOTLAND PLC,
New York Branch

CONSENT ORDER UNDER
NEW YORK BANKING LAW § 44

WHEREAS, The Royal Bank of Scotland pic ("RBS" or "the Bank"), a wholly owned subsidiary of The Royal Bank of Scotland Group pic ("RBSG"), is a major international banking and financial services institution, with assets totaling $1.85 trillion, that is licensed by the Department of Financial Services ("DFS" or "the Department") to operate as a foreign bank branch in New York;

WHEREAS, from at least 2002 to 2011, RBS conducted more than 3,500 transactions valued at approximately $523 million through New York correspondent banks involving Sudanese and Iranian customers and beneficiaries, including a number of entities on the Specially Designated Nationals ("SDN") list of the Office of Foreign Assets Control ("OFAC"), which RBS has self-identified and voluntarily disclosed to DFS;[①]

WHEREAS, to enable its sanctioned customers and beneficiaries to gain access to the U.S. financial system with anonymity, RBS established and implemented a procedure for processing U.S. dollar payments whereby information that could be used to identify sanctioned parties to a given transaction would be omitted from payment messages sent to correspondent banks in New York;

WHEREAS, to ensure the efficiency and accuracy of this procedure, RBS provided employees in payment processing centers in the United Kingdom written instructions containing a step by step guide on how to create and route U.S. dollar payment messages involving sanctioned entities through the United States to avoid detection. These instructions stated in relevant part:

> IMPORTANT: FOR ALL US DOLLAR PAYMENTS TO A COUNTRY
> SUBJECT TO US SANCTIONS, A PAYMENT MESSAGE CANNOT
> CONTAIN ANY OF THE FOLLOWING: 1. The sanctioned country
> name. 2. Any name designated on the Office of Foreign Asset Control
> (OFAC) restricted list, which can encompass a bank name, remitter or
> beneficiary...[②]

---

① To a lesser extent, RBS also processed U.S. dollar transactions for sanctioned clients from Burma, Cuba, and Libya.

② Nearly identical written instructions existed for processing U.S. dollar payments for Libyan state-owned banks.

WHEREAS, these instructions were included in RBS's Business Support Manual and made available to all relevant employees, posted on RBS's Intranet and periodically disseminated to RBS's International Banking Center payment processors;

WHEREAS, senior RBS employees, including RBS's Group Head of Anti-Money Laundering, as well as the Head of Operational Risk, Global Transaction Services, and the Head of Global Banking Services for Europe, Middle East and Africa, were fully aware of and in some instances even provided such instructions to employees;[1]

WHEREAS, despite official bank policies to the contrary adopted in July 2006, RBS continued to process transactions through New York in a non-transparent manner using these and other means;

WHEREAS, RBS's conduct was at odds with U.S. national security and foreign policy and raised serious safety and soundness concerns for regulators, including the obstruction of governmental administration, failure to report crimes and misconduct, offering false instruments for filing, and falsifying business records.[2]

WHEREAS, beginning in 2010, RBS initiated an internal investigation focused on these practices and voluntarily disclosed its findings to relevant authorities, including the Department, the Federal Reserve Bank of Boston, and its primary regulator, the UK Financial Services Authority;

WHEREAS, RBS cooperated with the Department by conducting a historical review and identifying in writing transactions that appeared to violate OF AC sanctions regulations or that involved apparent non-transparency;

WHEREAS, the Department recognizes RBS's cooperation with the Department's investigation, the disciplinary action taken by the Bank, including against individual wrongdoers,[3] and the remedial measures put in place to address weaknesses in the Bank's antimoney laundering and economic sanctions compliance programs;

NOW, THEREFORE, the Parties are willing to resolve the matters cited herein as follows:

SETTLEMENT PROVISIONS

Monetary Payment;

1. RBS shall make payment of a civil monetary payment to the Department pursuant to Banking Law § 44 in the amount of $50 million U.S. dollars ($50,000,000). RBS shall pay the entire amount within ten (10) days of executing the Consent Order.

Breach of the Consent Order:

2. In the event that the Department believes RBS to be materially in breach of the Consent

---

[1] For example, on at least one occasion, the Head of Operational Risk warned all Payment Processing Center Heads via email to: "Please take care when making [payments]... to ensure that there is no wording within the message that could potentially lead to the payment being stopped e.g. reference to a sanctioned country i.e. Sudan, Iraq."

[2] See P.L. § 195.05; 3 N.Y.C.R.R. § 300.1; P.L. § 175.35; and P.L. § 175.10.

[3] The Bank's Disciplinary Review Committee dismissed four current employees, including the Head of Asia, Middle East & Africa, Global Banking Services; the Senior Relationship Manager - Middle East; the Relationship Manager - Shipping; and the Head of the Money Laundering Prevention Unit, Corporate Markets. In addition, eight employees were subject to bonus clawbacks.

Order ("Breach"), the Department will provide written notice to RBS of the Breach and RBS must, within ten (10) business days from the date of receipt of said notice, or on a later date if so determined in the sole discretion of the Department, appear before the Department to demonstrate that no Breach has occurred or, to the extent pertinent, that the Breach is not material or has been cured.

3. The Parties understand and agree that RBS's failure to make the required demonstration within the specified period is presumptive evidence of RBS's Breach. Upon a finding of Breach, the Department has all the remedies available to it under New York Banking and Financial Services Laws and may use any and all evidence available to the Department for all ensuing hearings, notices, orders and other remedies that may be available under the Banking and Financial Services Laws.

Waiver of Rights:

4. The Parties further understand and agree that no provision of the Consent Order is subject to review in any court or tribunal outside the Department.

Parties Bound by the Consent Order:

5. It is further understood that the Consent Order is binding on the Department and RBS, as well as their successors and assigns that are within the supervision of the Department, but it specifically does not bind any federal or other state agencies or any law enforcement authority.

6. No further action will be taken by the Department against RBS for the conduct set forth in the Consent Order, provided that RBS complies with the terms of the Consent Order.

7. Notwithstanding any other provision contained in the Consent Order, however, the Department may undertake action against RBS for transactions or conduct that RBS did not disclose to the Department in the written materials that RBS submitted to the Department in connection with this matter.

Notices:

8. All communications regarding this Order shall be sent to:

> Jean Walsh
> Acting Executive Deputy Superintendent
> Banking Division
> New York State Department of Financial Services
> One State Street
> New York, NY 10004

> Regina Stone
> Deputy Superintendent of Foreign and Wholesale Banks
> Banking Division
> New York State Department of Financial Services
> One State Street
> New York, NY 10004

> RBS pic
> 36 St Andrew Square
> Edinburgh, EH2 2YB
> United Kingdom

Miscellaneous:

9. Each provision of the Consent Order will remain effective and enforceable until stayed, modified, terminated or suspended in writing by the Department.

10. No promise, assurance, representation, or understanding other than those contained in the Consent Order has been made to induce any party to agree to the provisions of the Consent Order.

《和解令》中文译文

纽约州金融服务局
关于
苏格兰皇家银行纽约分行

和解令①
根据《纽约银行法》第44条

鉴于，苏格兰皇家银行（以下称RBS或银行），苏格兰皇家银行集团全资所有子公司，系一家主要的国际银行与金融服务机构，总资产共185 00亿美元，经金融服务局（以下称DFS或服务局）授权在纽约开设分支机构；

鉴于，从2002年至2011年，RBS通过纽约代理行操作了涉及苏丹和伊朗客户和受益人超过3 500个交易，这些交易价值约5.23亿美元。这些客户和收款人中包括一些在海外资产控制办公室（OFAC）的特别指定国民名单之列的实体，这些实体系RBS自行确认并自愿向DFS披露②；

鉴于，为了使其受制裁的客户和受益人能够匿名进入美国金融系统，RBS建立和实施了一套处理美元支付的程序。通过该程序，可以用来识别从事特定交易的受制裁方的信息将被从发送给纽约代理行的支付信息中删除；

鉴于，为确保这一程序的效率和准确性，RBS向位于英国的支付处理中心的雇员提供书面指示。该书面指示包括如何创建涉及受制裁实体的美元支付信息和如何使该信息路经美国，从而避开侦测的逐步指南。这些指示在相关部分表述如下：

重要：对于所有的向受美国制裁国家的美元支付，支付信息不能包含以下任何信息：1.受制裁国家的名称；2.被列入海外资产控制办公室（OFAC）限制名单中的任何名称，这些名称可能包括银行名称、汇款人或收款人……③

① 资料来源：纽约州金融服务局官方网站，https://www.dfs.ny.gov/about/ea/ea131211_rbs.pdf。
② RBS至少还处理了来自缅甸，古巴和利比亚的受制裁客户的美元交易。
③ 对于处理利比亚国有银行的美元支付也存在几乎相同的书面指示。

　　鉴于，这些指示被包含在RBS的业务支持手册中，被提供给所有相关雇员，被发布在RBS的内部网络上，并定期被散发给RBS国际同业中心支付处理人员；

　　鉴于，RBS的高级雇员，包括RBS集团反洗钱负责人、操作风险负责人、全球交易服务负责人，以及欧洲、中东和非洲全球同业业务负责人，均完全知悉并在一些情况下向雇员提供这些指示；①

　　鉴于，尽管在2006年7月调整并采用了相反的官方银行政策，但RBS通过这些或其他途径以非透明方式继续通过纽约进行交易；

　　鉴于，RBS的行为违背了美国的国家安全政策和对外政策，并引发了监管者严重的安全性和稳健性担忧，这些担忧包括妨碍政府行政管理、报告犯罪和不端行为失败、提供错误档案文件、伪造商业记录。②

　　鉴于，从2010年开始，RBS开展了针对这些实践的内部调查，并自愿将调查结果向相关部门披露，这些部门包括纽约金融服务局、波士顿联邦储备银行，及其主要监管者英国金融服务局；

　　鉴于，RBS与纽约金融服务局进行合作，进行历史审查，并以书面形式确认看起来违反OFAC制裁法规的交易或者具有明显不透明性的交易；

　　鉴于，纽约金融服务局认可RBS在服务局调查中的合作，认可RBS采取的纪律惩戒，包括对失范者个人的惩戒③，认可RBS采取的解决银行反洗钱和经济制裁合规项目薄弱环节的补救措施；

　　双方特此愿意通过如下方式解决问题：

协议条款

货币支付：

　　1.RBS应根据《银行法》第44条向纽约金融服务局作出民事货币支付，金额为5 000万美元。RBS应在和解令执行之日起十日内支付全部款项。

---

① 例如，至少有一次，操作风险负责人通过电子邮件向所有支付处理中心负责人提出警示："作出支付时请注意……确保在信息中不存在可能导致支付被阻止的措辞，如提及被制裁的国家，如苏丹、伊拉克。"
② 见P.L. § 195.05; 3 N.Y.C.R.R. § 300.1; P.L. § 175.35; and P.L. § 175.10.
③ 银行的纪律检查委员会开除了四名现有雇员，包括全球银行服务亚洲、中东和非洲负责人、中东高级船务客户关系经理、预防反洗钱与公司市场部负责人。另外，八名雇员受到奖金追回惩戒。

和解令违反：

2.如果纽约金融服务局相信RBS实质性违反和解令，服务局将向RBS发出书面通知。RBS必须在收到上述通知之日起十个工作日内，或者经服务局决定的之后日期到服务局解释，证明其没有违反和解令，或者违反是非实质性的，或者违反已经得到补救。

3.双方理解并同意，RBS如果未能在特定期间内做出要求的解释将构成RBS违反和解令的推定证据。如果认定RBS违反和解令，服务局享有纽约银行和金融服务法律下的所有救济，并可以在后续的银行和金融服务法律规定的所有听证、通知、命令和其他救济中使用其可以获得的所有证据。

权利的放弃：

4.双方进一步理解和同意，该和解令所有条款不受服务局之外的任何法院或特别法庭的审查。

受和解令约束的主体：

5.双方进一步理解，该和解令约束服务局和RBS，以及双方承继者和在服务局监督之下的受让人，但该和解令不约束任何联邦或者州机构或者任何法律执行机关。

6.只要RBS遵守和解令中的条款，服务局不应针对RBS和解令中列明的上述行为采取其他措施。

7.然而，勿论和解令中的任何条款，服务局可以针对RBS未在书面材料中向服务局披露的与此和解令相关的交易或行为采取措施。

注意事项：

8.关于该和解令的所有通讯应发送至：

Jean Walsh

Acting Executive Deputy Superintendent

Banking Division

New York State Department of Financial Services

One State Street

New York， NY 10004

Regina Stone

Deputy Superintendent of Foreign and Wholesale Banks

Banking Division

New York State Department of Financial Services

One State Street

New York，NY 10004

RBS plc

36 St Andrew Square

Edinburgh，EH2 2YB

United Kingdom

其他事项：

9.除非被服务局以书面形式中止、修改、终止或暂停，该和解令所有条款均保持有效和可执行。

10.在和解令之外不存在引诱任何一方同意和解令条款的承诺、保证、陈述，或者谅解。

本协议各方已于2013年12月11日正式签署本协议，特此为证。

苏格兰皇家银行

Chris Campbell

苏格兰皇家银行授权代表

纽约州金融服务局

Benjamin M. Lawsky

局长

6.

棍棒下的"孝子"
——摩根大通银行案例

　　2014年1月，摩根大通银行与纽约州南区检察院和多家金融监管机构达成和解协议及延期起诉协议，累计支付了20.5亿美元的罚款，主要的原因是摩根大通银行违反了《银行保密法》并被发现反洗钱合规方案中存在缺陷，同时为客户提供获取麦道夫投资策略的机会。其中，与美国货币监理署达成了和解协议，支付罚款3.5亿美元；与纽约州南区检察院达成延期起诉协议，支付罚款17亿美元，罚款将全部用于补偿麦道夫案的受害者。与此同时，美国金融犯罪执法网络局对摩根大通银行罚款4.61亿美元，这部分罚款包含在了支付给检察院的17亿美元罚款中，因此共计20.5亿美元。

　　美国监管机构对美资银行的监管处罚毫不手软，仅在违反银行保密法和反洗钱合规条例一方面，美联银行于2010年收到了两份和解令以及5 000万美元罚单；花旗银行分别于2012年和2017年收到了两份和解令以及7 000万美元的罚单，富国银行于2015年收到了和解令等。

　　本篇以摩根大通银行的案例看看美国监管机构是如何管教"自己的孩子"。

摩根大通集团与摩根大通银行概述

摩根大通集团是美国实力最强的金融集团之一，旗下的摩根大通银行是资产排名第一的美资银行。它的历史可以追溯到1799年，连接着摩根财团、摩根士丹利、大通曼哈顿银行、化学银行和贝尔斯登等一个个昔日闪耀的金融巨头。

1799年，曼哈顿公司创立，随后200年时间里，通过不断地合并或收购兼并，主要包括1955年与大通国民银行合并成立大通曼哈顿银行和1996年被化学银行收购（但保留了大通曼哈顿银行的名称），成为了当时美国最大的银行集团。大通曼哈顿银行是一家为大众服务的商业银行。

传奇的摩根财团是美国十大财团之一，其支柱公司是JP摩根公司，它控制着外国37个商业银行、开发银行、投资公司和其他企业的股权。它曾两度使美国金融起死回生。特别是1907年在美国发生金融危机时刻，它承担了美国中央银行的职责，以一己之力帮助整个金融业渡过了危机。这随后才诞生了美国联邦储备委员会。

JP摩根公司前身是成立于1838年的一家商人银行。1895年更名为JP摩根公司。1933年，美国出台《格拉斯—斯蒂格尔法案》，禁止金融机构同时提供商业银行和投资银行业务。因此在1935年，JP摩根公司被分拆为两部分，一部分为投资银行，名为摩根士丹利，业界称大摩，另一部分主要经营商业银行业务，业界称小摩。小摩的主要客户群体是政府、大集团公司和富豪家族。

2000年，小摩与大通曼哈顿银行合并，正式更名为摩根大通银行集团。至此，小摩、大通和化学银行终于合为一体，并缔造了美国按资产排名最大的金融帝国。两者的合并是强强联合，达到了较好的优势互补和协调效应。

随后到了2008年金融危机期间，多家美资大银行遭受重创，而摩根大通银行由于其在危机大规模爆发前就采取了一系列的措施，不仅成功渡过难关，还在政府的引导下，以2.4亿美元收购了投资银行贝尔斯登（当时该公司的总市值是35.4亿美元），随后又以19亿美元收购了倒闭的地方性银行——华盛顿互惠银行。

现在，摩根大通银行仍是美国以资产排名第一的银行，在国际金融市场上有着深远的影响力，业务范围涵盖商业银行、投资银行、资产管理等，可以为客户提供全方位的银行服务。截至2017年末，总资产为2.5万亿美元，净利润244亿美元，业务遍及60多个国家，全球雇员达到了24万人。

案件回顾

2014年1月，摩根大通银行与纽约州南区检察院和多家金融监管机构达成和解协议及延期起诉协议，累计支付了20.5亿美元的罚款。其中，摩根大通集团旗下的摩根大通银行等三家金融机构由于违反了《银行保密法》并被发现反洗钱合规方案中存在缺陷，同时为客户提供获取麦道夫投资策略的机会，在2014年1月7日与美国货币监理署达成了和解，同意支付罚款3.5亿美元。此外，摩根大通银行等三家银行由于违反了银行保密法，在2014年1月6日与纽约州南区检察院达成延期起诉协议，同意支付罚款17亿美元，罚款将全部用于补偿麦道夫案的受害者。与此同时，该行也是由于违反银行保密法，未能充分上报麦道夫投资骗局的可疑交易，美国金融犯罪执法网络局在2014年1月7日对摩根大通银行罚款4.61亿美元，这部分罚款包含在了支付给检察院的17亿美元罚款中。因此，共计20.5亿美元。

上述三项强制行动中，纽约州南区检察院和美国金融犯罪执法网络局主要关注了摩根大通银行在美国麦道夫案的违法行为，罚金主要用来赔偿案件的受害者，因此，在本文中不再详述和解读。

涉及摩根大通银行违法银行保密法和存在反洗钱合规的缺陷是美国货币监

理署签发的2014-001号民事罚款和解令。说到这份和解令的时候，其第二段提到了2013年1月还签发一份和解令，并在监理官的调查结果，也就是条款一中多次提出"银行未能纠正先前发现的……"，由此引到了2013-002号和解令。

2013年1月14日，由于发现摩根大通银行在遵循保密法及反洗钱合规的缺陷，货币监理署向摩根大通签发2013-002号和解令，虽然长达26页，但和解令并未对摩根大通进行罚款，仅要求银行进行全面的整改。

巧合的是，2013-002号和2014-001号和解令签发的同时，媒体和外界将灯光聚焦到了2013年发生的CIO导致的60亿美元损失事件和2014年发生的麦道夫欺诈案上，对摩根大通银行涉及银行保密法和反洗钱合规的和解令报道少之又少。

存在的主要漏洞和缺陷

2013-002号和解令主要从以下方面提出了摩根大通银行在银行保密法/反洗钱合规方面存在问题和不足，并提出了解决的目标：

一是管理体系和责任分工方面。监理署对摩根大通提出了较为具体的整改目标，主要涉及合规委员会的人员组成的要求、工作职能、责任分工、授权。监理署要求首先董事会至少任命三名董事担任合规委员会的成员，且需按月召开例会；其次合规委员会每季度向董事会提交书面的整改进度报告，详细说明遵守和解令的每项条款所采取的措施；再次摩根大通银行应在合规管理人员和具体业务人员都有清晰的授权以及明确的责任分工，以便顺畅履行合规管理的义务；复次摩根大通银行确保各管理层能够有效履行保密法和反洗钱规定设定的合规义务；最后还应制定有效的评价方法，以衡量负责合规的相关人员工作的有效性。

二是合规风险评估方面。监理署要求摩根大通银行提交反洗钱合规有效性的评价报告，内容应包括反洗钱合规管理的组织架构、全行范围内的有效性、管理的能力、问责、人员需求、内部控制、客户尽职调查流程，风险评估流程，可疑交易监测系统，审计/独立测试等方面的内容。此外，还应评估每条业务线、不同的客户反洗钱风险量化有效性、时效性等。

三是客户尽职调查方面。监理署要求摩根大通银行在和解令生效后90天内应确保制定适当的客户尽职调查政策、程序和流程。

四是交易监控、识别和报告方面。监理署要求摩根大通银行在和解令生效后60天内应制定政策和程序，以便对可疑交易进行预警。在30天内，摩根大通应向独立咨询师进行咨询，以评估本行的可疑交易的识别的有效性，并提供详细的评估报告，主要涵盖交易监测系统的完整性、适当的处理风险能力、可根据客户的行为识别可疑活动或行为等方面的内容。

五是可疑活动、账户和交易的回溯重检方面。监理署要求可疑交易回溯需接受独立咨询师的认证、账户的回溯也需具有专业知识的机构独立顾问进行监督和认证，全部的可疑交易都已经上报。

六是独立测试和审计方面。监理署要求摩根大通在和解令发布90天内，制定反洗钱合规和制裁合规的审计计划，审计计划应包括内部控制方案是否充足、重点关注高风险客户和产品等要素。还应评估内部控制措施的时效性和有效性，应向合规高级管理人员报告存在缺陷的具体情况。

七是新业务发展方面。监理署要求摩根大通在开展新产品和服务前，接受高级合规管理人员的审查和批准；且银行不得进入新的高风险行业，银行基本不得新扩大现有高风险业务线。

2014—001号和解令是基于2013年和解令作出的。货币监理署发现，摩根大通银行不仅未按照2013年签发和解令要求进行整改，还发现了七方面的新问题：

一是该行未对其境外分支机构制订适当的反洗钱合规和尽职调查方案；

二是该行未对代理行业务、远程存款和光票托收三项产品实施适当的反洗钱方案和尽职调查，控制不力的结果导致部分客户在正常的反洗钱监控和制裁筛查外开展业务，因此无法及时提交可疑交易报告；

三是该行在大通汽车金融和学生贷款未能提交可疑交易报告；

四是卷入麦道夫诈骗事件中——该行通过多个"联结基金"为客户提供投资麦道夫投资产品的机会，虽然伦敦分行向英国监管机构提交了可疑交易报告，但是美国在获知此情况下，并未向美国提交任何可疑交易报告；

五是该行与委内瑞拉银行在波多黎各设立的分支机构存在账户行关系，虽然提交了可疑交易报告，但报告不充分，涉及20亿美元。

六是该行未能对一家被代理行开展的4.5亿美元大额现金交易进行充分的监控，并及时提交可疑交易报告；

七是银行未能对另一家被代理行开展的47.168万美元的可疑交易进行充分监控并提交补充可疑交易报告。

其中第四至第七造成的问题是重大的。

事件的影响和后续

违反银行保密法和反洗钱合规的和解令对摩根大通银行影响深远，从2012年开始，摩根大通银行集全集团力量和资源对其缺陷进行整改。主要表现在以下方面：

一方面是摩根大通退出部分重要的代理行业务。早在2012年，由于监管日趋严格，该行大大提高了对客户尽职调查的标准，导致每一客户的平均合规成本攀升到5万~10万美元，因此，摩根大通不再为业务量较少或收入不能覆盖成本的境内中小商业银行提供美元等其他外币清算业务，被清退的银行达到了40多家。随后，摩根大通银行于2013年6月正式退出光票托收业务，这原本是美元账户服务的重要组成部分。

另一方面是摩根大通银行对前台人员发展新的客户、产品和业务出台了严格的规定，和解令专门用了一整个条款对新增客户和业务的限制：一是"银行应确保在开展新产品和服务前，接受高级合规管理人员的审查和批准"，高管人员要具体到审查业务合规风险的数值、风险管理的质量和风险管理人员配备的问题；二是在没有进行风险评估、没有确定合规人员配置的影响、没有至少30天前通知监理署主管审查员开展此类行动的情况下，"银行不得进入新的高风险行业，银行不得新扩大现有高风险业务线"。根据华尔街日报的报道，2013年8月，摩根大通向内部员工发送了一份备忘录，备忘录主要内容包括："为加强风险控制，应监管部门要求，摩根大通银行决定未来将不会与国外银行机构建立更多的代理合作机制。"上述规定导致摩根大通银行从2013年起至2018年初几乎未增加与新代理行客户和老客户的新业务。众所周知，银行代理行业务是摩根大通核心业务之一，摩根大通也因此在业内被称为"银行的银行"。

此外，摩根大通银行反洗钱相关的系统，如客户尽职调查系统、可疑交易筛查和报告系统等也经过了多次的调整和完善，投入巨大。新招募的反洗钱专业从业人员成倍增长。反洗钱政策和流程也在不断更新过程当中。

案件的影响及教训

2008年金融危机发生后，美国监管当局面临的公众压力倍增，不断对加强对金融机构的监管和处罚力度。不仅仅是对欧洲或亚洲的银行，美国监管机构也没有放松对"自己孩子"的调查，调查的重点集中在消费者欺诈和反洗钱合规方面，调查的主导机构是美联储、货币监理署、司法部和金融犯罪执法网络局。

在违反银行保密法和反洗钱方面，对美国本土银行的调查主要由OCC主导并实施，除前面提到的摩根大通银行外，原美联银行于2010年收到了两份和解令以及5 000万美元罚单。根据媒体报道，货币监理署通过调查原美联银行海外代理行业务，发现其在遵循《银行保密法》和反洗钱合规方面存在缺陷，因此处以5 000万美元的罚金。花旗银行分别于2012年和2017年收到了和解令以及7 000万美元的罚单。据报道，由于花旗银行未能达到2012年和解令的要求，美国货币监理署处以7 000万美元的罚金。2012年监理署就发现花旗银行在遵循《银行保密法》和反洗钱合规方面存在缺陷，如该行合规体系未能覆盖反洗钱合规的所有要素，该行客户尽职调查不充分且未能及时上报部分业务领域的可疑交易等方面。2017年5月，花旗集团又收到9 744万美元罚单，承认了旗下墨西哥子行从2007年至2012年间违反了《银行保密法》，花旗集团与美国司法部和美国联邦检察官办公室达成和解，签订了不起诉协议。

可以看出，监管机构在违反银行保密法和反洗钱合规方面，对美资大行罚没的金额不及欧洲或其他地区的银行，主要是考虑到这些银行未被怀疑故意对不法分子提供洗钱的支持，虽然如此，但是，监管机构仍然未放松对"自己孩子"看管和教育。总体来看，美国监管机构对本土银行处罚时间较早，整改目标覆盖全面。整改要求较高。

以摩根大通银行的和解令为例，监理署提出的整改措施涵盖反洗钱合规的各个方面，可疑交易报告、交易监控、客户尽职调查、风险评估、内部控制、独立测试等，而不是将焦点集中在某一类客户或业务方面，而整改的目标都用"适当的appropriate""有效的effective"来表示，而不是具体的量化的指标，这相当于要求银行对其全行的反洗钱合规体系重构。和解令签发后，笔者感受到美资大行这几年一直不遗余力地对整个集团的反洗钱合规方方面面进行整改,从管理框架、到制度和流程、到人员和系统,最后到达具体的业务。监管机构还是定期对其整改效果进行评估和检查,检查不仅在美国本土检查,后来延伸到欧洲,2017年甚至来到香港,并要求大陆一线业务人员出差到香港进行了面谈。截止到作者发稿,仍未对这些巨头们撤销上述和解令。

2018年1月,花旗银行因为反洗钱政策缺陷未解决被处以7 000万美元的罚款。看来,美国监管机构对"自家孩子"的监管和处罚不仅没有放松,而是不断的完善和加强。而且,随着监管机构不断更新反洗钱新规,整改目标不断在更新。2018年4月11日,美国监管当局又出台了反洗钱新规,要求金融机构在企业开立账户时就应确认其真正的所有者。

对于我国的银行来说,金融业处在由高速发展转为稳健发展的转型阶段,由于监管不到位、经营理念和考核体系一时难以转变等多方面原因,对利润的追求更胜于合规经营的策略,因此,更应该吸取这些银行的经验教训,处理好业绩增长和合规经营的关系。从全球金融业发展趋势来看,防范风险和加强监管是趋势,我国也不例外。

附录1：

《和解令》英文原文

#2013-002

UNITED STATES OF AMERICA
DEPARTMENT OF THE TREASURY
COMPTROLLER OF THE CURRENCY

In the Matter of:

JPMorgan Chase Bank, N.A.
Columbus, OH

JPMorgan Bank and Trust Company, N.A., San
Francisco, CA

AA-EC-13-04

Chase Bank USA, N.A.,
Newark, DE

CONSENT ORDER

WHEREAS, the Comptroller of the Currency of the United States of America ("Comptroller"), through his national bank examiners and other staff of the Office of the Comptroller of the Currency ("OCC"), has conducted examinations of JPMorgan Chase Bank, N.A., Columbus, Ohio; JPMorgan Bank and Trust Company, N.A., San Francisco, California; and Chase Bank USA, N.A., Newark, Delaware (collectively referred to as "Bank"). The OCC has identified deficiencies in the Bank's overall program for Bank Secrecy Act/Anti-Money Laundering ("BSA/AML") compliance and has informed the Bank of the findings resulting from the examinations.

WHEREAS, the Bank, by and through its duly elected and acting Boards of Directors (collectively referred to as "Board"), has executed a "Stipulation and Consent to the Issuance of a Consent Order," dated January 14th , 2013, that is accepted by the Comptroller ("Stipulation"). By this Stipulation and Consent, which is incorporated by reference, the Bank has consented to the issuance of this Consent Cease and Desist Order ("Order") by the Comptroller, pursuant to 12 U.S.C. § 1818(b). The Bank has begun corrective action, and has committed to taking all necessary and appropriate steps to remedy the deficiencies identified by the OCC, and to enhance the Bank's BSA/AML compliance program.

ARTICLE I
COMPTROLLER'S FINDINGS

The Comptroller finds, and the Bank neither admits nor denies, the following:

(1) The OCC's examination findings establish that the Bank has deficiencies in its BSA/ AML compliance program. These deficiencies have resulted in the failure to correct a previously reported problem and a BSA/AML compliance program violation under 12 U.S.C. § 1818(s) and its implementing regulation, 12 C.F.R. § 21.21 (BSA Compliance Program). In addition, the Bank has violated 12 C.F.R. § 21.11 (Suspicious Activity Report Filings).

(2) The Bank has failed to adopt and implement a compliance program that adequately covers the required BSA/AML program elements due to an inadequate system of internal controls, and ineffective independent testing. The Bank did not develop adequate due diligence on customers, particularly in the Commercial and Business Banking Unit, a repeat problem, and failed to file all necessary Suspicious Activity Reports ("SARs") related to suspicious customer activity.

(3) The Bank failed to correct previously identified systemic weaknesses in the adequacy of customer due diligence and the effectiveness of monitoring in light of the customers' cash activity and business type, constituting a deficiency in its BSA/AML compliance program and resulting in a violation of 12 U.S.C. § 1818(s)(3)(B).

(4) Some of the critical deficiencies in the elements of the Bank's BSA/AML compliance program, resulting in a violation of 12 U.S.C. § 1818(s)(3)(A) and 12 C.F.R. § 21.21, include the following:

(a) The Bank has an inadequate system of internal controls and independent testing.

(b) The Bank has less than satisfactory risk assessment processes that do not provide an adequate foundation for management's efforts to identify, manage, and control risk.

(c) The Bank has systemic deficiencies in its transaction monitoring systems, due diligence processes, risk management, and quality assurance programs.

(d) The Bank does not have enterprise-wide policies and procedures to ensure that foreign branch suspicious activity involving customers of other bank branches is effectively communicated to other affected branch locations and applicable AML operations staff. The Bank also does not have enterprise-wide policies and procedures to ensure that on a risk basis, customer transactions at foreign branch locations can be assessed, aggregated, and monitored.

(e) The Bank has significant shortcomings in SAR decision-making protocols and an ineffective method for ensuring that referrals and alerts are properly documented, tracked, and resolved.

(5) The Bank failed to identify significant volumes of suspicious activity and file the required SARs concerning suspicious customer activities, in violation of 12 C.F.R. § 21.11. In some of these cases, the Bank self-identified the issues and is engaged in remediation.

(6) The Bank's internal controls, including filtering processes and independent testing, with respect to Office of Foreign Asset Control ("OFAC") compliance are inadequate.

NOW, THEREFORE, IT IS ORDERED that:

ARTICLE II
COMPLIANCE COMMITTEE

(1) The Board shall appoint and maintain a Compliance Committee of at least three

(3) directors, of which a majority may not be employees or officers of the Bank or any of its subsidiaries or affiliates. The names of the initial members of the Compliance Committee shall be submitted in writing to the Examiner-in-Charge for a written determination of no supervisory objection. In the event of a change of the membership, the name of any new member shall be submitted in writing to the Examiner-in-Charge at the Bank ("Examiner-in-Charge") for a written determination of no supervisory objection. The Compliance Committee shall be responsible for coordinating and monitoring the Bank's adherence to the provisions of this Order. The Compliance Committee shall meet at least monthly and maintain minutes of its meetings.

（2）Within ninety (90) days of this Order, and quarterly thereafter, the Compliance Committee shall submit a written progress report to the Board setting forth in detail the actions taken to comply with each Article of this Order, and the results and status of those actions, including improvements to the BSA/AML Program.

（3）The Board shall forward a copy of the Compliance Committee's report, with any additional comments by the Board, to the Deputy Comptroller for Large Bank Supervision ("Deputy Comptroller") and the Examiner-in-Charge within ten (10) days of receiving such report.

ARTICLE III
COMPREHENSIVE BSA/AML ACTION PLAN

（1）Within sixty (60) days of this Order, the Bank shall submit to the Deputy Comptroller and the Examiner-in-Charge a plan containing a complete description of the actions that are necessary and appropriate to achieve full compliance with Articles IV through XI of this Order ("BSA/AML Action Plan"). The Bank shall implement the BSA/AML Action Plan upon the Deputy Comptroller's issuance of a written determination of no supervisory objection. In the event the Deputy Comptroller requires the Bank to revise the plan, the Bank shall promptly make and the Board shall approve necessary and appropriate revisions and resubmit the BSA/AML Action Plan to the Deputy Comptroller and Examiner-in-Charge for review and determination of no supervisory objection. Following implementation, the Bank shall not take any action that will cause a significant deviation from, or material change to, the BSA/AML Action Plan unless and until the Bank has received a prior written determination of no supervisory objection from the Deputy Comptroller.

（a）The Board shall ensure that the Bank achieves and thereafter maintains compliance with this Order, including, without limitation, successful implementation of the BSA/AML Action Plan. The Board shall further ensure that, upon implementation of the BSA/AML Action Plan, the Bank achieves and maintains an effective BSA/AML compliance program, in accordance with the BSA and its implementing regulations. In each instance in this Order in which the Board is required to ensure adherence to or undertake to perform certain obligations of the Bank, it is intended to mean that the Board shall: Authorize and adopt such actions on behalf of the Bank as may be necessary for the Bank to perform its obligations and undertakings.

（b）Require the timely reporting by Bank management of such actions directed by the Board to be taken under this Order;

（c）Require corrective action be taken in a timely manner for any noncompliance with such actions; and

（d）Follow-up on any non-compliance with such actions in a timely and appropriate manner.

（2）The BSA/AML Action Plan must specify timelines for completion of each of the requirements of Articles IV through XI of this Order. The timelines in the BSA/AML Action Plan shall be consistent with any deadlines set forth in these Articles, unless modified by written agreement with the Deputy Comptroller or the Examiner-in-Charge.

（3）Upon request by the Deputy Comptroller or the Examiner-in-Charge, the Bank shall modify the BSA/AML Action Plan to address any Matters Requiring Attention concerning BSA/AML matters, or citations of violations of law concerning BSA/AML matters, which the OCC may issue to the Bank following the effective date of this Order.

（4）The Bank shall ensure that it has sufficient processes, personnel, and control systems to implement and adhere to this Order. The BSA/AML Action Plan must specify in detail budget outlays and staffing, including aggregated staff compensation information in a format acceptable to the Examiner-in-Charge, that are necessary to achieve and maintain full compliance with Articles IV through XI of this Order.

（5）Any independent consultant or auditor engaged by the Bank or the Board to assist in the assessment of the BSA/AML Action Plan or other compliance with this Order must have demonstrated and specialized experience with the BSA/AML matters that are the subject of the engagement, and must not be subject to any conflict of interest affecting the consultant's or auditor's independence.

（6）Within ten (10) days of this Order, the Bank shall designate an officer to be responsible for coordinating and submitting to the OCC the written plans, reports, and other documents required to be submitted under the terms and conditions of this Order.

ARTICLE IV
MANAGEMENT AND ACCOUNTABILITY

（1）The Bank shall ensure there are clear lines of authority and responsibility for BSA/AML and OFAC compliance with respect to lines of business and corporate functions, and that competent and independent compliance management is in place on a full-time basis.

（2）The Bank shall ensure that compliance staff has the appropriate level of authority to implement the BSA/AML Compliance Program and, as needed, question account relationships and business plans. Compliance staff shall maintain independence from the business line. The Bank shall follow any applicable guidance addressing independence issued by the OCC or the FFIEC.

（3）The Bank shall ensure that senior management and line of business management are accountable for effectively implementing bank policies and procedures, and fulfilling BSA/AML/OFAC obligations. The Bank shall incorporate BSA/AML and OFAC compliance into the performance evaluation process for senior and line of business management. Additionally, written Bank policies and procedures shall clearly outline the BSA/AML/OFAC responsibilities of senior management and relevant business line employees, including, but not limited to, relationship managers, business banking, commercial banking, correspondent banking and private banking personnel, and legal and business development staff.

（4）The Bank shall develop appropriate objectives and means to measure the effectiveness of compliance management officers and compliance management personnel within each line of business and for those with responsibilities across lines of business.

（5）The Board shall not permit any other party, including but not limited to the Bank's holding company, to perform any act on behalf of the Bank which is the subject of this Order, unless the Bank requires that party to perform such act in the manner and under safeguards and controls as least as stringent as required by the Bank under the terms of this Order as implemented by the Bank.

ARTICLE V
BSA/AML AND OFAC COMPLIANCE PROGRAM EVALUATION AND RISK ASSESSMENT

(1) Within 60 days of this Order, the Bank shall provide an action plan for the completion of an evaluation of the Bank's BSA/AML and OFAC Compliance Programs to the Examiner-in-Charge for no supervisory objection. If the Examiner-in-Charge recommends changes to the evaluation, the Bank shall incorporate those changes or suggest alternatives that are acceptable to the Examiner-in-Charge.

(2) The evaluation required pursuant to Paragraph (1) of this Article shall be completed and submitted to the Examiner-in-Charge within 90 days following the nonobjection of the Examiner-in-Charge to the action plan referred to in Article V(1). This evaluation shall include assessments of the BSA/AML and OFAC Compliance Programs' organizational structure, enterprise-wide effectiveness, competency of management, accountability, staffing requirements, internal controls, customer due diligence processes, risk assessment processes, suspicious activity monitoring systems, audit/independent testing, and training. The evaluation shall include recommendations for enhancements needed to achieve remediation of any deficiencies identified in the evaluation.

(3) This evaluation shall also include a comprehensive assessment of the Bank's BSA/AML risk, including detailed quantification of risk to accurately assess the level of risk and the adequacy of controls. The comprehensive assessment shall include:

(a) An assessment of the AML risk associated with each line of business, and an enterprise-wide assessment of AML risk. This evaluation shall include, but not be limited to, an assessment of the risk associated with correspondent banking, pre-paid cards and mobile banking, cash-intensive businesses, remote deposit capture, business, commercial, and private banking, and other higher risk products, services, customers, or geographies. The purpose of the enterprise-wide assessment is to identify systemic AML risk that may not be apparent in a risk assessment focused on line of business or assessment units;

(b) Evaluation of the Bank's current methodology for identifying and quantifying the level of BSA/AML risk associated with categories of customers and for specific customers. The methodology should ensure that the relationships are reviewed holistically, across lines of business, taking into consideration the risk within the Bank. This evaluation shall result in the development of a comprehensive approach to quantifying BSA/AML risk for new and existing customers. The quantification of risk shall encompass a customer's entire relationship with the Bank, include the purpose of the account, actual or anticipated activity in the account (e.g., type, volume, and value (number and dollar) of transaction activity engaged in), nature of the customer's business or occupation, customer location (e.g., customers' geographic location, where they transact business, and have significant operations), types of products and services used by the customer, material changes in the customer's relationship with the Bank, as well as other factors discussed within the FFIEC BSA/AML Examination Manual;

（c）The identification of specific lines of business, geographies, products or processes where controls are not commensurate with the level of AML risk exposure;

（d）The risk assessment shall be refreshed periodically, the timeframe for which shall not exceed twelve months, or whenever there is a significant change in AML risk within the Bank or line of business. The AML risk assessments shall also be independently reviewed by the Bank's internal audit function for the adequacy of identification of risk; control plan to manage identified risks; gap analyses where controls are not sufficient; and action plans to address gaps; and

（e）The aggregation of the Bank's enterprise-wide AML risk shall be logical and clearly supported in the work papers. The work papers and supporting documentation shall be readily accessible for OCC review.

（4）OFAC risk shall be included within the BSA/AML risk assessment, using the same criteria as described above in paragraphs 2(a) through (e) of this Article.

ARTICLE VI
<u>CUSTOMER DUE DILIGENCE</u>

（1）Within 90 days of this Order, the Bank shall ensure that appropriate customer due diligence policies, procedures, and processes are developed. These controls shall be implemented and applied on a Bank-wide basis. Minimum corporate standards shall provide general guidance, and individual lines of business and AML compliance management shall develop standards based on their client base, products, services, geographic risk, and other AML risk factors. Customer due diligence shall be commensurate with the customer's risk profile, and sufficient for the bank to develop an understanding of normal and expected activity for the customer's occupation or business operations. The customer due diligence process shall include the following items:

（a）Information regarding the client's/customer's relationships with the Bank, all lines of business within the Bank, and all Bank subsidiaries or affiliates (that are subject to management control by the Banks' holding company). This includes accounts within other lines of business, regions, and countries (as permitted by jurisdiction). The relationship includes its owners, principals, signers, subsidiaries, affiliates, and parties with the ability to manage or control the account or client;

（b）An electronic due diligence database, which includes information specified in subparagraph (a) above, that is readily accessible to the relationship manager or other parties responsible for the customer relationship, AML compliance personnel, suspicious activity monitoring alert analysts and investigators, and quality control and assurance personnel;

（c）Customer due diligence shall be periodically updated to reflect changes in the customer's behavior, activity profile, derogatory information, periodic reviews of the customer relationship, or other factors that impact the AML risk for the client and shall include any remediation required by the standards required by the Article. The frequency of the periodic update of due diligence shall be based on risk with the update performed at least annually for high- risk relationships, triennially for low-risk business relationships, and as appropriate for low-risk individuals. The periodic updates shall be documented, and subject to quality assurance processes;

(d) The client relationship AML risk shall be detailed in the customer due diligence record, along with the supporting factors, including transaction activity, geographies involved, and suspicious activity monitoring alert and filing history, among others;

(e) Specialized or enhanced due diligence for higher risk clients and/or products and services shall be implemented enterprise-wide. These due diligence standards shall comply with the FFIEC BSA/AML Examination Manual, the Interagency Guidance on Beneficial Ownership Information (OCC 2010-11), as well as industry standards; and

(f) Management processes to periodically review, based on the relationship risk, the type, volume, and value of customer activities in relation to normal and expected levels. The purpose of these reviews shall be to determine if the customer's activity is reasonable, that customer due diligence is current and complete, and the customer risk rating is accurate. These reviews shall be documented and quality assurance processes must ensure the reviews are comprehensive and accurate. Standards and processes shall be established for elevating reviews for additional management consideration regarding increased monitoring, additional due diligence, or account closure/

(2) The Bank shall submit its policies and procedures for customer due diligence to the Examiner-in-Charge for prior no supervisory objection. If the Examiner- in-Charge recommends changes to the policies or procedures, the Bank shall incorporate those changes or suggest alternatives that are acceptable to the Examiner-in-Charge.

ARTICLE VII
<u>SUSPICIOUS ACTIVITY IDENTIFICATION AND REPORTING</u>

(1) Within 60 days of this Order, the Bank shall develop and thereafter shall maintain a written program of policies and procedures to ensure, pursuant to 12 C.F.R. § 21.11, the timely and appropriate review and disposition of suspicious activity alerts, and the timely filing of Suspicious Activity Reports ("SARs").

(2) Within 30 days of this Order, the Bank shall retain or continue an existing or newly revised relationship with one or more independent consultants acceptable to the Examiner-in-Charge to evaluate its suspicious activity identification processes to ensure they are effective and provide comprehensive coverage to the Bank. This evaluation shall include an assessment of the capabilities of any surveillance and transaction monitoring systems used; the scope of coverage provided by the systems; and the management of those systems. Upon completion, the Bank shall submit this evaluation to the Examiner-in-Charge for no supervisory objection. The evaluation shall address, but not be limited to, the following issue:

An assessment of the functionality of automated transaction monitoring systems used to determine if the systems are sufficiently robust to provide for the timely identification of potentially suspicious activity. A comprehensive listing of weaknesses or deficiencies in the system and the risks presented by these deficiencies shall be highlighted for management consideration;

(3) Management's implementation of each surveillance and transaction monitoring system shall ensure the following:

(a) The integrity of data feeding the transaction monitoring systems;

(b) The system has been sufficiently tailored to the Bank's risk profile and operations;

(c) The system's functionality is being utilized to appropriately address risk, including the ability to aggregate data across platforms, lines of business, and relationships; and

(d) The business logic units, parameters, rules, or other factors selected for automated monitoring are appropriate and effective in identifying client activity that is unreasonable or abnormal given the nature of the client's occupation or business and expected activity. In addition, there shall be:

(i) Sufficient management information and metrics to manage and adjust the system, as necessary; and

(ii) Statistically valid processes to validate and optimize monitoring system settings and thresholds, and to measure the effectiveness of the automated system and individual scenarios, where appropriate.

(4) Management implementation of the alert investigation processes shall ensure the following:

(a) The adequacy of staffing to investigate and clear alerts;

(b) The quality and completeness of information available to analysts working transaction monitoring alerts and conducting investigations;

(c) The standards for dispositioning different types of alerts are reasonable, communicated in writing to relevant staff, and are adhered to by the alert investigators;

(d) Adequate documentation is maintained to support the disposition of alerts;

(e) The availability and adequacy of information to investigate potentially suspicious activity, including, if applicable, information from multiple lines of business a customer transacts with or information from bank subsidiaries or affiliates (that are subject to management control by the Banks' holding company), and information concerning foreign suspicious activity reports involving United States customers;

(f) Standards that ensure accounts with high volumes of alerts are identified, elevated, and properly categorized as high risk, and subject to enhanced due diligence and monitoring; and

(g) Sufficient quality control processes to ensure the surveillance and transaction monitoring system, alert management process, and SAR decisioning and filing are working effectively and according to internal standards.

ARTICLE VIII
SUSPICIOUS ACTIVITY REPORT REVIEW ("SAR LOOK-BACK")

(1) Within 30 days of this Order, the Banks shall provide to the Examiner-in-Charge for prior no supervisory objection an action plan to review the quality of SAR filings ("SAR look-back"). The purpose of the SAR look-back is to review the quality of SARs filed and determine whether corrections or amendments are necessary to ensure that the suspicious activity identified was accurately reported in accordance with 12 C.F.R. § 21.11, and whether additional SARs should be

filed on additional subjects or for continuing suspicious activity.

(2) The SAR look-back must be supervised and certified by independent consultant(s) acceptable to the Examiner-in-Charge with expertise in conducting lookback reviews for large institutions.

(3) Upon completion of the SAR look-back: (i) the Bank shall ensure that SARs have been filed, in accordance with 12 C.F.R. § 21.11, for any previously reported suspicious activity identified during this review; (ii) the written findings shall be reported to the Board; and (iii) the Bank will provide the Examiner-in-Charge with a report, containing relevant information, including the number of modified or amended SARs and any additional or continuing activity SARs filed as a result of the review.

(4) Based upon the results of the SAR look-back, the OCC may expand the scope of the independent review or require a longer SAR look-back period. If an additional SAR look-back is deemed appropriate by the OCC, the Bank shall complete the SAR look-back in accordance with this Article.

ARTICLE IX
ACCOUNT/TRANSACTION ACTIVITY AND SUSPICIOUS ACTIVITY REPORT REVIEW ("ACCOUNT AND TRANSACTION LOOK-BACK")

(1) Within 30 days of this Order, the Bank shall provide to the Examiner-in-Charge for prior no supervisory objection an action plan to conduct an independently supervised review of account and transaction activity ("account and transaction lookback") covering non-bank financial institutions, as defined in the FFIEC BSA/AML Examination Manual.

(2) The purpose of the account and transaction look-back is to determine whether suspicious activity was timely identified by the Bank, and, if appropriate to do so, was then timely reported by the Bank in accordance with 12 C.F.R. § 21.11.

(3) The account and transaction look-back must be supervised and certified by independent consultant(s) with expertise in conducting look-back reviews for large institutions. The account and transaction look-back shall be risk-based, including the risks identified in the Bank's risk assessment as revised under Article V, and shall identify the sampling, software screening, or analytical techniques used to identify transactions that are subject to review for suspicious activity.

(4) Upon completion of the account and transaction look-back: (i) the Bank shall ensure that SARs have been filed, in accordance with 12 C.F.R. § 21.11, for any previously unreported suspicious activity identified during this review; (ii) the written findings shall be reported to the Board; and (iii) the Bank will provide the Examiner-in-Charge with a report, containing relevant information, identifying any SARs filed as a result of previously unreported suspicious activity.

(5) Based upon the results of the account and transaction look-back, the OCC may expand the scope of the independent review or require a longer account and transaction look-back period. If an additional account and transaction look-back is deemed appropriate by the OCC, the Bank shall complete the account and transaction look-back in accordance with this Article.

ARTICLE X
INDEPENDENT TESTING AND AUDIT

(1) Within 90 days of this Order, the Bank shall develop and maintain an effective program

to audit the Bank's BSA/AML and OFAC Compliance Programs ("Audit Program"). The Audit Program shall include, at a minimum:

(a) A formal process to track and report upon Bank management's remediation efforts to strengthen the Bank's BSA/AML/OFAC compliance program;

(b) Testing of the adequacy of internal controls designed to ensure compliance with BSA and OFAC, and their implementing regulations;

(c) A risk-based approach that focuses transactional testing on higher- risk clients, products, geographies, and significant relationships; and

(d) A requirement for prompt management response and follow-up to audit exceptions or other recommendations of the Bank's auditor.

(2) The Audit Program shall evaluate internal controls and effectively and timely identify non-compliance with policy, laws, rules, and regulations across lines of business and within each line of business. At least annually, the Audit Program shall evaluate the adequacy of the Bank's BSA Program based on the results of the independent testing, and considering changes in the quantity of AML risk or AML risk management.

(3) The Bank's audit function shall be adequately staffed with respect to experience level, specialty expertise regarding BSA/AML and OFAC, and number of the individuals employed.

(4) The Bank's Audit Program shall report all internal audit- and OCC- identified deficiencies to the Compliance Committee, the Bank's Audit Committee, and to senior compliance management. The reports shall indicate the severity of the deficiencies, the risks, the corrective actions, and timeframes. Corrective actions must be followed-up by internal audit within a reasonable period of time until closed. Monthly status reports on corrective action status shall be provided to the Compliance Committee and the Bank's Audit Committee.

(5) The Board and senior compliance management shall receive adequately detailed information about the Bank's compliance management program in light of their respective obligations to oversee the Bank and to fulfill their fiduciary responsibilities and other responsibilities under law. Deficiencies in the program shall be identified and highlighted along with the risks.

(6) Within 90 days of this Order, the Bank shall submit the Audit Program to the Examiner-in-Charge for prior no supervisory objection. If the Examiner-in-Charge recommends changes to the Audit Program, the Bank shall incorporate those changes or suggest alternatives that are acceptable to the Examiner-in-Charge.

ARTICLE XI
NEW ACCOUNTS, PRODUCTS, SERVICES, OR MARKET
SEGMENT S/INDUSTRIES

(1) The Bank shall ensure that new products and services are subject to senior level compliance review and approval. These reviews must consider the quantity of BSA/AML and OFAC risk of the new product or service as well as the quality of risk management. At a minimum, these reviews must assess the ability of the Bank's compliance program to manage the risk, the anticipated growth in both the business and the compliance function, and the ability of alert investigators' to manage any anticipated increase in alert volume as a result of the new business.

(2) The Bank shall not enter into a new high-risk (inherent quantity) market segment/industry,

enter into new or expand existing high-risk (inherent quantity) lines of business, without conducting a risk assessment, a determination of compliance staffing impact, and without providing prior notification of at least 30 days to the Examiner-in-Charge of such proposed actions.

ARTICLE XII
APPROVAL, IMPLEMENTATION AND REPORTS

(1) The Bank shall submit the written plans, programs, policies and procedures required by this Order for review and determination of no supervisory objection to the Deputy Comptroller and the Examiner-in-Charge within the applicable time periods set forth in Articles III through XI. The Board shall approve the submission and cause the Bank to submit the plans, programs, policies and procedures to the Deputy Comptroller and Examiner-in-Charge for prior written determination of no supervisory objection. In the event the Deputy Comptroller asks the Bank to revise the plans, programs, policies or procedures, the Board shall promptly make necessary and appropriate revisions and resubmit the materials to the Deputy Comptroller and Examiner-in-Charge for review and determination of no supervisory objection. Upon receiving written notice of no supervisory objection from the Deputy Comptroller, the Board promptly shall adopt the plans, programs, policies and procedures and direct and cause the Bank to implement and thereafter adhere to the plans, programs, policies and procedures. Following implementation of the plans, programs, policies and procedures, the Board shall ensure that the Bank does not take any action that will cause a significant deviation from, or material change to the plans, programs, policies and procedures, unless and until the Board has received prior written determination of no supervisory objection from the Deputy Comptroller.

(2) During the term of this Order, the Bank shall revise the required plans, programs, policies and procedures as necessary to incorporate new, or changes to, applicable legal requirements and supervisory guidelines following the procedures above.

(3) The Board shall ensure that the Bank has processes, personnel, and control systems to ensure implementation of and adherence to the plans, programs, policies and procedures required by this Order.

(4) Within thirty (30) days after the end of each calendar quarter following the date of this Order, the Bank shall submit to the OCC a written progress report detailing the form and manner of all actions taken to secure compliance with the provisions of this Order and the results thereof. The progress report shall include information sufficient to validate compliance with this Order, based on a testing program acceptable to the OCC that includes, if required by the OCC, validation by third-party independent consultants acceptable to the OCC. The OCC may, in writing, discontinue the requirement for progress reports or modify the reporting schedule.

(5) All communication regarding this Order shall be sent to:

× × ×

× × × ×

Large Bank Supervision

Office of the Comptroller of the Currency

250 E Street, SW

Washington, DC 20219

Scott N. Waterhouse

Examiner-in-Charge
National Bank Examiners
1166 Avenue of the Americas, 21st Floor
New York, NY 10036

or such other individuals or addresses as directed by the OCC.

ARTICLE XIII
CLOSING

(1) Although this Order requires the Bank to submit certain actions, plans, programs, policies and procedures for the review or prior written determination of no supervisory objection by the Deputy Comptroller or the Examiner-in-Charge, the Board has the ultimate responsibility for proper and sound management of the Bank.

(2) If, at any time, the Comptroller deems it appropriate in fulfilling the responsibilities placed upon him by the several laws of the United States to undertake any action affecting the Bank, nothing in this Order shall in any way inhibit, estop, bar or otherwise prevent the Comptroller from so doing.

(3) This Order constitutes a settlement of the cease and desist proceeding against the Bank contemplated by the Comptroller, based on the unsafe or unsound practices and violations of law or regulation described in the Comptroller's Findings set forth in Article I of this Order. The OCC releases and discharges the Bank from all potential liability for a cease and desist order that has been or might have been asserted by the OCC based on the practices and violations described in the Comptroller's Findings set forth in Article I of the Order, to the extent known to the OCC as of the effective date of the Order. Provided, however, that nothing in the Stipulation or this Order shall prevent the Comptroller from instituting other enforcement actions against the Bank or any of its institution-affiliated parties, including, without limitation, assessment of civil money penalties, based on the findings set forth in this Order, or any other findings, and nothing in the Stipulation or this Order shall preclude or affect any right of the OCC to determine and ensure compliance with the terms and provisions of the Stipulation or this Order.

(4) This Order is and shall become effective upon its execution by the Comptroller, through his authorized representative whose hand appears below. The Order shall remain effective and enforceable, except to the extent that, and until such time as, any provision of this Order shall be amended, suspended, waived, or terminated in writing by the Comptroller.

(5) Any time limitations imposed by this Order shall begin to run from the effective date of this Order, as shown below, unless the Order specifies otherwise. The time limitations may be extended in writing by the Deputy Comptroller for good cause upon written application by the Board. Any request to extend any time limitation shall include a statement setting forth in detail the special circumstances that prevent the Bank from complying with the time limitation, and shall be accompanied by relevant supporting documentation. The Deputy Comptroller's decision regarding the request is final and not subject to further review.

(6) The terms and provisions of this Order apply to JPMorgan Chase Bank, N.A., Columbus, OH; JPMorgan Bank and Trust Company, N.A., San Francisco, CA; and Chase Bank USA, N.A., Newark, DE and all their subsidiaries, even though those subsidiaries are not named as parties to this Order. The Bank shall integrate any activities done by a subsidiary into its plans, policies,

programs and processes required by this Order. The Bank shall ensure that its subsidiaries comply with all terms and provisions of this Order.

(7) This Order is intended to be, and shall be construed to be, a final order issued pursuant to 12 U.S.C. § 1818(b), and expressly does not form, and may not be construed to form, a contract binding the Comptroller or the United States. Without limiting the foregoing, nothing in this Order shall prevent any action against the Bank or its institution-affiliated parties by a bank regulatory agency, the United States Department of Justice, or any other law enforcement agency.

(8) The terms of this Order, including this paragraph, are not subject to amendment or modification by any extraneous expression, prior agreements, or prior arrangements between the parties, whether oral or written.

IT IS SO ORDERED, this 14 day of San , 2013.

《和解令》中文译文

美国财政部 货币监理署

和解令
第2013 002号

鉴于，美国国家货币监理官（Comtroller，以下简称监理官）通过货币监理署（以下简称监理署）工作人员，对摩根大通银行、摩根大通信托公司和大通银行（以下简称银行）进行检查。监理署发现了上述银行在遵循保密法及反洗钱合规（以下简称BSA／AML）的缺陷并已通知检查的结果。

鉴于，上述银行通过其董事会，已执行于2013年1月14日发出的Stipulation and Consent to the Issuance of a Consent Order（Stipulation1），并得到了监理官的认可。根据12 U.S.C. 1818（b）§，通过签署Stipulation1，银行已接受监理官签发的和解令。银行已开始采取纠正措施，并承诺采取一切必要和适当的措施纠正由监理署中发现的缺陷，并提高银行的BSA／AML的合规管理。

条款一

监理官发现，且上述银行既不承认也不否认以下情况：

（1）监理署的检查结果发现上述银行在遵守BSA／AML方面存在缺陷。这些情况导致未能纠正先前报告的问题，同时，根据12 U.S.C. 1818（S）及其实施条例12 C.F.R 21.21，违反了BSA／AML的合规制度。此外，还违反了12 CFR 21.11（可疑交易报告制度）。

（2）由于内部控制体系不健全以及无效的独立测试，上述银行未能采纳并执行一个涵盖BSA／AML要素的合规方案。上述银行没有对客户，尤其是商业银行业务条线经营的客户，进行充分的尽职调查，同时，未能将所有可疑客户活动相关联的可疑交易（以下简称"SARs"）上报。

（3）上述银行未能纠正先前确定的系统性弱点，即客户尽职调查的充分性和根据客户的现金活动和商业活动的类型监测的有效性。这是BSA／AML合规管理缺陷，并违反了12 U.S.C. § 1818（S）（3）（b）。

（4）一些BSA／AML合规管理重要缺陷，违反了12 U.S.C. 1818（S）（3）（A）和12 CFR § 21.21，包括以下内容：

（a）上述银行内部控制和独立测试体系不健全；

（b）上述银行缺乏符合要求的风险评估程序，该程序没有为管理层识别、管理和控制风险提供决策依据；

（c）上述银行在交易监控系统、尽职调查程序、风险管理和质量保证计划方面存在系统缺陷；

（d）上述银行没有覆盖全行的政策和程序，以确保在境外分支机构发生的与其他分支机构客户有关的可疑活动，有效地传达给受影响的分支机构和相关的反洗钱人员。上述银行也没有覆盖全行的政策和程序，以确保在为防范风险，对境外分支机构的客户交易进行评估、汇总和监测。

（e）上述银行在可疑交易拟定决策方面存在重大缺陷，缺乏有效的方法来确保适当地记录、跟踪和解决产生的预警及转递。

（5）上述银行违反了12 CFR § 21.11，未能识别大量的可疑交易活动以及未能上报与上述客户的可疑行为相关的可疑交易。在其中一些案例中，银行自身查明了问题并正在从事补救工作。

（6）上述银行的内部控制措施是不够的，包括渗透程序和独立测试，以及与外国资产控制办公室（以下简称OFAC）相关的合规管理。

因此，现在命令：

条款二

合规委员会

（1）董事会应任命并保持含有至少3名董事的合规委员会，其中多数可不担任本行或其任何附属机构的雇员或职员。合规委员会初始成员的姓名应以书面形式提交给主管监查员（Examiners-in-Charge），以书面确定不存在监督异议。如遇成员变动，任何新成员的姓名应以书面形式提交给主管监查员。合规委员会应负责协调和监督银行遵守本和解令条款的规定。合规委员会应至少每月召开1次会议，并保持其会议记录。

（2）在本和解令正式生效后的90天内，合规委员会应每季向董事会提交一份书面整改进度报告，详细说明为遵守和解令的每项条款所采取的行动，以及这些行动的结果和状态，包括对BSA／AML项目的改进情况。

（3）董事会应在收到合规委员会报告的10日内，向负责大型银行监管的副监理官（Deputy Comptroller）和主管监查员提交这份报告，如有意见，应附上董事会对报告的意见。

条款三

全面的BSA／AML行动计划

（1）在和解令正式生效后的60天内，上述银行应根据和解令的条款四和条款十一，向副监理以及主管监查员提交一份完整的如何实施必要并正确的全面合规管理行动计划（以下简称BSA／AML行动计划）。在副监理签发无监管异议的书面决定后，银行应执行的BSA／AML的行动计划。当副监理要求银行更新计划，银行应及时更新，在董事会批准必要和适当的更新后重新提交给副监理，以便副监理和主管监查员进行评审。实施后，银行不应采取任何导致原行动计划显著偏离或发生重大改变，除非上述银行事先收到了副监理无监管异议的书面材料。

（a）董事会应确保银行达到并保持对本和解令的遵守，包括但不限于成功地执行BSA／AML行动计划。董事会应进一步确保通过执行BSA／AML行动计划，上述银行能够根据BSA及其实施条例，达到并保持有效的BSA/AML合规管理。在任何情况下，董事会须确保遵守或承诺履行银行的义务，由于银行有必要履行其义务和承诺，这意味着董事会应授权并采取行动；

（b）要求银行管理层及时报告董事会依据本和解令已采取的整改行动；

（c）对于不合规的做法，需要及时采取正确的行动；

（d）及时、适当地跟进任何不合规的行为。

（2）为达到条款四和条款十一的要求，BSA／AML的行动计划需制定明确的时间表，除非副监理和主管监查员事前通过书面协议进行修订，行动计划不得超出上述条款要求的最后期限。

（3）根据副监理或主管监查员的要求，银行应修改BSA／AML的行动计划以解决需引起注意的事项，或关于BSA／AML的违法行为。上述要求可能由监理署在和解令生效后向银行正式发出。

（4）银行应确保足够的流程、人员和控制系统来执行并遵守本和解令。BSA / AML的行动计划涉及的预算支出和人员编制必须详细注明，包括汇总员工补偿信息应以主管监查员接受的格式，这是实现和保持完全符合本和解令条款四和条款十一必要的。

（5）任何由上述银行或董事会聘用的协助评估BSA / AML的行动计划或本和解令涉及的其他合规事项的外部独立咨询师和审计师必须证明自身在BSA / AML领域的专业经验，并有不受任何利益和冲突影响的独立性。

（6）在本和解令生效后十天内，银行应指定人员负责协调并向监理署提交遵循本和解令条款的书面计划、报告及其他文件。

条款四
管理和责任

（1）银行应确保在BSA / AML和OFAC合规管理方面有清晰的授权以及关于业务条线和公司职能的责任分工，确保胜任且独立的合规管理人员各司其职。

（2）银行应确保合规工作人员具有适当的授权，以实施BSA / AML合规整改计划，并根据需要，质疑账户关系和业务计划。合规人员应保持与业务条线保持独立。银行应遵守任何监理署或FFIEC（Federal Financial Institutions Examination Council）发布为保持独立性的指引。

（3）银行应确保高级管理层和业务线管理层有效地实施银行政策和程序的责任，并履行BSA / AML /OFAC的义务。银行应当将BSA / AML和OFAC合规纳入高管层和业务条线管理层评价过程。此外，银行政策和流程应将高级管理人员和普通员工承担的BSA/AML/OFAC合规职责列明，普通员工包括但不限于客户关系经理，零售银行业务，商业银行业务，代理行和私人银行业务经理，以及法律和业务发展人员。

（4）银行应制定适当的目标和方法，以衡量合规官以及业务条线和跨业务条线的合规管理人员工作的有效性。

（5）银行的董事会不得允许任何第三方，包括但不限于本行的控股公司，代表银行履行本和解令项下的任何义务，除非银行要求，且以同样严格标准来执行。

条款五

BSA/AML AND OFAC合规及风险评估

（1）在本和解令生效后60天内，主管监查员表示无监管异议的情况下，银行应提供BSA /AML和OFAC合规完成情况的评估。如建议对评估情况作出改变，银行应将这些变更合并或提出主管监查员接受的备选方案。

（2）根据本条款第（1）条所要求的评估应在主管监查员根据本条款第（1）条无异议后90天内提交给监察员。评估的内容应包括BSA /AML和OFAC合规管理的组织架构、全行范围内的有效性、管理的能力、问责、人员需求、内部控制、客户尽职调查流程，风险评估流程，可疑交易监测系统，审计/独立测试和训练。评估还应包括为改进缺陷所需的建议。

（3）该评估还应包括对银行BSA/AML风险的全面综合评估，包括详细的风险量化，以准确评估风险水平和控制的充分性。综合评估应包括：

（a）对每条业务线的反洗钱风险的评价，以及对反洗钱风险的全行评价。评估还应包括但不限于代理行业务、预付卡和移动银行业务、现金密集型业务、远程存款、商业银行和私人银行业务，以及其他高风险产品、服务、客户或地理区域的风险。全行范围评价的目的是识别系统性反洗钱风险，这种风险在业务条线或业务单元的风险评估中可能并不明显；

（b）对银行目前用于识别和计量与客户类别和特定客户相关的BSA / AML风险水平的方法的评估。该方法应确保客户关系被全面审查、跨业务条线并且纳入银行风险水平。对于新老客户，这种评估会导致制定出综合性的方法来量化BSA / AML风险的综合方法。风险量化应涵盖客户与银行的全面关系，包括账户的目的，账户中的实际或预期活动（例如从事交易活动的类型，业务笔数和业务量（数量和美元），客户的业务或职业的特性，客户的位置（例如，客户的地理位置，他们和哪里进行业务交易，是否有重要的业务），客户使用的产品和服务类型，客户与银行关系的重大变化以及作为FFIEC BSA / AML考试手册中讨论的其他因素；

（c）对控制水平与AML风险暴露程度不相称的业务、地理位置、产品或流程的识别；

（d）银行内部或业务条线的反洗钱合规风险如发生重大的变化，风险评估应定期更新，其期限不得超过十二个月。为充分确定风险，银行内审应独立对AML风险的评估进行审查；管理已识别风险的控制计划；控制不足的缺口分析；以及解决差距的行动计划；以及

（e）全行反洗钱风险的汇总应符合逻辑并在工作文件中得到明确支持。工作文件和辅助文件应随时可供监理署审查。

（4）根据本条款2（a）至（e）段描述相同的标准，OFAC风险应包括在BSA／AML的风险评估里。

条款六
客户尽职调查

（1）在本和解令生效后的90天内，银行应确保制定适当的客户尽职调查政策、程序和流程。这些控制应在银行范围内实施和实施。全行范围内应提供综合指引。各个业务线和反洗钱合规管理应根据客户基础、产品、服务、地理风险和其他反洗钱危险因素制定标准。客户尽职调查应与客户的风险状况相匹配，足以使银行了解客户的职业或业务进行的正常活动并预测将来。客户尽职调查过程应包括下列项目：

（a）关于客户与银行关系的信息、银行内部所有业务条线的信息，以及所有银行附属公司或附属机构的信息（受持股公司的管理控制）。这包括其他业务、区域和国家的账户（管辖权允许）。账户关系应包括其所有者、委托人、签署人、子公司、附属机构以及具有管理或控制客户账户能力的当事人；

（b）包括上述（a）条款内容的尽职调查的数据库，应随时可由客户关系经理或其他负责客户关系的人员、反洗钱合规人员、可疑活动监测预警分析和调查人员，以及质量控制和质量保证人员调阅；

（c）客户尽职调查应定期更新，以反映客户行为、活动概况、贬损信息、定期审查客户关系，或影响客户的反洗钱风险的其他因素，并应包括本条确定的标准的补救措施。尽职调查周期性更新的频率应基于风险，至少每年对高风险的关系，每三年为低风险的业务关系或个人更新。定期更新应保留记录，并经质量保证程序检验；

（d）客户关系反洗钱风险应在客户尽职调查记录中详细列出，以及支持因素：包括交易活动、地理区域以及可疑活动监测警报和存档记录等；

（e）对高风险客户和/或产品及服务进行加强型尽职调查应在全行范围实施。尽职调查的标准应当遵守FFIEC BSA／AML检查手册，跨部门所有人信息引导（the Interagency Guidance on Beneficial Ownership Information 监理署 2010-11）以及行业标准；和

（f）定期重检的管理程序应依据风险因素、客户正常和预期活动的类型、数量和价值。重检的目的应确定客户的活动是否合理，客户尽职调查是否及时完整，客户风险评级是否准确。重检内容应记录在案，质量保证程序必须确保重检全面准确。

（2）在已经无监管异议的前提下，银行应将其客户尽职调查的政策和程序提交给主管监查员。如果主管监查员建议修订该政策或程序，银行应将这些修订合并或提出可供主管监查员接受的备选办法。

条款七
可疑交易识别和报告

（1）在本和解令生效后60天内，根据12 CFR §21.11，银行应制定书面的政策和程序，以便及时并正确评审和处置可疑活动的预警，及时提交可疑交易报告（以下简称SARs）；

（2）在本和解令生效后30天内，在主管监查员认可的情况下，银行应保留或继续与一个或多个独立的咨询师，以评估其可疑的活动识别过程，以确保其有效并覆盖全行。该评估应包括对所使用的任何监视和交易监控系统能力的评估；系统的覆盖范围；以及对系统的管理。完成后，银行应向主管监查员提交此项评估以排除监管异议。评价应能够说明，但不限于，下列问题：

如果系统有足够的能力，应提供自动交易监测功能的评估，以便及时识别潜在可疑交易。应全面列出系统弱点或缺陷以及这些缺陷所带来的风险，以供管理层考虑；

（3）对每个监视和交易监控系统的实施，管理层应确保以下内容：

（a）输入交易监测系统的数据的完整性；

（b）该系统已充分适用银行的风险状况和运营；

（c）该系统应有适当地处理风险的能力，包括整合跨平台、跨业务线和跨关系数据的能力；以及

（d）自动监控能根据正常的客户职业、商务活动和预期行为，来选择业务逻辑单元、参数、规则或其他因素，这对于识别客户不合理或不正常的行为是适当和有效的。此外，还包括：

（Ⅰ）根据足够的管理信息和度量标准管理和调整系统；以及

（Ⅱ）有效的过程，以验证和优化监控系统的设置和阈值，并在适当情况下可衡量自动系统和个人方案的有效性。

（4）调查过程预警的管理实施应确保下列内容：

（a）配备充足的调查和解除预警的人员；

（b）有高质量完整的信息以便对交易监测预警并进行调查；

（c）有合理的用于处置不同类型预警的标准，标准应在相关人员以书面形式进行沟通，调查人员遵守预警标准；

（d）预警处置应保留足够的档案记录；

（e）有充足的信息用于调查潜在的可疑交易，如果适用，应包括以下内容，从多个业务线的客户交易信息或从银行子公司或附属公司信息（由银行持股公司管理控制），及涉及美国客户的境外可疑交易报告的信息；

（f）在加强型的尽职调查和监控下，有相关的标准确保出现大量预警的账户被识别、提升，并适当地归为高风险；以及

（g）充分的质量控制过程以确保监控和交易监测系统、预警管理过程和可疑交易报告决策和档案保存工作有效且符合内部标准。

条款八
可疑交易报告的审查（SAR 回溯重检）

（1）在本和解令生效后30天内，银行应向主管监查员提供无监管异议的审查可疑活动报告质量的行动计划（可疑交易报告回溯重检，以下简称SAR look-back）。SAR look-back的目的是检查可疑交易上报的质量并确定修改或修订是否必要的，以确保根据12 CFR 21.11§准确报告了被识别出来的可疑交易，以及是否有额外的或持续存疑的可疑交易应被上报。

（2）在专门负责对大型机构进行回顾性审查的主管监查员接受的情况

下，SAR look-back必须接受独立的咨询师的监督和认证。

（3）在SAR look-back完成后：（i）根据12 CFR§21.11，银行应确保在本次审查中识别出来的所有SARs已经上报；（ii）书面调查结果应向董事会报告；及（iii）银行应向主管监查员提供一份报告，包含如下相关信息，已修改或修订SARS数量和本次审查到的额外或持续的SARS。

（4）基于SAR look-back，监理署可能扩大独立审查的范围或需要更长的时间。如果监理署认为应开展额外的SAR look-back时，银行应根据本条款完成本次SAR look-back。

条款九
账户/交易活动和可疑交易报告检查（账户和交易回溯重检）

（1）在本和解令生效后的30天内，根据"FFIEC BSA / AML考试手册"所定义的，银行应向主管监查员提供无监管异议的行动计划，以对账户和交易活动（涵盖非银行金融机构）进行独立审查（账户和交易回溯重检）。

（2）账户和交易回溯重检的目的是确定银行是否及时发现可疑交易，并在适当情况下，根据12 C.F.R§21.11，银行是否及时报告。

（3）账户和交易回溯重检必须由具有专业知识的大型机构进行回溯审查的独立顾问进行监督和认证。账户和交易回溯重检应基于风险，包括在条款五新提出的银行风险评估中识别的风险，并应识别分析交易所用的样本，软件筛查或分析技术。

（4）账户和交易回溯重检完成后：（i）对于此次审查中发现的任何以前未报告的可疑交易，银行应确保可疑交易报告已按照12 C.F.R§21.11的规定上报，（ii）书面调查结果应向董事会报告；及（iii）银行将向主管监查员提供一份报告，其中应包含识别以前未报告的可疑交易进行了上报了的相关信息。

（5）账户和交易回溯重检，监理署可能会扩大独立审查的范围或需要更长的账户和交易回顾期。如果监理署认为附加账户和交易回溯是合适的，银行应根据本条完成账户和交易回溯。

条款十
独立测试和审计

（1）本和解令发布后90天内，银行应制定并维持一个有效的计划，以审计银行的BSA／AML和OFAC合规计划（审计计划）。审计计划至少应包括：

（a）正式提交为加强银行BSA／AML／OFAC合规，跟踪和报告银行管理层实施的补救措施的流程；

（b）测试旨在确保BSA和OFAC，及其实施条例而采取的内部控制是否充足；

（c）一种基于风险的方法，将交易测试的重点放在高风险客户、产品、地理区域和重要关系上；以及

（d）对银行审计的例外情况或审计时提出的其他建议进行及时管理响应和后续审计的要求。

（2）审计计划应对内部控制进行评估，并有效和及时地识别不合规的跨业务条线和业务线内的政策、法律、规则和条例。审计计划应至少每年根据独立测试的结果评估银行BSA计划的是否充足，并考虑反洗钱风险或反洗钱风险管理数值的变化。

（3）银行的审计部门应配备经验水平、BSA／AML和OFAC领域专家，以及足够雇员。

（4）银行的审核程序应向合规委员会，审计委员会和合规高级管理人员报告所有的内部审计和监理署认定不足。报告应指出的不足的严重程度、风险，纠正措施和时间安排。内部审计应在合理时间跟进纠正措施直至完成。应向合规委员会和审计委员会提供纠正措施的月度进展报告。

（5）根据其应监督银行并履行其管理责任及法律规定的其他责任的义务，董事会和合规高级管理人员应获得充分详细的银行合规管理信息。合规管理中的缺陷应与风险一起进行揭示。

（6）在和解令生效的90天内，银行应将审计计划提交主管监查员，以便事先确认无监督异议。如主管监查员建议对审计计划进行更改，银行应将这些更改并入或提出可供主考者接受的备选方案。

条款十一

新账户，产品，服务或行业

（1）银行应确保在开展新产品和服务前，接受高级合规管理人员的审查和批准。这些审查必须考虑新产品或服务的BSA／AML和OFAC风险的数值以及风险管理的质量。审查必须至少评估银行合规管理把控风险及预期业务和合规职能的增长的能力，以及预警人员能管理由于新业务而导致的预警量增加的能力。

（2）银行不得进入新的高风险（固有数量）行业，在没有进行风险评估、没有确定合规人员配置的影响、没有至少30天前通知主管监查员开展此类行动的情况下，银行不得新扩大现有高风险（固有数量）业务线。

条款十二
批准，实施和报告

（1）银行应在条款三至条款十一规定的适用期限内提交本和解令所要求的书面计划，方案，政策和程序，以便副监理官和主管监查员确定无监管异议。董事会应批准提交的文件，并促使银行在事先书面确定无监管异议的情况下，向副监理官和主管监查员提交计划，方案，政策和程序。如果副监理官要求银行修改计划，方案，政策或程序，董事会应及时作出必要和适当的修改，并将材料重新提交副监理官和主管监查员以便审查和确定无监管异议。在收到副监理官无监管异议的书面通知后，董事会应及时采纳计划，方案，政策和程序，指导和促使银行执行并随后遵守计划，方案，政策和程序。在执行计划，方案，政策和程序后，董事会应确保银行不会采取任何会导致计划，方案，政策和程序出现重大偏差或重大变更的行动，直至董事会收到副监理官的书面无监管异议。

（2）在本和解令期限内，根据适用法律和监管指南要求的新内容或变更，银行应按照上述程序修改所需的计划，方案，政策和程序。

（3）董事会应确保银行拥有流程，人员和控制系统，以确保执行和遵守本和解令所要求的计划，方案，政策和程序。

（4）在本和解令生效后的每季度结束后的30天内，银行应向监理署提交书面进度报告，详细说明为确保遵守本和解令条款而采取的所有行动的形式和方式，以及其结果。基于监理署可接受的测试计划，进度报告应包括足以验证遵守本和解令的信息，如果监理署要求，监理署可接受的第三方独立顾问进行验证。监理署可以书面形式停止进度报告要求或修改上报的时间安排。

（5）有关此命令的所有通信均应发送至：

×××××. ×××××××，×××××，大银行监管局，监理署，250 E 街，审计软件华盛顿特区20219

×××××. ×××××××，×××××××，全国性银行监管，1166 美洲大道，第21楼，纽约，NY 10036

或其他监理署指定的个人或地址

条款十三
终止

（1）虽然本和解令要求银行提交一定的行动、计划、方案、政策和程序为审查或书面确定由副主任或负责监督考官没有异议的政策和程序，董事会应对适当、健全的管理银行承担最终责任。

（2）在任何时候，如果监理官认为美国法律赋予他应当履行的责任将会对银行产生影响，本和解令中的任何内容均不得以任何方式阻碍、反对、禁止或以其他方式阻止监理官从这样做。

（3）基于本和解令条款一中描述的由监理官发现的不安全或不健全以及违反法律的做法，本和解令为监理官考虑停止或终止对银行诉讼提供了解决方案。监理署豁免了银行所有潜在的责任，这些潜在的责任是由监理署在本和解令生效日期前基于本和解令条款一中发现的违规行为已经或可能已经声明的内容。但是，Stipulation1和本和解令不得妨碍监理官基于本和解令中的发现或任何其他调查结果，对银行或其任何机构关联方采取其他强制措施，包括但不限于民事罚款。同时，Stipulation1和本和解令中的任何内容均不得排除或影响监理署确定并确保遵守Stipulation1或本和解令的条款和规定的权利。

（4）本和解令在监理官通过其授权代表执行后生效，其授权代表出现在下面。除非本和解令的任何规定由监理官进行书面修改，暂停，放弃或终止，本和解令一直有效并应强制执行。

（5）除非本和解令另有规定，否则本和解令的任何时间限制均应从本和解令的生效日期开始执行，如下所示。时间限制可由副监理官根据董事会的书面申请以良好的理由以书面形式延长。任何延长时限的请求均应包括一份声明，详细说明妨碍本行遵守时限的特殊情况，并附有相关证明文件。副监理官对该申请的决定是最终决定，不需要进一步审查。

（6）本命令的条款适用于JPMorgan Chase Bank，N.A.，Columbus，OH; JPMorgan Bank and Trust Company，N.A.，San Francisco，CA; 和 Chase Bank USA，N.A.，Newark，DE及其所有子公司，尽管这些子公司并未被列为本和解令。银行应将子公司的任何活动纳入本和解令所要求的计划、政策、方案和程序中。银行应确保其子公司遵守本和解令所有条款。

（7）本和解令旨在并应被解释为根据12U.S.C§1818（b）颁布的最终命令，并明确不构成，并且不得构成对监理官或美国政府法律约束性的文件。本命令中的任何内容均不构成未来阻止银行监管机构，美国司法部或任何其他执法机构对银行或其附属机构采取任何行动的限制。

（8）本和解令的条款，包括本款，不接受任何口头或书面的、来源于其他表述、事前协议或当事人之间的事先安排的修改。

该令于2013年1月14日正式签发。

附录2:

《和解令》英文原文

#2014-001

UNITED STATES OF AMERICA
DEPARTMENT OF THE TREASURY
COMPTROLLER OF THE CURRENCY

In the Matter of:

JPMorgan Chase Bank, N.A.
Columbus, OH

JPMorgan Bank and Trust Company, N.A.
San Francisco, CA

AA-EC-13-109

Chase Bank USA, N.A.
Wilmington, DE

CONSENT ORDER FOR THE ASSESSMENT OF A CIVIL MONEY PENALTY

The Comptroller of the Currency of the United States of America ("Comptroller"), through his national bank examiners and other staff of the Office of the Comptroller of the Currency ("OCC"), has conducted examinations of JPMorgan Chase Bank, N.A., Columbus, Ohio; JPMorgan Bank and Trust Company, N.A., San Francisco, California; and Chase Bank USA, N.A., Wilmington, Delaware (collectively referred to as "Bank"). The OCC has identified deficiencies in the Bank's Bank Secrecy Act/anti-money laundering ("BSA/AML") compliance program, resulting in violations of 31 U.S.C. § 5318(i) and its implementing regulation, 31 C.F.R. § 1010.610(a), (b) and (c); 12 U.S.C. § 1818(s) and its implementing regulation, 12 C.F.R. § 21.21(c); and 12 C.F.R. § 21.11(c) and (d). The Bank is also the subject of a prior OCC Consent Cease and Desist Order issued on January 14, 2013 ("January 2013 Order").

Examinations conducted subsequent to the issuance of the January 2013 Order have revealed additional deficiencies in the Bank's BSA/AML compliance program, which resulted in the citation of additional violations of law and regulation. The Bank has been notified of the findings of these examinations.

The Bank, by and through its duly elected and acting Boards of Directors, has executed a "Stipulation and Consent to the Issuance of a Consent Order for the Assessment of a Civil Money Penalty," dated January 7, 2014, that is accepted by the Comptroller ("Stipulation"). By this Stipulation, which is incorporated herein by reference, the Bank has consented to the issuance of this Consent Order for the Assessment of a Civil Money Penalty ("Consent Order") by the Comptroller.

On January 6, 2014, the Bank entered into a Deferred Prosecution Agreement ("DPA") with the United States Attorney's Office for the Southern District of New York. In the DPA, the Bank admitted to certain facts concerning the failure to file a Suspicious Activity Report ("SAR") in the United States on Bernard L. Madoff Investment Securities, LLC ("Madoff").

ARTICLE I
COMPTROLLER'S FINDINGS

The Comptroller finds the following:

The Comptroller incorporates the following findings from Article I of the January 2013 Order:

(1) The OCC's examination findings establish that the Bank has deficiencies in its BSA/AML compliance program. These deficiencies have resulted in the failure to correct a previously reported problem and a BSA/AML compliance program violation under 12 U.S.C. § 1818(s) and its implementing regulation, 12 C.F.R. § 21.21 (BSA Compliance Program). In addition, the Bank has violated 12 C.F.R. § 21.11 (Suspicious Activity Report Filings).

(2) The Bank has failed to adopt and implement a compliance program that adequately covers the required BSA/AML program elements due to an inadequate system of internal controls and ineffective independent testing. The Bank did not develop adequate due diligence on customers, particularly in the Commercial and Business Banking Unit, a repeat problem, and failed to file all necessary SARs related to suspicious customer activity.

(3) The Bank failed to correct previously identified systemic weaknesses in the adequacy of customer due diligence and the effectiveness of monitoring in light of the customers' cash activity and business type, constituting a deficiency in its BSA/AML compliance program and resulting in a violation of 12 U.S.C. § 1818(s)(3)(B).

(4) Some of the critical deficiencies in the elements of the Bank's BSA/AML compliance program, resulting in a violation of 12 U.S.C. § 1818(s)(3)(A) and 12 C.F.R. § 21.21, include the following:

(a) The Bank has an inadequate system of internal controls and independent testing.

(b) The Bank has less than satisfactory risk assessment processes that do not provide an adequate foundation for management's efforts to identify, manage, and control risk.

(c) The Bank has systemic deficiencies in its transaction monitoring systems, due diligence processes, risk management, and quality assurance programs.

(d) The Bank does not have enterprise-wide policies and procedures to ensure that foreign branch suspicious activity involving customers of other bank branches is effectively communicated to other affected branch locations and applicable AML operations staff. The Bank also does not have enterprise-wide policies and procedures to ensure that on a risk basis, customer transactions at foreign branch locations can be assessed, aggregated, and monitored.

(e) The Bank has significant shortcomings in SAR decision-making protocols and an ineffective method for ensuring that referrals and alerts are properly documented, tracked, and resolved.

(5) The Bank failed to identify significant volumes of suspicious activity and file the required SARs concerning suspicious customer activities, in violation of 12 C.F.R. § 21.11. In some of these cases, the Bank self-identified the issues and is engaged in remediation.

(6) The Bank's internal controls, including filtering processes and independent testing, with respect to Office of Foreign Asset Control ("OFAC") compliance are inadequate.

The Comptroller further finds, for purposes of this Consent Order:

(7) The Bank has not established adequate BSA/AML and due diligence programs for its foreign branches, offices, or affiliates in violation of 31 U.S.C. § 5318(i) (implementing Section 312 of the USA PATRIOT Act, Pub. L. No. 107-56, § 312(a), 115 Stat. 272, 312 (2001)), and 12 C.F.R. § 21.21(c). This violation includes the Bank's failure to conduct suspicious activity monitoring of transactions between the Bank and certain of the Bank's affiliates.

(8) The Bank did not establish and implement an adequate BSA/AML program for correspondent banking and remote deposit capture ("RDC") and international cash letter ("ICL") products or adequate internal controls, including the Bank's due diligence programs, in the correspondent banking and RDC/ICL areas. Inadequate controls resulted in certain special accommodation clients in the Bank that operated outside of the normal AML monitoring and OFAC screening controls. For these reasons, the Bank is in violation of 31 U.S.C. § 5318(i), 12 U.S.C. § 1818(s), 12 C.F.R. § 21.21(c), and 31 C.F.R. § 1010.610(a), (b), and (c). These failures also caused the Bank to fail to file SARs and to do so timely in violation of 12 C.F.R. § 21.11(c) and (d).

(9) The Bank has failed to correct previously reported problems in several areas, including Asia Private Banking, and with respect to one of its correspondent bank relationships, resulting in additional violations of 12 U.S.C. § 1818(s).

(10) The Bank's SAR filing processes and procedures for SAR filing in the areas of Chase Auto Finance and Student Lending were inadequate, and the Bank further failed in certain instances to file SARs related to suspected fraud by employees, resulting in violations of 12 C.F.R. § 21.11(c).

(11) Between 2006 and 2008, the Bank created, sold and made a secondary market for structured products that provided customers access to Madoffs investment strategy through several "feeder funds." Prior to Bernard L. Madoffs arrest, the Bank developed concerns about Madoff and a distributor of Madoff-linked investments created by the Bank. These concerns caused the Bank's London branch to file a suspicious activity report with the United Kingdom's Serious Organised Crime Agency on October 29, 2008. Aware that Madoff was a client of the Bank in the U.S., U.K.-based Bank employees conveyed these concerns to U.S.-based Bank employees. Despite the fact that these concerns caused the Bank to file a suspicious activity report in the U.K., the Bank did not file a SAR in the U.S. based on these concerns. The failure to file a SAR on this activity and to do so timely is significant and a violation of 12 C.F.R. § 21.11(c) and (d).

(12) The Bank maintained a correspondent banking relationship with a Puerto-Rican-chartered affiliate of a Venezuelan bank. Although the Bank filed SARs relating to this correspondent account, the Bank did not investigate additional suspicious activity, totaling over $2 billion, pertaining to counterparties that flowed through the account at the Bank. The failure to file SARs on this activity and to do so timely is significant and in violation of 12 C.F.R. § 21.11(c) and (d).

(13) From 2004 to 2010, the Bank failed to adequately monitor, investigate and file SARs on approximately $450 million of suspicious bulk cash transactions in an account at the Bank for another of its correspondents. The failure to file SARs on this activity and to do so timely is significant and in violation of 12 C.F.R. § 21.11(c) and (d).

(14) From February 2013 to March 2013, the Bank failed to adequately monitor and file a

supplemental SAR on ongoing activity relating to $471,680 in suspicious transactions in an account at the Bank for a third correspondent. The failure to file SARs on this activity and to do so timely is significant and in violation of 12 C.F.R. § 21.11(c) and (d).

ARTICLE II
ORDER FOR A CIVIL MONEY PENALTY

Pursuant to the authority vested in him by the Federal Deposit Insurance Act, 12 U.S.C. § 1818(i), the Comptroller orders, and the Bank consents to, the following:

(1) The Bank shall make payment of a civil money penalty in the total amount of three hundred and fifty million dollars ($350,000,000), which shall be paid upon the execution of this Consent Order:

(a) If a check is the selected method of payment, the check shall be made payable to the Treasurer of the United States and shall be delivered to: Comptroller of the Currency, P.O. Box 979012, St. Louis, Missouri 63197-9000.

(b) If a wire transfer is the selected method of payment, it shall be sent in accordance with instructions provided by the Comptroller.

(c) The docket number of this case (AA-EC-13-109) shall be entered on the payment document or wire confirmation and a photocopy of the payment document or confirmation of the wire transfer shall be sent immediately, by overnight delivery, to the Director of Enforcement and Compliance, Office of the Comptroller of the Currency, 400 7th Street, S.W., Washington, D.C. 20219.

(2) This Consent Order shall be enforceable to the same extent and in the same manner as an effective and outstanding order that has been issued and has become final pursuant to 12 U.S.C. § 1818(h) and (i).

ARTICLE III
OTHER PROVISIONS

(1) This Consent Order is intended to be, and shall be construed to be, a final order issued pursuant to 12 U.S.C. § 1818(i)(2), and expressly does not form, and may not be construed to form, a contract binding on the Comptroller or the United States.

(2) This Consent Order constitutes a settlement of the civil money penalty proceeding against the Bank contemplated by the Comptroller, based on the violations of law and regulation described in the Comptroller's Findings set forth in Article I of this Consent Order. The OCC releases and discharges the Bank from all potential liability for a civil money penalty that has been or might have been asserted by the Comptroller based solely on the violations of law and regulation as described in the referenced findings, to the extent known to the Comptroller as of the effective date of the Consent Order. Provided, however, that nothing in the Stipulation or this Consent Order shall prevent the Comptroller from instituting enforcement actions against the Bank or any of its institution-affiliated parties, including, without limitation, assessment of civil money penalties, based on any other findings, including, but not limited to, findings related to required look backs or reviews conducted by or on behalf of the Bank. The violations of law and regulation described in Article I of this Consent Order may be utilized by the Comptroller in other future enforcement actions against the Bank or its institution-affiliated parties, including, without limitation, to establish a pattern or practice of violations or unsafe and unsound practices, or the continuation of a

pattern or practice of violations or unsafe or unsound practices. Nothing in this Consent Order shall preclude or affect any right of the Comptroller to determine and ensure compliance with the terms and provisions of the Stipulation or this Consent Order.

(3) The terms of this Consent Order, including this paragraph, are not subject to amendment or modification by any extraneous expression, prior agreements, or prior arrangements between the parties, whether oral or written.

IT IS SO ORDERED, this 7th day of January 2014.

《和解令》中文译文

XXXXXX XXXXXXX

副监理官

大型银行监管办公室

监理署

美国财政部

货币监理署

第2014-001号

民事罚款和解令

鉴于，美国国家货币监理官通过货币监理署（以下简称监理署）工作人员，对摩根大通银行、摩根大通信托公司和大通银行（以下简称"银行"）进行检查。监理署发现银行在遵循银行保密法/反洗钱（BSA／AML）合规方案存在不足之处，违反了31U.C.§5318（i）及其实施条例，31 C.F.R.§1010.610（a）、（b）和（c）；12 U.S.C.§1818（s）及其实施条例，12 C.F.R.§21.21（c）和12 C.F.R.§21.11（c）和（d）。银行也是2013年1月14日发布的监理署和解令（"2013年1月和解令"）的主体责任人。

发布2013年1月和解令后进行的检查揭示了银行在BSA／AML合规方案中的其他缺陷，导致更多的违法和违规行为。银行已收到这些检查结果的通知。

通过其正式当选的执行董事会，银行于2014年1月7日签署了"Stipulation and Consent to the Issuance of a Consent Order for the Assessment of a Civil Money Penalty"（以下简称Stipulation2），监理官已接受。通过签署Stipulation2，该银行已同意监理官签发的本和解令。

2014年1月6日，该银行与美国纽约南部区检察官办公室签订了暂缓起诉协议（DPA）。在DPA中，该银行承认了未能提交Bernard L. Madoff投资证券有限责任公司（Madoff）可疑交易（SAR）的某些事实。

条款一
监理官的调查结果

监理官发现：

监理官包括了2013年1月签发的和解令条款一的内容：

（1）监理署的检查结果表明，银行在其BSA／AML合规方案中存在缺陷。这些缺陷导致未能纠正之前报告的问题，同时，根据12U.S.C.§1818（s）及其实施条例，12 C.F.R.§21.21，导致违反BSA／AML合规方案的情况（BSA合规方案）。此外，银行还违反了12CFR§21.11（可疑交易报告制度）。

（2）由于内部控制系统不足和独立测试无效，银行采取和实施合规方案不能充分涵盖BSA／AML所要求的要素。银行没有对客户进行充分的尽职调查，特别是在零售银行部门，这是一个重复问题，并且未能提交与可疑客户活动有关的所有必要的报告。

（3）银行未能纠正先前发现的，对客户进行充分的尽职调查以及根据客户的现金活动和行业划分对客户进行有效监控方面的系统性弱点，这构成了BSA／AML合规方案的不足之处，并违反了12 USC§1818（s）（3）（B）。

（4）银行BSA／AML合规方案要素中的一些关键缺陷导致违反了12USC§1818（s）（3）（A）和12 C.F.R.§21.21，包括以下内容：

（a）银行内部控制和独立检测系统的不足；

（b）银行的风险评估程序不尽如人意，无法为管理层识别，管理和控制风险提供充分的基础；

（c）银行在交易监控系统，尽职调查流程，风险管理和质量保证方面存在系统性缺陷；

（d）银行没有全行范围内的政策和程序，以确保海外分行涉及的其他银行分支机构的客户可疑交易被有效地传达给其他受影响的分支机构和适用的反洗钱操作人员。银行也没有全行范围的政策和程序，以确保在风险的基础上，可以评估，汇总和监控外国分行的客户交易。

（e）银行在可疑交易报告决策方面存在重大缺陷，并且无法有效确保转介和预警得到适当记录、追踪和解决。

（5）银行未能识别大量的可疑交易活动并提交涉嫌可疑客户活动所需的

L5B-3IT0

可疑交易报告，这违反了12C.F.R.§21.11。在其中一些情况下，银行自行发现了问题并正在进行补救。

（6）银行内部控制措施，关于OFAC合规方面的，包括过滤流程和独立测试是不充分的。

为了本和解令的目的，监理官进一步发现：

（7）银行尚未为其境外分支机构，办事处或关联机构制定适当的BSA／AML和尽职调查方案，违反了31 U.S.C.§5318（i）（美国爱国者法案第312节实施章节，Pub L.107-56，§312（a），115 Stat.272，312（2001））和12 C.F.R.§21.21（c）。违规行为包括银行未能对本行和关联公司之间的交易进行可疑交易的监控。

（8）银行没有为代理行业务和远程存款（"RDC"）和光票托收（"ICL"）产品建立并实施适当的BSA／AML方案以及充足的内部控制（包括银行的尽职调查计划），在RDC／ICL产品没有充分的客户尽职调查方案。控制不力导致银行中的某些特殊客户在正常的反洗钱监控和OFAC筛查控制之外运营。由于这些原因，银行违反了31U.C.§5318（i），12 U.S.C.§1818（s），12 C.F.R.§21.21（c）和31 C.F.R.§1010.610（a），（b）和（c）。这些也导致本行无法及时提交可疑交易报告，这违反了12 C.F.R.§21.11（c）和（d）。

（9）银行未能纠正之前几个领域报告的问题，包括亚洲私人银行在内，关于其代理银行关系之一的业务，导致违反12U.S.C.§1818（s）。

（10）银行在大通汽车金融和学生贷款等领域的可疑交易报告的程序和流程不足，在某些情况下，银行又未能提交员工涉嫌欺诈案件可疑交易报告，导致违反12C.F.R.§21.11（c）。

（11）在2006年至2008年，银行设立，出售并建立了结构性产品的二级市场，该产品通过多个"联结基金"为客户提供获取麦道夫投资策略的机会。在Bernard L. Madoff（以下简称Madoff）被捕之前，银行对Bernard以及银行设立的Madoff相关投资的分销商产生了担忧，这些担忧导致银行的伦敦分行于2008年10月29日向英国严重有组织犯罪署提交了一份可疑交易报告。由于Madoff美国的银行的客户，英国员工将这些担忧转达给美国。尽管这些担忧导致银行在英国提交可疑交易报告，但银行并未在美国提交报告。未能就此活动及时提交报告的问题是重大的，违反了12 C.F.R. §21.11（c）和（d）。

（12）该银行与委内瑞拉银行的在波多黎各设立的分支机构有账户行关系。尽管银行提交了与本代理账户有关的可疑交易报告，但银行并未调查通过本行账户与代理行有关的总额超过20亿美元的其他可疑交易。没有对此及时提交可疑交易报告的问题是重大的，违反了12 C.F.R. §21.11（c）和（d）。

（13）从2004年到2010年，未能对其中一家被代理行通过银行开展的约4.5亿美元大额的现金交易进行充分监控，调查和提交可疑交易报告。没有对此及时提交可疑交易报告的问题是重大的，违反了12 C.F.R. §21.11（c）和（d）。

（14）从2013年2月至2013年3月，银行未能对另一家被代理行通过银行开展的47.168万美元可疑交易进行充分监控并提交补充可疑交易报告。没有对此提交可疑交易报告的问题是重大的，违反了12 C.F.R. §21.11（c）和（d）。

条款二
民事罚金令

根据"联邦存款保险法"12 U.S.C. §1818（i）授予他的权力，监理官命令，银行同意如下：

（1）银行应支付总额为3.5亿美元（350 000 000美元）的民事罚款，并应在执行本和解令时支付罚款：

（a）如果选择支票作为付款方式，支票应付给美国司库，邮寄地址：××××。

（b）如果选择电汇作为付款方式，则应按照监理官的指示发送。

（c）该案件的案卷号码（AA-EC-13-109）应记录在付款文件或电汇确认单上，付款文件或电汇确认单的复印件应立即通过快递发送给×××，地址：××××。

（2）本和解令的执行方式和效果应与已经签发生效的和解令相同，并作为根据12U.S.C.§1818（h）和（i）的最终裁决。

条款三
其他规定

（1）本和解令旨在成为并应解释为根据12U.S.C.§1818颁布的最终命令，这明确的不构成，且不得被解释为构成对监理官或美国政府有约束力的合同。

（2）根据本和解令条款一监理官所述的违反法律和法规的情况，该和解令构成监理官审议的针对银行的民事罚款解决方案。从和解令生效日期起，基于前述调查结果所描述的违反法律和法规的行为，通过民事罚金，监理署解除了银行应该承担的所有潜在责任。但是，若有其他的发现，包括但不限于对银行必需的回溯重检，各项条款或本和解令均不得妨碍监理官对银行或其任何附属关联方采取执法行动，包括但不限于民事罚款。本和解令条款一所述的违反法律和法规的行为可能会被监理官用于其他将来针对银行或其附属关联方的执法行为，包括但不限于建立违规、不安全或不健全的模式或做法，或继续存在违规、不安全或不健全的模式或做法。本和解令中的任何内容均不排除或影响监理官确定并确保遵守各项条款或本和解令条款的权利。

（3）本和解令的条款，包括本款，不接受任何口头或书面的、来源于其他表述、事前协议或当事人之间的事先安排的修改。

本和解令于2014年1月7日签发

×××××××

大银行监管部

7.

■ **天价罚单落地始末**
—— 法国巴黎银行案例

　　2014年6月30日，一纸和解令（详见附录X.1，X.2）落地。高达89.7亿美元的罚款金额创下了至今无人打破的最高纪录，也引发了各界的广泛关注。欧洲金融行业翘楚法国巴黎银行缘何遭此厄运？对该行和整个金融行业有何影响？天价罚单的背后是否有迹可循？其他金融机构又能否从中获益一二？带着诸多问题，让我们走近法国巴黎银行的案例，尝试一一解开谜题。

法国巴黎银行概况

法国巴黎银行的前身可以追溯到19世纪，近两百年间见证了欧洲工业革命的繁盛、1848年法国革命和经济衰退、第一次世界大战和大萧条等重要历史变革。为了刺激经济，1966年由法国政府主导法国国民工商银行（Banque Nationale pour le Commerce et I'Industrie）与巴黎贴现国民金库（Comptoir National d'Escpmpte de Paris）合并成立了法国巴黎国民银行（Banque National de Paris），自此，BNP首次以法国银行业领跑者的身份亮相。2000年以后，法国巴黎银行通过数次收购逐步扩大在欧洲的地位和影响力，2005年收购了土耳其的TEB银行，2006年收购了意大利的BNL银行，2009年收购了比利时富通银行和卢森堡的BGL银行，2014年先后收购了波兰的BGZ银行、专门从事消费者贷款的Laser Cofinoga和德国的Dab银行。得益于风险控制、审慎均衡的收购安排和业务策略，该行在2008年金融危机后也罕见地在国际性银行中保持了连续盈利的佳绩。

目前该行是法国和欧洲按资产排名第一的全球性银行及金融服务机构，全球排名第六位，集团拥有庞大国际网络，覆盖全球74个国家和地区。该行两大主要业务板块分别为零售银行与服务和公司与机构业务。其中零售银行与服务分为本土市场和国际金融服务两个部分，本土市场包括集团4个欧元区零售网络（法国零售银行FRB、收购比利时富通银行后整合的BNP Fortis、意大利的BNL、卢森堡的LRB）和4个专业条线（包括专门从事长期公司交通工具租赁的全方位服务的Arval、提供租赁和融资解决方案的BNP租赁、运用最新技术通过Compte-Nickel提供实时账户管理服务的新数字业务和提供在线储蓄和中介服务的BNP个人投资者）。国际金融服务包括多样互补的业务活动，覆盖BNP个人融资、集团在非欧元区15个国家的零售银行组成的国际零售银行、提供储蓄和保险解决方案的BNP Cardif、BNP财富管理、BNP投资伙伴、BNP房地产等。而公司与机构业务包括公司业务、全球市场（固定收益、货币与大宗商品、股票和精选服务）和BNP证券服务三个条线，提供资本市场、证券服务、融资、财务与金融顾问等服务内容，致力于连接公司客户的融资需求和机构投资者的投资需求。

案例回顾

2014年6月30日，法国巴黎银行宣布就接受调查的涉及受制裁的某些当事方的美元清算交易与美国司法部、美国纽约州南区联邦检察官办公室、纽约郡地区检察官办公室（DANY）、美国联邦储备理事会（FED）、纽约州金融监管局（DFS）以及美国财政部海外资产控制办公室（OFAC）等多家美国当局机构达成一项综合和解令。

根据该项和解令，法国巴黎银行承认其在针对苏丹、伊朗、古巴等国家的经济制裁和相关银行记录保存操作中确有违反美国相关法律和法规的行为。为此，法国巴黎银行同意接受以下处罚：

（1）**罚款：**同意向多家美国当局机构支付总共89.7亿美元的和解费用（具体细分请见表1）；

（2）**暂停美元清算服务：**同意暂停通过法国巴黎银行纽约分行进行美元清算服务，为期一年，于2015年1月1日开始，2015年12月31日终止，包含：

A. 暂停由其纽约分行代表法国巴黎银行日内瓦、巴黎和新加坡为石油、天然气、能源和大宗商品融资业务进行的所有美元清算；

B. 暂停其纽约分行代表法国巴黎银行米兰为石油和天然气贸易融资业务和其他贸易融资业务的所有美元清算；

C. 暂停其纽约分行代表法国巴黎银行罗马为石油和天然气相关客户的所有美元清算；

D. 暂停其纽约分行代表非附属第三方银行在法国巴黎银行伦敦的存款的所有美元清算。

此外，该行同意从和解令生效日起24个月内禁止其纽约和伦敦为非附属的第三方代理银行进行美元清算。

（3）**独立顾问延期**：同意在该行、其纽约分行和纽约州金融监管局于2013年8月19日达成的谅解备忘录中关于在纽约分行现场安排独立顾问审查其在分行落实的BSA／AML、OFAC合规项目、政策和流程的基础上，将独立顾问的期限额外延长两年。除2013年谅解备忘录的条款之外，独立顾问还将监督、评估和测试法国巴黎银行的补救工作、法国巴黎银行精简其通过纽约分行的全球美元清算的实施工作，以及前述暂停美元的要求。

（4）**处罚相关人员**：同意以包括终止雇佣、减薪、降级、强制培训和警告等方式处理包括首席运营官在内的共45名相关人员。

至此，法国巴黎银行与美国多家监管机构旷日持久的谈判终于画上了一个句号。

法国巴黎银行天价罚款后续反响

法国巴黎银行的天价罚款创下了至今无人打破的最高纪录，也引发了金融市场的广泛关注和担忧。

作为欧洲排名第一、当时全球排名第四的金融机构，89.7亿美元（约合65.5亿欧元）的罚款超过了法国巴黎银行2013年全年的税后净收入（约54.4亿欧元）。剔除2013年该行为可能的罚款计提的8亿欧元的拨备，该行在2014年财报中直接计入57.5亿欧元的损失，导致税后净收入跌至5.07亿欧元。

在和解协议正式落锤前，法国政府也曾多方努力，希望避免该国第一大银行受到美国监管机构的严厉处罚，影响到该行对法国经济的支持。据了解，包括法国总统奥朗德、法国财政部长萨潘、法国央行行长诺亚等在内的多位法国高层官员均在此前为法国巴黎银行和解一事奔走斡旋，试图降低冲击。

而在受罚不可避免的事实面前，法国人也很难咽下这口气。法国央行行长诺亚在公开讲话中表示："法国企业尽可能多地使用他国货币，符合法国企业的利益最大化。比如中国和欧洲间的贸易，我们可以用欧元和人民币，停止使用美元。"而在其后的2014年6月28日，法国央行与我国央行正式签署了《中国人民银行与法兰西银行备忘录》，并根据备忘录安排在9月授权中国银行巴黎分行担任巴黎人民币清算行。法国财长萨潘其后也公开表示："美国重罚法国巴黎银行的事件促使我们认识到使用（美元以外）其他货币的必要性。未来几周，我们将就去美元化继续展开讨论"。

美国监管机构对欧资金融机构的巨额罚款也引发了整个欧洲区的忧虑。2014年7月7日，在比利时首都布鲁塞尔欧盟总部举行的欧元区财长会议上，"如何提升欧元在国际贸易中的地位"首次被列为正式议题。受此天价罚款影响，欧洲央行其后在对金融机构的压力测试中甚至考虑添加一项内容，以评估银行拨备是否足以应对美国调查银行涉嫌行为不当而导致的不断增加的费用。

法国巴黎银行案例分析与借鉴

金融危机之后的几年间，美国监管部门对在受美制裁的国家积极开展业务的欧洲金融机构进行大力调查和重罚，在法国巴黎银行之前，包括英国巴克莱银行、瑞士信贷银行、渣打银行、汇丰银行等欧资银行均因违反美国对某些敏感国家的制裁规定而受罚，累计缴纳了超50亿美元的罚金。此次法国巴黎银行的罚款更是创下了至今无人打破的最高纪录。现试就此次案例的特点分析如下：

罚款金额巨大

在法国巴黎银行和解令尘埃落定前的各种传闻中，对罚款金额的猜测从10亿美元到160亿美元，众说纷纭，最终确定的89.7亿美元虽不是最坏的结果，但也已经相当严厉。OFAC发言人曾表示，本次和解是OFAC史上最大的一笔，也再次印证了OFAC加强美国制裁规则与监管的决心。

很难想象如果不是法国巴黎银行这样实力雄厚、盈利能力强的金融机构如何能负担这样巨额的罚款，如何能从处罚的重创中快速恢复。但据法国巴黎银行2015年年报显示，该行税后净收入实现70.44亿欧元，仅用了短短一年的时间就回到了比处罚前更高的水平。

据报道，天价罚金背后的原因可能包括以下三方面：

一是法国巴黎银行涉嫌违反美国制裁令的交易量巨大。据监管机构调查报告显示，从2002年至2012年，法国巴黎银行为苏丹，伊朗和古巴受制裁方提供价值超过1 900亿美元的美元清算服务，远远超出其他机构的涉违规交易规模。

二是多家政府机构和部门都同期介入了对法国巴黎银行的调查和处罚，其中包括美国司法部、纽约南区检察官办公室、美国财政部、纽约曼哈顿地区检察官办公室和纽约金融服务局等，表1是各相关主体对应的罚款金额。

表1　美国各监管机构处罚金额明细表

类别	主体	金额（百万美元）
没收非法所得（Forfeiture）	Federal Reserve	508.00
	Department of Financial Services	2 243.40
	New York County District Attorney	2 243.40
	OFAC	963.00
	未明确	2 875.80
罚款（Fine）	未明确	140.00
合计		8 973.60

从上表的构成可以看出，罚款的大部分其实是源自非法交易的所得，罚款只有1.4亿美元。而从表面上看，没收非法所得中各家监管机构似乎实施了多重处罚，很有可能谈判的空间主要也是集中在非法交易所得的计量方式上。

三是调查中有初步证据显示个别法国巴黎银行高层人员和合规人员知晓并容忍了这种行为的存在，这可能也是处罚措施中第三条专门针对人员处罚背后的原因。

另有外媒报道称，针对法国巴黎银行的罚单其实2009年就开好了，该行一直尝试与美国当局交涉，但未能达成一致。而5年后，美国当局不但没有减少罚金，还希望借此劝阻法国政府取消向俄出售两艘西北风级两栖攻击舰，在法国政府未中止合同履行的情况下，把罚金进一步升级。

首次动用了暂停美元清算的临时性处罚

美国监管机构在针对法国巴黎银行的处理中首次动用了暂停部分美元清算业务的手段。当然，为期一年暂停该行在某些地区石油、天然气能源和大宗商品融资业务的美元直接清算的象征意义似乎大于实质——法国巴黎银行毕竟保住了各项业务牌照，绝大部分运营和业务能力没有受到影响，仅涉及某些地区的石油、天然气能源和大宗商品融资业务的美元直接清算被暂停一年。而同时该行争取到6个月的过渡期，足以将受影响的业务平稳过渡，转由第三方银行代理处理。法国巴黎银行公开表示，预计和解安排对银行的经营以及为绝大多数客户提供服务的业务能力均不构成影响。

尽管法国政府官员在公开场合表示"去美元化"，考虑提升欧元、人民币等的使用，但短时间内，无论是美元的绝对主导地位，或是美国市场本身的重要意义都使得像法国巴黎银行这样的全球性金融机构在巨大罚款的威胁之下仍然难以割舍。

作为极少数在美国同时拥有个人业务网络和证券牌照的欧洲银行之一，法国巴黎银行2014—2016年营收增长至少10%的承诺其实主要依赖其在美国、亚洲和德国的业务增长。法国巴黎银行首席执行官Jean-Laurent Bonnafe也特别指出北美是具有战略意义的市场，未来该行计划在北美进一步发展零售、资产管理和企业及投资银行业务。

提升内控合规先行到位

法国巴黎银行首席执行官Jean-Laurent Bonnafe在和解令公布后即公开表示对过去的不当行为导致此项和解深感遗憾，并表示调查曝光的失当行为与法国巴黎银行一直追寻的经营原则背道而驰。他表示将加强内部控制和流程，与美国监管当局以及法国监管机构保持密切合作，确保达到负责任行为的高标准，并要求与法国巴黎银行有关的每个人都能够达到这种高标准。

在达成和解以前，法国巴黎银行已经制定了新的、强有力的合规和控制流程。许多流程已付诸实施，这给集团的业务流程带来了重大变化。具体如下：

（1）新建立了总部位于美国纽约的集团金融安全部门，是集团合规部门的一部分，旨在确保法国巴黎银行能够在全球遵守美国监管当局制订的国际制裁和禁令方面的规定。

（2）整个法国巴黎银行集团的所有美元资金将最终通过法国巴黎银行纽约分行进行处理和控制。

2014年集团还计提了2.5亿欧元的拨备作为与和解令相关的整改方案实施成本，2015年又将这笔费用调增了1亿欧元。

归根结底，和解令和天价罚款都只是警示手段，美国监管机构和政府当局的最终目标是维护其法律法规、经济制裁和金融体系不受侵犯，和解谈判只能解决过往问题，全面提升合规管理水平才是未来稳健经营的根本。

敲响警钟，合规无小事

法国巴黎银行的案例中，一端是某些条线、某些受制裁客户的以美元计价的汇款，另一端是高达89.7亿美元，罚没法国巴黎银行其是全年税后净收入的罚款。没有这样残酷的事实摆在面前，可能很多金融从业人员都完全无法在这两个事件之间建立联系。

利用这些过往案例敲响警钟，充分强化合规意识，让各家机构、各个条线、每一个从业人员都能充分认识到触碰合规红线可能带来的严重后果，才能够建立真正有效、全面的合规防线，这也许也是这些案例的正面价值的一个侧面。

心怀敬畏，严格遵守监管规定

在法国巴黎银行的和解令中可以看到有些操作规程中对运营人员的指示是在规避监管规定动作，有些内部合规和管理人员在邮件措辞中显示他们虽然清楚业务不合规，但仍在维护客户关系和保留业务的驱动下，未能及时纠正，构成了违反法律和监管规定的书面证据，这可能在一定程度上也是巨额罚款背后的原因。

对于合规工作的管理，每家金融机构都在致力于满足各国监管的要求，但是出于机构规模、资源配置、合规管理成熟程度等方面的不同，在实际执行效果的层面必定存在差异，但是至少应该在合理范围内做到尽职尽责。此外，针对当前欠缺的方面制定逐步完善、逐级递进的实施计划，这样在监管面前做到既对当前的阶段有充分的认识，又对未来的发展有合理的规划，应该可以争取到相对理想的自我辩护地位。

附录：

《和解令》英文原文

NEW YORK STATE DEPARTMENT OF FINANCIAL SERVICES

_____X

In the Matter of

CONSENT ORDER UNDER

NEW YORK BANKING LAW § 44

BNP PARIBAS, S.A.

New York Branch

_____X

The New York State Department of Financial Services ("the Department" or "DFS") and BNP Paribas S.A., Paris, France ("BNP Paribas" or "BNPP" or the "Bank") stipulate that:

WHEREAS, BNP Paribas is a foreign bank with complex operations and multiple business lines and legal entities in many countries worldwide;

WHEREAS, BNP Paribas conducts operations in the United States through various subsidiaries and entities including its branch in New York, New York (the "New York Branch");

WHEREAS, the Department is the licensing agency of the New York Branch, pursuant to Article II of the New York Banking Law ("NYBL") and is responsible for its supervision and regulation.

WHEREAS, BNP Paribas is pleading guilty to a one-count information filed in the U.S. District Court for the Southern District of New York on June 30, 2014, which accuses the Bank of conspiracy to commit an offense against the United States in violation of Title 18, United States Code, Section 371, by conspiring to violate the International Emergency Economic Powers Act ("IEEPA"), codified at Title 50, United States Code, Section 1701 et seq., and regulations issued thereunder, and the Trading with the Enemy Act ("TWEA"), codified at Title 50. United States Code Appendix. Section 1 et seq., and regulations issued thereunder.

WHEREAS, BNP Paribas is pleading guilty to one count of Falsifying Business Records in the First Degree, pursuant to New York Penal Law Section 175.10, and one count of Conspiracy in the Fifth Degree, pursuant to New York Penal Law Section 105.05(1).

WHEREAS, in connection with the federal and state charges listed above, BNP Paribas admitted certain facts and conduct, including:

- that BNPP developed and implemented policies and procedures for processing U.S. dollar-denominated transfers through the New York Branch and unaffiliated U.S. financial institutions in a manner that was designed to conceal relevant information regarding Sudan, Iran and Cuba that would permit the institutions and their regulators to determine whether the transactions were lawful and consistent with New York State and U.S. laws and regulations; and

- that BNPP's conduct allowed sanctioned countries and entities, including Specially Designated Nationals,[①] to access the U.S. financial system and engage in billions of dollars worth of U.S. dollar-based financial transactions, significantly undermining the U.S. sanctions and embargos.

WHEREAS, BNP Paribas' conduct violated U.S. national security and foreign policy and raised serious safety and soundness concerns for regulators, including the obstruction of governmental administration, failure to report crimes and misconduct, offering false instruments for filing, and falsifying business records.

NOW, THEREFORE, the parties agree to the following:

1. From at least 2002 through 2012, BNP Paribas provided U.S. dollar clearing services on behalf of Sudanese, Iranian, and Cuban parties ("Sanctioned Parties") with a value of more than $190 billion which were settled through the New York Branch and other New York-based financial institutions.[②]

2. The transactions with the Sanctioned Parties were identified during the Bank's internal review of its U.S. dollar transactions for the period of 2002-2009 (the "Review Period").

3. In processing transactions on behalf of these Sanctioned Parties, BNP Paribas engaged in a systematic practice, as directed from high levels of the Bank's group management, of removing or omitting Sudanese, Iranian, or Cuban information from U.S. dollar- denominated payment messages that it sent through the New York Branch and other non- affiliated New York-based U.S. financial institutions to "guarantee the confidentially of the messages and to avoid their disclosure to any potential investigatory authorities."

4. The Bank's written instructions included warnings to personnel and Sanctioned Parties such as the one contained in a *Memorandum to the Operations Center* that advised with respect to a Cuban transaction, "Attention Cuba: please do not mention Cuba on the [MT-] 202 [SWIFT Messages]."[③]

5. From as early as 1995 through at least 2007 memoranda were circulated to the Bank's operations staff with the blanket directive for U.S. dollar denominated transactions involving Iran: "Do not stipulate in any case the name of Iranian entities on messages transmitted to American banks or to foreign banks installed in the U.S.A."

6. In addition to the Bank's group-wide policy instructions, individual payment instructions

---

① A Specially Designated National ("SDN") appears on a list of individuals, groups, and entities subject to economic sanctions by the United States Treasury and the Office of Foreign Assets Control ("OF AC"). SDNs are individuals and companies, specifically designated as having their assets blocked from the U.S. financial system by virtue of being owned or controlled by, or acting for on behalf of, targeted countries, as well as individuals, groups, and entities, such as terrorists and narcotics traffickers, designated under sanctions programs that are not country- specific.

② U.S. dollar clearing is the process by which U.S. dollar-denominated payments between counterparties are made through a bank in the United States.

③ The Society of Worldwide Interbank Financial Telecommunications ("SWIFT") is a vehicle through which banks exchange wire transfer messages with other financial institutions, including U.S. correspondent banks. SWIFT messages contain various informational fields.

for Sanctioned Parties contained admonitions to the Bank's staff to refrain from using identifying information. For example, one payment message for a Sudanese party was stamped "URGENT," "ATTENTION EMBARGO" and cautioned, "! Transfer in $ without mentioning [Sudanese Bank] to the USA!!!"

New York

7. Compliance staff at the New York Branch operated knowing that they did not have adequate legal and compliance authority to ensure that activities conducted from BNP Paribas offices outside of the United States complied with New York and U.S. laws and regulations. This practice was intentional. In a January 2006 email addressing the question of whether or not the Bank's Energy, Commodities, Export & Project ("ECEP") group ran the risk of an allegation of circumventing the U.S. embargo, a BNPP employee described an "omission" procedure as follows: "A practice exists which consists in omitting the Beneficiaries/Ordering party's contact information for USD transactions regarding clients from countries that are under U.S. embargo: Sudan, Cuba, Iran. This avoids putting BNPP NY in a position to uncover these transactions, to block them, and to submit reports to the regulator."

8. Even the highest levels of the compliance division for the New York Branch recognized and accepted that amending, omitting and stripping was widespread among foreign banks transmitting funds through the U.S. When a settlement with U.S regulators and Dutch bank ABN AMRO was announced for violations of U.S. sanctions law, the Head of Ethics and Compliance North America wrote in an email to another employee, "the dirty little secret isn't so secret anymore, oui?"

9. In response to an email from the compliance office of the New York Branch, which raised concerns about employing cover payments to make a transaction nontransparent, BNPP compliance officers in Paris discussed how best to deal with the matter. According to documents obtained by the U.S. Department of Justice, the Parisian compliance officers weighed the costs and benefits of deceiving the New York Branch as opposed to an unaffiliated U.S. bank:

> If [the New York head of ethics and compliance] only offers the choice between abandoning the [cover payments] for movement in favor of clientele or promising BNPP NY we do not wire transfer in USD concerning Cuba, Iran, Sudan or Syria, I only see the solution of going through another bank than BNPP NY for all transactions to these destinations. The other, less gratifying alternatives are to stop working in USD in these zones or to disguise the reality with the no win situation between telling stories to BNPP NY or to [the unaffiliated U.S. bank].

Sudan

10. During the Review Period, BNP Paribas, through the Geneva branch of its Swiss subsidiary, BNP Paribas (Suisse) S.A. ("BNPP Geneva"), created deceptive schemes and transaction structures to conceal thousands of illegal Sudanese transactions from scrutiny by U.S. financial institutions, regulators and authorities. These transactions were valued at more than $20 billion dollars.

11. BNPP Geneva developed deceptive policies, procedures and transaction structures in order to process U.S. dollar-denominated funds transfers through the New York Branch and other

U.S. financial institutions for sanctioned Sudanese parties.

12. In BNPP Geneva's back office, there was policy to strip, amend and omit elements of U.S. dollar payment messages that could serve to identify Sanctioned Parties, including most prominently, those related to Sudan. An internal policy for processing U.S. dollar payments involving Sudan stated: "Do not list in any case the name of Sudanese entities on messages transmitted to American banks or to foreign banks installed in the U.S."

13. This policy intentionally prevented U.S. institutions from performing required screening for the presence of Sanctioned Parties on U.S. dollar-denominated transactions and hid from U.S. regulators and authorities the participation of Sudanese entities in U.S. dollar-denominated transactions.

14. Among these Sanctioned Parties were 18 Sudanese SDNs, of which six were clients of BNPP. During the period used by the Justice Department to calculate the volume of Federal Violations, BNPP executed approximately $4 billion dollars in transactions for these SDNs. For the most part, these transactions were processed for a financial institution owned by the Government of Sudan. During the entire Review Period, there were over $6 billion dollars in transactions processed for SDNs.

15. BNPP Geneva managed or financed billions of dollars worth of U.S. dollar-denominated letters of credit for Sudanese parties. In order to transmit the payment messages associated with the letters of credit through New York financial institutions, BNPP Geneva stripped and omitted references to Sudan in the messages to prevent the transaction from being blocked in the U.S. These transactions were designed to avoid the detection of sanctions violations by U.S. regulators.

16. Soon after the imposition of U.S. sanctions against Sudan in 1997, BNPP Geneva established account relationships with unaffiliated regional banks ("Regional Banks") located in Africa, Europe and the Middle East, eventually nine in all, some with no other business purpose than to clear payments for Sudanese clients.[①] The accounts with the Regional Banks were created and established to provide a means to circumvent U.S. sanctions.

17. Specifically, BNPP Geneva utilized the Regional Banks in a two-step process designed to enable BNPP Geneva's Sudanese clients to evade U.S. sanctions. In the first step, a Sudanese bank seeking to move U.S. dollars out of Sudan transferred funds internally within BNPP Geneva to a BNPP Geneva account specifically maintained by a Regional Bank to facilitate U.S. dollar transfers from Sudan. In the second step, the Regional Bank transferred the money to the Sudanese bank's intended beneficiary through a U.S. bank without reference to the Sudanese bank. As a result, it appeared to the U.S. bank that the transaction was coming from the Regional Bank rather than a Sudanese bank.

18. A similar process enabled sanctioned Sudanese banks to receive U.S. dollars without being detected: the originator of the transaction sent a wire transfer through the United States to the Regional Bank's account at BNPP Geneva without reference to Sudan, and the Regional Bank then transferred the money to the Sudanese bank via internal transfer at BNPP Geneva. Moreover, in order to further disguise the true nature of the Regional Bank transactions, employees at BNPP

---

① In the account opening documentation for these banks the following notation appeared: "As requested, we hereby confirm that we wish to open the account to facilitate transfers of funds for our mutual Sudanese customers."

Geneva frequently worked with the Regional Banks to wait between one and two days after the internal transfer before making a dollar-for-dollar, transaction-by-transaction, clearing of funds through the United States, delinking the U.S. transfer of funds from the prior transfer involving the Regional Banks so that financial institutions in the United States and U.S. authorities would be unable to link the payments to the involved Sanctioned Party.

19. In fact, BNPP employees internally proposed to BNPP Geneva compliance staff that they should get the Regional Banks "accustom [ed]... to spacing out the gap between covers they execute with their U.S. correspondents to the extent possible." Ultimately, BNPP Geneva successfully used the Regional Bank structure, which had no business purpose other than to help BNPP's Sudanese clients evade the U.S. embargo, to process thousands of U.S. dollar transactions, worth billions of dollars in total.

20. The use of Regional Banks to facilitate U.S. dollar transactions with Sudanese Sanctioned Parties was widely known within BNPP Geneva. For example, in a 2004 email to a BNPP Geneva front office employee, a Regional Bank requested "to open an account at BNP Paribas Genev[a] to be used mainly for the USD Transfers to and from Sudanese Banks." This email was forwarded to another BNPP Geneva front office employee who recommended opening the account, as "the opening of this account fits in the framework of our activity in Sudan." Referencing this exchange, another BNPP Geneva employee commented that: "we have advised [Regional Bank] for a long time to open a VOSTRO account to facilitate the transactions which this institution has with countries with which we are also active."

21. BNPP compliance officers warned the BNPP business employees of their concerns regarding the Sudanese business. In an August 2005 email, a senior compliance officer warned, "[We] have a number of Arab Banks (nine identified) on our books that only carry out clearing transactions for Sudanese banks in dollars...This practice effectively means that we are circumventing the U.S. embargo on transactions in USD by Sudan." The BNPP business managers were more concerned with BNPP's "goodwill in the Sudan," and therefore the business continued despite the warnings from compliance officers.

22. In September 2005, senior compliance officers at BNPP Geneva arranged a meeting of BNPP executives "to express, to the highest level of the bank, the reservations of the Swiss Compliance office concerning the transactions executed with and for Sudanese customers." The meeting was attended by several senior BNPP Paris and Geneva executives, including BNPP's Chief Operating Officer ("COO") at the time. At the meeting, the COO dismissed the concerns of the compliance officials and requested that no minutes of the meeting be taken.

23. BNPP's compliance personnel continued to warn against BNPP's use of Regional Banks to process transactions with Sanctioned Parties. For example, a 2005 compliance report described the scheme as follows:

> The main activity of certain BNPP customers is to domicile cash flows in USD on our books on behalf of Sudanese banks. These arrangements were put in place in the context of the U.S. embargo against Sudan...The accounts of these banks were therefore opened with the aim of "facilitating transfers of funds in USD for Sudanese banks." This comment was made on the account opening application forms of these banks. The funds in question were then transferred, on the same day or at latest D+1 or 2 by the [Regional Banks] to [U.S.

correspondent banks].

24. Despite the warnings, BNPP's senior compliance personnel agreed to continue the Sudanese business and rationalized the decision by stating that "the relationship with this body of counterparties is a historical one and the commercial stakes are significant. For these reasons, Compliance does not want to stand in the way of maintaining this activity for ECEP..."

25. Asa result of BNPP's conduct, the Government of Sudan and numerous banks connected to the Government of Sudan, including SDNs, were able to access the U.S. financial system and engage in billions of dollars' worth of U.S. dollar-based financial transactions, significantly undermining the U.S. embargo.

26. As the principal foreign bank for the Government of Sudan, BNPP Geneva had an essential role in the Government of Sudan's financial stability. BNPP Geneva held accounts for a financial institution owned by the Government of Sudan since 1997 for, among other purposes, illicit U.S. dollar clearing.

27. Internal Bank memoranda regarding BNPP's Sudanese business that discussed the political environment and the "crisis in Darfur" also discussed the economic environment and the Sudanese oil industry's "financial dynamism." In fact, many senior executives at BNPP were well aware of the crisis in Darfur and the illicit role Sudan has played in international issues of concern. BNPP officials have described Darfur as a "humanitarian catastrophe," and, while discussing the Sudanese business, noted that certain Sudanese banks "play a pivotal part in the support of the Sudanese government which.. .has hosted Osama Bin Laden and refuses the United Nations intervention in Darfur."

Iran

28. From at least 2002 through November 2012, several BNP Paribas branches, including Paris, London, Geneva, Rome and Milan, developed and implemented policies and procedures to systematically conceal at least $160 billion in U.S. dollar- denominated payments on behalf of Iranian customers. These transactions were processed by the New York Branch and other New York-based financial intuitions by use of a cover payment method.

29. BNP Paribas used policy directives, such as those contained in the February 2007 *Operating Application for Filtering of Transactions under the Group Policy on Iran*, to ensure that SWIFT MT 202 cover payment messages meant to be processed through New York from BNPP reflected only the identity of the "receiving institution (and not the [ultimate] Iranian beneficiary institution!)" (emphasis in the original).

30. By making these transactions nontransparent, BNPP rendered its New York Branch and other New York-based financial institutions incapable of making and maintaining records of any such U.S. dollar payment transaction that cleared through the institution, and accordingly prevented review of such records by regulators and authorities. In this way, BNPP also rendered its New York Branch and other New York-based financial institutions helpless to detect payments that should have been rejected or blocked under U.S. law.

31. Using its concealment practices, BNPP Paris was able to maintain its relationship with at least one Iranian-controlled petrochemical client ("Iranian Petrochemical Client") from 2006 through most of 2012, processing payments on its behalf in the amount of approximately one half

billion U.S. dollars. ① These payments were made in connection with three letters of credit BNPP issued in 2006, 2008 and 2011.

32. BNPP's "know your customer" ("KYC") documentation for Iranian Petrochemical Client demonstrated that while it was registered as a corporation in Dubai, it was wholly owned by an Iranian energy group based in Tehran, Iran, which was in turn fully controlled and owned by an Iranian citizen.

33. In 2010, BNPP revealed to its regulators that it had commenced an internal investigation into its compliance with U.S. sanctions, pledging immediate remedial efforts and its full cooperation with U.S. and New York regulators and authorities. Nevertheless, the Bank continued to process U.S. dollar-denominated transactions on behalf of Iranian Petrochemical Client despite the warnings from two financial institutions that had rejected transactions for Iranian Petrochemical Client as prohibited.

Cuba

34. Beginning from at least as early as 2000 and continuing through 2010, BNPP participated in eight Cuban Credit Facilities that involved U.S. dollar clearing valued at more than $7 billion and that were not licensed by OFAC. The Cuban Credit Facilities were managed out of BNPP Paris, and each facility processed hundreds (and in some cases thousands) of U.S. dollar transactions in violation of U.S. sanctions. One such credit facility involved U.S. dollar loans for one of Cuba's largest state-owned commercial companies which was an SDN.

35. BNPP was fully aware of the legal risks. In a January 2006 internal email, one employee at BNPP Paris asked a BNP Paribas compliance officer, "when we lend money to the Cubans, the loans are generally made out in [d]ollars...[c]ould we be reprimanded, and if so, based on what?" The compliance officer responded to that employee and others, including a senior manager at BNPP Paris: "These processing transactions obliges us to obscure information regarding the USD (BNPP NY) Clearer, and it is a position which BNPP is not comfortable with, and which, of course, offers a risk to its image and, potentially, a risk for reprisals from US authorities if this behavior was discovered..."

36. With a book-to-book, bank-to-banlc scheme, BNPP Paris and its sanctioned Cuban clients obscured from regulators and authorities the access provided to the U.S. financial system. In an April 2000 credit application for one of the Cuban Credit Facilities, two BNPP Paris employees acknowledged in at least one case that the sole motivating factor for using these deceptive structures was the "[l]egal risk linked to the American embargo."

37. BNPP Paris and its Cuban clients each held accounts at an unaffiliated French bank so that a transaction between a Cuban party's account and an account held at the same bank by BNPP Paris was recorded as a book-to-book funds transfer. Such transactions created no evidence of BNPP's funds clearing in U.S. dollars for the Sanctioned Cuban Parties. In a separate step, however, BNPP Paris transferred the U.S. dollars (cleared on its own behalf through its New York Branch or another

---

① By November 2008 there was no legal method by which Iranian Petrochemical Client could have accessed the U.S. financial system; nevertheless, by covertly processing U.S. dollar transactions for it, BNPP facilitated Iranian Petrochemical Client' s ability to trade in U.S. dollars through November 2012. Consequently, all transactions between November 2008 and November 2012 were in direct violation of U.S. sanctions.

New York-based financial institution). They went from BNPP Paris' account at the unaffiliated French bank to a transit account held at BNPP's Paris branch in a bank-to-bank transfer. Sometimes skipping the step of depositing U.S. dollar funds into the transit account, BNPP Paribas would either initially — or within a brief period of time — forward those funds to the Cuban Parties' accounts.

38. For the most part, wire messages for the Cuban Credit Facilities that were processed through BNPP's New York Branch made no reference to Cuba or a Sanctioned Cuban Party. BNPP Paris gave Cuban clients and other participants of the credit facilities clear instructions to refrain from doing so. In one email communication, a BNPP Paris employee directed the representative of a Sanctioned Cuban Party to omit the name of a Cuban bank on a SWIFT payment message; otherwise, the BNPP Paris employee warned, "these funds risk to be stopped by United Statefs] further to the embargo." Taking heed, the employee of the Sanctioned Cuban Party replied that he would indeed cancel the existing wire message, and execute one "following your instructions."

39. When references to Cuba accidentally appeared in three payment instructions dispatched to the U.S., BNPP staff stripped references to Cuba and resubmitted SWIFT messages to replace those that had been detected and blocked. A replacement message, now void of any reference to Cuba was then sent by BNPP to an unaffiliated U.S. bank.

40. The Bank structured resubmitted payments so that dollar amounts could not be matched and once again blocked in the U.S. To ensure that their resubmissions were not detected by the U.S., BNPP Paris staff, on at least one occasion, combined the dollar amounts of three payments into just one stripped message, aggregating the total value of the original three in the resubmitted replacement message. This prevented the possibility of matching the dollar- amount match to the three previously rejected messages. The extent of the Bank's deception was demonstrated by one senior attorney at BNPP's Paris headquarters in early 2006: "[m]y concern comes from the fact that we cannot rule out that we would have to explain to OFAC that this is part of a long standing facility with Cuban entities. Could that trigger a retroactive investigation of all prior payments...?"

41. In late 2006 and early 2007, BNPP Paris compliance personnel tried to persuade the Bank to convert the U.S. dollar Cuban Credit Facilities to another currency, such as Euros. Nevertheless, some of the Cuban Credit Facilities remained denominated in U.S. dollars for several years, with one operating in U.S. dollars until 2010. Senior employees at BNPP Paris, including the Bank's then-Group Plead of ECEP, allowed these credit facilities to operate in U.S. dollars, in violation of U.S. law, due to BNPP's long relationships with the Cuban Parties and calculated costs to the Bank in attempting to convert their credit facilities to Euro- denominated loans. In a memo issued at the end of 2009, one ECEP employee referenced an existing Cuban Party as a "historic client," a "major player in the Cuban economy," and a "strategic customer with whom we intend to arrange new financing secured by offshore flows."

42. In January 2007, the head of compliance at BNPP Paris received a memorandum entitled *Respect of Cuban Embargo*, acknowledging that BNPP had been systematically bypassing the U.S. sanctions against Cuba by permitting Cuban Parties to borrow U.S. dollars. The memorandum concluded that "[t]otal transparency is not currently possible" because "[c]hanging the payment currency during the process with a pool of participants would be long and costly." Just a few months later, a compliance officer at BNPP Paris sent a memo to senior BNPP Paris compliance and ECEP personnel entitled *Compliance with the Cuba embargo*. The memo set forth two possibilities for dealing with a Cuban Credit Facility that was still dollar denominated: (1) "[s]et this facility

aside from the official inventory with regard to the US so long as it cannot be converted into Euros or another currency;" or (2) "[i]f Group Compliance needs to be totally transparent with regard to the US authorities, the facility currency will have to be modified...[T]his option would trigger off an onerous process of negotiations with the banks and the borrowers, and ECEP will not have total control over the outcome: our decision to be OFAC compliant is a minor concern for the other parties." In the end, the memo concluded, "[g]iven its marginal character, we suggest that this facility should be kept silent, it is totally discreet and is reimbursed via internal wire transfers."

Violations of the Banking Law and Regulations

43. BNPP failed to maintain or make available at its New York Branch true and accurate books, accounts and records reflecting all transactions and actions in violation of Banking Law § 200-c.

44. BNPP officers, directors, and employees made false entries in BNPP's books, reports and statements and willfully omitted to make true entries of material particularly pertaining to the U.S. dollar clearing business of BNPP at its New York Branch with the intent to deceive the Superintendent and examiners of the Department and representatives of other U.S. regulatory agencies who were lawfully appointed to examine BNPP's conditions and affairs at its New York Branch in violation of Banking Law § 672.1.

45. The Department's regulation, 3 NYCRR § 300.1, requires BNPP to submit a report to the Superintendent immediately upon the discovery of fraud, dishonesty, making of false entries and omission of true entries, and other misconduct, whether or not a criminal offense, in which any BNPP employee was involved. It knowingly failed to do so for several years.

46. In 2004, a joint examination by the Department's predecessor agency and the Federal Reserve Bank of New York ("FRB-NY") identified systemic failures in BNPP's compliance with Bank Secrecy Act and Anti-Money Laundering (BSA/AML) requirements. Of particular note were deficiencies in monitoring by BNPP's New York Branch of the Bank's correspondent banking relationships with overseas clients, including its processing of U.S. dollar-denominated transactions. Based on the regulators' findings, BNPP voluntarily entered into a Memorandum of Understanding, dated September 16, 2004 (the "2004 MOU"), with the Department and the FRB-NY, vowing to remediate, among other things, BNPP's systems for compliance with BSA/AML requirements.

47. Instead, the Bank concealed its continuing violations from the regulators and authorities in New York. During that same 2004 period, internal documents obtained from the Bank demonstrate that BNPP's most senior operations, compliance and legal staff knew of the Bank's serous illegal conduct in violation of laws and regulations, and, rather than report the conduct to the Bank's regulators, actively supported it.

48. In 2004, BNPP executives from its Paris headquarters and its Geneva branch met on the subject of U.S. embargoes "against sensitive countries (Sudan, Libya, Syria...)" and their impact on BNPP's business. To shield the New York Branch from potential regulatory enforcement actions, BNPP officials fashioned a solution whereby BNPP Geneva would use an unaffiliated U.S. bank to conduct illicit U.S. dollar-denominated transactions for Sanctioned Parties. In this way, "the problem" of violating U.S. sanctions "shifted" to the unaffiliated U.S. bank.

49. Although BNPP Geneva executives were warned by a BNPP Geneva compliance officer that clearing through an unaffiliated U.S. bank in this manner could be viewed as a "serious breach" and a "grave violation," the practice continued throughout the Review Period.

50. On March 3, 2008, the Department and FRB-NY terminated the 2004 MOU finding the Bank compliant in all cited areas of concern. The termination letter was addressed to, among others, BNPP's then-Group Head of Compliance. The Bank was fully aware that the 2004 MOU's termination was based on falsified facts. The then-Group Head of Compliance knew and remained silent about BNPP's continuing and longstanding efforts to conduct secret transactions for Sanctioned Parties, such as Cuba. In September 2008, a more junior compliance officer emailed the then-Group Head of Compliance and other compliance staff that "[The Cuban Credit Facility], for which [BNPP had] for two years now been putting pressure on ECEP to have the USD reference abandoned, is more or less at a dead-end, and we know it will be impossible to modify without giving up something in exchange...[T]he subsistence of [the Cuban Credit Facility] in USD [ ] prevents [BNPP's] situation on Cuba from being totally 'compliant.'"

Settlement Provisions

Monetary Payment:

51. BNP Paribas shall make payment of a civil monetary penalty to the Department pursuant to Banking Law § 44 in the amount of $2,243,400,000.00. BNP Paribas shall pay the entire amount within thirty (30) days of executing the Consent Order. BNP Paribas agrees that it will not claim, assert, or apply for a tax deduction or tax credit with regard to any U.S. federal, state or local tax, directly or indirectly, for any portion of the civil monetary penalty paid pursuant to this Consent Order.

52. Additionally, BNPP shall make payment of reparations and restitution to the Department and the State of New York in the amount of $1,050,000,000.00 for injury caused by its wrongful conduct. This amount will be satisfied by the Bank's payment to the New York County District Attorney ("DANY") pursuant to the June 30, 2014 plea agreement between the Bank and DANY. The forfeiture of such funds is pursuant to CPLR § 1349 and any subsequent distribution of such funds shall be governed by the terms of the June 30, 2014 Agreement to Escrow and Distribute Forfeiture Funds entered into between DANY and the State of New York.

Suspension of U.S. Dollar Clearing:

53. On the effective date of this Order, BNP Paribas shall begin taking steps to implement the one year-long suspension of U.S. Dollar clearing services through its New York Branch described in this section (the "Suspension"). The Suspension shall begin on January 1, 2015 and terminate on December 31, 2015 and shall encompass the following:

   A. Suspension of all U.S. dollar clearing by the New York Branch on behalf of BNPP Geneva, BNPP Paris and BNPP Singapore for the oil and gas Energy & Commodity Finance business;

   B. Suspension of all U.S. dollar clearing by the New York Branch on behalf of BNPP Milan for its oil and gas Trade Finance business and for other Trade Finance business at BNPP Milan;

   C. Suspension of all U.S. dollar clearing by the New York Branch on behalf of BNPP's Rome operation for oil and gas related clients; and

   D. Suspension of all U.S. dollar clearing by the New York Branch of deposits by unaffiliated third-party banks at BNPP London.

54. Additionally, the Bank agrees to a prohibition, for a period of twenty-four (24) months

from the date of this Agreement, of U.S. dollar clearing as a correspondent bank for unaffiliated third party banks in New York and London.

55. Avoidance of Suspension:

- BNPP shall not avoid or circumvent the Suspension by using any BNPP branch, affiliate, subsidiary or entity in which BNPP has a controlling interest in the United States for U.S. Dollar Clearing.

- BNPP shall not avoid or circumvent the Suspension by moving, or causing to be moved, any client relationship or business to any other business line, branch or affiliate of BNPP.

Extension of Independent Consultant:

56. The Bank, the New York Branch and the Department entered into a Memorandum of Understanding, dated August 19, 2013 (the "2013 MOU") to install an independent consultant ("IC") on site at the New York Branch to conduct a review of the BSA/AML and OFAC compliance programs, policies and procedures in place at the Branch. The parties now agree to extend the IC's engagement for an additional two years. In addition to the terms and conditions of the 2013 MOU, the IC will oversee, evaluate and test BNPP's remediation efforts, the implementation of BNPP's efforts to streamline the global U.S. dollar clearing through the New York Branch and the U.S. dollar suspension requirements contained in this agreement.

Discipline of BNP Paribas Employees:

57. At the direction of the Department, the following individuals were terminated by or separated from the Bank as a result of the investigation: (1) the former Group Head of Compliance; (2) the former Group Chief Operating Officer; (3) the former Head of Ethics and Compliance North America; (4) the former Group Head of Structured Finance for the Corporate Investment Bank ("CIB") and former Group Head of ECEP; (5) the former Group Head of Debt Capital Markets; (6) a former attorney of BNP Paribas's CIB Legal Department; (7) a former front office employee in Paris and Geneva with responsibility for an Iranian client; (8) a former relationship manager in Geneva with responsibility for a client engaged in Sudanese business; (9) a former front office supervisor in Geneva with responsibility for a client engaged in Sudanese business; (10) a former manager in Geneva with responsibility for a client engaged in Sudanese business; (11) a former senior employee in Geneva with responsibility for clients engaged in Iranian business; (12) a former employee of ECEP with responsibility for clients engaged in Sudanese business, and (13) a former account officer in Geneva with responsibility for a client engaged Sudanese business. In total, the Bank disciplined 45 employees in connection with this investigation, with levels of discipline ranging from termination, to cuts in compensation, demotion, mandatory training sessions and warnings.

58. BNPP shall not in the future, directly or indirectly, retain any of the individuals referenced in the paragraph above, as either an officer, employee, agent, consultant, contractor of BNPP, or any affiliate of BNPP, or in any other capacity. This restriction also applies to any current or former employee who is either separated from the Bank or whose employment is terminated by the Bank as a result of any future formal disciplinary action in connection with this investigation.

Breach of the Consent Order:

59. In the event that the Department believes BNPP to be materially in breach of the Consent Order ("Breach"), the Department will provide written notice to BNPP of the Breach and BNPP must,

within ten (10) business days from the date of receipt of said notice, or on a later date if so determined in the sole discretion of the Department, appear before the Department to demonstrate that no Breach has occurred or, to the extent pertinent, that the Breach is not material or has been cured.

60. The Parties understand and agree that BNPP's failure to make the required demonstration within the specified period is presumptive evidence of BNPP's Breach. Upon a finding of Breach, the Department has all the remedies available to it under New York Banking and Financial Services Law and may use any and all evidence available to the Department for all ensuing hearings, notices, orders and other remedies that may be available under the New York Banking and Financial Services Laws.

Waiver of Rights:

61. The Parties further understand and agree that no provision of the Consent Order is subject to review in any court or tribunal outside the Department.

Parties Bound by the Consent Order:

62. It is further understood that the Consent Order is binding on the Department and BNPP, as well as their successors and assigns that are within the supervision of the Department, but it specifically does not bind any federal or other state agencies or any law enforcement authority.

63. No further action will be taken by the Department against BNPP for the conduct set forth in the Consent Order, provided that BNPP complies with the terms of the Consent Order.

64. Notwithstanding any other provision contained in the Consent Order, however, the Department may undertake action against BNPP for transactions of conduct that BNPP did not disclose to the Department in the written materials that BNPP submitted to the Department in connection with this matter.

Notices:

65. All communications regarding this Order shall be sent to:

> Elizabeth Nochlin
> Assistant Counsel
> Banking Division
> New York State Department of Financial Services
> One State Street
> New York, NY 10004

> Megan Prendergast
> Assistant Counsel
> Banking Division
> New York State Department of Financial Services
> One State Street
> New York, NY 10004

> Georges Dirani
> Group General Counsel
> BNP Paribas S.A.
> 12 Rue Chauchat
> 75450 Paris CEDEX 09, France

Miscellaneous:

66. Each provision of the Consent Order will remain effective and enforceable until stayed, modified, terminated or suspended in writing by the Department.

67. No promise, assurance, representation, or understanding other than those contained in the Consent Order has been made to induce any party to agree to the provisions of the Consent Order.

《和解令》中文译文

纽约州金融服务部（该部门或DFS）和总部位于法国巴黎的法国巴黎银行（BNP Paribas或BNPP或该银行）明确：

鉴于法国巴黎银行是一家运营复杂、拥有遍布全球许多国家的多条业务线和法人实体的外资银行。

鉴于法国巴黎银行通过各子公司和实体，包括其在纽约的纽约分行（该行纽约分行）在美国开展业务。

鉴于该部门是根据纽约银行法（"NYBL"）第二条为该行纽约分行发放牌照的机构并负责其监督和监管。

鉴于法国巴黎银行对2014年6月30日在美国纽约南区地区法院提交的一项指控表示认罪，该指控称该银行阴谋违反《美国法典》第18卷第371节，通过密谋违反《国际紧急经济权力法》（IEEPA），《美国法典》第50卷第1701节等及其下列条款，以及《敌国贸易法》（TWEA），《美国法典》第50卷附录第1节及其下列条款。

鉴于法国巴黎银行就根据《纽约刑法》第175.10条规定的一级伪造商业记录罪和《纽约刑法》第105.05（1）条规定的五级共谋罪认罪。

鉴于上述联邦和州的指控，法国巴黎银行承认了某些事实和行为，包括：

法国巴黎银行制定和实施了通过其纽约分行和其他非附属金融机构处理美元汇款的政策和程序，其制定的方式旨在隐藏与苏丹、伊朗和古巴相关的信息，而这些信息本可使各机构及其监管机构能够确定这些交易是否符合纽约州和联邦的法律法规；和法国巴黎银行的行为允许受到制裁的国家和实体，包括特别指定国民①接入美国的金融体系，参与数以十亿美元计的、基于美元的金融交易，严重破坏了美国的制裁和禁运。

鉴于法国巴黎银行的行为侵犯了美国的国家安全和外交政策，并引起监管机构对于安全和稳健的严重担忧，包括妨碍政府管理，未能报告犯罪和不当行为，提供虚假工具存档以及伪造商业记录。

因此，双方现就以下几点达成一致：

1.从2002年至2012年，法国巴黎银行为苏丹，伊朗和古巴各方（"受制裁方"）提供价值超过1 900亿美元的美元清算服务，这些服务通过纽约分行和其他基于纽约的金融机构进行结算②。

2.该银行在对2002—2009年美元交易进行内部审查（"审查期"）期间已经发现了与受制裁方进行的交易。

3.在代表这些受制裁方处理交易的过程中，法国巴黎银行根据该行集团管理层的高层指示，在该行通过其纽约分行和其他非附属的纽约的美国金融机构发送的、以美元计价的支付报文中系统性地删除或省略了苏丹、伊朗或古巴的国民信息，以"保证信息的机密性，并避免向任何潜在的调查机构披露信息"。

4.该行书面指示中包括向雇员和受制裁方提出警告，例如《运营中心备忘录》中所载的就古巴交易的建议："注意古巴：请不要在MT202 SWIFT报文中提及古巴。"③

5.从1995年起，直到2007年，分发给该行运营人员的备忘录中就以美元计价的涉伊朗交易概括指示为："在任何情况下，不要将伊朗实体的名称明确在发送给美国银行或在美运营外国银行的报文中。"

6.除该行集团层面的政策指示外，针对受制裁方的单独付款指示中告诫该行雇员不要使用识别信息。例如，一个给苏丹主体的支付报文上加盖了"紧急"，"注意禁

---

① 特别指定国民（"SDN"）出现在受美国财政部和外国资产管制办公室（OFAC）经济制裁的个人，团体和实体名单中。 SDN是个人和公司，被指定为拥有，控制或代表目标国家以及代表目标国家的个人，团体和实体（如恐怖分子）阻止他们的资产从美国金融体系中被阻止以及根据制裁方案指定的非国家特定毒品贩运者。

② 美元清算是通过美国的银行在交易对手之间进行以美元计价的付款。

③ 环球同业银行金融电讯协会（"SWIFT"）是银行与其他金融机构，包括美国代理银行，交换汇款信息的中枢。 SWIFT报文包含各种信息字段。

运"的印章，并提示："! 美元汇款不要向美国方提起[苏丹银行]!!!"

纽约

7.纽约分行的合规雇员知道他们没有足够的法律和合规授权来确保法国巴黎银行在美国境外机构开展的活动符合纽约和美国的法律和法规。这种做法是故意的。在2006年1月的一封电子邮件中，针对该行能源、商品、出口和项目（ECEP）团队是否存在规避美国禁运的指控风险，法国巴黎银行一名员工对"省略"的程序描述如下："存在的做法是针对涉及美国禁运的苏丹、古巴和伊朗等国客户的美元交易，省去受益方/发起方的联系报文，这样可以避免将法国巴黎银行纽约分行置于能够发现这些交易，阻拦它们，并向监管机构提交rep01的境地。"

8.即使是纽约分行合规部门的最高级别也认识到并接受这种修改、省略和剥离在外国银行通过美国转移资金的过程中普遍存在的现实。当荷兰银行ABN AMRO与美国监管机构宣布就违反美国制裁法达成和解时，北美道德与合规负责人在给另一名雇员的电子邮件中写道："这肮脏的小秘密不再那么秘密了，是吧？"

9.针对纽约分行合规办公室发出的一封担忧使用隐蔽付款使交易不透明的电子邮件，法国巴黎银行巴黎的合规人员在回复中讨论了处理此事最好的方式。

根据美国司法部获得的文件，巴黎的合规人员权衡了欺骗纽约分行或是一家非附属的美国银行的成本和效益：

如果[纽约道德与合规负责人]仅提供两个选择，放弃给受益人客户群体的隐蔽汇款或是向法国巴黎银行纽约分行承诺不再办理涉古巴、伊朗、苏丹或叙利亚的美元汇款，在我看来唯一的解决方案就是通过法国巴黎银行纽约分行以外的另一家银行完成所有涉及这些目的的交易。不那么令人满意的选择包括在这些区域停止美元服务，或者掩盖现实，在"无盈"情况下选择向法国巴黎银行纽约分行或[非附属的美国银行]编造故事。

苏丹

10.在审查期间，法国巴黎银行通过其瑞士子行日内瓦分行（法国巴黎银行日内瓦）构造欺骗计划和交易结构，向美国金融机构、监管机构和当局隐瞒了数千笔非法的苏丹国民交易。这些交易价值超过200亿美元。

11. 法国巴黎银行日内瓦制定了欺骗性政策、流程和交易结构，以便通过纽约分行和其他美国金融机构为受制裁的苏丹主体方处理以美元计价的资金转移。

12. 在法国巴黎银行日内瓦的后台，有旨在剥离、修改和省略美元支付报文元素的政策，这些信息本可用来识别受制裁方，包括最突出的与苏丹有关的内容。处理涉及苏丹的美元付款的内部政策规定："在任何情况下，在发送给美国的银行或在美运营的外国银行的报文中都不要列出苏丹实体名称"。

13. 该政策刻意妨碍美国机构按要求筛查以美元计价的交易中存在的受制裁主体，并向美国监管机构和当局隐瞒苏丹实体参与以美元计价的交易。

14. 在这些受制裁主体中有18个是苏丹的SDN，其中6个是法国巴黎银行的客户。在司法部用于计算该行违反联邦法规的期间，法国巴黎银行为这些SDN执行了大约40亿美元的交易。这些交易大部分是为苏丹政府拥有的金融机构处理的。在整个审查期，为SDN处理的交易总额超过60亿美元。

15. 法国巴黎银行日内瓦为苏丹主体价值数十亿美元的美元信用证提供管理或融资。为了通过纽约金融机构传递与这些信用证相关的付款报文，法国巴黎银行日内瓦在报文中剥离和省略了其中提及苏丹的内容，以防止交易在美国被拦截。这些交易的设计旨在避免被美国监管机构发现违反制裁规定。

16. 1997年美国对苏丹实施制裁后不久，法国巴黎银行日内瓦与位于非洲、欧洲和中东的无附属关系的区域性银行（区域银行）建立了账户关系，最终共有9家，其中几家仅出于为苏丹客户处理清算付款的商业目的[①]。在区域银行创建和开立账户是为了避开美国制裁。

17. 具体而言，法国巴黎银行日内瓦利用区域银行，设计了分两步的流程，目的是使法国巴黎银行日内瓦的苏丹客户能够避开美国制裁。第一步，试图将美元转出苏丹银行在法国巴黎银行日内瓦内部先将资金转移到法国巴黎银行日内瓦由区域银行专门维护的账户，以便将美元从苏丹转移出去。第二步，区域银行通过一家美国银行将这笔钱转给苏丹银行的指定受益人，而不提及苏丹银行。这样，在美国的银行看来，这笔交易来自区域银行而不是苏丹银行。

---

① 在这些银行的开户文件中，出现了以下表述："按要求，我们在此确认，我们希望开设账户以方便为我们共同的苏丹客户完成资金转移。"

18.类似的流程可以让受制裁的苏丹银行接收美元而不被发现：交易的发起人通过美国将汇款转入区域银行在法国巴黎银行日内瓦的账户，而不提及苏丹，然后区域银行通过法国巴黎银行日内瓦内部转移将钱转给苏丹银行。此外，为了进一步掩盖区域银行交易的实质，法国巴黎银行日内瓦的员工经常与区域银行合作，在内部转移后等待一至两天后再通过美国进行美元对美元、逐笔交易的资金清算，隔离美国的资金转移与此前区域银行参与的资金转移，这样美国金融机构和美国当局就无法将付款与参与的受制裁方联系起来。

19.事实上，法国巴黎银行的员工内部向日内瓦合规工作人员建议，他们应该让区域银行"习惯于……尽可能地将其执行的隐蔽交易与其美国代理行间隔开来"。最终，法国巴黎银行日内瓦成功使用了区域银行的结构处理了上千笔美元交易，总价值达数十亿美元。而该结构的商业目的仅在于帮助法国巴黎银行的苏丹客户逃避美国禁运。

20.利用区域银行完成与苏丹受制裁主体的美元交易在法国巴黎银行日内瓦内部广为人知。例如，2004年，一家区域银行在2004年发给法国巴黎银行日内瓦前台员工的电子邮件中，要求"在法国巴黎银行日内瓦开立一个账户主要用于向苏丹银行进行美元转账"。这封电子邮件被转发给另一位法国巴黎银行日内瓦前台员工，后者建议开立账户，因为"开立该账户符合我们在苏丹的活动框架"。另一位法国巴黎银行日内瓦员工引用这段内容并称："我们长期以来一直建议[区域银行]开设账户，以完成在该机构与我们都活跃的国家的交易。"

21.法国巴黎银行合规官向业务人员提示对苏丹业务的担忧。在2005年8月的一封电子邮件中，一位高级合规官员警告说："我们账上有数家阿拉伯银行（已确定的有9家），只为苏丹银行进行美元清算交易……这种做法实际上意味着我们在规避美国禁止苏丹进行美元交易的规定。"法国巴黎银行的业务人员更关心法国巴黎银行"在苏丹的商誉"，因此，尽管合规官提出警告，业务仍在继续。

22.2005年9月，法国巴黎银行日内瓦高级合规官安排了法国巴黎银行高层会议"向银行最高层表达瑞士合规办公室就与苏丹客户执行交易的保留意见"。巴黎和日内瓦的几位高级管理人员，包括法国巴黎银行的首席运营官（以下简称首席运营官）当时出席了会议。在这次会议上，首席运营官驳回了合规官员的担忧，并要求不做会议记录。

23.法国巴黎银行的合规人员继续警告法国巴黎银行使用区域银行处理与受制裁方的交易。例如，2005年的合规报告对该做法进行如下描述：法国巴黎银行某些客户的主要活动是代表苏丹银行在我们账上处置美元现金流。这些安排是在美国对苏丹实行禁运的背景下进行的。因此，这些银行的账户是为了"便利向苏丹银行进行美元资金转移"而开立的。上述评论被写在这些银行的开户申请表上。相关资金其后于当天或最迟1至2天后由[区域银行]转移至[美国代理行]。

24.尽管有这些警告，法国巴黎银行的高级合规人员同意继续苏丹业务并合理化该决策称"与交易对手的关系是有历史的，而且商业利害关系显著，出于上述原因，合规部门不希望阻碍为ECEP维持这些业务活动……"

25.由于法国巴黎银行的行为，苏丹政府和许多与苏丹政府有关联的银行，包括SDN，都能够进入美国的金融体系，参与价值达数十亿美元的基于美元的金融交易，严重破坏了美国的禁运。

26.作为苏丹政府主要的外国银行，法国巴黎银行日内瓦在苏丹政府的金融稳定方面发挥了关键作用。自1997年以来，法国巴黎银行日内瓦为苏丹政府拥有的一家金融机构开立账户，用于非法美元清算以及其他目的。

27.关于法国巴黎银行苏丹业务的银行内部讨论政治环境和"达尔富尔危机"的备忘录中也探讨了经济环境和苏丹石油工业的"金融活力"。事实上，法国巴黎银行的许多高级管理人员都深知达尔富尔危机以及苏丹在国际关注问题上所扮演的不当角色。法国巴黎银行官员称达尔富尔为"人道主义灾难"，并在讨论苏丹业务时指出，某些苏丹银行"在支持苏丹政府……接纳乌萨马·本·拉登并拒绝联合国干预达尔富尔方面发挥了关键作用"。

伊朗

28.从2002年至2012年11月，包括巴黎，伦敦，日内瓦，罗马和米兰在内的若干法国巴黎银行分行制定并实施了政策和流程，以系统性地隐瞒其代表伊朗客户进行的至少1 600亿美元的美元付款。这些交易由纽约分行和纽约的其他金融机构通过隐蔽付款处理。

29.法国巴黎银行采用政策指令，例如2007年2月集团政策下的交易过滤操作应用中所载的针对伊朗的内容，来确保从法国巴黎银行发出，将通过纽约处理的SWIFT MT 202拨付报文的付款信息仅反映"接收机构（而不是[最终]伊朗受益机构）的身份！"（原件中强调）。

30.通过使这些交易变得不透明，法国巴黎银行使其纽约分行和其他纽约金融机构无法生成和保存通过该机构清算的任何此类美元付款的交易记录，从而避免监管机构和当局对这些记录进行审查。通过这种方式，法国巴黎银行也使纽约分行和其他纽约金融机构无法检测根据美国法律应该被拒绝或拦截的付款。

31.通过隐瞒操作，从2006年至2012年的大部分时间，法国巴黎银行能够保持与至少一名伊朗控制的石化客户（以下简称伊朗石化客户）的关系，代其处理大约十五亿美元的付款①。这些付款牵涉2006年，2008年和2011年法国巴黎银行开出的三张信用证。

32. 法国巴黎银行对伊朗石化客户的"了解你的客户"（KYC）文件表明，虽然它是一家注册在迪拜的公司，但它由位于伊朗德黑兰的伊朗能源集团全资拥有，而伊朗能源集团由伊朗公民控制和持有。

33. 2010年，法国巴黎银行向监管机构透露，其已经开始针对美国制裁的合规情况进行内部调查，承诺立即采取补救措施并与美国和纽约监管机构及当局全面合作。然而，尽管两家金融机构拒绝了应被禁止的伊朗石化客户的交易，并提出警告，该银行仍继续代伊朗石化客户处理美元计价交易。

古巴

34.至少从2000年开始到2010年，法国巴黎银行参加了8个古巴信贷项目，涉及价值超过70亿美元的美元清算，而且没有获得OFAC的许可。古巴的信贷项目是由法国巴黎银行管理的，每个项目都处理了数百笔（有时甚至是数千笔）违反美国制裁的美元交易。其中一项信贷项目涉及给古巴最大的国有商业公司之一，也是SDN主体发放美元贷款。

35. 法国巴黎银行充分认识到法律风险。在2006年1月的一封内部电子邮件中，法国巴黎银行的一名员工向合规官询问："当我们借钱给古巴人时，贷款一般都是用美元发放的……我们会否受到谴责，如果会，是基于什么理由？"合规官对该员工和其他人员，包括一位法国巴黎银行高级经理作出的回应为：

---

① 截至2008年11月，伊朗石化客户再无合法途径接入美国金融体系；尽管如此，通过隐蔽处理美元交易，法国巴黎银行助长了伊朗石化客户在2012年11月之前以美元进行贸易的能力。因此，2008年11月至2012年11月间的所有交易都直接违反了美国的制裁。

"这些处理的交易使得我们有必要隐瞒有关美元（法国巴黎银行纽约）清算机构的信息，这是法国巴黎银行不愿置身的情境，当然也会给它的形象带来风险，如果这种行为被发现，还可能招致美国当局报复……"

36.通过账面和银行转换的安排，法国巴黎银行及其受制裁的古巴客户避开监管和当局的视线接入美国金融系统。在2000年4月的一份古巴信贷项目申请中，两名巴黎员工承认，在至少一起个案中使用这些欺骗性结构的唯一动机就是"与美国禁运有关的法律风险"。

37.法国巴黎银行及其古巴客户各自在一家非附属法国银行开立账户，以便古巴主体的账户与法国巴黎银行在同一家银行开立的账户之间的交易记录为账面资金转账。这样的交易不会构成法国巴黎银行为古巴受制裁方美元清算的证据。不过，在另一个步骤中，法国巴黎银行转移美元资金（通过其纽约分行或另一家纽约金融机构以自己名义清算）。他们从法国巴黎银行在非附属法国银行的账户进行一笔到法国巴黎银行巴黎分行过渡账户的银行间划拨。有时会跳过将美元资金存入过渡账户的步骤，法国巴黎银行或直接或在短时间内将这些资金转入古巴主体的账户。

38.在大部分情况下，通过法国巴黎银行纽约分行处理的古巴信贷项目报文信息都没有提及古巴或受制裁的古巴主体。法国巴黎银行向古巴客户和其他信贷机构的参与者明确指示不要提及。在一封电子邮件中，一名法国巴黎银行工作人员指示古巴受制裁主体的代表在SWIFT付款报文中省去了一家古巴银行的名字；否则，法国巴黎银行的员工警告说，"这些资金有可能被美国拦截不能进入禁运国家。"接受提示的古巴受制裁主体人员答复说，他会取消目前的汇款报文，并"遵照你的指示"另行发送一条报文。

39.当三份发给美国的付款指令中意外地提到古巴时，法国巴黎银行的工作人员剥离提及古巴的内容，并重新提交SWIFT报文，以取代那些已经被发现和拦截的报文。然后，法国巴黎银行将没有提及古巴的替代报文发给一家非附属的美国银行。

40.该行结构性地重新提交付款，使美元金额无法匹配，从而不会在美国被再次拦截。为了确保他们重新提交的报文不被美国发现，法国巴黎银行的工作人员至少一次将三笔美元付款加总为一条剥离信息的报文，重新提交的替代报文总金额是原来三笔的总和。这种做法避免了将美元金额与之前三笔被拒绝的报文匹配的可能性。法国巴黎银行巴黎总部的一位高级律师在2006年初证明了该行欺诈的程度："我担心的是，我们不能排除下述情况的可能性，即我们可能不得不向OFAC解释这是对古巴实体长期信贷安排的一部分。而这是否会引发对此前所有付款的回溯调查……？

41.在2006年末和2007年初，法国巴黎银行的合规人员试图说服该行将古巴美元信贷安排转换为另一种货币，如欧元。尽管如此，一些古巴信贷项目仍然以美元计价数年，其中一个以美元计价直到2010年。考虑到法国巴黎银行与古巴主体的长期关系，加上该行将他们的信贷转换为以欧元计价贷款的成本计算，法国巴黎银行的高级雇员，包括当时集团ECEP的负责人，允许这些信贷项目违反美国法律以美元执行。在2009年底发布的一份备忘录中，一名ECEP员工将一个存量古巴主体称为"老客户""古巴经济中的主要参与者"，以及"我们打算基于离岸资金流安排新融资的战略客户"。

42.2007年1月，法国巴黎银行的合规负责人收到了一份题为"尊重古巴禁运"的备忘录，承认该行允许古巴主体借入美元，系统性规避美国对古巴的制裁。该备忘录的结论是"目前完全透明是不可能的"，因为"与一揽子参与者在过程中改变付款币种将是漫长而昂贵的。"几个月后，法国巴黎银行的一名合规官向法国巴黎银行高级合规及ECEP人员发送了一份题为"遵守古巴禁运"的备忘录。该备忘录提出了两种处理仍然以美元计价的古巴信贷的可能性：（1）"只要不能将其转换为欧元或其他货币，就将该贷款与美国相关的官方存量设置在不同的地方"；或者（2）"如果集团合规需要对美国当局完全透明，将不得不修改贷款货币……这种选择会触发与其他银行和借款人之间烦琐的谈判进程，而且ECEP将无法完全控制结果：我们决定遵守OFAC规定对其他参与方来说只是小问题。"最后，备忘录总结说：'鉴于其边缘性质，我们建议应该对该信贷项目保持沉默，保持完全谨慎，并通过内部汇款转移进行偿付。'"

违反银行法律和监管规定

43.法国巴黎银行未能在其纽约分行保留或提供真实、准确的、可反映所有交易和行为的报表、账户和记录，违反银行法第200条c款。

44.法国巴黎银行的官员、董事和雇员在法国巴黎银行的报表、报告和陈述中制造虚假条目，并故意遗漏真实条目，特别是与法国巴黎银行纽约分行的美元清算业务相关的资料，意图欺骗主管和部门审查人员以及其他美国监管机构的代表，这些代表依法被指定在纽约分行审查法国巴黎银行的情况和事务，违反银行法第672.1条。

45.该部门监管规定3NYCRR第300.1条规定要求法国巴黎银行在发现任何法国巴黎银行雇员涉及欺诈、不诚实行为、虚假记录和遗漏真实记录以及其他不当行为时，不论是否属于刑事犯罪，应立即向主管提交报告。该行数年故意未履行上述要求。

46. 2004年，该部前身机构和纽约联邦储备银行（FRB-NY）联合进行了一次审查，发现法国巴黎银行在遵守《银行保密法》和反洗钱（BSA/AML）要求方面存在系统性不足。特别值得注意的是，法国巴黎银行纽约分行在监测本行与海外客户之间的代理行关系，包括处理以美元计价的交易方面存在缺陷。根据监管机构的调查结果，法国巴黎银行自愿于2004年9月16日与该部门和FRB-NY签署了一份谅解备忘录（2004年谅解备忘录），承诺弥补法国巴黎银行的合规体系以符合BSA / AML要求及其他内容。

47.相反，该行隐瞒其持续违反纽约监管机构和当局的行为。同样是在2004年，从银行获得的内部文件显示，法国巴黎银行最高级的运营、合规和法律人员知晓该行的严重违法违规行为，而且，并没有向银行监管机构报告，反而积极支持这些行为。

48. 2004年，巴黎总部和日内瓦分行的法国巴黎银行高管就对敏感国家（苏丹、利比亚、叙利亚等）的美国禁运及其对法国巴黎银行业务的影响举行了会议。为了保护纽约分行免受潜在的监管强制执行，法国巴黎银行官员制定了一个解决方案，通过法国巴黎银行日内瓦使用一家非附属的美国银行为受制裁主体进行以美元计价的非法交易。这样一来，违反美国制裁的"问题"就"转移"到了非附属的美国银行。

49.尽管法国巴黎银行日内瓦高级管理人员受到日内瓦合规官的警告，以这种方式通过一家非附属的美国银行清算可能被视为"严重违规"，但这种做法持续了整个审查期。

50. 2008年3月3日，部门和FRB-NY终止了2004年的谅解备忘录，认定该行在所有引述的关注领域内均合规。终止函发给了法国巴黎银行当时的集团合规主管等人。该行充分了解2004年谅解备忘录的终止是基于伪造的事实。当时的集团合规负责人了解法国巴黎银行长期以来持续为古巴等受制裁主体进行秘密交易的做法，并对此保持沉默。 2008年9月，一位初级合规官在给当时的集团合规负责人和其他合规工作人员的电子邮件说，两年来[法国巴黎银行]就[古巴信贷项目]向ECEP施加压力，要求不要提及美元，目前或多或少是条死胡同，我们都清楚在不放弃某些东西的前提下是不可能的……古巴信贷项目赖以美元维持生计，这使得法国巴黎银行的古巴局面无法完全"合规"。

和解条款

货币支付：

51.法国巴黎银行应根据《银行法》第44条向该部门支付民事罚款2 243 400 000.00美元。法国巴黎银行应在执行和解令后三十（30）日内支付全部金额。法国巴黎银行同意，不会就依据本和解令支付民事罚款的任何部分，直接或间接索取、主张或申请任何美国联邦、州或地方税的抵扣或减免。

52.此外，法国巴黎银行应就其不当行为造成的损失向该部和纽约州赔偿和补偿1 050 000 000.00美元。根据2014年6月30日该行与纽约县地区检察官（DANY）之间的认罪协议，该行将向DANY支付这笔款项。没收上述资金的依据是CPLR§1349，该笔资金后续的任何分配应遵照DANY与纽约州之间签订的托管和分配没收资金协议的条款进行。

暂停美元清算：

53.在本和解令生效日，法国巴黎银行应按照本节所述开始逐步实施暂停通过其纽约分行进行美元清算服务（暂停），为期一年。暂停将于2015年1月1日开始，并于2015年12月31日终止，并应包含以下内容：

A. 暂停由纽约分行代表法国巴黎银行日内瓦、巴黎和新加坡为石油、天然气、能源和大宗商品融资业务进行的所有美元清算；

B. 暂停纽约分行代表法国巴黎银行米兰为石油、天然气贸易融资业务和其他贸易融资业务的所有美元清算业务；

C. 暂停纽约分行代表法国巴黎银行罗马为石油和天然气相关客户的所有美元清算；

D. 暂停纽约分行代表非附属第三方银行在法国巴黎银行伦敦的存款的所有美元清算。

54. 此外，该行同意从本协议生效日起二十四（24）个月内禁止纽约和伦敦为非附属的第三方代理银行进行美元清算。

55. 规避暂停：

- 法国巴黎银行不得通过使用法国巴黎银行在美国拥有控股权的任何法国巴黎银行分行、附属机构、子公司或实体来规避或绕道暂停美元清算的安排。

- 法国巴黎银行不得通过将任何客户关系或业务移动或转移至法国巴黎银行的任何其他业务线，分行或附属公司来避免或规避暂停。

独立顾问延期：

56. 该行、其纽约分行和该部门于2013年8月19日达成一项谅解备忘录（2013年谅解备忘录），在纽约分行现场安排独立顾问（IC）审查其在分行到位的BSA/AML、OFAC合规项目、政策和流程。

各方现同意将独立顾问的参与额外延长两年。除2013年谅解备忘录的条款之外，独立顾问还将监督、评估和测试法国巴黎银行的补救工作、法国巴黎银行精简其通过纽约分行的全球美元清算的实施工作，以及本协议包含的暂停美元的要求。

法国巴黎银行员工处罚：

57. 根据该部门指示，经调查，以下人员终止雇佣或离开该行：（此处略去涉及机构及个人）。

该行共处罚了与此调查有关的45名员工，处罚方式包括终止雇佣、减薪、降级、强制培训和警告。

58. 法国巴黎银行未来不得直接或间接保留上一段提及的任何个人，作为法国巴黎银行的高级职员、雇员、代理、顾问、法国巴黎银行承包商或其任何附属机构，或任何其他身份。这一限制也适用于任何因与本次调查有关的任何未来正式处分而离开该行或被终止雇佣的现任或前任雇员。

违反和解令：

59.如果该部门认为法国巴黎银行实质性违反了和解令（"违反"），则该部门将向法国巴黎银行提出违约的书面通知，法国巴黎银行必须在收到所述通知的10个工作日内，或在该部门酌情决定的较晚日期，现身该部门来证明没有发生违规行为，或在相关情况下，证明违规行为不具实质性或已改正。

60.双方理解并同意，如法国巴黎银行未能在规定期限内按要求进行证明，将被作为法国巴黎银行违规的推定证据。在发现违规之后，该部门拥有《纽约银行业和金融服务法》所有可用的补救措施，并可使用该部门可用的全部和任何证据进行所有依据《纽约银行和金融服务法》可能的听证、通知、命令和其他补救措施。

放弃权力：

61.双方进一步理解并同意，和解令的任何条款均不受该部门以外的任何法院或仲裁庭审查约束。

62.双方进一步理解和解令对该部门和法国巴黎银行以及在该部门监督下的继承人和受让人具有约束力，但是它并不约束任何联邦或其他州立机构或任何执法机构。

63.如法国巴黎银行遵照和解令的条款，则该部门不会就和解令所陈述的行为对法国巴黎银行采取进一步行动。

64.尽管和解令中任何其他条款规定如上，但该部门可对法国巴黎银行就该行向该部门提交的与此相关的书面材料中没有披露的交易行为采取行动。

注意事项：

65.关于本和解令的所有通讯应发送至：

（此处略去涉及机构及个人）

杂项：

66.和解令的每一个条款将保持有效和可执行，直到该部门保留、修改、终止或以书面形式中止。

67.除和解令包含的内容外，没有作出任何的承诺、保证、陈述或理解诱使任何一方同意和解令条款。

特此证明，各方自2014年6月29日起执行本和解令。

8.

■ ## 此"德"非彼"德"，双德被罚
——德意志银行和德国商业银行洗钱案例

　　德意志是一片神奇的土地，在全球经济动荡时期，虽几经跌宕，德国一直是发达经济体中的一枝独秀。作为欧洲最大的经济体和贸易大国，德国金融业一直以安全和稳健著称。德国两大金融巨头——德意志银行和德国商业银行不仅是德国金融界的标志，也在世界舞台上占据了重要位置。

然而，近些年德意志银行和德国商业银行纷纷被美国监管机构开出巨额罚单，引发市场一片哗然。更有声音认为，美国在全力阻击德国金融，从金融入手打击德国经济进而打击欧盟，攻击欧元。

德意志银行和德国商业银行不论从事件背景还是事件缘由来看都存在很多共同的特点，值得一起研究。让我们一同走近德国两家大型银行被处罚事件，到底是阴谋论？还是事出有因？我们一探究竟。

德国银行体系概观

一直以来，德国的银行体系是其最具活力的经济部门，它的健康发展对促进整个社会经济和就业起到了相当大的作用。但德国的银行体系有其独特性，与我国存在着较大的差别。在介绍两家银行处罚事件之前，有必要对德国的银行体系有一个了解。

统计显示，德国合法独立的金融机构有3 200家，银行的就业率占总就业率的3%。德国的银行体系大体上可以分为两大部分：专业型银行和综合型银行。专业型银行顾名思义是以其"专业属性"区别于其他机构的银行，如抵押银行、建房信贷联会等。综合型银行包括储蓄银行、合作银行和商业银行。德国的储蓄银行一般都归当地市政所有，是由各州政府出资、为地方政府和各州经济提供融资的银行。这类银行区域性特点明显，主要服务于中小型客户，比如德国复兴信贷银行就是由国家和政府出资，以国家信用为背景的储蓄银行；合作银行在德国本土市场占据比较重要的位置，其采用三级合作银行体系，若自下而上进行区分的话，第三级合作银行由农民、城市居民、个体私营企业、合作社企业和其他中小企业入股组成，由入股股东拥有；第二级是区域合作银行，是由地方合作银行入股组成并拥有的；第一级合作银行是中央合作银行，由区域合作银行和地方合作银行入股组成。德国的商业银行都是混业经营的全能型银行，比如本文提到的德意志银行和德国商业银行就是商业银行的代表。与储蓄银行和合作银行相比，德国的商业银行更加国际化，更加具有国际影响力。这也就是美国监管机构的合规处罚主要涉及德国的商业银行的原因。

案件回顾

无独有偶，德意志银行（以下简称德银）和德国商业银行（以下简称德商）均于1870年成立。1876年，德意志银行收购德意志联合银行和柏林银行协会，成为德国最大的银行。1905年，德国商业银行和柏林银行合并，1958年迁移至法兰克福，成为德国三大银行之一。

2015年3月，纽约州金融服务局在对德商调查时发现，该行合规框架存在缺陷，同时存在向伊朗、苏丹等受制裁国家转移资金以及间接助长奥林巴斯株式会社重大会计欺诈等合规问题。当月，德商同意向美国纽约州金融服务局（以下简称金融服务局）支付约6.1亿美元罚款，以和解上述违规行为。两年后，德银同样因合规管理存在缺陷为由被金融服务局处以4.25亿美元罚款。同时，监管机构指出其纽约、莫斯科、伦敦三家分行未能发现受制裁的俄罗斯客户利用镜像交易（Mirror Trading）涉嫌跨境洗钱等违法犯罪行为也是被处罚的关键原因。

德国大型银行连续被罚，市场一片哗然。有声音认为，美国希望阻击德国由来已久。他们认为美国最终目标就是欧元，从1999年欧元出现时，美国就一直坐立不安，美国希望通过打击德国经济进而打击欧盟，攻击欧元。只有德国银行业倒下，欧元才会被美元打倒。德国大型银行被罚后，德国西门子、巴斯夫、戴姆勒等众多知名企业纷纷站出来对德国银行表示支持。甚至有声音认为是德国对美国的集体反抗。一时间各种阴谋论此起彼伏不绝于耳。

德国这两家银行被处罚至今已经尘埃落地，当事过境迁，一切沉淀下来之后，更容易清楚的看清事件本质。抛开欧洲其他银行被罚的案例不谈，仅在美国，就已经有美银、大通、花旗等好几家美国本土大行被罚。在金融服务局开出的处罚和解令中，清晰地陈列了被处罚的原因以及事件的前前后后，两家银行存在很多相似点。我们不妨一起走近监管机构对于这两家银行的指控，一同探寻其中奥秘。

监管机构的指控

有缺陷的合规框架

合规框架是合规管理的筋骨，而合规框架的核心是合规流程和机制，合规流程的不通畅，必然导致合规框架的瘫痪。在美国监管机构对两家机构实施检查的过程中发现，两行的合规流程均存在脱节。在如今快节奏且紧密交互的金融网络中，全球金融机构是防御非法金融交易的第一道防线。纽约及联邦法律要求金融机构设计、实施和执行相关合规、反洗钱政策制度以对非法金融交易起到防范和杜绝的作用。两行合规框架缺陷包括以下原因：

第一，在战略布局和业务部署全球化的同时，合规的全球化管理存在缺陷。分支机构间合规流程和角色定位不清晰，没有设立相应绩效考核机制，存在互相推诿情况。

金融服务局在和解令中描述："德银AML政策在制定时重点关注区域特性而非全球层面。例如，德银莫斯科的管理人员主要关注俄罗斯当地监管要求，忽视国际或其他国家管制要求。与很多全球性银行一样，很多业务条线是需要双重报告的，即有些德银莫斯科交易员需要向德银莫斯科主管报告的同时，也需要向德银伦敦的主管有虚线的汇报责任，莫斯科交易员在实际工作中只对莫斯科主管负责，从未向德银伦敦上报过任何可疑交易活动，管理框架形同虚设。"

监管机构在审查德商时，重点描述了其合规流程的问题。如德商纽约分行发现某客户的可疑交易，但该客户的管理隶属于另外一家分行，纽约分行合规人员只能向另一家分行问询该客户信息。然而，由于没有相应健全的机制，该机构人员通常很长时间都不回复纽约职员的这些请求，大多结果是不了了之，有些仅仅是得到不足够或不充分的回复，这使得纽约分行的人员对可疑交易无法进行充分调查。分支机构间没有必要的信息共享机制，在无法从其他机构获取相关客户信息后，纽约职员只基于自身不够权威的网上搜索及在公共数据库的搜索就"解除"或关闭警报；另外，流程冗余烦琐也是全球合规管理存在缺陷的原因。比如，纽约的合规职员曾试图将他们判断为高风险的特定外国分支机构的客户姓名/名称加入他们的交易监控过滤中，以确保这些客户的交易受到额外审查，但是由于该客户隶属于法兰克福分行，法兰克福的客户经理要求纽约的合规职员在采取此类行动前必须咨询德国的业务人员，使得本可以实现自动化的流程，被人为干预，使得整个流程拖沓冗余。

第二，部分合规审查流于形式，缺乏深入研究，只限于文档和材料的堆砌。

如果说合规框架是合规管理的筋骨，那么合规调查的信息就是合规管理的血肉。监管机构在对德商的调查中指出，该行纽约分行为德商的外国分支机构维护代理账户，但其没有维护或没有调查这些分支机构之客户的尽职调查信息，没有对外国代理银行业务有关的风险进行适当的合规审查和管理。有些客户的尽职调查和合规审查只停留在基本信息的收集，没有信息的分析和加工。许多客户经理没有按照符合美国法规的方式维护客户尽职调查及"了解你的客户"材料，在纽约的职员开展调查时，缺乏可共享的正式文档。德银莫斯科同样没有用于KYC信息的中央储存库，文件分布散落。有些客户开户文件并不充分，在客户被纳入后也未采取任何行动对他们进行定期审核。美国监管机构在对其进行审查时指出，部分KYC系统仅发挥检查单的功能，只是机械地罗列。雇员机械地关注确保相关文档的收集，而非从潜在客户提供的信息中发现关键信息。

不完美的合规系统

系统对于反洗钱合规管理来说，可谓是重中之重。一家商业银行如果脱离了系统，那么就无从谈论合规管理。

监管机构在和解令中明确指出，德银监测可疑证券交易的监控系统存在不足。监管机构对系统问题的重视，是完全可以理解的。在业务量、业务复杂性的逐年提升，人工检测已经远远不能满足发展需要的情况下，业务监测系统就显得尤为重要。系统的建设一定是以合规为中心，不能为了建设而建设，做面子工程。需要设计严密和精准的警报筛查标准，精准定位问题，减少因为人为原因造成的漏报和错报。

与德银的系统问题相比，德商在系统设计上的缺陷似乎更值得关注。德商首席执行官在公开致歉中重点提到了该行的合规系统："我们严重违规，并对此深表歉意，我们已经并将继续改进我们的系统，培训员工应对不足。"德商一把手的明确表态，足以见得系统的重要性。金融服务局在和解令中提到该行在设计合规流程和工具时，对交易监控系统进行了改动，有意减少应有的报警数量，漏掉了这些本应该产生的报警和后续必要的调查；该行在设计监控软件时并不是基于发现可疑交易并排除无关警报的目的，而是从警报输出的数量出发，基于不产生"太多警报"的期望而设置的。

技术和系统本应是合规管理的有利支撑，但如果合规流程和工具不以风险和合规为重，而是为了应付差事而做的表面工程，使合规流程和工具成为摆设，不仅不会对合规管理产生有益的作用，反而会起到不良效果，颠覆合规的根基。

"丰厚收益"的代价

长久以来，商业银行业务发展和合规管理一直存在着一种微妙的博弈关系。毋庸置疑，商业银行是以营利和股东价值最大化为核心的企业，发展并获得效益是商业银行的根本目标。但商业银行的本质是经营风险，如果只重业务、重效益，轻风险、轻合规，后果不堪设想，德国的这两家机构的相关问题，值得我们深究。

像很多金融机构一样，德银莫斯科十分重视效益，年均收益可观。但自2008年全球金融危机和德银内部重组后，该行年收入减少了至少一半，交易员人人自危，为了业绩压力该行交易员竟然铤而走险，采用了一种收益丰厚的交易形式——镜像交易。交易员帮助某些客户定期开立订单以购买俄罗斯蓝筹股，并一直使用卢布支付，此后不久——实际上是购买后当天的某个时间——相关交易方通过德银伦敦以相同数量和相同价格出售相同的俄罗斯蓝筹股，以美元结算。许多出售交易方是在塞浦路斯或英属维尔京群岛等离岸领土进行登记的。因此，通过本计划，交易方能通过德银偷偷地将卢布兑换为美元。"镜像交易"均未显示出任何正当的经济理由。特定证券的买入或卖出一般对于交易方没什么分别，重要的是存在有配对交易。

轻松获得佣金对于德银莫斯科的交易员是很有吸引力的。监管机构的和解令中提到一个例子：在被德银莫斯科交易员告知没有俄罗斯联邦储蓄银行的股份可供镜像交易时，一个交易方代表立马将订单转向俄罗斯天然气工业股份公司的股份。此转向没有显而易见的理由，也没给出交易假说。

几年间，多家可疑公司客户（有共同受益人、管理者、代理人或者注册地址相同，特定的个体拥有几种不同的身份），通过德银莫斯科进行镜像交易。作为久经沙场、经验丰富的交易员，识别出这些"无明显交易目的的证券"是非常容易的，此类交易可以实现资本外逃、逃税或其他潜在的非法目的。但交易员选择视而不见，并乐此不疲的进行着这些交易。有位交易员承认他们没有有力地对这些可疑交易提出质疑，是因为当时交易大幅减缓，他们要趁机赚取佣金。一个交易员承认在"市场清淡"时交易员主要"关注佣金"，且尽管存有疑虑，他们还是持续开展这些交易，因为这些交易产生"丰厚的佣金"。

与对于违规行为视而不见相比更严重的是德银莫斯科的一名主管涉嫌受贿。这名主管的近亲属接受镜像交易的主要交易对手的贿赂款项。自以为天衣无缝的贪婪计划在监管机构的审查下暴露无遗。

如果说德银某些员工在业绩压力下铤而走险，那德商某些员工则是因为贪图"诱人"的中间收益而引发合规定时炸弹。从两家银行共同的问题可以看出，商业银行因业务而牺牲合规并非个案，这是一种长久遗留下来固有思维模式。从1999年起，德商就卷入奥林巴斯会计欺诈事件中。在该欺诈存续期间，多个位于新加坡的德商雇员对业务和相关交易提出担忧，但是这些担忧并没有引起对该业务的有效调查。尽管曾有合规专员注意到该业务的结构是"复杂的"具有洗钱、欺诈、资产拆卖、市场操纵、及衍生的税务犯罪的嫌疑，但业务人员以"收益丰厚"为由，消极对待质疑，使得相关审查停滞不前。业务人员经常以影响业务发展，阻碍集团盈利为由，漠视合规的重要性。多名在新加坡担任合规专员的职员，均曾表示新加坡合规是"一个随时会爆炸的定时炸弹"。但没有人将这一质疑抬出水面，认为业务盈利是第一位的，结果"丰厚收益"带来了惨痛代价。长远来看，以稳健的合规为代价的、允许通过不当行为进行短期获利的企业文化反而会让机构付出更昂贵的监管成本、声誉成本和其他代价。

浮出水面的"粉饰太平"

在监管机构作出的和解令中有这样的描述：当德银莫斯科多个交易员担忧这些镜像交易背后没有任何经济理由时，主管却对他们的担忧不屑一顾。可以看出，在德银莫斯科已经默许了这种业务模式的存在，并对这种掩耳盗铃的"太平"习以为常。德银错过了多个发现并制止镜像交易计划的机会。比如，因合规问题俄罗斯联邦金融市场服务局暂时吊销了德银莫斯科的客户A的营业执照。但德银莫斯科没有对此作出AML审查或上报;一家主流的俄语商业杂志随后对客户A作出特别报道,暗示了其镜像交易计划的存在,德银莫斯科没有启动合规审查;面对其他机构对于可疑客户的质疑,德银莫斯科的相关主管却保证该客户已通过了本行的KYC(了解你的客户)程序,且认为没有担心的理由。从德银莫斯科镜像交易的做法来看, 他们关于美国对俄罗斯的制裁情况是非常了解的,正是因为清楚某些交易应该是被禁止的,才想出运用镜像交易淡化问题的手段。虽然抵消交易本身并不违法,但多次、高频、均无明显交易目的高度暗示了金融犯罪的存在。对于经验丰富的交易员来说,识别出这种可疑交易并不复杂,我们可以作出故意为之的这种假设。可是利用这种交易模式嵌套真实目的,这样的粉饰太平最终是要付出代价的。

与德银类似,德商在追寻利润的同时,也采取了一些"包装"行为。从2002年到2008年间,德商用不透明的方法和做法代表伊朗及苏丹等受美国制裁的实体和个体,开展了估值逾2 530亿美元的约60 000笔以美元结算的交易。该行通过改动的或不透明的付款报文,代表受美国经济制裁的客户经由纽约处理了数万笔交易。为了发展其与伊朗客户的业务关系,该行制定了用于处理美元付款的内部程序以使这些客户(包括国有控股的金融机构,如伊朗赛帕银行和伊朗国家银行)能在不被发现的情况下通过美国金融体系结算美元款项。该银行甚至指定了一队特别雇员去人工处理伊朗交易——具体来说,是从SWIFT付款报文中消除与制裁有关的任何识别信息。该银行的雇员通过邮件传达正式书面指示和非正式指导,指示下级职员在发送付款报文给美国结算银行前从电汇报文中消除可能识别受制裁有关方的信息。

此外,该银行发现由于美国的制裁,其他国际金融机构拒绝处理苏丹的美元交易,因此苏丹可能是个有利可图的市场。至少从2002年到2006年,该银行为多达17家苏丹银行(包括五家位于SDN上的)维护美元账户,并用不透明的方法为这些客户和其他苏丹实体经由美国处理了估值超过2.24亿美元的约1 800笔美元交易。

不论掩饰工作做得如何天衣无缝,始终是纸包不住火。恰恰正是因为伪造商业记录、提供虚假文件进行备案、没有维护有效的BSA/AML计划及没有检测和上报可疑交易,阻碍了监管机构和当局的有效审查。使得本错得不轻的德商错上加错。监管机构并不会因为没有留下详细的交易记录就放松审查，该行为反而会引发监管机构的怀疑和反感，提高审查力度，加大处罚措施。

改进缓慢，惹火监管

监管机构的处罚并不是没有征兆的，两家银行面对多个负面检查报告，忽视监管机构警告，继续听之任之，没有任何补救措施，使得监管机构终于开出巨额罚单。两家银行均在被正式处罚之前，从内部审计师和监管机构收到了多个与其BSA/AML合规缺失有关的警告和批评，但是并没有补救其有缺陷的BSA/AML合规计划。德商在2008年收购德累斯顿银行时，监管机构曾指出其BSA/AML存在的问题，但该行并没有进行有效的解决。2009年，德商集团审计部对纽约分行的合规计划开展了审计。该审计发现，纽约分行的AML合规计划在多个重要方面存在缺失。该报告详细说明了交易监控、客户信息监控、及"了解你的客户"程序中存在的缺陷，以及影响AML计划的一般IT基础设施缺失。接下来一年，在监管机构对该行2009年5月协议条款的遵守进度进行检查时，检查员再次发现多个重要的BSA/AML缺陷。然而，该银行的BSA/AML合规问题还是持续存在。监管机构对银行的合规审查一定不是以罚款作为最终目的的，但监管机构的权威性不容动摇，有些银行对监管机构的提示和警告置若罔闻，必然会招致更大的处罚。

案件的影响及教训

在我国商业银行纷纷进行全球布局的今天，国际大行的合规事件值得引起我们深思，以此为鉴。

第一，正确理解业务与合规的关系，合规管理为业务的平稳发展保驾护航。商业银行的本质是经营风险，风险是商业银行的核心，脱离风险的企业文化都是无根之木，无源之泉。经营风险的特性决定了合规经营是商业银行得以长足发展的唯一道路。合规是银行的立行之本，合规文化是银行企业文化建设的重要组成部分。

现在很多金融机构都存在着对合规管理漠视的情况。重视合规仅仅还是停留在口头上。企业文化是一家银行的"魂"，没有企业文化的商业银行就像丢了魂的行尸走肉，早晚出事。纵观当今全球银行，几乎没有一家银行不把合规经营的口号放在企业文化里面，但是，真正把合规文化深深植入日常经营的商业银行少而又少。大多数商业银行只是把合规作为一句空口号，喊喊而已。高层在做战略、定目标的时候，不应只是各种业务指标，也要设定有份量且落地的合规绩效指标。

合规文化建设是一项系统工程。对于我国商业银行来说，目前的当务之急是树立自上而下"合规先行"的企业文化。受罚银行因缺乏健康的合规文化，在清楚地意识到合规风险隐患的情形下，仍置合规问题于不顾，贪恋佣金短期获利，终将合规定时炸弹引爆。随着全球金融网络关联化程度加强，跨境新型金融业务和产品日益增多，各国金融机构都必须时刻保持警惕，在集团上下营造合规、稳健经营的企业文化，妥善处理业务创新发展和合规风险防范之间、短期获利和长期稳健经营之间的关系，业务创新时认真评估其洗钱风险隐患，采取风险防范措施，有效打击洗钱和其他网络犯罪及国际恐怖主义的活动。

第二，建立全球反洗钱政策框架体系，加大合规资源投入，明确流程和岗位职责，将各个岗位的合规职能纳入绩效管理。

目前，几乎所有的大银行都在谈论国际化、全球化。可是，合规框架却没有达到国际化和全球化的基本要求。就像德商的案例中提到的，其纽约机构识别出问题，但问题客户属于其他机构，这里没有一个清晰的合规协调机制，流程的不顺畅，使得很多问题往往不了了之。对于跨国金融机构，在集团内部建立统一的反洗钱政策，对全集团采取统一指引，承认区域的特殊性，要求境外分支机构结合所在国的监管规定执行孰严原则，严格执行反洗钱监管规定，防范海外执法风险。此外，梳理明确的全球合规管理流程图，明确界定集团总部与海外分支行之间及各部门的反洗钱岗位职责，将各个岗位的合规职能纳入绩效管理，防止合规管理脱节。加大对合规资源和内审人力资源的投入力度。监管机构在其制度中明确表示，金融机构必须聘用足够数量的受训合规专业人员，以确保其制度正常运行。金融服务局在和解令中对两行合规人力资源不足均有描述。在各个业务风险增加的情况下，合规人员配置不充足。其中提到一段描述，"有一个高级合规职员一再指出，他不得不"乞求、借用和偷用"以获得适当的资源，导致现有人员不得不一人扮演多个角色。""同样地，在某一时刻，没有任何合规背景的一个律师竟同时担任德银莫斯科的合规负责人、法务负责人及AML官。许多在AFC、AML和合规小组担任领导的雇员缺乏必要经验或培训。"此外，加大对合规条线人员的培训力度至关重要，合规形势变化多样，合规从业人员能及时了解国际新局势，新规定至关重要，要多维度提高合规人员业务素质和能力。

第三，以合规为中心，构建严密的合规监控系统。

系统对于合规管理的重要性不言而喻，打造金融机构全方位风险防范的"免疫系统"势在必行。系统的建设一定是以合规为中心，不能为了建设而建设，做面子工程。严密和精准的设计警报筛查标准，精准定位问题，减少因为人为原因造成的漏报和错报。此外，随着监管机构和银行内部对合规的进一步重视，很多法规和制度应运而生，在系统建设时，需要满足金融机构对外规和内规制度进行维护、查询、解析等需求，形成内外规库。可根据条线、流程、产品、岗位、关键字等多维度查询所需的法律法规和规章制度，做到"有法可依、有规可查"。在合规管理中，经常会遇到员工对合规流程模糊和不清晰的情况。在系统中，对合规流程做图形化流程管理，以流程为中心，完成流程与内外规、岗位、产品的关联，完成合规风险点和控制点的识别、评估与整改。建立科学的可疑交易监测规则，实现对客户和可疑交易行为的全面监控。在系统中建立客户关系树，存储客户信息，并建立科学流程，设立控制点，保留浏览痕迹，在必要时客户经理可授权其他机构进行合规查询。

第四，构建统一的风险评价标准体系。

目前，世界主要国家和经济体纷纷加大了反洗钱监管力度，"严管重罚"的监管态势愈演愈烈。美国、英国、日本、欧盟等先后公布了制裁黑名单，对防范不力的金融机构，采取了严厉的惩戒措施，处以了高额甚至"震慑性"的巨额罚款。这要求商业银行在全行范围内统一国别风险评价标准，允许各家海外分支机构根据当地监管要求采取孰严原则，对部分国家风险级别进行调整。定期对风险评估情况进行审查确保风险评估科学准确。对高风险客户采取加强型尽职调查措施和持续性身份识别措施。根据业务量和风险情况对境外金融机构客户进行梳理，对于业务量低、无发展潜力且高风险客户，可以考虑进行逐步退出政策。

　　最后，了解了美国监管机构对两家德国银行的处罚细节，大家对当前严峻的国际监管形势有了更加深入的了解。正所谓练兵千日，用在一时，在面对监管机构的合规审查时，更是需要厚积薄发。合规是一项系统的大工程，需要日常的积累，面对检查，突击准备和临时抱佛脚的做法不会起任何作用。在美元主导的当今世界，如果希望继续参与美元清算系统，遵守美元规则恐怕是一个不得已而必须作出的决定。现在已不是利润至上的单纯年代，国际局势的复杂多变，阴晴不定，和动荡不安使很多经济利益必然掺杂着政治利益与目的。 在参与国际竞争的同时，必须要了解国际规则，避免我行我素，掩耳盗铃的侥幸心理。一方面，需静下心来抓紧时间研究国际新形势，按国际游戏规则参与全球竞争。另一方面，需加强自身发展，提高参与国际规则的制定权与话语权。

附录1:

《和解令》英文原文

NEW YORK STATE DEPARTMENT OF FINANCIAL SERVICES

In the Matter of:

DEUTSCHE BANK AG and
DEUTSCHE BANK AG NEW YORK BRANCH

CONSENT ORDER UNDER
NEW YORK BANKING LAW §§ 39, 44 and 44-a

The New York State Department of Financial Services (the "Department"), Deutsche Bank AG and Deutsche Bank AG New York Branch (the "New York Branch"), (together, "Deutsche Bank," or the "Bank"), agree:

Introduction

The Culture of Compliance in the Age of Risk

1. Global financial institutions serve as the first line of defense against illegal financial transactions in today's fast-paced, interconnected financial network. New York and federal law require these institutions to design, implement, and execute policies and systems to prevent and detect illegal financial transactions. The Bank Secrecy Act ("BSA"), for example, requires these institutions to report suspicious transactions (via "Suspicious Activity Reports" or "SARs") to the U.S. Treasury Department's Financial Crimes Enforcement Network ("FinCEN"), enabling law enforcement to conduct investigations that result in the future interdiction of these transactions and, ultimately, prosecution or the blocking of bad actors. The BSA likewise requires financial institutions to have adequate anti-money laundering ("AML") systems in place.

2. New York law imposes these same requirements on its regulated financial institutions.[1] Specifically, the law obligates financial institutions to devise and implement systems reasonably designed to identify and block suspicious activity and transactions prohibited by law. Each institution is expected to configure a system based on the particular risks faced by the institution, considering such factors as its size, geographical reach, and specific lines of business. Moreover, the institution must employ or engage sufficient numbers of trained compliance professionals to ensure that its systems run properly.

3. To strengthen anti-money laundering efforts, New York law imposes additional requirements on regulated institutions, obligating them to maintain effective programs to monitor and filter transactions to screen for money laundering and bar transactions with sanctioned entities. [2]Additionally, to both

---

[1] *See, e.g.*, Part 115 of the Superintendent's Regulations (3 NYCRR 115), Part 116 (3 NYCRR 116), Part 416 (3 NYCRR 416) and Part 417 (3 NYCRR 417).

[2] See Part 504 of the Superintendent's Regulations (3 NYCRR 504).

protect consumers and the safety and soundness of financial institutions, the Department has proposed regulations requiring regulated entities to adopt a series of measures to prevent against cyber attacks.[1]

4. Ultimate responsibility for design and implementation of such policies and systems belongs at the institution's top echelon. The board of directors and senior management must devote careful study to the design of the anti-money laundering and other compliance systems that lie at the core of this first line of defense, and must ensure sufficient resources to undergird these systems and structures. Adequate staffing must be put in place, and training must be ongoing.

5. **Summary of Findings:** As set forth more fully below, this Consent Order addresses serious compliance deficiencies identified in the Department's investigation that spanned Deutsche Bank's global enterprise. These flaws allowed a corrupt group of bank traders and offshore entities to improperly and covertly transfer more than $10 billion out of Russia, by conscripting Deutsche Bank operations in Moscow, London and New York to their improper purpose.

6. The suspicious security trading schemes identified - termed "mirror trades" - permitted this corrupt consortium to move very large sums of money out of Russia under the radar and without the scrutiny of Deutsche Bank's compliance function. By converting rubles into dollars through security trades that had no discernible economic purpose, the scheme was a means for bad actors within a financial institution to achieve improper ends while evading compliance with applicable laws.

7. Afflicted with inadequate AML control policies, procedures, and structures, Deutsche Bank missed several key opportunities to identify and interdict this scheme. Moreover, the suspicious mirror-trading machinations occurred at a time Deutsche Bank was on clear notice of numerous deficiencies in its BSA/AML systems and management, and yet the steps it took to remediate the situation proved seriously inadequate.

8. For these reasons, the Department has entered into this Consent Order with the consent and agreement of Deutsche Bank to resolve this matter as set forth below and without further proceedings.

Factual Findings

The Mirror-Trading Scheme at Deutsche Bank's

Moscow. London and New York Offices

9. **The "Minor-Trading" Scheme**: The "mirror trading" scheme at issue here was simple and effective. Deutsche Bank Trust Company of the Americas ("DBTCA"), an entity located at 60 Wall Street, New York, New York which is licensed and supervised by the Department, was the entity through which the U.S. dollar payments flowed to the suspicious entities involved here.

10. Operating through the securities desk at Deutsche Bank's Moscow affiliate ("DB-Moscow"), certain companies that were clients of that desk routinely issued orders to purchase Russian blue chip stocks, always paying in rubles. The size of the typical order ranged in value from $2 to $3 million.

11. Shortly thereafter - indeed, sometimes the very same day - a related counterparty would sell the identical Russian blue chip stock in the same quantity and at the same price through Deutsche Bank's London branch ("DB-London"). The counterparties to the trade were actually

---

[1] *See* Part 500 of Title 23 of the Superintendent's Regulations (23 NYCRR 500 eff. March 1,2017).

closely related on both sides, such as through common ownership.

12. None of these "mirror trades" demonstrated any legitimate economic rationale. The counterparties frequently lost money on these trades, due to fees and commissions that were substantially credited to DB-Moscow by Deutsche Bank pursuant to the brokerage arrangements between Moscow and London.

13. For example, typically, it made no difference to the counterparties the particular security to be bought or sold. All that mattered was that there was a matching trade available. In one instance, a counterparty representative, who was buying shares for one counterparty and selling the identical shares for a related counterparty, told a DB- Moscow trader, *"I have a billion rouble today. ... Will you be able to find a security for this size?"*

14. In another case, a counterparty representative, when told by a DB-Moscow trader there were no Sberbank Russian shares available for a mirror trade, immediately switched the order to Gazprom Russian shares. No rationale for this switch was apparent; no trading hypothesis was offered.

15. Moreover, a number of the selling counterparties were registered in offshore territories, like Cypras or the British Virgin Islands.[①] The seller would be paid for its shares in U.S. dollars, which were routinely cleared through DBTCA. Thus, by virtue of this scheme, the counterparties were able to surreptitiously convert rubles into U.S. dollars using Deutsche Bank.

16. While offsetting trades are not inherently illegal, where - as here - they lack obvious economic purpose and could be used to facilitate money laundering or other illicit conduct, they are highly suggestive of financial crime.

17. The scheme was well-developed, running between 2011 and early 2015. At least 12 entities were involved in these suspicious trading activities, and the entities were closely related, linked, for example, by common beneficial owners, management, or agents. Certain individuals were employed by several of the different counterparties. For example, one person was the chairman of the Board of Directors of one entity, as well as the beneficial owner of another entity - which was itself the 100 percent shareholder of the first counterparty. Similarly, several counterparties were registered at the same address.

18. **"One-Legged" Trades**: The DB-Moscow securities desk also facilitated a second type of suspicious trading activity with the same suspect counterparties - trades that appeared to be one leg of a mirror trade that may have involved a second (unidentified) financial institution to execute the

---

① Conducting business with counterparties registered in offshore territories can be risky, and offshore registration may, in and of itself, warrant enhanced due diligence measures. In general, offshore financial centers are lightly regulated, are historically reputed to be "tax havens," and permit customers a far greater amount of confidentiality than financial institutions in onshore jurisdictions, especially as to the identity of ultimate beneficial owners. Thus, offshore financial centers often have been associated with illegal money laundering activity and typically warrant higher levels of scrutiny. *See, e.g.*, Department of the Treasury, *National Money Laundering Risk Assessment* (2015), https://www.treasury.gov/resource-center/ terrorist- illicit-finance/Documents/National%20Money%20Laundering%20Risk%20Assessment%20 %E2%80% 93%2006-12-2015.pdf; U.S. Department of State' s International Narcotics Control Strategy Report, *Money Laundering and Financial Crimes* (Mar. 1, 2001), https://www.state.gov/j/inl/rls/ nrcrpt/2000/959.htm.

other leg ("one-legged trades"). These trades were almost entirely buy transactions involving the same counterparties involved in the mirror trades.

19. Roughly the same group of traders involved with the DB-Moscow securities desk also performed these one-legged trades. Moreover, the payments made by Deutsche Bank for these counterparties - which likewise flowed through DBTCA - were made almost entirely to accounts at banks outside of Russia and the U.K.

20. **Active Facilitation by DB-Moscow Traders**: The evidence is clear that DB-Moscow traders knowingly and actively facilitated both of these trading schemes.

21. For example, most of the subject trades were placed by a single trader representing both sides of the transaction. The DB-Moscow trader would execute the sell side of the trade, helping the suspicious Russian counterparty acquire Russian securities, settled in rubles. The same DB-Moscow trader then would buy the identical quantity of the same stock from DB-London's customer as an over-the-counter trade, settled in U.S. dollars. The DB-Moscow trader would directly book the trade to the DB-London trading book via a remote booking function.

22. This "remote-booking" feature was central to the scheme, permitting the Moscow traders to carry out the mirror trades without any effective supervision or compliance review in London. This way, the scheme stayed under the radar.

23. Traders on the DB-Moscow desk sometimes would go to significant lengths to facilitate the suspicious trades. When Deutsche Bank suspended one of the counterparties involved in the scheme, for example, DB-Moscow traders continued to effectuate the mirror trades by pre-arranging the timing of the bid and offers with the suspended counterparty on the Russian Moscow Exchange (MICEX).

24. When one trader on the Moscow desk expressed concern about the lack of any economic rationale behind these numerous trades, colleagues on the desk assured the concerned trader that these trades had been sanctioned by a supervisor. When other traders raised similar issues about the suspicious trading activity, the supervisor was dismissive of their concerns.

25. **Greed and Corruption Motivated the DB-Moscow Traders**: In 2006 and 2007, the yearly revenues generated for Deutsche Bank by the Russian business line at issue here approximated €169 million and €123 million, respectively. Following the global financial crisis in 2008 and Deutsche Bank's internal restructuring, that profit decreased at least by half, putting pressure on traders to increase revenue.

26. An easy commission scheme was attractive for the traders on the Moscow securities desk. Traders conceded they did not forcefully question these suspicious trades, because they were earning commissions at a time when trading had dramatically slowed. One trader admitted that the trader was largely "focused on [] commission" during this time of "slow markets" and continued conducting these trades despite misgivings because they generated a "good commission."

27. Furthermore, a supervisor on the Moscow desk appears to have been paid a bribe or other undisclosed compensation to facilitate the schemes. The supervisor's close relative, who apparently had a background in historical art, and not finance, was also the apparent beneficial owner of two offshore companies, one each located in the British Virgin Islands and Cyprus (both high-risk jurisdictions for money laundering). In April and again in June 2015, one of the key counterparties involved in the mirror-trading scheme made payments totaling $250,000 to one of the companies owned by this close relative, allegedly pursuant to a "consulting agreement." Payments to one of

these two companies, totaling approximately $3.8 million, were almost exclusively identified for the purported purpose of "financial consulting," and largely originated from two companies registered in Belize.

28. These suspicious payments, too, were cleared through DBTCA in New York.

29. The above demonstrates that a corporate culture that allows for short-term profiteering through improper conduct, at the expense of robust compliance, turns out to be much more expensive in the long run to an institution in regulatory, reputational, and other costs.

In Excess of $10 Billion of Scheme Proceeds Flowed Through New York

30. As noted above, DBTCA is a U.S. subsidiary of Deutsche Bank located on Wall Street that, among other things, conducts correspondent banking and U.S. dollar clearing activity for customers of the Bank, including other financial institutions. [①]DBTCA is chartered pursuant to Article III of the New York Banking Law and subject to the supervision and regulation by the Department.

31. Every single one of the U.S. dollar payments involved in the mirror trading and one-legged trading activity discussed above flowed through DBTCA. *In total, payments exceeding $10 billion were transmitted from London and through New York as a result of the trading conduct facilitated by the scheme*.

32. Deutsche Bank thus caused New York State to become a key conduit in a long-running artifice involving highly suspicious financial activity. Deutsche Bank has represented that it has been unable to identify the actual purpose behind this scheme. It is obvious, though, that the scheme could have facilitated capital flight, tax evasion, or other potentially illegal objectives.

Deutsche Bank Missed Repeated Opportunities to Detect the Long-Running Mirror-Trading Scheme

33. Deutsche Bank missed a number of key opportunities to detect and interdict the mirror-trading scheme (both one and two-legged). These chances arose early on in the scheme and continued until Deutsche Bank's discovery of this scheme in February 2015. The failure to detect or escalate this misconduct reflects pervasive deficiencies at each level of the Bank's compliance function.

34. For example, a first opportunity arose in November 2011. DB-Moscow entered a 900 million ruble trade on behalf of DB-London with one of the suspect counterparties ("Counterparty A") that failed to settle because the Russian Federal Service for Financial Markets ("FSFM") had suspended Counterparty A's license to operate. Although a well-established red flag, no AML review or escalation occurred.

35. A second and strikingly clear warning arose shortly thereafter in November 2011, when a mainstream Russian-language business journal noted that the FSFM had suspended the operating licenses of several financial firms for engaging in suspicious trading. The article described an artifice very similar to the instant mirror trade scheme:

---

① Correspondent banking involving U.S. dollar clearing is the process by which U.S. dollar-denominated transactions are satisfied between counterparties through a U.S. bank. While it is essential to bank customers engaged in international commerce, U.S. dollar clearing may be a potentially high-risk business line for many banks, as it may be used by bad actors to launder money or facilitate terrorist transactions.

According to an intelligence officer, the scheme operated as follows: a client wish ing to move the money transferred the funds to a brokerage firm which then bought blue chips .... Then the shares were sold in favor of a company-non- resident . . . which then sold the securities on the market and transferred the money minus the commission fee to the client abroad. The law enforcement authorities believe that approximately 100 billion rubles were siphoned abroad in this manner this year.

Notably, Counterparty A was identified in the article.

36. The business journal article led to an e-mail circulated to several members of management, in both Moscow and London, requesting that certain trading accounts be suspended. The e-mail also contained a link to the article, and its recipients included a senior compliance staffer in London, along with several chief operating officers for various interested divisions. Numerous responsible managers were thus on notice of this serious AML controls issue.

37. Further, senior Deutsche Bank employees continued to discuss, for several months, how to obtain payment for the failed trades involving the suspended counterparty, which apparently cost the bank about $1.5 million in profit. Despite these conversations, at no time did anyone at the Bank undertake to escalate or investigate the basis for the revocation of a customer's operating license, or its connection to the money laundering scheme specified in the article.

38. Yet a third opportunity to detect the suspicious mirror trading activity occurred in January 2014, when a European financial institution (the "European Bank") sent a Request for Assistance ("RFA") to DB-London. The European Bank had been prompted to send the RFA after reviewing 20 transactions originating with Deutsche Bank and involving another of the suspicious counterparties ("Counterparty B"). Seeking more information about the relationship between and transactions involving DB-London and Counterparty B, the European Bank specifically asked whether DB-London had *"any reason to believe that the transactions [with Counterparty B] are in any way of a suspicious nature."*

39. Upon receiving no response, the European Bank sent several reminders to DB-London. Eventually, the DB-Moscow supervisor (the one whose close relative received substantial undisclosed and suspicious payments) responded by reassuring the European Bank that Counterparty B *"ha[s] passed through our KYC [know-your- customer] procedures"* and that Deutsche Bank *"seefsj no reason for concern here"* Not a single Deutsche Bank compliance staffer was ever involved in the response to this RFA provided by the corrupt supervisor to the European Bank.

40. Notably, only days before this response was sent to the European Bank by the supervisor at DB-Moscow, DBTCA's AML Compliance unit sent its own RFA to the European Bank inquiring about Counterparty B. DBTCA's information request had been spurred by an alert generated by a transaction monitoring system located at DBTCA.[1] Based on the DB-Moscow supervisor's

---

① "Transaction monitoring" is the process by which an institution monitors financial transactions after their execution for potential BSA/AML violations and Suspicious Activity Reporting. While this process may be carried out manually, larger institutions such as Deutsche Bank often employ electronic systems using advanced software to monitor transactions and, in the first instance, screen them even before execution for possible violations of federal sanctions laws. See Part 504 of the Superintendent's Regulations, 3 NYCRR § 504.

assurances, the European Bank relayed back to DBTCA that it had no adverse information about Counterparty B.

41. Subsequently, in light of the contradictory information about Counterparty B received from two different components of Deutsche Bank (which did not communicate with each other), the European Bank contacted a senior Anti-Financial Crime ("AFC") employee at DBTCA who supervised special investigations, in an attempt to reconcile these concerns. The senior compliance employee never responded to the European Bank. Nor did the employee take any steps to investigate the basis for the European Bank's inquiry, later explaining this omission on the ground that *the employee had "too many jobs " and "had to deal with many things and had to prioritize."*

42. Just as troubling, through a leak apparently originating with Deutsche Bank, Counterparty B was informed of the European Bank's RFA. This was a very serious breach of anti-money laundering and corruption policies and practices. Yet when the leak came to the attention of senior DB-Moscow management, no action to investigate the leak was taken.

43. A fourth opportunity to detect the mirror-trading scheme occurred several months later. In approximately April 2014, Deutsche Bank identified problematic trading involving another of the counterparties ("Counterparty C"). About the same time, Deutsche Bank received information from a Russian regulator that Counterparty C was involved in a money laundering and tax evasion scheme. Trading with Counterparty C was suspended, and some preliminary investigation identified suspicious trading with additional counterparties. Flowever, no further escalation occurred, despite the emergence of an unmistakable pattern of suspicious trading at the securities desk at DB-Moscow.

44. Subsequently, between April and September 2014, DB-Moscow identified additional suspicious mirror trading activity involving several other counterparties ("Counterparties D and E"). Although DB-Moscow suspended trading with Counterparties D and E, and a certain level of escalation occurred involving the AFC Unit at DB-London, Deutsche Bank again failed at the time to conduct a broader investigation that would have uncovered the entirety of the scheme. [①]

Numerous Compliance Deficiencies Allowed for the
Mirror-Trading Scheme to Flourish at Deutsche Bank

45. Numerous compliance failures at Deutsche Bank allowed for the mirror- trading scheme to flourish. The deficiencies are extensive and are catalogued only generally below.

46. **Flaws in KYC Policies and Procedures**: During the relevant period Deutsche Bank suffered from widespread and well-known weaknesses in its KYC processes for onboarding new clients. KYC procedures were manual and functioned merely as a checklist, with employees mechanically focused on ensuring documentation was collected, rather than shining a critical light on information provided by potential customers.

47. Even so, inadequate documentation typically characterized many of the onboarding files at DB-Moscow's securities desk. Nor were any steps taken to periodically review and verify clients once brought in. Notably, Deutsche Bank's Russia operations scored the worst out of 28 countries

---

① In addition to the missed opportunities delineated above, certain systems at Deutsche Bank had the capacity to detect the mirror trading activity but were not oriented to do so. For example, "dbCAT," a reporting tool that collects and displays a wide array of trade data, could have identified both legs of the mirror trades had the proper filters been applied.

whose KYC procedures were reviewed by Deutsche Bank in an internal report released to senior management in early 2014.

48. Virtually all of the KYC files for the counterparties implicated here were insufficient. Moreover, because no central repository for KYC information existed at Deutsche Bank, when the Bank suspended a counterparty for suspicious trading, a related counterparty was able to get onboarded and resume trading activity without raising any red flags.

49. Further, the Moscow supervisor who oversaw the mirror trading was actively involved in the onboarding and KYC documentation of counterparties involved in the scheme. Bank onboarding staff experienced hostility and threats from the supervisor on several occasions when it appeared they had not moved quickly enough to facilitate transactions.

50. Distressingly, this was a fact about which senior management at DB- Moscow was aware, yet management's response was inadequate. Indeed, although deficiencies in KYC policies and procedures were well known for many years, Deutsche Bank; did not take sufficient action to implement genuine reform until 2016.

51. **Flaws in the AML Risk Rating System**: Deutsche Bank failed to accurately rate its AML country and client risks throughout the relevant time period. The Bank lacked a global policy benchmarking its risk appetite, resulting in material inconsistencies and no methodology for updating the ratings. Nor was Deutsche Bank in line with peer banks, which rated Russia as high risk well before Deutsche Bank did in late 2014.

52. Although Deutsche Bank Group Audit specifically identified deficiencies in the Bank's risk rating methodology in a Global Anti-Money Laundering Report prepared in 2012, DB-Moscow resisted adopting modified risk rating procedures because most of their clients would be re-classified as high risk, and the office lacked the operational resources required to handle the increased compliance workload.

53. **Inadequate Compliance and Internal Audit Resources:** These deficiencies were exacerbated by Deutsche Bank's ineffective and understaffed AFC, AML, and Compliance Units. At a time that it was increasing risk in various business segments, the Bank's intense focus on headcount reduction between 2010 and 2012 prevented the AFC and Compliance units in DB-Moscow and elsewhere from being staffed with the resources necessary to function effectively.

54. A senior compliance staffer repeatedly stated that he had to "beg, borrow, and steal" to receive the appropriate resources, leaving existing personnel scrambling to perform multiple roles. Similarly, at one point in time, a single attorney who lacked any compliance background served as DB-Moscow's Head of Compliance, Head of Legal, and as its AML Officer - all at the same time. And a number of employees with leadership positions in the AFC, AML, and Compliance groups lacked necessary experience or training.

55. Nor did Deutsche Bank have an automated system to monitor suspicious securities transactions, which added to the risks of utilizing the remote booking model. Moreover, Deutsche Bank's Group Audit also lacked in a number of ways that prevented it from fulfilling its key role as a third line of defense behind the business and compliance units.

56. **Flaws in Corporate Structure and Organization:** Also responsible for the breakdown in compliance here is Deutsche Bank's decentralized AML framework, which caused confusion in policies, roles, and responsibilities. This decentralized model caused AML policies to be set at the regional, rather than global, level, resulting in the inconsistent formulation and application of

policies and procedures.

57. As relevant here, DB-Moscow management focused primarily on local regulatory requirements imposed by Russian authorities. Little or no attention was paid to the implementation or adherence to controls designed to comply with international or other country requirements. And where such policies did exist, they were frequently ill designed and insufficient to meet the demands of the business lines involved.

58. Additionally, a dual reporting structure and lack of clarity in job responsibilities led to an over-reliance upon the supervisor for management of trading activity on the DB-Moscow securities desk. A number of trading employees directly reported to this supervisor, and while the trading employees also had dotted line reporting to individuals at DB-London, no concerns relevant to the suspicious trading activities were ever escalated out of Moscow.

59. Nor was there any effective oversight of the Moscow securities supervisor. His local manager, who was assigned to a different business group, did not understand such oversight to be part of his responsibilities. Moreover, the Moscow supervisor's direct supervisor in London failed to exercise any reasonable oversight over the Moscow supervisor; compliance topics generally were not discussed during regular business calls or meetings, and the Moscow supervisor's superiors failed to review reports with an eye towards non-compliant or suspicious activity.

60. Indeed, the supervisor's direct manager praised the work of the supervisor for engaging local clients with global products - creating the pernicious culture that gave rise to the improper trading scheme and permitted it to continue uninterrupted for a five-year stretch. In short, Deutsche Bank's AML control failures were longstanding and enterprise-wide, enabling the mirror trade scheme to flourish and persist.

Deutsche Bank's Substantial History of Regulatory Violations Placed It On Firm Notice That Schemes Like Mirror Trading Might Occur

61. Deutsche Bank has a substantial history of regulatory violations over the last decade - one that placed it squarely on notice of the need to address potential compliance issues that permitted the mirror-trading scheme to fester.

62. In October 2005, DBTCA entered into a Written Agreement with the Department (via its predecessor agency) after anti-money laundering and compliance programs related to its correspondent banking and dollar-clearing services were found to be substantially deficient Deutsche Bank agreed to make a variety of reforms designed to create an effective control environment for these business lines.

63. In April 2015, Deutsche Bank entered into a Consent Order with the Department arising out of its failure to employ relevant and specific systems and controls to prevent manipulation of the LIBOR and IBOR rate-setting process. The conduct at issue occurred for the time period 2005 through 2009 - right after entry of DBTCA's Written Agreement with the Department - and was systemic. The LIBOR manipulation issues had been known to the Bank from at least 2008, and even after being placed on notice, the Bank failed to address the absence of relevant systems and controls. The Bank paid a penalty of $600 million to the Department, and agreed to install an independent monitor to recommend and implement important compliance reforms.

64. On November 3, 2015, the Bank entered into another Consent Order with the Department, arising out of the Bank's use of non-transparent methods and practices to conduct nearly $11 billion in dollar-clearing transactions on behalf of Iranian, Libyan, Syrian, Burmese, and Sudan financial

institutions and other entities subject to U.S. economic sanctions.' The conduct at issue occurred during the time period 1999 through 2006. One of the main purposes of the non-transparent practices at issue was to keep the Bank's U.S. staff in the dark about sanctions connections of the payments they were processing through New York. The Bank paid a penalty of $200 million to the Department, and again agreed to engage an independent monitor to "conduct a comprehensive review of the Bank's existing BSA/AML and OFAC sanctions compliance programs, policies, and procedures in place at the Bank that pertain to or affect activities conducted by or through Deutsche Bank New York"; which included a review of the "thoroughness and comprehensiveness of the Bank's current global BSA/AML and OFAC compliance program."

65. In light of this regulatory history, the suspicious mirror trading activity, which commenced in 2011 and continued until as recently as February 2015, occurred after the Bank was on clear notice of serious and widespread compliance issues dating back a decade.

66. Once the mirror trade scheme became sufficiently elevated within Deutsche Bank's investigation function (in March 2015), the Bank commenced an internal investigation designed to identify the background of the suspicious trades, as well as understand to what extent Bank employees were aware of these activities and its associated risks.

67. The Bank timely self-reported its initial assessment of the internal investigation to the Department. Since then, it appears to the Department that the Bank has conducted an internal investigation consistent with the stated mission, and has done so in a serious manner and timely fashion, keeping the Department informed of its findings. While much more remains to be done, the Bank has taken certain necessary steps toward remediation.

68. In setting forth the violations and remedies below, the Department recognizes and credits the forthright manner in which Deutsche Bank performed its internal investigation, and its timely communications with the Department.

Violations of Law and Regulation

69. Deutsche Bank has conducted its banking business in an unsafe and unsound manner, in violation of New York Banking Law §§ 44, 44-a.

70. Deutsche Bank failed to maintain an effective and compliant anti-money laundering program, in violation of 3 N.Y.C.R.R. § 116.2.

71. Deutsche Bank failed to maintain and make available true and accurate books, accounts and records reflecting all transactions and actions, in violation of New York Banking Law § 200-c.

Settlement Provisions

Monetary Payment

72. Deutsche Bank shall pay a civil monetary penalty pursuant to Banking Law §§ 39, 44 and 44-a to the Department in the amount of $425,000,000 as a result of the conduct and violations set forth above. The Bank shall pay the entire amount within ten (10) days of executing this Consent Order. Deutsche Bank agrees that it will not claim, assert, or apply for a tax deduction or tax credit with regard to any U.S. federal, state, or local tax, directly or indirectly, for any portion of the civil monetary penalty paid pursuant to this Consent Order.

Independent Monitor

73. Within sixty (60) days of this Order, Deutsche Bank, DBTCA and the New York Branch shall engage an independent monitor (the "Independent Monitor") to: conduct a comprehensive

review of the Bank's existing BSA/AML compliance programs, policies and procedures in place at the Bank that pertain to or affect activities conducted by or through (a) DBTCA and (b) the New York Branch.

74. The Independent Monitor will be selected by the Department in the exercise of its sole discretion, and will report directly to the Department. The term of the Independent Monitor will be up to two years. The Department will consider whether one of the two existing independent monitors currently in place at Deutsche Bank may expand its assignment to include the work contemplated in this Order; provided, however, that nothing herein shall so require the Department to expand any such assignment of any other independent monitor, and the Department reserves the right in its sole discretion to require engagement of an additional independent monitor.

75. Within thirty (30) days of the selection of the Independent Monitor, Deutsche Bank, DBTCA and the New York Branch shall jointly submit to the Department for approval an engagement letter that provides, at a minimum, for the Independent Monitor to review and report on:

> a. The elements of the Bank's corporate governance that contributed to or facilitated the improper conduct discussed in this Consent Order and that permitted it to go on, relevant changes or reforms to corporate governance that the Bank has made since the time of the conduct discussed in this Consent Order, and whether those changes or reforms are likely to significantly enhance the Bank's BSA/AML compliance going forward;

> b. The thoroughness and comprehensiveness of the Bank's current global BSA/AML compliance programs, including, but not limited to, compliance programs designed to address the conduct discussed in this Consent Order;

> c. The organizational structure, management oversight, and reporting lines that are relevant to BSA/AML compliance, and an assessment of the staffing of the BSA/AML compliance teams globally, including the duties, responsibilities, authority, and competence of officers or employees responsible for the Bank's compliance with laws and regulations pertaining to BSA/AML compliance;

> d. The propriety, reasonableness and adequacy of any proposed, planned, or recently-instituted changes to the Bank's BSA/AML compliance programs; and

> e. Any corrective measures necessary to address identified weaknesses or deficiencies in the Bank's corporate governance or its global BSA/AML compliance programs.

76. On a date to be agreed upon in the engagement letter, the Independent Monitor shall submit to the Bank a written report on its findings and recommendations (the "AML Compliance Report").

77. Within sixty (60) days of receiving the AML Compliance Report, the Bank will submit to the Department a written plan to improve and enhance the current global BSA/AML compliance programs that pertain to or affect activities conducted by or through DBTCA and the New York Branch, including, but not limited to, activities of the kind discussed in this Consent Order (the "Action Plan").

78. The Action Plan will provide recommendations for enhanced internal controls and updates or revisions to current policies, procedures, and processes in order to ensure full compliance with all applicable provisions of the BSA, related rules and regulations, and applicable New York law and regulations, and the provisions of this Consent Order, incorporating the corrective measures identified in the AML Compliance Report.

79. The Action Plan shall also provide recommendations to improve and enhance management oversight of BSA/AML compliance programs, policies, and procedures now in place at the Bank, to provide a sustainable management oversight framework, incorporating the corrective measures identified in the AML Compliance Report.

80. Should the Bank take the position that any of the corrective measures identified by the Independent Monitor should not be adopted by the Bank, the Bank shall, within forty-five (45) days of receiving the Compliance Report, so notify the Independent Monitor and the Department, specifying in writing the grounds for this position.

81. In consultation with the Independent Monitor, the Department will review and determine, in its sole discretion, whether to require the Bank to adopt the recommendations to which the Bank has objected, whether to agree with the Bank, and/or whether some other action should be taken by the Bank to achieve the remediation contemplated by this Consent Order.

82. The Independent Monitor will thereafter oversee the implementation of any corrective measures undertaken pursuant to the AML Compliance Report and/or plans discussed above in Paragraphs 73 through 81.

83. The Independent Monitor will assess the Bank's compliance with its corrective measures and will submit subsequent progress reports and a final report to the Department and the Bank, as determined by the Department in its sole discretion. The Department may, in its sole discretion, extend any reporting deadline set forth in this Order.

84. The term of the Independent Monitor's engagement will extend for up to two years from the date of its formal engagement by the Bank; provided, however, that the term may be extended further, in the Department's sole discretion, if Deutsche Bank fails to cooperate.

85. Any dispute as to the scope of the Independent Monitor's authority or mandate will be resolved by the Department in the exercise of its sole discretion, after consultation with the Bank and the Independent Monitor.

Full and Complete Cooperation of Deutsche Bank

86. Deutsche Bank and the New York Branch each agree that they will fully cooperate with the Independent Monitor and Department, and support the Independent Monitor's work by, among other things, providing it with access to all relevant personnel, consultants and third-party service providers, files, reports, or records, wherever located, consistent with applicable law.

Breach of Consent Order

87. In the event that the Department believes the Bank to be in material breach of the Consent Order, the Department will provide written notice to the Bank and the Bank must, within ten business days of receiving such notice, or on a later date if so determined in the Department's sole discretion, appear before the Department to demonstrate that no material breach has occurred or, to the extent pertinent, that the breach is not material or has been cured.

88. The parties understand and agree that the Bank's failure to make the required showing

within the designated time period shall be presumptive evidence of the Bank's breach. Upon a finding that the Bank has breached this Consent Order, the Department retains all remedies and relief available to it under the New York Banking and Financial Services Laws, and may use any evidence available to the Department in any ensuing orders, hearings or notices.

Waiver of Rights

89. The parties understand and agree that no provision of this Consent Order is subject to review in any court or tribunal outside the Department.

Parties Bound by the Consent Order

90. This Consent Order is binding on the Department and Deutsche Bank and the New York Branch, as well as any successors and assigns that are under the Department's supervisory authority. This Consent Order does not bind any federal or other state agency or law enforcement authority.

91. No further action will be taken by the Department against Deutsche Bank for the specific conduct set forth in this Order, provided that the Bank fully complies with the terms of this Order. Notwithstanding the foregoing or any other provision in this Consent Order, however, the Department may undertake additional action against the Bank for transactions or conduct of which Deutsche Bank had knowledge prior to the execution of this Consent Order, but that Deutsche Bank did not disclose to the Department in the written materials Deutsche Bank submitted to the Department in connection with this matter.

Notices

92. All notices or communications regarding this Consent Order shall be sent to:

> For the Department:
>
> Terri-Anne Caplan
> Assistant Deputy Superintendent
> for Enforcement
> One State Street
> New York, NY 10004
>
> Christine Tsai
> Attorney
> One State Street
> New York, NY 10004
>
> For Deutsche Bank:
>
> Christof von Dryander
> Co-General Counsel
> Deutsche Bank AG
> Taunusanlage 12
> 60325 Frankfurt am Main, Germany
>
> Dr. Mathias Otto
> Co-General Counsel Germany
> Deutsche Bank AG
> Taunusanlage 12

60325 Frankfurt am Main, Germany

Samuel W. Seymour

Sullivan & Cromwell LLP

125 Broad Street

New York, N Y 10004

Miscellaneous

93. Each provision of this Consent Order shall remain effective and enforceable until stayed, modified, suspended, or terminated by the Department.

94. No promise, assurance, representation, or understanding other than those contained in this Consent Order has been made to induce any party to agree to the provisions of the Consent Order.

[Remainder of page intentionally left blank]

IN WITNESS WHEREOF, the parties have caused this Consent Order to be signed this 30th day of January, 2017.

《和解令》中文译文

纽约州金融服务局和解令
德意志银行股份公司
德意志银行股份公司纽约分行

和解令
——《纽约州银行法》第39节、第44节及第44-a条

纽约州金融服务局（以下简称本部门）、德意志银行股份公司和德意志银行股份公司纽约分行（以下简称纽约分行）（统称为德意志银行或该银行）同意：

简介

风险时代的合规文化

1.在如今快节奏、互联的金融网络中，全球金融机构作为防御非法金融交易的第一道防线。纽约及联邦法律要求这些机构设计、实施和执行相关政策制度以对非法金融交易进行检测并防止其产生。比如，《银行保密法》（以下简称BSA）要求这些机构（通过可疑活动报告，SAR）将可疑交易报告给美国财政部金融犯罪执法网络局（以下简称FinCEN），使执法机关能开展调查，以在未来禁止此类交易并最终起诉或阻拦危险份子。BSA也要求金融机构设立适当的反洗钱（以下简称AML）制度。

2.纽约法律也对其所监管的金融机构施加上述要求①。具体来说，法律要求金融机构有义务合理设计并实施相应制度，以识别并阻拦可疑活动及法律禁止的交易。每家机构应基于其所面临的特定风险、并考虑其规模、地理影响范围及具体业务范围等因素以进行制度配置，此外，其必须聘用足够数量的受训合规专业人员，以确保其制度正常运行。

3.为加强反洗钱工作，纽约法律对所监管的机构施加额外要求，使其有义

---

① 见（比如）《监管者条例》第115部分（《纽约州准则、法规及条例》第3篇第115节）、第116部分（《纽约州准则、法规及条例》第3篇第116节）、第416部分（《纽约州准则、法规及条例》第3篇第416节）及第417部分（《纽约州准则、法规及条例》第3篇第417节）。

务维护有效的程序去对交易进行监控和过滤，从而筛选洗钱行为并禁止与被制裁实体开展交易。[①]此外，为保护消费者及金融机构的安全稳健，本部门提出了有关法规，要求受监管实体采取一系列措施以防止网络攻击。[②]

4.金融机构的高层人员对上述政策制度的设计和实施负最终责任。董事会和高级管理人员必须仔细研究作为第一道防线核心的反洗钱和其他合规制度的设计，必须确保配置充足的资源以由底层巩固这些制度和结构。必须设置足够的人员，且必须持续开展培训。

5.调查结果摘要：（在下文有更全面的说明）本和解令述及在本部门对德意志银行的全球机构开展的调查中所发现的严重合规缺失，这些缺陷使得一群腐败的银行交易员和离岸实体能通过利用德意志银行在莫斯科、伦敦和纽约的业务部不当且隐秘地从俄罗斯转出100多亿美元，以满足自身的不当目的。

6.所发现的可疑证券交易计划——被称为"镜像交易"——使得这一腐败团体能在没有引人注意且未受德意志银行合规职能部门的审查的情况下，从俄罗斯移出大笔资金。通过无明显经济目的的证券交易，该计划将卢布兑换为美元，使得金融机构内的危险分子在达到不当目的同时规避对适用法律的遵守。

7.由于AML控制政策、程序和结构的不足，德意志银行错过了几次识别并制止该计划的关键机会。而且，可疑镜像交易的图谋行动发生时德意志银行已被明确告知其BSA/AML制度和管理存在多个缺失，然而，其为补救该情况所采取的行动却是严重不足的。

8.因此，本部门征得德意志银行的同意订立了本和解令，以按下述方式解决本问题。

事实调查结果

在德意志银行莫斯科、伦敦及纽约机构进行的镜像交易计划

9."镜像交易"计划：这里所讨论的镜像交易计划是一个简单但有效的计划。德意志银行美洲信托公司（以下简称DBTCA）为一家位于纽约州纽约市

---

① 见《监管者条例》第504部分（《纽约州准则、法规及条例》第3篇第504节）。

② 见《监管者条例》第23篇第500部分（《纽约州准则、法规及条例》第23篇第500节，于2017年3月1日起生效）。

华尔街60号的实体，获本部门签发的执照并受本部门监督，美元款项正是由该实体经手流入本文所涉及的可疑实体。

10.作为德意志银行莫斯科附属机构（简称德银莫斯科）证券专柜客户的某些公司，通过该专柜进行操作，定期开立订单以购买俄罗斯蓝筹股，并一直使用卢布支付。一般订单的价值为200万~300万美元。

11.此后不久——实际上是购买后当天的某个时间——相关交易方通过德意志银行伦敦分行（以下简称德银伦敦）以相同数量和相同价格出售相同的俄罗斯蓝筹股。该交易中的交易双方确实是密切相关的，比如通过共同所有权而密切相关。

12.这些镜像交易均未显示出任何正当的经济理由。由于德意志银行依据莫斯科和伦敦间的经纪安排将大量手续费和佣金计入德银莫斯科贷方，使得交易方在这些交易中频频亏钱。

13.比如，特定证券的买入或卖出一般对于交易方没什么分别，重要的是存在有配对交易。有一次，为一个交易方买入股份并为其相关交易方卖出相同股份的一个交易方代表告诉德银莫斯科交易员："我今天有十亿卢布……你能找到与此大小匹配的证券吗？"

14.在另一情况下，在被德银莫斯科交易员告知没有俄罗斯联邦储蓄银行的股份可供镜像交易时，一个交易方代表立马将订单转向俄罗斯天然气工业股份公司的股份。此转向没有显而易见的理由，也没给出交易假说。

15.此外，许多出售交易方是在塞浦路斯或英属维尔京群岛等离岸领土进行登记的。[①]卖方的股份以美元支付，并定期通过DBTCA结算。因此，通过本计划，交易方能通过德意志银行偷偷地将卢布兑换为美元。

16.虽然抵消交易本身并不违法，但在本例中，它们没有明显经济目的且可被用于促进洗钱或其他非法行为，因此它们高度暗示了金融犯罪的存在。

---

① 与在离岸领土注册的交易方开展业务是有风险的，对于离岸注册本身可能需要强化尽职调查措施。一般而言，离岸金融中心受到宽松监管，向来被誉为"避税天堂"，能为客户提供大大超出岸上管辖区金融机构所能提供的机密性，尤其是最终实益拥有人的身份。因此，离岸中心一般与非法洗钱活动联系在一起，一般需要更高级别的审查。见（比如）财政部《国家洗钱风险评估》（2015），https://www.treasury.gov/resource-center/terrorist-illicit-finance/Documents/National%20Money%20Laundering%20Risk%20Assessment%20E2%80%93%202006-12-2015.pdf；美国国务院的国际毒品管制战略报告《洗钱与金融犯罪》（2001年3月1日），https://www.state.gov/j/inl/rls/nrcrpt/2000/959.htm。

17.该计划从2011年到2015年初取得良好发展。至少12个实体参与了这些可疑交易活动,这些实体通过(比如)共同实益拥有人、管理者,或代理而密切相关。某些不同交易方雇用了相同的某些个体。比如,某一人士为某一实体的董事会主席,也作为另一实体(该实体本身是持前一个交易方实体100%股份的股东)的实益拥有人。同样地,几个交易方均注册同一个地址。

18."单边"交易:德银莫斯科的证券专柜也促成了与同一群可疑交易方的第二类可疑交易活动——在镜像交易中它们似乎作为交易的一边,而另一边可能由第二家(未识别的)金融机构执行("单边交易")。这些交易几乎全部为镜像交易中所涉及的同一群交易方的买入交易。

19.德银莫斯科证券专柜的交易员执行这些单边交易。此外,德意志银行支付给这些交易方的款项(同样由DBTCA经手)几乎全部支付到俄罗斯和英国以外的银行账户中。

20.有证据清楚表明,德银莫斯科的交易员故意主动地为这两个交易计划提供便利。

21.比如,大多数标的物交易由代表交易双方的单一交易员下单。德银莫斯科的交易员执行交易的卖出,帮助可疑俄罗斯交易方取得俄罗斯证券,并以卢布结算;然后所述德银莫斯科的交易员以场外交易的形式从德银伦敦的客户处购买相同数量的相同股票,并以美元结算;所述德银莫斯科的交易员其后通过远程簿记功能直接将该交易登记到德银伦敦的交易账户中。

22.该"远程簿记"功能对此计划很重要,能使莫斯科交易员在不经伦敦任何有效监督或合规审查的情况下开展镜像交易。通过该方式,该计划得以掩人耳目地进行。

23.德银莫斯科的交易员有时会竭尽全力地促进可疑交易。比如,在德意志银行暂停了计划中涉及的某一交易方时,德银莫斯科的交易员将预先安排买卖的时间,以在俄罗斯莫斯科交易所(MICEX)继续进行与被暂停交易方的镜像交易。

24.当莫斯科专柜的某个交易员担忧这些交易背后没有任何经济理由时,专柜的其他同事则向该担忧的交易员保证说这些交易已经主管批准。在其他多个交易员对可疑交易活动提出同样的问题时,主管却对他们的担忧不屑一顾。

25.贪婪及腐败是德银莫斯科交易员的动机:2006年及2007年,本文所述的俄罗斯业务部为德意志银行产生的年收入分别约为1.69亿英镑和1.23亿英镑。在2008年全球金融危机和德意志银行内部重组后，该年收入减少了至少一半，对交易员增加收入产生了压力。

26.能够轻松获得佣金的计划对于莫斯科证券专柜的交易员是很有吸引力的。交易员承认他们没有有力地对这些可疑交易提出质疑，因为当时交易大幅减缓，他们要趁机赚佣金。一个交易员承认在"市场清淡"时交易员主要"关注佣金"，且尽管存有疑虑，他们还是持续开展这些交易，因为这些交易产生"丰厚的佣金"。

27.此外，莫斯科专柜的一名主管似乎接受了贿赂或其他未披露的报酬以利便本文所述的计划。该主管的一名近亲属（其明显具有历史艺术背景而非金融背景）显然是两家离岸公司的实益拥有人，这两家一家位于英属维尔京群岛一家位于塞浦路斯（均为洗钱高风险管辖区）。2015年4月及6月，镜像交易计划所涉的主要交易方之一，支付总计250 000美元给该名近亲属所拥有的一家公司，据称是依据"咨询协议"进行支付。给这两家公司其中一家的付款总计约为380万美元，几乎都是出于所声称的"财务咨询"目的，且大部分来自两家注册于伯利兹的公司。

28.这些可疑付款也是通过纽约DBTCA进行结算的。

29.上述表明，长远来看，以稳健的合规为代价的、允许通过不当行为进行短期获利的企业文化反而会让机构付出更昂贵的监管、声誉和其他代价。

逾100亿美元计划所得收益由纽约经手

30.如上所述，DBTCA是德意志银行位于华尔街的美国子公司，为该银行的客户（包括其他金融机构）开展代理银行和美元结算活动等。[①]DBTCA依据《纽约州银行法》第三条特许建立，并受本部门的监督和监管。

31.上述镜像交易和单边交易活动所涉的所有美元款项均由DBTCA经手。导致总计超过100亿美元从伦敦转出并由纽约经手。

32.德意志银行因此导致纽约州成为涉及高度可疑金融活动的漫长诡计中的一

---

① 代理银行的美元结算指由美国银行完成交易双方以美元标价的交易之过程。虽然美元结算对从事国际商务的银行客户来说至关重要，不过美元结算对许多银行来说可能是具有潜在高风险的一项业务，因为危险分子可能用于洗钱或便利恐怖分子交易。

个关键渠道。德意志银行已表示其未能发现该计划背后的实际目的，尽管很明显地，该计划可能促成资本外逃、逃税，或其他潜在非法目的。

德意志银行错过了多个发现漫长镜像交易计划的机会

33.德意志银行错过了多个发现并制止镜像交易计划（单脚和双边）的机会，这些机会产生于计划早期，且直到德意志银行于2015年2月发现该计划时持续存在。未能发现或上报该不端行为体现了该银行每一级都存在着合规职能普遍缺陷。

34.比如，第一个机会出现于2011年11月。德银莫斯科代表德银伦敦与可疑交易方之一（以下简称交易方A）进行9亿卢布的交易，但未能进行结算，因为俄罗斯联邦金融市场服务局（以下简称FSFM）已暂时吊销了交易方A的营业执照。尽管出现了明显的“示警红旗”，但仍未有AML审查或上报。

35.第二个清楚了然的警告出现于同月其后不久，一家主流的俄语商业杂志注意到FSFM暂时吊销了几家金融公司从事可疑交易的营业执照。文章描述了高度类似即将发生的镜像交易计划：

根据情报人员所述，计划的运作如下：想要移动资金的客户将资金转入经纪公司，该经纪公司随后购买蓝筹股……之后股份以非居民公司为受益人进行出售……之后在市场上出售证券并将扣除佣金的款项转给国外客户。执法机构认为今年有约1 000亿卢布以此方式转到国外。

值得注意的是，该文章指出了交易方A。

36.由于该商业杂志的文章，莫斯科和伦敦管理层的若干成员收到了一封电邮，要求暂停有关的交易账户。该邮件也含有文章的链接，其收件人包括伦敦的高级合规职员以及各相关部门的几个首席运营官。因此，多个责任经理均被告知了此严重的AML管制问题。

37.此外，德意志银行的高级雇员就如何获得与被吊销交易方有关的失败交易的费用（显然耗费了银行约150万美元的利润）持续讨论了数月。尽管如此，整个过程中，该银行没有任何人员上报或调查客户营业执照被吊销的依据或做相应反洗钱调查。

38.第三个发现可疑镜像交易活动的机会出现于2014年1月，当时欧洲一家金融机构（以下简称欧洲银行）向德银伦敦发出协助请求（以下简称RFA）。在审查来自德意志银行的、涉及另一个可疑交易方（以下简称交易方B）的20个交易后，欧洲银行发出RFA。为了寻求更多有关德银伦敦和交易方B之间关系和交易的信息，欧洲银行特别问及德银伦敦是否有"任何理由相信[与交易方B的]交易在任何方面具有可疑性"。

39.在未收到回复的情况下，欧洲银行多次向德银伦敦发出了提醒函。最终，德银莫斯科的上述主管（其近亲属收到大笔未披露的可疑款项）在回复中向欧洲银行保证交易方B"已通过了本行的KYC［了解你的客户］程序"且德意志银行"认为没有担心的理由"。在该名腐败主管提供给欧洲银行的这封RFA回复中未提及任何一名德意志银行的合规职员。

40.值得注意的是，在德银莫斯科的该主管向欧洲银行发出该回复前仅数日，DBTCA的AML合规小组自行向欧洲银行发送了RFA，询问有关交易方B的信息。DBTCA的信息请求是在DBTCA的交易监控系统发出警报的情况下提出的。[①]根据德银莫斯科主管的保证，欧洲银行在向DBTCA的反馈中提到其没有关于交易方B的不良信息。

41.然后，鉴于从德意志银行两个不同机构处（彼此未进行交流）收到的关于交易方B的矛盾信息，欧洲银行联系了DBTCA的一名高级反金融犯罪（"AFC"）雇员（其负责对特别调查进行监督），以试图调和这些问题。然而，该高级合规雇员未曾回复欧洲银行，也未采取任何行动调查欧洲银行的质疑，后来为该不作为提供的解释是该雇员有"太多工作要做""有太多事务要处理，而只能进行优先排序"。

42.同样令人不安的是，通过显然产生于德意志银行的泄露，交易方B被告知了欧洲银行的RFA，该行为严重违反了反洗钱和反腐败政策做法，然而在德银莫斯科的高级管理层注意到该泄露后，并未展开调查该泄露的行动。

43.第四个发现镜像交易计划的机会出现于几个月后。大约2014年4月时，德意志银行发现了涉及另一交易方（以下简称交易方C）的有问题交易。大约

---

① "交易监控"指机构在调查潜在BSA/AML违规和进行可疑活动报告后对金融交易进行监控的过程。虽然该过程可手动开展，如德意志银行等大型机构通常使用电子系统的高级软件进行交易监控，并在调查对于联邦制裁法可能的违反前首先进行筛选。见《监管者条例》第504部分（《纽约州准则、法规及条例》第3篇第504节）。

在同一时间，德意志银行收到俄罗斯监管机构的信息，指出交易方C参与一个洗钱和逃税计划。然后与交易方C的交易被暂停，且某个初步调查发现了与其他交易方的可疑交易。然而，即便在德银莫斯科的证券专柜出现了明显的可疑交易模式，也并未有进一步的上报。

44. 其后，在2014年4月到9月间，德银莫斯科发现了涉及多个其他交易方（以下简称交易方D和交易方E）的其他可疑镜像交易活动。德银莫斯科暂停了与交易方D和交易方E的交易，并未开展深入调查。①

合规管理不足滋生了德意志银行的镜像交易计划

45.德意志银行的多个合规缺失使得镜像交易计划发展壮大，这些缺失具有广泛性，一般分为以下类别。

46.KYC政策和程序的缺陷：相关期间内，德意志银行用于新客户开户的KYC流程存在广泛且众人皆知的缺陷。其KYC程序为手动程序，仅发挥检查单的功能，雇员机械地关注确保相关文档的收集，而非从潜在客户提供的信息中发现关键信息。

47.即使如此，德银莫斯科证券专柜的许多客户开户文件并不充分，在客户被纳入后也未采取任何行动对他们进行定期审核。值得注意的是，2014年初发布给高级管理人员的内部报告显示，在德意志银行对其位于28个国家的业务部所进行的KYC程序审查中，德意志银行俄罗斯业务部的得分最低。

48.本文所涉交易方的几乎所有KYC文件均是不充分的。此外，由于德意志银行没有用于KYC信息的中央储存库，在该银行暂停一个交易方的可疑交易时，其相关交易方能够开户并继续该交易活动，而不产生任何"示警红旗"。

49.此外，对镜像交易进行监督的莫斯科主管主动参与计划所涉交易方的开户和KYC文档。银行负责开户的职员在未能迅速促进交易进行的多个情况下，感受到了来自主管的敌意和威胁。

50.令人苦恼的是，德银莫斯科的高级管理人员知悉该事实，然而管理人员的应对并不充分。实际上，虽然KYC政策和程序的缺陷多年来已众所周知，德

---

① 除了上述错失的机会，德意志银行的某些制度能够检测镜像交易活动，但却没有被如此使用。比如，"dbCAT"是收集和显示一系列交易数据的报表工具，假如运用适当的过滤，本可发现镜像交易的两边。

意志银行在2016年之前并未采取充分行动进行真正的改革。

51.AML风险评级制度中的缺陷：相关期间内德意志银行未能准确地对其AML国家和客户的风险进行评级。该银行缺乏一个全球性政策规定其风险偏好基准。德意志银行亦没有与同业银行一致，在德意志银行在2014年末将俄罗斯评为高风险之前，同业银行早已这样做了。

52.虽然德意志银行集团审计在2012年制定的《全球反洗钱报告》中具体识别了该银行风险评级方法中的缺陷，德银莫斯科却抵制采用经修改的风险评级程序，因为若采用，其大多数客户将被重新分类为高风险，且该办事处没有所需的经营资源去处理增加的合规工作量。

53.合规和内部审计资源不足：这些缺失由于德意志银行有瑕疵、人员不足的AFC、AML和合规小组而更加恶化。在各个业务分部的风险增加时，该银行在2010年到2012年却集中关注人员编制削减，导致德银莫斯科和其他地方的AFC和合规小组未被配置有效运行所必备的资源。

54.一个高级合规职员一再指出，他不得不"乞求、借用和偷用"以获得适当的资源，导致现有人员不得不一人扮演多个角色。同样地，在某一时刻，没有任何合规背景的一个律师竟同时担任德银莫斯科的合规负责人、法务负责人及AML官。许多在AFC、AML和合规小组担任领导的雇员缺乏必要经验或培训。

55.德意志银行也不具备对可疑证券交易进行监控的自动化系统，而增加了使用远程簿记模式的风险。此外，德意志银行的集团审计在许多方面也都有缺陷，使得其没有履行作为业务和合规小组背后第三道防线的关键角色。

56.公司结构和组织的缺陷：德意志银行分散的AML框架也应对本文所述的合规不足承担责任，该框架导致了政策、角色和责任的混淆。该分散框架导致AML政策在区域而非全球层面进行制定，使得政策和程序的制定和应用不一致。

57.此外，德银莫斯科的管理人员主要关注俄罗斯当地监管要求，几乎或完全忽视国际或其他国家管制要求。这些政策通常没有得到良好设计且不足以满足所涉业务的要求。

58.此外，双重报告结构及工作职责的模糊导致在管理德银莫斯科证券专柜的交易活动时，对主管的过于依赖。许多交易雇员直接向该主管报告，虽然交易雇员对于德银伦敦的个体也有虚线报告责任，但是莫斯科从未上报与可疑交易活动有关的疑虑。

59.莫斯科证券主管也未进行任何有效的监督，他的地方经理（被派到另一个业务组）未意识到此类监督是其责任的一部分。此外，该莫斯科主管在伦敦的直接主管未能对莫斯科主管进行任何合理的监督。总之，德意志银行的AML管制失效是长期存在且覆盖全企业的，使得镜像交易计划发展壮大并持续。

对于德意志银行的长期监管历史明确警示镜像交易等计划可能会发生

60.德意志银行在过去十年存在实质的违反监管历史，明确警示其需要解决会导致镜像交易计划的潜在合规问题。

61.2005年10月，在与DBTCA代理银行和美元结算服务有关的反洗钱和合规计划被发现存在实质缺陷后，DBTCA与本部门（经由其先前的代理机构）签订了书面协议：德意志银行同意开展旨在为这些业务创造有效控制环境的一系列改革。

62.2015年4月，由于德意志银行未能使用相关具体的制度和控制去防止对LIBOR（伦敦银行同业拆放利率）和IBOR（银行间拆放利率）制定过程的操纵，其与本部门订立了一个和解令。所述行为发生于2005年到2009年——就在DBTCA与本部门签订书面协议后——且是全局性的。至少2008年起该银行就知悉LIBOR操纵问题，然而即使在被警告后，该银行仍未能解决相关制度和控制的缺失。该银行向本部门支付6亿美元罚款，并同意设置独立监控官以对重要合规改革进行建议和实施。

63.2015年11月3日，由于该银行用不透明的方法和做法代表伊朗、利比亚、叙利亚、缅甸及苏丹金融机构及受美国经济制裁的其他实体进行近110亿美元的结算交易，该银行与本部门订立了另一个和解令。所述该银行的行为发生于1999年到2006年。这些不透明做法的一个主要目的是不让该银行的美国职员知道他们经由纽约分行所处理的款项与制裁的关联。该银行向本部门支付2亿美元罚款，并再次同意设置独立监控官以"全面审查与德意志银行纽约分行所开展或经手活动有关的或影响这些活动的该银行现有的BSA/AML和OFAC（海外资产控制办公室）制裁合规计划、政策和程序"，包括审查"该银行当前全球BSA/AML和OFAC合规计划的彻底性和全面性。"

64.在有上述监管历史的情况下，2011年起开始并持续到最近2015年2月的可疑镜像交易活动还是发生了，就在该银行被明确告知可追溯到十年前的严重和普遍的合规问题之后。

65.镜像交易计划在德意志银行的调查职能部门内充分上报后（2015年3月），该银行启动了旨在识别可疑交易背景以及了解银行雇员对这些活动及其相关风险的知悉程度的内部调查。

66.该银行及时自行将内部调查的初步评估报告给本部门。自那时起，在本部门看来，该银行认真及时地开展了符合所述任务目的的内部调查，并将其调查发现及时通报本部门。虽然尚有许多工作要做，该银行已采取了必要的补救措施。

67.下述为该银行的违规及其补救措施，本部门认可及肯定德意志银行在开展内部调查的有效性以及与本部门沟通的及时性。

违反法律和法规

68.德意志银行未安全稳健地开展其银行业务，违反了《纽约州银行法》第44节及第44-a节。

69.德意志银行未能维持有效和合规的反洗钱计划，违反了《纽约州准则、法规及条例》第3篇第116.2节。

70.德意志银行未能维持和提供体现所有交易和行为的真实准确账簿、账目和记录，违反了《纽约州银行法》第200-c节。

和解条款

罚款

71.由于上述行为，德意志银行应根据《纽约州银行法》第39节、第44节及第44-a节向本部门支付425 000 000美元民事罚款，应在签署本和解令的十（10）日内支付全部款项。德意志银行同意，对于依据本和解令支付的民事罚款的任何部分，其将不会直接或间接要求、主张或申请税额扣减或与任何美国联邦、州或地方税有关的税收抵免。

独立监控官

72.在本和解令日期后的六十（60）日内，德意志银行、DBTCA和纽约分行应聘请独立监控官（以下简称独立监控官）以：全面审查与（a）DBTCA及（b）纽约分行所开展或经手活动有关的或影响这些活动的该银行现有的BSA/AML合规计划、政策和程序。

73.独立监控官将由本部门全权酌情进行选任，且直接向本部门报告。独立监控官的任期为两年。本部门将考虑是否将德意志银行现有的两个独立监控官其中之一的任务扩展为包含本令所指的工作，本部门保留全权酌情要求聘用额外独立监控官的权利。

74.在独立监控官选择后的三十（30）日内，德意志银行、DBTCA和纽约分行应共同向本部门提交一份聘用函以供批准，该聘用函应至少规定由独立监控官审查和报告以下内容：

a.导致或促使产生本和解令中不当行为且使该等行为持续发酵的原因，自本和解令所述行为发生起该银行对公司治理进行的相关变革或改革，及这些变革或改革是否能显著提升该银行的BSA/AML合规；

b.该银行现有的全球BSA/AML合规计划的彻底性和全面性，包括但不限于旨在解决本和解令所述行为的合规计划；

c.与BSA/AML合规有关的组织结构、管理监督和汇报关系，及对BSA/AML合规团队全球人员配置的评估，包括评估负责该银行遵守BSA/AML合规法律法规的高级职员或雇员的职责、责任、权限和胜任能力；

d.对该银行的BSA/AML合规计划所建议、规划，或最近颁布实行的变革之适当性、合理性和充分性；及

e.对于解决该银行公司治理或其全球BSA/AML合规计划中所发现缺陷或缺失所必要的任何纠正措施。

75.独立监控官应于聘用函所约定的日期向该银行提交与其调查发现和建议有关的书面报告（AML合规报告）。

76.在收到AML合规报告后的六十（60）日内，该银行应向本部门提交一份书面计划，以改善和加强与DBTCA及纽约分行所开展或经手活动有关的或影响这些活动的现有全球BSA/AML合规计划，包括但不限于本和解令中讨论

的那类活动（以下简称"行动计划"）。

77.该行动计划应提供对于增强内部控制的建议及对当前政策、程序和过程的更新或修订，以确保完全遵守BSA的所有适用规定、相关的规章制度、适用的纽约法律法规及本和解令的规定，并包含AML合规报告中识别的纠正措施。

78.该行动计划也应提供改善和加强该银行现有BSA/AML合规计划、政策和程序之管理监督的建议，以提供实质的管理监督框架，并包含AML合规报告中识别的纠正措施。

79.如果该银行认为其不应采纳独立监控官识别的任何纠正措施，该银行应在收到合规报告的四十五（45）日内，将之通知给独立监控官和本部门，书面指出其理由。

80.在与独立监控官磋商后，本部门将审查并全权酌情决定是否要求该银行采纳其所反对的那些建议，是否与该银行进行约定、和/或该银行是否应采取其他行动以实现本和解令所预期的补救。

81.独立监控官其后将监督依据第73到第81段所述的AML合规报告和/或计划所开展的任何纠正措施的实施情况。

82.独立监控官将评估该银行对于其纠正措施的遵守情况，且将提交后续的进度报告和最终报告给本部门和该银行（由本部门全权酌情决定）。本部门可全权酌情决定延长本令规定的任何报告截止期限。

83.独立监控官的任期为被该银行正式聘用之日起的两年，但是，如果德意志银行未能提供配合，本部门可全权酌情决定进一步延长该任期。

84.与独立监控官的权限或授权有关的任何争议将由本部门在与银行和独立监控官协商后全权酌情进行解决。

德意志银行的全面完整配合

85.德意志银行及纽约分行均同意，它们将全面配合独立监控官及本部门，并依照适用法律提供措施，使独立监控官接触到所有相关人员、顾问和第三方服务提供商，及文件、报告，或记录（无论位于何处）等，以支持独立监控官的工作。

违反和解令

86.如果本部门认为该银行重大违反本和解令，本部门将向该银行发出书面通知，该银行必须在收到此类通知的十个营业日或本部门全权酌情决定的较晚的日期内前往本部门以证明未出现重大违反，或（相关时）该违反非属重大违反或已被补救。

87.各方理解并同意，如果该银行未能在指定的期限内按要求出席，这将作为该银行违反的推定证据。在发现该银行已违反本和解令的情况下，本部门保留纽约银行和金融服务法律下可获得的所有补救措施和救济，且可在任何随后的命令、听证会或通知中使用可获得的任何证据。

弃权

88.各方理解并同意本和解令的任何规定均不受本部门以外的任何法院或审判处之审查。

受和解令约束的各方

89.本和解令约束本部门及德意志银行及纽约分行，以及受本部门监督的任何继承者和受让者。本和解令不约束任何联邦或其他州机关或执法机构。

90.本部门将不会就本和解令规定的具体行为对德意志银行采取进一步的行动，但前提是该银行完全遵守本和解令的条款。尽管有前述规定或本和解令中的任何其他规定，对于德意志银行在签署本和解令前知悉的、但在就本文事项提交给本部门的书面材料中未披露的交易或行为，本部门可对该银行采取其他行动。

通知

91.与本和解令有关的所有通知或通信应发到：

本部门：

执法助理副局长

纽约州纽约市

One State Street，邮编10004

律师

纽约州纽约市

One State Street，邮编10004

德意志银行：
联合法务总顾问
德意志银行股份公司
德国法兰克福
Taunusanlage 12号，邮编60325

德国联合法务总顾问
德意志银行股份公司
德国法兰克福
Taunusanlage 12号，邮编60325

律师
纽约州纽约市
Broad Street 125号，邮编10004

其他

93.除非由本部门延缓、修改、中止，或终止，本和解令的每项规定应保持有效和可强制执行。

94.除了本和解令所含的内容，未有诱使任何一方同意本和解令规定的其他承诺、保证、陈述或理解。

附录2：

《和解令》英文原文

NEW YORK STATE DEPARTMENT OF FINANCIAL SERVICES

In the Matter of: COMMERZBANK AG, COMMERZBANK AG NEW YORK BRANCH	CONSENT ORDER UNDER NEW YORK BANKING LAW §§ 39 and 44

The New York State Department of Financial Services (the "Department"), Commerzbank AG New York Branch ("New York Branch"), and Commerzbank AG (collectively with New York Branch, "Commerzbank" or "the Bank") stipulate that:

WHEREAS Commerzbank is a major international banking institution with more than 53,000 employees and total assets exceeding $670 billion that is licensed by the Department to operate a foreign bank branch in New York State;

WHEREAS Commerzbank failed to maintain sufficient controls, policies, and procedures to ensure compliance with the Bank Secrecy Act and other anti-money laundering laws and regulations ("BSA/AML") of the United States and New York;

WHEREAS the Bank maintained ineffective compliance procedures relating to due diligence on its foreign branches and its customers, failed to share information about customers or transactions necessary for BSA/AML compliance with the appropriate New York-based compliance personnel, and constructed its monitoring processes and tools so as to reduce the number of alerts that would be generated and require further investigation;

WHEREAS examinations of the Bank by the Department and other regulators concluded that the Bank's BSA/AML compliance program was deficient due to, among other things, weaknesses in its transaction monitoring system and failure to implement internal controls to appropriately manage risks relating to foreign correspondent banking business;

WHEREAS despite repeated negative examination reports from the Department and other regulators that cited BSA/AML-related problems, the Bank failed to remedy its deficient BSA/AML compliance program;

WHEREAS one result of these deficiencies was Commerzbank's facilitation of numerous payments through the Bank's New York Branch that furthered a massive accounting fraud by a large international corporation;

WHEREAS in addition, from at least 2002 to 2008, Commerzbank used non-transparent methods and practices to conduct approximately 60,000 U.S. dollar clearing transactions[1] valued at

---

[1] U.S. dollar clearing is the process by which U.S. dollar-denominated payments between counterparties are made through a bank in the United States.

over \$253 billion on behalf of Iranian and Sudanese entities[1] subject to U.S. economic sanctions, including entities and individuals on the Specially Designated Nationals List ("SDN") of the Office of Foreign Assets Control ("OFAC");

WHEREAS by knowingly processing these transactions for entities subject to U.S. sanctions using non-transparent methods, Commerzbank failed to maintain accurate records as to those transactions, vitiated its New York Branch's and correspondents' controls that were designed to detect possibly illegal transactions, and prevented effective review by regulators and authorities;

WHEREAS Commerzbank's conduct ran counter to U.S. foreign policy and national security interests, constitutes potential violations of New York law and regulations, and raises serious regulatory safety and soundness concerns, including concerns as to the falsification of business records, the offering of false instruments for filing, the failure to maintain books and records, the failure to maintain an effective BSA/AML program and to detect and report suspicious transactions, the obstruction of governmental administration, and the failure to report misconduct;

WHEREAS the Bank is entering into a Deferred Prosecution Agreement with the U.S. Department of Justice, in which Commerzbank AG admits that it violated Title 18, United States Code, Section 371, by conspiring to violate the International Emergency Economic Powers Act, and that Commerzbank AG New York Branch also violated Title 31, United States Code, Sections 5318(g), 5318(h), and 5318(i), because Commerzbank AG New York Branch, acting through certain employees located in New York, willfully (i) failed to maintain an adequate anti- money laundering program; (ii) failed to establish due diligence for foreign correspondent accounts; and (iii) failed to report suspicious transactions relevant to a possible violation of law or regulations, as required by the Secretary of the Treasury.

NOW THEREFORE, to resolve this matter without further proceedings pursuant to the Superintendent's authority under Section 44 of the Banking Law, the Department and Commerzbank agree to the following:

Failure to Maintain an Effective BSA/AML Compliance Program

1. Commerzbank willfully failed to maintain an adequate BSA/AML compliance program for a number of years, in violation of U.S. and New York laws and regulations.

The Bank's Compliance Program Suffered From Structural and Procedural Deficiencies

2. While Commerzbank Group Compliance had ultimate oversight of the Bank's global legal and regulatory compliance, compliance personnel in Commerzbank's New York Branch were responsible for BSA/AML compliance.

3. Commerzbank's New York Branch maintained correspondent accounts for Commerzbank's foreign branches, but it did not maintain or have access to due diligence information about those branches' customers, which information was necessary to conduct effective BSA/AML monitoring.

4. Foreign branches often transmitted payment requests to Commerzbank's New York Branch using non-transparent SWIFT payments messages[2] that did not disclose the identity of the remitter

---

[1]   Commerzbank also processed a number of U.S. dollar transactions involving Burmese and Cuban entities subject to U.S. sanctions from 2002 to 2007.

[2]   The Society of Worldwide Interbank Financial Telecommunications, or SWIFT, provides an international network through which banks exchange electronic wire transfer messages. SWIFT messages contain various informational fields.

or beneficiary. As a result of not having a complete picture of the transactions, Commerzbank's New York Branch's compliance processes and controls were ineffective, and fewer alerts or red flags were raised than would have been if full information had been shared.

5. The Bank's global compliance program also suffered from serious deficiencies and contributed to significant failings. Even when transactions from foreign branches did trigger alerts in New York, the New York compliance staff did not have access to the customer information necessary to investigate the alert; they had to request relevant information directly from the foreign branch or from the Home Office in Frankfurt.

6. Overseas personnel, however, often did not respond to those requests by New York staff for many months or sent inadequate or insufficient responses. This practice prevented Commerzbank's New York Branch personnel from adequately investigating alerts and led to alert backlogs.

7. For example, a member of the New York compliance staff told investigators that many foreign relationship managers did not maintain customer due diligence and know-your-customer material in a manner consistent with U.S. regulations, keeping little formal documentation that could be shared with New York staff when they needed to investigate alerts. And many overseas employees were uncooperative or did not respond to requests for more information by those investigating alerts - they felt that New York compliance staff were simply "crying wolf" when they raised BSA/AML compliance issues.

8. On some occasions, because information from overseas offices was not provided, New York staff "cleared" or closed alerts based on its own perfunctory internet searches and searches of public source databases, without ever receiving responses to its requests for information from the foreign offices.

9. In some instances, when compliance personnel in New York attempted to strengthen the transaction monitoring filters, business personnel in Frankfurt overruled those efforts. For example, New York compliance staff reported that on at least two occasions they sought to add the names of particular foreign branch clients, whom they judged to be high-risk, to their transaction monitoring filters, so as to ensure that those clients' transactions received extra scrutiny. But employees in Germany initially overruled those steps and forbade the New York Branch from adding client names to its filters on its own initiative, instead demanding that New York compliance staff consult with business-side personnel in Germany before taking such actions. Eventually, after consultation between New York compliance staff and business-side personnel in Germany, those customer names were added to the transaction monitoring filters.

10. Furthermore, a New York compliance staff member (discussed below in Paragraphs 12 and 13) told investigators that when he joined the bank in late 2009, the compliance department in New York did not have an adequate number of employees or sufficiently experienced personnel.

Compliance Management Altered the Transaction Monitoring System to Reduce Alert Output

11. In an interview with investigators, a New York-based vice president in compliance who was involved in establishing the thresholds used by Commerzbank's New York Branch's monitoring software in effect until 2010 reported that, while the goal of the threshold- setting process was to identify suspicious transactions and exclude irrelevant alerts, the threshold floors were driven by the volume of the output of alerts - that is, the threshold floors were set based on a desire not to generate "too many alerts."

12. In addition, the New York compliance staff member charged with overseeing the

implementation of a new transaction monitoring tool told investigators that the Head of Regional Compliance for Commerzbank's New York Branch (who is also discussed below, in Paragraph 22) required a weekly update as to the number of alerts generated by the transaction monitoring system.

13. Furthermore, the compliance staff member reported that in 2011, both the Head of Regional Compliance and the Head of AML Compliance asked him to change the thresholds in the automated system to reduce the number of alerts generated. The compliance staff member reported that he refused to do so.

Compliance Failings Resulted in the Bank's Facilitation of a Massive Fraud by an Overseas Affiliate's Customer

14. Commerzbank's BSA/AML compliance deficiencies allowed a customer to operate a massive corporate accounting fraud through the Bank, during which time some senior bank officials in Singapore - two of whom later held senior positions in Commerzbank's New York Branch while the fraud was ongoing - had suspicions about the business but failed to convey those suspicions to compliance personnel in Commerzbank's New York Branch or take adequate steps to stop fraudulent transactions.

15. From in or about the late 1990s through in or about 2011, the Olympus Corporation, a Japanese optics and medical device manufacturer, perpetuated a massive accounting fraud designed to conceal from its auditors and investors hundreds of millions of dollars in losses. Olympus perpetuated its fraud through Commerzbank's private banking business in Singapore, known as Commerzbank (Southeast Asia) Ltd. ("COSEA"), and a trusts business in Singapore, Commerzbank International Trusts (Singapore) Ltd., and the New York Branch, through its correspondent banking business. Among other things, the fraud was perpetuated by Olympus through special purpose vehicles, some of which were created by Commerzbank - including several executives based in Singapore - at Olympus's direction, using funding from Commerzbank. One of those Singapore-based Commerzbank executives, Chan Ming Fong - who was involved both in creating the Olympus structure in 1999 while at COSEA, and who later on his own managed an Olympus-related entity in 2005-2010 on behalf of which Chan submitted false confirmations to Olympus's auditor - subsequently pled guilty in the United States District Court for the Southern District of New York to conspiracy to commit wire fraud.

16. Starting as early as 1999 and continuing intermittently until 2010, Commerzbank facilitated numerous transactions through New York, totaling more than $1.6 billion, that supported the accounting fraud by Olympus.[①]

17. Over the life of the fraud, numerous Commerzbank employees in Singapore raised concerns about the Olympus business and related transactions. But those concerns did not lead to effective investigation of the business and were not shared with relevant staff in New York responsible for BSA/AML compliance, even as numerous transactions in furtherance of the fraud were processed through New York. Indeed, certain Commerzbank personnel who investigated the compliance issues relating to the Olympus business in Singapore or who had otherwise been made aware of the concerns about the Singapore affiliates' business with Olympus later held senior positions at Commerzbank's New York Branch, yet they never related their concerns to New York compliance staff.

---

① The corporation and three of its former executives pled guilty to criminal charges in Japan relating to the years-long fraud in 2012.

18. For example, when Commerzbank sent a London-based compliance officer on special assignment to Singapore in 2008 to analyze and help enhance compliance efforts there, he was told by the Bank's Asian Regional Head of Compliance and Legal to pay particular attention to the Olympus-related business. The Regional Head of Compliance warned him that, while the business yielded "very substantial" fees for Commerzbank, the structure of the business was "complex" and "extraordinarily elaborate and redolent of layering" and that it raised suspicions of money laundering, "fraud, asset stripping, market manipulation, and derivative Tax offences."

19. The compliance officer did investigate the Olympus-related business that Commerzbank's Singapore affiliates were conducting; he became "concerned about the complex nature" of the business and concluded that Commerzbank "may have to terminate the relationship if we can't get to the bottom of the structure." He ordered Singapore staff to meet with Olympus representatives to get more information about the business, and he criticized those employees when they dragged their feet and urged them to get more information quickly. By the time he left Singapore, however, the issue was not resolved.

20. During his time in Singapore, he also learned of more general compliance deficiencies there. He learned that the compliance controls there had been weak for some time, ever since management-directed cost cutting significantly reduced compliance resources. He discovered that relationship managers were slow to conduct customer due diligence he requested. Indeed, the compliance officer criticized staff in Singapore for their lax attitude toward customer due diligence. And he and others noted that recent departures of compliance staff and relationship managers had left the Singapore affiliates "very very weak in regards to control and support."

21. Soon after his special assignment in Singapore concluded in late 2008, the compliance officer took over as head of compliance in Commerzbank's New York Branch in approximately April 2009. Yet despite all he had learned about compliance deficiencies in Singapore generally and about the suspicious Olympus-related business specifically, at no time during his tenure in New York did the compliance officer convey negative information or raise any issues about Olympus or any related entity to the New York Branch.

22. A new staff member was installed as Head of Regional Compliance for the New York Branch in approximately June 2010. He, too, had spent time at Commerzbank's Singapore affiliates before coming to New York. And he, too, was aware of the compliance deficiencies in Singapore and of the suspicious nature of the Olympus-related business, which he also knew involved wire transactions through New York. For example, while he was working in Singapore, a resigning compliance staff member told him that Singapore compliance was "a time bomb ready to go off." And after the previous compliance officer's special assignment ended in late 2008, he was made aware of the specific suspicions surrounding the Olympus-related business. Yet after moving to the New York Branch, he also failed to share any concerns with the New York compliance staff who would have been in a position to scrutinize the fraudulent transactions being processed through New York.

23. Between 1999 and 2010, Commerzbank's New York Branch processed transactions worth more than $1.6 billion that supported or helped facilitate the Olympus fraud. Most of those transactions did not trigger alerts in the New York Branch's transaction monitoring system and thus were not scrutinized by New York compliance staff.

24. Alerts were triggered, however, regarding two large transactions in March 2010. In

response to the alerts, compliance officers in New York sent a request for information directly to Singapore as well as to a dedicated mailbox for information requests in Frankfurt, asking for information about the identities of the ultimate originator and recipient of the transactions, the main business of the parties, and the purpose of the transactions. Compliance officers in Singapore had previously identified the same two Olympus-related transactions as potentially suspicious and investigated and closed the alerts. In response to the New York Branch's request for information, however, compliance personnel in Singapore did not relay any of the concerns about the Olympus-sponsored structures or transactions. Instead, the only response to the request for information came in the form of a brief email. New York staff eventually cleared the alerts as not suspicious.

Internal and External Reviews Repeatedly Highlighted Compliance Failures

25. The Bank received numerous warnings and criticisms about its BSA/AML compliance deficiencies from internal auditors, the Department, and other regulators in the United States during the relevant time period, but the Bank failed to remedy its deficient BSA/AML compliance program.

26. The Bank recognized it faced BSA/AML challenges arising from its 2008 acquisition of Dresdner Bank, which had been subject to a Cease and Desist Order issued by the Department and the Board of Governors of the Federal Reserve System. The Bank hired a consultant to advise about integration issues. The consultant identified various aspects of BSA/AML compliance that needed to be addressed and identified enhancements that the Bank should make to the transaction monitoring process, including the implementation of a new transaction monitoring system. The Bank committed to enhancing its BSA/AML compliance in a joint letter agreement with the Department and the Federal Reserve Bank of New York ("NYFRB") in May 2009 and reported regularly to regulators about its integration progress.

27. In 2009, Commerzbank Group Audit conducted an audit of the New York Branch's compliance program. The overall assessment of the New York Branch's AML compliance program was "fair," which equated to a score of three on a five-point scale. According to numerous Commerzbank New York Branch compliance officials, the 2009 AML audit report of New York Branch was among the most negative internal audit reports in memory. The audit found the New York Branch's AML compliance program lacking in several important ways. The report detailed weaknesses in transaction monitoring, customer profile monitoring, and know-your-customer processes, as well as general IT infrastructure deficiencies that affected the AML program.

28. The following year, a joint examination by the Department and NYFRB analyzed the Bank's progress in meeting the terms of the May 2009 agreement. The examiners once again found several significant BSA/AML weaknesses, concluding that the BSA/AML program was "adequate, but require[d] management's further focused attention to certain areas that need improvement." For example, the examination team concluded that while the Bank had implemented some changes to its transaction monitoring system recommended by the outside consultant described above in Paragraph 26, the monitoring system lacked "other fundamental rules typically used to monitor wire activity" and that these failings "heightened the risk that [the Bank] did not detect suspicious activity for approximately nine months." The examiners also pointed out weaknesses in other areas such as alert investigation and customer due diligence.

29. The Bank's BSA/AML compliance problems persisted, however. A NYFRB examination that concluded in May 2012 found yet more deficiencies and lapses in the BSA/AML program, this time relating to Commerzbank's New York Branch's involvement in the banknotes business

conducted by the Home Office in Germany. That finding led to formal supervisory action by the NYFRB. As late as July 2014, however, the NYFRB found that the Bank had not yet satisfied or only partially satisfied most of the remedial measures that it required as a result of its negative assessment of the Bank's deficiencies in monitoring the (now closed) banknotes business.

30. Despite the deficiencies identified in this string of negative reports by internal auditors and outside regulators and the series of remedial efforts ordered and undertaken as a result, BSA/AML compliance problems persisted. A joint examination by the Department and NYFRB, concluded in July 2013, found continued inadequacies in the core BSA/AML compliance program elements at Commerzbank's New York Branch. The Department and NYFRB concluded that "management has failed to implement internal controls to appropriately identify, mitigate, and manage BSA/AML risks associated with the branch's foreign correspondent banking business." The examiners' report also criticized management for failing to conduct appropriate due diligence on Commerzbank's foreign branches, for whose customers business was conducted through the New York Branch. And they found "violations of BSA/AML laws and regulations that were the result of systemic internal control weaknesses with the branch's customer risk rating, [customer due diligence], and suspicious activity monitoring programs" that helped "increase the branch's risk to money laundering activities."

Use of Wire Stripping and Non-Transparent Cover Payments to Disguise Transactions

31. Commerzbank also used altered or non-transparent payment messages to process tens of thousands of transactions through New York on behalf of customers subject to U.S. economic sanctions.

32. In an effort to grow its business relationships with Iranian customers in the early 2000s, Commerzbank created internal procedures for processing U.S. dollar payments to enable those clients, which included state-controlled financial institutions such as Bank Sepah and Bank Melli, to clear U.S. dollar payments through the U.S. financial system without detection.

33. From at least May 2003 to July 2004, Commerzbank altered or stripped information from wire messages for payments involving Iranian parties subject to U.S. sanctions so as to hide the true nature of those payments and circumvent sanctions-related protections.

34. The Bank designated a special team of employees to manually process Iranian transactions - specifically, to strip from SWIFT payment messages any identifying information that could trigger OFAC-related controls and possibly lead to delay or outright rejection of the transaction in the United States. Bank employees circulated both formal written instructions and informal guidance via email directing lower-level staff to strip information that could identify sanctioned parties from wire messages before sending the payment messages to U.S. clearing banks.

35. The Bank advised customers subject to U.S. sanctions to omit sanctions-related information from payment messages, to complement Commerzbank's special processing. And some customers included notes such as "do not mention our name in USA" in their payment requests so as to ensure Bank employees applied special processing before sending those payment requests to U.S. correspondents.

36. This conduct continued into July 2004 because senior management failed to institute effective controls or procedures to ensure the practice ceased even after announcing a prohibition on wire stripping in 2003.

37. From at least 2002 to 2007, Commerzbank also relied heavily on the use of non-transparent cover payments to process tens of thousands of U.S. dollar transactions for Iranian and other clients subject to U.S. sanctions as part of a strategy to evade scrutiny in the U.S.

38. Employees followed Bank instructions that required them to split incoming payment messages into two outgoing messages - one message that was sent directly to the beneficiary's bank and a second MT202 cover message that was sent to the U.S. clearing bank, which did not require or contain any information about the remitter - with the intent of preventing such transactions from being detected and possibly frozen, blocked, or delayed in the United States.

39. Commerzbank usually processed U.S. dollar payments for sanctioned customers through its own New York Branch; however, in some instances involving Iranian clients, Commerzbank refrained from processing the payment through its own New York Branch and in one instance routed the payment through a U.S. correspondent bank so that their "own branch would not be involved" in case "the going [got] tough."

40. Beginning in 2005, Commerzbank processed U.S. dollar payments for an Iranian subsidiary of the Islamic Republic of Iran Shipping Lines ("IRISL") using the accounts of a different, non-Iranian IRISL affiliate in order to avoid detection by correspondents and regulators in the U.S. Later, after the Bank instituted a policy limiting its business with Iranian customers in 2007, Hamburg branch employees moved the accounts of two Iranian IRISL subsidiaries into sub-accounts under the account of one of IRISL's European affiliates and also changed the country identification codes for certain IRISL affiliates in the Bank's internal records so as to obfuscate these entities' true Iranian relationship.

41. In addition, the Bank recognized that other international financial institutions declined to process Sudanese U.S. dollar transactions, due to U.S. sanctions, and therefore that Sudan represented a potentially profitable market. From at least 2002 to 2006, the Bank maintained U.S. dollar accounts for as many as 17 Sudanese banks, including five SDNs, and processed approximately 1,800 U.S. dollar transactions valued at more than $224 million through the U.S. using non-transparent methods for these clients and other Sudanese entities.

42. Commerzbank's New York Branch also helped hide the true nature of the Bank's U.S. dollar clearing activities by failing to act on numerous indications that payment requests were being submitted in a non-transparent manner; in 2004, an employee even called upon the Frankfurt office to "suppress" the creation of MT210s[1] relating to payments ordered by Iranian banks because "authorities could view our handling of them as problematic."

Violations of Law and Regulations

43. Commerzbank AG and Commerzbank's New York Branch failed to maintain an effective and compliant anti-money laundering program and OFAC compliance program, in violation of 3 NYCRR § 116.2.

44. Commerzbank failed to maintain or make available at its New York Branch true and accurate books, accounts, and records reflecting all transactions and actions, in violation of New York Banking Law § 200-c.

45. Commerzbank employees knowingly made and caused to be made false entries in the

---

①   MT210 messages advised the New York Branch of an incoming payment.

Bank's books, reports, and statements and omitted and caused to be omitted therefrom true entries of material particular pertaining to the U.S. dollar clearing business of Commerzbank at its New York Branch, with the intent to deceive the Superintendent and examiners of the Department and representatives of other U.S. regulatory agencies who were lawfully appointed to examine the Bank's condition and affairs at its New York Branch, in violation of 3 NYCRR § 3.1.

46. Commerzbank failed to submit a report to the Superintendent immediately upon discovering fraud, dishonesty, making of false entries and omission of true entries, and other misconduct, whether or not a criminal offense, in violation of 3 NYCRR §300.1.

SETTLEMENT PROVISIONS

Monetary Payment

47. Commerzbank shall pay a civil monetary penalty pursuant to Banking Law § 44 to the Department in the amount of $610,000,000. Commerzbank shall pay the entire amount within ten days of executing this Consent Order. Commerzbank agrees that it will not claim, assert, or apply for a tax deduction or tax credit with regard to any U.S. federal, state, or local tax, directly or indirectly, for any portion of the civil monetary penalty paid pursuant to this Consent Order.

Independent Monitor

48. Commerzbank will engage an independent monitor, selected by the Department in the exercise of its sole discretion, to conduct, consistent with applicable law, a comprehensive review of the BSA/AML and OFAC compliance programs, policies, and procedures now in place at the bank that pertain to or affect activities conducted by or through Commerzbank's New York Branch. The monitor will report directly to the Department.

49. Among other things, the monitor will review and report on:

a. The elements of the Bank's corporate governance that contributed to or facilitated the improper conduct discussed in this Consent Order and that permitted it to go on, relevant changes or reforms to its corporate governance that the Bank has made since the time of the conduct discussed in this Consent Order, and whether those changes or reforms are likely to significantly enhance the Bank's BSA/AML and OFAC compliance going forward;

b. The thoroughness and comprehensiveness of the Bank's current global BSA/AML and OFAC compliance program;

c. The organizational structure, management oversight, and reporting lines that are relevant to BSA/AML and OFAC compliance, and an assessment of the staffing of the BSA/AML and OFAC compliance teams, including the duties, responsibilities, authority, and competence of officers or employees responsible for the Bank's compliance with laws and regulations pertaining to BSA/AML or OFAC compliance;

d. The propriety, reasonableness, and adequacy of any proposed, planned, or recently-instituted changes to the Bank's BSA/AML and OFAC compliance programs;

e. Any corrective measures necessary to address identified weaknesses or deficiencies in the Bank's corporate governance or its global BSA/AML and OFAC compliance program.

50. Commerzbank agrees that it will fully cooperate with the monitor and support its work by, among other things, providing the monitor with access to all relevant personnel, consultants and third-party service providers, files, reports, or records, whether located in New York, Germany, or elsewhere, consistent with applicable law.

51. Within 90 days of the date of formal engagement, the monitor will submit to the Department and Commerzbank's Board of Directors a preliminary written report of findings, including proposed corrective measures.

52. Within 30 days of receiving the monitor's preliminary written report of findings, Commerzbank will submit to the Department a written plan designed to improve and enhance current global BSA/AML and OFAC compliance programs that pertain to or affect activities conducted by or through Commerzbank's New York Branch, incorporating any relevant corrective measures identified in the monitor's report (the "Action Plan"). The Action Plan will provide for enhanced internal controls and updates or revisions to current policies, procedures, and processes in order to ensure full compliance with all applicable provisions of the BSA and related rules and regulations, OFAC requirements and rules, and the provisions of this Consent Order. Upon receipt of written approval from the Department, Commerzbank will begin to implement the changes.

53. Within 30 days of receiving the monitor's preliminary written report of findings, Commerzbank will submit to the Department a written plan to improve and enhance management oversight of BSA/AML and OFAC compliance programs, policies, and procedures now in place at the Bank that pertain to or affect activities conducted by or through Commerzbank's New York Branch (the "Management Oversight Plan"). The Management Oversight Plan will address relevant matters identified in the monitor's written report of findings and provide a sustainable management oversight framework. Upon receipt of written approval from the Department, Commerzbank will begin to implement the changes.

54. The monitor will thereafter oversee the implementation of corrective measures set out in the Bank's Action Plan and Management Oversight Plan. Finally, the monitor will assess the Bank's compliance with those measures. The monitor will submit subsequent progress reports and a final report to the Department and to Commerzbank's Board of Directors at intervals to be determined by the Department. The Department may, in its sole discretion, extend any reporting deadline set out in this section.

55. The term of the monitor's engagement will extend for two years from the date of formal engagement. Any dispute as to the scope of the monitor's authority or mandate will be resolved by the Department in the exercise of its sole discretion, after appropriate consultation with Commerzbank and the monitor.

Termination of Commerzbank Employees

56. While several of the Bank employees who were centrally involved in the improper conduct discussed in this Consent Order no longer work at the Bank, several such employees do remain employed by the Bank.

57. The Department orders the Bank to take all steps necessary to terminate the following four

employees, who played central roles in the improper conduct discussed in this Consent Order but who remain employed by the Bank: a relationship manager in the Financial Institutions Department who was assigned the code number 6; a front office staff member in the Interest, Currency & Liquidity Management Department who was assigned the code 402; and two back office staff members in the Cash Management & International Business Department, who were assigned the codes 131 and 430. If, after taking whatever action is necessary to terminate these employees, a judicial or regulatory determination or order is issued finding that such action is not permissible under German law, then these employees shall not be allowed to hold or assume any duties, responsibilities, or activities involving compliance, U.S. dollar payments, or any matter relating to U.S. operations.

58. The Department's investigation has also resulted in the resignation from Commerzbank of the former Head of AML, Fraud, and Sanctions Compliance for Commerzbank's New York Branch, who played a central role in the improper conduct described in this Consent Order.

Breach of Consent Order

59. In the event that the Department believes Commerzbank to be in material breach of the Consent Order, the Department will provide written notice to Commerzbank and Commerzbank must, within ten business days of receiving such notice, or on a later date if so determined in the Department's sole discretion, appear before the Department to demonstrate that no material breach has occurred or, to the extent pertinent, that the breach is not material or has been cured.

60. The parties understand and agree that Commerzbank's failure to make the required showing within the designated time period shall be presumptive evidence of Commerzbank's breach. Upon a finding that Commerzbank has breached this Consent Order, the Department has all the remedies available to it under New York Banking and Financial Services Law and may use any evidence available to the Department in any ensuing hearings, notices, or orders.

Wavier of Rights

61. The parties understand and agree that no provision of this Consent Order is subject to review in any court or tribunal outside the Department.

Parties Bound by the Consent Order

62. This Consent Order is binding on the Department and Commerzbank, as well as any successors and assigns that are under the Department's supervisory authority. But this Consent Order does not bind any federal or other state agency or any law enforcement authority.

63. No further action will be taken by the Department against Commerzbank for the conduct set forth in the Consent Order, provided that Commerzbank complies with the terms of the Consent Order.

64. Notwithstanding any other provision in this Consent Order, however, the Department may undertake additional action against Commerzbank for transactions or conduct that Commerzbank did not disclose to the Department in the written materials Commerzbank submitted to the Department in connection with this matter.

Notices

65. All notices or communications regarding this Consent Order shall be sent to:

For the Department:

        James Caputo
        Senior Counsel
        One State Street
        New York, NY 10004

For Commerzbank:

        Volker Barth
        Divisional Board Member, Compliance
        Hafenstrasse 51
        60261 Frankfurt am Main, Germany

        Gunter Hugger
        General Counsel
        Kaiserstrasse 16
        60261 Frankfurt am Main, Germany
        Armin Barthel
        Managing Director - Head of Legal North America
        225 Liberty Street
        New York, NY 10281

Miscellaneous

66. Each provision of this Consent Order shall remain effective and enforceable until stayed, modified, suspended, or terminated by the Department.

67. No promise, assurance, representation, or understanding other than those contained in this Consent Order has been made to induce any party to agree to the provisions of the Consent Order.

《和解令》中文译文

纽约州金融服务局

德国商业银行股份有限公司

德国商业银行股份有限公司纽约分行

和解令

——《纽约州银行法》第39节及第44节

纽约州金融服务局（以下简称本部门）、德国商业银行股份有限公司纽约分行（以下简称纽约分行），及德国商业银行股份有限公司（与纽约分行统称为德国商业银行或该银行）规定：

鉴于德国商业银行为拥有53 000多名雇员及逾6 700亿美元总资产的一家大型国际银行机构，获本部门颁发的执照在纽约州开立一家外国银行分行；

鉴于德国商业银行未能维持充分的控制、政策和程序，以保证符合《银行保密法》和美国及纽约的其他反洗钱法律法规（以下简称"BSA/AML"）要求；

鉴于该银行没有对其外国分支机构和客户开展有效的尽职调查，该银行没有将对于BSA/AML合规来说必要的客户或交易信息报告给相应的纽约合规人员。此外，该行在设计合规流程和工具时，有意减少应有的报警数量，规避了这些本应该产生的报警和后续必要的调查；

鉴于本部门及其他监管机构对该银行的检查结论为：由于其交易监控系统的缺陷以及其内部控制缺失不能对外国代理银行业务有关的风险进行适当管理等原因，该银行的BSA/AML合规计划存在缺陷；

鉴于尽管本部门和其他监管机构所给出的多个负面检查报告已指出了BSA/AML相关问题，该银行仍未能补救其有缺陷的BSA/AML合规计划；

鉴于德国商业银行在其纽约分行所经手的多次付款交易中存在上述缺陷，这些付款促成了一家大型国际公司的重大会计欺诈；

鉴于此外，至少从2002年到2008年，德国商业银行用不透明的方法和做法代表受美国经济制裁的伊朗及苏丹实体[①]，包括海外资产控制办公室（以下简

[①] 德国商业银行2002年到2007年也处理了涉及受美国制裁的缅甸和古巴实体的多个美元交易。

称OFAC）特别指定国民名单（以下简称SDN）上的实体和个体，开展了估值逾2 530亿美元的约60 000笔以美元结算的交易[1]；

鉴于德国商业银行故意使用不透明方法为受美国制裁的实体处理这些交易，其没有保留与这些交易有关的准确记录，阻碍了纽约分行及代理银行的对旨在检测潜在非法交易的控制，且阻止了监管机构和当局的有效审查；

鉴于德国商业银行的行为违反了美国的外交政策及国家安全利益，构成对纽约法律法规的潜在违反，且引起了严重的监管安全和稳健问题，包括以下有关的问题：伪造商业记录、提供虚假文件进行备案、没有维持账户和记录、没有维护有效的BSA/AML计划及没有检测和上报可疑交易、阻碍政府行政部门及没有报告不当行为；

鉴于该银行正与美国司法部签订延缓起诉协议，在该协议中，德国商业银行股份有限公司承认其由于密谋违反《国际紧急经济权力法》而违反了《美国法典》第18篇第371节，且德国商业银行股份有限公司纽约分行亦违反了《美国法典》第31篇第5318（g）节、第5318（h）节和第5318（i）节，因为该分行通过纽约的某些雇员而故意（i）不维持充分的反洗钱计划；（ii）不对外国代理账户进行尽职调查；及（iii）不按照财政部长的要求上报可能违反法律或法规的可疑交易。

因此，依据《银行法》第44节下的局长授权，为解决本问题而不再引起更多诉讼程序，本部门与德国商业银行同意如下：

未能维护有效的BSA/AML合规计划

1.德国商业银行多年故意不维护适当的BSA/AML合规计划，违反了美国及纽约的法律法规。

该银行的合规计划存在结构和程序缺失

2.虽然德国商业银行集团合规部对该银行的全球法务与监管合规承担最终监督，但德国商业银行纽约分行的合规人员对BSA/AML合规承担责任。

3.德国商业银行纽约分行为德国商业银行的外国分支机构维护代理账户，但其没有维护或没有调查这些分支机构之客户的尽职调查信息，而所述信息对于开展有效的BSA/AML监控是必要的。

---

① 美元结算指由美国境内银行完成交易双方以美元标价的交易之过程。

4.外国分支机构通常使用不披露汇款人或受益人身份的不透明银行SWIFT付款报文①来向德国商业银行纽约分行传输付款申请。由于不了解交易的全貌，德国商业银行纽约分行的合规流程和控制弱化，所引起的警报或"示警红旗"少于充分信息共享下可引起的数量。

5.该银行的全球合规计划也存在严重的缺失，导致重大失效。即使外国分支机构的交易触发了在纽约的警报，纽约的合规职员还是无法访问调查该警报所必需的客户信息，他们只能直接向外国分支机构或法兰克福总行请求相关信息。

6.然而，海外人员通常多个月都不回复纽约职员的这些请求或只发送不足够或不充分的回复，这一做法阻止了德国商业银行纽约分行的人员对警报的充分调查并导致警报积压。

7.比如，一名纽约合规职员告诉调查员，许多国外客户经理没有按照符合美国法规的方式维护客户尽职调查及"了解你的客户"材料，在纽约的职员需要调查警报时，几乎没有可共享的正式文档。在要求提供这些警报调查所需的更多信息时，许多海外雇员不配合或不回复——他们觉得纽约的合规职员在提出BSA/AML合规问题时，仅仅是在发假警报。

8.在某些情况下，由于海外办事处未提供信息，在从未于海外办事处收到信息请求回复的情况下，纽约职员只基于自身不够权威的网上搜索及在公共源数据库的搜索就"解除"或关闭警报。

9.在某些情况下，当纽约的合规人员试图加强交易监控过滤时，却被法兰克福的业务人员否决了。比如，纽约的合规职员报告说，至少有两次，他们寻求将他们判断为高风险的特定外国分支机构的客户姓名/名称加入他们的交易监控过滤中，以确保这些客户的交易受到额外审查，但是德国的雇员起初否决这些行动并禁止纽约分行自行将客户的姓名/名称加入其过滤，反而要求纽约的合规职员在采取此类行动前应咨询德国的业务人员。最终，在纽约合规职员与德国业务人员协商后，这些客户的姓名/名称被加入了交易监控过滤。

10.此外，一名纽约的合规职员（见以下第12段和第13段）告诉调查员，在他于2009年末加入该银行时，纽约的合规部门并没有足够数量的员工或富有经验的人员。

---

① 环球银行金融电信协会，即SWIFT，提供了一个国际网络，经由该网络，银行进行电汇报文的交换。SWIFT报文含有多个不同信息栏。

11.在接受调查员的访问时，一个纽约合规副总裁，其参与了为德国商业银行纽约分行的监控软件（到2010年前仍有效）确定阈值的工作，报告说，虽然阈值设定的目标是发现可疑交易并排除无关警报，但为了不产生太多警报，在设计阈值时，做了一些不该做的调整。

12.此外，负责监督一个新交易监控工具实施的一名纽约合规职员告诉调查员，德国商业银行纽约分行的地区合规负责人（也在以下第22段中述及）要求对交易监控系统所产生的警报数量进行每周更新。

13.此外，该合规职员报告说，2011年，地区合规负责人及AML合规负责人要求他将自动化系统的阈值进行变更，以减少所产生的警报数量。该合规职员报告说，他拒绝了该要求。

14.德国商业银行的BSA/AML合规缺失使得一名客户能够通过该银行施行重大公司会计欺诈，在该欺诈进行期间，新加坡的某些银行高级官员（其中两个后来在德国商业银行纽约分行担任高级职位，而当时欺诈还在持续进行）对于该业务有过怀疑，但没有将这些疑虑传达给德国商业银行纽约分行的合规人员或采取适当行动以阻止欺诈交易。

15.从大约20世纪90年代后期到大约2011年，日本光学及医疗器械制造商奥林巴斯株式会社为了对其审计师和投资者隐瞒数亿美元的亏损而持续开展重大会计欺诈。奥林巴斯通过德国商业银行（东南亚）有限公司（以下简称"COSEA"）、德国商业银行国际信托（新加坡）有限公司及纽约分行的代理银行业务而持续开展其欺诈。奥林巴斯通过特殊目的实体等手段开展欺诈，其中某些特殊目的实体由德国商业银行（包括位于新加坡的数个高管）经奥林巴斯指示且利用德国商业银行的资金进行创建。

16.最早从1999年起，断断续续地到2010年，德国商业银行经由纽约促成了多个交易，总计超过16亿美元，这些交易支持了奥林巴斯的会计欺诈。[①]

17.在该欺诈存续期间，多个位于新加坡的德国商业银行雇员对奥林巴斯业务和相关交易提出担忧，但是这些担忧并没有引致对该业务的有效调查，且未报告给纽约负责BSA/AML合规的相关职员，即使促成该欺诈的多个交易经由纽约处理。实际上，某些德国商业银行人员（在新加坡调查与奥林巴斯业务有

① 该公司及其三名前高管于2012年在日本，就该长达数年的欺诈，承认犯有相关刑事指控。

关的合规问题或以其他方式对在新加坡的附属机构与奥林巴斯之间业务产生疑虑）后来在德国商业银行纽约分行担任高级职位，然而他们从未将自身的疑虑告知纽约的合规职员。

18.比如，德国商业银行在2008年派遣一名伦敦的合规官员到新加坡开展特殊任务以分析和帮助增强当地的合规工作，他被该银行的亚洲地区合规和法务负责人告知要特别注意与奥林巴斯有关的业务。该地区合规负责人警示他，虽然该业务为德国商业银行产生了"非常丰厚的"费用，但该业务的结构是"复杂的"且"及其煞费苦心且令人联想到（洗钱中的）多层化"，产生洗钱、"欺诈、资产拆卖、市场操纵、及衍生的税务犯罪"的嫌疑。

19.该合规官员调查了德国商业银行新加坡附属机构正在开展的与奥林巴斯有关的业务；他对该业务的"复杂性质产生担忧"，得出结论认为德国商业银行"可能需要终止该段关系，因为我们无法了解其中结构的底细"。他命令新加坡职员与奥林巴斯代表见面以了解该业务的更多信息，并在这些职员拖延时批评他们，督促他们加快速度获取更多信息。然而在他离开新加坡时问题并未解决。

20.在他停留新加坡时，他也了解到当地更多的一些合规缺陷。他了解到，自从由管理指示的成本削减造成合规资源显著减少，一段时间以来，当地的合规控制都较薄弱。他发现客户经理在开展他所要求的尽职调查时动作缓慢。实际上，该合规官员由于新加坡职员对于客户尽职调查的松懈态度而批评他们。他和其他人注意到，近来合规职员和客户经理的离职使得新加坡附属机构的"控制和支持非常薄弱"。

21.在新加坡特别任务于2008年末结束后不久，该合规官员大约在2009年4月接任了德国商业银行纽约分行合规负责人一职。然而尽管他已大体得知新加坡的合规缺失以及具体了解与奥林巴斯有关的可疑业务，但他在纽约任职期间从未向纽约分行传达奥林巴斯或任何相关实体的负面信息或提出与它们有关的任何问题。

22.大约2010年6月一名新职员任职纽约分行地区合规负责人，在去纽约之前，他也在德国商业银行的新加坡附属机构任过职，也知道新加坡的合规缺失及与奥林巴斯有关业务的可疑性质，他还知道该业务涉及经由纽约的电汇交易。比如，当他在新加坡工作时，一名离职的合规职员告诉他，新加坡合规是

"一个随时会爆炸的定时炸弹"。在前述合规官员的特别任务于2008年末结束时，他也听到了围绕奥林巴斯有关业务的具体怀疑声音。然而，在移到纽约分行后，他也没有将任何担忧告知纽约合规职员，否则他们本可详细检查正经由纽约处理的欺诈交易。

23.1999年到2010年间，德国商业银行纽约分行处理了价值超过16亿美元的交易，这些交易支持或帮助促成了奥林巴斯欺诈。这些交易大多数未触发纽约分行的交易监控系统的警报，因此未被纽约合规职员详细检查。

24.不过2010年3月发生的两起大型交易倒是触发了警报。为应对这些警报，纽约的合规官员直接向新加坡以及法兰克福专用于信息请求的邮箱发送信息请求，询问相关交易的最初发起人和接受人的身份、各方的主要业务，及交易目的。新加坡的合规官员先前将这两个与奥林巴斯有关的交易识别为具有潜在可疑性，并调查和关闭了警报。不过在回复纽约分行的信息请求中，新加坡的合规人员未传达与奥林巴斯结构或交易有关的任何疑虑，唯一的信息请求回复中只使用了简短邮件的形式。纽约职员最终将这些警报作为不可疑进行解除。

内外部审查多次凸显了合规缺失

25.该银行在相关期间从内部审计师、本部门及美国的其他监管机构收到了多个与其BSA/AML合规缺失有关的警告和批评，但是该银行没有补救其有缺陷的BSA/AML合规计划。

26.该银行在2008年收购德累斯顿银行时意识到其面临着BSA/AML挑战，该收购受到了本部门及美国联邦储备委员会发出的终止及停止令。该银行聘用了一名顾问对整合问题提供建议，该顾问发现BSA/AML合规的多个方面问题需要进行解决，且该银行需对交易监控过程进行改进，包括实施新的交易监控系统。该银行在2009年5月与本部门和纽约联邦储备银行（以下简称"NYFRB"）的共同协议中承诺改善其BSA/AML合规，并定期向监管机构报告其整合进程。

27.2009年，德国商业银行集团审计部对纽约分行的合规计划开展了审计。纽约分行的AML合规计划整体被评估为"中等"，相当于五分制中的三分。多个德国商业银行纽约分行的合规官员认为，纽约分行的2009年AML审计报告是记忆中最负面的内部审计报告之一。该审计发现,纽约分行的AML合规计划在多个重要方面存在缺失。该报告详细说明了交易监控、客户信息监控及"了解你的客户"程序中存在的缺陷,以及影响AML计划的一般IT基础设施缺失。

28.接下来一年,本部门和NYFRB的共同检查分析了该银行对于2009年5月协议条款的遵守进度。检查员再次发现多个重要的BSA/AML缺陷,认为BSA/AML计划"是适当的,但需管理层进一步关注某些不完善的领域"。

29.然而,该银行的BSA/AML合规问题还是持续存在。NYFRB于2012年5月完成的一次检查发现了BSA/AML计划的更多缺失和失误,这次是与德国商业银行纽约分行所参与的德国总行开展的钞票业务有关。这一检查结果引起NYFRB的正式监督行动。但是直到2014年7月,NYFRB发现该银行仍未满足或只部分满足被要求采取的补救措施,由于该银行在监控(现已关闭的)钞票业务中的缺陷得到NYFRB的负面评估,而被要求采取所述补救措施。

30.尽管在这一连串内部审计师和外部监管机构的负面报告中发现了缺陷,且因此被命令和开展一系列补救工作,BSA/AML合规问题还是持续存在。本部门与NYFRB在2013年7月完成的一个联合检查发现德国商业银行纽约分行BSA/AML合规计划的核心要素持续存在不足。本部门和NYFRB的检查结论为"管理人员未能实施内部控制以适当发现、降低并管理与分行外国代理银行业务有关的BSA/AML风险"。检查员的报告也批评上述管理人员未能对德国商业银行外国分支机构(由纽约分行为它们的客户开展业务)开展适当的尽职调查。他们认为"由于分行客户风险评级、[客户尽职调查],及可疑活动监控计划的系统性内控缺陷(所述缺陷导致"增加分行承受洗钱活动的风险")而造成了对于BSA/AML法律法规的违反"。

利用电汇信息消除和不透明拨付对交易进行掩盖

31.同时,通过改动的或不透明的付款报文,德国商业银行代表受美国经济制裁的客户经由纽约处理了数万个交易。

32.2000年早期,为了发展其与伊朗客户的业务关系,德国商业银行制定了用于处理美元付款的内部程序以使这些客户(包括国有控股的金融机构,如伊朗赛帕银行和伊朗国家银行)能在不被发现的情况下通过美国金融体系结算美元款项。

33.至少从2003年5月到2004年7月，德国商业银行对涉及受美国制裁的伊朗有关方付款电汇报文中的信息进行了修改或消除，以隐藏这些款项的真实性质并规避与制裁有关的防护。

34.该银行指定了一队特别雇员去人工处理伊朗交易——具体来说，是从SWIFT付款报文中消除可触发OFAC相关管制且可能导致在美国境内交易被延迟或断然拒绝的任何识别信息。该银行的雇员通过邮件传达正式书面指示和非正式指导，指示下级职员在发送付款报文给美国结算银行前从电汇报文中消除可能识别受制裁有关方的信息。

35.该银行建议受美国制裁的客户在付款报文中略去与制裁有关的信息，以与德国商业银行的特别处理形成互补。某些客户在其付款申请中包含如"请勿在美国提及我方名称"等附注，以确保该银行雇员在发送这些付款申请给美国代理行前进行特别处理。

36.即使2003年宣布禁止电汇信息消除，由于高级管理人员未能采取有效控制或程序以确保终止该做法，上述行为还是持续到了2004年7月。

37.至少从2002年到2007年，德国商业银行还大量使用不透明拨付为伊朗和受美国制裁的其他客户处理数万个美元交易，构成逃避美国境内审查策略的一部分。

38.雇员遵从该银行的指示：要求他们将发来的付款报文分成两个发出的报文——一个直接发给收款行，另一个MT202拨付发给美国结算银行，此类报文不要求或含有与汇款人有关的任何信息——意在防止此类交易被发现及可能在美国境内被冻结、拦截或延迟。

39.德国商业银行通常经由其自身的纽约分行处理受制裁客户的美元付款；但是，在涉及伊朗客户的某些情况下，德国商业银行没有通过其纽约分行进行付款处理，且有一次是通过一家美国代理银行进行款项处理，以使在"事情不顺"时它们"自身的分行不受牵连"。

40.2005年起，德国商业银行通过使用另一家非伊朗伊斯兰共和国航运公司（以下简称"IRISL"）附属机构的账户，为IRISL的一家伊朗子公司处理美元付款，以避免被代理银行和美国监管机构发现。后来，在该银行于2007年实施限制与伊朗客户业务往来的政策后，汉堡分行的雇员将两家伊朗IRISL子公司的账户移入IRISL一家欧洲子公司账户的子账户中并变更了某些IRISL子公司在该银行内部记录中的国家识别代码，以模糊这些实体的真实伊朗关系。

41.此外，该银行发现由于美国的制裁，其他国际金融机构拒绝处理苏丹的美元交易，因此苏丹可能是个有利可图的市场。至少从2002年到2006年，该银行为多达17家苏丹银行（包括五家位于SDN上的）维护美元账户，并用不透明的方法为这些客户和其他苏丹实体经由美国处理了估值超过2.24亿美元的约1800个美元交易。

42.在多个迹象显示付款申请正在以不透明的方式提交时，德国商业银行纽约分行没有采取行动，从而帮助隐藏该银行美元结算活动的真实性质；2004年，一名雇员呼吁法兰克福办事处"制止"创建与伊朗银行所要求付款有关的MT210①，因为"当局可能会认为我们对于它们的处理是有问题的"。

违反法律和法规

43.德国商业银行股份有限公司和德国商业银行纽约分行未能维持有效和合规的反洗钱计划及OFAC合规计划，违反了《纽约州准则、法规及条例》第3篇第116.2节。

44.德国商业银行未能在其纽约分行维持和提供体现所有交易和行为的真实准确账簿、账目和记录，违反了《纽约州银行法》第200-c节。

45.德国商业银行雇员故意自行及让人在该银行的账簿、记录和报表中作出虚假条目，在其中省略及让人省略与德国商业银行纽约分行美元结算业务有关的要项的真实条目，以在本部门局长和检查员及其他美国监管机构的代表被依法委任检查该银行的状况及其纽约分行的事务时欺骗他们，违反了《纽约州准则、法规及条例》第3篇第3.1节。

46.德国商业银行在发现欺诈、不诚实、作出虚假条目及省略真实条目及其他不当行为（无论是否属于刑事犯罪）时没有立即提交报告给局长，违反了《纽约州准则、法规及条例》第3篇第300.1节。

---

① MT210报文用于向纽约分行告知相关汇入款。

和解条款
罚款

47.德国商业银行应根据《纽约州银行法》第44节向本部门支付610 000 000美元民事罚款，应在签署本和解令的十日内支付全部款项。德国商业银行同意，对于依据本和解令支付的民事罚款的任何部分，其将不会直接或间接要求、主张或申请税额扣减或与任何美国联邦、州或地方税有关的税收抵免。

独立监控官

48.德国商业银行应聘请一名由本部门全权酌情选择的独立监控官，以依据适用法律全面审查与德国商业银行纽约分行所开展或经手活动有关的或影响这些活动的该银行现有的BSA/AML及OFAC合规计划、政策和程序。

49.该监控官将审查和报告以下内容等：

a.导致或促进本和解令中所述不当行为开展且使其持续进行的该银行的公司治理要素，自本和解令所述行为发生起该银行对公司治理进行的相关变革或改革，及这些变革或改革是否能显著提升该银行的BSA/AML及OFAC合规；

b.该银行现有的全球BSA/AML及OFAC合规计划的彻底性和全面性；

c.与BSA/AML及OFAC合规有关的组织结构、管理监督和汇报关系，及对BSA/AML及OFAC合规团队人员配置的评估，包括评估负责该银行遵守BSA/AML或OFAC合规法律法规的高级职员或雇员的职责、责任、权限和胜任能力；

d.对该银行的BSA/AML及OFAC合规计划所建议、规划，或最近颁布实行的变革之适当性、合理性和充分性；及

e.对于解决该银行公司治理或其全球BSA/AML及OFAC合规计划中所发现缺陷或缺失来说必要的任何纠正措施。

50.德国商业银行同意，其将全面配合该监控官，支持监控官的工作，并依照适用法律，使监控官能接触到所有相关人员、顾问和第三方服务提供商及文件、报告，或记录（无论是否位于纽约）等。

51.在正式聘用日期后的90日内，该监控官将向本部门和德国商业银行的董事会提交一份初步调查结果书面报告，包括所建议的纠正措施。

52.在收到监控官的初步调查结果书面报告后的30日内，德国商业银行应向本部门提交一份书面计划，以改善和加强与德国商业银行纽约分行所开展或经手活动有关的或影响这些活动的现有全球BSA/AML及OFAC合规计划，并包含监控官报告中指出的任何相关纠正措施（以下简称行动计划）。该行动计划应包括增强内部控制的建议及对当前政策、程序和过程的更新或修订，以确保完全遵守BSA的所有适用规定、相关的规章制度、OFAC的要求和规则及本和解令的规定。在收到本部门的书面批准后，德国商业银行应开始实施变革。

53.在收到监控官的初步调查结果书面报告后的30日内，德国商业银行应向本部门提交一份书面计划，以改善和加强对于与德国商业银行纽约分行所开展或经手活动有关的或影响这些活动的BSA/AML及OFAC合规计划之管理监督（以下简称"管理监督计划"）。该管理监督计划应解决监控官初步调查结果书面报告中发现的相关问题，并提供可持续的管理监督框架。在收到本部门的书面批准后，德国商业银行应开始实施变革。

54.监控官其后将监督该银行行动计划和管理监督计划中所规定纠正措施的实施情况。最终，监控官将评估该银行对于这些措施的遵守情况。监控官将以本部门决定的时间间隔提交后续的进度报告和最终报告给本部门和德国商业银行董事会。本部门可全权酌情决定延长本节规定的任何报告截止期限。

55.该监控官的任期为正式聘用之日起的两年。与该监控官的权限或授权有关的任何争议将由本部门在与德国商业银行和监控官适当协商后全权酌情进行解决。

德国商业银行雇员的终止雇用

56.虽然集中参与本和解令所述不当行为的该银行的一些雇员已不在该银行工作，但还是有几个此类雇员仍受雇于该银行。

57.本部门命令该银行采取所有必要行动去终止雇用以下四名雇员，他们在本和解令所述不当行为中扮演核心角色且仍受雇于该银行：金融机构部的一名客户经理，代码为××；互联网、货币及流动性管理部的一名前台职员，代码为××；现金管理与国际业务部的两名后台职员，代码为××和××。如果在采取任何必要行动终止雇用这些员工后，所发出的相关司法或监管裁定或命令认为此类行动不被德国法律所允许，那么这些雇员不得担任或开展涉及合规、美元付款，或与美国业务有关的任何事项之任何职务、职责或行动。

58.本部门的调查也致使前任德国商业银行纽约分行的AML、诈骗及制裁合规负责人从德国商业银行离职，其在本和解令所述的不当行为中扮演核心角色。

违反和解令

59.如果本部门认为德国商业银行对本和解令有重大违反，本部门将向德国商业银行发出书面通知，该银行必须在收到此类通知的十个营业日或本部门全权酌情决定的较晚的日期内前往本部门以证明未出现重大违反，或（相关时）该违反非属重大违反或已被补救。

60.各方理解并同意如果德国商业银行未能在指定的期限内按要求出席，这将作为该银行违反的推定证据。在发现德国商业银行已违反本和解令的情况下，本部门保留《纽约银行和金融服务法》下可获得的所有补救措施，且可在任何随后的听证会、通知或命令中使用可获得的任何证据。

弃权

61.各方理解并同意本和解令的任何规定均不受本部门以外的任何法院或审判处之审查。

受和解令约束的各方

62.本和解令约束本部门及德国商业银行，以及受本部门监督的任何继承者和受让者。本和解令不约束任何联邦或其他州机关或任何执法机构。

63.本部门将不会就本和解令规定的行为对德国商业银行采取进一步的行动，但前提是该银行完全遵守本令的条款。

64.尽管有前述规定或本和解令中的任何其他规定，对于德国商业银行在就本文问题提交给本部门的书面材料中未披露给本部门的交易或行为，本部门可对该银行采取其他行动。

通知

65.与本和解令有关的所有通知或通信应发到：

本部门：

高级法律顾问

纽约州纽约市

One State Street，邮编10004

德国商业银行：

负责合规的分部董事会成员

德国法兰克福

Hafenstrasse 51号，邮编60261

法务总顾问

德国法兰克福

Kaiserstrasse 16号，邮编60261

常务董事兼北美法务负责人

纽约州纽约市

自由街225号，邮编10281

其他

66.除非由本部门延缓、修改、中止，或终止，本和解令的每项规定应保持有效和可强制执行。

67.除了本和解令所含的内容，未有诱使任何一方同意本和解令规定的其他承诺、保证、陈述或理解。

以兹证明，各方于2015年3月11日签署本和解令。

德国商业银行股份有限公司　纽约州金融服务局

负责合规的分部董事会成员　金融服务局局长

9.

■ **任性的孩子**
——兆丰银行被罚事件

2016年8月，因违反保密法与反洗钱防治法，台湾兆丰金控旗下兆丰国际商业银行与美国纽约州金融服务局（New York Department of financial Services，DFS）签署《和解令》（见附录）。作为《和解令》的一部分，兆丰国际商业银行认缴罚款1.8亿美元（约合56.9亿新台币或12亿元人民币），创台湾地区金融史上罚款总额之最。

　　兆丰银行被重罚，并非因为该行存在明确的洗钱行为。兆丰银行管理层"喊冤"，台湾地区监管当局也表示处罚过重。这次并非兆丰银行第一次被监管机构处罚，回溯过往，兆丰银行依靠其特殊的股东背景，长期忽视作为商业银行的反洗钱合规职责，面对问题有恃无恐任性而为，凡此种种，值得玩味并引以为戒。

兆丰银行概述

兆丰国际商业银行（以下简称兆丰银行）成立于1984年8月21日，是台湾兆丰金融控股股份有限公司（以下简称兆丰金控）旗下全资子公司。兆丰银行前身是中国商银及交通银行，两家均为台湾地区历史悠久的银行。中国商银前身"中国银行"可溯至清光绪时期之户部银行及大清银行。"中央银行"成立前，"中国银行"被赋予代理国库及发行钞券的职责，"中央银行"成立后则被指定为政府特许的国际贸易及汇兑专业银行。交通银行创立于1916年，初期奉命与"中国银行"共同掌管国库收支及办理钞券发行。交通银行历年来致力配合经济政策及经建计划，协助策略性及重要工业发展。

兆丰银行经营地域范围以亚洲地区为中心，并拓展其他地区，地理分散性较台湾当地其他同业佳。截至2016年底，该行在台湾地区共有108家分行（含海外部），台湾地区以外分行22家、支行5家、代表处（含营销办事处）5处，加上在泰国、加拿大的转投资子银行及分行，合计海外网点39处。

根据BANKSCOPE最新数据，截至2017年12月31日，兆丰银行总资产92 148百万美元，资产规模在台湾地区商业银行中排名第5位，世界排名第235位。

兆丰银行发展初期是台湾地区当局指定的外汇业务主办银行，也是台湾地区美元和欧元清算银行，在台湾地区金融体系及外汇市场占据重要地位。由此，兆丰银行得以维持稳定的客户结构与营收来源，并以稳固的企业客户为基础开拓海外业务，凭借海外业务的优势，在利差幅度较大的外币放款业务方面持续成长。兆丰银行的净利息收益率优于台湾地区其他同业，为该行的业务与资金结构奠定了良好的基础。

兆丰国际商业银行股权结构图：

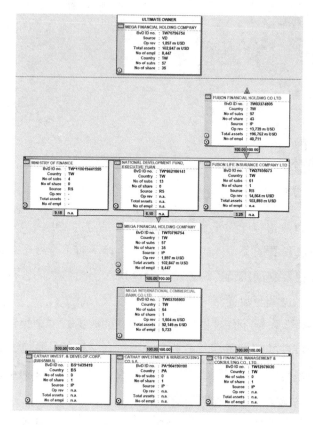

图1　兆丰银行股权结构

兆丰银行是兆丰金控利润的主要来源，对兆丰金控的利润贡献度约为80%。由于台湾"财政部"持有兆丰金控8.4%的股份，作为旗下全资子公司，兆丰银行也成为台湾当局推动外汇政策最主要的支持配合银行。S&P对兆丰银行的信用评级为A。台湾地区最大评级公司中华信评认为，该行在面临市场剧烈变动压力时，应可以获得来自"政府"方面的潜在支持。2015年兆丰银行获得兆丰金融控股公司241亿新台币（折合7.79亿美元）注资，作为未来兆丰银行在海外布局所需的资金。根据未来业务发展需要，母公司兆丰金控将持续支持兆丰银行的资本与各项业务资源。

兆丰银行未来发展战略包括六部分：

（1）强化授信的贷后管理，并透过完整的授信资产报酬率分析，了解客户的利润贡献度，作为后续授信的参考，提升经营效益。

（2）持续强化财富管理系统交易平台，推展数字营销，透过虚实通路及社群媒体之整合，提供全通路之营销机制，争取数字金融之新商机。

（3）积极寻找适切之策略联盟伙伴，或评估参股投资其他海外金融机构，以深化国际化经营。

（4）配合金管会"打造数字金融环境3.0"计划，持续进行通讯技术应用于金融之研发及创新，开发新客群、新利基。

（5）扩大投资领域，积极寻找金融科技（Fintech）、大数据分析、云端应用及物联网概念等相关产业之合适投资目标，协助数字金融发展的进程。

（6）由2016年增设的"洗钱防制中心"负责规划及推动全行洗钱防制机制的有效实施，协助各单位落实洗钱防制/反恐融资作业、确保台湾地区内、外单位洗钱防制/反恐融资相关规范能符合各地区的最新法令及监理要求。

兆丰银行被罚事件始末

事件经过

2016年8月19日，美国纽约州金融服务局（NEW YORK STATE DEPARTMENT OF FINANCIAL SERVICES，DFS）以违反银行保密法及反洗钱法（BSA/AML[1]）相关规定为由，重罚台湾兆丰金控旗下兆丰国际商业银行（以下简称兆丰银行）纽约分行1.8亿美元（约合56.9亿新台币或12亿元人民币），罚金数额之高创台湾地区金融业的海外受罚纪录。兆丰银行认缴高额罚金是该行与美国纽约州金融服务局于2016年8月签署的《和解令》（见附录）的一部分。

美国纽约州金融服务局主管在新闻稿中指出，检查发现，兆丰银行纽约分

---

[1] "BSA" stands for the Bank Secrecy Act, 31 U.S.C. § § 5311 et seq. "AML" stands for "anti-money laundering." The Bank Secrecy Act, the rules and regulations issued thereunder by the U.S. Department of the Treasury, 31

行的合规项目只是"一个空壳","完全缺乏对一个必要的法令遵循结构的根本理解","DFS不会容忍对反洗钱法的公然漠视,并将采取果断和强硬的行动,反对任何机构不实施合规计划,以防止非法交易","DFS在兆丰银行纽约分行发现的合规缺失是严重的、持续的,影响了整个兆丰银行。它们表明该行根本不理解强有力的合规基础设施的重要。"

兆丰银行遭美重罚一事震惊台湾地区金融界。台湾"财政部"随即邀集公股①金控及银行召开会议,了解公股银行海外分支机构内部稽核及法令遵循的情形。台行政当局还要求"金融管理委员会"召集"财政部""法务部"等组成专案督导小组着手调查,追究兆丰银行相关人员的可能责任。台湾"金融管理委员会"于同年对兆丰银行开出1 000万新台币罚单,并要求解除总经理等多人职务。

兆丰银行曾于2016年8月5日在董事会期间将此案作为重大议题讨论,并请相关人士到会说明。美国纽约州金融服务局调查期间,兆丰银行前董事长蔡友才闪辞。2016年8月16日,兆丰银行前总经理徐光曦正式就任兆丰金控兼兆丰银行董事长。徐光曦曾亲赴兆丰银行美国分行所在地金融监理机关说明有关情况,希望降低损失,维护信誉。但此行被媒体称为"徐光曦查徐光曦",无助问题的澄清。徐光曦返台后暨辞去集团内所有职务。兆丰金控暨兆丰银行总经理吴汉卿曾于22日口头请辞以示对案件负责,但被挽留。

据资深媒体人曝料,兆丰银行牵涉2003年10月底萨尔瓦多前政府本票事件。本票是在萨尔瓦多前总统弗朗西斯柯·弗洛雷斯卸任前以其全名开具。弗朗西斯柯·弗洛雷斯趁出席纽约联合国大会期间拿着这张兆丰银行纽约分行的黄色本票前去兑付并转账,从而导致哥斯达黎加、危地马拉、尼加拉瓜在内的另外三位前总统被美国参政部反洗钱中心监测并抓在当场。马英九上台后,以此为戒,将改由巴拿马分行开出。

兆丰银行被罚原本是一个简单的金融事件,一个多月后却逐渐升级为政治案件。台媒名嘴和绿营②政治人物大肆宣传这是国民党党产的洗钱,从马英九、周美青到金溥聪,再加蓝营执政时的财政官员,都被点名是幕后黑手。另

---

① 台湾金融机构一度以公营银行为主。1989年7月17日公布实施银行法部分条文修正案,开放民营银行的设立。除新设民营银行外,还出现一批由信托投资与信用合作社改制及原公营私有化的民营银行。
② 台湾蓝绿阵营是指国民党和民进党。国民党的党旗颜色是蓝色为主,民进党的党旗是以绿色为主。

一方面，绿营内部趁机争权夺位，猛攻绿营现任的财政官员。有关人士指出，林全[①]团队上台后，背后存有各方派系角力，对于兆丰金控董事长迟迟无法拍板。除徐光曦外，绿营里也有一股力量挺台"财政部"前负责人吕桔诚出任兆丰金控董事长，这也是导致兆丰金控董事长拖延数月才敲定的原因。兆丰银行纽约分行出问题的时间是从2010年到2014年，即马英九执政时期。由于马妻周美青在2008年退休以前长期任职兆丰银行，于是媒体名嘴和绿营政治人物就把马英九、周美青、金溥聪和前朝的蓝营财政金融官员全部牵拖进来，大肆抨击。其实纽约州金融服务局早已把疑似洗钱交易的名单交给"金融管理委员会"，"金融管理委员会"主任丁克华却迟迟不公布名单内容，任由简单的金融案件演变成复杂的政治风暴。名单内容公布后，疑似洗钱交易的名单内并无台湾政治人物，而且可疑的汇款全都不是由台湾汇出，所有指控一下都成了空穴来风、子虚乌有，令人啼笑皆非。

各方较量，终于造成"金融管理委员会"主任丁克华去职和六位前、现任财政金融官员被移送"监察院"追究责任。兆丰银行方面，由于董事长长期缺位，总、分行对美方不予积极回应，以及银行自身长期以来对反洗钱合规的漠视和任性而为，最终招致美监管当局重罚。

细数兆丰银行的六项失误

美国纽约州金融服务局在《和解令》中详细陈述了其对兆丰银行纽约分行的检查结果。据此，笔者概括了兆丰银行在此次事件中的六项失误：

1. 内控合规的缺失

兆丰银行在反洗钱内控合规的制度、人员、系统等方面存在一系列缺失。

首先，合规制度缺失。兆丰纽约缺乏可疑交易预警制度和处理流程。反洗钱内控合规的制度与流程、交易监控和客户尽职调查的制度与流程严重不一致，缺乏可疑交易预警制度和处理流程。

其次，缺乏合格的合规人员。兆丰银行虽然在总部和分支机构都设置了首席合规官（CCO）一职，但任职者均不熟悉美国的监管要求。兆丰纽约首席合规官同时兼任关键业务运营职责，存在职责冲突。合规人员在任职期间培训不足。

---

① 林全：中国台湾地区前"行政院长"。

再次，系统的缺失。兆丰银行总部和分支机构的合规人员未能定期审查旨在发现可疑交易的监测监控过滤标准；兆丰纽约交易监控系统、可疑活动告警、案例管理系统等制度和流程存在缺失。

2. 未对可疑交易进行申报

2010—2014年，兆丰银行未申报其巴拿马-科隆自由贸易区分行大量的可疑交易。有证据表明，有大量的客户在巴拿马的莫萨克·冯塞卡（Mossack Fonseca）律师事务所协助下，在兆丰银行其他分行开立或曾经开立账户，而这家律师事务所的主要业务正是为客户设立空壳公司，目的可能是为避开金融或税务上的法律规定。兆丰银行没有依据法令、防制洗钱及可疑交易等规定对这些交易进行申报。

3. 对客户的尽职调查不足

巴拿马被认为是洗钱的高风险地区。兆丰银行在巴拿马城和巴拿马-科隆自由贸易区均设有分支机构，有义务将涉及巴拿马的交易按照最高级别进行客户尽职调查和防控，然而兆丰银行总部和纽约分行漠视此类交易风险：1）未按规定对包括代理行在内的高风险客户进行加强型尽职调查（Enhanced Due Diligence）；2）客户信息收集不充分；3）没能就其代理行业务的交易实质进行合理解释；4）作为"可疑交易"的中间行，兆丰纽约的工作人员未能对交易给出合理的解释。

4. 风险评估不足

兆丰纽约的总体风险评估存在严重缺陷，缺乏对分行客户、产品、服务和地理位置的全面BSA/AML风险评估。

5. 季报未按规定报送总行

兆丰纽约没有将季度合规会议记录转发总部合规部门。而且，兆丰纽约经常以会议议程代替会议记录。此外，兆丰纽约的季度合规报告缺失关键信息，阻碍了总部合规部门对于兆丰纽约的合规充分程度的评估。

6. 漠视监管机构且态度不佳

兆丰银行前董事长蔡友才在得知此事后闪辞，此后，董事长职位空窗期长达4个多月。期间，代理董事长吴汉卿被质疑未积极处理此事。台湾"金融管理委员会"、"财政部"也是后续才知道此事，然后才成立项目小组开展专职调查。2016年2月，美方已向兆丰银行指出兆丰银行纽约分行存在内控不佳、巴拿马分行存在未上报可疑交易、未恰当执行客户尽职调查、风险评估政策，以及总行监督职能不足等问题，但兆丰银行直到3月24日才予以回复，而且非但不接受调查结果反而反驳纽约州金融服务局的若干检查发现，并表示某些交易并非可疑交易。时任总经理的蔡友才事发后闪电离职，兆丰银行也不再特别响应，以上态度均让美方觉得不满。

另外，在《和解令》中，DFS两次提到兆丰银行关于交易监控的大量文件没有从中文翻译成英文，妨碍了监管机构的有效审查，足见其对兆丰银行的漠视和不积极配合的态度极其不满。

兆丰被罚事件的影响和教训

据悉，此次DFS对兆丰银行开出的1.8亿美元（约合56.9亿新台币）的罚金，是台湾"央行"行长彭淮南亲自出面与美方交涉后谈下来的"优惠价"，否则罚金会更高。

被罚事件造成了兆丰银行一系列的开支和损失。2016年8月19日《和解令》正式签署后，22日一开市，兆丰金控股价跳水，台股一度跌破9 000点关卡。除缴纳1.8亿美元的高额罚款外，兆丰银行还必须按照《和解令》的要求聘请美国纽约州金融服务局认可的独立顾问和独立监察员，并支付高额的顾问费。高额罚款与顾问费，约占兆丰银行全年获利的两成以上。兆丰银行是兆丰金控的主要获利机构，兆丰银行遭罚对兆丰金控影响甚巨。据台媒报道，1.8亿美元的罚款约占兆丰金控2015年获利六分之一。兆丰金控表示，兆丰银行纽约分行平均每年获利约2 500万美元，这次遭罚的金额需要超过7年才赚得回来。

2016年兆丰银行遭美方处罚后，台湾"金融管理委员会"于同年对其开出1 000万新台币罚单，美国联邦储备银行（FRB）也于同年对兆丰银行在美国的4家分行（纽约、芝加哥、洛杉矶和硅谷）进行金融检查。2018年，由于纽约分行、芝加哥分行及硅谷分行在防制洗钱制度等未达当地标准，兆丰银行被美国联邦储备委员会（FED）罚款2 900万美元，并被要求委任独立第三方机构就兆丰纽约2015年1至6月间的美元清算交易进行审查及回溯调查并提交改善计划。这是2016年兆丰银行遭美国纽约州金融服务局罚款1.8亿美元后，该银行再度遭美方罚款。兆丰银行此次遭罚并非因为兆丰纽约在事件后出现了新的缺失，而是缘于美国联邦储备委员会及地方监管机构有权对银行同一时期的缺失可以分别进行处罚。

除缴纳外部罚款以外，兆丰银行在内部整改方面也花费颇多。兆丰银行董事会于2016年9月30日就被罚事件进行相关授权，在总行的常务董事会直接设置美国纽约州和解令应对委员会：于2016年12月31日前立即执行相关加强整改措施，包括强化董事会督导管理功能、改进总行对海外分行的监督管理、改进海外分行的法规制度、强化内部稽核功能、在纽约分行成立独立的专职法务部门，聘请富有经验的洗钱防制主管（BSA officer）等整改措施，落实防制洗钱工作。据悉，2016年受罚以来，兆丰银行已投入超过10亿新台币进行整改。

按照双方签署的《和解令》，兆丰银行需在《和解令》生效后10天内，在美国纽约州金融服务局指定范围内聘请独立顾问，弥补其合规政策和流程的缺失，并立即纠正纽约分行的合规缺陷。《和解令》还要求兆丰银行于30天内在美国纽约州金融服务局指定范围内聘请独立监察员，对兆丰纽约合规计划的有效性进行全面审查。独立监察员将开展一项与OFAC制裁相关的审查，以确定在2012年至2014年期间兆丰银行是否违反了OFAC法规，存在涉及高风险客户及交易的可疑活动，是否对此类客户和交易进行了适当的确认和报告。

有台湾媒体指出，兆丰被罚事件可能冲击台湾地区整体银行业的海外交易。最令台湾地区"主管机关"及银行业者担心的，就是2018年亚太防制洗钱组织将对台湾进行第三轮反洗钱评测，兆丰被罚事件很可能影响评测分数。若评测结果不佳，届时所有从台湾地区进出海外的款项，都可能被严格审查，严重影响交易效率。

纵观《和解令》，美国纽约州金融服务局在没有查到兆丰银行确切洗钱证据的情况下，直接按照当地监管规定予以重罚，其背后一系列故事及事件本身值得各家正在"走出去"的商业银行借鉴。

首先，在商言商，商业银行的反洗钱内控合规不能任性而为。

兆丰银行是兆丰金控的全资子公司。兆丰金控8.4%的股份由台湾"财政部"所持有，兆丰银行也成为台湾当局推动外汇政策最主要的支持配合银行。兆丰银行未能先行制定符合海外标准的内部合规框架及政策制度，而是依靠股东背景，长期忽视商业银行的反洗钱合规职责，漠视当地监管规定。一位兆丰金控董事表示，该行纽约分行与巴拿马分行长期协助台湾地区"巩固"中南美邦交国。如今兆丰银行被美重罚，台行政当局非但不予祖护反而组成专案督导小组着手调查，并追究兆丰银行相关人员的可能责任，丝毫不给面子。

其实，事件初期，美国纽约州金融服务局早已把疑似洗钱交易的名单交给台湾"金融管理委员会"，由于某些原因"金融管理委员会"迟迟不宣布名单内容，任由简单的金融案件不断升级。事后，台湾"金融管理委员会"还特别发表声明，称依据国际洗钱防制规定，如果在金融交易过程中有疑似洗钱的情况，银行必须先向当地洗钱防制中心提出申报，兆丰银行纽约分行未依据规定提出申报因而遭到重罚。台北"地检署"更是兵分三路"搜索"兆丰银行总部、金融主管部门与财政部门，调阅相关资料，传讯前任和现任董事长。

兆丰银行在反洗钱合规方面确实存在漏洞。此次并非兆丰银行首次被罚，该行海外分支机构"有前科"。兆丰银行在2013年年报中已载明巴拿马分行2010年便违反洗钱规定，但从总行到台当局金融主管部门均未重视。2008年，兆丰银行澳洲分行也曾因内控缺失，遭当地监管机构调查，面临撤行危机，足见兆丰银行内控缺失问题严重。鉴于从商业银行的角度，任性的兆丰银行确实存在反洗钱合规方面的严重问题和缺失，面对1.8亿美元重罚后台当局的所作所为，兆丰银行也只能哑巴吃黄连，有苦难言。

其次，商业银行应该培养并储备合格的反洗钱合规人员，充分了解当地法令法规。

兆丰银行轻视了金融行业国际化所具有的难度，忽视了文化认知差异，在海外高端人才储备方面，存在明显不足，缺乏既熟悉国际反洗钱法律法规又懂当地反洗钱要求的专业人才。美国纽约州金融服务局在《和解令》中表示，兆丰银行总部和分支机构的首席合规官均不熟悉美国的监管要求。兆丰纽约的合规负责人由台湾总部派过去，被美国纽约州金融服务局认为对美国反洗钱要求不甚了解。由于不熟悉美国的监管要求，兆丰纽约分行分管反洗钱的负责人同时分管运营等支持部门，服务资金运营、信贷等业务条线，一人"身兼数职"的情况长年无法改善，利益冲突无法回避，这也是引发美国纽约州金融服务局不满的另一个原因。

作为当今商业银行的管理者以及合规人员，不具备相当的反洗钱合规知识和头脑，不仅无助于企业抵御合规风险，反而会招致当地监管部门的不满，严重的甚至累及自己的职业生涯。本案中，兆丰金控前董事长以及现任董事长先后被约谈到案说明。前董事长蔡友才被约谈后，遭限制出境、出海及"小三通"，并由"他字案"转列"侦字案"被告。相关人员也被台当局要求予以处理。

最后，可疑交易监测系统很重要。

美国纽约州金融服务局最引以为豪的，就是其对可疑交易监测系统的高度重视，并作出了两项制度创新。本来反洗钱在美国搞了几十年，已经比较成熟，主要制度架构都是以联邦的为主，州层级的机构不必出台什么新的制度，抄联邦的就行。2016年之前都是这样，翻看美国纽约州金融服务局的要求，与联邦层级的要求并无大的不同。但2016年之后不一样了，美国纽约州金融服务局说他们过去的经验发现，可疑交易监测系统对于反洗钱十分重要，因此，不论这个监测系统是完全人工的系统，还是建立在计算机程序的基础之上，都需要满足一些共同的要求。这些要求成为美国纽约州金融服务局引以自豪的第一项创新。

在此基础上，美国纽约州金融服务局提出第二项创新，公司董事及高管要定期向美国纽约州金融服务局报承诺书，承诺反洗钱监测系统符合美国纽约州金融服务局的具体要求。而兆丰银行则是哪壶不开提哪壶。美国纽约州金融服务局说可疑交易监测系统有问题，有些可疑交易没有报，兆丰回应说根据相关法规，那些交易不应作为可疑交易上报。

当前，合规监管形势日趋严峻，商业银行应按商业原则，审慎决策、自担风险、后果自负，金融机构要增强政治敏感度，消除侥幸心理，做好相关问题的应对预案。任性而为只能自食其果。

附录：

《和解令》英文原文

NEW YORK STATE DEPARTMENT OF FINANCIAL SERVICES

In the Matter of:

MEGA INTERNATIONAL COMMERCIAL
BANK CO., LTD. and
MEGA INTERNATIONAL COMMERCIAL BANK
CO. LTD. - NEW YORK BRANCH

CONSENT ORDER UNDER
NEW YORK BANKING LAW 39 and 44

The New York State Department of Financial Services (the "Department" or "DFS"), Mega International Commercial Bank Co., Ltd. ("Mega International"), and Mega International Commercial Bank Co., Ltd. New York Branch ("Mega-New York" or the "New York Branch") (together, the "Bank") are willing to resolve the matters described herein without further proceedings;

WHEREAS, Mega International is an international banking institution with more than 100 branches, 5,000 employees and assets totaling approximately $103 billion, and is licensed by the Department to operate a foreign bank branch in New York State;

WHEREAS, Mega-New York has assets totaling approximately $9 billion and has operated a correspondent banking business for many years;

WHEREAS, in 2015, the Department and another regulator conducted an examination of the New York Branch, as of September 30, 2014;

WHEREAS, in February 2016, the Department provided its Report of Examination describing its findings; and in March 2016, Mega International and Mega-New York provided their written response to this report. The Department finds as follows:

The Department's Findings
After Examination and Additional Investigation

Mega International

1. Mega International is based in Taipei, Taiwan. As of year-end 2015, Mega International had 107 domestic branches, and 22 branches, 5 sub-branches, and 4 representative offices internationally abroad. Mega International also has wholly-owned subsidiaries in Thailand and Canada, bringing the total number of overseas branches and offices to 39 in total.[1]

2. Mega International has branches located in major U.S. cities, including New York,

---

[1] *See* https://www.megabank.com.tw/en/about.asp.

Chicago, Los Angeles and Silicon Valley. Mega International also has two branches in Panama, one located in the Colon Free Trade Zone ("FTZ") and the other in Panama City.

3. Mega International has approximately 5,400 employees worldwide. At present, Mega International holds total assets of approximately $103 billion; assets held at Mega-New York are approximately $9 billion. In other words, Mega International is an important institution in the world financial system.

The New York Branch's Poor Internal Controls

4. From January through March 2015, examiners from DFS conducted an examination of Mega-New York as of September 2014. The examination focused on the New York Branch's risk management, operational controls, compliance, and asset quality. The examiners also evaluated any corrective actions undertaken by management to address the issues from a prior examination conducted as of 2013.

5. The Department issued its Report of Examination in February 2016. The Bank submitted its response on March 24, 2016.

6. What the examiners found was extremely troubling. They discovered numerous deficiencies in Mega-New York's compliance function.

7. The examination found that the position of BSA/AML Officer[1] in the New York Branch was held by a person from the Mega International Head Office who possessed little familiarity with U.S. regulatory requirements. Similarly, the Chief Compliance Officer ("CCO") for the New York Branch lacked adequate knowledge of U.S. BSA/AML and the Office of Foreign Assets Control of the United States Department of Treasury ("OFAC") requirements, as well as the supervisory expectations relating to these requirements.

8. The examiners also found that the compliance structure at Mega-New York was significantly flawed because the compliance and operational functions were comingled as a result of the dual conflicting responsibilities of certain compliance personnel. For example, the Branch's Vice President and Deputy General Manager also served as the Branch's CCO. The CCO provided support to all Branch operations, including its funding division, the business division, the correspondent banking division, the loan division, and also served as the Information Technology Security Officer.

9. Thus, the New York CCO devoted insufficient time and effort to important compliance responsibilities and, in any event, was conflicted in these responsibilities, since the CCO had a key business and operational role, along with the compliance role.

10. Similarly, the Branch's BSA/AML Officer also served as operations manager of the Business Division; this presented a clear conflict of interest between his compliance and business responsibilities.

11. A clear conflict of interest also existed with respect to the Branch's OFAC Officer, because

---

① "BSA" stands for the Bank Secrecy Act, 31 U.S.C. §§ 5311 *el seq*. "AML" stands for "anti-money laundering." The Bank Secrecy Act, the rules and regulations issued thereunder by the U.S. Department of the T reasury, 31 C.F.R. Chap. X; and the requirements of Regulation K of the Board of Governors of the Federal Reserve System to report suspicious activity and to maintain an adequate BSA/AML compliance program, 12 C.F.R. §§ 211.24 (f) and (j), all require a robust compliance structure in the New York and other branches of each regulated institution.

that person also served as the Operations Manager for the Foreign Correspondent Banking Division.

12. To compound these structural deficiencies, the examination also discovered that both the BSA/AML Officer and the CCO received inadequate training subsequent to their assignment to Mega-New York.

13. The examination also uncovered serious deficiencies in the New York Branch's transaction monitoring systems and policies. For example, compliance personnel — either at the Branch level or the Flead Office - failed to periodically review surveillance monitoring filter criteria, required to evaluate the appropriateness of filter criteria and thresholds. Moreover, for a number of the criteria or key words purportedly used to detect suspicious transactions, branch management was unable to explain the validation process or justification of the selection of the criteria being used. And a number of documents relied upon in the transaction monitoring process remained un-translated from the Chinese language, precluding effective examination by regulators.

14. The examination discovered that the New York Branch had inadequate policies and procedures governing the processing of suspicious activity alerts and its case management system. Although compliance staff researched alerts, it failed to adequately maintain the documentation necessary to support decisions made by compliance personnel during the investigation of alerts - in many cases the only documentation maintained was in the case of an actual determination to file a Suspicious Activity Report ("SAR").

15. Similarly, Branch procedures provided little guidance concerning the requirements for reporting continuing suspicious activity, and the notation of the latter in the Branch's SAR log book.

16. The examination also concluded that the New York Branch's BSA/AML policies and procedures lacked consistency and unity of purpose. Deficiencies included, without limitation, (a) substantial inconsistencies between policies and procedures for the Business Division and the Correspondent Banking Division; (b) inconsistent policies and procedures concerning transaction monitoring, customer on-boarding and OFAC compliance; and (c) that written guidelines failed to properly incorporate federal regulatory guidance for reviews of Customer Due Diligence, Enhanced Due Diligence, and diligence concerning Politically Exposed Persons.

17. The New York Branch did not perform adequate reviews of the Bank's affiliates' correspondent banking activities at the Branch. For example, New York Branch officials failed to (a) determine whether foreign affiliates had in place adequate AML compliance processes and controls; (b) ensure the New York Branch has an understanding of the effectiveness of the AML regime of the foreign jurisdictions in which its foreign correspondent banking customers operate; and (c) follow up on account activity and transactions that did not fit the foreign affiliates' customers' strategic profile.

Suspicious Activity Involving Mega International's Panama Branches

18. The compliance failures found at the New York Branch are serious. They indicate a lack of understanding by both Mega International and the New York Branch of the need for a vigorous compliance infrastructure.

19. These deficiencies make it all the more concerning given that Mega International operates branches in Panama City and the Colon FTZ. Panama has historically been recognized as a high-risk jurisdiction for money laundering, and only earlier in this year was it announced that

Panama is no longer subject to the Financial Action Task Force's monitoring process.① Moreover, the publication of the "Panama Papers" and information about the Mossack Fonseca Law firm emphasize Panama as a high-risk jurisdiction. Accordingly, Mega International is obligated to treat transactions running between its New York and Panama Branches with the highest level of diligence and scrutiny, yet compliance failures occurring at the New York Branch demonstrated that this did not occur.

20. This failure was serious in light of the significant amount of financial activity running between Mega International's New York and Panama Branches. For example, according to the Bank's records, the dollar value of credit transactions between the New York Branch and the Colon FTZ totaled $3.5 billion and $2.4 billion in 2013 and 2014, respectively. Corresponding figures for the Panama City branch were $1.1 billion and $4.5 billion.

21. Mega's International's Head Office has acted with indifference towards the risks associated with such transactions. The DFS examination found a number of concerning issues related to Mega International transactions involving its Panama Branches indicative of possible money laundering and other suspicious activity. For example:

a. Mega-New York rated its Panama Colon FTZ Branch at high risk for AML purposes. It purports to conduct a quarterly enhanced due diligence ("EDD"), yet the Branch's responses to the DFS examination team indicated that this has not been implemented effectively.

b. Despite repeated requests, the Bank has not provided an adequate explanation about the nature of its correspondent banking activities on behalf of its Panama City and Colon FTZ branches, as requested in DFS's Report of Examination and at the regulatory close-out meeting held with the Bank in February 2016.

c. Mega-New York acted as an intermediary paying bank in connection with suspicious and unusual "debit authorizations" (or payment reversals) received from its Panamanian branches that reversed wire payments processed on behalf of various remitters (the "Suspicious Payment Reversals"). When asked about this in connection with the examination, New York Branch personnel provided explanations that did not address the examiners' concerns.

d. A significant number of reported debit authorizations processed by Mega- New York between 2010 and 2014 occurred when the Panamanian beneficiary accounts identified in the underlying transactions were closed by the Colon FTZ Branch because of inadequate Know-Your-Customer ("KYC") documentation received by that Branch - a highly suspicious level of activity. Moreover, most of these accounts were open for less than two years; a number were open even less than one year - further evidence of very questionable activity. The suspicious nature of this activity is compounded by the fact that the remitters and beneficiaries associated with many of the Suspicious Payment Reversals were identical parties; in some cases, the original payment instructions were sent months after the beneficiary accounts already had been closed. Moreover, the Suspicious Payment Reversals continued at least into 2015.

---

① *See, e.g.*, http://www.state.gOv/j/inl/rls/nrcrpt/2013/vol2/204062,htm; 11Up://www,Fatf-»all.ora/ conntrics/a- c/atghan i stan/doc i nnen ts/tatr-cornpl iance-f ebruary-2016.html.

e. Examiners also noted that many of the Colon FTZ Branch accounts involved with the Suspicious Payment Reversals were opened with closely ranged account numbers - another compelling indicator of suspicious activity.

22. Further, an account held in the name of a corporate customer of the Colon FTZ Branch that received funds remitted by Mega-New York and its reported beneficial owner have been the subject of significant adverse comment in the media. Among other things, the beneficial owner apparently has been linked to violations of U.S. law concerning the transfer of technology. Despite numerous requests by DFS, Mega International has failed to provide any meaningful explanation of its due diligence regarding this customer's account.

Failure to Conduct Adequate Customer Due Diligence

23. The DFS examination also found that Mega-New York Branch personnel failed to follow established policies and procedures for enhanced due diligence, an increased level of scrutiny for high-risk customers. For example, the New York Branch failed to conduct a comprehensive review of such customers on a quarterly basis, as required by its own policies and procedures. Nor did New York Branch personnel regularly engage in periodic vetting of medium and low-risk customers in a timely manner to identify any increase in the risk profile of such customers.

24. Similarly, the examination found that the New York Branch failed to perform adequate customer due diligence when taking in a correspondent account for a foreign financial institution.

25. Furthermore, a review of 30 customer files indicated that approximately one-third of them lacked adequate information on beneficial ownership. The lack of such information seriously compromises the New York Branch's Know-Your-Customer ("KYC") processes.

Inadequate Risk Assessment Policies and Procedures.

26. The examination also found serious flaws in the New York Branch's overall risk assessments. For example, the New York Branch's risk assessment for BSA/AML issues lacked a thorough review of Branch customers, products, services, and geographic locations served. It likewise was insufficient in its methodology, for, among other reasons, having been conducted for a six month period, and not a year-long period as recommended.

27. The New York Branch's risk assessment for OFAC concerns was found to be flawed for similar reasons.

Lack of Diligent Oversight by the Head Office

28. In addition, with respect to the New York Branch's reporting to the Head Office about the compliance function, DFS examiners found that quarterly compliance meeting minutes were not forwarded to Head Office compliance; and that the New York Branch regularly substituted a meeting agenda in lieu of proper meeting minutes. Additionally, the New York Branch's report on quarterly compliance meetings provided insufficient information on the compliance environment, and critical information concerning SARs filed during prior periods were omitted. These failings prevented Head Office compliance from properly evaluating the compliance adequacy of the New York Branch.

29. Additionally, Head Office compliance did not ensure that numerous documents employed and stored by the New York Branch were translated from Chinese to English, thereby preventing effective examination by regulators.

**Mega-New York Branch's Troubling and
Dismissive Response to the DFS Examination**

30. In its March 24, 2016 response to the February 2016 DFS examination report, the Bank has refuted a number of the examination findings.

31. Perhaps most egregious, Mega International and the New York Branch, in its March 2016 response to the examination, declared that certain types of activity were not suspicious. As justification, the Bank's March 2016 examination response claimed that there is "no AML regulatory guidance related to filing [Suspicious Activity Reports] on these types of transactions" and that therefore such "transactions do not constitute suspicious activity."

32. This is a complete misstatement of well-established BSA law.

33. Moreover, the Bank did not act quickly to remedy the acute shortcomings as directed in the February 2016 Report of Examination. For example, despite communications between the Department and the New York Branch in the Spring of 2016, the Bank has not taken sufficient steps to demonstrate material improvement in the quality of its compliance program.

NOW THEREFORE, to resolve this matter without further proceedings pursuant to the Superintendent's authority under Sections 39 and 44 of the Banking Law, the Department and the Bank hereby stipulate and agree to the terms and conditions listed below requiring further review of the Bank's activities, for remediation, and for imposition of a penalty:

Violations of Law and Regulation

34. Mega International and Mega-New York failed to maintain an effective and compliant anti-money laundering program and OFAC compliance program, in violation of 3 N.Y.C.R.R. § 116.2.

35. Mega International and Mega-New York failed to maintain and make available at its New York Branch true and accurate books, accounts and records reflecting all transactions and actions, in violation of New York Banking Law § 200-c.

36. Mega International and Mega-New York failed to submit a report to the Superintendent immediately upon discovering fraud, dishonesty, making of false entries and omission of true entries, and other misconduct, in violation of 3 N.Y.C.R.R. § 300.1.

Settlement Provisions

Monetary Payment

37. Mega International shall pay a penalty pursuant to Banking Law § 44 to the Department in the amount of $180,000,000.00 as a result of having an inadequate and deficient compliance program as set forth above. The Bank shall pay the entire amount within ten (10) days of executing this Consent Order. Mega International agrees that it will not claim, assert, or apply for a tax deduction or tax credit with regard to any U.S. federal, state, or local tax, directly or indirectly, for any portion of the penalty paid pursuant to this Consent Order,

Immediate Compliance Consultant and Independent Monitor

38. **Compliance Consultant:** Mega International and the New York Branch shall engage an independent third party of the Department's choosing, within ten (10) days of the Department's selection of such third party, to immediately consult about, oversee and address deficiencies in Mega-New York's compliance function, including, without limitation, compliance with BSA/AML requirements, compliance with federal sanctions laws, and compliance with New York laws and

regulations (the "Compliance Consultant").

39. The Compliance Consultant shall work with the Department, Mega International and Mega-New York to implement changes or modifications to policies, procedures or personnel that may be made immediately to address any identified deficiencies in the New York Branch's compliance function.

40. The term of the Compliance Consultant's engagement shall extend for a period of up to six months, at the sole discretion of the Department, to be extended in the sole discretion of the Department should Mega International fail to cooperate as required.

41. **Independent Monitor:** Within thirty (30) days of the Department's selection thereof, Mega International and Mega-New York shall retain an independent monitor (the "Independent Monitor") to: (i) conduct a comprehensive review of the effectiveness of the Branch's program for compliance with BSA/AML requirements, laws and regulations (the "Compliance Review"); and (ii) prepare a written report of findings, conclusions, and recommendations (the "Compliance Report").

42. The Independent Monitor will be selected by the Department in the exercise of its sole discretion, and will report directly to the Department.

43. Within ten (10) days of the selection of the Independent Monitor, but prior to the Compliance Review, Mega International and Mega-New York shall jointly submit to the Department for approval an engagement letter that provides, at a minimum, for the Independent Monitor to:

   a. identify all of the Branch's business lines, activities, and products to ensure that such business lines, activities, and products are appropriately risk-rated and included in the Branch's BSA/AML compliance program, policies, and procedures;

   b. conduct a comprehensive assessment of the Branch's BSA/AML compliance program, policies, and procedures;

   c. complete the Compliance Review within 60 days of the Department's approval of the engagement letter;

   d. provide to the Department a copy of the Compliance Report at the same time that the report is provided to the Bank and the Branch; and

   e. commit that any and all interim reports, drafts, workpapers, or other supporting materials associated with the Compliance Review will be made available to the Department.

44. The Independent Monitor shall also conduct a review of Mega-New York's U.S. dollar clearing transaction activity from January 1, 2012 through December 31, 2014, to determine whether transactions inconsistent with or in violation of the OFAC Regulations, or suspicious activity involving high risk customers or transactions or possible money laundering at, by, or through the Branch were properly identified and reported in accordance with the OFAC Regulations and suspicious activity reporting regulations and New York law (the "Transaction and OFAC Sanctions Review") and to prepare a written report detailing the Independent Monitor's party's findings (the "Transaction and OFAC Sanctions Review Report") for the Department.

45. Within ten (10) days of the engagement of the Independent Monitor, but prior to the commencement of the Transaction and OFAC Sanctions Review, Mega International and Mega-New York shall jointly submit to the Department for approval additional terms in the engagement letter that set forth:

a. the methodology for conducting the Transaction and OFAC Sanctions Review, including any sampling procedures to be followed;

b. the expertise and resources to be dedicated to the Transaction and OFAC Sanctions Review;

c. the anticipated date of completion of the Transaction and OFAC Sanctions Review and the Transaction and OFAC Sanctions Review Report; and

d. a commitment that supporting material and drafts associated with the Transaction and OFAC Sanctions Review will be made available to the Department upon request.

46. The Independent Monitor shall provide to the Department a copy of the Transaction and OFAC Sanctions Review Report at the same time that the report is provided to Mega International and Mega-New York.

47. Throughout the Transaction and OFAC Sanctions Review, Mega International and Mega-New York shall ensure that all matters or transactions required to be reported that have not previously been reported are reported in accordance with applicable rules and regulations.

BSA/AML Compliance Program

48. Within sixty (60) days of the submission of the Compliance Report, Mega Bank and Mega-New York shall jointly submit a written revised BSA/AML compliance program for the Branch acceptable to the Department. At a minimum, the program shall provide for:

a. a system of internal controls designed to ensure compliance with the BSA/AML Requirements and the State Laws and Regulations;

b. controls designed to ensure compliance with all requirements relating to correspondent accounts for foreign financial institutions;

c. a comprehensive BSA/AML risk assessment that identifies and considers all products and services of the New York Branch, customer types, geographic locations, and transaction volumes, as appropriate, in determining inherent and residual risks;

d. management of the New York Branch's BSA/AML compliance program by a qualified compliance officer, who is given full autonomy, independence, and responsibility for implementing and maintaining an effective BSA/AML compliance program that is commensurate with the New York Branch's size and risk profile, and is supported by adequate staffing levels and resources;

e. identification of management information systems used to achieve compliance with the BSA/AML Requirements and the State Laws and Regulations and a timeline to review key systems to ensure they are configured to mitigate BSA/AML risks;

f. comprehensive and timely independent testing for the New York Branch's compliance with applicable BSA/AML Requirements and the State Laws and Regulations; and

g. effective training for all appropriate Branch personnel and appropriate Mega International personnel that perform BSA/AML compliance-related functions for the New York Branch in all aspects of the BSA/AML requirements, state laws and regulations, and internal policies and procedures.

Suspicious Activity' Monitoring and RetKn tiiij;

49. Within sixty (60) days of the submission of the Compliance Report, Mega International

and Mega-New York shall jointly submit a written program to reasonably ensure the identification and timely, accurate, and complete reporting by the New York Branch of all known or suspected violations of law or suspicious transactions to law enforcement and supervisory authorities, as required by applicable suspicious activity reporting laws and regulations acceptable to the Department. At a minimum, the program shall include:

    a. a well-documented methodology for establishing monitoring rules and thresholds appropriate for the New York Branch's profile which considers factors such as type of customer, type of product or service, geographic location, and foreign correspondent banking activities, including U.S. dollar clearing activities;

    b. policies and procedures for analyzing, testing, and documenting changes to monitoring rules and thresholds;

    c. enhanced monitoring and investigation criteria and procedures to ensure the timely detection, investigation, and reporting of all known or suspected violations of law and suspicious transactions, including, but not limited to:

        i. effective monitoring of customer accounts and transactions, including but not limited to, transactions conducted through foreign correspondent accounts;

        ii. appropriate allocation of resources to manage alert and case inventory;

        iii. adequate escalation of information about potentially suspicious activity through appropriate levels of management;

        iv. maintenance of sufficient documentation with respect to the investigation and analysis of potentially suspicious activity, including the resolution and escalation of concerns; and

        v. maintenance of accurate and comprehensive customer and transactional data and ensuring that it is utilized by the New York Branch's compliance program.

Customer Due Diligence

    50. Within sixty (60) days of the submission of the Compliance Report, Mega International and Mega-New York shall jointly submit a written enhanced customer due diligence program acceptable to the Department. At a minimum, the program shall include:

    a. policies, procedures, and controls to ensure that the New York Branch collects, analyzes, and retains complete and accurate customer information for all account holders, including, but not limited to, affiliates;

    b. a plan to remediate deficient due diligence for existing customers accounts;

    c. a revised methodology for assigning risk ratings to account holders that considers factors such as type of customer, type of products and services, geographic locations, and transaction volume;

    d. for each customer whose transactions require enhanced due diligence procedures to:

        i. determine the appropriate documentation necessary to verity the identity and business activities of the customer; and

        ii. understand the normal and expected transactions of the customer.

e. policies, procedures, and controls to ensure that foreign correspondent accounts are accorded the appropriate due diligence and, where necessary, enhanced due diligence; and

f. periodic reviews and evaluations of customer and account information for the entire customer base to ensure that information is current, complete, and that the risk rating reflects the current information, and if applicable, documenting rationales for any revisions made to the customer risk rating.

Corporate Governance and Management Oversight

51. Within sixty (60) days of the submission of the Compliance Report, Mega International's board of directors and the management of Mega-New York shall jointly submit to the Department a written plan to enhance oversight, by the management of the Bank and New York Branch, of the New York Branch's compliance with the BSA/AML Requirements, the State Laws and Regulations, and the regulations issued by OF AC acceptable to the Department. The plan shall provide for a sustainable governance framework that, at a minimum, addresses, considers, and includes:

a. actions the board of directors will take to maintain effective control over, and oversight of, Branch management's compliance with the BSA/AML Requirements, the State Laws and Regulations, and the OF AC Regulations;

b. measures to improve the management information systems reporting of the Branch's compliance with the BSA/AML Requirements, the State Laws and Regulations, and the OFAC Regulations to senior management of the Bank and the Branch;

c. clearly defined roles, responsibilities, and accountability regarding compliance with the BSA/AML Requirements, the State Laws and Regulations, and the OFAC Regulations for the Bank's and the Branch's respective management, compliance personnel, and internal audit staff;

d. measures to ensure BSA/AML issues are appropriately tracked, escalated, and reviewed by the Branch's senior management;

e. measures to ensure that the person or groups at the Bank and the Branch charged with the responsibility of overseeing the Branch's compliance with the BSA/AML Requirements, the State Laws and Regulations, and the OFAC Regulations possess appropriate subject matter expertise and are actively involved in carrying out such responsibilities;

f. adequate resources to ensure the New York Branch's compliance with this Order, the BSA/AML Requirements, the State Laws and Regulations, and the OFAC Regulations; and

g. a direct reporting line between the Branch's BSA/AML compliance officer and the board of directors or committee thereof.

Full and Complete Cooperation of Mega International

52. Mega International and Mega-New York each agrees that it will fully cooperate with the Immediate Compliance Consultant and the Independent Monitor and support the work of each by, among other things, providing each with access to all relevant personnel, consultants and third-party service providers, files, reports, or records, whether located in New York, Taiwan, Panama, or any other location sought, consistent with applicable law.

53. The Independent Monitor will thereafter oversee the implementation of any corrective

measures undertaken pursuant to the Action Plan and Management Oversight Plan.

54. The Independent Monitor will assess the Bank's compliance with its corrective measures and will submit subsequent progress reports and a final report to the Department and the Bank, at intervals to be determined by the Department. The Department may, in its sole discretion, extend any reporting deadline set forth in this Order.

55. The term of the Independent Monitor's engagement will extend for two years from the date of its formal engagement by the Bank, to be extended in the Department's sole discretion if Mega International fails to cooperate. Any dispute as to the scope of the Independent Monitor's authority or mandate will be resolved by the Department in the exercise of its sole discretion, after appropriate consultation with the Bank and the Monitor.

Interaction with the Department

56. Within 30 days of the submission of the Compliance Report, the Bank and the Branch shall jointly submit written policies and procedures that govern the conduct of the Branch's personnel in all supervisory and regulatory matters, including, but not limited to, interaction with and requests for information by examiners for the Branch, acceptable to the Department. The policies and procedures shall, at a minimum, ensure that all Branch personnel provide prompt, complete, and accurate information to examiners and provide for employee training that emphasizes the importance of full cooperation with banking regulators by all employees.

Breach of Consent Order

57. In the event that the Department believes the Bank to be in material breach of the Consent Order, the Department will provide written notice to the Bank and the Bank must, within ten (10) business days of receiving such notice, or on a later date if so determined in the Department's sole discretion, appear before the Department to demonstrate that no material breach has occurred or, to the extent pertinent, that the breach is not material or has been cured.

58. The parties understand and agree that the Bank's failure to make the required showing within the designated time period shall be presumptive evidence of the Bank's breach. Upon a finding that the Bank has breached this Consent Order, the Department has all the remedies available to it under New York Banking and Financial Services Law and may use any evidence available to the Department in any ensuing hearings, notices, or orders.

Waiver of Rights

59. The parties understand and agree that no provision of this Consent Order is subject to review in any court or tribunal outside the Department.

Parties Bound by the Consent Order

60. This Consent Order is binding on the Department and the Bank, as well as any successors and assigns that are under the Department's supervisory authority. This Consent Order does not bind any federal or other state agency or law enforcement authority.

61. No further action will be taken by the Department against the Bank for the conduct set forth in this Order, provided that the Bank complies with the terms of the Order.

Notwithstanding any other provision in this Consent Order, however, the Department may undertake additional action against the Bank for transactions or conduct that comes to the attention of the Department, either as a result of the Transaction and OFAC Sanctions Review, or in some other manner.

Notices

62. All notices or communications regarding this Consent Order shall be sent to:

For the Department:

Jeffrey Waddle
Elizabeth Nochlin
Megan Prendergast
New York State Department of Financial Services
One State Street
New York, NY 10004

For Mega International and Mega-New York:

Jui-Chung Chuang
Mega International Commercial Bank Co., Ltd.
10F, No. 123, Sec. 2 Jhongsiao E. Rd.
Taipei 10058, Taiwan, R.O.C.

Vincent S.M. Huang
Mega International Commercial Bank Co., Ltd - New York Branch
65 Liberty Street
New York, NY 10005

Miscellaneous

63. Each provision of this Consent Order shall remain effective and enforceable until stayed, modified, suspended, or terminated by the Department.

64. No promise, assurance, representation, or understanding other than those contained in this Consent Order has been made to induce any party to agree to the provisions of the Consent Order.

IN WITNESS WHEREOF, the parties have caused this Consent Order to be signed this 19th day of August, 2016.

《和解令》中文译文

和解令

纽约州金融服务局

就

兆丰国际商业银行有限公司

和

兆丰国际商业银行有限公司纽约分行

依据纽约银行法第39条和第44条和解令

纽约州金融服务局（以下简称本属或DFS）、兆丰国际商业银行有限公司（以下简称兆丰国际）和兆丰国际商业银行有限公司纽约分行（以下简称兆丰纽约或纽约分行）（合称为银行）同意就本文所述事项达成最终和解。

鉴于兆丰国际是一家国际性银行，拥有100多家分支机构，5 000名员工，资产总额约为1 030亿美元，并由DFS授权在纽约州开设一家外资银行分行；

鉴于兆丰纽约资产总额约为90亿美元，已经营代理行业务多年；

鉴于2015年，DFS和另一个监管机构对兆丰纽约截至2014年9月30日的业务进行了检查；

鉴于2016年2月，DFS提交了检查报告，描述了检查所见；2016年3月，兆丰国际和兆丰纽约递交了他们对检查报告的书面回应。DFS检查发现问题如下：

检查结果和附加调查

兆丰国际

1. 兆丰国际总部位于台湾台北。截至2015年底，兆丰国际在台湾设有107家分支机构，在台湾以外设有22家分支机构，5家二级支机构，4家代表处。兆丰国际在泰国和加拿大拥有全资子公司，海外分支机构和代表处总计39家。

2. 兆丰国际在美国主要城市设有分支机构，包括纽约、芝加哥、洛杉矶和硅谷。兆丰国际在巴拿马也有两个分支机构，一个位于科隆自由贸易区

（FTZ），另一个位于巴拿马城。

3. 兆丰国际在全球拥有大约5 400名员工。目前，兆丰国际的总资产约为1 030亿美元；兆丰纽约的总资产约为90亿美元。简而言之，兆丰国际是世界金融体系中的一个重要机构。

兆丰纽约的内部控制很差

4. 2015年1月至3月，DFS检查官对兆丰纽约截至2014年9月的业务进行了检查。检查的重点是兆丰纽约的风险管理、业务控制、合规和资产质量。检查官还评估了管理层为解决2013年之前进行的检查所采取的所有改正措施。

5. 2016年2月，DFS发布检查报告。2016年3月24日，银行提交了反馈。

6. 检查官的检查所见极其棘手。他们发现兆丰纽约在合规方面存在大量缺失。

7. 检查发现，兆丰纽约的BSA/AML职位是由一名来自兆丰国际总部的人担任，该人员完全不熟悉美国的监管要求。同样，兆丰纽约的首席合规官（"CCO"）对美国BSA/AML和美国财政部外国资产管理办公室（"OFAC"）的要求以及与这些要求有关的监管目的缺乏足够了解。

8. 检查还发现，由于某些合规人员兼具运营工作，合规和运营职能设置冲突，致使兆丰纽约的合规结构存在明显缺陷。例如，兆丰纽约的副行长和副总经理同时担任兆丰纽约的首席合规官（CCO）。CCO对兆丰纽约的所有运营提供支持，包括其筹资部门、业务部门、代理行部门、贷款部门，并同时担任信息技术安全保障一职。

9. 因此，兆丰纽约CCO在重要的合规责任方面投入的时间和精力不足，由于其同时在主要业务以及运营中担任重要职务，在任何情况下，均与其合规责任发生冲突。

注："BSA"代表银行保密法案，31日事项§§5311节。"AML"代表"反洗钱"。《银行保密法》，美国财政部颁布的规章和条例，31。

C.F.R. X章;和监管的要求K理事会报告可疑活动的联邦储备系统和维持一个适当的BSA／AML合规计划，12 C.F.R.§§211.24（f）和U），都需要一个健壮的合规结构在纽约和其他各监管机构的分支。

10. 类似地，兆丰纽约BSA/AML人员同时兼任业务部门的经理；这些人员的合规职责和业务职责之间存在明显的利益冲突。

11. 兆丰纽约的OFAC检查官也同样存在着明显利益冲突，此人还同时担任了境外代理行业务的业务经理。

12. 基于这些结构性缺陷，检查还发现，兆丰纽约的BSA/AML检查官和CCO在任职期间接受的培训不足。

13. 检查还发现兆丰纽约在交易监控系统和政策方面存在严重缺陷。例如，无论兆丰纽约还是其总行的合规人员，都没有定期重检监视监测标准，没有被要求评估其监测标准和阈值的合理性。此外，对于一些据称用于监测可疑交易的标准或关键字，分行管理人员无法解释验证过程或选择使用的标准的合理性。而在交易监控过程中所依赖的一些文件仍为未被翻译的中文，从而妨碍了监管机构进行有效检查。

14. 检查发现，兆丰纽约在可疑交易预警的处理政策和过程方面存在不足。尽管合规人员研究了警告，但未能充分保存必要的文件，以支持合规人员对警告作出决定，在许多情况下，唯一留存的文件是SAR实际决定需要的表格。

15. 同样地，兆丰纽约的监管流程对于可以交易的持续监控以及SAR日志本上的表示方法未能提供指导。

16. 检查还得出结论，兆丰纽约的BSA/AML政策和程序缺乏一致性和统一的目的。缺陷包括但不限于，（a）业务部门和代理行部门的政策和程序之间的严重不一致；（b）关于交易监控、客户登记和OFAC合规的政策和程序不一致；（c）对于客户尽职检查、加强尽职检查和对PEP尽职调查的书面指导方针未能合理的与联邦监管指保持一致。

17. 兆丰纽约没有对自身相关的代理行业务进行重检。例如，兆丰纽约检查官未能（a）确定外国关联公司是否有足够的AML合规流程和控制；（b）确保兆丰纽约了解其境外代理行客户在外国管辖区内的AML制度的有效性；（c）跟进不符合外国关联公司客户战略配置文件的账户活动和交易。

涉及兆丰国际巴拿马分行的可疑交易

18. 在兆丰纽约发现的合规缺失是严重的。它们表明，兆丰国际和兆丰纽约均对强有力的合规基础设施建设的必要性缺乏足够的认识。

19. 这些缺失使兆丰国际巴拿马城分行和科隆FTZ分行的运营备受关注。

巴拿马历来被认为是洗钱的高风险区域，今年早些时候，刚刚宣布巴拿马不再受金融行动特别工作组监督程序的管辖。此外，《巴拿马文件》的出版和莫萨克·丰塞卡律师事务所的资料都强调巴拿马是一个高风险的司法管辖区。因此，兆丰国际有义务将其纽约和巴拿马分行之间的交易按照最高级别尽职检查和防控处理，然而兆丰纽约在合规方面的缺失导致该责任没有履行。

20. 兆丰国际的纽约分行和巴拿马分行之间大量金融交易活动的合规监控缺失问题严重。例如，银行记录显示，2013年和2014年，兆丰纽约和科隆FTZ之间的贷记交易的总计分别为35亿美元和24亿美元，与巴拿马城分行之间的相应交易为11亿美元和45亿美元。

21. 兆丰国际总部对此类交易的风险无动于衷。DFS检查发现大量与兆丰国际有关的可疑交易，其巴拿马分行牵涉其中，显示可能存在洗钱和其他可疑活动。例如：

a.兆丰纽约将其巴拿马科隆FTZ分行定为反洗钱高风险级别。它声称要进行季度加强型尽职检查（EDD），但兆丰纽约对DFS检查小组的回馈显示，这一措施并没有有效实施。

b.尽管一再提出要求，但兆丰纽约并没有按照DFS的检查报告和2016年2月在该银行举行的监管闭会会议上的要求，对其代理行业务的实质作出合理的解释。

c.兆丰纽约作为巴拿马分行与发出的各种汇款人（可疑付款）可疑交易和非正常"借记授权"（或付款转帐）交易的中间行，当被检查询问有关的问题时，兆丰纽约工作人员提供的解释没有解决考官的担忧。

d.兆丰纽约报告2010年至2014年该行经手处理了大量"借记授权"业务，这些业务的巴拿马受益人账户由于缺乏足够的尽职检查而被科隆FTZ分行关闭。此事属于高度可疑交易。而且，这些账户大部分都是开了不到两年的；有的账户甚至开立不到一年——这进一步证明了这些是非常可疑的交易。事实上，由于汇款人与受益人与许多可以交易的各方完全相同，导致这些可疑交易的性质非常复杂；在某些交易中，最初的付款指示是在受益人账户已经关闭几个月后发出的。此外，可疑付款至少持续到了2015年。

e. 检查官还注意到，科隆FTZ分行的许多涉嫌可疑交易的账户密切关联，这足以引起高度怀疑。

22. 此外，一个以科隆FTZ分行某公司客户名义开设的账户，接收汇自兆丰纽约的款项，其受益人是媒体关注的重大不良对象。在其他事项中，该受益人明显涉及技术性规避美国法律禁止的交易。尽管DFS多次要求，兆丰国际并没有提供对该客户的账户进行尽职检查的合理的解释。

未能进行充分的客户尽职检查

23. DFS检查还发现，兆丰纽约的人员未能遵循既定的政策和程序开展加强型尽职检查，一项更高层面的对高风险客户的尽职调查。例如，兆丰纽约没有按照其既定政策和程序要求，按季度对这些客户进行全面重检。兆丰纽约的人员也没有定期对中、低风险客户进行定期核实，以确定这些客户的风险状况是否有所增加。

24. 同样地，检查发现，兆丰纽约在接受外国金融机构的代理账户业务时，未能进行充分的客户尽职检查。

25. 此外，对30个客户文件进行的重检显示，大约三分之一的客户没有足够的关于实际所有权情况的资料。这些信息的缺乏严重损害了兆丰纽约的"了解你的客户"（"KYC"）流程。

风险评估政策和程序的不足

26. 检查还发现，兆丰纽约的总体风险评估存在严重缺陷。例如，兆丰纽约对BSA/AML问题的风险评估缺乏对分行客户、产品、服务和地理位置的全面检查。其方法论也同样不足，因为，除其他原因外，仅进行了6个月的时间，而不是建议的一年。

27. 兆丰纽约关于OFAC的风险评估也由于类似的原因而存在缺陷。

总部缺乏尽职检查的预见性

28. 此外，关于兆丰纽约向总部汇报的合规职能的情况，DFS检查员发现，季度合规会议记录没有被转发到总部合规部门;而且，兆丰纽约经常以会议议程代替会议记录。此外，兆丰纽约在季度合规会议上的报告仅提供了关于合规环境的部分信息，并忽略了在前一段期间提出的有关SARs的关键信息。这些缺失阻碍了总部合规部门对于兆丰纽约的合规充分程度的评估。

29. 此外，总部合规部门没有确保兆丰纽约使用和存储的大量文件由中文翻译成英文，从而妨碍了监管机构的有效检查。

兆丰纽约的问题以及对DFS检查轻视

30. 兆丰纽约在其2016年3月24日提交的反馈中对DFS 2016年2月检查报告涉及的大量已发现问题予以了驳斥。

31. 最令人震惊的是，在2016年3月对检查报告的反馈中，兆丰国际和兆丰纽约均宣称，某些类型交易并非可疑交易。据此，兆丰纽约在其2016年3月的反馈中称，"没有与提交（可疑活动报告）有关此类交易的AML监管指导"，因此此类"交易不构成可疑活动"。

32. 这完全是对公认的BSA法的错误解读。

33. 此外，兆丰纽约并没有迅速采取行动，纠正2016年2月检查报告中所指出的严重缺陷。例如，除了2016年春季兆丰纽约与DFS的沟通以外，银行没有采取足够措施提高其合规业务纸质材料的质量。

因此，为解决这个问题，依据银行法39和44项的规定，DFS和银行在此申明并同意下列银行业务重检、修正及处罚：

违反法律法规的行为

34. 兆丰国际和兆丰纽约未能有效开展反洗钱合规业务和OFAC合规项目，违反了N.Y.C.R.R. § 116.2的3项规定。

35. 兆丰国际和兆丰纽约未能在其兆丰纽约保有和提供真实、准确的台账、反映所有交易和行为的账户和记录，违反纽约银行法 § 200 - c。

36. 兆丰国际和兆丰纽约未能立即向监管者提交报告，报告期发现的欺诈、不诚实、对欺诈条款的修改、隐瞒真实信息、其他不当行为，违反3 N.Y.C.R.R. § 300.1。

争议解决

罚款支付

37. 由于前述在合规方面的缺失和不足，根据银行法 § 44，兆丰国际应当向DFS支付罚款180 000 000.00美元。银行应在本和解令生效后十（10）日内支付全部款项。兆丰国际同意不会就和解令涉及的全部或部分罚款追索、主张或申请任何美国联邦、州或地方税中直接或间接减税或税收抵免。

即时合规顾问和独立监督

38. 合规顾问：兆丰国际和兆丰纽约应当在十（10）天在DFS提供的范围内聘请独立第三方机构，即时对兆丰纽约合规问题开展咨询，监督和解决，包括但不限于遵守BSA／AML要求，遵守联邦法律的制裁法律，遵守纽约法律法规（合规顾问）。

39. 合规顾问应与DFS、兆丰国际和兆丰纽约合作，完善和修改政策、流程或人员安排，以解决兆丰纽约合规职能中存在的可以立即修正的缺陷。

40. 合规顾问的聘任期限最长可达六个月，由DFS自行决定，如兆丰国际未按要求进行合作，DFS有权自行延长期限。

41. 独立监督：自DFS选定后三十（30）天内，兆丰国际和兆丰纽约应保留独立监督机构（独立监督人）开展：（i）全面检查兆丰纽约的项目是否符合BSA/AML要求、法律及规例（合规重检）；并（ii）准备一份检查结果、结论和建议的书面报告（合规报告）。

42. 独立监督员将由DFS全权选择决定，并将直接向DFS报告。

43. 在选择独立监察机构后的十（10）天内，在合规重检之前，兆丰国际和兆丰纽约应联合向DFS提交一份聘书，至少为独立监督人提供：

 a.确定兆丰纽约的所有业务线、活动和产品，以确保这些业务线、活动和产品由适当的风险评级，并包括在兆丰纽约的BSA/AML合规计划、政策和流程中；

 b.对兆丰纽约的BSA/AML合规计划、政策和程序进行全面评估；

 c.在DFS批准聘书的60天内完成合规重检；

 d.向DFS提供一份合规报告的副本，同时向银行和分行提供报告；并

 e.承诺向DFS提供所有与合规检查有关的临时报告、草案、工作文件或其他支持性材料。

44. 独立监督员还应对2012年1月1日至2014年12月31日期间兆丰纽约的美元结算交易活动进行重检，以确定按照AC法规和可疑活动报告法规和纽约法

（交易和交流制裁检查），通过兆丰纽约进行的交易是否违反OFAC规定，或涉及高风险客户或交易或潜在的洗钱风险被正确的识别和报告，并为DFS准备一份详细的、独立的作为独立监督人的书面报告。

45. 在独立监督员任职后十（10）天内，在交易和OFAC制裁重检之前，兆丰国际和兆丰纽约应联合向DFS提交聘书，保函以下条款：

    a.进行交易和OFAC制裁重检的方法，包括应遵循的任何抽样程序；

    b.对交易和OFAC制裁重检的专家和资源；

    c.完成交易和OFAC制裁重检的预计日期和报告日期；以及

    d.承诺，按照DFS要求提供与交易和OFAC制裁重检相关的材料和草案。

46. 独立监督员应向DFS提供一份交易和OFAC制裁重检报告，同时向兆丰国际和兆丰纽约提供该报告。

47. 在整个交易和OFAC制裁重检期间，兆丰国际和兆丰纽约应确保所有需要报告而以前没有报告的事项或交易按照适用的规章制度进行报告。

BSA/AML 合规项目

48. 在提交合规报告后的六十（60）天内，兆丰国际和兆丰纽约将联合提交一份DFS能够接受的关于兆丰纽约BSA/AML合规计划的书面修订。该计划应至少包含：

    a.为确保符合BSA/AML要求和国家法律法规而设计的内部控制系统；

    b.旨在确保符合与外国金融机构往来账户有关的所有要求的控制；

    c. 关于BSA/AML的综合风险评估，涵盖兆丰纽约所有产品和服务、客户类型、地理位置和交易数量，并酌情确定其固有和剩余风险；

    d.由一名合格的合规官负责纽约兆丰的BSA/AML合规计划管理，该合规官享有充分的自主权、独立性并负责实施和维护CO的有效BSA/AML合规计划的责任，对兆丰纽约的规模和风险状况进行检查，并得到足够的人员编制和资源支持；

    e.能够识别遵守BSA/AML要求以及国家法律法规的管理信息系统，重检关键系统的时间表，以确保减轻BSA/AML风险；

    f.对兆丰纽约遵守适用的BSA/ AML要求和国家法律法规的全面和及时的

独立测试；和

g.按照BSA/AML的要求、国家法律法规和内部政策和流程，对兆丰国际与兆丰纽约合规相关人员以及兆丰纽约自身执行BSA/AML合规职能的所有相关人员进行有效的培训。

可疑交易监测和报告

49.合规报告提交后六十（60）天内，兆丰国际和兆丰纽约应当联合提交一份书面计划，合理确认，兆丰纽约及时准确的按照适用的可疑活动报告法律法规以及DFS认可的法规完成了所有已知或疑似违反法律或可疑交易执法和监管机构的报告。该计划应至少包括：

a.建立一套完善的适用于兆丰纽约的档案监测规则的方法，以及兆丰纽约在该方法下开展业务时客户类型、产品或服务类型、地理位置和包括美元清算业务在内的国外代理行业务的准入门槛；

b.分析、测试和记录更改监控规则和阈值的政策和程序；

c.加强型的监测和检查标准和程序以确保及时发现、检查和报告所有已知或可疑的违规和可疑交易，包括但不限于：

（1）有效监控客户账户和交易，包括但不限于通过国外代理行账户进行的交易；

（2）适当分配资源以管理机警和个案盘存；

（3）通过合适的管理积累潜在可疑活动的信息；

（4）保存检查和分析潜在的可疑活动的充分信息，包括解决和决议升级；和

（5）保存准确、全面的客户和交易数据，并确保其被纽约兆丰纽约的合规计划所使用。

客户尽职检查

50.合规报告提交后六十（60）天内，兆丰国际和兆丰纽约应当联合提交一份书面DFS认可的客户尽职检查计划，大型国际和Mega-New纽约应当共同增强客户尽职检查计划提交一份书面接受。该计划至少应包括：

a. 政策、流程和控制，以确保兆丰纽约收集、分析，并保留对所有账户持有人完整、准确的客户信息，包括但不限于子公司；

b. 对存量客户账户的尽职检查的不足进行纠正的计划；

c. 经修订的对账户持有者进行风险分类的方法，考虑因素包括客户类型、产品和服务类型、地理位置和交易量；

d. 为每个需要进行加强型尽职检查的客户：

i. 判断客户交易活动和核实身份必需的文件和

ii. 了解客户的正常和预期交易。

e. 政策、流程和控制，以确保国外代理行账户给予适当的尽职检查，在必要时，给予加强型尽职检查；和

f. 定期评审和评估整个客户群和账户信息，确保信息是及时更新的，完整的，风险评级反映了当前情况，如果适用，记录客户风险修订情况。

公司监管和监督

51. 合规报告提交后六十（60）天内，兆丰国际和兆丰纽约应当联合向DFS提交一份书面计划，在兆丰纽约符合BSA／AML需求、州法律法规，以及DFS接受的OFAC的管理规定的前提下，加强兆丰国际和兆丰纽约监督。该计划应提供一个可持续的治理框架，该框架至少应考虑到，并包括：

a. 董事会将采取的行动，以保持对兆丰纽约管理层遵守BSA/AML要求、国家法律法规和AC法规的有效控制和监督；

b. 改进管理信息系统的措施，用于向兆丰国际和兆丰纽约的高级管理层报告兆丰纽约遵守BSA/AML要求，国家法律法规，以及OFAC法规；

c. 明确规定了遵守BSA/AML要求、国家法律法规、银行和分行各自的管理、合规人员和内部审计人员的职责、职责和责任；

d. 确保BSA/AML问题得到适当的跟踪、升级，并由兆丰纽约的高级管理人员检查的措施；

e. 有效措施，以确在兆丰国际和兆丰纽约负责BSA／AML合规要求、国家法、法规和受法规监督的个人或组织具有适当的专业技能和积极参与实施

这样的责任；

　　f.充足的资源，以确保兆丰纽约遵守本和解令、BSA/AML要求、国家法律法规，以及OFAC法规;和

　　g.兆丰纽约BSA/AML合规官与董事会或委员会之间的直接汇报路线。

兆丰国际全面完整的合作

52．兆丰国际和兆丰纽约同意将立即全力配合合规顾问和独立监督检查官并支持其工作，除此之外，按照规定为位于纽约，中国台湾、巴拿马，或任何其他位置的所有相关个人、顾问和第三方服务提供者提供文件、报告或记录。

53．独立监督员将监督执行根据行动计划和管理监督计划所采取的任何纠正措施。

54．独立监督员将介入兆丰国际的合规工作，是否遵守其纠正措施，并将向DFS和兆丰国际提交后续进度报告和最终报告，由DFS自行酌情延长本订单所规定的任何报告期限。

55．独立监督员的任期为从其正式签约之日起两年，如果兆丰国际不合作，则由DFS全权决定是否延期。在与银行和监督员进行适当磋商后，有关独立监察机构职权范围或任务范围的任何争议将由本部门自行决定。

与DFS的互动

56．合规报告提交后30天内，兆丰国际和兆丰纽约应当共同提交书面的政策和程序，管理部门的人员的行为在所有监管问题，包括但不限于，DFS认可的与检查兆丰纽约的人员信息互动。政策和程序应至少确保所有部门人员向检查人员提供及时、完整和准确的信息，并提供员工培训，强调所有员工与银行监管机构充分合作的重要性。

违反同意令

57．如果DFS认为，兆丰国际书面违反本和解令，DFS将书面通知兆丰国际，兆丰国际必须在收到书面通知十（10）工作日，或在DFS认可的时间出庭，直到DFS认为没有书面违反本和解令，或者相关的违反不是书面的或已被纠正。

58．各方理解并同意，兆丰国际未能在规定的时间内作出必要的回应，应成为兆丰国际违约的假定证据。一旦发现兆丰国际违反本和解令，本署在纽约

银行法和金融服务法下拥有所有可用的补救措施，并可在随后的聆讯、通知或命令中使用任何可用的证据。

放弃的权利

59．双方理解并同意，本同意令的任何条款均不得在DFS以外的任何法院或法庭进行检查。

受和解令约束的当事人

60．本和解令对本署及兆丰国际及本署监管当局的任何继承人及受让人均有约束力。该和解令不约束任何联邦或其他国家机构或下属执行机构。

61．如果兆丰国际和兆丰纽约遵守本和解令，DFS将不采取进一步的行动，对该银行的行为进行处罚。然而，尽管在本同意令中有其他规定。但是，DFS可对兆丰国际和兆丰纽约的引起DFS注意的交易或行为采取额外的行动，以作为交易和OFAC制裁检查的结果，或以其他方式处理。

提示

62．本和解令的所有通知或通讯均应发送至：

For the Department:

Jeffrey Waddle Elizabeth Nochlin Megan Prendergast New York State Department of Financial Services One State Street New York， NY 10004

For Mega International and Mega-New York:

Jui-Chung Chuang Mega International Commercial Bank Co.， Ltd. l0F， No. 123， Sec. 2 Jhongsiao E. Rd. Taipei 10058， Taiwan， R.O.C.

Vincent S.M. Huang Mega International Commercial Bank Co.， Ltd -New York Branch 65 Liberty Street New York， NY 10005

其他未尽事宜

63．除非DFS保留、修改、暂停或终止，本和解令的每一项条款将持续有效。

64．除本和解令条款以外，各方不承诺、同意、表示或理解和解令外的任何内容。

兹证明，双方于2016年8月19日签署本协议。

本和解令当事人：

纽约州金融监管局

兆丰国际商业银行有限公司

兆丰国际商业银行有限公司纽约分行

10.

好学生同样会犯错
——意大利联合圣保罗银行洗钱案例

2016年12月，意大利最大零售银行联合圣保罗银行因反洗钱不利和违反银行保密法被美国监管当局处罚。美国纽约州金融服务局指控该银行及其纽约分行对交易监控系统管理不善，未能发现涉及空壳公司的可疑交易。此外，还培训员工处理伊朗交易，并故意对银行稽核人员隐瞒信息。最终，被美国纽约州金融服务局罚款2.35亿美元。

这家行事风格一直秉承严谨低调的欧元区大型银行为何在反洗钱方面栽了大跟头，值得我们引以为戒。

意大利联合圣保罗银行概况

意大利联合圣保罗银行（Intesa Sanpaolo S.p.A.）成立于2007年1月1日，是由意大利联合商业银行Banca Intesa和意大利圣保罗银行Sanpaolo IMI合并成立的新银行集团。新的意大利联合圣保罗银行集团目前是意大利第二大银行，仅次于意大利联合信贷银行之后；它也是欧元区第三大银行，拥有688亿欧元的资产规模。银行集团总部设立在意大利都灵，在米兰也设有次级银行总部。

原意大利联合商业银行成立于1998年1月1日，由两家私人商业银行Cariplo和Banco Ambrosiano Veneto合并而成。1999年，意大利商业银行（Banca Commerciale Italiana）加入Intesa集团。2001年5月，随着BCI正式并入Banca Intesa，该集团更名为Intesa Bci。2002年12月，股东大会决议将公司名称变更为Banca Intesa，并于2003年1月1日起生效。

原意大利圣保罗银行成立于1998年，由都灵圣保罗银行（Bancario sanpaolo di Torino）和伊米银行（IMI BANK）合并而成，这两家银行具有很强的互补性。都灵圣保罗银行是一家专门从事零售贷款业务的机构；IMI银行成立于1931年，是一家领先的商业和投资银行，旨在支持国家工业体系的重建。

2006年8月，意大利联合商业银行和意大利圣保罗银行共同声明了合并事宜，并于同年12月实施具体合并工作。2007年1月1日，意大利联合圣保罗银行正式成立。

意大利联合圣保罗银行目前的业务经营范围主要划分为六大部分，其中，在零售业务、公司业务及财富管理业务方面已跻身于欧元地区顶级银行之列。

零售银行是其核心业务，该行在意大利大部分地区的市场份额不低于

12%，其零售业务覆盖超过70%的意大利家庭财富；公司企业银行服务方面，该行主要向公司客户提供从借贷、结构融资及咨询等一系列服务；银行保险业务方面，其旗下的国际保险公司（Assicurazioni Internazionali di Previdenza）是意大利人寿保险第三大公司；金融服务和资产管理方面，在意大利名列前茅，拥有意大利五分之一的市场份额；投资银行业务方面，通过集团IMI银行的分行以及分布在米兰、伦敦、纽约和其他金融中心的子行经营；公共财务管理方面，通过OPI银行经营；商业银行方面，通过圣保罗私人银行经营。此外，在资产管理、个人理财以及基础设施融资领域也表现相当活跃。

意大利联合圣保罗银行在意大利本土拥有广泛的业务网络，约有4 700家分支机构遍布全国，向1 230万客户提供服务，在意大利大部分地区的市场份额不低于12%。该行86%的贷款客户来自于意大利，77%的收入来自欧洲。

该行的海外分支机构网络遍布24个国家，在美国、巴西、俄罗斯、印度和中国等设有分行或代表处。但海外业务还是主要集中在欧洲中东部，中东和北非地区，通过所设立的零售网点和商业银行在13个国家开展业务，拥有大约1 100家分行和760万名客户。

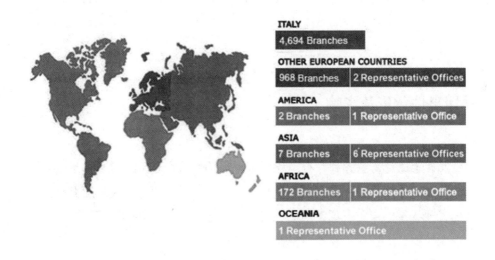

图1　全球网络情况

意大利联合圣保罗银行进入中国还要追溯到1981年，该行是第一家在北京设立代表处的意大利银行。20世纪80年代，银行的战略目标是面向在中国开展业务的意大利公司提供全面的运营和咨询支持。1984年香港分行成立。随后1987年又成立了上海代表处，1997年上海代表处升级为全面银行业务的分行。2002年9月，该行成为第一家被批准开展人民币业务的意大利银行。

近年来，该行通过多种不同的方式加强与中国的业务合作关系。2005年，该行与中国银行合作，出资成立上海华意达商务咨询有限公司，向在中国开展工业及商业项目的意大利企业提供商务咨询和协助。2007年2月，旗下子公司欧利盛金融集团收购合众人寿保险公司19.9%的股份，进入中国人寿保险市场。在该收购交易后仅几周，收购了中国鹏华基金管理有限公司的49%的股份。自2006年起，与国家开发银行和中国进出口银行合作投资曼德琳基金，该基金是为支持在中国和意大利市场拓展业务而设立的私募基金。2008年，意大利联合圣保罗银行认购青岛银行的增资，使持股比例达到20%，总对价约为1.35亿美元。

意大利联合圣保罗银行集团与多家推动中意两国文化、商业、技术和科学交流的组织合作，积极支持中国意大利商会各项工作，并且是当代中国高级研究中心以及意中基金会的创始成员。

处罚事件背景及影响

2016年12月，意大利联合圣保罗银行因反洗钱行动不力以及违反银行保密法被美国纽约州金融服务局罚款2.35亿美元。主要合规缺陷包括对其交易监控系统管理不善，未能发现涉及空壳公司的可疑交易。此外，银行还对伊朗交易作特殊处理，使其真实背景不易被了解和监控。

纽约金融服务局部门负责人Maria Vullo在其声明中表示，"这家银行的疏忽行为可能会促进国际犯罪活动行为，从而严重危及国际金融体系的安全"。

除了支付罚款外，联合圣保罗银行还需继续聘请独立顾问，对反洗钱合规、可疑活动监控、客户尽职调查、内部审计、公司治理和管理层监督等方面进行整改，以及提交纽约金融服务局认可的书面报告。

这笔罚金是纽约州金融服务局2016年的收官之作。据统计，自2012年以来，仅因反洗钱和制裁政策违规而导致的案件，纽约州金融服务局即针对数十家银行的纽约分支机构处以了合计68亿美元的天价罚款。

经验教训的总结和启示

事实上，意大利尽管作为世界第八大经济体，但世界知名的意大利银行却少之又少，银行业长期处于萎靡不振的状态。根据权威杂志《银行家》的排名，自2000年以来，世界前二十五大银行也仅有意大利联合圣保罗银行能够勉强几次出现在榜单上。该行是意大利资本状况最好的银行，是意大利银行业中的"好学生"。2016年6月，意大利政府拿出170亿欧元（约合190亿美元）用于救助濒临破产的维琴察大众银行与威尼托银行两家地方性银行。两家银行的优质资产和不良资产被分割，高质量资产以1欧元象征性价格卖给意大利联合圣保罗银行。随后，政府提供52亿欧元的立即援助资金来维持两家银行的运作，并提供给意大利联合圣保罗银行 120 亿欧元的风险亏损补助，以达成对两家银行的收购。

那么，作为在意大利银行业中的翘楚，该行为何在反洗钱方面栽了大跟头，经过对该案例及监管部门和解令的分析，带给我们如下几方面的启示。

（1）有效且高效的交易监测筛查系统是必不可少的利器

意大利联合圣保罗银行受罚的主要罪证之一是交易监控的缺陷，DFS在和解令的开篇即对交易监控及系统的定义和重要性予以说明，"交易监控是一个机构在执行可能的BSA/AML违规和可疑活动报告后监控金融交易的过程。"虽然这一过程可能是人工进行的，但较大的机构通常会使用先进的软件来监控交易，并在第一时间筛选出来。

当前，反洗钱合规要求日趋严苛，制裁形式和名单越来越复杂，仅以名单筛查为例，OFAC规定，SDN名单上的实体或个人拥有50%或以上所有者权益的实体被视为被制裁对象；2014年，OFAC为实施对俄制裁，首次发布SSI名单（Sectoral Sanctions Identifications， OFAC的行业制裁名单），并发布制裁措施指令，只允许为此名单内的制裁对象提供特定类型和特定期限的服务。

在反洗钱形势日趋严峻的情况下，每天从大量的交易数据中甄别可疑交易已非易事，即使涉嫌洗钱行为被发现，也为时已晚、鞭长莫及。目前，一些银行资金交易不受时间、空间限制，资金能够被瞬间转移，线索很容易被切断。不法分子可通过频繁转账、频繁更换交易对象、多次存取等手段割裂资金链条，将资金转移到安全的地方。在这种形势下，金融机构要满足合规要求，就必须结合自身实际设计使用先进的交易监测系统，并定期审视，通过新技术的运用不断提高可疑报告管理与数据统计分析质量。

（2）强调高级管理层的合规责任

和解令中就意大利联合圣保罗银行对公司治理和管理监督方面的整改提出了明确的要求，要求该行总行和纽约分行管理层加强反洗钱合规的监督并提供书面计划。

2016年6月30日，纽约州金融服务局颁布了最新的反洗钱监管条例《银行业机构交易监控与过滤程序及证实管理条例（BANKING DIVISION TRANSACTION MONITORING AND FILTERING PROGRAM REQUIREMENTS AND CERTIFICATIONS）》。其中，最为引人注目的即是所有受其监管的金融机构的董事会成员或高级合规官以后每年必须要做一次保证，保证该金融机构的交易监控和过滤系统完全符合上述法规的要求。如果一旦作出虚假或错误的保证，则其董事会成员或高级合规官个人可能要承担刑事责任。

该条例自2017年1月1日起生效，所有纽约金融机构的董事会成员和高级合规官们都需要非常地了解公司的反洗钱合规体系，包括反恐怖主义融资和制裁，并且保证该体系完全符合法律的要求，且没有漏洞和瑕疵。一旦存在任何制度上的脆弱，导致违法情形出现，监管机构很有可能就认为该公司的合规体系不符合法律的要求，进而认定该公司的董事会成员或高级合规官们所做的保证不够准确，甚至有可能被视为不诚信。结果就会依据条例要求董事会成员和高级合规官们承担个人的民事乃至刑事责任。

之所以要出台如此严厉的政策，说明纽约州金融服务管理局旨在通过年度报告的方式来向公司的高级管理层施压，以督促其在公司层面推行落实完整恰当的反洗钱以及合规体系。

（3）远离制裁名单完善内控制度

在意大利圣保罗银行的和解令中也出现了处理涉及伊朗的交易，并故意隐瞒稽查人员。细数近年来被美国因反洗钱法处罚的金融机构，或许会让人感到震惊，他们中绝大多数都涉及与制裁名单中的国家有业务往来，可见制裁名单不可小觑。金融机构为逐利不惜铤而走险、明知故犯，故意接纳制裁国家及高风险客户帮助其清洗黑钱，最终的后果只能属于罪有应得。

2001年"9·11事件"后，美国颁布《爱国者法案》（The USA Patriot Act of 2001）以建立全球金融反恐和反洗钱监管架构。在该法案第317条，"对外国洗钱者行使长臂司法管辖权"的规则被确立下来。由于任何犯罪通常都需资金支持或通过金融机构进行结算，而任何国家的银行，只要其经营国际业务，就离不开美元和美国的金融机构，因此，如果哪国银行不执行美国的反恐和反洗钱措施，其国际业务就可能因此被美国限制甚至关闭，损失必然难以估量。在当前美元强势地位下，各国银行都只能乖乖就范，远离联合国和美国监管的制裁名单。

此外，完善反洗钱内控工作尤为重要，一旦反洗钱内控出现漏洞，甚至内部员工故意违规，那么银行的合规将面临致命的威胁。充分提高反洗钱内控工作的重视程度，强化监测系统，加强内部核查体系，有效防范洗钱犯罪。

近年来，意大利银行业资产负债规模收缩，利润大幅下滑，不良贷款快速攀升，评级、股价等市场指标急剧恶化。意大利经济依旧疲弱，负利率政策短期难以扭转局面，意大利国内政权更迭造成动荡，这些都会加大银行的经营风险。意大利联合圣保罗银行占据着意大利银行业的主导位置，在这种不利的大环境下，要进一步加强合规管理工作，特别是反洗钱和涉嫌为恐怖主义融资方面，吸取经验，建立完备的反洗钱制度，防范洗钱风险。

同时，这类大型金融机构洗钱丑闻更像一面镜子，照着我们并给予警示，应以它为鉴，防止犯下相同的错误。

附录:

《和解令》英文原文

NEW YORK STATE DEPARTMENT OF FINANCIAL SERVICES

In the Matter of

INTESA SANPAOLO S.p.A.
INTESA SANPAOLO S.p.A.
NEW YORK BRANCH

CONSENT ORDER UNDER
NEW YORK BANKING LAW SS 39 and 44

The New York State Department of Financial Services (the "Department" or "DFS"), Intesa Sanpaolo S.p.A. ("Intesa-Milan"), and Intesa Sanpaolo S.p.A. New York Branch ("Intesa- New York" or the "New York Branch") (together, "Intesa" or the "Bank") stipulate that:

INTRODUCTION

The Culture of Compliance in the Age of Risk

1.Global financial institutions serve as the first line of defense against illegal financial transactions in today's fast-paced, interconnected financial network. Federal and New York law require these institutions to design, implement, and execute policies and systems to prevent and detect illegal financial transactions. The Bank Secrecy Act ("BSA"), for example, requires these institutions to report suspicious transactions (via "Suspicious Activity Reports" or "SARs") to the U.S. Treasury Department's Financial Crimes Enforcement Network ("FinCEN"), enabling law enforcement to conduct investigations that result in the future interdiction of these transactions and, ultimately, prosecution or the blocking of bad actors. TheBSA likewise requires financial institutions to have adequate anti-money laundering ("AML") systems in place.

2.New York law imposes these same requirements on its regulated financial institutions.[①] Specifically, the law obligates financial institutions to devise and implement systems reasonably designed to identify and block suspicious activity and transactions prohibited by law. Each institution is expected to configure a system based on the particular risks faced by the institution, considering such factors as its size, geographical reach, and specific lines of business. Moreover, the institution must employ or engage sufficient numbers of trained compliance professionals to ensure that its systems run properly.

---

① See, e.g., Part 115 of the Superintendent's Regulations (3 NYCRR 115), Part 116 (3 NYCRR 116), Part 416 (3 NYCRR 416) and Part 417 (3 NYCRR 417).

Transaction Monitoring - An Essential Compliance Tool

3.One such system is known as "transaction monitoring." This is the process by which an institution monitors financial transactions after their execution for potential BSA/AML violations and Suspicious Activity Reporting. While this process may be carried out manually, larger institutions often employ electronic systems using advanced software to monitor transactions and, in the first instance, screen them even before execution for possible violations of federal sanctions laws.

4.Attention to detail in the operation of these monitoring and filtering systems is essential. A system must be designed to address the specific risks encountered by the institution in conducting its business. Effective transaction monitoring and filtering also necessitates a system that can be adjusted to changes in risk profiles, and which can be audited routinely. Skilled, adequately-trained staff is also necessary to operate and oversee these systems competently.

5.Ultimate responsibility for the design and implementation of a transaction monitoring system lies at the top echelon of the financial institution. The board of directors and senior management must adequately oversee the compliance, infrastructure, and other personnel that design, implement, operate and (as necessary) modify a transaction monitoring system.

6.In both past investigations and routine examinations, the Department has identified significant shortcomings in transaction monitoring and filtering programs of a number of major financial institutions. The Department found that such deficiencies generally were attributable to a lack of robust governance, oversight, and accountability at senior levels. These findings have resulted in a number of enforcement actions, and have led the Department to issue a new regulation (effective January 1,2017) governing transaction monitoring and filtering systems. Among other things, the regulation creates an obligation for a covered institution's chief compliance officer (or functional equivalent) to certify compliance with this regulation, thereby encouraging institutions to proactively ensure compliance with existing federal and state anti-money laundering and sanctions requirements. The Department views effective transaction monitoring systems as an essential tool in the battle against illicit transactions and terrorist financing in this age of risk.

Summary of Findings

7.This Consent Order first addresses compliance failures at the New York Branch over the last several years arising from deficiencies in the implementation and oversight of the transaction monitoring system located at the New York Branch.

8.Additionally, the Bank suffered a separate compliance failure in 2005-2006 arising from the processing of thousands of transactions bearing strong indicia of shell company activity or other possible money laundering activity, which were cleared through the New York Branch or other U.S. banks or branches. From 2008 to 2012, the Bank discontinued relationships with approximately 5,400 clients to remediate this compliance failure.

9.Further, from approximately 2002 to 2006, Intesa used non-transparent practices to process payments on behalf of Iranian clients and other entities. While these transactions may very well have been legally permissible "U-Turn" transactions under federal law and regulations in effect at the time, they involved non-transparent payment messages. Consequently, the Bank deprived the Department of the opportunity to learn of the true nature of these transactions when carrying out its supervisory responsibilities.

10.The Bank made the decision to discontinue this practice in 2006. In addition, the Bank reached a settlement with the U.S. Treasury Department's Office of Foreign Asset Control ("OFAC") in 2013 in which it paid $2.9 million for apparent violations of federal sanctions laws and regulations related to processing certain U.S. dollar transactions that terminated in the United States for Iranian, Sudanese, and Cuban entities.

FACTUAL FINDINGS

Background on Intesa

11.Intesa is a major international banking institution headquartered in Milan, Italy. The Bank has over 4,000 branches globally. Additionally, it has approximately 1,200 branches belonging to subsidiaries in Central and Eastern Europe, the Middle East, North Africa, Asia, and the United States. The Bank employs more than 90,000 people across the globe.

12.Intesa's financial services businesses include retail lending, wealth management, asset management, and corporate and investment banking. The Bank holds total assets exceeding $761 billion; assets at the New York Branch total approximately $18 billion. It remains one of the top banks in Italy by total assets, and is a key player in the world financial system.

13.The Department supervises and regulates Intesa's New York Branch as a foreign bank branch in New York State. According to the Bank, the New York Branch clears approximately $4 trillion each year through its correspondent banking relationships. This enormous volume of transactions poses significant risks for money laundering and other illicit transactions that need to be properly mitigated by the Bank's leadership.

The 2007 Written Agreement with the Department

14.Following a joint examination by the Department and Federal Reserve Bank of New York ("FRBNY"), the Department (via its predecessor, the Banking Department) and FRBNY commenced a public enforcement action against the Bank and the New York Branch pursuant to a Written Agreement (the "Agreement") dated March 2, 2007. The Agreement sought to address multiple deficiencies identified by the Department in Intesa's BSA/AML compliance.

15.Among other things, the Agreement required important and material improvements in Intesa's BSA/AML compliance, Suspicious Activity Reporting, and Customer Due Diligence efforts. The Agreement also required a limited transaction "look-back" for a six month period in 2006 (the "Initial Look-Back"), to determine the extent of compliance failures at the New York Branch. The Bank hired an independent consultant to assist in its efforts to remediate deficiencies identified in the Written Agreement and to conduct the Initial Look-Back.The Initial Look-Back was concluded, and a comprehensive written report by the independent consultant was submitted to the Department and FRBNY in 2009.

16.Upon consideration of the results from the Initial Look-Back, the Department required Intesa in December 2013 (the "December 2013 Order") to (1) conduct an expanded look-back for the period of 2005 through 2006, focusing on possible shell company activity first identified during the Initial Look-Back (the "Expanded Look-Back"), and (2) review the existing AML/BSA compliance systems utilized by the New York Branch and make recommendations for correcting any deficiencies.

17.The term "shell company" typically refers to privately-held corporations, limited liability companies (LLCs), and trusts that frequently have no physical presence (other than a post office box), and generate little or no independent economic value. Shell companies have become common tools for money laundering and other financial crimes, primarily because they are easy and inexpensive to form and operate. Ownership and transactional information on these entities can readily be concealed from regulatory and law enforcement authorities, because most states do not collect or otherwise require disclosure of ownership information at the formation stage or thereafter.[1]

18. Under its December 2013 Order, the Department and the Bank selected a new independent consultant (the "Second Independent Consultant") to (1) perform the Expanded Look-Back concerning shell company activity in 2005 through 2006, and (2) conduct the comprehensive review of all existing AML/BSA compliance systems utilized by the New York Branch and make recommendations to correct any deficiencies. The Second Independent Consultant has conducted an investigation since 2014 to further the Department's supervisory and enforcement efforts, and the Second Independent Consultant's investigative efforts have continued to the present.

The Transaction Monitoring System at the New York Branch Is Deficient

19. The Bank'.v System and Governing Policies/Procedures: The Bank's transaction

monitoring system is divided between two electronic programs. The first program - known as "GIFTS-EDD" - employs keywords and algorithms to identify suspicious transactions. When there is a hit on a keyword or when the algorithm is satisfied, the program generates an electronic "alert."[2]

20. An alert may be prompted by such factors as the presence of key terms within a payment message; a relationship to other payments by the same originator or beneficiary; unusual criteria such as round-dollar payments or frequent repetitive payments that appear unrelated to a party's legitimate business purposes; a potential match with persons or entities appearing on lists of persons or entities specifically prohibited from conducting transactions ("specially-designated national" or "SDN" lists); involvement of parties who appear on lists of people who have governmental positions that may subject them to attempts at bribery ("politically-exposed persons" or "PEP" lists); or certain combinations of these indicia.

21. The second program - known as "Casetracker" - is a case management system .According to the New York Branch's General Transaction Monitoring Procedures (the "Monitoring Procedures"), each and every alert generated by GIFTS-EDD is supposed to be loaded into Casetracker by compliance personnel.

---

[1] See FinCEN Advisory, Potential Money Laundering Risks Related to Shell Companies (FIN-2006-G014, Nov. 9, 2006), at https://www.fmcen.gov/resources/statutes-regulations/guidance/potential-money-laundering-risks-related-shell-companies. Indeed, because of concerns about shell company activity, FinCEN recently expanded its efforts to prevent money laundering and terrorist financing by issuing a Geographic Targeting Order that requires title insurance companies to identify natural persons who are behind shell companies that pay all cash for high-end residential real estate in six major metropolitan areas. See FinCEN Expands Reach of Real Estate "Geographic Targeting Orders" Beyond Manhattan and Miami (FinCEN July 27, 2016), at https://www.fmcen.gov/news/news-releases/fincen-expands- reach-real-estate-geographic-targeting-orders-beyond-manhattan.

[2] An alert is not a suspicious transaction in itself. Rather, it is a transaction that contains indicia of potentially suspicious activity and must be investigated to exclude or confirm the existence of suspicious features.

22.Indeed, for keyword-based alerts, the Monitoring Procedures specifically mandate that each alert be loaded into the case management system even if an alert appears to be a "false positive," that is, a transaction that alerts due to language in a transaction message that is not actually the term or word intended.[①]

23.Once done, New York Branch compliance staff are required to review each alert and decide whether it warrants further investigation or escalation - including the filing of a SAR - or whether it should be cleared and closed. The reviewer must document the determination whether to investigate, escalate, or close, and the factual basis for this decision. Documentation is critical to effective analysis and auditing of transaction monitoring systems.

24.GIFTS-EDD and Casetracker do not interface with each other directly. Accordingly, the New York Branch's written procedures require compliance personnel to load each and every alert generated by GIFTS-EDD into the Casetracker program manually. The compliance staffer is required to create what is essentially a spreadsheet containing all of the alerts generated by each keyword each month, and then load those spreadsheets into Casetracker for review.

25.Deviations front the Bank's Poiicies/Procedures: The New York Branch's policies and procedures were clear and unambiguous in requiring each alert to be loaded into Casetracker for review. Nonetheless, the New York Branch's designated anti-money laundering compliance officer (the "AML Officer") allowed the staff he supervised to decide, on their own, how they would accomplish this alert transfer from GIFTS-EDD to Casetracker for keyword alerts. The AML Officer reported that he simply left it to individual reviewers to decide which process "works best" for them, without standardization, for keyword alerts.

26.More egregiously, in or about 2012, the AML Officer and his staff began reviewing and "clearing" significant volumes of keyword-based alerts without loading them into Casetracker, as expressly required by written policy. For example, if a staff member believed an alert was a "false positive," based on nothing more than a cursory review of the alert, the staffer would omit the alert from the spreadsheet loaded into Casetracker. As such, it was never subject to any subsequent re-review, investigation, documentation, or internal audit.

27.This unauthorized "clearing" process was executed by compliance staff members and interns - and even the AML Officer himself. While the AML Officer claimed to have provided some guidance to staff on how to carry out this unauthorized clearing process, no formal training on this unauthorized clearing process was ever provided or documented.

28.From sometime in 2012 until at least mid-2014, these alerts were cleared outside of Casetracker without any formal investigation or the creation of reviewable records. This meant that no one at the Bank had the ability to formally re-review the alerts in Casetracker, nor was there an audit trail in Casetracker of any of the thousands of unauthorized clearances of alerts.[②]

---

① For example, if the keyword is "silver," which seeks to identify transactions that reference the precious metal, the system will generate an alert on the term, "Silverstar Plumbing Company." Because that term is not actually the term the system is searching for, this alert would likely be deemed a "false positive."

② In or about mid-2014, compliance staff began to create some brief documentation of the unauthorized alert clearing process within the GIFTS-EDD system itself, but it was inadequate because, among other reasons, it was not compliant with express written procedures; it was ad hoc and irregular; and it was kept in GIFTS-EDD, not in Casetracker, such that anyone who wanted to audit or review these decisions would have had to look in a different system.

29.Moreover, for two months, none of the keyword-based alerts were migrated from GIFTS-EDD to Casetracker. There is simply no record of these alerts in the case management system, and the Bank could not find any documentation confirming such transfers.

30.Accordingly, in 2014 alone, approximately 10,000 of the keyword-based alerts generated by GIFTS-EDD - approximately 92 percent of the total keywords generated - were never loaded into Casetracker for formal review, either because they were ignored, or were cleared with no formal review or documentation.

31.The unauthorized clearing practice and repeated failure to properly load alerts into Casetracker continued until approximately March 2016, when the Second Independent Consultant discovered it and brought it to the attention of the Department. The Department immediately instructed the Bank to cease this misconduct.

32.The AML Officer subsequently justified the unauthorized clearing practice on the basis that there purportedly was a very high volume of "false positives" being generated by GIFTS-EDD. The AML Officer claimed this unauthorized clearing method was "more efficient" than the procedure prescribed by the New York Branch's written policies. According to the AML Officer, because the Bank allegedly employed a "risk-based approach," this unauthorized process was acceptable, because a risk-based policy meant (at least to him) that "if you miss one, you miss one."

33.In fact, the New York Branch did not track many thousands of alerts. The Independent Consultant determined that, in 2014 alone, approximately 41 percent of the alerts improperly closed through the unauthorized and ad hoc clearing process were not "false positives" but were proper alerts that required further investigation, of which some may have required further escalation.

34.Deficiencies in the GIFTS-EDD Rule book: In addition to the disregard of the New York Branch's policies and procedures described above, the GIFTS-EDD system itself contained a number of flaws that went undetected by the Bank.

35.First, some keyword alerts had been incorrectly programmed into the software, thereby failing to capture numerous alerts that the Bank intended to identify and review. One example arose when, in writing the script for a particular keyword search, a third-party programmer (apparently inadvertently) added an extra space into the query. This caused the system to search for an incorrect combination of letters and spaces, and for several years the system did not generate one type of important alert.

36.The consequences of this error were material. In 2014 alone, the system generated alerts from this keyword for only 12 transactions; the Independent Consultant's review determined, however, that - if programmed correctly - this search would have generated more than 1,400 alerts.

37.Second, the algorithms designed to conduct searches in GIFTS-EDD contained other programming errors. As one example, algorithms intended to search for certain country- name information were programmed to generate an alert only if the official country name appeared in the transaction message, neglecting to search for commonly-used short forms of the country names. For example, the system searched for "Russian Federation" - but not "Russia": the system searched for "Libyan Arab Jamahiriya" - but not "Libya."

38.For 2014 alone, the Second Independent Consultant's review determined that, if these algorithms have been programmed correctly, at least $9 billion worth of additional transactions would have been subject to alerts and review by compliance staff.

39.Third, an algorithm intended to search for three or more transactions within a ten- day period instead only generated an alert when three or more transactions occurred in a single day. This programming error alone caused the omission of at least 1,136 alerts during 2014 alone.

40.Fourth, certain properly-functioning algorithms nonetheless were applied only to a subset of the transactions intended - rather than the full universe of transactions.

41.These programming errors were compounded by flawed decision-making from compliance personnel. New York compliance staff decided to modify the suite of algorithms employed by GIFTS-EDD based on a mistaken understanding of system operations. Three pattern algorithms running in the program for a period of time, for example, were eliminated based on a mistaken belief they were duplicative of other algorithms also running. These decisions created material gaps in the Bank's transaction surveillance, causing numerous transactions to go unreviewed.

42.Failure to Upload Large Numbers of Alerts Into Casetracker: The collection of human and machine errors described above substantially diminished the effectiveness of the transaction monitoring system. Unfortunately, the deficiencies did not end there.

43.The Independent Consultant discovered that many of the alerts generated by pattern- or list-based algorithms in GIFTS-EDD were never migrated into Casetracker, for reasons not yet apparent.

44.In sum, due to the breakdowns in the transaction monitoring systems at the New York Branch, the Bank failed to review at least 17,000 alerts, totaling approximately $16.6 billion in transactions during 2014 alone (equaling approximately 13% of the alerts that the system was designed to capture). Deficiencies at the New York Branch, however, occurred before then, and continued until at least March 2016, when discovered by the Independent Consultant. Thus, the total number of missed alerts is far larger.

45.Breakdown in Audit and Management Oversight. As noted above, faults in the New York Branch's transaction monitoring system came to light only recently due to the extensive investigation conducted by the Department's Second Independent Consultant.

46.Senior management in New York and at the Head Office in Milan were unaware of such weaknesses, despite the existence of facts that could have led to their discovery. For example, an internal auditor at the New York Branch stated he was aware, through discussions with compliance staff, that some alerts never made it into Casetracker - even though this practice stood against the Bank's written policies.

47.Similarly, in 2014, a compliance manager who conducted a quarterly quality control review of transaction monitoring, learned from compliance staff about the existence of the unauthorized clearance process outside of Casetracker. The compliance manager noted this deviation in a quarterly report, but it was never escalated for higher-level review. This compliance manager's report prompted no further scrutiny or follow-up from senior management, and the practice continued until the Independent Consultant uncovered it two years later.

48.Equally problematic is the fact that Head Office received reports from the New York CCO, as well as the quarterly quality control reports mentioned above. None of the departures from written policy concerning screening of alerts caught the attention of anyone in New York or Milan charged with overseeing compliance.

49.Poor oversight also led to faulty efforts by compliance staff and their managers in the day-to-day review process. One example: a transaction that cleared through the New York Branch in May 2014 generated an alert because one of the parties to the transaction was a possible match to someone listed as a "politically-exposed person" or "PEP."

50.A "politically-exposed person" is defined as an individual entrusted with a prominent public function. It is recognized that many such persons, due to their position and influence, are in a position that may be abused for the purpose of committing money laundering, bribery, or facilitating terrorist financing.[1]

51.For this reason, a New York Branch compliance staffer investigated the matter to determine whether the identified party was the same individual listed on the PEP list. The investigation revealed that, while the identified party to the transaction was not a politically- exposed person, the party did have known possible links to organized crime.[2]

52.Nonetheless, the analyst "cleared" and closed the alert as non-suspicious, because the alert had only been generated as a potential match for a politically-exposed person.

Shell Company Activity Indicative of Potentially Suspicious Transactions

53.The deficiencies in transaction monitoring were among several AML deficiencies identified by the Second Independent Consultant. The Expanded Look-Back covering the entire 2005-2006 period confirmed the findings of the Initial Look-Back covering a portion of 2006 - namely, that Intesa cleared thousands of transactions through the New York Branch, totaling hundreds of millions of dollars, which bore indicia of potentially suspicious activity in relation to shell companies.

54.As noted above, transactions involving "shell companies" may be suspicious. Ownership and transactional information on these entities can be concealed from regulatory and law enforcement authorities, because many jurisdictions do not collect or otherwise require disclosure of ownership information at any point in time. And shell companies are oftentimes located in an off-shore or other jurisdiction separate from the jurisdiction in which the bank holding the account is located.

55.With this and the findings of the Initial Look-Back in mind, the Second Independent Consultant determined that, during the period 2005 through 2006, one of Intesa's subsidiaries (which had been wholly-owned by Intesa since 1999 and was located in Hungary) handled more than 2,500 transactions in relation to potential shell company activity valued at at least $124.4 million. Yet the Bank processed at least $21 million of these transactions through the New York Branch and is unable to show that it took reasonable steps to determine that these transactions were not suspicious at the time that they were processed.

56.The Expanded Look-Back also uncovered examples of suspicious activity involving government agents or other politically-exposed persons, as well as unusual payment patterns, both of which also may be indicative of money laundering, bribery or other illicit conduct.

57.For example, Intesa's Hungarian subsidiary processed a series of transactions in 2005-2006 on behalf of a corporate customer registered in the British Virgin Islands and that [3] used

---

[1] See Financial Action Task Force, Politically Exposed Persons, at 3 (June 2013).

[2] As part of the investigation, the analyst secured a report from a third-party vendor that maintains databases of high-risk individuals and organizations. That report indicated that the party's name returned hits on risk criteria for "organized crime" and "military" relationships.

[3] As part of the investigation, the analyst secured a report from a third-party vendor that maintains databases of high-risk individuals and organizations. That report indicated that the party's name returned hits on risk criteria for "organized crime" and "military" relationships.

a Swiss mailing address - both of which are well-known secrecy jurisdictions. Two individuals who had applied to receive bankcards linked to that customer account were politically-exposed persons connected to the government of Angola. Intesa's corporate accountholder made payments to a beneficiary who was also a well-known public official of the Angolan government, but that beneficiary held accounts at three different banks in three different countries. Intesa processed these transactions without developing information to show that these troubling criteria were not in fact suspicious.

58.Another representative example involved a corporate customer of Intesa's Hong Kong branch, on whose behalf the New York Branch processed transactions in 2005 - 2006 totaling approximately $70 million. The company was controlled by a billionaire businessman of an Asian nation. Many of the payments processed by the New York Branch involved entities controlled by this billionaire owner on both sides of the transaction; many involved shell companies with no obvious business operations; and many involved round-dollar payments to counterparties organized in known secrecy jurisdictions like the British Virgin Islands.

59.There are additional examples involving other Intesa branches. In 2006, Intesa's Luxembourg subsidiary processed one transaction through the New York Branch for a customer registered at a known shell company address in Panama. This shell company address is associated with the Mossack Fonseca law firm. Mossack Fonseca is a Panamanian firm centrally involved in shell company formation around the globe. These shell companies are possibly designed in some instances to skirt banking and tax laws worldwide, including U.8. laws designed to fight money laundering.

60.Suspicious indicia include the fact that the shell company client of Intesa's Luxembourg subsidiary existed only for about 14 months before dissolution; and that the shell company's transactions included a large round-dollar payment to another apparent shell company doing its banking in Monaco, which was processed through the New York Branch.

The Department's investigation determined that the Panamanian shell company was beneficially owned by Italian shipping magnates who were linked, in 2012, to allegations concerning money laundering and tax evasion schemes.

61.Another example concerns a customer of Intesa's Slovakian subsidiary that engaged in apparent "pass-through" activity. In 2005-2006, this customer regularly received payments from one entity and then immediately paid a similar amount to a different entity. In a one-week period, for example, the Intesa customer received three different payments from a company registered in Cyprus that did its banking in Russia. Each time, the Intesa customer immediately paid out a similar amount to a business registered in Panama with a bank account in Latvia. Intesa processed these payments, including through the New York Branch, but cannot show that the New York Branch took reasonable steps to determine that these transactions were not suspicious.

62.The Independent Consultant uncovered at least 6,600 SWIFT messages, totaling at least $319 million, processed by Intesa during 2005-2006 period that bore strong indicia of possible shell company activity. Of this amount, Intesa processed at least $130 million through the New York Branch without appropriate review or investigation.

Non-Transparent Payment Processing

63.Beginning in 2002, payments for Intesa's financial institution clients were processed through Intesa's operations center in Parma, Italy ("Intesa-Parma"). From 2002 to 2006, a special process was used to clear thousands of Iranian transactions through the New York Branch at a time when Iran was subject to OFAC economic sanctions.

64.Certain Iranian transactions, however, were permitted under the U.S. Department of Treasury's "U-Turn General License" in effect at the time. While the transactions subject to this special process at Intesa had the structure of permissible "U-Turn" transactions under U.S. law and regulations in effect at the time, they involved non-transparent payment messages, because they omitted a possible connection to Iran from the payment messages sent to the U.S.

65.More specifically, from 2002 to 2006, Intesa-Parma divided payment instructions, known as "SWIFT" messages, [1] involving Iranian bank treasury transactions or customer payments into two message streams.

66.The first SWIFT message included all details about the transaction, and Intesa- Parma would send it directly to the Iranian beneficiary's bank. Intesa-Parma would then send a second message, known as an MT202 or "cover payment" message, to Intesa-New York. The cover payment message did not include details about the underlying parties to the transaction and was sent in order to accomplish a transaction to be settled in U.S. dollars.

67.This process was designed to omit details included in the payment message sent to the New York Branch that might have been flagged by human or electronic scrutiny for possible OF AC violations, and which might have led the U.S. bank to delay or block the transaction. Nor would the Department be able to learn of the true nature of these transactions when carrying out its supervisory responsibilities.

68.Indeed, in a 2006 e-mail, an employee with the Head Office Compliance Department in Milan summarized the fundamental problem with Intesa's non-transparent processes: "if we don't show the underlying links, we take away all possibility of controls by the authorities and/or the intermediary banks."

69.Between approximately 2002 and 2006, the Bank conducted more than $ 11 billion of U.S. dollar transactions for Iranian entities through its non-transparent protocol. While such transactions may very well have been permissible under federal law and regulations at the time, New York and U.S. regulators were not able to thoroughly supervise the processing of these transactions because of the transactions' non-transparent nature.

70.Additionally, in conduct that occurred in the period October 2004 through March 2008, Intesa handled approximately $9 million of U.S. dollar transactions for Iranian, Sudanese and Cuban entities in apparent violation of federal sanctions laws and regulations. According to its settlement for $2.9 million with OFAC,

> Intesa had reason to know that one of its customers met the definition of the [Government of Iran under federal sanctions law], and that payments which terminated in the United States for this customer constituted apparent violations of [sanctions regulations]; Intesa's conduct resulted in harm to the integrity of U.S. economic sanctions programs; Intesa is

---

[1] The Society of Worldwide Interbank Financial Telecommunications ("SWIFT") provides an international network through which banks exchange electronic wire transfer messages. The SWIFT network offers various message types that can be used to transfer funds between banks; each type of message includes various informational fields.

a commercially sophisticated international financial institution; and Intesa did not at the time of the apparent violations, maintain an adequate program to ensure that it was in compliance with U.S. economic sanctions. Substantial mitigation was provided to Intesa due to the following factors: OFAC concluded that the apparent violations did not constitute a willful or reckless violation of the law; OFAC also determined that no Intesa managers or supervisors had actual knowledge or awareness of these matters within the meaning of the Guidelines; Intesa provided substantial cooperation to OFAC, including signing a tolling agreement and multiple extensions; Intesa took remedial action in response to the apparent violations and now has a more robust compliance program in place; and Intesa has not received a penalty notice or Finding of Violation from OFAC in the five years preceding the date of the transactions giving rise to the apparent violations.[1]

71.In early 2006, Intesa began revising its policies, and eventually blocked and then closed all of its Iranian U.S. dollar accounts between May and October 2007.

Violations of Law and Regulations

72.Intesa Sanpaolo S.p.A. and Intesa Sanpaolo S.p.A. New York Branch failed to maintain an effective and compliant anti-money laundering program and OF AC compliance program, in violation of 3 NYCRR § 116.2.

73.Intesa failed to maintain and make available at its New York Branch true and accurate books, accounts, and records reflecting all transactions and actions, in violation of New York Banking Law § 200-c.

74.Intesa failed to submit a report to the Superintendent upon discovering omissions of true entries in violation of 3 NYCRR § 300.1.

75.Intesa failed to fully comply with the 2007 Written Agreement, which required Intesa to implement and maintain an effective BSA/AML compliance program.

Settlement Provisions

Monetary Payment

76.Intesa shall pay a civil monetary penalty pursuant to Banking Law § 44 to the Department in the amount of $235,000,000. Intesa shall pay the entire amount within ten days of executing this Consent Order. Intesa agrees that it will not claim, assert, or apply for a tax deduction or tax credit with regard to any U.S. federal, state, or local tax, directly or indirectly, for any portion of the civil monetary penalty paid pursuant to this Consent Order.

Independent Consultant

77.Intesa shall extend the engagement of the Second Independent Consultant for the sole purpose of analyzing and testing the Bank's efforts to remediate the identified shortcomings in its BSA/AML compliance program and audit the Bank's transaction review efforts. All findings and other results from this extended engagement of the Second Independent Consultant, including the

---

[1] See https://www.treasury.gov/resource-center/sanctions/CivPen/Documents/20130628_intesa.pdf (penalty of approximately $3 million for conducting approximately 150 transactions).

reports, transaction review and audit described in Paragraphs 78-81, below, are intended for the sole purpose of informing the Bank's remediation efforts. Except as specified in Paragraphs 78-83, below, the Second Independent Consultant's work on the Expanded LookBack shall be considered complete as of the execution of this Consent Order and payment of the civil monetary penalty by Intesa.

78.Within 60 days of full execution of this Consent Order, the Second Independent Consultant shall submit to the Department a report that summarizes its findings and conclusions concerning the Expanded Look Back (the "Look Back Report"). The Department shall make the Look Back Report available to Intesa for review and inspection.

79.Within 60 days of the full execution of this Consent Order, the Second Independent Consultant shall submit to the Department and the Bank a report that summarizes its findings, conclusions and recommendations concerning the effectiveness of Intesa-New York's compliance with applicable federal and state laws, rules and regulations relating to anti-money laundering policies and procedures, including but not limited to, under the BSA and Part 300 of the Superintendent's Regulations (the "Compliance Report").

80.The Second Independent Consultant shall prepare a written report assessing the implementation of the various remediation plans described in Paragraphs 84-88, below, within 60 days after receiving notice from the Bank that it has completed the remediation implementation.

81.The Bank will conduct a review of transactions processed by or through, or that otherwise pertain to or affect activities conducted by, the New York Branch, to identify and review missed alerts of the type described in Paragraph 44 and additional omissions or deficiencies in transaction monitoring, if any, subsequently identified by the bank for the period 2014 to present, sufficient to reasonably ensure its compliance with all relevant laws, rules and regulations, including, but not limited to, the Bank Secrecy Act, federal sanctions laws, and New York laws, rules and regulations. The Independent Consultant shall perform a reasonable audit of those efforts and report on its audit to the Bank and the Department.

82.In connection with the Bank's obligations under Paragraph 81 above, Intesa shall take reasonable and necessary steps to ensure that all matters or transactions required by law to be reported, and that have not previously been reported, are duly reported in accordance with applicable laws, rules and regulations.

83.The extended term of the Independent Consultant shall be determined in the sole discretion of the Department in light of the remediation obligations set out in Paragraphs 77-88, but will not exceed two years. However, the Department retains the right to extend the term of the engagement if, in its sole discretion, it determines that an extension is necessary for the Bank to complete the remediation plans described in Paragraphs 84-88 below.

BSA/AML Compliance Program

84.Within sixty days (60) of the submission of the Compliance Report, Intesa-Milan and Intesa-New York shall jointly submit to the Department a written revised BSA/AML compliance program for Intesa-New York, acceptable to the Department. The program shall provide for:

      a.a system of internal controls designed to ensure compliance with the BSA/ AML Requirements and the state laws and regulations;

      b.controls designed to ensure compliance with all requirements relating to correspondent accounts for foreign financial institutions;

c.a comprehensive BSA/AML risk assessment that identifies and considers ail products and services of the New York Branch, customer types, geographic locations, and transaction volumes, as appropriate, in determining inherent and residual risks;

d.management of the New York Branch's BSA/AML compliance program by a qualified compliance officer, who is given full autonomy, independence, and responsibility for implementing and maintaining an effective BSA/AML compliance program that is commensurate with the New York Branch's size and risk profile, and is supported by adequate staffing levels and resources;

e.identification of management information systems used to achieve compliance with the BSA/AML requirements and the state laws and regulations and a timeline to review key systems to ensure they are configured to mitigate BSA/AML risks;

f.comprehensive and timely independent testing for Intesa-New York's compliance with applicable BSA/AML requirements and state laws and regulations; and

g.effective training for all appropriate Branch personnel and appropriate personnel of affiliates that perform BSA/AML compliance-related functions for Intesa-New York in all aspects of the BSA/AML requirements, state laws and regulations, and internal policies and procedures.

Suspicious Activity Monitoring and Reporting

85.Within sixty days (60) of the submission of the Compliance Report, Intesa-Milan and Intesa-New York shall jointly submit a written program to reasonably ensure the identification and timely, accurate, and complete reporting by Intesa-New York of all known or suspected violations of law or suspicious transactions to law enforcement and supervisory authorities, as required by applicable suspicious activity reporting laws and regulations, acceptable to the Department. The program shall include:

a.a well-documented methodology for establishing monitoring rules and thresholds appropriate for the New York Branch's profile which considers factors such as type of customer, type of product or service, geographic location, and foreign correspondent banking activities, including U.S. dollar clearing activities;

b.policies and procedures for analyzing, testing, and documenting changes to monitoring rules and thresholds;

c.enhanced monitoring and investigation criteria and procedures to ensure the timely detection, investigation, and reporting of all known or suspected violations of law and suspicious transactions, including, but not limited to:

i. effective monitoring of customer accounts and transactions, including but not limited to, transactions conducted through foreign correspondent accounts;

ii. appropriate allocation of resources to manage alert and case inventory;

iii.adequate escalation of information about potentially suspicious activity through appropriate levels of management;

iv.maintenance of sufficient documentation with respect to the investigation and analysis of potentially suspicious activity, including the resolution and escalation of concerns; and

v.maintenance of accurate and comprehensive customer and transactional data and ensuring that it is utilized by Intesa-New York's compliance program.

Customer Due Diligence

86.Within sixty days (60) of the submission of the Compliance Report, Intesa-Milan and Intesa-New York shall jointly submit a written enhanced customer due diligence program, acceptable to the Department. The program shall include:

a.policies, procedures, and controls to ensure that Intesa-New York collects, analyzes, and retains complete and accurate customer information for all account holders, including, but not limited to, affiliates;

b.a plan to remediate deficient due diligence for existing customer accounts;

c.a revised methodology for assigning risk ratings to account holders that considers factors such as type of customer, type of products and services, geographic locations, and transaction volume;

d.for each customer whose transactions require enhanced due diligence procedures to:

i. determine the appropriate documentation necessary to verily the identity and business activities of the customer; and ii. understand the normal and expected transactions of the customer;

e.policies, procedures, and controls to ensure that foreign correspondent accounts are accorded the appropriate due diligence and, where necessary, enhanced due diligence; and

f.periodic reviews and evaluations of customer and account information for the entire customer base to ensure that information is current, complete, and that the risk rating reflects the current information, and if applicable, documenting rationales for any revisions made to the customer risk rating.

Internal Audit

87.Within sixty days (60) of the submission of the Compliance Report, Intesa-Milan and Intesa-New York shall jointly submit a written revised internal audit program for Intesa-New York acceptable to the Department that shall provide for:

a.completion, at least annually, of a written Board of Directors-approved, risk-based audit plan that encompasses all appropriate areas of audit coverage;

b.timely escalation and resolution of audit findings and follow-up reviews to ensure completion of corrective measures; and

c.comprehensive tracking and reporting of the status and resolution of audit and examination findings to the Bank's Board of Directors.

Corporate Governance and Management Oversight

88.Within sixty days (60) of the submission of the Compliance Report, Intesa- Milan's board of directors and the management of Intesa-New York shall jointly submit to the Department a written plan to enhance oversight, by the management of Intesa-Milan and Intesa- New York, of Intesa-New York's compliance with BSA/AML requirements, state laws and regulations, and the regulations issued by OFAC acceptable to the Department. The plan shall provide for a sustainable governance framework that addresses, considers, and includes:

> a.actions the board of directors will take to maintain effective control over, and oversight of, Intesa-New York's management's compliance with the BSA/AML requirements, state Laws and regulations, and OF AC regulations;
>
> b.measures to improve the management information systems' reporting of Intesa-New York's compliance with BSA/AML requirements, state laws and regulations, and OFAC regulations to senior management of Intesa-Milan and Intesa-New York;
>
> c.clearly defined roles, responsibilities, and accountability regarding compliance with BSA/AML requirements, state laws and regulations, and OFAC regulations for Intesa-Milan's and Intesa-New York's respective management, compliance personnel, and internal audit staff;
>
> d.measures to ensure BSA/AML issues are appropriately tracked, escalated, and reviewed by Intesa-New York's senior management;
>
> e.measures to ensure that the person or groups at Intesa charged with the responsibility of overseeing the Intesa-New York's compliance with BSA/AML requirements, state laws and regulations, and OFAC regulations possess appropriate subject matter expertise and are actively involved in carrying out such responsibilities;
>
> f.adequate resources to ensure Intesa-New York's compliance with this Order, BSA/AML requirements, state laws and regulations, and OFAC regulations; and
>
> g.a direct reporting line between the Head Office compliance officer and the board of directors or committee thereof.

Breach of Consent Order

89.In the event that the Department believes Intesa to be in material breach of the Consent Order, the Department will provide written notice to Intesa, and Intesa must, within ten business days of receiving such notice, or on a later date if so determined in the Department's sole discretion, appear before the Department to demonstrate that no material breach has occurred or, to the extent pertinent, that the breach is not material or has been cured.

90.The parties understand and agree that Intesa's failure to make the required showing within the designated time period shall be presumptive evidence of the Bank's breach. Upon a finding that Intesa has breached this Consent Order, the Department has all the remedies available to it under New York Banking and Financial Services Law and may use any evidence available to the Department in any ensuing hearings, notices, or orders.

Waiver of Rights

91.The parties understand and agree that no provision of this Consent Order is subject to review in any court or tribunal outside the Department.

Parties Bound by the Consent Order

92.This Consent Order is binding on the Department and Intesa, as well as any successors and assigns. This Consent Order does not bind any federal or other state agency or any law enforcement authority.

93.No further action will be taken by the Department against Intesa for the conduct set forth in the Consent Order, provided that the Bank complies with the terms of this Consent Order.

Notices

94.All notices or communications regarding this Consent Order shall be sent to:

For the Department:

> Megan Prendergast One State Street New York, NY 10004
>
> James Caputo One State Street New York, NY 10004
>
> Christine Tsai One State Street New York, NY 10004

For Intesa:

> Piero Boccassino Intesa Sanpaolo S.p.A. Corso Inghilterra, 3 10138 Torino Italy
>
> Pierpaolo Monti Intesa Sanpaolo S.p.A. Corso Matteotti, 1 20121 Milano Italy
>
> Giuseppe La Sorda Intesa Sanpaolo S.p.A. Corso Inghilterra, 3 10138 Torino Italy
>
> Elisabetta Lunati Intesa Sanpaolo S.p.A. Via Verdi, 8 20121 Milano Italy

Miscellaneous

95.Each provision of this Consent Order shall remain effective and enforceable until stayed, modified, suspended, or terminated by the Department.

96.No promise, assurance, representation, or understanding other than those contained in this Consent Order has been made to induce any parly/ to agree to the provisions of the Consent Order.

IN WITNESS WHEREOF, the parties have caused this Consent Order to be signed this 15lh day of December, 2016

《和解令》中文译文

和解令

纽约银行法§§39和44款项下

纽约州金融服务部门（部门或DFS），Intesa Sanpaolo S.p.A.（Intesa-milan），Intesa Sanpaolo S.p.A.，纽约分行（Intesa-New York或纽约分行）（联合，Intesa或银行）规定：

风险时代的合规文化

1. 在当今快节奏、相互关联的金融网络中，全球金融机构是抵御非法金融交易的第一道防线。联邦和纽约法律要求这些机构设计、应用和执行政策和系统，以防止并发现非法的金融交易。例如，银行保密法案（BSA）要求这些机构向美国财政部金融犯罪执法网络（FinCEN）报告可疑交易（通过可疑活动报告，SARs），使执法部门可以进行调查，以制止未来同类交易，并最终起诉或阻止不法分子。BSA同时要求金融机构拥有可以胜任这一任务的反洗钱（AML）系统。

2. 纽约法律对受其监管的金融机构提出了同样的要求。特别是，法律规定金融机构必须设计并应用合理设计的系统，以识别和阻止法律禁止的可疑活动和交易。每个机构都要根据其面临的特定风险来配置一个系统，考虑到的因素包括机构规模、地域范围和具体业务线等。此外，该机构必须雇用或聘用足够数量的训练有素的合规专业人员，以确保其系统正常运行。

交易监控——一个基本的合规工具

3. 交易监控是一个机构在执行可能的BSA/AML违规和可疑活动报告后监控金融交易的过程。虽然这一过程可能是人工进行的，但较大的机构通常会使用先进的软件来监控交易，并在第一时间筛选出来。

4. 在这些监测和过滤系统的运行中注意细节是至关重要的。必须设计一个系统，以解决机构在开展业务时遇到的特定风险。要做到有效的交易监控和过滤也需要该系统可以根据风险条件变化进行调整，并且定期审视。也必须有熟练的、训练有素的员工对这些系统进行操作和监控。

5．交易监控系统的设计和实施的最终责任在于金融机构的高管层。董事会和高级管理人员必须充分监督设计、实施、操作和修改（必要时）交易监控系统的合规、基础设施和其他人员。

6．在过去的调查和例行检查中，DFS发现了许多主要金融机构的交易监控和过滤体系的重大缺陷。DFS发现，这些缺陷一般是由于缺乏强有力的管理、监督和高层的问责制。这些发现导致了一系列的执法行动，并使DFS发布了一项监管交易监控和过滤系统的新规定（2017年1月1日生效）。除其他事项外，该规例为其所监管的金融机构的首席合规官（或职能相同的管理者）制定了一项义务，即保证遵守本条例，从而鼓励各机构积极地确保遵守现有的联邦和国家反洗钱和制裁要求。DFS认为有效的交易监测系统是在这个风险年代打击非法交易和恐怖主义筹资的重要工具。

调查结果概要

7．第一，这份和解令第一次指向过去几年中，纽约分行在实施和监督位于纽约分行的交易监控系统方面存在的缺陷所导致的合规失败。

8．第二，该银行在2005—2006年还遭遇了另一项合规失败，即处理了数千笔明显涉及空壳公司活动或其他可能的洗钱活动的交易，这些交易通过其纽约分行或其他美国银行或分支机构进行了清算。2008年到2012年，该行与大约5 400名客户中断了关系，以弥补这一合规失败。

9．第三，从大约2002年到2006年，Intesa利用非透明的做法为伊朗客户和其他实体处理汇款。虽然在当时的联邦法规框架下，这些交易很可能在法律上是被允许的"U-Turn"交易，但它们涉及不透明的支付信息。因此，DFS在履行其监管职责时，被剥夺了了解这些交易的真实性质的机会。

10．该银行在2006年决定停止这种做法。此外，2013年，因处理某些在美国禁止进行的对于伊朗、苏丹和古巴实体的美元交易而明显违反了联邦制裁法律法规，该银行与美国财政部外国资产控制办公室（OFAC）达成和解，并支付了290万美元罚款。

调查事实

意大利联合银行背景

11．Intesa是一家总部设在意大利米兰的大型国际银行机构。该行在全球有4 000多家分支机构。此外，它在中东欧、中东、北非、亚洲和美国的子公司拥有约1 200家分支机构。该银行在全球有超过9万名员工。

12．Intesa的金融服务业务包括零售贷款、财富管理、资产管理、企业和投资银行业务。银行总资产超过76.1亿美元;纽约分行的资产总额约为180亿美元。该行是意大利资产规模最大的银行之一，并且是世界金融体系的重要参与者。

13．Intesa纽约分行作为纽约州的一家外资银行分支机构受DFS监管。根据该银行数据，其纽约分行通过代理银行业务每年清算大约4万亿美元。大量交易引来巨大洗钱和其他非法交易风险，这些风险必须得到银行领导层的关注以适当规避。

2007年与DFS达成的整改协议

14．2007年3月2日，在DFS和纽约联邦储备银行（FRBNY）的联合检查之后，DFS（通过其前身，银行部）和FRBNY与该银行及其纽约分行达成书面协议（协议），并据此开始公共执法行动。协议试图解决DFS发现该行存在的多项BSA / AML合规缺陷。

15．该协议首先要求该银行就其BSA/AML合规、可疑活动报告、客户尽职调查等作出重要且实质性的改进。协议还要求对于2006年中6个月的交易进行"回溯"（初始回溯），以确定纽约分行合规失败的程度。银行雇佣了独立顾问协助开展初始回溯并对书面协议中识别的缺陷进行整改。2009年，初始回溯结束，独立顾问完成了一份全面的书面报告并提交给DFS和FRBNY。

16．对初始回溯结果进行评估后，DFS于2013年（2013年12月令）要求联合商业银行（1）对2005年到2006年期间交易进行扩展回溯，重点关注首次回溯中第一次发现的可能的壳公司活动，和（2）重检纽约分行现有的AML / BSA合规系统，并提出纠正缺陷的建议。

17．"壳公司"一词通常是指私营企业、有限责任公司（LLCs）和信托公司，且通常没有物理存在（除了一个邮政信箱），并产生很少或没有独立的经济价值。空壳公司已经成为洗钱和其他金融犯罪的常用工具，主要因为他们可以方便且低成本的设立和运作。这些实体的所有权和交易信息在可以很容易地向监管和执法当局隐瞒，因为大多数州在公司设立和之后，不收集或不要求披露所有权信息。

18．根据2013年12月令，DFS和该银行选择了一个新的独立顾问（第二家独立顾问）以（1）执行2005年到2006年有关壳公司活动的扩展回溯，和（2）全面重检纽约分行现有的AML／BSA合规系统，并提出纠正缺陷的建议。自2014年以来，第二家独立顾问进行了调查以推进DFS的监督执法工作，第二家独立顾问的调查工作一直持续到现在。

纽约分行的交易监控系统存在缺陷

19．该银行的系统和管理政策/程序:该银行的交易监控系统分为两个程序。第一个程序被称为GIFTS-EDD，使用关键字和算法来识别可疑交易。当触及关键字或算法被满足时，程序生成一个电子"警报"。

20．警报被触发的因素包括，一笔支付信息中触及关键字;同一汇款人或受益人出现在多笔支付中;其他条件还包括，与当事人合法的商业目的无关的循环美元付款或经常性重复付款;与出现在特别禁止进行交易的个人或实体名单（specially-designated national 或 SDN名单）上的个人或实体的潜在匹配;付款中的一方拥有可能会使他们受到贿赂的在册的政府职位（politically-exposed persons或PEP名单）;或者是这些条件的组合。

21．第二个程序被称为Casetracker，是一个案例管理系统。

根据纽约分行的一般交易监控程序（监控程序），每一个由GIFTS-EDD生成的警报都需要由合规人员导入Casetracker系统。

22．的确，对于基于关键字的警报，监控程序特别要求每个警报被加载到案例管理系统，即使警报是一个"误报"，也就是说，一笔交易被警报是由于交易信息中的拼写，而并不是实际上想要筛查的词或字。

23．一旦完成，纽约分行的合规工作人员被要求审查每一个警报，并决定是否需要进一步调查或升级——包括对一个SAR的归档——或者是否应该清除和关闭。审查人必须记录调查、升级或关闭的决定，以及作出该决定的事实依据。文档对于有效的分析和审计事务监控系统至关重要。

24．GIFTS-EDD和Casetracker不直接交互。因此，纽约分行的书面程序要求合规人员手动加载每一个由GIFTS-EDD生成的警报。合规工作人员需要创建一个电子表格，其中包含每个月每个关键字生成的所有警报，然后将这些电子表格加载到Casetracker中进行审核。

25．银行的政策/程序的偏离：纽约分行的政策和程序是明确的，明确的要求每一个警报都要装进Casetracker进行审查。尽管如此，纽约分行指定的反洗钱合规官（AML官员）允许他监督的员工自行决定如何完成从GIFTS-EDD到Casetracker的警报转移。合规官报告说，针对关键字警报，他只是交由每一个审核人员决定哪些流程"最适合"他们，而没有标准化。

26．更严重的是，在2012年，AML官员和他的员工开始审查和"清除"大量关键字警报，而不是按书面政策明确要求的那样，把它们装载到Casetracker中。例如，如果一名员工仅仅基于对警报的粗略检查，而认为警报是"误报"，该员工就可以将其从装入Casetracker的警报汇总表格中删除。这样，这个警报后续就无法被重新审查、调查、存档或内部审计。

27．这一未经授权的"清除"过程由合规员工和实习生——甚至是AML官员本人——执行。虽然AML官员声称对如何执行这一未经授权的清除过程提供了一些指导，但从未提供或记录这一未经授权的清除过程的正式培训。

28．从2012年的某个时候到2014年中期，这些警报在没有任何正式调查或可查看记录的情况下在Casetracker之外被清除。这意味着，银行里没有人有能力对Casetracker的警报进行正式的重新审查，Casetracker中数千条未授权的警报清除，也没有任何审计记录。

29．而且，有两个月，没有一条基于关键字的警报从GIFTS-EDD装载到Casetracker。在案例管理系统中没有这些警报的记录，银行也找不到任何证实这种转移的文件。

30．因此，仅在2014年，就有大约1万件由产生的基于关键词的警告——大约占关键词警报总数的92%——从未被载入到Casetracker中被正式审查，要么是因为它们被忽略了，要么是在没有正式审查或记录的情况下被清除了。

31．未经授权的对警报的清除以及反复出现的未能正确地将警报装入Casetracker的情况一直持续到2016年3月，直到第二家独立顾问发现并提交DFS。DFS立即指示该银行停止这种不当行为。

32．AML官员随后提出未经授权的清除警报的理由，是GIFTS-EDD产生的举报据称有大量为"误报"。AML官员声称，这种未经授权的清除方式比纽约分行的书面政策所规定的程序"更有效"。根据AML官员的说法，因为银行据称采用了一种"风险为本的方法"，这种未经授权的流程是可以接受的，因为基于风险的政策意味着（至少对他来说），"如果你错过了一个，你就错过了一个。"

33．事实上，纽约分行没有跟踪成千上万条警报。独立顾问认定，仅在2014年，通过未经授权的和特别的清除流程被不正确地结案的警报中，大约有41%并不是"误报"，而是适当的警报，需要进一步调查，其中一些可能需要进一步的升级。

34. GIFTS-EDD系统操作手册的缺陷：除了以上提到的对纽约分行的政策和程序的忽视，GIFTS-EDD系统本身包含了许多银行未发现的缺陷。

35．首先，一些关键字警报被错误地编入软件中；因此，未能捕捉到银行打算识别和审查的大量警报。一个例子是，在为特定的关键字搜索编写程序时，第三方程序员（显然是无意中）在查询中添加了一个空格。这导致了系统搜索字母和空格的错误组合，而多年间，系统都没有生成一个重要的警报。

36．这种错误的后果是实质性的。仅在2014年，系统从这个关键字生成的警报仅涉及12个交易；然而，独立顾问的审查认定，如果程序正确的话，这个搜索将会产生超过1 400个警报。

37．其次，在GIFTS-EDD中进行搜索的算法包含了其他编程错误。例如，为了搜索特定的国家名称信息而编写的算法只有在交易消息中出现官方名称时才会发出警报，而忽略了搜索常用的国家名称的缩写形式。例如，该系统搜索的是"俄罗斯联邦"，而不是"俄罗斯"；搜索"阿拉伯利比亚民众国"，而不是"利比亚"。

38．仅在2014年，第二家独立顾问的审查认定，如果这些算法被正确编程，至少额外价值90亿美元的交易将会触发警报并受到合规人员的审查。

39．再次，一个本应搜索在10天内出现三笔或更多交易的算法，变成只有一天内发生三笔或以上交易才会发出警报。仅在2014年，单单这个编程错误就导致了至少1136个警报的遗漏。

40．最后，某些功能正确的算法只被应用于交易的一个子集——而不是整个交易。

41．这些编程错误被由合规人员的错误决策进一步加重。纽约的合规人员决定根据对系统操作的错误理解，修改GIFTS-EDD所使用的算法套件。例如，在一段时间内同时运行的三种模式算法被删除，因为他们被错误地认为是其他算法的重复。这些决策在银行的交易监控中造成了实质性的空白，导致大量交易未经审查。

42．大量警报未能上传到Casetracker：上面描述的人为和机器错误大大降低了交易监控系统的有效性。不幸的是，缺陷不止如此。

43．独立顾问发现，GIFTS-EDD中，基于模式或列表的算法生成的许多警报从未迁移到Casetracker中，原因尚不清楚。

44．总而言之，由于纽约分行的交易监控系统的问题，仅在2014年，该银行未能审查至少17 000个警报，总计约166亿美元（相当于该系统被设计用来捕获的警报的约13%）。然而，纽约分行的缺陷在那之前就发生了，直到2016年3月才被独立顾问发现。因此，错过警报的总数要大得多。

45．审计和管理监督失职：如上文所述，由于DFS第二家独立顾问进行了广泛的调查，纽约分行的交易监控系统缺陷最近才得以曝光。

46．纽约的高级管理层和米兰的总部都没有意识到这些弱点，尽管他们本应通过一些事实发现。例如，纽约分行的一名内部审计员表示，通过与合规人员的讨论，他意识到一些警告从未进入到Casetracker——尽管这种做法违反了银行的明文规定。

47．相似地，在2014年，一名合规经理对交易监控进行了季度质量控制重检，从合规人员那里了解到存在未经授权的在Casetracker之外的清除做法。合规经理在季度报告中指出了这一问题，但它从未被升级为更高级别的审查。这一合规经理的报告没有引起高级管理层的进一步审查或跟进，这种做法一直延续到两年后独立顾问发现为止。

48．同样有问题的是，总部收到了纽约分行首席合规官的报告，以及上面提到的季度质量控制报告。有关违反规定屏蔽警报的问题没有引起纽约或米兰负责合规监管人员的注意。

49．监督不力也导致合规人员及其管理人员在日常审查过程中作出了错误的努力。一个例子是，2014年5月通过纽约分行的一笔交易引起了一个警报，因为交易的一方可能与被列为"政治敏感人物"或"PEP"的人匹配。

50."政治敏感人物"是指被赋予重要公共职能的个人。由于他们的地位和影响，许多这样的人被认为，可能利用职权从事洗钱、贿赂或协助恐怖融资。

51.出于这个原因，纽约分行的一名合规人员调查了这个问题，以确定被确认的当事人是否是在PEP名单上的同一个人。调查显示，虽然该交易的被确认方不是一个政治敏感人物，但该当事人确实有可能与有组织的犯罪团伙有联系。

（作为调查的一部分，分析人员从维护高风险个人和组织的数据库的第三方供应商那里获得了一份报告。该报告指出，该当事人的名字未能通过"有组织犯罪"和"军事"关系的风险标准。）

52.尽管如此，分析人士"清除"并关闭了警报，因为该警报只是作为一个潜在的政治敏感人物而产生的。

空壳公司活动意味着潜在的可疑交易

53.交易监控的缺陷是第二家独立咨询公司所发现的几个反洗钱缺陷之一。对2005年至2006年交易的扩展回溯证实了对2006年部分是间断的初始回溯的调查结果，即Intesa通过纽约分行清算了大量与空壳公司相关的潜在可疑交易，总计达数亿美元。

54.如上所述，涉及"空壳公司"的交易可能是可疑的。这些实体的所有权和交易信息可以隐藏于监管和执法部门，因为许多司法管辖区在任何时候都不收集或要求披露所有权信息。而空壳公司通常位于与开户银行所在的管辖区不同的离岸或其他管辖区。

55.结合初始回溯的结果，第二家独立咨询公司认为，2005年到2006年期间，一家Intesa的子公司（1999年起被其全资拥有，位于匈牙利）处理了超过2 500笔与潜在的空壳公司活动有关的交易，至少价值1.244亿美元。然而该行通过纽约分行处理了其中至少2 100万美元的交易，并且无法证明他们采取了合理的步骤来确定这些交易在处理过程中并不可疑。

56.扩展回溯还发现了涉及政府机构或其他政治敏感人士的可疑交易案例，以及不正常的支付方式，这两种情况也可能指向洗钱、贿赂或其他非法行为。

57.例如，Intesa的匈牙利子公司在2005—2006年为一个在英属维尔京群岛注册同时使用瑞士通信地址的企业客户处理了一系列交易，这两个国家/地区都是著名的保密辖区。曾申请领取与该客户账户关联的银行卡的两个个人是与安哥拉政府有关的政治人士。Intesa的公司客户账户曾向一位受益人付款，该受益人也是安哥拉政府的一位著名的官员，但该受益人在三个不同国家的三家不同银行持有账户。Intesa在没有信息证实这些令人不安的关联实际上并不可疑的情况下，处理了这些交易。

58.另一个有代表性的例子涉及Intesa香港分行的一个公司客户。2005—2006年，纽约分行为其处理的交易总额约为7 000万美元。该公司由一个亚洲国家的亿万富商控制。纽约分行处理的许多款项涉及的交易双方都是由这位富商所控制的实体;许多涉及空壳公司，没有实质的业务操作;许多涉及（round-dollar payment）美元汇款给注册于保密管辖区（如英属维尔京群岛）的交易对手。

59．还有一些其他的例子涉及其他的Intesa分支机构。2006年，Intesa的卢森堡子行通过纽约分行处理了一笔交易，客户注册在巴拿马知名的一个空壳公司地址。这个空壳公司地址与莫萨克·冯塞卡律师事务所关联。莫萨克·冯塞卡是一家巴拿马公司，主要从事全球范围内的空壳公司设立业务。这些空壳公司可能是为了规避全球范围内的银行和税法而设计的，包括旨在打击洗钱的美国法律。

60.可疑的线索包括Intesa卢森堡子行的该空壳公司客户只存在了大约14个月就解散了;而该公司所作的业务包括支付一笔大额美元给另一个在摩纳哥开户的空壳公司，这笔业务通过纽约分行处理。DFS调查认定，巴拿马的空壳公司的有权受益者为意大利航运巨头，他们在2012年被指控涉嫌洗钱和逃税。

61.另一个例子涉及Intesa斯洛伐克子行的一个客户，该客户涉及明显的"pass-through"活动。在2005—2006年，该客户定期收到来自一个实体的付款，然后立即向另一个实体支付类似的金额。例如，在一周的时间内，该客户从一家在塞浦路斯注册而在俄罗斯开户的公司获得了三笔不同的付款。每一次，该客户都立即向一家在巴拿马注册而在拉脱维亚开户的公司支付类似的金额。Intesa通过其纽约分行等处理了这些付款，但不能证明纽约分行采取了合理的步骤来确定这些交易非可疑。

62．独立顾问发现，在2005—2006年Intesa处理的信息中，至少6 600条

SWIFT信息，总计至少3.19亿美元，存在明显的线索指向潜在空壳公司活动。在这些交易中有至少1.3亿美元由Intesa通过纽约分行处理，且没有经过适当的审查或调查。

不透明的付款操作

63. 从2002年开始，Intesa的金融机构客户的付款通过Intesa在意大利帕尔马的运营中心（Intesa-Parma）进行。从2002年到2006年，在伊朗受到OFAC经济制裁的情况下，采用了一个特殊的流程通过其纽约分行清算了数千笔伊朗交易。

64. 在当年执行的美国财政部的"U-Tum通用许可证"项下，某些伊朗交易是被允许的。虽然Intesa通过这一特殊流程处理的交易，具有当时美国法律法规允许的"U-Tum"交易结构，但是它们涉及不透明的支付信息，因为他们从这些向美国发送的付款信息中清除了可能的与伊朗的关联。

65. 更具体地说，从2002年到2006年，Intesa-Parma将涉及伊朗的银行交易指令或客户支付指令，即"SWIFT"报文，分成两条报文发送。全球银行间金融电信协会（SWIFT）提供了一个国际网络，银行通过该网络交换电子电汇信息。SWIFT网络提供了各种信息类型，可以用来在银行间转移资金;每种类型的消息都包含各种信息字段。

66. 第一条SWIFT报文包含了交易的所有细节，Intesa-Parma直接将其发送给伊朗的受益人银行。然后，Intesa-Parma将发送第二条报文给Intesa纽约分行，称为MT202报文或"支付头寸"报文。支付头寸报文不包括交易的基础各方的细节，只是被用来完成该笔交易的美元头寸结算。

67. 这一过程旨在去除发送到纽约分行的支付信息中包含的细节信息，这些信息可能被人工或电子审查标记为可能违反OFAC规定，并可能导致美国的银行延迟或阻止交易。同时，DFS在执行监督职责时，也不能了解这些交易的真正性质。

68. 事实上，在2006年的一封电子邮件中，米兰总部合规部门的一名员工总结了该行的非透明流程的根本问题："如果我们不显示潜在的关联，我们就剥夺了监管当局和/或中间行控制的可能性。"

69. 大约2002年到2006年之间，该银行通过其非透明流程为伊朗实体处理了超过110亿美元的交易。尽管根据当时的联邦法律和法规，这种交易很可能是被允许的，但因为交易的不透明性质，纽约和美国的监管机构无法对这种交易进行彻底的监管。

70. 此外，在2004年10月至2008年3月期间，Intesa为伊朗、苏丹、古巴的实体处理了大约900万美元的美元交易，明显违反了联邦制裁法律法规。根据OFAC对该行处以290万美元的协议，Intesa有理由知道，它的一个客户符合[根据联邦制裁法]对[伊朗政府]的定义，而为该客户付款到美国显然违反了[制裁条例]；Intesa的行为损害了美国经济制裁计划的完整性;Intesa是一个商业上成熟的国际金融机构；而Intesa并没有在明显违反规定的时候，维持适当的程序以确保它符合美国的经济制裁。由于下列因素，对Intesa的处罚的导显著减轻：OFAC认定，明显的违反行为不构成故意或不计后果的违法行为；OFAC还确定，任何Intesa的管理人员或监督者在制定指导方针的角度都不知晓或未意识到这些问题；Intesa为OFAC提供了大量的实质性合作，包括签署了费用协议和多个扩展文件；Intesa采取了补救行动，以应对明显的违规行为，并且现在有了更健全的合规体系；同时，Intesa在此次违规交易之日前的5年内未收到任何处罚或违规行为通知。

71. 2006年初，Intesa开始修改其政策，在2007年5月至10月冻结并关闭了所有伊朗的美元账户。

违反法律法规事实

72. Intesa Sanpaolo S.P.A.和Intesa Sanpaolo S.P.A.纽约分行未能保持一个有效的、合规的反洗钱体系和OFAC合规体系，违反了3 NYCRR§116.2。

73.Intesa未能在其纽约分行维护和提供真实、准确的账簿、账户和记录反映所有交易和行为，违反纽约银行法§200 - c。

74.Intesa在发现遗漏真实交易信息时，未能向监管提交报告，违反3 NYCRR§300.1。

75.Intesa未能完全遵守2007年的书面协议，该协议要求Intesa实施并维持有效的BSA/AML合规体系。

结算条款

货币支付

76. 根据银行法§44，联合商业银行应当向DFS支付民事罚款235 000 000美元。Intesa应在本和解令生效后10天内付清全部款项。Intesa同意，不会根据该和解令支付的任何部分的民事罚款，向美国联邦、州或地方税收中直接或间接地声称、主张或申请税收减免或税收抵免。

独立顾问

77. Intesa将扩大第二家独立顾问的工作，以达到分析和测试该银行在其BSA/AML合规体系中识别的缺陷，并审计该银行的交易审查工作的唯一目的。

在下文第78~81段所述的报告、交易审查和审计报告中所述的所有调查结果和其他结果，都是为了报告银行的整改工作的唯一目的。除第78~83段所述外，随着本和解令的执行和Intesa民事罚款的支付，第二家独立顾问在扩展回溯方面的工作应被视为完成。

78.本和解令正式生效后60天内，第二家独立顾问应向DFS提交一份报告，总结扩展回溯的调查结果和结论（"回溯报告"）。DFS应向Intesa提供回顾报告，供审查和检查。

79.本和解令正式生效后60天内，第二家独立顾问应向DFS和Intesa提交一份"合规报告"，就Intesa纽约分行在遵守适用的有关反洗钱政策和流程的联邦和州的法律、法规方面，总结其调查结果、结论和建议，法律法规包括但不限于，BSA项下的和监管规定300部分。

80.第二家独立顾问应在收到Intesa完成整改的通知后60天内，草拟一份书面报告，评估第84~88段所述各项整改计划的执行情况。

81. 银行将对2014年至今纽约分行处理、通过或影响活动的交易进行审查，以识别和审查第44段中描述的错过的警报和交易监控中其他的遗漏或缺陷，如果有的话，审查应足以确保其合理符合所有相关法律、规章制度，包括但不限于银行保密法案，联邦制裁法和纽约的法律、规章制度。独立顾问应对这些努力进行合理的审计，并向银行和DFS报告其审计工作。

82. 根据上文第81段所述的银行的义务，Intesa应采取合理和必要的步骤，确保根据适用的法律、规则和条例应该被报告而未报告过的一切事项或交易，根据适用的法律规定要求得到及时报告。

83.独立顾问的延期由DFS根据第77至88段所述的整改义务决定，但不超过2年。然而，DFS保留全权决定延长独立顾问期限的权利，以决定是否有必要延长期限，以完成下文第84~88段所述的整改计划。

BSA / AML合规方案

84.在提交合规报告后的60天内，Intesa-Milan和Intesa-New York将联合向本部门提交一份经修订的纽约分行BSA/AML合规方案，该方案应为本部门所接受的。该方案应提供：

a. 为确保符合BSA/AML要求和国家法律法规而设计的内部控制系统；

b. 旨在确保符合与代理外国金融机构往来账户有关的所有要求的内部控制；

c. 全面BSA/AML风险评估，识别并考虑纽约分行所有产品和服务、客户类型、地理位置和交易金额，以确定其固有和剩余风险；

d. 一个合格的合规官管理纽约分行的BSA / AML合规工作，合规官应是完全自主，独立的，负责实现和维护一个与纽约分行的规模和风险状况相称的有效的BSA / AML合规机制，并应得到充足的人力和资源支持；

e. 管理信息系统的识别，以达到遵守BSA/ AML要求以及国家法律法规的目的，以及审查关键系统的时间表，以确保它们被配置为减轻BSA/ AML风险；

f. 全面和及时的独立测试，以确保纽约符合适用的BSA/ AML要求和国家法律法规；和

g.对所有分行相关人员和附属机构相关人员的有效培训，这些人员在BSA/AML规定、州法律法规、内部政策和程序方面，履行纽约分行BSA/AML合规相关职能。

可疑活动监控和报告

85.在提交合规报告后的60天内，Intesa-Milan和Intesa-New York将共同提交书面方案，以根据适用的可疑活动报告法律法规要求，合理确保识别和及时、

准确和完整地向监管当局报告所有已知的或涉嫌违法的或可疑的交易。该方案应得到DFS的认可。该方案应包括：

a. 一种完备的方法，用来建立监测规则和阈值，以适用于纽约分行的特征，要考虑客户类型、产品或服务类型、地理位置和国外代理行业务，包括美元清算业务；

b. 分析、测试和记录更改监控规则和阈值的策略和过程；

c. 升级监测调查标准和程序，以确保及时发现、调查和报告所有已知或可疑的违法和可疑交易，包括但不限于：

1）有效监控客户账户和交易，包括但不限于通过外国代理行账户进行的交易；

2）合理分配资源以管理警报和案例；

3）通过适当的管理水平适当增加潜在可疑活动的信息；

4）保留足够的调查和分析潜在的可疑活动的档案，包括疑问的解决和升级；和

5）维护准确和全面的客户和交易数据，并确保它被Intesa纽约分行的合规体系所应用。

客户尽职调查

86. 在提交合规报告后的60天内，Intesa-Milan和Intesa-New York将共同提交一份书面的增强客户尽职调查方案，该项目应被DFS认可。该方案应包括：

a.政策、程序和控制，以确保Intesa-New York收集、分析和保留所有账户持有人的完整和准确的客户信息，包括但不限于关联公司的；

b.对不充分的现有客户账户尽职调查整改的计划；

c.修整过的账户持有人风险等级分类，考虑因素应包口客户类型、产品类型、服务、地理位置和交易量等；

d.对于其交易需要加强尽职调查的客户：

i.确定可以核实客户的身份和业务活动的必要文件；

ii.了解客户的正常和预期交易；

e.政策、程序和控制，以确保外国代理行账户得到适当的尽职调查，或必要的加强尽职调查；和

f.对整个客户基础的客户和账户信息进行定期检查和评估，以确保信息是最新的、完整的，并且风险评级反映了当前的信息，如果适用的话，对客户风险评级作出任何修订的合理记录。

内部审计

87.在提交合规报告后的60天内，Intesa-Milan和Intesa-New York应共同提交一份书面修订的对纽约分行的内部审计方案，并为DFS所认可，应包括：

a. 完成至少每年一次，由董事会批准的，基于风险的，包括审计范围的所有适当领域的审计计划，

b. 及时上报和解决审计结果和后续审查，以确保纠正措施的完成；

c. 对审计和审查结果进行全面跟踪并向银行董事会报告。

公司治理和管理监督

88．在提交合规报告后的60天内，Intesa总行董事会和纽约分行管理层应当共同提交一份书面计划，在纽约分行遵守BSA／AML规定，纽约州法律法规，OFAC规定方面，加强总行和纽约分行管理层的监督。该计划应为DFS认可，应提供一个可持续的治理框架，针对、考虑和包括：

a. 董事会将采取的行动，以保持对纽约管理层遵守BSA/AML要求、国家法律法规和OFAC规定的有效控制和监督；

b. 改进管理信息系统报告的方法，向总行和分行管理层报告纽约分行遵守BSA／AML规定，纽约州法律法规，OFAC规定的情况；

c.对总行和纽约分行的各自管理层、合规人员和内部审计人员的，在遵守BSA／AML规定，纽约州法律法规，OFAC规定方面的明确的岗位、职责和责任；

d.措施，以确保BSA/AML问题得到适当的跟踪、升级，并由纽约分行高级管理层进行审查；

e.措施，以确保Intesa负责监督纽约分行遵守BSA/AML要求、纽约州法

律法规，以及OFAC规章的个人或团体，具有适当的专业知识，并积极参与执行这些职责；

f.足够的资源以确保纽约分行执行本和解令、BSA/AML规定、纽约州法律法规和OFAC规定；

g.总行合规官与董事会或其委员会之间的直接汇报关系。

违反和解令

89. 如果部门认为Intesa实质性违反了和解令（违反），则部门将向银行提出违约的书面通知，银行必须在收到所述通知的10个工作日内，或在部门酌情决定的较晚日期，现身部门来证明没有发生违规行为，或在相关情况下，证明违规行为不具实质性或已改正。

90.双方理解并同意，如Intesa未能在规定期限内按要求进行证明，将被作为Intesa违规的推定证据。在发现违规之后，部门拥有《纽约银行业和金融服务法》所有可用的补救措施，并可使用部门可用的全部和任何证据进行所有依据《纽约银行和金融服务法》可能的听证、通知、命令和其他补救措施。

放弃的权利

91.双方理解并同意，和解令的任何条款均不受部门以外的任何法院或仲裁庭审查约束。

受和解令约束的主体

92.和解令对部门和Intesa以及在部门监督下的继承人和受让人具有约束力，但是它并不约束任何联邦或其他州立机构或任何执法机构。

93. 如Intesa遵照和解令的条款，则部门不会就和解令所陈述的行为对法国巴黎银行采取进一步行动。

11.

捉迷藏
——HBL被罚案例

2017年8月24日，美国纽约州金融服务局（New York State Department of Financial Services，DFS）公告要求巴基斯坦HBL（Habib Bank Ltd，HBL）出席于2017年9月举行的听证会。2017年9月7日，DFS与HBL签署《和解令》（见附录），决定吊销其纽约分行的金融许可，并处以2.25亿美元的罚款，理由是HBL在过去10年涉嫌53项违规行为。

　　HBL一方则宣称：由于与美国纽约州金融监管部门就其是否已完善反洗钱合规程序存在争执，该行将关闭其纽约分行。

　　DFS对HBL的处罚和《和解令》的最终签署均发生于美巴两国关系发生变化的时期。按照2017年9月7日《和解令》，HBL应于《和解令》生效后14日内支付全部款项。

巴基斯坦HBL概况

巴基斯坦HBL（HabibBank Ltd）成立于1941年，总部最初位于印度孟买，1947年在穆罕默德·阿里·真纳①的要求下将其业务迁往巴基斯坦，总部迁至卡拉奇。1974年HBL被收归国有。

1956年巴基斯坦建国后，逐渐建立了政府主导的国有银行体系，对银行实施严格的管制。从20世纪70年代初期到90年代初期，巴基斯坦处于严重的金融抑制状态。为提高金融机构效率，促进经济发展，巴基斯坦开始实施金融改革，国有银行私有化是改革的主要内容之一。2003年12月，巴基斯坦私营化委员会宣布，政府已正式将HBL所持股份的51%（224 090亿欧元，约合3.89亿美元）转让给阿加可罕经济发展基金（Aga Khan Fund for Economic Development，AKFED）。2004年2月，银行的管理控制权移交给了AKFED。截至2015年4月，巴基斯坦政府通过巴基斯坦私有化委员会将其41.5%的股份全部剥离，AKFED继续持有HBL 51%的股权，其余股权由个人、本地及外国机构及基金持有，其中包括持有5%股份的CDC Group和持有3%股份的国际金融公司。HBL正式成为巴基斯坦最大的私人银行。

HBL在巴基斯坦境内设有1 425家分支机构和2 000家ATM，客户基本超过1 000万。多年来，HBL致力于扩大在主要国际市场的业务，在遍及四大洲的25个国家设立了55家分支机构，包括：阿富汗、澳大利亚、孟加拉、比利时、加拿大、中国、法国、中国香港、伊朗、肯尼亚、黎巴嫩、尼泊尔、荷兰、尼日

---

① "巴基斯坦国之父"。

利亚、阿曼、新加坡、斯里兰卡、土耳其、阿联酋、英国和美国等。

作为目前巴基斯坦资产排名第一位的商业银行，HBL是巴基斯坦银行业的领跑者，提供广泛的商业银行产品和服务，如公司业务、零售业务、现金管理、金融市场业务、资产管理、为中小企业和农业贷款项目提供银行服务等。该行在投资银行业务方面也十分活跃。依托自身四大洲25个国家的境外机构网络，HBL跨国汇款业务在巴国内独占鳌头。

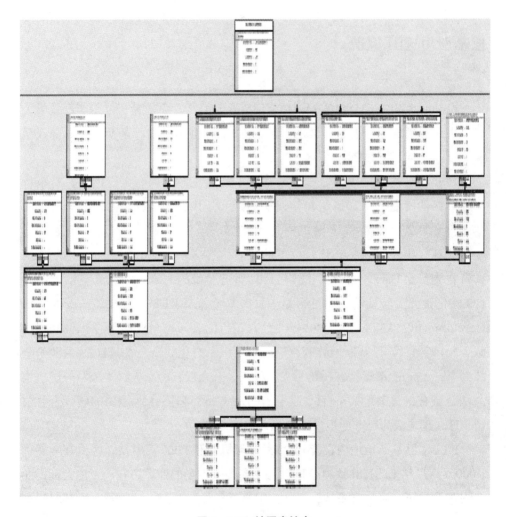

图1 HBL 被罚案始末

事件经过

2017年8月24日，美国纽约州金融服务局（New York State Department of Financial Services，DFS）公告称巴基斯坦HBL存在严重不合规问题，该行在过去10年涉嫌53项违规行为，打算对其处以6.296亿美元罚款，并要求HBL出席于2017年9月举行的听证会。8月29日，HBL对外宣布由于与纽约州金融监管部门就其是否已完善反洗钱合规程序存在严重分歧，该行将关闭其纽约分行。

不久，2017年9月7日，双方正式签署《和解令》（见附录）。按照《和解令》，HBL纽约分行被DFS处以2.25亿美元的罚款。不仅如此，HBL纽约分行还被DFS评为最低级别"5"，通常该级别的金融机构不允许继续存在和经营。

DFS称，早在2006年，HBL就被监管发现在制裁合规管理方面存在不足，当时HBL接受并同意进行改正。在2015年的检查中，DFS发现HBL纽约分行不但未进行有效改正，情况反而更为严重，于是责令HBL聘请外部独立顾问对其过往的美元清算交易进行回溯调查，以确认是否有违反制裁的情况。2016年，DFS再次对HBL纽约分行进行检查，发现其对之前的警告置若罔闻，在合规培训、客户尽职调查和风险划分、黑名单数据、黑名单监控系统审核、审计方面未有好转，HBL反洗钱和反恐融资措施存在严重缺失，例如：HBL为沙特私人银行Al Rajhi Bank开立了账户，但未对通过Al Rajhi Bank账户汇款的最终客户进行有效识别，从而产生了极危险的"套嵌账户交易"行为。而HBL为Al Rajhi Bank处理的数十亿美元的交易据称与恐怖组织"基地组织"有关，但HBL未采取足够的反洗钱/反恐融资措施。DFS还发现，有1.3万千笔汇款交易未经过有效的制裁黑名单扫描，并且HBL还很不妥当的创造并在"黑名单"监控系统中使用了"白名单"（good-guy list），直接导致与制裁实体、中资军火公司和伊朗原油运输船只的交易均未被监测出来。更为严重的是，HBL还对一笔收款方为美国制裁个人的汇款指令进行篡改，故意将该制裁个人姓名从付款指令中隐去，从而达到躲避监控的目的。DFS认为HBL的黑名单监控机制已经"薄弱到危险的程度"。

DFS认为，HBL违反了纽约州法律法规；开展了超权限和不安全的业务；在不稳妥不安全的情况下运营；尽管HBL被给予了充分的机会修正过失，但其没有及时修正，表明HBL要么不具备整改能力，要么固执地不愿整改，或者两者兼具。HBL则坚持认为，HBL纽约分行设立于1978年，至今已有40年历史。自2015年美国联邦储备委员会和DFS下令整改以来，HBL采取了真诚、广泛的整改措施，但DFS仍不理解、不认可其纽约分行取得的明显进步，DFS的处罚不公平、随意、不合理，得不到事实或法律支持，且不符合时效。

HBL纽约分行主要提供美元清算服务，对HBL整体的贡献度有限。鉴于目前情况下，纽约分行的收益已难以覆盖合规成本，HBL将关闭纽约分行。

关于事件

当一系列特殊事件集中出现在某个历史时期时，往往引发人们的好奇、联想和各种猜测。

在美国纽约州金融服务局（DFS）正式发布对HBL公告的前几日，即美国当地时间2017年8月21日晚，美国总统特朗普宣布了美国新的阿富汗和南亚战略，表明美国不仅不会从阿富汗撤军，还要向该国继续增兵。显然，美国增兵的目的在于加大对塔利班、"伊斯兰国"和"哈卡尼网络"等极端组织的打击力度和军事威慑，维持美国在阿富汗的影响力。对于阿富汗的重要邻国巴基斯坦，特朗普则充满批判之词，指责巴基斯坦在反恐事务上出力不足，为阿富汗塔利班和其他武装分子提供"避风港"，美国已经开始调整未来对巴基斯坦的援助。美国还暗示，将对涉嫌与武装分子有联系的巴基斯坦官员进行制裁。

除了不从阿富汗撤军，特朗普还在其演讲中的南亚战略方面提到了印度，特朗普在演讲中表示，"（美国）在南亚战略的另一个关键部分是进一步发展与印度的战略伙伴关系"，称希望印度能为阿富汗的地区经济援助和发展出力，并表示美国愿进一步发展与印度的战略伙伴关系。其实，尽管巴基斯坦自身也遭受着恐怖主义的巨大威胁，但是近年来巴基斯坦在阿富汗安全事务上依然发挥着非常重要甚至是不可替代的作用。巴基斯坦不支持印度过多插手阿富汗事务，这也成为美巴两国间一个突出的矛盾点。

特朗普的"南亚新战略"公布后，巴外交政策顾问、安全官员和政府高层工作人员举行头脑风暴，以制定对策，逐步减少对美国的依赖。美巴两国关系出现恶化趋势。

特朗普发表演讲后仅三天，8月24日，美国纽约州金融服务局（DFS）即发布公告，要求HBL出席于2017年9月举行的听证会，称HBL 10年来有53项违规，打算对其处以6.296亿美元罚款。

DFS偏偏选择在2017年8月24日这一特殊时点公告对巴基斯坦第一大商业银行在美机构进行处罚，难免使人联想到几天前刚刚宣布的美国"南亚新战略"，似乎此次针对HBL的举动是有目的、有计划的配合行动。

其实早在2006年，DFS就已发现HBL纽约分行涉及OFAC制裁法律规定方面的问题而且在BSA/AML方面存在严重不足，双方当年已就此达成书面协议。在10年后即2016年的检查中，DFS也曾发现HBL纽约分行管理层仍然没有进行有效的改进和管理BSA/AML和OFAC风险，包括但不限于：

- BSA/AML合规不足；
- 培训不足；
- 客户风险分类不足，包括有风险的外资代理尽职调查的缺失；
- 加强型客户尽职调查文件缺失；
- 高级人力资源管理和总部管理、监管和记录文件不足；
- 缺乏足够的OFAC和制裁筛查；
- BSA/AML独立测试和内部审计薄弱，包括内部审计方法论的薄弱；和
- 数据映射和整合的薄弱。

此外，在2017年的《和解令》中，DFS提到了HBL纽约分行在对待Al Rajhi Bank方面的失察。Al Rajhi Bank是沙特阿拉伯最大的私人银行，HBL纽约分行为该行开立了代理行账户并代理其美元清算业务。2012年7月17日U．S．SENATE PERMANENT SUBCOMMITTEE曾报告称，有证据表明，Al Rajhi Bank及其一些所有者与恐怖袭击和恐怖融资有联系。"9·11"事件发生于2001年，直至2017年，DFS方在《和解令》中细述"Al Rajhi代理行账户显示HBL银银行被利用从事高风险反恐融资和洗钱活动……"。或许HBL纽约分行太熟悉国际惯例，并十分了解美国的监管规则，以至于隐藏16年而不被发现。

关于罚款的总金额，据称最初为6.296亿美元。然而，在双方最终达成的《和解令》中，罚款总金额实际为2.25亿美元。此前曾有媒体称，因不满巴基斯坦在反恐方面的作为，特朗普政府正在考虑掐断对巴基斯坦2.55亿美元的反恐资金援助。或许这也仅仅是一种巧合。

按照《和解令》，HBL应于《和解令》生效后14日内支付全部款项。目前，罚款是否已经缴纳、营业执照是否已交回均不得而知。

HBL的专业所在

作为曾被"巴基斯坦之父"特别关注过的银行，作为巴基斯坦第一家商业银行，作为目前总资产排名巴国第一位的商业银行，作为巴国长期致力于拓展国际市场业务的商业银行，HBL具有相当的国际经验。HBL纽约分行在美国也已经营40载，对当地的监管要求理应非常了解。《和解令》中对于HBL检查结果的描述充分印证了HBL是一家具有相当经验的国际性商业银行。

发明并使用"白名单"

与当地监管部门发布的"黑名单"相对，HBL制定了"白名单"，HBL将列入"白名单"的客户定义为低风险客户，并应用于监测系统。HBL的"白名单"中有154个字段涵盖在SDN名单和禁止交易人员名单（SDN名单）中，被美国财政部明确禁止交易。由于不合理的所谓"白名单"的存在，HBL纽约分行至少2 500亿美元交易没有进行实时监控。而且，不断有客户被不恰当的列入"白名单"。

对信息进行技术处理

HBL纽约分行的工作人员不合理清除监测系统发出的报警提示，包括对交易受益人或者其他潜在信息截停的指令。该行曾取消了一个客户交易金额为11 226 796巴基斯坦卢比（约合107 000美元）的SWIFT付款指令，目的是隐去被制裁当事人的名字后重新发送付款指令，因为该笔付款的收款人是美国财政部禁止交易的个人。

总金额超过27 000美元的多笔付款被发送给HBL总部的一个被FBI认定为非法的账户。账户持有人于2012年被列入FBI'S CYBER CRIMES MOST WANTED LIST（FBI网络犯罪红通名单），然而，这些汇款均于2014年10月6日至11月28日期间通过纽约分行予以清算，完全不考虑广为人知的账户持有人的负面新闻。而且，该可疑账户持有人在2012年被列入FBI红通名单后仍开立了五个账户中的四个账户，包括2014年4月的美元清算账户。银行没有按照"了解你的客户"流程对客户进行尽职调查。结果，当这些交易的金额超过美元监控门槛引发实时监控系统报警时，HBL纽约分行不合理地清除了报警，貌似该交易没有显示可疑。在HBL总行也发生了对于账户持有人同样的报警，原因是账户持有人因FBI'S CYBER CRIMES MOST WANTED LIST而被列入反洗钱黑名单。然而，这份黑名单没有被HBL纽约分行实时监测系统使用。而且，抛开公共信息，一位HBL总行的分析师不合理的将与此网络犯罪相关的交易警报列为"假性相关（报错）"并予以删除。

HBL被罚的经验和教训

抛开种种扑朔迷离的猜想，HBL被罚事件还是有值得商业银行借鉴和参考之处的。

首先，作为商业银行，应根据反洗钱法律法规的规定，制定详细的政策和流程，确保有效进行黑名单筛查和交易实施监控。

在2017年《和解令》中，DFS首先详细陈述了HBL纽约分行极其薄弱的合规功能，称：2006年以来，HBL就发现的存在涉及OFAC经济制裁法律问题，并且自身BSA/AML项目方面严重不足。在2015年进行的检查中，DFS发现哈比银行的合规功能进一步恶化，确认HBL纽约分行在风险管理能力方面的重大缺陷。HBL纽约分行提供的几个金融产品缺乏制裁筛查证据，新的案例与内部审计项目的分类方法论薄弱有关。HBL和其纽约分行没能维护有效合规的反洗钱项目和OFAC合规项目，违反了NYCRR116.2第3款。

其次，银行高层管理人员要强调反洗钱合规的重要性，并保持对其运作的监督和控制。DFS在2016年的检查确认了纽约分行在风险管理能力方面的重大缺陷，提到尽管已对纽约分行的风险管理表现进行了不断批评，但HBL管理层仍然没有进行有效的改进和管理BSA/AML和OFAC风险。导致一系列合规方面的严重缺失。

附录:

《和解令》英文原文

NEW YORK STATE DEPARTMENT OF FINANCIAL SERVICES

In the Matter of:

HABIB BANK LIMITED and

HABIB BANK LIMITED, NEW YORK BRANCH

CONSENT ORDER UNDER
NEW YORK BANKING LAW 39,44 and 60S

The New York State Department of Financial Services (the "Department"). Habib Bank Limited, and the New York Branch of Habib Bank Limited (the "New York Branch") (together, "Habib Bank" or "the Bank") arc willing to resolve the matters described herein without further proceedings.

WHEREAS, Habib Bank is an international banking institution with assets totaling approximately S24 billion and Is licensed by the Department to operate a foreign branch In New York State;

The Department findsas follows:

Introduction

This Consent Order addresses the circumstance where a banking institution, Habib Bank and its New York Branch, has failed to comply with New York laws and regulations designed to combat money laundering, terrorist financing, and other illicit financial transactions. Due to serious failures in the bank's anti-money laundering compliance function and its processes to screen out prohibited transactions, Habib Bank, through its New York Branch, has facilitated transact ions that pose a grave threat to the people of this State and the financial system as a whole. Among other things, Habib Bank, through its New Yak Branch:

- facilitated billions of dollars in transactions with a Saudi private bank, the Al Rajhi Bank, with reported links to al Qaeda, without adequate anti-monoy laundering and counter-terrorist financing controls;

- failed to adequately identify customers of the Al Rajhi Bank that might be using the Al Rajhi account at Habib Bank to transfer funds through New York, thus permitting unsafe "nested activity";

- more generally, allowed for at least 13,000 transactions to flow through the New York Branch that potentially omitted information adequate to properly screen for prohibited transactions or transactions with sanctioned countries;

- improperly used a "good guy" list - a list of customers who supposedly presented a low risk of illicit transactions - to permit transactions by an identified terrorist, an international arms dealer, an Iranian oil tanker, and other potentially sanctioned porsons and entities; and

• granted the request of a customer to cancel an instruction to send funds through the New York Branch to a person who was blocked from using the U.S. financial system, so that the instruction could be resent by intentionally omitting the prohibited party's name.

As detailed more folly below, the Department has determined that the Bank's compliance function is dangerously weak. Head Office screening, which the Branch has repeatedly relied on to augment its anti-money laundering safeguards, appears to be as weak as that of the Branch itself -- if not even more Inadequate. For these reasons, the Department's most recent compliance examination determined that the Branch should receive the lowest possible rating, a score of "5." This tyjx of conduct by on Institution licensed by the Depertment cannot and will not be allowed to persist.

The above conclusions arise from an investigation that the Department has been conducting concerning serious deficiencies identified in the New York Branch's program devoted to complying with New York and Federal laws and regulations concerning anti-money laundering ("AML") compliance, including the Bank Secrecy Act ("BSA"). This investigation lias been undertaken pursuant to the December 15, 2015 Consent Older among the Department, the Bank and the Branch (the "2015 Consent Order"), which had identified previous significant deficiencies in the Bank's BSA/AML. compliance. Additionally, the Department conducted an examination of the New York Branch of Habib Bank for the period closing March 3, 2016.

Although the Bank has been given more than sufficient opportunity to rectify its deficiencies, it has failed to do so. As set forth below, the Bank has committed violations of New York laws attd regulations; has conducted its business in an unauthorized or unsafe manner; and has operated in an unsound or unsafe condition to transact its business. This Consent Order ensures that his misconduct will now cease.

The Department's. Findings After Examination amd Additionl Investigation

The Bank

1. Habib Bank is a Pakistani Bank headquartered in Karachi. With $1 billion in total revenues in 2016, and $24 billion in total assets, Habib Bank is Pakistan's largest bank. Habib Bank was majority owned by the government of Pakistan until 2004. Presently, the government has no ownership interest m the Bank, and its shares are publicly traded on the Pakistan Stock Exchange.

2. The New York Branch has been licensed by the Department since 1978. Habib Bank established the Branch primarily to offer U.S. dollar clearing services, including hinds transfer, check clearing, and collection, trade finance, overnight sweeps, and corporate term and employee loans. For the year ending December 31, 2015, the Branch processed correspondent banking transactions for a total of approximately $287 billion. It is the Bank's only US. branch, and it has served as an important correspondent for the Bank for a substantial period of time.

The New York Branch's Extremelv Poor Complicnce Function

3. **The 2006 Written Agreement.** In December 2006, Hablb Bonk and the New York Branch entered into a Written Agreement with the Department and the Federal Reserve Board of Governors (the "Board") arising out of significant deficiencies identified within the Bank's programs intended to maintain compliance with the economic sanctions laws overseen by the U.S. Office of Foreign Assets Control ("OFAC") and with its BSA/AML compliance (the "2006 Written Agreement") (attached hereto as Exhibit A).

4. Since 2006. the New York Branch has struggled to comply with the 2006 Written

Agreement and the requirements of New York Banking laws and regulations. Repeated breakdowns in the Bank's BSA/AML and OF AC compliance programs have plagued the Bank. Violations of the 2006 Written Agreement and or New York Banking law have occurred almost every year since 2006.

5. **The 2015 Consent Older:** Another examination conducted in 2015 by the Department and Board demonstrated that Habib Bank's compliance function had deteriorated even further. As a consequence, in December 2015, Habib Bank and the New* York Branch entered into the 2015 Consent Order with the Department (attached as Exhibit B), along with a parallel Consent Cease and Desist Order with the Board. The 2015 Consent Order required the Branch to undertake extensive remedial actions to comply with New York and federal law.

6. The 2015 Consent Order also required the Bank to engage an independent consultant to conduct a review of the New York Branch's U.S. dollar clearing transaction activity from October 1. 2014 through March 31. 2015, to determine whether transactions inconsistent with or in violation of OF AC regulations, or suspicious activity involving high risk customers or transactions, facilitated through the New York Branch were properly identified and reported in accordance with OFAC Regulations and suspicious activity reporting regulations (the "Lookback").

7. Further, Paragraph 7(b) of the 2015 Consent Order provided that the Superintendent, based on the Department's evaluation of the Lookback results, could (in her sole discretion) expand the scope of the Lookback to additional time periods.

8. **The 2016 Examination,** The Department and the Board Jointly conducted another examination in 2016, reviewing information and financial data as of March 31,2016 (the "2016 Exam"). The Department determined that the New York Branch continued to suffer from severe weaknesses in its risk management and compliance with BSA/AML and OF AC laws. The 2016 Exam noted tltat Habib Bank had been under either joint or separate enforcement actions by the Department and Board for 10 consecutive examination cycles.

9. The 2016 Exam identified significant weaknesses in the Branch's risk management capabilities. It also found that, despite the Department's repeated criticism of the Branch's performance, management had yet to implement effective controls to mitigate and manage BSA/AML and OFAC risks at the Branch. Overall, serious deficiencies identified by the Department in the 2016 Exam include (without limitation):

- insufficient BSA/AML compliance;
- Insufficient training;
- Insufficient customer risk ratings, including insufficient risk-based foreign correspondent due diligence;
- Insufficient documentation for enhanced due diligence customers;
- Insufficient senior management and head office governance, oversight, and documentation;
- Lack of evidence for adequate OFAC and sanctions screening;
- Weaknesses in BSA/AML independent testing and the Branch's audit program, including weaknesses in the internal audit program's rating methodology; and
- Weaknesses in data mapping and integrity.

10. The 2016 Exam further discovered 855 "batch-waived" transaction alerts that were

cleared by Branch staff without review or rationale for the failure to review the alerts. "Batch waiver" results when a group of alerts arc disposed of summarily, purportedly for a uniform reason. When questioned by the Department's examiners, the Bank's management was unable to provide written approval of the batch waive process by Head Office or local management.

11. The 2016 Exam also identified new issues with the OFAC compliance program that relate to the Branch's compliance with provisions within the 2015 Consent Order, including a lack of evidence of sanctions screening for several financial products offered at the Branch, and new weaknesses related to the internal audit program's rating methodology.

The Rkltv Al Ritllil Bunk Relationship

12. The Branch's deficiencies arc all the more concerning given that one of hs largest U.S. dollar clearing accounts has been Al Rajhi Bank ("Al Rajhi"). Al Rajhi is the largest private bank in Saudi Arabia.

13. Previously, Al Rajhi has been linked through negative media to Al Qaeda and terrorism financing. Por example, a report released on July 17, 2012 by the U.S. Senate Permanent Subcommittee on Investigations, of tlic Committee on Homeland Security and Governmental Affairs (the "Senate Report"),[1] stated that,

> After the 9/11 terrorist attack…evidence began to emerge that Al Rajhi
> Bank and some of its owners had links to organizations associated with
> financing terrorism, including that one of the bank's founders was an
> early financial benefactor ofal Qaeda.

(Senate Report at 189.) The Senate Report goes on to provide significant detail of, among other things, "lajllcgcd Al Rajhi links to Terrorism." (Id. at 194-203.) '

14. As such, this Al Rajhi correspondent account presented Habib Bank with a significant risk of being used for terrorist financing and money laundering. Since approximately 2014, AI Rajhi transactions represent approximately 24 percent of the total number of transactions conducted through the New York Branch.

15. The 2016 Exam identified a range of control deficiencies in the documentation and administration of the Bank's customer due diligence program as a whole and, In particular, for existing foreign correspondent customers, including Al Rajhi. The customer due diligence file did not include sufficient information about Al Rajhi's own customers, or a thorough review of Al Rajhi's expected versus actual transactional activity. The Department's examination concluded that Al Rajhi was engaging in downstream correspondent clearing activities for several of Al Rajhi's own affiliates, particularly the Al Rajhi branches in Malaysia and Jordan.

16. This type of "nesting" activity was unknown to management at the New York Branch, as it was not captured in the customer file, in any correspondence with the customer, nor was the activity triggered by the Branch's transaction monitoring systems.

17. Furthermore, the 2016 Exam determined that bi-weekly calls administered between Branch and Compliance senior management and Al Rajhi senior management for purposes of maintaining compliance were not meaningful. Examiners' review of the minutes and agenda for these calls indicate that they are primarily administrative and do not address current BSA/AML,

---

[1] See https://Avww.hsga.sena!e.gov/downloadfrcport-us-vulncrabililies-to-money-drugs-and-terrorist-financlng-bsbc case-history.

related risks or issues posed by the customer relationship.

18. The 2016 Exam concluded that, overall, Habib Bank and the Branch's management failed to establish an appropriate BSA/AML control environment to manage the Brandi's high- risk client base, and that the Branch management's risk appetite substantially exceeds the control measures in place at the Branch.

19. On or about July 10, 2017, the New York Branch terminated its correspondent banking relationship with Al Rajhi - but only after the Department requested that Habib Bank do so.

Additional Findings of the Department's Investigation

20. The Department's investigation has identified significant additional concerns relating to lapses in the Bank's BSA/AML and OFAC compliance. For example (and without limitation), the investigation has uncovered:

- More than 13,000 transactions with SWIFT payment messages that omitted essential information, such as the identities of the ultimate originator and beneficiary of each transaction; and
- Multiple instances where multiple SWIFT payment messages were improperly aggregated into a single message for processing through the Branch, thereby preventing the Branch from effectively screening these messages for suspicious or prohibited activity.

21. The Department's investigation also revealed that Head Office completely excluded screening of more than 4,000 transactions, apparently because the partios involved were listed on what is known as a so-called "good guy" list - a list of customers who purportedly have been screened and identified as very low risk. The Department's investigation determined that a substantial number of parties were improperly included on the Habib Dank "good-guy" list, or that the transactions had other indicia that should have required them to be screened by the Bank.

22. The Department's investigation determined that transactions went un-reviewed because of inclusion of transacting parties on the good-guy list, but where:

- 154 terms included in Habib Bank's "good guy" list corresponded to identical entries that were included on the Specially Designated Nationals and Blocked Persons List (the "SDN List"), which is a list of panics prohibited from transactions by the U.S. Treasury Department; and
- terms on the "good-guy" list include prohibited persons and entities identified on the SDN List corresponding to:
- a transaction that involved the leader of a Pakistani terrorist group;
- a transaction that involved a known international arms dealer; an individual on the Specially Designated Global Terrorist list;
- the former Deputy Prime Minister of Iraq under Saddam Hussein; and
- an Iranian oil tanker involved in a transaction.

23. To date, the Department's investigation has determined that at least $250 million in transactions havo flowed through the Now York Branch without any screening due to the apparent improper inclusion on the so-called "good guy" list.

24. The Department's investigation has also identified breakdowns in the Branch's transaction monitoring processes, including instances where the Branch's screening terms are wholly

insufficient to identify all of the activity the term is intended to Identify. One example of this deficiency is the keyword "Embassy of Pakistan," which failed to Identify the payment messages containing the phrase "Pakistan Embassy."

25. Additionally, the Department's investigation has uncovered instances where alerts generated by the Branch's transaction monitoring system were improperly cleared because, while certain factors suggested they might be false positives, other suspicious characteristics warranted escalation for further review by compliance staff, including instructions to withhold the name of a transaction's beneficiary or other pertinent information.

26. One such instance involved a payment to a Chinese weapons manufacturer that was subject to U.S. non-proliferation sanctions. The Department's Investigation determined that the originals of certain trade finance documents had been altered to conceal that the goods shipped were explosives.

27. Another instance concerned an instruction from a customer of the Bank to cancel a SWIFT payment message to an individual included on the U.S. Treasury Department's list of blocked persons and entities, in the amount of 11,226,796 Pakistani rupees (approximately $107,000), so that the message could be recent by intentionally omitting the prohibited party's name.

28. The Department's investigation further uncovered several payments totaling more than $27,000 that were sent to an account at the Bank's Head Office associated with an alleged cybercriminal wanted by the Federal Bureau of Investigations ("FBI"). The account holder was charged with wire fraud, identity theft and theft of $50 million on June 29,2012 in a warrant issued by the U.S. District Court for the District of New Jersey. The account holder was added to the FBI's Cyber Crimes Most Wonted List in 2012, and was arrested in Pakistan in February 2015. Nevertheless, these payments to the alleged cybercriminal were all cleared through the New York Branch between October 6 and November 28, 2014, despite tho widespread availability of this negative information on the account holder.

29. Moreover, this same suspicious account holder opened four of his five accounts after being added to the FBI most wanted list in 2012, Including a U.S. dollar account which was opened in April, 2014. The Bank failed to conduct sufficient due diligence in its Know Your Customer ("KYC") file. Subsequently, when a transaction monitoring alert was generated when one these transactions amounts exceeded a dollar threshold applied to the account, the New York Branch improperly cleared the alert, finding that the activity did not appear suspicious.

30. Further more, a review of Head Office data from Habib Bank found that the same activity involving the account holder was alerted at Head Office specifically because the account holder was on an AML blacklist, resulting from his placement on the FBI Cyber Crimes Most Wanted List in 2012. Nonetheless, this blacklist entry was not used in the course of the New York Branch's screening process. Moreover, despite tltc publicly-available nature of the information, a Head Office analyst improperly ruled the suspicious alcrt concerning this cybercriminal's transactions as a "false positive" and cleared the alert.

31. Moreover, five Deportment's investigation has identified nearly 200 additional instances of suspicious activity that were never identified or reported by the Branch. These transactions include a variety of suspicious characteristics, such as (i) payments lacking economic purpose (e.g.. a payment to a technology company for leather goods); (ii) instances of structuring; (iii) shell company activity; and (iv) politically exposed person activity. These additional cases sometimes

revealed negative media associated with the parties and/or their beneficial owners, including allegations of terrorist financing, black market trading, drug trafficking, smuggling and fraud.

The Notice of Hearing, Expanded Lookback Order and ,Surrender Order

32. In connection with • the Department's Investigation in this matter, the Superintendent issued two orders pertaining to Habib Bank and the New York Branch.

33. **The Exnnnded Lookback Order.** First, in light of the troubling information developed by the Independent consultant during the existing Lookback, the Superintendent exercised her authority on August 24, 2017 to expand the scope of the Lookback as provided for in Paragraph 7(b) of the 2015 Consent Order (the "Expanded Lookback Order") (attached as Exhibit C). The Expanded Lookback Order requires Habib Bank to expand the scope of the Lookback to cover the additional periods of October I, 2013 through September 30, 2014; and April 1,2015 through July 31,2017. The Expanded Lookback Order further requires Habib Bank to continue to engage the independent consultant, previously approved by the Department, to conduct this expanded review.

34. **The Surrender Order:** Also in connection with the Department's investigation. Habib Bank expressed an interest in surrendering its license to operate the New York Branch. Accordingly, the Deportment issued a second Order, also on August 24, 2017, that provides for Habib Bank to notify the Department within 30 days of whether it would surrender its license (the "Surrender Order") (attached as Exhibit D). Tire Surrender Order imposes a scries of conditions upon Habib Bank and the New York Branch pursuant to Banking Law § 605 in connection with the orderly wind down of the affairs of the New York Branch. Among those conditions are the requirement that the Bank engage and pay for an independent consultant of the Department's selection (in its sole discretion) to assist the Bank in the safe, sound and lawful wind down of the affairs of the New York Branch.

35. The Surrender Order also provides that, should Habib decline to inform the Department that it was voluntarily surrendering its license (as it had expressed it would do), then the Department could seek revocation of that liccnso in a hearing.

36. **The Notlee of Hearing:** Simultaneously with issuance of the Expanded Lookback and Surrender Orders, the Department issued a Notice of Hearing and Statement of Charges against Habib Bank and the New York Branch (the "Notice of Charges"). The Notice of Charges set forth more than 53 separate violations of New York laws and regulations committed by Habib Bank and/or the New York Branch, for the period January l, 2007 to the present. The offenses included violations ofNew York Banking Law, the 2006 Written Agreement, and the 2015 Consent Order. The hearing was scheduled for September 27,2017.[1]2

NOW THEREFORE, to resolve this matter without further proceedings pursuant to the Superintendent's authority under Sections 39, 44 and 605 of the New York Banking Law, the Department, Habib Bank and the New York Brandi hereby stipulate and agree to the following terms and conditions:

Violations ofl.-am mul Kcmilntlojw

37. Hubib Bank and the New York Branch failed to maintain an effective and compliant anti-money laundering program and OFAC compliance program, in violation of 3 NYCRR § 116.2.

---

① The Notice of Charges may be found at http://www.<lfi.nv.cov/aboni/c»^en 17082du.ndf. They are being dismissed as pail of this resolution of the enforcement action on consent.

38. I labib Bank and the New York Branch failed to maintain tme and accurate books, accounts, and records reflecting all transactions and actions, in violation of New York Banking Law § 200-c.

39. Habib Bank and tire New York Branch conducted their bonking business in an unsafe and unsound manner, in violation of New York Banking Law §§ 44, 44-a.

40. Habib Bank and lire New York Branch violated multiple provisions of the 2006 Written Agreement, which required the Bank, inter alia, to implement and maintain an effective BSA/AML compliance program and transaction monitoring system.

41. Habib Bank and the New York Branch violated multiple provisions of the 2015 Consent Order, which required the Bank, inter alia, to implement and maintain an effective BSA/AML compliance program and transaction monitoring system.

Settlement Provisions

Monetary Payment

42. Habib Bank shall pay a civil monetary penalty pursuant to Banking Law § 44 to the Department in the amount of $225,000,000. Habib Bank shall pay the entire amount within fourteen (14) days of executing this Consent Order.

43. Habib Bank agrees that it will not claim, assert, or apply for n tax deduction or tax credit with regard to any U.S. federal, state, or local tax, directly or indirectly, for any portion of the civil monetary penalty paid pursuant to this Consent Order.

Expansion of the LooltbncU Pursuant to the 2015 Consent Order

44. Habib Bank and the New York Branch hereby affirm, acknowledge and agree that (a) they shall ftilly comply with the Expanded Lookback Older, (b) that Paragraph 7(b) of the 2015 Consent Order shall remain in full force and effect, and that (c) as a result, under the Transaction and OF AC Sanctions Review conducted pursuant to Paragraph 7(b) of the 2015 Consent Order, Habib Bonk and the New York Branch shall (i) expand the Transaction and OFAC Review to cover the additional time periods of (A) October 1,2013 to September 30,2014; and (B) April 1, 2015 to July 31,2017; and (ii) continue to engage the Independent third party, previously approved by the Department, to conduct this expanded review until the expanded Transaction and OFAC Review is completed to the satisfaction of the Superintendent.

Surrender of License and Orderly Wind Down of Affairs of the New York Branch

45. On August 31, 2017, pursuant to the Surrender Order, Habib Bank and the New York Branch offered, in writing, to surrender to the Department the license to operate the New York Branch. Habib Bonk and the New York Branch hereby affirm and acknowledge that they will fully comply with the Surrender Order.

46. The Department will accept the surrender of the license to operate the New York Branch upon fulfillment of the conditions set forth in the Surrender Order and completion, to the satisfaction of the Superintendent, of the orderly wind down of the affairs of the New York Branch pursuant to the requirements of the New York Banking Law.

47. Habib Bank and the New York Branch shall promptly commence the safe, sound and orderly wind down of the affairs of the New York Branch pursuant to New York Bonking Law.

48. Habib Bank and the New York Brand) shall immediately engage and pay for an independent consultant of the Department's selection (in its sole discretion) to assist the Bank in the

safe, sound and lawful wind down of the affairs of the New York Branch.

49. Habib Bank and the New York Branch shall preserve all documents and information in their possession, custody or control that relates, directly or indirectly, to the affairs, operations or business of the New York Branch until further Order of the Superintendent, inter alia, to facilitate full and complete compliance with the 2015 Consent Order, including, but not limited to, the Transaction and OFAC Sanctions Review conducted pursuant to Paragraph 7(b) of the Consent Order, as well as the terms and conditions of this Consent Order. This paragraph is not intended to modify or alter any other obligation Habib Bonk or the New York Branch may have to preserve documents and information pursuant to applicable law.

50. Habib Bank and the New York Branch shall maintain the level of the asset maintenance and asset pledge requirements of thc Department currently imposed on the New York Branch. Such asset maintenance and asset pledge requirements shall continue in full force and effect until completion of the orderly wind down of the affairs of the New York Branch to the Department's satisfaction. Furthermore, no assets or properties, whether real, personal or mixed, and whether tangible or intangible, situated In New York, or wherever situated if constituting part of the business of the New York Branch, stall be transferred or moved out of any such location without the prior written approval of the Department.

Survival of the 2006 Written Agreement

51. Upon completion of the orderly wind down of the affairs of the New York Branch to the satisfaction of the Superintendent, the 2006 Written Agreement shall remain in full force ar.d effect, but with its terms suspended unless and until Habib Bank re-establishes a branch, agency, representative office, or a banking subsidiary within the State of New York.

52. In the event that Habib Bank re-establishes a branch, agency, representative office, or a banking subsidiary within the State of New York, Habib Bank, the New York Branch, and any such branch, agency, representative office, or banking subsidiary shall fully comply with ail terms and conditions of the 2006 Written Agreement, which terms and conditions shall remain effective and enforceable until stayed, modified, terminated or suspended in writing by the Department.

Survival of the 2015 Consent Order:

53. Upon completion of the orderly wind down of the affairs of the New York Branch to the satisfaction of the Superintendent, and with the exception of Paragraph 7(b) of the 2015 Consent Order, os provided in Paragraph 44 above of this Consent Order, the 2015 Consent Order shall remain in full force and effect, but with its terms suspended unless and until Habib Bank reestablishes a branch, agency, representative office, or a banking subsidiary within the Stale of New York.

54. In the event that Habib Bank re-establishes a branch, agency, representative office, or a banking subsidiary within the State of New York, Habib Bank, the New York Branch, and any such branch, agency, representative office, or banking subsidiary, shall fully comply with all terms and conditions of the 2015 Consent Order, which terms and conditions shall remain effective and enforceable until stayed, modified, terminated or suspended in writing by the Department.

Waiver of Rights

55. 'The parties understand and agree that no provision of this Consent Order is subject to review in any court or tribunal outside the Department.

Parties Bound by the Consent Order

56. This Consent Order is binding on the Department, Habib Bank and the New York Branch, as well as any successors and assigns. This Consent Order docs not bind any federal or other state agency or any law enforcement authority.

57. No further action will be taken by the Department against Hubib Bank or the New York Branch for the conduct set forth in this Consent Order, provided that the Bank complies with the terms of this Consent Order.

Breach of Consent Order

58. In the event that the Department believes Habib Bank or the New York Branch to be in breach of this Consent Order, the Department will provide written notice to Habib Bank, and the Bank must, within three (3) business days of receiving such notice, or on a later date if so determined in the Department's sole discretion, appear before the Department to demonstrate that no breach has occurred or, to the extent pertinent, that the breach has been cured.

59. The parties understand and agree that Habib Bank's failure to make the required showing within the designated time period shall be presumptive evidence of the Bank's breach. Upon a finding that Habib Bank has breached this Consent Order, the Department has all the remedies available to it under New York Banking and Financial Services Laws, as well as any other state or federal luw, and may use any evidence available to the Department in any ensuing hearings, notices, or orders. Habib Bank and the New York Brandi agree to the binding authority of this Consent Order and every provision hereof.

60. Habib Bonk and the New York Branch waive any challenge to jurisdiction or venue in any action or proceeding brought by the Department before any agency, tribunal or court, whether federal or state, to enforce (a) this Order, (b) tire 2015 Consent Order, or (c) the 2006 Written Agreement.

Notices

61. All notices or communications regarding this Consent Order shall be sent to:

For the Department:

> Elizabeth Nochlin, Esq.
> New York State Department of Financial Services
> One State Street
> Now York, NY 10004

> Hadas Jacobi, Esq.
> Now Yoik State Department of Financial Services
> One Stato Street
> New York, NY 10004

> Jeremy Schildcrout, Esq.
> New York Slate Department of Financial Services
> One State Street
> New York, NY 10004

For Habib Bank:

> Nausheen Ahmad

Company Secretary and Head of Legal
Habib Bank Limited
HBL Plaza
1.1 Chundrigar Road
Karachi, Pakistan

Manochere Alamglr
Country Manager
Habib Bank Limited New York Branch
60 B. 42nd Street, No. 535
New York, NY 10165

Miscellaneous

62. c Each provision of this Consent Order shall remain effective and enforceable untile stayed, modified, suspended, or terminated by the Department.

63. e No promise, assurance, representation, or understanding other than those containede in this Consent Order has been made to induce any party to agree to the provisions of the Cbnscnt Order.

EXHIBIT A

UNITED STATES OF AMERICA
BEFORE THE
BOARD OF GOVERNORS OF THE FEDERAL RESERVE SYSTEM
WASHINGTON, D.C.

NEW YORK STATE BANKING DEPARTMENT
NEW YORK, NEW YORK

Written Agreement by and among:

HABIB BANK LIMITED
Karachi, Pakistan

HABIB BANK LIMITED
NEW YORK BRANCH
New York, New York

FEDERAL RESERVE BANK OF NEW YORK
New York, New York

and

NBW YORK STATE BANKING DEPARTMENT
New York, New York

Docket Nos. 06-027-WA/RB-FU
06027-WA/RB-FBR

WHEREAS, Habib Bank Limited, Karachi, Pakistan (the "Bank"), a foreign bank as defined in section I (b)(7) of (be International Banking Act (12 U.S.C. $ 3101(7)), and the New York, New York branch of the Bank (the "New York Branch") are taking steps to address deficiencies relating to the New York Branch's compliance with applicable federal and state laws, rules, and regulations relating to aoti-money laundering ("AML") policies and procedures, including tbe Bank Secrecy Act (the "BSA") (31 U.S.C. § 5311 g scq.L the rules and regulations issued thereunder by the U.S. Department of the Treasury (31 C.P.R. Part 103); the AML requirements of Regulation K of the Board of Governors of the Federal Reserve System (the "Board of Governors") (12 C.F.R. §§ 211.24 (0 and 21 i.24) j»; and those of the New York State Banking Department (the "Department") (3 N.Y.C.R.R. Port 300);

WHBREAS, the New York Branch provides correspondent banking services to its respondent banks, including non-U.S. banks and the Bank's non-U.S. branches and affiliates, and also conducts U.S. dollar funds transfer clearing, and examiners have identified compliance and risk management deficiencies at the New York Branch in these operational areas;

WHEREAS, it is the common goal of the Board of Oovemors, the Federal Reserve Bank of New York, the Department, the Bank, and the New York Branch to ensure that the Bank and the New York Branch fully address all deficiencies in the New York Branch's AML policies and procedures, customer due diligence practices, risk management processes, and internal control environment; and

WHEREAS, on December 7,2006, the board of directors of the Bank, at a duly constituted meeting, adopted a resolution authorizing and directing Nauman K. Dar and Faiq Sadiq, respectively, to enter into this Written Agreement (the "Agreement") on behalf of the Bank and the New York Branch, and consenting to compliance by the Bank, the New York Branch, and their institution-affiliated parties, as defined in sections 3(u) and 8(b)(4) of the Federal Deposit Insurance Act. os amended (12 U.S.C. §§ 1813(u) and 18180(b)(4)). with each and every provision of this Agreement.

NOW, THEREFORE, the Reserve Bank, the Department (collectively, the "Supervisors"), the Bank, and the New York Branch hereby agree os follows:

Primary Contact

1. Within 10 days of this Agreement, the Bank and the New York Branch shall designate an officer to be responsible for coordinating and submitting to the Supervisors the written programs, plans, procedures, and engagement letter required under the terms and conditions of this Agreement.

Anti-Money Laundering Compliance

2. Within 60 days of this Agreement, the Bank and the New York Branch shall jointly submit to the Supervisors an acceptable written BSA/AML compliance program for the New York Branch that is designed to improve the New York Branch's internal controls to ensure compliance with ail applicable provisions of the BSA and the rules and regulations issued thereunder, including the requirements of Regulation K of the Board of Governors (12 C.F.K. § 211.24(j)). The program shall include provisions for updates on an ongoing basis os necessary to incorporate amendments to the BSA and the rules and regulations issued thereunder. At a minimum, the program shall include:

> (a) Improvements to the New York Branch's system of internal controls for correspondent banking and funds transfer clearing activities, including controls to ensure compliance with all recordkeeping and reporting requirements;

> (b) policies and procedures designed to ensure identification and verification of (be identity of account holders and transactors in accordance with applicable regulations;

> (c) controls designed to ensure compliance with all requirements relating to correspondent accounts for non-U.S. persons, including but not limited to, the prohibition on correspondent uccounts for foreign shell banks (31 C.F.R. § 103.177) and special due diligence requirements for certain correspondent accounts (31 C.F.R. § 103.176);

> (d) an assessment of legal and reputational risks associated with the New York Branch's correspondent banking and funds transfer clearing activities; and

> (e) adequate resources for the BSA compliance officer, including sufficient staff levels, to implement and maintain an effective program for compliance with all applicable BSA/ AML requirements and the institution's internal policies and procedures.

Suspicious Activity Reporting and Customer Due Dillgence

3. Within 60 days of this Agreement, the Bank and the Now York Branch shall jointly submit to the Supervisors an acceptable written customer due diligence program designed to reasonably ensure the identification and timely, accurate, and complete reporting of all known or suspected violations of law against or involving the New York Branch and suspicious transactions at the New York Branch to law enforcement and supervisory authorities as required by applicable suspicious activity reporting laws and regulations. At a minimum, the program shall include:

> (a) A methodology for assigning risk levels to the New York Branch's customer base,

including correspondent account holders, that considers factors such as type of customer, type of product or service, and geographic location;

(b) a risk-focused assessment of the New York Branch's customer base that:

(i) identifies the categories of customers, transactions, and banking activities that arc routine and usual; and

(ii) determines the appropriate level of enhanced due diligence necessary for those categories of customers that pose a heightened risk of conducting potentially illicit activities at or through the New York Branch.

(c) for each customer whose transactions require enhanced due diligence, procedures to:

(i) determine the appropriate documentation necessary to verity the identity and business activities of the customer; and

(ii) understand the normal and expected transactions of the customer;

(d) enhancements to the customer identification program to ensure compliance with the requirements of 31 C.F.R. § 103.121 and 12 C.F.R. § 211.24(jX2);

(e) for correspondent accounts established, maintained, administered, or managed in the United States for a non-U.S. financial institution (including any non-US. branch or affiliate of the Bank), procedures that arc designed to ensure compliance with applicable due diligence and other requirements (including the provisions of 31 C.F.R. §§ 103.176 and 103.177), and that, at minimum, provide for:

(i) obtaining and maintaining appropriate information about the respondent, its business operations, markets served, customer base, and its AML procedures, particularly with regard to its customer relationships that may present a heightened risk of money laundering or other concerns; and

(ii) ensuring that correspondent banking services provided by the Now York Branch arc reviewed and approved by appropriate levels of management, and are subject to appropriate ongoing review; and

(f) establishment of procedures and appropriate monitoring criteria to ensure proper detection and reporting of all known or suspected violations of law and suspicious or unusual transactions, including, but not limited to:

(i) effective monitorin g of customer accounts and transactions, including transactions conducted through correspondent accounts;

(ii) appropriate participation by New York Branch senior management in the process of identifying, reviewing, and reporting potentially suspicious activity;

(iii) adequate referral of information about potentially suspicious activity through appropriate levels of management, including a policy for determining action to be taken in the event of multiple filings of Suspicious Activity Reports ("SARs") on the same customer or where a customer fails to provide due diligence information;

(iv) adequate procedures to ensure the timely and complete preparation and filing of SARs and Currency Transaction Reports; and

(v) maintenance of sufficient documentation with respect to the investigation and analysis of suspicious activity, including the resolution and escalation of concerns.

Independent Testing

4. Within 60 days of this Agreement, the Bank and the New York Branch shall jointly submit to the Supervisors an acceptable written plan for independent testing of the New York Branch's compliance with all applicable BSA/AML requirements. At a minimum, the pliui shall include:

(a) Procedures to evaluate the adequacy and effectiveness of the New York Branch's compliance with the BSA, the rules and regulations issued thereunder, and all other applicable AML requirements, including monitoring of customer activity to ensure reporting of suspicious activity;

(b) provisions for independent testing to be perfoimed on a regular basis by qualified parties (which may include internal audit) who are independent of the Bank's and the New Yotk Branch's business lines and compliance function, provided, however, that the first independent test of the New York Branch's BSA/AML compliance shall be conducted by a qualified independent firm acceptable to the Supervisors;

(c) procedures for the review of independent testing results by senior Bank and New York Branch management and escalation to the board of directors of the Bank in appropriate circumstances;

(d) procedures to ensure that senior Bank and New York Branch management institute and complete oppropriatc actions in response to the independent testing results; and

(e) procedures to ensure that independent testing results are communicated to the Supervisors on a regular basis and retained for subsequent supervisory review.

Training

5. Within 60 days of this Agreement, the Dank and the New York Branch shall jointly submit to the Supervisors an acceptable written plan to improve the training of all appropriate personnel at tbe Now York Branch including, but not limited to, correspondent account relationship personnel, employees involved in (he funds transfer clearing operations, and customer contact personnel. Tbe training should extend to all aspects of regulatory and internal policies and procedures related to the BSA and the identification and reporting of suspicious transactions and be updated on a regular basis to reasonably ensure that all personnel arc trained in the most current legal requirements and the New York Branch's risk management processes.

Transaction Monitoring System

6. (a) Within 45 days of this Agreement, the Bank and the New York Branch shall jointly submit to the Supervisors an acceptable written plan, including a timetable, for the full testing and activation of the New York Branch's proposed new transaction monitoring system. The plan shall also include a methodology and target date for determining that the transaction monitoring system is effective.

(b) Within 60 days of this Agreement, the Bank and the New York Branch shall jointly submit to the Supervisors acceptable written policies and procedures for the monitoring of customer accounts and transactions that are designed to effectively manage Iegal and reputational risks and ensure compliance with regulatory requirements. Tire acceptable policies and procedures shall take effect upon the determination by a competent independent outside consultant acceptable to the Supervisors that the new transaction monitoring system is fully effective. Documentation to support (he determination that the new transaction monitoring system is fully effective shall be retained for subsequent supervisory review.

Transaction Review

7. (a) Within 30 days of this Agreement, the Bank and the New York Branch shall jointly engage a qualified independent firm (the "Independent Pirm") acceptable to the Supervisors to conduct a review of account and transaction activity for the time period from January 1,2005 to December 31,2005 to determine whether suspicious activity involving accounts or transactions at, by, or through the New York Branch was properly identified and reported in accordance with applicable suspicious activity reporting regulations (the "Transaction Review"). The Transaction Review shall encompass all transaction activity including, but not limited to, funds transfers, cash letters, and international drafts for both customers and non- customers of the New Vork Branch.

   (b) Based on the Supervisors' evaluation of the results of the Transaction Review, the Supervisors may direct the New York Branch to engage the Independent Firm to conduct an additional review for the time period Grom January 1,2006 to the date of this Agreement, with the scope and methodology for Chat time period to be determined in the same manner as described in paragraph S.

8. Within 10 days of the engagement of the Independent Fum, but prior to the commencement of the Transaction Review, the Bank and the New York Branch shall jointly submit to the Supervisors for approval an engagement letter that sets forth:

   (a) The scope of the Transaction Review, including the types of accounts and transactions to be reviewed;

   (b) the methodology for conducting tire Transaction Review, including any sampling procedures to be followed;

   (c) the expertise and resources to be dedicated to the Transaction Review;

   (d) the anticipated date of completion of the Transaction Review; and

   (e) a commitment that any interim reports, drafts, workpapers, or other materials associated with the Transaction Review will be made available to the Supervisors upon request.

9. Upon completion of the Transaction Review, the Bank and the New York Branch shall provide to the Supervisors a copy of the Independent Firm's report detailing the findings of the Transaction Review at the same time that the report is provided to the Bank and the New York Branch.

10. Throughout the Transaction Review, the Bank and the New York Branch shall ensure that all matters or transactions required to be reported that have not previously been reported are reported in accordance with applicable rules and regulations.

Approval, Implementation, and Progress Reports

11. (a) The Bank and the New York Branch shall jointly submit written programs, plans, policies, procedures, and an engagement letter that are acceptable to the Supervisors within the applicable time periods set forth in paragraphs 2,3,4,5,6, and 8 of this Agreement. An Independent Firm acceptable to the Supervisors shall be retained by the Bank and the New York Branch within the period set forth in paragraph 7(a) of this Agreement.

(b) Within 10 days of approval by tbc Supervisors, the Bank and the New York Branch shall adopt the approved programs, plans, policies, procedures, and engagement letter. Upon adoption, the Bank and the New York Branch shall implement the approved programs, plans, policies, and procedures and thereafter fully comply with them.

(c) During tbc term of this Agreement, the approved programs, plans, procedures, and engagement letter shall not be amended or rescinded without the prior written approval of the Supervisors.

12. Within 20 days after the end of each month following tbc date of this Agreement, the Bank and the New York Branch shall jointly submit to the Supervisors written progress reports detailing the form and manner of all actions taken to secure compliance with the provisions of this Agreement and the results thereof. Management responses to any audit reports covering BSA/ AML matters prepared by internal and external auditors shall be included with the progress reports. The Supervisors may, in writing, discontinue tbc requirement for progress reports or modify the reporting schedule.

Notice

13. All communications regarding this Agreement shall be sent to:

    (a) Mr. Daniel Muccia
        Senior Vice President
        Federal Reserve Bank of New York
        33 Liberty Street
        New York, New York 10045

    (b) Mr. David S. Freds: all
        Deputy Superintendent
        New York State Banking Department
        One State Street
        New York, New York 10004

    (c) Mr. Nauman K. Dnr
        Group Executive
        International Banking Group
        Habib Bank UK
        63 Mark Lane
        London EC3R7NQ, England

    (d) Mr. Faiq Sadiq
        Senior Vice President and Country Manager
        Habib Bank Limited
        New York Branch
        60 East 42nd Street
        New York, New York 10165

Miscellaneous

14. The provisions of this Agreement shall be binding on the Bank, the New York Branch, and each of their institution-affiliated pasties in their capacities ns such, and their successors and assigns.

15. Each provision of this Agreement shall remain effective and enforceable until stayed, modified, terminated or suspended in writing by the Supervisors.

16. Notwithstanding any provision of this Agreement, the Supervisors may, in their sole discretion, grant written extensions of time to the Bank and the New York Branch to comply with any provision of this Agreement.

17. The provisions of this Agreement shall not bar, estop or otherwise prevent the Board of Governors, the Supervisors, or any other federal or stale agency from taking any further or other action affecting the Bank, the New York Branch, or any of their current or former institution-affiliated parlies or their successors or assigns.

18. This Agreement is a "written agreement" for the purposes of, and is enforceable by the Board of Governors as an order issued under, section 8 of the Federal Deposit Insurance Act and by the Department pursuant to Section 39 of the New York State Banking Law.

IN WITNESS WHEREOF, the parties hereto havo caused this Agreement to be executed as of this 19th day of December, 2006.

EXHIBIT B

NEW YORK STATE DEPARTMENT OF
FINANCIAL SERVICES

In the Matter of

HABIB BANK LIMITED
Karachi, Pakistan

and

HABIB BANK LIMITED NEW YORK BRANCH
Now York, New York

ORDER ISSUED
UPON CONSENT
PURSUANT TO SECTION 39
OF THB NEW YORK
BANKING LAW

WHEREAS, Habib Bank Limited, Karachi, Pakistan (the "Bank") Is a foreign bank that conducts operations In the United States through a branch In Now York, New York (the "Branch");

WHEREAS, the New York State Deportment of Financial Services (the "Deportment") is the licensing agency of the Branch pursuant to Articlo II of the New York Banking Law ("NYBL") and is responsible for its supervision and regulation;

WHEREAS, the most recent examination of the Branch conducted by tho Federal Reserve Bank of New York (the "Reservo Bank") and the Department identified significant breakdowns in tho Branch's risk management and compliance with applicable federal ar.d state laws, rules, end regulations relating to anti-money laundering ("AML") compliance, including the Bank Secrecy Act ("BSA") (31 U.S.C. $ 5311 et seq.); tho rules and regulations issued thereunder by the United States Department of the Treasury (31 C.F.R. Chapter X); the requirements of Regulation K of the Board of Govomors of the Federal Reserve System (the "Board of Governor") to report suspicious activity and to maintain an adequate BSA/AML compliance program (12 C.F.R. §§211.24(f) and 211.24(j)) (collectively, the "BSA/AML Requirements") resulting in a compliance program violation; and the laws and regulations of the Department (NYBl, § 200-c and 3 N.Y.C.R.R. Parts 116 and 300) (the "State Laws and Regulations");

WHEREAS, on December 19,2006 the Bank and the Branch entered into a Written Agreement with the Roserve Bank and the predecessor of the Department, the New York State Banking Department, designed to correct certain deficiencies in the Brnnch's compliance with the BSA/AML Requirements and the State Laws and Regulations;

WHEREAS, the Bank and the Branch have not achieved full compliance with each and every provision of the Written Agreement;

WHEREAS, it is the common goal of the Department, the Bank and the Branch that the Branch operates in compliance with all applicable federal and state laws, rules, and regulations;

WHEREAS, the Bank, the Branoh, and the Department have mutually agreed to enter into this Consent Order (the "Order"); and

WHEREAS, on December3, 2015, tho board of directors of the Bank, at a duly constituted meeting, adopted a resolution authorizing and directing Mf respectively, and consenting to compliance with each and every provision of this Order by the Bank and the Branch, and waiving at) rights that the Bank and the Branch may have, including, but not limited to: (i) the issuance of a notice of charges on any and all matters set forth In this Order; (ii) a hearing for the purpose of taking evidence on any matters set forth in this Order; (iii) judicial review of this Order; and (iv) challenge or contest, in any manner, the basis, Issuance, validity, terms, effectiveness or enforceability of this Order or any provision hereof.

NOW, THERKPORB, IT IS HEREBY ORDERED that, before the filing of any notices, or taking of any testimony or adjudication of or finding on any issues of fact or law herein, and solely for the purpose of settling this matter without a formal proceeding being filed and without the necessity for protracted or extended hearings or testimony, the Bank and the Branch shall not engage in unsafe or unsound banking practices and not commit apparent violations of tho law and/ or regulation.

IT IS FURTHER ORDERED that the Bank, tho Branch, their institution-affiliated parties, and their successors and assigns, shall take affirmative action as follows:

Corporate Governance and Management Oversight

1. Within 60 days of this Order, the Bank's board of directors and the Branch's management shall Jointly submit to tho Department a written plan to enhance oversight, by the management of the Bank and Branch, of the Branch's compliance with tho BSA/AML Requirements, the State Laws and Regulations, and the regulations issued by the Office of Foreign Assets Control of the United States Department of the Treasury ("OFAC") (31 C.P.R. Chapter V) (the "OFAC Regulations") acceptable to the Department. The plan shall provide for a sustainable governance framework that, at a minimum, addresses, considers, and includes:

(a) actions the board of directors will take to maintain effective contr ol over, and oversight of, Branch management's compliance with the BSA/AML Requirements, tho State Laws and Regulations, and the OFAC Regulations;

(b) measures to Improve the management Information systems reporting of the Branch's compliance with the BSA/AML Requirements, the State Laws and Regulations, and the OFAC Regulations to senior management of the Bank and the Branch;

(c) clearly defined roles, responsibilities, and accountability regarding compliance with the BSA/AML Requirements, the Stato Laws and Regulations, and the OFAC Regulations for the Bank's and the Branch's respective management, compliance personnel, and Internal audit staff;

(d) measures to ensure BSA/AML issuos aro appropriately tracked, escalated, and reviewed by the Branch's senior management;

(e) measures to ensure that the person or groups at tho Bank and the Branch charged with the responsibility of overseeing the Branch's compliance with the BSA/AML Requirements, the State Laws and Regulations, and tho OFAC Regulations possess appropriate subject matter expertise and are actively involved in carrying out such responsibilities;

(f) adequate resources to ensure the Branch's compliance with this Order, the BSA/AML Requirements, the State Laws and Regulations, and the OFAC Regulations; and

(g) a direct reporting line between the Branch's BSA/AML compliance officer and the board of directors or committee thereof.

BSA/AML Compliance Review

2. Within 60 days of this Order, the Bank and the Branch shall retain an independent third

party acceptable to the Department (Use "Compliance Review Consultant") to: (i) conduct a comprehensive review of the effectiveness of the Branch's program for compliance with the BSA/AML Requirements and the State Laws and Regulations (the "Compliance Review"); and (ii) prepare a written report of findings, conclusion), and recommendations (the "Compliance Report").

3. Within 10 days of the engagement of the Compliance Review Consultant, but prior to the Compliance Review, the Dank and Branch shall jointly submit to the Department for approval an engagement letter that provides, at a minimum, for the Compliance Review Consultant to:

(a) identify all of the Branch's business lines, activities, and products to ensure that such business lines, activities, and products are appropriately risk-rated and included In the Branch's BSA/AML compliance program, policies, and procedures;

(b) conduct a comprehensive assessment of the Branch's BSA/AML compliance program, policies, and procedures;

(c) complete the Compliance Review within 60 days of the Department's approval of the engagement letter;

(d) provide to the Department a copy of the Compliance Report at the same time that the report Is provided to the Bank and the Branch; and

(e) commit that any and all interim reports, drafts, workpapers, or other supporting materials associated with the Compliance Review will be made available to the Department upon request.

BSA/AML Compliance Program

4. Within 60 days of the submission of the Compliance Report, the Bank and die Branch shall jointly submit a written revised BSA/AML compliance program for the Branch acceptable to the Department. At a minimum, the program shall provide for:

(a) a system of internal controls designed to ensure compliance with the BSA/AML Requirements and the State Laws and Regulations;

(b) controls designed to ensure compliance with all requirements relating to correspondent accounts for foreign financial institutions;

(c) a comprehensive BSA/AML risk assessment that identifies and considers all products and services of the Branch, customer types, geographic locations, and transaction volumes, os appropriate, in determining inherent and residual risks;

(d) management of the Branch's BS A/AML compliance program by a qualified compliance officer, who is given full autonomy, independence, and responsibility for implementing and maintaining an effective BSA/AML compliance program that is commensurate with the Branch's size and risk profile, and is supported by adequate staffing levels and resources;

(e) Identification of management information systems used to achieve compliance with the BSA/AML Requirements and the State Laws and Regulations and a timeline to review key systems to ensure they are configured to mitigate BSA/AML risks;

(f) comprehensive and timely independent testing for the Branch's compliance with applicable BSA/AML Requirements and the State Laws and Regulations; and

(g) effective training for all appropriate Branch personnel and appropriate personnel of affiliates that perform BSA/AML compliance-relatcd functions for the Branch in all aspects of the BSA/AML Requirements, the State Laws and Regulations, and internal policies and procedures.

Customer Due Dlligcnce

5. Within 60 days of the submission of the Compliance Report, the Bank and the Branch shall jointly submit a written enhanced customer due diligence program acceptable to tire Department. At a minimum, the program shall include:

(a) polioies', procedures, and controls to ensure that the Branch collocts, analyzes, and retains complete and accurate customer information for all account holders, including, but not limited to, affiliates;

(b) a plan to remediate deficient due diligence for existing customers accounts;

(c) a revised methodology for assigning risk ratings to account holders that considers factors such as type of customer, type of products and services, geographic locations, and transaction volume;

(d) for each customer whose transactions require enhanced due diligence, procedures to;

(i) determine the appropriate documentation necessary to verify the Idontity and business activities of the customer; and

(ii) understand the normal and expected transactions of the custemer,

(e) policies, procedures, and controls to ensure that foreign correspondent accounts are accorded the appropriate due diligence and, where necessary, enhanced due diligence; and

(f) periodic reviews and evaluations of customer and account information for the V entire customer base to ensure that information is current, complete, and that tire risk rating reflects the current information, and If applicable, documenting rationales for any revisions made to tho customer risk rating.

Suspicious Activity Monitoring and Reporting

6. Within 60 days of the submission of the Compliance Report, tho Bank and the Branch shall jointly submit a written program to reasonably ensure the identification and timely, accurate, and complete reporting by the Branch of all known or suspected violations of law or suspicious transactions to law enforcement and supervisory authorities, as required by applicable suspicious activity reporting laws and regulations acceptable to the Department. At a minimum, the program shall include:

(a) a well-documented methodology for establishing monitoring rules and thresholds appropriate for the Branch's profile which considers factors such as typo of customer, type of product or service, geographic location, and foreign correspondent banking activities, including U.S. dollar clearing activities;

(b) polioles and procedures for analyzing, testing, and documenting changes to monitoring rules and thresholds;

(c) enhanced monitoring and investigation criteria and procedures to ensure the timely detection, investigation, and reporting of all known or suspected violations of law and suspicious transactions, including, but not limited to:

(i) effective monitoring of customer accounts and transactions, including but not limited to, transactions conducted through foreign correspondent accounts;

(ii) appropriate allocation of resources to manage alert and case inventory;

(iii) adequate escalation of information about potentially suspicious activity through appropriate levels of management;

(iv) maintenance of sufficient documentation with respect to the investigation and analysis of potentially suspicious activity, Including the resolution and escalation of concerns; and

(v) maintenance of accurate and comprehensive customer and transactional data and ensuring that it is utilized by the Branch's compliance program.

Transaction and OFAC Sanctions Review

7. (a) Within 20 days of this Order, the Bank and the Branch shall engage an independent third party acceptable to the Department to conduct a review of the Branch's U.S. dollar clearing transaction activity from October 1,2014 to March 31,2015 to determine whether transactions inconsistent with or in violation of the OPAC Regulations, or suspicious activity involving high risk customers or transactions at, by, or through the Branch were properly identified and repotted in accordance with the OFAC Regulations and suspicious activity repotting regulations (the "Transaction and OPAC Sanctions Review") and to prepare a written % report deluding (he independent third party's findings (the "Transaction and OPAC Sanctions Review Report") to be shared will) the Department and the Reserve Bank.

(b) Based on the Department's evaluation of the results of the Transaction and OPAC Sanctions Review, the Department may direct the Bank and tho Branch to engage the independent third party to conduct a review of the types of transactions and activity described in paragraph 7(a) for additional time periods.

8. Within 10 days of the engagement of the Independent third party, but prior to the commencement of the Transaction and OPAC Sanctions Review, the Bank and the Branch shall Jointly submit to the Department for approval an engagement letter that sets forth:

(a) the scope of the Transaction and OFAC Sanctions Review;

(b) the methodology for conducting the Transaction and OFAC Sanctions Review, inoluding any sampling procedures to be followed;

(c) the expertise and resources to be dedicated to the Transaction and OF AC Sanctions Review;

(d) the anticipated date of completion of the Transaction and OFAC Sanctions Review and the Transaction and OFAC Sanctions Review Report; and

(c) a commitment that supporting material and drafts associated with the Transaction and OPAC Sanctions Review will be made available to the Department and the Reserve Bank upon request.

9. The Bank and the Branch shall provide to the Department and the Reserve Bank a copy of the Transaction and OFAC Sanctions Review Report at the same time that the report is provided to tho Bank and the Branch.

10. Throughout the Transaction and OFAC Sanctions Review, the Bank and the Branch shall ensure that all matters or transactions required to be reported that have not previously been reported are reported in accordance with applicable rules and regulations.

U.S. Dollar Clearing Activities Growth

11. (a) Tho Branch shall not, without tho prior written approval of the Department, take any action that would result in an increase in the aggregate dollar value of the Branch's U.S. dollar clearing activities above tho aggregate dollar value balanco as of the date of this Order.

(b) The Branch shall not, without the prior written approval of the Department, take any action that would result in an increase (n the aggregate transaction volume of the Branch's U.S. dollar clearing activities above the aggregate transaction volume as of the date of this Order.

(c) As of the date of this Order, the Branch shall not, without the prior written approval of the Department, accept any new foreign correspondent accounts or new customer accounts for U.S. dollar clearing.

(d) For the purposes of this Order, U.S. dollar clearing activities include, but are not limited to, wire transfers, letters of credit, and trade finance activities undertaken on behalf of the Bank, its affiliates, customers thereof, or third parties.

(e) The restrictions of paragraphs 11 (a), (b), and (c) of this Order shall continue In force and effect until the Bank and the Branch:

(i) submit to the Department the written plan and programs described In paragraphs I, 4, 5, and 6 of thi9 Order and a written plan to manage the growth In tho Branch's U.iS. dollar clearing activities;

(ii) are notified in writing by tho Department that the aforesaid plans and programs are acceptable;

(iii) adopt and fully implement the aforesaid plans and programs; and (iv) arc notified in writing by tho Department that all the above-described conditions have been met.

(f) Within 10 days after the end of each calendar month following tho date of this Order, t)>c Bank and tho Branch shall jointly submit to the Department written reports detailing the aggregate transaction U.S. dollar value and the aggregate transaction volume of the Branch's U.S. dollar clearing activities.

Interaction with Regulatory Authorities

12. Within 30 days of this Order, the Bank and the Branch shall jointly submit written policies and procedures that govern the conduct of tho Branch's personnel in all supervisory and regulatory matters, including, but not limited to, Interaction with and requests for Information by examiners for the Branch, acceptable to the Department. The policies and procedures shall, at a minimum, ensure that all Branch personnel provide prompt, complete, and accurate Information to examiners and provide for employee training that emphasizes the importance of fall cooperation with banking regulators by all employees.

OFAC Compliance

13. Within 30 days of this Order, the Bank and the Branch shall jointly submit a plan to

enhance the Bank's compliance with the OFAC Regulations acceptable to the Department, including but not limited to enhanced OFAC screening procedures, an improved methodology for assessing OFAC risks, timeliness of resolving alerts, and enhanced policies and procedures to ensure compliance with the OFAC Regulations.

Primary Contact

14. Within 10 days of this Order, the Bank and the Branch shall designate an officer to be responsible for coordinating and submitting to the Department the written plan, programs, and engagement letters required under the terms of this Order.

Approval and Implementation of Plan and Programs, and Progress Reports

15. (a) The Bank and the Br anch shall jointly submit the written plan and programs that are acceptable to the Department within the applicable time periods set forth in paragraphs), 4, 5,6, 11, 12, and 13 of this Ordor. Each plan or program shall contain a timeline for full implementation of the plan or program with speoifle deadlines for the completion of each component of the plan or program. Independent third parties acceptable to the Department shell be retained by the Bank and the Branch within the time periods set forth In paragraphs 2 and 7(a) of this Order. Engagement letters acceptable to the Department shall be submitted within the time periods set forth in paragraphs 3 and 8 of this Order.

(b) Within 10 days of approval by the Department, the Bank and the Branch, as applicable, shall adopt the approved plan and programs. Upon adoption, the Bank and the Branch, as applicable, shall promptly implement the approved plan and programs, and thereafter fully comply with them.

(c) During the term of this Order, the approved plan, programs, and engagement letters shall not be amended or rescinded without the prior written approval of the Department.

16. Within 30 days after the end of each calondar quaiter following the date of this Ordor, the Bank and the Branch shall jointly submit to the Department written progress reports detailing the form and manner of all actions taken to secure compliance with this Order, a timetable and schedule to implement specific remedial actions to bo taken, and the results thwrcof. The Department may, in writing, discontinue the requirement for progress reports or modify the reporting schedule.

Communications

17. All communications regarding this Ordcr shall be sent to:

(a) Mr. Jeffrey G. Raymond
Deputy Superintendent
New York State Department of Financial Services
One State Street
New York, New York 10004

(b) Ms. Hadas A. Jacobi
Office of General Counsel
Now York State Department of Financial Services
One State Street
New York, New York 10004

(c) Ms. Elizabeth Nochlin

Senior Enforcement Counsel
Now York State Department of Pinancial Services
One State Street
New York, New York 10004

(d) Ml. Megan Prendergast
Sonior Enforcement Counsel
New York State Department of Financial Services
One State Street
New York, New Yoik 10004

(e) Mr. Nauman K. Dar
President and Chief Executive Officer
Habib Bank Limited
Habib Bank Plaza
1.1 Chundrigar Road
Karachi-75650
Pakistan

(f) Mr. Manochcrc Alamgir
General Manager and Country Head
Habib Bank Limited
New York Branch
60 East 42nd Street, Suite S35
New York, New York 10165

Miscellaneous

18. Notwithstanding any provision of this Order to the contrary, the Department may, In its sole discretion, grant written extensions of time to the Bank and the Branch to comply with any provision of this Order.

19. The provisions of this Order shalt be binding on the Bank and the Branch, and each of their institution-affiliated parties, as defined in section 3(u) and 8(b)(4) of the FD1 Act (12 U.S.C. §§ I813(u) and 1818(bX4)), in their capacities as such, and their successors and assigns.

20. Each provision of this Older shall remain effective and unforceable until stayed, modified, terminated, or suspended in writing by the Department.

21. The provisions of this Order shall not bar, estop, or otherwise prevent the Department, or any other federal or state agency from taking any other action affecting the Dank, the Branch, any of their subsidiaries, or any of Choir current or former instltution-affliated parties and their successors and assigns.

EXHIBIT C

NEW YORK STATE DEPARTMENT OF FINANCIAL SERVICES

In the Matter of

HABIB. BANK LIMITED and
HABIB BANK LIMITED, NEW YORK BRANCH

ORDER PURSUANT TO
NEW YORK BANKING LAW

Pursuant to the statutory powers vested in Maria T. Vullo, Superintendent of the New York State Department of Financial Services (tho "Department") by the People of the State of New York; and, further, pursuant to the Consent Order, dated December 3, 2015, between the Department, Habib Bank Limited and the New York Branch of Habib Bank Limited (the "New York Branch"), the Superintendent hereby issues the following Order with respect to Habib Bank Limited and the New York Branch:

Following the Department's evaluation of the results, to date, of the Transaction and OKAC Sanctions Review conducted pursuant to Paragraph 7(b) of the December 3, 2015 Consent Order, the Department hereby directs and orders Habib Bank and the New York Branch to:

(a) expand the Transaction and OFAC Review to cover the additional time periods of (i) October 1,2013 to September 30,2014; and (ii) April 1,2015 to July 31,2017; and

(b) continue to engage the independent third party, previously approved by the Department, to conduct this expanded review.

By Order of the Superintendent, this ^fday of August, 2017. New York, New York MARIA T.VULLO Superintendent of Flnanclul Services.

EXHIBIT D

NEW YORK STATE DEPARTMENT OP FINANCIAL SERVICES

In the Matter of

HABIB BANK LIMITED and
HABIB BANK LIMITED, NEW YORK BRANCH

ORDER PURSUANT TO
NEW YORK BANKING LAW

Pursuant to the statutory powers vested in Maria T. Vullo, Superintendent of the New York State Department of Financial Services (the "Department") by the People of the State of New York, the Superintendent hereby issues the following Order with respect to Habib Bank Limited and the New York Branch of Habib Bank Limited (the "New York Branch") (together, the "Bank"):

Habib Bank and the New York Branch have expressed to the Department their intontion to surrender to the Department the foreign bank branch license to operate the New York Branch. In connection with such surrender, and pursuant to the New York Banking Law, including, but not limited to, Sections 10, 14, 39 and 605, the Superintendent hereby imposes the following conditions in connection with the surrender by the Bank of its license to operate the New York.

Branch:

1. In order to effectuate such surrender, within thirty (30) days of service of this Order, Habib Bank and the New York Branch shall, in writing, offer to surrender to the Department the license to operate the New York Branch. The Department will accept the surrender of the license upon fulfillment of the conditions set forth in this Order and completion, to the satisfaction of the Superintendent, of ihc orderly wind down of the affairs of the New York Branch pursuant to the requirements of the New York Banking Law.

2. Upon submitting to the Department written notice of the offer to surrender the license to operate the New York Branch, Habib Bank and the New York Branch shall promptly commence the orderly wind down of the affairs of the New York Branch pursuant to the procedures set forth in the New York Banking Law.

3. Upon completion of the orderly wind down of the affairs of 1hc New York Branch to the satisfaction of the Superintendent, and with the exception of Paragraph 7(b) of the Consent Order-dated December 3, 2015 between and among the Department, Habib Bank and the New York Branch (the "Consent Order") as provided In Paragraph 4 of this Order below, the Consent Order shall remain in lull force and effect, but with its terms suspended unless and until Habib Bank re-establishes a branch, agency, representative office, or a banking subsidiary within the United States of America.

4. Paragraph 7(b) of the Consent Order shall remain in full force and effect, and Habib Bonk and the New York Branch shall immediately comply with the expansion of the Transaction and OFAC Review set forth in Paragraph 7(b) to include the additional time periods indicated, as set forth in the Superintendent's separate Order of same date.

5. Upon completion of the orderly wind down of the affairs of the Now York Branch to the

satisfaction of the Superintendent, thc Written Agreement dated December 19, 2006 between and among the Department, the Federal Reserve Bank of New York, Habib Bank and the New York Branch (the "Written Agreement") shall remain in full force and effect, but with its terms suspended unless and until Habib Bank re-cstablishcs a branch, agency, representative office, or a banking subsidiary within the United States of America.

6. Habib Dank and the New York Branch shall immediately engage and pay for an independent consultant of the Department's selection (in its sole discretion) to assist the Bank in tho safe, sound and lawful wind down of the affairs of the New York Branch.

7. Habib Bank and the New York Branch shall preserve all documents and information in their possession, custody or control that relates, directly or indirectly, to the affairs, operations or business of the New York Branch until further Order of the Superintendent, Inter alia, to facilitate full and complete compliance with the Consent Order, including, but not limited to, the Transaction and OFAC Sanctions Review conducted pursuant to Paragraph 7(b) of the Consent Order. This paragraph is not intended to modify or alter any other obligation Habib Bank or the New York Branch may have to preserve documents and information pursuant to applicable law.

8. In the event Habib Bank and the New York Branch fall to offer to surrender the license to operate tho New York Branch within thirty (30) days of service of this Order, the Department shall exercise its full authority to suspend or otherwise limit the activities of the New York Brunch, pursuant to New York Banking Law § 40(2), on grounds including those set forth in the separate Notice of Hearing and Statement of Charges of same date.

9. Service of this Order shall have no effect on the level of the asset maintenance or on the level of the asset pledge requirements of the Department currently imposed on the New York Branch, and such asset maintenance and asset pledge requirements shall continue in full force and effect until completion of the orderly wind down of the affairs of the New York Branch to the Department's satisfaction. Furthermore, no assets or properties, whother real, personal or mixed, and whether tangible or intangible, situated in New York, or wherever situated if constituting part of the business of the New York Branch, shall be transferred or moved out of any such location without the prior written approval of the Department.

10. Habib Bank and the New York Branch shall comply with such other conditions the Superintendent deems appropriate in connection with the orderly wind down of the affairs of the New York Branch, in order to ensure the safe, sound and lawful conduct of such wind down and otherwise protect tho public intorest.

《和解令》中文译文

美国纽约州金融服务局

就

哈比比银行有限公司

和

哈比比银行有限公司纽约分行

纽约银行法39项、44项和605款《和解令》

纽约州金融监管局（以下简称本属或DFS），哈比比银行有限公司和哈比比银行有限公司纽约分行（以下简称纽约分行）（合称哈比比银行或银行）同意就解决下述事宜达成最终和解。

鉴于，哈比比银行是一家总资产约240亿美元的国际性银行，并被DFS颁发营业执照在纽约开设外资银行分行；

本属发现如下：

简介

本《和解令》描述了银行机构——哈比比银行和其纽约分行没有按照纽约法律法规规定反击反洗钱、反恐融资以及其他非法金融活动。由于银行的反洗钱措施违法交易和监测的严重缺失，哈比比银行通过其纽约分行为对本国人民和整个金融系统构成威胁的交易提供便利。在这方面，哈比比银行通过其纽约分行：

1. 为某沙特私人银行Al Rajhi银行数亿美元的交易提供便利，而没有充分地进行反洗钱、反恐融资调查，据悉Al Rajhi银行与基地组织有联系；

2. 未能充分识别Al Rajhi银行的客户利用Al Rajhi银行在哈比比纽约分行的账户汇款，从而纵容了不安全的"嵌套活动"；

3. 总体上，允许至少13 000笔交易通过纽约分行清算，交易信息有意省略制裁所涉及的内容或被制裁国家名称；

4．滥用"白名单"——一份特意定制的低风险非法交易客户名单，允许恐怖分子国际武器交易商、伊朗石油商和其他遭制裁分子和机构进行交易；

5．指导客户取消付款指令，在付款指令中省略受制裁方的名称后通过纽约分行重新发送，支付给禁止使用美元清算系统的个人。

细节如下，本属认为银行的反洗钱合规职能非常薄弱。纽约分行所依赖的总行的监测系统与纽约分行自身的系统一样薄弱，甚至更为薄弱。鉴于此，本属最新的合规检查认为纽约分行应该被评为最低级别，即"5"级，本属对于该级别金融机构将不允许继续使用营业执照。

以上结论来自本属近期的调查，该调查是关于纽约分行致力于按照纽约州。反洗钱法律法规，包括银行保密法BSA的合规项目严重缺失的调查。该调查依照本属2015年12月15日的《和解令》进行，银行及纽约分行（2015年《和解令》）被认定在银行BSA/AML合规方面严重缺失。另外，本属就纽约分行截至2016年3月31日的业务进行了调查。

尽管银行被给予了充分的机会来修正其缺失，但是银行没有及时修正。如下所述，银行违反了纽约法律法规；开展了超权限和不安全的业务；在不稳妥不安全的情况下运营；本《和解令》确保此类错误的终止。

本属检查和额外检查结果

银行

1．哈比比银行是一家巴基斯坦的银行，总部位于卡拉奇，截至2016年总利润10亿美元，总资产240亿美元。哈比比银行是巴基斯坦最大的银行。截至2004年，该行主要为巴基斯坦政府所有。目前，政府已不再持有该行股份，该行在巴基斯坦股票交易所正式上市交易。

2．本属于1978年正式向纽约分行颁发营业执照。哈比比银行开设纽约分行主要提供美元清算服务，包括资金划转、支票兑付和托收、贸易融资、隔夜掉期、公司贷款。截至2015年12月31日，纽约分行持有代理行交易总计约2 870亿美元。纽约分行是银行在美国的唯一机构，并在相当时间段内是重要的代理行机构。

纽约分行极其薄弱的合规功能

3．2006年书面协议　2006年12月哈比比银行及其纽约分行与本属和Federal Reserve Board of Governors（the Board）达成书面协议，就发现的银行涉及OFAC经济制裁法律和自身BSA/AML项目方面的严重不足达成一致意见（详见附件A）。

4．2006年以来，纽约分行竭力按照纽约银行法律法规及2006年书面协议去做。

不断违反银行BSA/AML以及合规项目困扰着银行。甚至自2006年以来一直在违反2006年书面协议和/或纽约银行法。

5．2015年《和解令》在本属和the Board 2015进行的检查中，发现哈比比银行的合规功能进一步恶化。因此，2015年12月，哈比比银行和纽约分行进入2015年《和解令》程序（详见附件B），同时进行和解终止以及终止令程序。2015年《和解令》要求纽约分行采取特别措施以符合纽约和联邦法。

6．2015年《和解令》还要求银行雇佣独立顾问对纽约分行自2014年10月1日到2015年3月31日的美元结算交易进行审查，确定交易是否符合或违反OFAC的规定，或可疑活动涉及高风险客户或交易，通过纽约分行的交易被按照OFAC的规定和可以交易报告规定（Lookback）正确的识别和报告。

7．此外，2015年《和解令》的7（b）款显示，基于DFS的回溯（Lookback）结果，监管人员可以（自主决定）额外延长回溯时间。

8．2016年调查2016年本属和the Board联合进行了另一项检查，对截至2016年3月31日的信息和财务数据进行了重检。本属认为，纽约分部在风险管理和遵守BSA/AML和OFAC法律方面依旧非常薄弱。在2016年的调查提示，哈比比银行已经接受了由本属和the Board联合或单独的强制措施下的10个连续的检查。

9．2016年的检查确认了纽约分行在风险管理能力方面的重大缺陷。它还发现，尽管本属对纽约分行的风险管理表现进行了不断批评，管理层仍然没有进行有效的改进和管理BSA/AML和OFAC风险。总之，在2016年的检查中，本属发现了严重的缺失，包括（但不限于）；

- BSA/AML合规不足；

- 培训不足；

- 客户风险分类不足，包括有风险的外资代理尽职调查的缺失；

- 加强型客户尽职调查文件缺失；

- 高级人力资源管理和总部管理、监管和记录文件不足；

- 缺乏足够的OFAC和制裁筛查；

- BSA/AML独立测试和内部审计薄弱，包括内部审计方法论的薄弱，和

- 数据映射和整合的薄弱。

10．2016年的检查进一步发现了855份"batch-waived"交易预警，纽约分行人员在没有核对或有合理理由拒绝核对的情况下予以清算。"batch-waived"结果来自于一组基于总结性、统一性的预警。当被本属检查人员询问时，银行的管理层无法提供总部或当地管理者的batch豁免流程的书面批准。

11．2016年的检查进一步发现了2015年《和解令》内容与OFAC合规项目相关的新案例，包括纽约分行提供的几个金融产品缺乏制裁筛查证据，新的案例与内部审计项目的分类方法论薄弱有关。

12．纽约分行的失职主要在于其最大的美元清算业务客户之一是Al Rajhi Bank（Al Rajhi）。Al Rajhi是沙特阿拉伯最大的私人银行。

13．前述，Al Rajhi与AI Qneda和恐怖主义融资联系在一起。例如，2012年7月17日U．S．SENATE PERMANENT SUBCOMMITTEE曾报告，关于国家安全和政府事件，如下：

9·11恐怖袭击后……有证据表明，Al Rajhi银行及其一些所有者的与恐怖融资有联系，包括一个银行的创始人是alQaedade资助者（Senote报告189）。

参议院的报告继续给出其他事情的重要细节AI RajhiIinks ω Terrorism。

14．因此，这个Al Rajhi代理行账户显示哈比比银行被利用从事高风险反恐融资和洗钱活动。自大概2014年起，Al Rajhi的交易占到纽约分行所有交易的约24%。

15．2016年调查确认一系列纸质文件管理不到位和银行客户尽职调查管理整体不足，特别是，对于包括Al Rajhi在内的存量境外代理行客户。客户尽职调查档案没有Al Rajhi自身客户资料，或者深入了解Al Rajhi真实交易背景。本

属调查认为，Al Rajhi为自己的关联方，特别是在马来西亚和约旦的分支进行代理清算活动。

16．纽约分行不知道这类"嵌套"交易，客户档案中没有记录，没有代理客户信息，也没有被纽约分行的交易监测系统预警。

17．更有甚者，2016年的调查显示，每两周一次的纽约分行、高级合规官和Al Rajhi管理层的电话会毫无意义。检查人员重检了这些电话的记录和日程表，显示只有基础信息，并没有包括客户关系带来现行的BSA/AML相关的风险事件。

18．2016年的调查显示，总体上，哈比比银行及其纽约分行管理层没有构建恰当的BSA/AML监管环境来管理分行的高风险客户，以至于分行管理层风险偏好超出并替代了管理手段。

19．2017年7月10日当日或前后，在本属的要求下纽约分行才终止了与Al Rajhi的代理行账户关系。

20．本属的调查还发现了众多与银行的BSA/AML和OFAC合规相关的疏忽。如下（但不限于）：

- 超过13 000个通过SWIFT付款的交易被省略基础信息，例如每一笔交易最终策划者和受益人确认信息；和

- 多笔交易不恰当的汇集为一笔交易通过纽约分行清算，以防止纽约分行进行有效的可疑交易或禁止交易监控。

21．本属的调查还发现，总行对4 000多笔交易没有进行实时监控，显然是因为交易当事方在其"白名单"上，列入名单的客户被有意定义为低风险客户。本属调查认为，不断有客户被不恰当的列入哈比比银行的"白名单"，或者这些客户的交易被显著标记本应该被银行实时监控。

22．本属的调查认为这些交易没有被重检源于交易的当事方在白名单里，但是：

- 哈比比银行的白名单中有154个字段涵盖在SDN名单和禁止交易人员名单中（SDN名单），被美国财政部明确禁止交易；并且白名单中的字段包含SDN确认的与下述相关的禁止交易的实体和个人：

§ 与巴基斯坦恐怖组织头目相关的交易；

§与已知的国际军火商相关的交易；

§一个在特别关注国际恐怖分子名单中的个人；

§伊拉克萨达姆候赛因政权前副总理；

§一个伊朗邮轮卷入某笔交易。

23．时至今日，本属的调查发现纽约分行已经办至少2 500亿美元交易，由于不合理的所谓"白名单"的存在，这些交易没有进行实时监控。

24．本属调查还发现，纽约分行交易监测的不连续性，包括分行的监测字段不完备无法识别所有交易的应识别字段。例如关键字Embassy of Pakistan，对于Pakistan Embassy无法识别。

25．另外，本属调查揭示了某些情况下纽约分行监测系统给出的报警提示被不合理清除掉，因为某些因素显示它们可能错误，其他需要合规人员进一步重检的可疑字段，包括对交易受益人或者其他潜在信息截停的指令。

26．其中的一个例子涉及一个对中国武器制造厂的付款，该交易按照美国制裁规定被禁止开展。

27．另一个例子涉及银行的一个客户取消一个SWIFT付款指令，该笔付款的收款人是美国财政部禁止交易的个人，交易金额为11 226 796巴基斯坦卢比（约合107 000美元），目的是隐去被制裁当事人的名字重新发送付款指令。

28．本属调查还发现，几个付款，金额超过27 000美元被发送给银行总部的一个被FBI认定为非法的账户。账户持有人被控网络犯罪、盗窃，曾于2012年6月29日被新泽西州美国地方法院判定盗窃总额5 000万美元。账户持有人于2012年被列入FBI'S CYBER CRIMES MOST WANTED LIST（FBI网络犯罪红通名单），2015年在巴基斯坦被捕。然而，这些汇款均于2014年10月6日至11月28日期间通过纽约分行予以清算，完全不顾广为人知的账户持有人的负面新闻。

29．而且，该可疑账户持有人在2012年被列入FBI红通名单后仍开立了五个账户中的四个账户，包括2014年4月的美元清算账户。银行没有按照"了解你的客户"流程对客户进行尽职调查。结果，当这些交易的金额超过美元监控门槛引发实时监控系统报警时，纽约分行不合理地清除了报警，貌似该交易没有显示可疑。

30．进一步，一份来自哈比比银行总行的重检资料显示，在总行也发生了对于账户持有人同样的报警，原因是账户持有人因FBI'S CYBER CRIMES MOST WANTED LIST（FBI网络犯罪红通名单）而被列入反洗钱黑名单。然而，这份黑名单没有被纽约分行实时监测系统使用。而且，抛开公共信息，一位总行的分析师不合理地将与此网络犯罪相关的交易警报列为"假性相关"（报错）并予以删除。

31. 本属调查确认了将近200宗额外的可疑交易案例，银行没有发现和上报。这些可疑交易涉猎广泛，例如（i）缺乏经济目的的付款（例如将皮货款项付给了一家技术公司）；（ii）结构性案例；（iii）空壳公司交易；（iv）政治敏感人物交易。这些交易显示与交易当事方和/或他们的实际控制人的负面信息，包括恐怖融资、黑市贸易、贩毒、走私和欺诈。

听证、延迟回溯令和放弃令的提示

32. 考虑到本属就此事的调查，the Superintendent向哈比比银行和纽约分行发布了两份指令。

33. 扩大的回溯令首先，鉴于现有回溯期间独立顾问引出的错误信息，2017年8月24日，the Superintendent行使职权，按照2015年《和解令》第7段b的内容扩大回溯范围（详见附件C）。扩大回溯令要求哈比比银行额外增加回溯范围由2013年10月1日至2014年9月30日；2015年4月1日至2017年7月31日。扩大回溯令进一步要求哈比比银行继续聘用DFS认可的独立顾问来执行这项扩大回溯。

34. 放弃令考虑到本属就此事的调查，哈比比银行有意放弃在纽约的营业执照。相应地，本属于2017年8月24日签发了第二份命令，允许哈比比银行在30天内向本属确认其是否放弃营业执照（详见附件D）。在纽约分行有秩序地停业方面，the Superintendent按照银行法第605款对哈比比银行和纽约分行设置了一系列条件，其中要求银行自费聘用一名本属认可的（唯一认可的）独立顾问帮助纽约分行安全、稳妥、合法的处理停业事宜。

35. 放弃令同时提出，如果哈比比银行没有同时本属其自愿放弃营业执照（如其前述），本属可在听证会中撤销该营业执照。

36. 听证会通知：在签发扩大回溯领和放弃令的同时，本属签署了听证会通知和对哈比比银行及纽约分行指控函（以下简称"指控函"）。指控函指出了自2007年1月1日至今，超过53项相互独立的哈比比银行和/或纽约分行违反纽约法律法规之处。损害内容包括违反纽约银行法、2006年书面协议、2015年《和解令》。听证会预定2017年9月27日举行。

因此，根据纽约银行法39项、44项和605款，在the Superintendent职责范围内解决此事件不留后患，本属、哈比比银行和纽约分行提议并一致同意：

违反法律法规

37．哈比比银行和纽约分行没能维护有效合规的反洗钱项目和OFAC合规项目，违反了NYCRR116．2第3款。

38．哈比比银行和纽约分行未能保留真实、准确的反映所有交易和活动的簿记、账户、记录，违反了纽约银行法200-c。

39．哈比比银行和纽约分行以不安全、不稳妥的方式开展银行经营，违反了纽约银行法44，44-a。

40．哈比比银行和纽约分行以不安全、不稳妥的方式开展银行经营，违反了纽约银行法44，44-a。

41．哈比比银行和纽约分行违反多项2015年《和解令》，该《和解令》要求银行，inter alia，维护一套BSA/AML合规项目和交易监测系统。

解决条款

款项支付

42．哈比比银行应按照银行法第44款向本属支付罚款总额225 000 000美元。哈比比银行应于本《和解令》生效后14日内支付全部款项。

43．哈比比银行同意不向任何美国联邦、州或地方税务机构直接或间接追索、加入或申请本《和解令》项下所交罚款的税收减免或税收抵免。

44．哈比比银行和纽约分行在此确认，承认并同意（a）完全遵守扩大的回溯令要求，（b）2015年《和解令》7（b）持续有效（c）相应地，按照2015年《和解令》7（b），在交易和OFAC制裁回溯要求，哈比比银行和纽约分行应（i）额外扩大交易和OFAC制裁回溯时间为（A）2013年10月1日至2014年9月30日；（B）2015年4月1日至2017年7月31日；并且（ii）继续聘用前述本属认可的第三方独立机构，直至该额外交易和OFAC制裁回溯完成并达到the Superintendent满意。

45．2017年8月31日，按照放弃令规定，哈比比银行和纽约分行书面提出的，向本属返还纽约分行营业执照。哈比比银行和纽约分行确认并承认将完全遵守放弃令。

46．按照纽约银行法的要求，一旦放弃令中规定的条款被完全无误地履行并达到the Superintendent满意，纽约分行停业事宜管有序完成，本属将收回纽约营业执照。

47．哈比比银行和纽约分行应该按照纽约银行法安全稳妥有序地开展纽约分行停业事宜。

48．哈比比银行和纽约分行应立即出资雇佣本属认可（唯一认可）的独立顾问协助银行安全稳妥有序地开展纽约分行停业事宜。

49．哈比比银行和纽约分行应保存、托管或控制相关进程中与此事、纽约分行运营直接或间接相关的所有文件和信息，直至the Superintendent下发进一步的指令，inter alia，以全面和完整符合2015年《和解令》要求，包括但不限于按照2015年《和解令》第7（b）的交易和OFAC制裁回溯，以及本《和解令》的条款。该段内容不意味着修改或去除哈比比银行和纽约分行按照准据法应该保存的文件和信息。

50．哈比比银行和纽约分行应当保持本属给出的纽约分行资产规模和资产抵押水平。该资产规模和资产抵押水平要求持续有效直至纽约分行停业事宜有序完成并达到本属满意。而且，未经本属事前书面同意，任何资产或财产，无论是实体、个人或固定，也无论有形或无形，位于纽约或其他地方但属纽约分行所有，均不能转移或搬离。

2006年书面协议的存续

51．即使纽约分行停业事宜有序完成并达到he Superintendent满意，2006年书面协议仍持续有效，除非直至哈比比银行在纽约州从新设立分行、代表机构，或子银行。

52．如果哈比比银行在纽约州从新设立分行、代表机构，或子银行，哈比比银行、纽约分行以及任何分支机构、代表机构，或子银行应完全遵守2006年书面协议，除非本属书面保持、修改、终止或暂停，2006年书面协议持续有效。

2015年《和解令》的存续

53．一旦纽约分行停业事宜有序完成并达到he Superintendent满意，按照本《和解令》第44款不考虑2015年《和解令》第7段（b），2015年《和解令》仍持续有效，除非并直至哈比比银行在纽约州从新设立分行、代表机构或子银行。

54．如果哈比比银行在纽约州从新设立分行、代表机构，或子银行，哈比比银行、纽约分行以及任何分支机构、代表机构，或子银行应完全遵守2015年《和解令》所有条款，除非本属书面保持、修改、终止或暂停，所有条款持续有效。

权利的放弃

55．当事人确认并一致同意本《和解令》不受本属以外的任何法庭或仲裁庭重审。

本《和解令》当事各方

56．本《和解令》对本属、哈比比银行和纽约分行，以及任何承继者有效。本《和解令》不适用于任何联邦或州代理机构或法律执行部门。

57．如果哈比比银行和纽约分行遵守本《和解令》，本属将不对哈比比银行和纽约分行采取进一步措施。

违反《和解令》

58．一旦本属确认哈比比银行和纽约分行违反本《和解令》，本属将书面通知哈比比银行，银行必须在接到通知后3个工作日内，或本属认定的后续日期出现在本属面前，对没有违反甚或违反了《和解令》作出解释。

59．双方理解并同意，哈比比银行没有在规定的时间出现将被认为是违反本《和解令》。一旦发现哈比比银行违反本《和解令》，本属可以按照纽约银行和金融服务法，以及其他州或联邦法律予以修正，并在听证会、通知，或命令中使用本属认可的证据。哈比比银行和纽约分行同意受本《和解令》管辖和约束。

60．为保证（a）本《和解令》（b）2015年《和解令》或（c）2006年书面协议的实施，哈比比银行和纽约分行放弃在任何代表机构、仲裁庭或法庭对本属任何行动和后续措施的抗辩，无论是联邦或州。

61．本《和解令》项下所有通知和往来函应送至：

本属：

×××××××

哈比比银行：

××××××××

其他事项：

62．除非本属书面保持、修改、终止或暂停，本《和解令》所有条款持续有效。

63．本《和解令》当事人仅同意本《和解令》内容，而非其他承诺、保证、代表或理解。

本《和解令》于2017年9月7日由当事人见证并签署。

纽约州金融服务局

哈比比银行有限公司

哈比比银行有限公司纽约分行

附录

反洗钱部分框架法案汇编

1. 银行保密法（*Bank Secrecy Act*）

《银行保密法》（BSA）作为世界上首部有关反洗钱的立法，最初于1970年由美国国会通过，该法案确立了对个人、银行和其他金融机构记录和报告的要求，以协助美国政府机构识别流入、流出美国或存入金融机构的现金或其他货币工具的来源、数量和变动情况。该法案力求通过要求个人、银行和其他金融机构向美国财政部提交现金交易报告，正确识别进行交易的人员，并通过保留适当的财务记录来保留文件线索。这些记录使执法和监管机构能够对犯罪、税务和监管违规行为进行调查，并提供有用的证据来起诉洗钱和其他金融犯罪。

《银行保密法》要求银行和其他金融机构对于涉及大额现金交易及其他可能意味着洗钱、逃税或其他犯罪活动的可疑活动的行为具有报告的义务。具体而言，对于超过1万美元的现金交易，金融机构必须向有关部门提交涉及存款、取款、现金兑换或者其他支付或转移的报告。在提交的现金交易报告中，还要求必须透露拥有账号的客户身份和客户资金的来源。同时，该法案还要求银行和其他金融机构具有报告可疑交易、保存交易记录等义务。①

1986年颁布的《洗钱控制法》（Money Laundering Control Act）通过在联邦存款保险法（FDIA）和联邦信贷联盟法（FCUA）中增加了相关章节内容，提升了BSA的法律效力。该法案禁止规避BSA要求的行为，对故意协助洗钱及构造交易规避报告义务的个人或金融机构追究刑事责任。同时，该法案指导银行需设立和保持合理的流程以确保和监测对BSA要求的报告和记录义务遵守情况。

1988年美国政府通过了《洗钱起诉改善法》（*Money Laundering Prosecution Improvement Act*），扩大了《银行保密法》中对"金融机构"的定义，将汽车、飞机和轮船的经销商以及从事房地产、美国邮政服务的人员，也列入金融机构的范畴②。

1992年的《阿农齐奥—怀利反洗钱法案》（*The 1992 Annunzio–Wylie Anti-Money Laundering Act*）加强了对违反BSA的处罚和美国财政部的作用。两

---

① 《反洗钱立法之发展》——王新（《比较法研究》2009年第2期）。

② 《美国法典》（31 U. S. Code，§5312（a）（2）（T）-（V））。

年后，国会通过了1994年的《洗钱抑制法》（*Money Laundering Suppression Act*），该法进一步解决了美国财政部在打击洗钱方面的法律支撑。

1996年4月，制定可疑活动报告（Suspicious Activity Report，SAR）供美国所有银行机构使用。只要银行检测到已知或疑似违反联邦法律或涉嫌洗钱活动或违反BSA的可疑交易，就必须提交SAR。

《银行保密法》随着全球反洗钱形势处于不断变化的状态，已经历多次修订，在后续修订的《爱国者法案》第三章中的规定，修改《银行保密法》来要求金融机构通过建立内部政策，程序和控制措施，指定合规官员，员工培训，独立审计制度，来设立反洗钱机制，[1]详细内容请见本章节第二条爱国者法案注释。

2. 爱国者法案（Patriot Act）

在9·11恐怖事件发生后不久，为了防止和惩罚美国境内外的恐怖分子行为，加强执法调查的手段[2]，美国时任总统布什于2001年10月26日签署《为拦截和阻止恐怖主义而提供适当手段以团结和巩固美利坚的法案》（*Uniting and Strengthening America by Provi-ding Appropriate Tools Required to Intercept and Obstruct Terrorism Act*），声称：该法是战胜恐怖主义的必要步骤，将会给情报和执法人员提供新的重要的工具，以便与眼前的危险做斗争。[3]若将该法案名称各词的第一个英文字母放在一起，就是"USA PATRIOT"，故简称为《爱国者法案》。其中，反洗钱和恐怖融资有关内容列入第三篇——"铲除国际洗钱和反恐怖融资法（2001）（*the International Money Laundering Abatement and Anti-Terrorist Financing Act of 2001*）"。

《爱国者法案》可以说是自《银行保密法》以来美国国会颁布的最重要的反洗钱法。《爱国者法案》将恐怖主义融资行为定为刑事犯罪，并扩大了现有的BSA框架，包括：加强客户身份识别流程；禁止金融机构与外国空壳银行开展业务；要求金融机构开展尽职调查流程，并在某些情况下对外资代理行和私

---

① Linn, Courtney J.（2010）. "Redefining the Bank Secrecy Act: Currency Reporting and the Crime of Structuring". *Santa Clara Law Review*. 50（2）: 407–513.

② 《爱国者法案》（PATRIOT Act, 115 Stat., p. 272）。

③ 布什总统在签署《爱国者法案》时的讲话[See 37 Weekly Comp. Pres. Doe. 1550（October 26, 2001）]。

人银行账户开展加强型尽职调查流程；增加金融机构与美国政府之间的信息共享。《爱国者法案》及其实施条例还包括：

- 扩充对"金融机构"的定义范围，将在美国境外经营的金融机构也纳入其中。
- 增加对洗钱的民事和刑事处罚。
- 给予财政部长对涉及"主要洗钱问题"的司法管辖区、机构或交易实施"特别措施"的权力。
- 要求银行为记录查看提供便利，并在120小时内回复监管要求提供的信息。
- 要求联邦银行业管理机构在审查银行兼并、收购和其他合并申请时考虑银行的反洗钱记录。
- 扩大了上游犯罪的范围，将海外腐败列为上游犯罪。
- 增加对外国洗钱者行使长臂司法管辖权。

3. 国家紧急状态法（NEA）

1976年9月14日签署的国家紧急状态法（*National Emergencies Act*）（Title 50 §1601-1651）旨在限制启动和结束国家紧急状态，并规定国会的权力以达到与总统的紧急权力产生一定制衡作用的目的。国会法对总统调用此类权力施加了某些程序性的手续，可看出对法律的需求源于在国家紧急状态时赋予行政机构特殊权力的法律的范围和数量。

在这两部法律的框架下，当美国总统认为国际上出现某一局势或者发生的某一事件对美国的国家安全、外交政策和经济利益构成"非同寻常威胁"时，可根据上述法律的授权和定义，在国会的批准下宣布进入应对威胁的紧急状态，从而采取对相关国家、实体、组织或特定群体和个人实施相应的金融制裁措施。而美国财政部则通过其专门的外国资产管理办公室（OFAC）负责具体的金融制裁活动。

4. 国际紧急经济权力法（IEEPA）

1977年10月28日颁布的国际紧急经济权力法（*The International Emergency*

Economic Powers Act）（United States CodeTitle 50 Chapter 35①）授权总统如存在对于"国际上出现某一局势或者发生的某一事件"对美国的国家安全、外交政策或经济而言存在"非同寻常的威胁"，有权宣布进入紧急状态。②该法案进一步授权总统在宣布进入应对威胁的紧急状态后，阻止交易并冻结资产以应对威胁。③如果发生对美国的实际袭击，总统也可以没收与援助袭击的国家、团体或个人有关的财产④，并包括采取其他金融制裁措施。

从吉米卡特开始回应伊朗人质危机之后，美国总统通过IEEPA法案冻结交战国政府⑤或某些海外的外国人的资产来维护美国的国家安全利益。继"9·11"恐怖袭击事件发生后，时任美国总统乔治·W.布什在IEEPA框架下签署了第13224号行政命令，以冻结恐怖组织的资产。⑥总统授予美国财政部领导的联邦机构的封锁权力。2001年10月，国会通过的爱国者法案，部分根据50U.S.C.§1702（a）（1）（B）加强了IEEPA资产封锁条款，允许在"调查未决期间"冻结资产⑦。

5. 国防授权法案（NDAA）

《国防授权法案》（*National Defense Authorization Act*）是一系列美国联邦法律的统称，每一财政年度由美国国会通过并由美国总统批准颁布，详细说明美国年度国防经费预算以及具体行使的国防职权。⑧其内容随着美国历年国家利益的变动而发生相应的调整，其中有许多与金融制裁紧密相关的条文。该法案为相应年度美国金融制裁的发起和实施提供补充性的导向依据以及参考标准。

---

① 50 U.S. Code Chapter 35 - INTERNATIONAL EMERGENCY ECONOMIC POWERS | LII / Legal Information Institute. Law.cornell.edu. Retrieved on 2014-06-16.

② 50 U.S.C. §1701（a）.

③ 50 U.S.C. §1702（a）（1）（B）.

④ 50 U.S.C. §1702（a）（1）（C）.

⑤ Executive Order 12170，44 C.F.R. 65，729.

⑥ Exec.Order.No.13224，Sec.1（a），http://www.gpo.gov/fdsys/pkg/FR-2001-09-25/pdf/01-24205.pdf.

⑦ 50U.S.C.§1702（a）（1）（B）.

⑧ National Defense Authorization Acts for 1996 - 2016.

6. 以制裁反击美国敌人法案（CAATSA）

源于对俄罗斯涉嫌干涉2016年美国总统大选及插手乌克兰危机的不满，2017年7月25日美国参议院以高票通过该法案，其中涉及对俄罗斯／克里米亚、伊朗和朝鲜实施新的制裁。2017年8月2日，美国总统特朗普签署该法案。与以往不同的是，该法案限制了美国总统的外交权限，要求总统必须获得国会批准后才能修改或接触法案中的制裁条款。

有关该法案对被制裁国家相关的制裁条款将在下一个注释章节详细阐述。

7. 敌国贸易法（*Trading with the Enemy Act of 1917*，TWEA）

《敌国贸易法》是1917年10月6日颁布的美国联邦法案，旨在限制与敌视美国的国家进行贸易，该法案曾经作为在战争时期或战前时期通过的一系列法律的通用名称，旨在禁止与外国公民进行商业活动，以及可能为敌方提供协助的行为[1]。在第一次世界大战期间，时任美国总统伍德罗·威尔逊使用该法案设立"外国财产管理局"，有权没收任何被认为可能对战争胜利造成威胁的个人或机构的财产。[2]

虽然该法案最初仅限于战时，第一次世界大战结束后，该法案也开始适用于国家紧急情况。美国财政部根据该法案，制定《外国资产管理条例》，冻结相关国家资产并禁止金融交易，而指定和解除列入敌国名单是政府的固有权限。在朝鲜问题上，美国早在1949年就开始对朝鲜实施经济制裁和贸易封锁，特别是自2005年10月以来，为迫使朝鲜"首先放弃核计划"，美国甚至对朝鲜以涉嫌"伪造货币"和"洗钱"等为由实行金融制裁，2008年6月27日，随着朝鲜提交核计划申报清单，美国终止对朝适用《敌国贸易法》。截至2017年，古巴是该法案的唯一受制裁国家。此前，伊朗、伊拉克、阿富汗等国也曾经位列制裁范围中。[3]

---

[1] Phelps, Shirelle and Lehman, Jeffrey（editors）（2005）"Aiding the enemy acts" West's Encyclopedia of American Law（2nd edition）Vol. 1. Gale, Detroit, Michigan, pp. 182–183.

[2] Gross, Daniel A. (28 July 2014)."The U.S. Confiscated Half a Billion Dollars in Private Property During WWI: America's home front was the site of interment, deportation,and vast property seizure". Smithsonian.Retrieved 6 August 2014.

[3] "Overview of Sanctions with North Korea".U.S. Treasury.Retrieved 22 November 2013.

8.纽约州银行法（*NEW YORK BANKING LAW*）

纽约州银行业务局（The New York State Banking Department）于1851年4月15日由纽约州立法机构设立，是美国历史最悠久的银行监管机构。该机构是国家许可和州特许金融机构的主要监管机构，包括美国国内银行、外国银行机构、其分支机构和代表处、储蓄机构和信托公司、信贷联盟和在纽约经营的其他金融机构，包括抵押贷款银行和经纪商、慈善机构、汇款机构和特许贷款机构等。

作为2011年国家计划的一部分，纽约州州长和纽约州立法机构将纽约州保险机构和纽约州银行业务机构合并，并于2011年10月3日成立纽约州金融服务局（The New York State Department of Financial Services）[1]。合并代理机构和建立金融服务部门的目的是通过该机构监督更广泛的金融产品和服务来实现监管现代化，保护公众以及存款人、债权人和股东的利益。

纽约州银行法属于纽约州综合法律的一部分，共分为十六个章节，对监管机构的职责、权力、处罚规定及流程等作出详细阐释，并分别对适用于此法律中定义的所有公司，非公司组织，合伙企业和个人等作出相应的规定和指引。

本书案例多以纽约州银行法第二章节中第39条、第41条为法律依据。

NY BANK §39. Orders of superintendent监督的命令：

- 出现并解释明显的违规行为。
- 停止未经授权或不安全的和不健全的操作。
- 使资金减值或确保符合财务要求。
- 保持充足的储备金。
- 按规定保存文件和账户。[2]

NY BANK §44.Violations; penalties违规和处罚

- 根据不同违规行为及具体情况对罚金数额进行细分规定。[3]

---

[1]　http://www.dfs.ny.gov/about/history.htm.

[2]　https://codes.findlaw.com/ny/banking-law/bnk-sect-39.html.

[3]　https://codes.findlaw.com/ny/banking-law/bnk-sect-44.html.

美国金融制裁名单（Sanctions Lists）与金融制裁方案（Sanctions Programs）合编：

美国财政部外国资产管理办公室（OFAC）根据美国的外交政策和国家安全目标，针对目标国家和政权、恐怖分子、国际毒品贩运者、从事大规模杀伤性武器扩散及对美国国家安全、外交政策或经济造成其他威胁有关活动的人员进行管理和实施经济及贸易制裁。其各项制裁计划主要落实于名单与对国家和地区的制裁，事实上对于国家和地区的制裁也是以制裁名单为依托的。比如我们所了解的，美国对于伊朗、俄罗斯、克里米亚、朝鲜等国家或地区均有不同程度的制裁措施，而这些制裁措施均是通过名单进行管理。所以归根结底，我们可以说美国金融制裁主要是基于制裁名单的制裁。

（1）SDN（Specially Designated Nationals，特别指定国民名单）：

这是一份由目标国家拥有、控制或代表目标国家行事的个人和公司名单，它还列出了并非针对具体国家的制裁个人，团体和实体的名单，例如对恐怖分子和毒品贩运者的制裁计划。OFAC 要求美国实体（包括美国公民、有永久居留权的外国人、在美国法下成立的机构（包括海外分支机构）及其他在美国境内的个人和机构对 SDN 名单上的实体采取冻结措施，不得提取、转让、出境、出口、支付、交易。

（2）Consolidated Non-SDN（整合非SDN名单）

这是一份为了整合OFAC各项制裁下的非SDN名单，该名单并不是SDN名单的一部分，列在Non-SDN名单中的人员也可能被列入到SDN名单中。在此章节，我们将通过梳理对俄罗斯／克里米亚，伊朗，朝鲜等国家及地区金融制裁的历史沿革，加以解释与被制裁国家相关的制裁名单，包括SSI（Sectoral Sanctions Identification）List，NS-ISA（Non-SDN Iran Sanctions Act List），FSE（Foreign Sanctions Evaders）List，第561条款名单，The 13599 list。

对乌克兰、俄罗斯相关制裁方案（UKRAINE/RUSSIA–RELATED SANCTIONS PROGRAM）

2014年3月，俄罗斯批准克里米亚加入俄罗斯联邦成为美国开始对其实施制裁的导火索，时任美国总统奥巴马签署一系列总统行政令，根据13660号，

13661号，13662号和13685号行政令列出或指定的人员或实体名称，其财产和财产权益被冻结，其信息会在联邦注册簿上公布，并纳入OFAC的SDN名单中。[①]根据13662号行政令中的1，2，3，4号指令由财政部长确认俄罗斯经济部门特定人员名单，OFAC制定了SSI（Sectoral Sanctions Identification）名单，即行业制裁名单，是美国针对俄制裁中创设，要求按照随名单同时发布的指令对名单人员和实体采取相应制裁措施。

对于SSI名单中的制裁对象，美国实体只需按照名单对应的指令采取相应措施，不需采取冻结措施。

指令1（2014年9月12日发布）：禁止为本指令制裁实体期限大于30天的新债务和新股权融资提供金融服务以及其他形式的交易，以及有意规避上述制裁措施的行为。

指令2（2014年9月12日发布）：禁止为本指令制裁实体期限大于90天的新债务和新股权融资提供金融服务以及其他形式的交易，以及有意规避上述制裁措施的行为。

指令4（2014年9月12日发布）：禁止直接或间接提供物品、服务（金融服务除外）、技术等相关的出口以及再出口服务，当上述物品、服务或技术可能被用于支持受制裁人员在俄罗斯联邦或其领土延伸海域的石油开采工作，以及有意规避上述制裁措施的行为。

2017年8月为了回应俄罗斯在美国选举中所谓的"干涉"及之前插手乌克兰危机颁布的《以制裁反击美国敌人法案》（CAATSA），重中之重是实施更严厉的对俄制裁。OFAC也根据CAATSA对SSI名单进行了更新。具体内容如下：

指令1，禁止为被制裁实体（SSI名单中标注Subject to Directive 1的实体）在制裁生效日后产生的期限大于14天的债务融资以及股权融资提供金融服务以及其他形式的交易，以及有意规避上述制裁措施的行为。

---

① UKRAINE/RUSSIA-RELATED SANCTIONS PROGRAM（OFAC）—Sectoral sanctions.

指令 1（2017 年 9 月 29 日）	
Period when the debt was issued	Applicable tenor of prohibited debt
2014 年 7 月 16 日（包含）至 2014 年 9 月 12 日	期限大于 90 天
2014 年 9 月 12 日（包含）至 2017 年 11 月 28 日	期限大于 30 天
2017 年 11 月 28 日起	期限大于 14 天

指令2，禁止为被制裁实体（SSI名单中标注Subject to Directive 2的实体）在制裁生效日后产生的期限大于60天的债务融资提供金融服务以及其他形式的交易，以及有意规避上述制裁措施的行为。

指令 2（2017 年 9 月 29 日）	
Period when the debt was issued	Applicable tenor of prohibited debt
2014 年 7 月 16 日（包含）至 2017 年 11 月 28 日期间	期限大于 90 天
2017 年 11 月 28 日起	期限大于 60 天

指令3，禁止为被制裁实体（SSI名单中标注Subject to Directive 3的实体）在制裁生效日后产生的期限大于30天的债务融资提供金融服务以及其他形式的交易，以及有意规避上述制裁措施的行为。

指令4，禁止直接或间接提供物品、服务（金融服务除外）、技术等相关的出口以及再出口服务，当上述物品、服务或技术可能被用于支持俄罗斯联邦或受制裁人员（SSI名单中标注Subject to Directive 4的实体）页岩油气的勘探和开发工作，以及有意规避上述制裁措施的行为。以及涉及指令4所指定的任何人士或该人士拥有至少为33%权益的任何财产或财产的权益。

"50法则"

OFAC还对2014年7月在乌克兰/俄罗斯相关制裁背景下制定的SSI名单上的实体适用50%的规定，即一个或多个受SSI名单限制的人合计拥有50%或以上的实体同样纳入制裁范围。在SSI名单限制的范围内，可确定哪些下属实体仅受SSI列表限制，但并不意味着应对这些实体实施任何其他操作（例如冻结）。2017年10月31日修订的指令4中提及"33%或更高的所有权"并没有改变OFAC在指令4背景下适用50%的规则。

列入SSI名单被制裁实例：俄罗斯外贸银行（VTB）

俄罗斯外贸银行（VTB）于1990年10月17日在莫斯科成立，1991年获得全面经营执照。2005年10月，该行将总部地址由莫斯科迁至圣彼得堡。2000年，该行收购了MOST-BANK（莫斯科极具实力的一家零售银行）。2011年，该行收购了BANK VTB NORTH-WEST OJSC。据该行2017年年报数据显示，截至2017年12月31日该行总资产达130亿美元，较2016年增长3.3%，净利润1.2亿美元，较2016年增长132.8%。

VTB是俄罗斯资产排名第二大的商业银行，一直以来得到俄罗斯联邦中央银行大力支持。作为"响应克里姆林官对乌克兰政策"美国制定了新制裁清单，即针对俄罗斯创立的SSI名单于2014年7月31日发布，并于次日生效，VTB开始被列入该名单。该制裁限制美国公民和法人不得购买VTB或与其有关的法人股权以及交易超过90天到期的债务。

美国对俄罗斯的长期制裁对俄罗斯银行业的影响是显而易见的，据俄罗斯央行数据，2016年俄罗斯银行业总利润下降了15%至7 900亿卢布，约合人民币。在VTB集团层面，制裁对以大型机构客户为主、业务主要涉及证券交易的VTB Bank影响较大，同时该银行的私有化进程也因制裁而被迫中止。而对于VTB集团的子公司VTB 24（PJSC），专门为个人和小型企业提供服务，列入制裁名单对其业务影响有限。首先，制裁只涉及俄罗斯国有银行在海外吸引金融资源。VTB24的业务模式由独立资金决定，专门在俄罗斯市场吸引资金。其次，所有VTB 24客户账户都位于俄罗斯联邦境内，不受任何限制，这同样适用于银行卡持卡人，无论在俄罗斯或国外不受使用限制。

自2018年1月《以制裁反击美国敌人法案》正式生效以来，美国进一步扩大对俄罗斯经济部门的制裁措施被视为宣布"经济战"，新的制裁被看作不仅是施加经济压力，更是政治压力。俄罗斯已经开始把VTB和Sberbank涉及国防工业的主要债权向其他国有银行转移，甚至为此设立军事银行，来削弱这两家在俄罗斯排名前两位的银行的战略业务，希望通过采取这一步骤保护这些银行可能免受新的一揽子制裁。

然而，相对于美国不断加码的制裁计划，俄罗斯银行对自己的保护措施只能说是杯水车薪。4月6日美国财政部宣布对俄罗斯实施更加严厉的制裁，以回应所谓的俄罗斯在全世界范围内的"全部恶意行为"。列入SDN制裁名单涉及

24名俄罗斯个人和14家经济实体，其中就包括VTB集团主席安德烈·列昂尼多维奇·柯斯金。此举随后对俄罗斯股市和卢布汇率造成强大冲击，4月9日，俄罗斯股市VTB报价下跌近8.8%。如今面对此新一轮更加严厉的制裁，俄罗斯方面底气的来源我们可从对VTB集团主席在今年年初达沃斯论坛上的一段采访中追寻到一些蛛丝马迹："我们与央行一同制定一揽子措施来应对已设想到的不同情况，对每种情况还制定了不同的行动方案。经历被制裁近四年时间，我们早已适应。如果有新制裁的话，我们会在新的制裁条件下开展业务，以确保经济的逐步发展。"

对伊朗制裁（IRAN SANCTIONS）：

截至目前OFAC已制定的整合非SDN名单（Consolidated Non-SDN），六中有四都与伊朗有关，包括NS-ISA（Non-SDN Iran Sanctions Act List），FSE（Foreign Sanctions Evaders）List，第561条款名单，The 13599 list，这一系列名单也体现了美国对伊制裁的历史沿革过程。

（1）NS-ISA（Non-SDN Iran Sanctions Act List）

1996年，美国通过《伊朗制裁法案》（Iranian Sanction Act）将美国公司以外的主体列入制裁措施的对象，即次级制裁（Secondary Sanctions），并由此制定NS-ISA（Non-SDN Iran Sanctions Act List）名单，此名单是在《伊朗制裁法案》第6章条款下的"非冻结"名单。

NS-ISA名单制裁内容：

美国国务卿选择对名单中的个人或实体实施制裁，禁止美国金融机构为其提供某些贷款或授信。OFAC禁止美国金融机构在12个月的期限内向名单中个人或实体提供总计超过1 000万美元的贷款或授信，参加人道主义援助活动的贷款或授信除外。NS-ISA名单与SDN名单的区别在于，此名单内的制裁对象其财产或财产权益不会被冻结，为此创建了代码[NS-ISA]。而那些财产或财产权益因《1996伊朗制裁法案》规定的其他制裁而被冻结的个人或实体将出现在特别指定国民名单上，代码为[ISA]。2016年1月16日是与伊朗达成的《联合行动计划》执行日，NS-ISA名单被清空。

（2）FSE（Foreign Sanctions Evaders）

FSE（Foreign Sanctions Evaders）名单，是OFAC根据13608号行政令，公

布的一份确定违反、试图违反、共谋违反或导致美国对叙利亚或伊朗制裁的外国个人和实体的名单。包含了违反美国对叙利亚和伊朗的制裁规定的外国实体，以及帮助被美国制裁的实体进行欺骗性交易的外国实体。名单还列出了帮助受美国制裁人员进行欺骗性交易的外国人。OFAC禁止美国实体和FSE名单上的实体交易或为其提供金融服务。

具体而言美国人一般被禁止直接或间接从事涉及FSE名单上个人或实体的所有如下交易：①商品、服务或技术在美国境内或计划运入美国的。②不论身在何处，商品、服务或技术由美国人提供或提供给美国人的。

（3）第561条款名单

2010年7月1日颁布《全面制裁伊朗，究责和撤资法案》（*Comprehensive Iran Sanctions, Accountability, and Divestment Act*，CISADA），该法案根据1996年的《伊朗制裁法案》延伸了对伊朗的经济制裁，对向伊朗出口石油制品或援助伊朗石油生产的公司和个人实施制裁。这种不断施压是针对伊朗核计划制裁活动的一部分，其目标是打压伊朗所依赖的别国对其石油进口需求。[①]

为了执行2010年CISADA法案、2012财年国防授权法案（NDAA）、2012年伊朗自由与反扩散法案（IFCA）以及一些相关的行政命令，OFAC制定Part 561 list名单，即外国金融机构第561条款名单（以下简称"第561条款名单"），主要针对涉嫌违反有关伊朗制裁法案和决议的外国金融机构，禁止美国金融机构与其建立或保持相应的代理行账户关系。

一旦美国财政部发现某家外国金融机构明知地参与美国联邦法律第31章第561条201款和203款的活动，则对此类金融机构在美国开立或维护代理账户或"过路账户"（payable-through account，指美国金融机构为外国金融机构的客户提供开立支票特权的存款账户）实施特定的禁止或限制措施。

列入涉伊制裁名单Part 561 list实例：昆仑银行

昆仑银行前身为成立于2006年6月6日的克拉玛依市商业银行，2009年4月，中国石油天然气集团公司增资控股克拉玛依市商业银行。2010年4月，克拉玛依市商业银行正式更名为昆仑银行。截至2017年末，昆仑银行资产总额3

---

① Lake, Eli（2009-04-28）. "Senators push for business sanctions". *Washington Times*. Retrieved 2009-09-10.

175亿元，存款余额1 510亿元，贷款余额1 510亿元，利润总额35.09亿元；资产收益率0.97%，资本收益率10.98%，资本充足率16.48%，不良贷款率1.57%。

2012年7月31日，针对昆仑银行与美国涉伊制裁法案指定的伊朗多家银行之间的持续关系，OFAC将其列入Part 561 list名单实施制裁。

根据OFAC得到的信息，发现昆仑银行有意为多家被美国当局指定与大规模杀伤性武器或恐怖主义有关的伊朗银行提供重大交易的便利，即涉及价值数亿美元的"关键金融服务"，包括维护账户、转移支付，以及担任美国指定的伊朗银行开立信用证的付款银行。在发现昆仑银行有意从事这些根据CISADA法案可予以制裁的活动时，时任美国财政部长禁止美国的银行在昆仑银行开设或维护代理账户以及禁止昆仑银行在美国的账户交易——切实切断昆仑银行直接进入美国金融体系，并要求任何持有该银行账户的美国金融机构必须在10天之内销户。

（4）The 13599 list

伊朗核问题转机出现在2013年10月，伊朗与伊核问题六国恢复中断已久的谈判，并于2015年7月14日达成历史性协议《联合行动计划》（JCPOA），该协议于2016年1月开始履行，也标志着2013年11月24日《联合行动计划》（JCPOA）的结束，包括根据JCPOA提供制裁救济。

The 13599 list名单为OFAC根据JCPOA创设的不属于SDN名单和二级制裁名单的Non-SDN名单，要求美国人仍需对该名单上的人员、实体、船舶等资产继续进行冻结。

2017年8月2日由现任美国总统特朗普签署的《以制裁反击美国敌人法案》（*Countering America's Adversaries Through Sanctions Act*，CATTSA），重新确认伊核制裁方案。CAATSA第105条要求根据行政令13224对伊朗伊斯兰革命卫队（IRGC）以及作为伊斯兰革命卫队官员，代理人或附属机构的外国人实施适用的制裁。根据CAATSA的要求和13224号行政令决议，OFAC于2017年10月13日指定IRGC为以前曾被指定用于支持各种恐怖主义团体的IRGC-Qods部队提供支持。此外，从2017年10月31日起OFAC修订了"全球恐怖主义制裁条例"（31 C.F.R. 第594部分），已被OFAC确定为IRGC的官员、代理人或附属机构的外国人的财产和股权将受到限制。

对北朝鲜制裁方案（NORTH KOREA SANCTIONS PROGRAM）

2008年，时任美国总统颁布了13466号行政令，宣布国家启动紧急状态以应对由于朝鲜半岛存在可用于武器的裂变材料而对美国的国家安全和外交政策构成的威胁，并继续对原先在《敌国贸易法》（TWEA）的管辖下实施对北朝鲜的某些限制。2008年至2017年间，美国总统发布了一系列行政命令，扩大了2008年的国家紧急情况并采取了额外措施，包括阻止某些人（个人和实体）的财产以及禁止某些类型的交易：

A.冻结财产及财产权益

根据13466号行政令及2000年6月16日的《敌国贸易法》（TWEA），被冻结至2008年6月26日的北朝鲜机构或其国民的财产和财产权益，继续被实施冻结。

13551号、13687号行政令分别冻结了对应行政令附件所列的人员财产和财产权益，并且冻结了财政部长与国务大臣协商确定人员的财产。

13722号行政令冻结了北朝鲜政府和北朝鲜劳动党的财产和财产权益，以及财政部长与国务大臣协商确定人员的财产和财产权益。

有关大规模毁灭性武器扩散者的13382号行政令冻结了所属附件中所列的三名北朝鲜人的财产和财产权益，以及财政部长与国务大臣协商确定人员的财产和财产权益。

在13551号行政令附件中列出的或13551号行政令指定被冻结其财产及财产权益的人员信息，会公布在联邦公报，并纳入OFAC的特别指定国民名单（SDN名单），标识符为"[DPRK]"；根据13687号行政令指定被冻结其财产及财产权益的人员信息，会公布在联邦公报，并纳入OFAC的SDN列表中，标识符为"[DPRK2]"。根据13722号行政令指定被冻结其财产及财产权益的人员信息，会公布在联邦公报，并纳入OFAC SDN清单中，标识符为"[DPRK3]"。13382号行政令指定被冻结其财产及财产权益的人员信息，会公布在联邦公报，并将其并入OFAC的SDN名单，标识符为"[NPWMD]"。

B.禁止与涉及北朝鲜船只交易

根据13466号行政令，禁止美国人在北朝鲜登记船只，或获得授权悬挂北朝鲜国旗的船只，以及拥有、出租、经营或保证任何有北朝鲜标记的船只。

C.禁止从北朝鲜进口

根据13570行政令，没有OFAC许可或适用豁免，来自北韩的货物、服务和技术可能不会直接或间接进口到美国。这种广泛的禁止条例适用于被第三国用作成品或转化来源的北朝鲜货物，服务和技术。

D.禁止出口北朝鲜

根据第13722号行政令，货物、服务和技术不得直接或间接地从美国或由美国人从任何地方出口或再出口到北朝鲜。为了出口到指定人员，美国人必须从OFAC和BIS获得许可证。

E.禁止在北朝鲜投资

根据13722号行政令，美国人禁止未经OFAC许可或豁免在北朝鲜进行新的投资项目。

北朝鲜导弹和核项目的重大进展，已经成为美国最为紧迫的外来威胁。对朝制裁作为2017年8月签署的《以制裁反击美国敌人法案》（CAATSA）第三部分内容，被命名为《朝鲜禁令及制裁现代化法案》（*Korean Interdiction and Modernization of Sanctions Act*）。该法案修改并增加了总统对违反某些联合国安理会有关北朝鲜决议的人实施制裁的权力。美国金融机构不得设立或维护外国金融机构用于向北朝鲜提供间接金融服务的代理账户。向北朝鲜提供或接收来自北朝鲜的防卫物品或服务的外国政府不得接受某些类型的美国协助。该法案确认针对下列情况的制裁：①北朝鲜的货物和运输，②全部或部分由北朝鲜罪犯或强迫劳动生产的货物，以及③雇用北朝鲜强迫劳工的外国人。

2017年9月特朗普签署13810号行政令《对北朝鲜实施附加制裁》（Imposing Additional Sanctions with Respect to North Korea）。13810号行政令向财政部长提供了在与国务卿磋商条件下的补充方式来破坏北朝鲜支持大规模杀伤性武器（WMD）和弹道导弹计划的能力，包括：①制定了若干项新的指定制裁人员标准；②禁止外国人拥有的飞机在从北朝鲜起飞后180天之内降落美国境内，并且禁止在过去180天之内停靠在北朝鲜港口或在过去180天之内与此类船舶进行船对船转运的外国人拥有的船舶停靠美国；③有权阻止任何资金流入美国境内或美国人拥有的与北朝鲜有关的账户；④有权对在命令日期或之后故意进行或促成的如下交易的外国金融机构实施制裁（ⅰ）代表某些被封锁人员进行重大交易或（ⅱ）与对北朝鲜贸易有关的任何重大交易。适用于外国金融机构的制裁可以是对通信账户或应付账款的限制或完全阻止制裁。

进入2018年北朝鲜因其导弹和核项目的重大进展已成为特朗普政府最为紧迫的外国威胁，2月23日特朗普在一个保守主义者大会上发表演讲时，宣布将对北朝鲜实施新一轮"史上最大规模"制裁。美国财政部随后对56个涉朝实体和个人实施制裁，旨在切断北朝鲜核项目的资金源，从而通过加大对北朝鲜施压，促使北朝鲜放弃核武器和导弹项目。

对苏丹及达尔富尔地区制裁（SUDAN AND DARFUR SANCTIONS）

以苏丹政府支持国际恐怖主义对美国的国家安全和外交政策构成的威胁为由，1997年11月3日时任美国总统克林顿签署关于冻结苏丹政府财产及禁止与苏丹进行交易（Blocking Sudanese Government Property and Prohibiting Transactions With Sudan）的13067号行政令，开启为期20年的对苏丹制裁计划。有关金融制裁的条款被写入第一部分：除了国际紧急经济权力法（IEEPA）中相关的条款范围，冻结所有苏丹政府在美国境内或之后汇入美国，或之后由美国公民包括其海外分支机构所有或控制的财产和权益。

2006年4月26日，美国时任小布什政府以苏丹达尔富尔地区持续发生暴力事件等问题为由，签署13400号行政令，冻结与苏丹达尔富尔地区冲突关联个人的财产（Blocking Property of Persons in Connection With the Conflict in Sudan's Darfur Region），扩大了在第13067号行政令中声明的国家紧急情况范围，添加大量对个人制裁的内容。使对苏丹政府和相关个人的制裁更加严格。

同年10月17日，同样针对苏丹达尔富尔地区持续冲突，时任美国总统小布什签署13412号行政令（Blocking Property and Prohibiting Transactions With the Government of Sudan），加强对苏丹石油工业和石化工业领域的限制。

由于美国财政部严格监管众多国际金融机构的涉苏丹行为，大量与苏丹进行贸易往来的第三国公司和个人也受到波及。2014年，法国巴黎银行就因涉嫌为遭美制裁的苏丹、伊朗等国转移资金，被迫向美国支付高达89.7亿美元的罚款。这导致绝大部分金融机构都对苏丹避而远之，苏丹难以获得外部资金信贷支持。

为解除长达20年的制裁枷锁，近年来苏丹政府不遗余力通过加强反恐合作、参加解决地区冲突等方式，谋求与美国改善关系。2017年初，因近六个月苏丹政府采取的政策和行动在与美国的关系和维护地区稳定上发挥积极作用，时任美国总统奥巴马在即将卸任之际，签署行政命令决定考虑解除对苏丹部分制裁，但却将生效日期延后至7月份，交由特朗普政府视苏丹政府表现最终定夺。这些行动包括显著减少进攻性的军事活动，最终承诺在苏丹冲突地区停止敌对行动，并采取措施改善整个苏丹的人道主义准入情况，并与美国合作解决区域冲突和恐怖主义的威胁。

自2017年10月12日起，根据2017年1月13日美国总统签署的第13761号行政令及随后修订并于2017年7月11日签署的第13804号行政令，美国财政部海外资产管理办公室（OFAC）解除部分自1997年以来对苏丹和苏丹政府实施的制裁，包括解除1997年11月3日签署的第13067号行政令第1款和第2款以及2006年10月13日签署的第13412号行政令全部条款的制裁内容。虽然美国宣布解除对苏制裁，而苏丹仍在美国的支持恐怖主义国家名单中，继续遭受美方武器禁运、取消经济援助及其他金融限制措施。解除的部分制裁措施不包括：根据2006年4月26日第13400号行政令以及根据13067号行政令宣布的国家紧急情况，OFAC对达尔富尔冲突实施的制裁；OFAC指定的13067号和13412号行政令以外的苏丹人制裁名单。

古巴制裁（CUBA SANCTIONS）

美国对古巴制裁可追溯至20世纪60年代初，美国与古巴断交，并开始对古巴实施经济金融封锁和贸易禁运。1963年7月8日美国财政部根据1917年《敌国贸易法》制定《古巴资产控制条例》（31 C.F.R. 515），该条例规定古巴与美国之间的关系总体规范（General Regulate Relations），是美国国内执行针对古巴禁运的主要机制。

《古巴民主法案》是美国国会议员罗伯特托里切利于1992年10月提出的一项法案，该法案禁止美国公司的外国子公司与古巴进行贸易，禁止美国公民前往古巴以及向古巴家属汇款。该法案为"通过对卡斯特罗政府实施制裁并支持古巴人民以促进古巴向民主和平过渡的法案"。该法案指出，"菲德尔卡斯特罗政府已展示一贯漠视国际公认的人权标准和民主价值"，并补充道"这里没有迹象表明卡斯特罗政权准备向民主作出任何重大让步或进行任何形式的民主开放"[1]。1993

---

① "Cuban Democracy Act（"CDA"）"（PDF）.United States Code - Title 22: Foreign Relations and Intercourse. Archive.org. Archived from the original（PDF）on November 8, 2004.

年7月时任美国总统签署12854号行政令，宣布该法案的实施，并说明了政府部分在执行该法案的职责分工。

1996年古巴自由民主团结法（被称为"赫尔姆斯—伯顿法"）延续并强化了美国对古巴的禁运。该法延长了最初禁运的领土适用范围，适用于与古巴进行贸易的外国公司，并对外国公司进行处罚，据称这些外国公司曾经"贩运"美国公民原来拥有但在古巴革命后被古巴没收的财产。该法还涵盖了曾经成为美国公民的古巴人所拥有的财产。[①]

时任美国总统乔治布什当选后，两国关系再次恶化。其在竞选期间呼吁古巴裔美国人反对菲德尔卡斯特罗政府，并支持更严格的禁运限制。在就职后约三个月，布什政府开始扩大旅行限制并对古巴进一步实行经济封锁的施压计划。

奥巴马政府上台后，有意与古巴缓解紧张关系，逐步修改对古巴的制裁条款和条例。2014年12月17日，奥巴马宣布进行一系列外交和经济变革，以绘制美国与古巴关系的新路线。由美国财政部和美国商务部修订出版的《古巴资产控制条例》（CACR）和《出口管理条例》（EAR），该条例同样于12月17日宣布实施由财政部外国资产管理办公室（OFAC）和商业工业和安全局（BIS）管理的制裁变化。

这些措施将允许某些实体转发授权汇款，提高限额并全面授权某些类别的汇款至古巴，允许美国金融机构在古巴金融机构开设代理账户以方便处理授权交易，授权与位于古巴境外的古巴国民进行某些交易，并允许其他一些与电信、金融服务、贸易和其他领域有关的其他活动运输。

与奥马巴不同，美国新一任总统特朗普再次收紧了对古巴政策，并扩大对古巴制裁事项及范围。特朗普总统2017年6月实施国家安全总统备忘录的修正案（National Security Presidential Memorandum，NSPM），加强了美国对古巴的政策。根据NSPM，国务院拟定一份由古巴军方、情报部门、安全部门或其人员来控制、代表或执行的实体和子公司清单，以及与将使古巴军方、情报部门、安全部门或其人员受益而损害古巴民众或古巴私营企业利益进行直接金融

[①] Hillyard，Mick；Miller，Vaughne（14 December 1998）．"Cuba and the Helms-Burton Act"（PDF）. House of Commons Library Research Papers. Great Britain. Parliament.House of Commons. 98（114）：3. Archived from the original（PDF）on August 19，2000. Retrieved 26 June 2014.

交易的对手清单。这份清单则为"古巴限制名单"（Cuba Restricted List）。根据NSPM，OFAC正在发布一项新的禁令，限制与"古巴限制名单"上的实体和子公司之间的直接金融交易。[①]

OFAC修订了关于附带交易（incidental transactions）的解释条款，并澄清通常许可交易（licensed transactions）中发生的授权交易（authorized transactions）不包括与此类实体和子公司之间的直接金融交易，条件是适用的一般或特定许可条款明确排除此类直接金融交易。[②]

目前，美国或受美国管辖的人员与古巴之间的大部分交易仍被禁止，OFAC将继续执行CACR的禁令。OFAC正在发布监管修正案，以实施NSPM中阐述的古巴制裁计划的变更。具体而言，OFAC将发布以下变更：限制在美国司法管辖区内的人员与国务院制定的与古巴有关联的受限实体和子公司名单（"古巴受限制名单"）中确定的实体和子公司进行直接金融交易。

---

① 31 CFR § 515.209.
② 31 CFR § 515.421.

后 记

《美国反洗钱合规监管风暴》一书即将付梓出版,感慨良多。

从有点想法到想法的逐步成型,从收集材料到分章节编写,从编写体例的变化到编写人员的遴选等等,很多领导、同事和朋友都给予鼓励和支持,尤其出版社的革军社长、智慧主任、雪珂编辑以及悉尼分行扬统总经理提供了全方位的指导和帮助。

在全书的编写过程,国际业务部鼎立支持、内控合规部持续给力,同事于雯做了很多协调工作,同事罗英燕虽然已经不再从事这方面的工作,但还是非常积极并介绍烟台大学法学院助理教授姜福晓博士参与进来,还有同事崔彤虽然未能参加具体章节的编写,也做了很多辅助性的有益的工作等等,在此一并感谢。

《美国反洗钱合规监管风暴》一书以事实为依据,尽可能为广大读者还原当前美国反洗钱合规监管的情势。为此,我们挑选了2012年至2017年间、罚款金额在1亿美元以上、震慑性的11个典型洗钱合规案例,以监管机构和银行达成的《和解令》公布的时间为序和核心进行详细解读。各章节执笔人情况如下:

引言:美国反洗钱合规监管风暴概述(岳留昌)

1. 制裁国家的业务碰不得——荷兰安智银行洗钱案例(杨志华)

2. 塞耳盗钟大福不再——汇丰银行洗钱案例(王淼)

3. 不认真整改的后果很严重——渣打银行洗钱案例(李拓)

4. 欲盖弥彰搞小动作的后果——三菱日联银行反洗钱合规案例分析（韩磊、郭芊）

5. 蓄意遮挡号牌的后果——苏格兰皇家银行洗钱案例（罗英燕、姜福晓）

6. 棍棒下的"孝子"——摩根大通银行案例（刘洁）

7. 天价罚单落地始末——法国巴黎银行案例（杨慧）

8. 此"德"非彼"德"，双德被罚——德意志银行和德国商业银行洗钱案例（于雯）

9. "任性"的孩子——兆丰银行被罚事件（叶小琳）

10. 好学生同样会犯错——意大利联合圣保罗洗钱案例（黄颖、王盛楠）

11. 捉迷藏——HBL被罚案例（叶小琳）

附录美国反洗钱合规监管法案汇总（李紫燕）

编者于2019年1月